REVOLUTIONARY WOMEN *in*

POSTREVOLUTIONARY MEXICO

||||||||||||||||||||||||||||||||||||||||||||||||||||||||||||||||||||||||||||||||

NEXT WAVE

New Directions in Women's Studies

A series edited by Inderpal Grewal,

Caren Kaplan, and Robyn Wiegman

REVOLUTIONARY
WOMEN
in POSTREVOLUTIONARY
MEXICO

|||||||||||||||||||||||||||||||||||||||||||||||||||||||||||||||||||||||||||||||

JOCELYN OLCOTT

|||||||||||||||||||||||||||||||||||||||||||||||||||||||||||||||||||||||||||||||

DUKE UNIVERSITY PRESS

Durham and London

2005

© 2005 Duke University Press

All rights reserved

Printed in the United States

of America on acid-free paper ∞

Designed by Amy Ruth Buchanan

Typeset in Carter & Cone Galliard

by Keystone Typesetting, Inc.

Library of Congress Cataloging-in-

Publication Data appear on the last

printed page of this book.

CONTENTS

ACKNOWLEDGMENTS

Over the years that I spent researching and writing this book, I have accumulated debts of every sort to research institutions, mentors, family, colleagues, and friends. Here, I hope to distract my creditors from the fact that I have little hope of ever repaying them.

This project enjoyed support from a Henry Hart Rice Fellowship (Yale Center for International and Area Studies), an International Pre-Dissertation Fellowship (Social Science Research Council), a Fulbright-García Robles Fellowship, a Mrs. Giles Whiting Dissertation Fellowship in the Humanities, a Junior/Senior/General Faculty Research Award (California State University, Fullerton), and a Donald D. Harrington Faculty Fellowship (University of Texas, Austin). Duke University also provided course relief during my first year to allow me to revise my manuscript. In Mexico, El Colegio de México and the Centro de Investigaciones y Estudios Superiores de Antropología Social (CIESAS) provided crucial institutional support.

Throughout my research, I relied on the tireless work of librarians and archivists. In particular, I thank Carlos Castañón Cuadros at the Instituto Municipal de Documentación, Torreón; Sergio Antonio Corona Páez at the Archivo Histórico of the Universidad Iberoamericana, Torreón; and Piedad Peniche at the Archivo General del Estado de Yucatán. Also, Citlali Rieder generously shared with me the unsorted papers of her grandmother Concha Michel. Alejandra García Quintanilla offered indispensable guidance about Yucatecan women's history. Working in many different archives and libraries also allowed me to develop enduring friendships with like-minded scholars. For their diversion, inspiration, and generosity, I am grateful to Chris Boyer, Sarah Buck, Karen Caplan, John Crider, Alec Dawson, Susan Gauss, Dan LaBotz, Stephanie Bryant Mitchell, and Sasha Schell. Daniela Spenser has been a friend, mentor, and colleague both in Mexico and in the United

States. Perhaps my greatest debt in Mexico is to Rodolfo González Ono and Javier Arroyo Rico — my *maestros y compañeros*.

This book results from intense engagements with many people whose intellectual passions fueled my own. Michael Jiménez, Miguel Centeno, and Arcadio Díaz Quiñones sparked my interest in Latin America as an undergraduate. Many of the ideas in this book reflect discussions in coffeehouses and graduate seminars in New Haven. David Montgomery and Jean-Christophe Agnew will, I hope, recognize the imprint of their teaching. Nancy Cott continues to press me to clarify my ideas and to consider the larger context of women's history. Emilia Viotti da Costa, who never fails simultaneously to terrify and inspire her students, sacrificed time from her well-deserved retirement to offer encouragement, advice, and incisive questions. Gil Joseph has patiently guided this project from start to finish, offering intellectual and professional support at critical moments and with his characteristic generosity.

My most important lessons came from my *compañeros* in the Graduate Employees and Teachers Organization (GESO) and the Hotel Employees and Restaurant Employees International (HERE). My experiences working with these extraordinary people helped me — more than rereadings of Foucault and Gramsci ever could — to understand the complex, mystified, and sometimes absurdly simple ways that power operates. GESO created a community of activist intellectuals that fostered reading and writing groups as well as organizing committees. Special thanks to Jessica and Eric Allina-Pisano, Lori Brooks, Peter Carroll, Greg Grandin, Michele Janette, Ben Johnson, Gordon Lafer, Shafali Lal, Kieko Matteson, Bryan McCann, Michelle Nickerson, Robert Perkinson, Corey Robin, David Sanders, Michelle Stephens, and Wendi Walsh, for their hard work, support, and friendship. Di Paton and Mark Lawrence both read the entire dissertation and offered thoughtful criticism leavened by affectionate boosterism.

At California State University, Fullerton, I enjoyed support from our department chair, Bill Haddad, as well as the members of our writing group: Clark Davis, Terri Snyder, Laichen Sun, and Roshanna Sylvester. While supported by a generous Harrington Faculty Fellowship at the University of Texas, Austin, I found a vibrant scholarly and social community with Susan Boettcher, Caroline Castiglione, Janet Davis, Carolyn Eastman, Julie Hardwick, Julia Mickenberg, Victoria Rodríguez, and Shirley Thompson. I also had helpful research assistance from Chris Albi and Heather Peterson. Since arriving at Duke, I have relished its engaged and dynamic intellectual atmosphere and especially the support of Ed Balleisen, Kathryn Burns, Sally Deutsch, Laura Edwards, John and Jan French, Esther Gabara, Lupe García, Cynthia Herrup, Claudia Koonz, Karen Krahulik, Wahneema Lubiano, Diane Nelson, Gunther Peck, Tom Rogers, Alejandro Velasco, and Priscilla Wald. Alvaro Jarrín assisted in the final preparation of this manuscript.

Others with no particular institutional connection or obligation have expended extraordinary energy reading parts of the manuscript or discussing it with me over e-mail and caffeine. They include Raphael Allen, Gabriela Cano, Elisabeth Friedman, Jim Green, Shelagh Kenney, Josh Miller, David Sartorius, Pete Sigal, Vanessa Taylor, and Mary Kay Vaughan. As many a Latin Americanist has already recognized, Valerie Millholland and the crew at Duke University Press labor overtime to help authors identify and realize the potential of their work. I also benefited tremendously from the detailed and constructive comments of the Duke University Press readers: Ben Fallaw, Heidi Tinsman, and Pamela Voekel.

During the time I revised my dissertation into a book, four friends died. Clark Davis, Michael Jiménez, Shafali Lal, and Michael Powell did not know each other, but they shared a talent for inspiring those around them to approach academic endeavors with both a sense of humor and a sense of purpose. I hope this book manages to reflect a fraction of that inspiration.

I suppose we can't blame our parents for everything, and mine aren't responsible for getting me into this racket. Phoebe and Neil Olcott are, however, "enablers" of this peculiar habit of historical research and writing. Their emotional and financial support allowed me the freedom to make my own choices; I can't imagine a more valuable gift.

INTRODUCTION

The Daughters of La Malinche:

Gender and Revolutionary

Citizenship

> Woman is a living symbol of
> the strangeness of the universe and
> its radical heterogeneity.
> — Octavio Paz,
> "Los hijos de la Malinche"[1]

In late January 1936, some 250 peasant women and their children invaded the Hacienda Santa Bárbara, the estate of Mexico's former president and political puppeteer Plutarco Elías Calles. Led by the intrepid activist and erstwhile Communist Party militant Concha Michel, the *campesinas* (rural women) claimed the ranch for a women's school for vocational and political skills, delivering the benefits of Mexico's 1910–17 revolution. They immediately faced Calles's menacing *guardias blancas*, the private militia charged with preventing such challenges. According to Michel's account, she assuaged the women's fears by explaining that Calles would find it "inconvenient" to massacre women and children.[2] A general in the revolution's Constitutionalist army and the *jefe máximo* (supreme chief) of postrevolutionary politics, Calles publicly aligned himself with the masses; surely he would not allow this encounter to degenerate into bloodshed by campesinas standing up for their revolutionary rights. As tensions mounted, Calles offered to negotiate, and Michel steeled herself to confront the man she had recently likened to Joseph Stalin for their shared betrayal of popular revolutions.[3] She viewed mass mobilizations as critical to revitalizing Mexico's receding revolution and, sensing imminent victory, hoped to inspire future land invasions. While Michel conferred with Calles, however, his guards forcibly removed the invaders, unilaterally terminating the negotiations.

Participants and observers alike understood the episode as a gender inversion. Challenging the jefe máximo by assuming the masculine personae of land invaders placed the campesinas outside the gender conventions of political action. Submitting photographs of the incident to Washington, U.S. Ambassador Josephus Daniels characterized the episode as "amusing but pathetic" and awkwardly translated Calles as saying, "Yes, in Mexico, when there is an issue to be made wherein the men have not the courage to sustain it, they invariably send out the women and children."[4] Calles, rather than attributing manly traits to the campesinas, impugned the masculinity of those he assumed had put them up to the act. Still, Michel relied on prevailing gender codes and Calles's own self-image as postrevolutionary paterfamilias to restrain his henchmen from using violence, as they presumably would have against a group of men. Pointing to the regime's own efforts to fashion campesinas into revolutionaries, Michel proclaimed that the school strove "not to divide the sexes in the class struggle but rather to link them more closely, raising consciousness about women's social responsibility for reproducing the species."[5]

Less than two years after this confrontation, in September 1937, President Lázaro Cárdenas (1934–40) called on Congress to amend Mexico's constitution, granting women the right to vote and to hold public office. Responding to a vocal and mobilized women's suffrage movement, the proposal inspired magnanimous speeches on the chamber floor, as one lawmaker after another emphasized the revolution's debt to women. The constitutional amendment, which contained a modest change to specify that "*mexicanos*" referred to both men and women, unanimously passed both houses of Congress. By mid-November 1938, enough states had ratified the amendment that the ruling party's newspaper carried a banner headline trumpeting, "Today the Declaration of the Feminine Vote Will Be Made."[6] Exploiting a constitutional loophole, however, legislators refused to publish the vote counts in the congressional record, rendering the amendment a dead letter. Despite repeated suffragist protests, women would not vote in a federal election until 1958.

Making sense of these two episodes and their resolutions calls for an excavation of the meanings of citizenship in postrevolutionary Mexico and, in particular, during the pivotal Cárdenas presidency. Bridging the authoritarian period of Calles's *maximato* (1928–34) and the conservative presidency of Manuel Avila Camacho, the Cárdenas government has earned the reputation, both in scholarship and in popular memory, as the presidency that most honored revolutionary ideals.[7] While this characterization remains subject to debate, most observers would agree that the historical conjuncture of January 1936 — the crisis of capitalism manifest in a worldwide Depression, the dawn of the Communist International's Popular Front campaign, and the growing appeal of both fascism and populism — made it a propitious moment for popular mobilization. Cárdenas fell within this international current, encouraging government-sponsored mass organizing to contain the effects of the global economic upheaval. He broke with Calles in June 1935, purging the Callista cabinet members and taking a sharp left turn in political style and substance. At the time of the Santa Bárbara incident, Calles was "between exiles," having returned from a six-month absence at the end of 1935 before leaving again in April 1936. His banishment continued until Cárdenas's successor, Avila Camacho, invited him to return. Thus, rather than an attack on the governing regime, the assault on Calles's property would have appeared to the Cárdenas government as endorsing its support for popular mobilizations.

Pierre Bourdieu has famously observed the permeability between formal politics and the quotidian practices that give them meaning, between conjuncture and habitus.[8] Episodes such as the Santa Bárbara invasion set in relief the articulation between high and low politics, offering particular insights for women's interventions and their place in defining both formal citizenship and what we have come to think of as civil society.[9] The actors who take center stage in this story of the mobilization and consolidation of postrevolutionary women's activism, progressive and radical women like Concha Michel, struggled to make the revolution meaningful for ordinary Mexicans. To be sure, these women stood apart in many ways; greater numbers of women supported the Catholic and conservative movements that celebrated women's domestic roles.[10] However, progressive and radical women's disproportionate representation among Mexico's "organic intellectuals" — especially teachers, journalists, and government employees — helped define postrevolutionary political culture. Like their ideological opposites in Catholic and conservative organizations, these women pushed the boundaries of women's organizing and political activities more generally.

Citizenship

Women activists faced a compounded challenge: they claimed revolutionary citizenship at a moment when the meanings of both citizenship and womanhood remained unstable and contested. As in other postrevolutionary societies, in Mexico debates over citizenship rights served as proxies for defining the parameters of the revolution itself, underscoring the contingency of this supposedly static, natural right.[11] Between the signing of the 1917 Constitution and Cárdenas's 1934 inauguration, the attributes of revolutionary citizenship underwent significant changes and reversals. And although the Constitutionalists came to power under the banner, "Effective Suffrage, No Reelection," it quickly became clear that effective suffrage remained limited to those who supported the governing regime, and no reelection often remained true only in the most literal sense. Arguments over the meanings of and qualifications for citizenship turned on two questions that have framed these debates for centuries: what is the proper balance between the rights and the obligations of citizenship, and to what extent is citizenship a status versus a practice? In postrevolutionary Mexico, these deliberations played out against a backdrop of an established tradition of political patronage, which, in quotidian practice, often trumped competing imaginaries of citizenship with its promise of (uneven) reciprocity.

Observers on all sides of the "woman question" assumed that the encounter between "women" and "politics" would have some identifiable effect similar to two solid objects colliding. Disagreements centered on whether women would redefine Mexican politics or political involvement would alter women's nature. Suffragists often contended that women would make political life less fraudulent, more family-oriented, and more humane, while antisuffragists insisted on the reverse effect — that politics would corrupt women, wrench them from their homes, and render them more callous. In short, the suffrage debate largely swirled around the question of whether women would feminize politics or political involvement would masculinize women.

Embedded within these deliberations lay the unspoken question of what these two categories — "women" (or, more often, the singular "woman") and "politics" (also singular, *la política*) — meant in everyday practice. At a moment witnessing the international emergence of the "new woman" and the "modern girl," along with welfare states and fascist-style corporatism, the definitions of women and of politics remained far less distinct, less solid, than contemporary observers implied. Interactions between women and politics more closely resembled a roughly choreographed dance than a collision. Most participants recognized certain moves; those less schooled in the political arts might misstep but still draw nearer to their objectives. Dancers changed partners and at times moved to entirely different rhythms. The increasing participation of a wide variety of women in a world formerly closed off to them as "civic life" or the "public realm" did not precipitate a political "big bang" but, rather, proceeded as a complex interplay that created new possibilities, further troubling the categories of "women" and "politics" even through their strategic invocation as clearly defined entities.

Through the 1920s and '30s—even as governments around the world granted women either partial or full citizenship rights and as articulate, well-placed Mexican women argued strenuously for women's suffrage, land and labor rights, and even mothers' wages—public intellectuals and policymakers highlighted the cognitive dissonance between Mexican womanhood and the citizen statesman. "The woman is called upon to intervene as an element of action and opinion in national endeavors," the ruling party's newspaper editorialized in 1931. "But while she prepares herself and organizes herself, we men prefer to continue ceding our seats on the buses, finding the soup hot in the household olla, and listening to the broom dancing under conjugal songs, than to hear falsetto voices in Parliament or to entrust the suffragist ballots to poetic hands."[12]

Feminist theorists and historians have exposed the masculinist assumptions of both liberal and civic-republic conceptions of citizenship, pointing to the ideological divide between public and private (or between the political and the nonpolitical), the insistence on universalism and impartiality, and the extent to which citizenship practices often conflict with women's customary duties.[13] However, the political and economic uncertainty of postrevolutionary Mexico offered a shaky foundation for constructing the type of citizenship that appears in political theories and histories based on Anglo-European or U.S. experiences. For if the rise of the nation-state gave birth to the citizen-subject, and the onset of industrial capitalism sharpened the public-private divide, then we must consider that Mexico, even by the 1930s, remained a tenuously consolidated nation-state and unevenly incorporated into capitalist production. As ideological conflicts heightened long-standing regional, ethnic, and political rivalries, the universal citizen-subject seems like a caricature. Men and women moved constantly between subsistence and market production and between households and meeting halls, ignoring the demands of a public-private divide. And at a moment when no one could agree on what constituted citizenship, the demands of women's

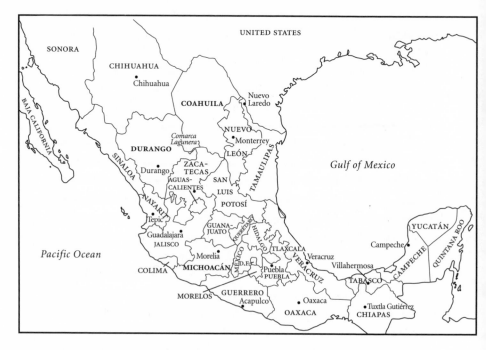

Map 1. "México." By Natalie Hanemann.

reproductive-labor duties constituted just one of many impediments to exercising it.

Any effort to make sense of secular women activists' frustrated bids for citizenship must first examine how they imagined this objective. This book argues that Mexicans — men and women alike — experienced revolutionary citizenship as contingent, inhabited, and gendered. In other words, the practice of citizenship depended on specific historical and political contexts, which had local and regional characteristics as well as national and transnational ones. Furthermore, people inhabited citizenship less as a collection of specific laws and exclusions than as a set of social, cultural, and political processes that both shaped and refracted contemporary political discourses and practices. Finally, deliberations over citizenship served as a battleground amid rapidly destabilizing gender ideologies. This perspective takes us some distance toward unraveling the riddle of Mexican women's suffrage bid. In the context of postrevolutionary Mexico, voting rights represented only a small slice — and a relatively unimportant one — of the ways in which people lived citizenship. The many collective, public, and deliberative ways in which men and women exercised revolutionary citizenship took precedence over this individual and well-circumscribed right. Women activists insisted, however, on revolutionary citizenship — on material revolutionary benefits, recognition as political, "public" actors, and official appreciation of their centrality to the new regime's revolutionary project.

"Many Mexicos" and the Contingencies of Revolutionary Citizenship

The language of citizenship dominated postrevolutionary political discourse, where the title *ciudadano* (citizen) designated one as a legitimate revolutionary, but the term's significance hinged on competing interpretations of the revolution's history and objectives. As Hannah Arendt chillingly reminds us, the "duties of a law-abiding citizen" do not stand above politics, culture, and history but, rather, remain firmly embedded within them.[14] If citizenship marks a boundary between those included and excluded from the polity, between those who enjoy representation and those who do not, then this designation of ciudadano carried more than symbolic weight. The revolution opened the possibility for moving the boundary that delineated, in the political theorist Sheldon Wolin's terms, the "circumscribed space in which likeness dwells," expanding the pool not only of those enjoying formal political rights but also of those whose actions registered as political interventions rather than simply chaos or criminality.[15] The "essence of State sovereignty," the political philosopher Giorgio Agamben contends, lies in the power to define — and constantly redefine — where that line of legitimacy falls.[16] Contenders for control over the postrevolutionary regime sought to seize that power of exclusion, the right to draw the lines of legitimacy.

But the authority to decide this exclusion — to designate, for example, certain land invasions as revolutionary and others as criminal — underscores citizenship's historical contingency. In the wake of the Santa Bárbara invasion, the minister of government declared that the guilty would "be brought to justice."[17] Unlike many land invasions orchestrated by men, this "amusing but pathetic incident" had crossed the bounds of revolutionary legitimacy. However, as Wolin argues, "revolutionary transgression is the means by which the demos makes itself political."[18] In transcending conventional limits, Michel sought both rights and political visibility for women; through such ordinary and extraordinary transgressions, Mexicans participated in defining the revolution from the bottom up.[19]

A process of negotiation ensued between the constant drawing and transgressing of these boundaries, reflecting both Mexico's national history and the world-historical moment of the 1920s and '30s. First and foremost, revolutionary citizens demonstrated patriotic loyalty, distinguishing themselves from the cosmopolitan *vendepatrias* (traitors) of the Porfiriato (1876–1910) — the dictatorship of Porfirio Díaz characterized by European tastes in culture and Anglo-American tastes in capital. Factions competed to define the terms of revolutionary nationalism, but, at minimum, they questioned loyalties not only to foreign governments and investors but also to international entities such as the Catholic church and, later, the Communist Party.

Second, the national and the international climates fostered class-centered discourses that structured both popular and legislative politics. If race has framed political debates in the post–Reconstruction United States — not only in discussions about segregation, miscegenation, and affirmative action but also in less explicitly racialized debates over poll taxes, gerrymandering, and diversity — class assumed an analogous place in postrevolutionary Mexico. The Depression fostered the intellectual ascendancy of historical materialism, and activists strove to identify themselves not only as nationalist but also as struggling on behalf of Mexico's "proletariat," a category that in popular usage extended to everyone from peasants and miners to teachers, tailors, and even, on occasion, housewives. The 1938 restructuring of Mexico's governing National Revolutionary Party (PNR) into the corporatist Party of the Mexican Revolution (PRM) formally inscribed class-based political discourses by structuring interactions with the state into four political sectors: the peasantry, the military, organized labor, and a more nebulous "popular" sector. Joining an affiliated organization such as the Mexican Labor Confederation (CTM) or National Peasant Confederation (CNC) meant automatic membership in the party, where decisions resulted not from individual votes but, rather, from negotiations among corporate representatives. Although women also joined these organizations, they remained at the margins, leading many women activists to demand women-only organizations. In other words, individuals exercised citizenship based on their ascribed class identity but with an implicit male subject; the workers and peasants of the corporatist imaginary were *obreros* (workingmen) and campesinos, not *obreras* (workingwomen) and campesinas.

Finally, national and transnational currents placed a premium on modernization efforts, including everything from industrialization and public education to sanitation and anticlerical campaigns. The emphasis on modernization — or "developmentalism," as the historian Alan Knight puts it — pulled against the emphases on class-based politics and revolutionary nationalism.[20] Although modernization efforts predated the revolution by at least a century, their postrevolutionary variant drew on international developments in the social sciences and welfare-state formation. Much like their predecessors, postrevolutionary policymakers generally saw themselves — overwhelmingly Anglo-European men of means — as embodying modernity and directed their efforts at remaking the poor, nonwhite, and female in their image. But modernization efforts did not remain the exclusive purview of white-shod statesmen; communists, labor organizers, peasant leaders, and schoolteachers all called for a more "modern" Mexico. Activists like Michel, agitating for a school to instruct women in political and vocational skills, tapped into this impulse to transform rural mestizas into productive citizens.

Unsurprisingly, given Mexico's notorious regional fragmentation, contingent citizenship reflected local and regional experiences and ideologies as well as national and transnational ones.[21] As the cases under consideration in this book demonstrate, the meanings of citizenship reflected local upheavals such as the Cristero Rebellion's (1926–29) challenge to postrevolutionary anticlericalism in the center-west, the 1936 general strike in the Comarca Lagunera, and postrevolutionary Yucatán's political maneuverings. Political fault lines followed locally defined courses, and even labels such as *agrarista* (agrarian radical) took on different connotations in these different settings. The political philosopher Joshua Foa Dienstag has demonstrated that "high" political theory, despite its pretense toward abstraction, rests on particular historical narratives, and the political theorist Seyla Benhabib draws on psychoanalytic theory to argue a similar point on a personal and community level.[22] "We are born into webs of interlocution or into webs of narrative," Benhabib asserts, "from the familial and gender narratives to the linguistic ones to the narratives of one's collective identity. We become who we are by learning to become a conversation partner in these narratives."[23] Mexico's organic intellectuals fashioned their own political theories — their political "common sense" in the Gramscian vein — out of local narratives that assumed their own boundaries of exclusion.

In the context of Mexico City's modernizing interventions, however, these "webs of interlocution" could not remain local. While some activists —

most notably, those seeking to protect religious freedom — viewed the new regime as an imperialist juggernaut, others anthropomorphized the revolution, incarnating it in the postrevolutionary state and its agents. The Cárdenas government, bent on fostering a unified national identity, came to appreciate the importance of regional concerns and power structures that limited the federal government's power. Local actors alternately resisted Mexico City's policies and invited the federal government into their communities to defend them against arbitrary local *caciques* (bosses); federal agencies' attempts to enforce the rule of law appealed to popular actors who persistently found themselves on the short end of local power struggles.[24] In particular, communications to Cárdenas, much like those to his U.S. counterpart Franklin Delano Roosevelt, often took on a "letter to the king" quality, indicating that once he realized that the revolution had not yet arrived in a certain village, he would rectify matters by distributing land, opening schools, and building irrigation systems. Many different actors at varying points in Mexico's political power structure — centralizing statesmen in Mexico City, regional political leaders, and local activists — sought, within the continual play between conjuncture and habitus, to define the contours of both revolution and citizenship.

If revolutionary citizenship hinged on place, it also depended on time. In his study of abolitionism in the postrevolutionary United States, the historian David Brion Davis points to the "perishability of revolutionary time" in which the "power of Revolutionary ideals depended upon the sense of a continuing Revolutionary time — a time not simply of completion and rounding out, but a time of creation, marked by the same contingency, fears, and openness of the Revolution itself."[25] Similarly, in postrevolutionary Mexico the new regime's architects struggled not only to paint themselves as the revolution's legitimate heirs but also to depict the revolution itself as ongoing and simultaneously both stable enough to inspire confidence and imperiled enough to justify extreme measures in its defense. Activists exploited official concerns about the revolution's recession into history, arguing that support for their efforts — for land reform, health clinics, or corn mills — would prolong the revolution by signaling its long-awaited arrival in their communities. Particularly after Cárdenas's 1935 break with Calles, petitions frequently indicated that Cardenismo promised a revolutionary renaissance. Practical conceptions of citizenship, then, depended on these specificities, on the competing narratives and webs of interlocution through which individuals imagined and reimagined themselves as revolutionary citizens.

These contingencies of time and place, however, tell us little about how ordinary Mexicans enacted that role. The historian Nancy Cott describes citizenship as "a political fiction, an identification that can be put on like new clothing by the properly readied wearer." Rather than seeing citizenship as a falsehood, she depicts it as "purposefully constructed," indicating that "the rewards and obligations it conveys may vary over time and among citizens." Citizenship, she continues, "represents an attachment to a political community, different from membership in a kinship group because the bonds are only figurative."[26] Citizenship, then, requires not only that one fulfill the contingent requirements of legitimate membership but also that one inhabit citizenship, donning its garb and giving it meaning. Mexican activists drew ecumenically from three seemingly contradictory modes of citizenship — liberal invocations of suffrage, traditional expectations of patronage, and revolutionary commitments to popular mobilization — to pursue an array of tangible benefits.

Lawmakers at the 1917 Constitutional Congress restricted citizenship to those who, "having the quality of being Mexican, also fulfill the following requirements: being eighteen years of age if married or twenty-one if not, and having an honest way of life."[27] Leaving the state considerable latitude in determining who possessed "the quality of being Mexican" and an "honest way of life," this article also reflected the new constitution's purpose in obligating the state and its citizenry rather than simply restricting them, as its 1857 predecessor had done. In the balance between rights and obligations, the new regime came down heavily on the side of obligations for both state and society. Revolutionary citizens would perform citizenship on a daily basis, and the new regime, in turn, would fulfill its revolutionary commitments. Both the performance and the commitments, of course, remained contested.

The performance of revolutionary citizenship derived from three traditionally masculine activities that purportedly instilled the consciousness of "sincere" and "authentic" revolutionaries and promoted a citizenship centered on collective well-being: military service, civic engagement, and labor. Military leaders dominated both formal and informal politics and prized military socialization. Similarly, participation in congresses and political organizations, the formation of political parties, and involvement with state agencies constituted civic engagement and indicated political consciousness.

Finally, the emphasis on workforce participation—meaning remunerated labor such as agricultural work, artisanal production, or industrial wage labor—reflected the widely held commitment to historical materialism and economic modernization. Across a broad range of ideologies, the notion that labor inculcated revolutionary consciousness became axiomatic. Revolutionary citizens, in addition to exhibiting the traits of nationalism, class-consciousness, and modernity, would engage in these three activities: military service, civic engagement, and paid labor.

For its part, the postrevolutionary state cultivated an institutional infrastructure upon which to hang this citizenship. Although this infrastructure did not always adhere to the state or the ruling party (which often became indistinguishable), official support promoted a mobilization-centered political culture that created both the ideological climate and the material conditions to facilitate activism. As Knight has pointed out, "Cárdenas' constant theme was, like Lenin's, 'organize.'"[28] Cardenista organizing programs explicitly sought to structure and "modernize" Mexican society in preparation for broader participation in governance. As paternalist and patronizing as these tactics appear in retrospect, they fostered mass political engagement and gave political voice to historically marginalized groups. This emphasis on mobilization and collective organizing over individualism and competition constituted one of Cardenismo's defining aspects within debates over revolutionary citizenship.

However, the Santa Bárbara episode and its disheartening denouement underscore the possibilities and limitations of this political culture of organizing. On one hand, the revolution itself—with its rhetoric of "land and liberty" and of popular enfranchisement—legitimated such mobilizations as the enactment of revolutionary citizenship. On the other, "organizing" implies not only mobilization and representation but also order and discipline. "Democracy carried along by revolution," Wolin reminds us, "comes to appear as surplus democracy when revolutions are ended and the permanent institutionalization of politics is begun."[29] Cárdenas and his allies encouraged mass organizations to secure the more radical gains of agrarian reforms and industrial nationalizations but endeavored to maintain strict control over those organizations. The ruling party forbade, for example, labor radicals from organizing peasants into their ranks, fearing that such an alliance would create too strong a bloc, a proscription that provoked intense conflicts over organizational jurisdiction as people moved among agricultural and industrial production and between wage and subsistence economies.[30]

The two aspects of organizing—mobilization and discipline—informed how people inhabited revolutionary citizenship. Policymakers struggled to differentiate "sincere revolutionaries" from "subversive agitators," finding particularly unsettling the idea that regime-supporting revolutionaries might become subversive agitators or that the two might even remain indistinguishable. To channel popular organizing in directions that regime leaders considered both revolutionary and "safe," they adroitly cast any gains made through popular struggle—whether in women's rights, land reform, or labor conditions—as the result of state benevolence and the victory of the "institutionalized revolution."

Still, organizational infrastructures, including official unions, party committees, and agrarian leagues, could only provide the warp into which was woven the woof of local experiences, producing a variegated and multi-textured political culture of organizing. Many foot soldiers of state formation—teachers, social workers, and agrarian- and labor-department representatives—sympathized with both local and national concerns and sought to mediate between the postrevolutionary regime and diverse communities. These men and, increasingly, women understood their jobs in multifaceted ways, as livelihoods, vocations, and missions. While the new rural federal schools provided many young women with professional identities and modest incomes (although they frequently protested that they did not receive their pay), as long as teachers faced violent assault and even assassination at the hands of "socialist" education's opponents, and as long as Agrarian Department agents endured harassment by landowners' guardias blancas, government posts did not always offer comfortable sinecures.

Government employees often entered communities with the condescension of the educated and the insensitivity of outsiders, but they also harbored a sense of purpose and the conviction that the Cárdenas government offered, at last, the opportunity for ordinary people to reap the dividends of a quarter-century of civil war and political strife. Amid the political currents of the 1930s, these activists and organic intellectuals regarded themselves not as agents of a leviathan state but, rather, as catalysts of revolutionary change and facilitators of revolutionary citizenship. They provided logistical and material support, offering not only personal contacts but also navigation through the emergent state bureaucracy, assisting locals with everything from typing petitions and recognizing solicitation protocols to framing petitions for land, credit, and social services.

Furthermore, these efforts bore the markings of individual teachers' and organizers' preferences and ordinary Mexicans' appropriations and reinterpretations. A teacher, for example, absorbed her normal-school training through the lens of her own values and ideologies, perhaps blending the Education Ministry's modernizing impulse with homegrown elements of communism or folk Catholicism.[31] She might practice her vocation in a cultural context quite foreign to her or encounter local political leadership that remained deeply ambivalent about federal interventions. The community where she taught would pick and choose from her agenda, supporting those activities that seemed sensible to its members and rejecting others; *comuneros* (collective landholders) might embrace the consumer cooperative and rebuff the sanitation committee. If the teacher seemed too strident in her "anti-fanaticism," the community might dismiss her altogether as a threat to one of its most dearly held institutions, the parish church. In short, organizing efforts emanating from Mexico City faced a long and tortuous road to reach their intended audiences and underwent many transformations en route, with uneven and unpredictable effects.

Activists and government agents also helped popular groups gain access to public space, which, as the Santa Bárbara invasion indicates, became a crucial marker of citizenship. Women activists stressed this demand, petitioning repeatedly to take over cantinas, billiard halls, and churches to transform them into schools, cooperatives, and child-care facilities. Controlling public space, after all, tangibly marked women's presence in the public realm not as itinerants or imposters but, rather, as permanent fixtures in civil society — as citizens. The Catholic church had traditionally provided women with their most important public venue, and new-regime Jacobins hoped to lure women away from the church by acceding to their entreaties. However, these reallocations, which often involved recoding masculine spaces as feminine, provoked some of the bitterest and most violent community conflicts.

The ruling party's 1938 restructuring emphasized the disciplinary aspects of organizing, reining in the "surplus democracy" generated by revolutionary citizenship. It also reinscribed the importance of labor, civic engagement, and military service as the activities that "properly readied" one to don the clothing of citizenship, mapping these activities onto the party's four branches — the peasant union, a labor confederation, the military, and the popular sector — and informing the relationship between citizenship and subjectivity, as all political identities now passed through its prism. Although the transformation did not take place all at once, efforts to remain outside of this construct increasingly resulted in relegation to a political hinterland beyond the reciprocal obligations of revolutionary citizenship.

Malinchismo *and the Gendering of Citizenship*

Arguably, nothing placed one outside citizenship's boundaries as surely as accusations of disloyalty to the *patria* and the *revolución*, but disloyalty assumed a particularly feminine guise. In the Mexican popular imagination, Hernando Cortés's mistress and translator La Malinche signifies, alternately, the victim of Spanish conquest, the betrayer of indigenous peoples, and the mother of the Mexican "race."[32] As Mexico's own iteration of the woman as victim/betrayer, layered over more universal archetypes such as the virgin/whore, La Malinche retains considerable force as a gender marker in Mexican culture, equating feminine with "fascinated, violated, or seduced."[33] The sons of La Malinche, in Octavio Paz's formulation, are the mestizo people — José Vasconcelos's *raza cósmica*. Born of this unequal marriage of European empires and American colonies, they spring from betrayal, tragedy, and exploitation. As popular groups and political leaders alike wrestled to define the legacy of Mexico's revolution, the question of betrayal hung in the air. Identifying the revolution's betrayers, after all, would go some distance toward defining the significance of the revolution itself.

Who were the Malinches of Mexico's new regime? Were these teachers, organizers, and activists Malinche's daughters, repeating her errors by translating the language of an imperial Mexico City into the lingua franca of Mexican communities, facilitating the co-optation of women's activism?[34] Or were they defiant daughters disdaining their mother's passivity and abjection, exerting control over this unequal encounter by preempting violent domination, only to find that they could not fully escape the world their mothers created? As in the Malinche narrative, women's purported revolutionary betrayal assumed both literal and metaphorical links to sexuality. Concerns that women might be "fascinated, violated, or seduced" by free-loving communists or lecherous clergy permeated public debate. Anticlerical periodicals ran cartoons and essays depicting lascivious priests enticing and even raping young, vulnerable women, while anticommunists accused their rivals of succumbing to the "concupiscence of foreigners."[35]

The faithless La Malinche did not monopolize depictions of femininity, however. *Abnegación* — selflessness, martyrdom, self-sacrifice, an erasure of

self and the negation of one's outward existence—became nearly synonymous with idealized Mexican femininity and motherhood. Factions on all
sides of the "woman question" claimed abnegación to advance their causes,
and arguments often turned on assumptions about women's essentially self-
sacrificing nature. Opponents of women's political rights argued that passive
and subjugated women did not merit the title of citizen, pointing to their
domestic devotion as evidence of their unsuitability to the public realm.
Advocates of women's rights, meanwhile, contended that precisely this sacrificing nature made women ideal citizens. A feminist editorial in the ruling party's newspaper argued, "The emancipation of woman prevails. Her
weapons? Perseverance, study, work, sacrifice, and abnegación, and the principal of all these, her own femininity."[36] A suffragist government employee
reassured her audience in 1938 that the female voter "would not leave off
being a loving mother and an abnegated wife."[37] An internal Communist
Party memo advised local committees to form cells of "the most abnegadas
and active laboring and peasant women of the revolutionary movement."[38]
Members of the Popular Front women's organization contended that precisely their qualities as long-suffering abnegadas made Mexican women the
model of femininity the world over, while an opposing women's group
maintained that it represented the true mujer abnegada.[39] The largest Catholic women's organization defined womanhood as "the paradigm of purity,
abnegación and sublimity."[40]

While the practical implications of this feminine archetype varied among
communities, classes, and ethnic groups and fluctuated over time, the persistent invocation of the mujer abnegada undeniably informed the ways that
ordinary Mexican women constituted themselves as political subjects, simultaneously elevating and subjugating them. "By abnegación we should understand not the acceptance of poor treatment, nor the complacent tolerance of
ruinous vices," explained the schoolteacher and former Communist Elena
Torres. "Woman's constructive abnegación consists in renouncing comforts
in favor of other family members."[41] Often paired with the word "wife" or
"mother," abnegación indicated not only personal characteristics but also
reproductive-labor obligations, and gender disruptions of the term drew
notice. In a congressional debate, for example, a suffrage proponent's repeated references to "compañeras abnegadas" provoked a rival to ask sardonically whether undereducated and apathetic male peasants should be
dubbed *abnegados*.[42]

The common language of abnegación reflected not the stability of gender identities but, rather, mounting anxiety about fragmenting conceptions of femininity. Both advocates and opponents of women's activism overwhelmingly sensed that Mexico stood at the threshold of dramatic changes. Women's revolutionary participation had added new archetypes, including the *soldadera* (camp follower) and the *soldada* (armed combatant), to La Malinche and *la madre* (mother) *abnegada* as available models of feminine identity, and the rise of *la chica moderna* (modern girl) and *la mujer nueva* (new woman) sparked controversy about the entire postrevolutionary modernization project.[43]

Women's intrusion into activities normally construed as masculine, such as wage labor, military engagement, and political machinations, provoked attacks against the instability of gender roles. Referring to the nefarious influence of "North American *flapperismo*," one editorialist lamented that the "most disconcerting effect that feminism produces through the current customs, styles, and manners is to feminize the masculine mentality. It can almost be said that today man thinks in the feminine. . . . Today, social ideas have no foundation in the power of rough, strong, deep, and transcendent virility. Everything is softness, fear, suspicion, and dread. There is a growing tendency to group together and find strength in numbers, to think socially and develop overly sentimental theories."[44] Women activists faced accusations not only of feminizing the masculine but also of masculinizing the feminine. Questioning the demands of abnegación quickly earned one the unfeminine label *marimacho*, a tomboy of dubious sexuality (dyke or butch in more contemporary parlance), as distinct from a "genuine" woman. Always used in the masculine form to highlight the gender subversion, the suffragist or feminist marimacho stood as an unmistakable counterpoint to the madre abnegada in depictions of women's activism.

The latter image proved far more palatable to most men and women alike; the former not only challenged traditional family formations and patriarchal control but also devalued time-honored ideas about femininity and women's social roles. Even the most radical women activists remained reluctant to forgo the legitimacy and recognition that accompanied this feminine ideal. However, while maternalist strategies promised an expedient route to political and economic opportunities, they also reinforced the expectation that "women's interests" remained indistinguishable from those of their families and communities. The persistent conflation of women and children in welfare policies, labor law, and public discourse perpetuated this conviction, compelling activists to invoke maternal obligation when formulating programs and leading even some public officials to note the pitfalls of maternalist strategies. The secretary of public assistance boasted in a 1939 Mother's Day pamphlet that "the Mexican mother synthesizes the highest virtues," but he cautioned against "allowing her innate resignation to convert her into a slave or her abnegación to make her endure the indifference with which she is treated on repeated occasions."[45]

Despite the prevalence of abnegación and maternalism, the endless disputes that fractured women's congresses and the sheer proliferation of women's organizations during the 1920s and '30s — from mothers' clubs, consumption cooperatives, and temperance leagues to women-only militia, motorcycle clubs, and labor unions — testify to the impossibility of establishing a common conception of womanhood. As the feminist theorist Judith Butler observes, efforts to "establish a normative foundation for what ought properly to be included in the description of women would be only and always to produce a new site of political contest. That foundation would settle nothing, but would of necessity founder on its own authoritarian ruse."[46] For Butler, this "permanent openness and resignifiability" of identity constitutes the democratic promise of feminist politics, the "ungrounded ground of feminist theory." However, activists on the ground in postrevolutionary Mexico, even those who welcomed a challenge to the "authoritarian ruse" of abnegación, struggled to fix a coherent feminine identity for the purposes of political interventions.[47]

Conflicts inevitably arose over what constituted something as subjective and intangible as "femininity." Even an identity as seemingly fixed and biological as motherhood varied significantly in its content between urban and rural women and wage earners and housewives, and across generational and cultural divides. Groups petitioned *as women* for items ranging from weapons to maternity clinics. Despite their efforts at unity, activists promoted heterodox gender ideologies, drawing selectively from images of modernist North American flapperismo or the traditional Mexican abnegación to define themselves as political subjects. These divisions often manifested themselves rhetorically as groups varied their names to reflect agendas and affiliations. The simple choice among the nearly synonymous adjectives *femenino* (feminine), *feminista* (feminist), and the more neutral *femenil* (women's) indicated orientation within the emerging debates over gender and politics.

Masculinity remained no less contested. Prerevolutionary dissonances persisted between elite and popular conceptions of masculinity and among various ethnic expressions of masculinity, remaining unresolved after the revolution.[48] During the 1917 Constitutional Congress and after, lawmakers deliberated over how to eliminate Mexico's "barbaric" masculine traditions, including cockfighting, pulque drinking, and wife beating. Like government efforts to discourage pious femininity by offering women alternatives to the church as spaces of sociability, officials promoted "cultural Saturdays" and non-blood sports such as baseball and basketball to encourage a more modern and refined (read "Anglo-European") masculinity. By the 1930s, bureaucratic and professional stature had begun to overtake military prowess as the hallmark of revolutionary masculinity, and professional statesmen replaced revolutionary generals as the country's political leaders.

This semantic and cultural instability served as a backdrop for the articulation between the unstable ideologies of gender and citizenship. Claiming revolutionary citizenship required women activists on the one hand to blunt accusations of malinchista disloyalty — to the church, the Communist Party, even placing one's family above the revolution — and on the other to fit themselves into the prevailing masculinist ideology of citizenship by appropriating and reshaping its terms. Although the 1917 Constitution did not explicitly exclude women from full citizenship rights, political practice did. Policymakers deliberated about the nationality of Mexican women who married foreigners, about whether female lawyers could serve as notaries, and, most prominently, about whether women could vote and hold public office. The 1917 Law of Family Relations gave women more control within their households but sparked conservative resistance. One legal scholar, referring to the law as a "destructive virus of the first order," saw it as another symptom of U.S. imperialism. "The growing feminism that is palpable to everyone is Yankee feminism; the rudeness and insolence of a certain part of the proletariat are also Yankee; the khakis and cowboy hats of the army demonstrate the sartorial impulses from the other side of the Bravo," he elaborated, underscoring the connections many conservatives made among different manifestations of social and cultural instability. "Our national way of life is evaporating and being substituted by a very dubious culture and morality, with the aggravation that we perhaps imitate the defects without the strengths."[49] Article 2 of the 1928 Civil Code stated bluntly that "juridical capacity is equal for men and women; the woman cannot be subjected, by reason of her sex, to any restriction in the acquisition and exercise of her civil rights."[50] Yet the Civil Code also allowed husbands to prevent their wives from working outside the home if it interfered with their "mission" of directing and caring for the household.

Mexican women activists, like their counterparts throughout the world, disagreed over whether and how to deploy notions of gender difference with regard to citizenship. Within the gendered division of cultural labor, women — particularly rural, indigenous women, wrapped in colorful *huipiles* (indigenous dress) and grinding corn on the traditional stone *metates* — embodied a bona fide *mexicanidad* that would seem to entitle them to revolutionary citizenship.[51] Although they faced commonplace representations as benighted peasants and Indians, rural women frequently claimed an "authentic" Mexican femininity, distinguishing themselves from the bobbed-hair flappers of the urban middle class. Further, women throughout Mexico raised the banner of feminine morality to argue that they would sanitize Mexico's notoriously dirty politics. Policymakers and public intellectuals celebrated Mexican feminine domesticity as part of the Mexican national patrimony, a treasure to be protected from the threat of foreign ideas. "From the moral perspective, the Mexican home is moral by tradition," boasted one ruling-party official. "Stability, vitality, and even maternal sacrifices are indisputable characteristics of the Mexican home, placing it above nearly all other homes in the world."[52] Cárdenas's populist commitment to *indigenismo* (celebration of indigenous cultures) and ethical commitment to political transparency seemed to give these claims considerable weight.

However, rather than trying to secure revolutionary citizenship through claims of gender difference, the more common strategy was to destabilize the exclusively masculine nature of its three cornerstones: military service, labor, and civic engagement. Much like their counterparts in postrevolutionary France, women activists in Mexico practiced citizenship through activities that, as the French historians Darline Gay Levy and Harriet B. Applewhite explain, "identified [them] as members of a sovereign body politic — *citoyennes* notwithstanding their exclusion from codified political rights of citizenship."[53] Mexican women activists sought to recode the cultural meanings of women's labor and community involvement, reframing them not as private, particular matters that left women unsuited for citizenship but, rather, as public, civic duties that demonstrated their political capacity. Such efforts pressed against the boundaries of revolutionary citizenship, expanding its foundation to support a broad range of women's customary activities.

Women activists also laid claim to military service, the most conspicuously masculine practice of citizenship, not only underscoring their widespread presence in the revolutionary armies but also creating networks of women's leagues intended to have the same socializing function as men's compulsory military service.[54] Organizations such as the Ejército de Mujeres Campesinas (Army of Rural Women) adopted military rhetoric, and members of a Michoacán Women's Resistance League prefaced their political demands by emphasizing that they "have fought in the ranks of the Revolution in the purest sense of the word."[55] The Confederation of Revolutionary Women asserted that "in no way should the feminine element be left on the margin in matters where the defense of the Patria are concerned, since, apart from underestimating her valuable qualities of sacrifice, abnegación, and ability, she would be left deserted by her lack of preparation." The group went on to call for women's compulsory military service, including firearms training.[56] Women who had served as armed combatants made claims as *veteranas*, and, particularly after the PRM's formation, women also demanded benefits as the wives, widows, and orphans of revolutionary veterans, highlighting the fluidity between roles of combatants and noncombatants during the revolution's armed phase.[57]

Women activists similarly highlighted their participation in congresses and "revolutionary" political organizations and parties to showcase their capacity for civic engagement, often casting this engagement as constitutive of, rather than merely incidental to, revolutionary citizenship. As one former militant recalled, "The women's leagues were the vanguard of the revolution, the custodians of the revolutionary process."[58] Although far more likely to engage in the informal politicking of patron-client relationships, women activists emphasized their involvement in "modern" political entities that would form the backbone of a more transparent, progressive, and democratic regime. The collaboration between activists and functionaries in these endeavors underscores both policymakers' perceived exigency to "prepare" women for citizenship and activists' understanding that their cooperation would secure political recognition.

Finally, women raised questions about what constituted "labor." Although many activists pointed to women's participation in wage labor, the vast majority of women spent most of their time performing the unremunerated household labor — or reproductive labor — on which Mexico's economic modernization depended. Juridically, civil codes and labor laws reinforced the importance of women's domestic labor, prohibiting wives from working outside the home without their husbands' permission and making women's primary labor responsibility to their families. When working-class women campaigned to secure membership in unions and "resistance" groups without their husbands' consent, middle-class critics dubbed the campaign "Bolshevik" and "smelling of suffragism," arguing that woman "as queen of the household should always be subject to the dispositions of her husband, sometimes out of affection and other times out of obedience to the head of the household."[59]

The postrevolutionary regime's vision, emphasizing commodity rather than subsistence production, demanded both a clear public-private divide and an active reproductive labor force. The ideal of feminine domesticity provided more than just stability and continuity amid rapid social change; it promised the everyday labor required to reproduce Mexico's modern labor force. Within prevailing gender codes, female wage earners "passed" in manly territory rather than subverted the distinction between the gendered spheres of productive and reproductive labor. Even the most progressive commentators contended that women must transform themselves from "factors of consumption" into "factors of production" to fashion the "more constant, more disinterested" modern woman.[60] In this formulation, women could transgress the boundaries of traditional womanhood, but labor traditionally marked as feminine remained either invisible or an impediment to political consciousness.

Rank-and-file members of women's organizations saw matters quite differently. To them, recognition of their reproductive labor — and the new regime's rhetorical commitment to improve its conditions — constituted the revolution's realization. Opportunities to secure child care, health clinics, and especially mechanized corn mills generated considerable enthusiasm, particularly among rural women; for officials and campesinas alike, corn mills became feminine emancipation. A *corrido* (ballad) printed in the Public Education Ministry's magazine called on women to abandon the "slavery" of the metate. "The metate is more jealous than your husband Miguel," the lyrics intoned, "after giving you no rest, it wants you to dream of it."[61] Ordinary women and government agents alike cast emancipation from slavery to the metate as a precondition for inhabiting revolutionary citizenship. Placing reproductive labor on par with industrial and agricultural labor as a foundation for citizenship claims carried truly revolutionary implications not only in legitimating women as revolutionary citizens but also in securing the benefits and protections enjoyed by other (paid) workers. Efforts to redefine "labor," therefore, sought more than an abstract notion of revolutionary affirmation; they sought the material and political gains that the new regime promised Mexico's "producing classes."

Cardenismo and the Co-optation of Revolutionary Citizenship

Considering the multifaceted, often creative ways women claimed revolutionary citizenship raises anew the nagging question of why this period of extraordinary mobilization within the women's movement also witnessed its co-optation, its blunting through absorption into the ruling party's machinery. As diverse groups of women increasingly organized *as women*, vocally demanding political and labor rights, welfare provision, and protection of religious freedom, officials sought to manage this activism as they did other popular mobilizations. Given the pace of social change in Mexico and abroad, Cárdenas most likely saw the writing on the wall for issues such as women's suffrage and religious tolerance and wanted the federal government to control the terms of those reforms. The Cárdenas government — in many ways the watershed between revolutionary political chaos and postrevolutionary regime consolidation — endeavored to fashion a hegemonic project that would incorporate competing factions under a unified, nationalist agenda.

In Ernesto Laclau's and Chantal Mouffe's formulation, hegemony emerges "precisely in a context dominated by the experience of fragmentation and by the indeterminacy of the articulations between different struggles and subject positions," and it fashions "chains of equivalence" to link subordinated groups, creating an internal frontier within a society.[62] The postrevolutionary regime, confronting fragmentation and indeterminacy, sought to connect popular groups together in a common project — overshadowing political rivalries, regional identities, religious convictions, sexual difference, and ethnic distinctions — to create a frontier between the "revolutionary" and the "antirevolutionary" or "counterrevolutionary."[63] But the creation of this frontier raised the stakes of demonstrating one's loyalty and of vanquishing Malinchismo.

The hegemonic effort presented women activists with both an opportunity and a hazard. Over the course of the 1920s and '30s, the postrevolutionary government's vast array of modernization and reform programs came to rely on women's support to transform Mexico into a more efficient and productive society. Mothers would decide whether or not to send their children to the new federal schools. Within their homes, they could choose to cultivate what the regime dubbed modern values of efficiency, progress, and independence or, conversely, so-called traditional values of piety, patronage, and conservatism. "Women's support, both as students and as mothers, was decisive in the rural organizers' efforts," explains the historian Alicia Civera Cerecedo. "In some pueblos and *rancherías* (settlements), the women refused even to talk to the agents. . . . To win over the women meant to enter the community, where they filled a fundamental role not only as those responsible for child-rearing but also as the nucleus of unity."[64] As Cárdenas himself often pointed out, women shaped future citizens. "Women's participation in the social struggle," he asserted, "is indispensable to making the Revolution follow its ascendant trajectory with new generations."[65]

Defining "chains of equivalence," however, also called the question of how secular women activists would resolve the relentless tensions within the concept of revolutionary citizenship. They struggled to demonstrate mobilization and consciousness on the one hand but loyalty and discipline on the other. They drew on the assertively internationalist ideologies of feminism and communism but invoked revolutionary nationalism and patriotic commitment. With the ascendancy of historical materialism, they emphasized women's participation in the "productive" labor force but also celebrated their maternal *abnegación* and morality. Amid far-reaching modernization efforts by state agencies and popular organizations, women simultaneously situated themselves as agents of progressive change and embodiments of cultural traditions.

To understand how women managed these tensions, this book follows the wrangling over postrevolutionary women's organizing — and, by extension, over the legacy of the revolution itself — during the period of "long Cardenismo," stretching from Cárdenas's 1928 investiture as Michoacán's governor until the 1940 inauguration of his successor, Avila Camacho, who abandoned radical politics and purged Communists from government and public education. While hewing closely to a conventional time line, this study is not strictly chronological. Other scholars have established the basic narrative of the Cárdenas presidency, and no single, unified thread would capture the diverse experiences recounted here.[66] Research beyond Mexico City reveals the jerky, stuttering, uneven progress of provincial women's organizing, and the standard periodization falls apart in places where major events in the center — such as the ruling party's restructuring or the battle over women's suffrage — mattered little in local politics. Moreover, women's activism developed in a nonlinear fashion, responding to shifts in the local political climate and to opportunities and obstacles in the realm of women's rights, rather than on a direct course of constant gains. Defeats and triumphs often looked strikingly similar, making them difficult to distinguish from one another. A narrative focusing too explicitly on the end—the defeat of the women's suffrage campaign and the co-optation of a vibrant women's movement—would ignore the small and large victories and their legacy for women's organizing.

Alternating between national perspectives and regional case studies, the chapters follow a loosely chronological sequence, although the case studies all include material covering the entire period. Rather than ethnohistorical vignettes or close social histories, these local studies illuminate the dynamic nature of revolutionary citizenship—the contingent, inhabited, and gendered aspects that made it a practice and a tool rather than simply a juridical structure of exclusion. The first chapter considers the roots of Mexico's national women's movement, beginning with the First Feminist Congress in 1916 in Yucatán and ending with the national women's congresses of the early 1930s, which exposed fault lines within activist circles and disagreements about not only ideology and tactics but also the very meanings of womanhood. The second chapter turns to Michoacán and the enduring imprint of conflicts between secular and religious radicals. The third chapter examines who populated the women's movement by the 1930s, giving particular attention to schoolteachers and Popular Front activists who strove to unite disparate factions of women's organizing. Chapter 4 investigates the labor mobilizations in the Comarca Lagunera, where, much in the way that religious violence defined women's organizing in Michoacán, labor conflicts did the same, creating opportunities for women's activism while closely defining its terms. Chapter 5 explores the militant but ultimately unsuccessful suffrage campaign, during which the ruling party transformed the meaning and practice of voting with its corporatist reorganization and eclipsed the suffrage battle with its internal political disputes. The final chapter, on Yucatán, considers how dramatic shifts in political climate and an often combative relationship between local and federal government agencies challenged activists' efforts to navigate the difficult and unpredictable political terrain, underscoring the contingencies of citizenship.

The fates of Concha Michel's Santa Bárbara invasion and the 1937 suffrage amendment demonstrate the stakes of the push and pull between popular efforts to exercise revolutionary citizenship and state efforts to contain "surplus democracy." Michel and her supporters practiced revolutionary citizenship—contingent, inhabited, and gendered—in both discourse and action, taking advantage of a particularly propitious opening and making demands squarely in line with official priorities. Having left the Communist

Party but remaining somewhat aloof from the ruling party, Michel lacked the institutional allies who would have not only given her greater leverage but also rendered her more legible within the postrevolutionary political landscape.[67] However, despite Calles's dismissal—using the well-practiced technique of simultaneously undermining and negotiating with popular organizations—the Cárdenas administration honored the group's request eighteen months later but changed the terms and conditions. In July 1937, Cárdenas's mentor, the radical elder statesman Francisco Múgica, endorsed the project and called on Cárdenas to support it via the bureaucratic structures of the Agrarian, Education, and Indigenous Affairs departments. Indicating that the efforts resulted from "the impulses of your doctrine and the program that the Agrarian Department developed in the Comarca Lagunera," Múgica informed Cárdenas, "I think you would find it very satisfying to see the fruits of the actions you initiated in [the Comarca Lagunera]; the enthusiasm of these women merits your respectable attention."[68] By this time, Michel served as the Mexican Peasant Confederation's "women's action" secretary, demonstrating her party loyalty and capacity for political discipline.

Múgica's imprimatur and Michel's new status transformed the project from one of rebellion that fell outside the boundary of legitimate, legible political activity, channeling it through structures of personal and bureaucratic patronage and discourses of regime loyalty. Like the successful suffrage amendment of the 1950s, which effaced its ties to the radical suffrage movement of the 1930s, Múgica's involvement and the time lapse after the Santa Bárbara incident separated the school's creation from the mobilization that inspired it, linking it instead to the paternalist wisdom of "the Revolution," as embodied in men like Cárdenas and Múgica. The new genealogy led back not to the campesinas at Santa Bárbara in January 1935 but, rather, to Cárdenas and the Agrarian Department's employees in the Comarca Lagunera in October 1936, itself an appropriation of a radical popular mobilization. Such a revision carried political implications, narrowing the boundaries of revolutionary citizenship and undermining women's claims to it.

ONE

"A Right to Struggle":
Revolutionary Citizenship and the
Birth of Mexican Feminism

The guns of the Mexican revolution had not yet fallen silent when women activists began agitating for expanded rights in the wake of the conflict. Indeed, women issued demands for expanded social, economic, and political rights almost immediately after Porfirio Díaz fled Mexico City.[1] The upheaval allowed society's "extras" — most notably, peasants, wage laborers, indigenous groups, and women — to land speaking parts in Mexico's political theater. In the years following the revolution's armed phase, women's activism pursued a trajectory similar to that of the revolution itself. The revolutionary leadership traced a loosely dialectical arc from the reformist Francisco Madero period to the more radical Zapatista/Villista period to the synthetic Constitutionalists, who bore the imprint of both antecedents. Similarly, the burgeoning women's movement had an ebb and flow both distinctly its own and inevitably informed by concomitant developments in postrevolutionary politics. A small but vocal and dynamic women's movement developed among liberal reformers and expanded to include more women from a broader spectrum of Mexican society, generating political tensions analogous to those within the revolutionary leadership. Women's organizing also paralleled the revolution geographically, shifting from localized and specific mobilizations to a national movement that endeavored to represent women from throughout the republic.

citizen ship [handwritten margin note]

Early feminist organizing—from the 1916 First Feminist Congress in Yucatán to the 1931 proposal to grant women suffrage rights—coincided with broader efforts to define revolutionary citizenship, linking it in particular with "productive" labor and military service. Women activists struggled among themselves and with political leaders over how women should define a space within this gendered notion of citizenship. Should they strive to create a place for the citizen-mother, or should they highlight women's service as soldiers and laborers? Two important developments informed these debates. First, the outbreak of religious violence in the center-west— the 1926–29 antigovernment Cristero Rebellion—heightened policymakers' concerns about women's presumed "fanaticism." Second, the Communist Party, formed in 1919, stepped up its organizing among women but rarely acknowledged gendered experiences of inequality, instead mobilizing women as workers or peasants. By the early 1930s, a national women's movement had developed that, while still fragmented and contentious, increasingly linked its strategies to these masculinized conceptions of revolutionary citizenship, abandoning early efforts to address gender-specific issues of women's sexuality, birth control, and unpaid reproductive labor. Revolutionary citizenship, it seemed, demanded "neutrality" of both locality and identity, requiring women to cast their agendas as benefiting patria and revolution rather than community, family, or themselves.

Imagining Community: The 1916 First Feminist Congress

The 1916 First Feminist Congress, gathering more than seven hundred women in Mérida, Yucatán, to debate political rights, gender roles, education, and prostitution, exemplified many of the tensions that characterized postrevolutionary women's activism and popular organizing more generally.[2] The congress occurred in a city noted for its regional orientation and historic animosity toward Mexico City's centralizing efforts, but it relied on the sponsorship of Salvador Alvarado (1915–18), the socialist governor imposed by the Constitutionalists.[3] Strategic and programmatic discussions sparked heated disputes about the meanings and duties of womanhood, the advisability of cooperating with men's organizations, and women's appropriate roles in political life. Despite egalitarian rhetoric, the congress remained under the control of relatively privileged, urban women—including a preponderance of schoolteachers, since registration required a primary-school education—who claimed to speak for the subaltern majority. And, in a strategy developed more fully by the 1930s, Alvarado sought both to mobilize and to direct women through congresses and women's leagues.

The very fact of holding an explicitly "feminist" congress carved out a new space within the Constitutionalist project, which had emerged as the dominant force within Mexico's civil war.[4] The feminist community remained ill-defined and divided—no unified "feminist perspective" grew out of the proceedings—but the congress's official sponsorship legitimated a political feminism that moved beyond individual commentary on juridical and social inequalities, instead making collective, public interventions to redefine women's roles. The congress, although contentious, directed from above, and limited in its aims, launched a transition among women activists from commentary to activism, participating in Mexico's emergent political culture of organizing.

Alvarado dictated the congress's principal themes and objectives, adopting a "revolutionary" approach to women's issues, but it remained a revolution not only "from without" but also from above.[5] The agenda, revealing its socialist-materialist roots, stressed the importance of labor experience and a strong state in "transforming" and "manumitting" women. The congress galvanized public debate, leading the newspaper *La Voz de la Revolución* to conduct a survey about the congress and its impact.[6] Many respondents, apparently handpicked by Yucatán's Department of Public Education, underscored the modernizing influences of "the progress of science," "the tendency toward improvement and liberty," the "fruits of the Revolution," and "a great step on the road toward social progress." The survey also inquired why women remained "a factor of consumption and not of production in society." Of eight respondents, the three women described women's "lack of preparation to earn their daily bread" and "inability to support [themselves] or to produce anything useful for society." Two of the five men, meanwhile, took issue with the question's premise. Pointing to women's child rearing, management of household budgets, and performance of "conjugal duties," they argued that it was "unjust to say that women are only good for spending money" and that "in general, the Yucatecan woman, especially the married woman, honorably fulfills the social law of labor." This reasoning highlights an important revolutionary legacy, especially in socialist Yucatán: the "social law of labor" held that labor—above property or literacy or status—made one a rights-bearing citizen. In this context, the matter of whether women's household labor constituted consumption or production took on new import.

This question of women's "productive" role persisted through the 1920s and '30s, indicating not only modernist and socialist emphases on labor and productivity but also feminist concerns with women's traditional and emerging economic roles. Policymakers, activists, and public intellectuals recognized the issue's centrality within larger discussions about women's rights and Mexico's gender order. In a front-page newspaper interview, Consuelo Zavala, an organizer of the congress, dubbed herself a "feminist" and proclaimed, "I think that the modern woman has a right to struggle, to be strong, to learn how to support herself without assistance from men in the hard struggles of life."[7] Although they challenge heteronormative assumptions of gender complementarity, such assertions reinscribed the notion that women required "assistance" from men but that men could countenance the "hard struggles of life" without women. In other words, women's reproductive labor remained invisible and dispensable within this formulation.

Much like subsequent women's congresses, the Mérida conference exposed rather than bridged the fault lines within this emergent feminist community. One of the congress's most notorious disputes exploded in response to an essay submitted by Hermila Galindo de Topete, personal secretary of the Constitutionalist leader Venustiano Carranza and an adamant women's suffrage advocate at the following year's constitutional congress.[8] A leading activist and editor of a weekly feminist magazine, *La Mujer Moderna*, Galindo viewed the Constitutionalist cause as the surest avenue to women's emancipation, describing feminism as an effort "to awaken woman to be a useful influence in her Patria, her town, and herself, and to help consolidate the government, giving the world an example of dedication to a culture of civilization and human rights proclaimed and sustained by the most noble and most just of the revolutions in Mexico."[9] She embodied a prominent *national* figure linking Yucatecan feminism and its congress to the consolidation of Constitutionalist power.

Galindo delivered more than a Constitutionalist allegiance, however; she interjected ideas about gender and sexuality that stood apart from revolutionary struggles over land and political succession. She shocked conference attendees with her statement that "the sexual instinct prevails in woman in such a way and with such irresistible resources that no hypocritical artifice can destroy, modify, or restrain it." A truly revolutionary society, therefore, would acknowledge and even embrace women's sexuality, offering universal education in human physiology and anatomy to enable girls and young women to avoid pregnancy. She also lambasted the sexual double standard that allowed men to proclaim their sexual conquests "with the majestic tone used by a revolutionary leader relating the capture of a plaza," while the women involved in these same encounters found themselves "relegated to disgrace, cut off from their futures, and dragged into desperation, misery, insanity, and suicide." Amid protests from the audience, Galindo's address described the growing number of women engaged in prostitution and asserted that men of "elastic conscience" could sit at the best tables and wear gentlemen's finery notwithstanding their "criminal and disgusting exploitation" of fallen women. More shameful still, foreigners "came to this land to make a real industry of the Mexican woman, taking advantage of her abnegation and ignorance."[10]

Coming from Mexico City and passing through several levels of mediation, Galindo's ideas provoked a particularly hostile reception. She had not consulted any local congress organizers, and, since the organizing committee had not issued the invitation and "did not even know her," its members relegated the address to a time outside the official program, proposing later to drop it entirely.[11] In the end, a male functionary from Yucatán's Department of Public Education read Galindo's essay aloud before the congress's official inauguration. Congress organizers demonstrated more concern about showcasing local leadership than the essay's contents, but the offending address precipitated disputes over whether it should appear in the congress's published proceedings.

Galindo's controversial ideas and Alvarado's hand in shaping the congress's agenda provided fodder for those who viewed feminism as an imported ideology contrary to Yucatecan regional identity. One congress organizer referred to an "invasion of modern feminism," and, although participants included native Yucatecas who remained prominent activists for the next quarter-century, the congress retained an imported flavor.[12] However, Galindo's essay also validated women who welcomed her ideas. Another participant, Candelaria Ruz, ardently endorsed Galindo's address and accused the congress organizers of provoking protests and scheming to make them appear spontaneous. Ruz's intervention generated "strenuous applause among the students occupying the higher rows," indicating that the controversy had generational as well as regional expressions.

The furor surrounding Galindo's essay highlights the instability of gender identities as the revolution contributed to the sense that dramatic social change was afoot.[13] Congress organizers and participants all came from *cabeceras* (head towns) or from Mérida itself and included no identifiably indigenous women, fostering a discussion that excluded the majority of Yucatecas. Yet even with such narrow participation, disagreements abounded regarding the contents of "femininity," as women adopted elements of seemingly divergent gender ideologies. Mercedes Betancourt de Albertos chastised the students in the galleries for dismissing the importance of women's modesty but went on to argue that, in postrevolutionary Mexico, "the weak woman will disappear and the strong, heroic woman will appear, knowing how to struggle in life. . . . Woman should be woman, but this word should not indicate weakness but rather a poem of love, abnegation, labor, strength, and patriotism."[14] The "impassioned" Ana María Espinosa, meanwhile, cautioned against tying women's rights and opportunities to motherhood, explaining that "not only mothers would play an important role in modern societies."[15]

These competing constructions of femininity carried political as well as social consequences. Gesturing toward the links between "productive" labor and revolutionary citizenship, the Education Department's survey followed its question about why women remained consumers with one about whether they should vote in municipal elections, indicating that a victorious revolution and successful consolidation of the regime made women's suffrage possible. However, the coming debates over women's citizenship rights would turn this logic on its head. By the following year, it had become clear that lawmakers viewed women's suffrage not as a sign of the revolution's triumph but as a threat to its future.

Masculine Citizenship: The 1917 Constitutional Congress

As they would repeatedly over the coming decades, lawmakers danced carefully, if somewhat awkwardly, around the thorny question of women's suffrage. Participants in the 1917 Consitutional Congress remained divided between moderates, who favored Carranza's program of a strong presidency and electoral reforms, and radicals, who called for more sweeping changes in education policy, land reform, and labor law. However, this divide often blurred when debates ranged outside these three issues.[16] If Galindo and the Yucatecan feminists saw room to destabilize gender codes, the constitutional deliberations would have disheartened them. Deploying the florid, metaphor-laden language of lawmakers, the constitution's authors convening in Querétaro invoked a monolithic femininity that signified physical, moral, and spiritual weakness. Participants warned each other not to "cry like a woman" or to "tremble like women."[17] Deliberations about laws affecting women focused on protective measures such as whether to bar women and children from working overtime and night shifts, or whether the crimes of rape and seduction should merit the death penalty. Even halfhearted efforts to engage women's concerns provoked derision. When one lawmaker pointed out that "many women work at night," his comment met with snickers from his peers and references to prostitutes.[18]

The Constitutional Congress came closest to deliberating women's citizenship status during discussions about the nationality of Mexican women who married foreigners.[19] Concerns centered on the nationality of children born from such a union rather than the women's status, since the constitution would bar foreigners' sons from holding public office.[20] Only Francisco Múgica, who would champion women's suffrage rights in the 1930s, questioned the provision's implications for women. Although "naturally subordinated" to men, who enjoyed greater representation before the law, he averred, "The woman would naturally have a more substantial part in children's formation than the man, and yet she has no right to pass down her nationality. This commits a great injustice, and we do not want this injustice in the Constitution because that is, señores, the reason we are reforming it."[21]

When the Congress turned its attention to the citizenship articles, women received scant consideration. Letters regarding women's rights from Galindo and Deputy S. González Torres passed to the committee on constitutional reforms without being read into the record, and the committee's report examining Articles 34–37 concentrated on whether to restrict suffrage through literacy requirements.[22] The committee recommended against restrictions, which, it argued, ran counter to a central tenet of the revolution. "If the revolution proposed to restrict the vote," the committee's report contended, "its enemies could accuse it of abandoning one of its principles, and it would be extremely dangerous to allow our enemies these weapons."[23]

Despite assertions of "effective suffrage," the report rejects women's suffrage in the paragraph that follows this sentence, indicating an essentialized and static conception of womanhood and establishing the parameters within which the struggle over women's citizenship would unfold in the coming decades. "The fact that some exceptional women have the necessary qualities for the satisfactory exercise of political rights," the committee stated, "does not justify the conclusion that these rights should be granted to women as a class. The difficulty of selection authorizes the denial." Notwithstanding lofty liberal rhetoric, the "satisfactory exercise of political rights" transparently entailed supporting the new government. Women, unlike men, could be understood "as a class" and, as the report continued, the "differences between the sexes" determined their levels of political involvement. While men unprepared for suffrage would be culled out by a clause that revoked suffrage rights from those who failed to exercise them, this restriction would not prove adequate with regard to women. As evidence of this assertion, the committee maintained that women's activities rested "within the domestic circle of the home," making their interests indistinguishable from those of their male family members. Disaggregating those interests threatened to "break up the family unit."

Ignoring women's participation in revolutionary combat, lawmakers assumed that the other critical difference between, for example, illiterate men (who would be allowed to vote) and women (who would not) lay in the fear that men might take up arms. As further confirmation that women did not need or even desire voting rights, the committee pointed to the "absence of any collective movement in this direction." This last argument underscored the fact that political rights derived not from nature or justice but from necessity. "Political rights are not based on human nature," the committee explained, "but in the State's regulatory function, in the functions that it should exercise to maintain the coexistence of the natural rights of all. Under the present conditions in Mexican society, there is no indication of the need to concede women the vote." These two justifications—that women remained essentially ill-suited for politics and that denying women's suffrage did not threaten the social peace—carried the committee's argument.

The ensuing discussions, however, belied the certainty of essential womanhood, family unity, and an absence of mobilization. In the debate about suffrage restrictions, concerns about political appeals to "sentimentalism" referred not to women's susceptibility to clerical influences but to the sway of "political agitators" over inadequately prepared men.[24] Women's adherence to the "domestic circle" rested more on an imagined domesticity than on the postrevolutionary Mexican reality, which, particularly during and after the civil war, included substantial numbers of female-headed households, women working in both the formal and informal sectors, and a wide variety of family structures. Félix F. Palavicini, editor of *El Universal* and a conservative from Tabasco, broached the question of what might happen if women's presumed political apathy gave way to mobilization. The radical Luis G. Monzón responded vaguely that the committee had declined to vote on the question "for reasons of tradition" and provoked laughter by indicating that Palavicini could "come to the defense of the feminine vote."

Palavicini had no such intentions, however. He simply pointed out that the generic noun ciudadanos, or citizens, did not explicitly exclude women. "I was asking the Committee to clarify women's condition," he explained, "and whether we are in danger if they organize to vote and be voted on." Monzón protested again, "We did not consider that women would also have the vote."[25]

In a subsequent intervention, Monzón eliminated any ambiguity in the committee's intentions. Responding to suggested literacy restrictions, Monzón called on "all the *señores diputados* (señores deputies) of a truly democratic impulse, all who felt a truly revolutionary soul beating within their chests" to confer suffrage rights on the *masas masculinas* (masculine masses). He went on to explain that Madero's revolutionary rallying cry of "Effective suffrage, no reelection!" had galvanized Mexican men. "From the mines, the workshops, the fields, the cities, the villages, the one-mule towns [*villorrios*], the mountains, and the valleys, surged thousands and thousands of patriots, strong and virile men, for the most part illiterate, who flew to the battlefields to offer their lives for effective suffrage."[26] Thus, to justify unrestricted *male* suffrage, Monzón explicitly effaced from his account the women who had served the revolutionary armies as battlefield provisioners and in armed combat, leaving aside all those who remained home to replace men's labor in fields and factories.

The rationalization for denying women's suffrage proved porous. Granting unrestricted male suffrage undermined the notion that literacy or "civic preparation" served as a litmus test. Moderates' concerns that "human nature" made people susceptible to the "sentimentality" of political appeals rendered gender-neutral an attribute often reserved for women and lachrymose men. Granting citizenship rights as a reward for military service fell within Mexican tradition but begged the question of how to reward women who joined revolutionary armies. Although no national campaign for women's suffrage existed in 1917, Palavicini's query about the possibility of such a movement recognized that history, not "nature," had forestalled such a development. The increasing radicalism of the U.S. suffrage movement made Palavicini's question quite relevant.[27] Perhaps Monzón's gesture toward "tradition" and the committee's concern for the "family unit" offer more insight, indicating the need for continuity amid dramatic social change.[28] The reinscription of gender hierarchy into the 1917 Constitution resulted not, as some scholars would have it, from an oversight on the convention's part but, instead, from a self-conscious effort to ward off the changes augured by the 1916 Feminist Congress.[29] Thus, even as the Constitution's authors found no stable or reliable characterization of "women" that validated their position, they passively but self-consciously upheld the women's exclusion from full citizenship.

The 1917 Constitution did contain important labor rights for women, including guarantees of equal pay for equal work, paid maternity leave, and lactation breaks. Although most often honored in the breach, such guarantees proved useful. Not six months after the congress concluded, women employees of the Secretariat of War and the Navy brandished the Constitution's Article 123 when Undersecretary Agustín Castro attempted to replace them with men, who ostensibly possessed superior "discipline and performance." In their impassioned plea to the Chamber of Deputies, the employees resorted to the same gendered imagery that lawmakers had used at the Constitutional Congress. After pointing out that they also had families to support, the employees argued, "The revolution, among its many promises, made a solemn vow to help the weak, and . . . it occurs to us to ask whether by your lofty criterion there is anything weaker than a woman . . . since our fears and the social prejudices have left us only the sewing machine and domestic service as resources for a livelihood."[30] Such anthropomorphizing appeals to revolutionary patriarchy bolstered prevailing gender codes even while protecting women's rights.

If the Constitutional Congress exposed anxieties about "preserving" feminine domesticity, it also demonstrated a desire to define the contours of acceptable masculinity. Debates over whether to abolish the vicious habits of alcohol consumption, gambling, and drug use revealed that congress participants distinguished their masculinity from that of the men they claimed to lead.[31] The Constitutionalist revolution, prohibitionists explained, had the "noble duty of awaking the light in all Mexicans who are delayed in civilization" and "making them understand that men could be neither great nor happy without unwavering resolve to do good." Efforts to promote physical wellness and to "develop men's minds and will" would be undermined if the "temple of vice" continued to be "not only tolerated but protected." Although these exhortations might seem simple turns of phrase, referring more broadly to "mankind," the ensuing discussion — describing workingmen and military men squandering their wages, beating their wives, and brawling in cantinas — underscores the concern about men's behavior.

Much like prerevolutionary Spencerian eugenicists, prohibitionists lamented behavior that "degenerated the race" and concentrated their deliberations on behaviors culturally linked with lower classes and indigenous groups.[32] Morality tales about alcohol almost invariably involved the abuse of pulque, a Mexican drink derived from the maguey cactus particularly associated with the indigenous groups of the central highlands. The proposal regarding gambling emphasized "games of chance, bullfights, cockfights, and every type of game or diversion that brings inescapable bloodshed." Although strict prohibition failed, derogating to the states the enforcement of anti-vice laws, this shared discourse of racial degeneration and deviant manhood exemplified Constitutionalists' ambition to refashion "backwards" (bloodletting, pulque-guzzling, peyote-smoking) Mexican men into "civilized" laborers, soldiers, and farmers. Even while recognizing the hypocrisy of their concerns — one participant pointed out the "curious fact" that "there could not be more than two or three of us here who have never been drunk in our lives" — many lawmakers believed the revolution created an opportunity to create a stronger, farther-reaching state machinery that would rebuild Mexican society, fulfilling the objectives of Porfirian positivism.

Communists, Feminists, and Eugenicists: Postrevolutionary Civil Society

The Constitutionalist government's commitment (or, at least, that of the powerful radical faction) to remaking Mexico from the bottom up — transforming everything from drinking habits to property rights — created opportunities for activists of varying ideological stripes and inspired new ones. Particularly in the years between the 1917 Constitutional Congress and the 1929 creation of the National Revolutionary Party (PNR), groups competed to define the revolution's meaning and objectives. A conflict with many phases and factions, the revolutionary struggle legitimated a broad array of movements vying to claim its authentic legacy. Policymakers, for their part, learned that implementing their ambitious social-reform and economic-modernization programs, such as a national public-education system and the movement of workers into the formal economy, required engagement with these proliferating non-state actors. As the postrevolutionary state's architects sought to harness and direct these mobilizational energies, women, although explicitly excluded from formal citizenship, gained limited access to political decision making by participating in organizations that managed to command government attention.

Through discipline and organization, the Mexican Communist Party

(PCM) cultivated an influence well out of proportion with its membership, obliging policymakers to turn their co-optative energies on the party. As the historian Barry Carr has pointed out, the PCM, established in November 1919, "oscillated violently between two extreme positions — an uncritical acceptance of the anticapitalist potential of the Mexican Revolution and of its associated governments ('pushing the revolution to the left') and a blunt, undifferentiated condemnation of these governments as 'despotic,' 'bourgeois,' 'capitulating to imperialism,' etc."[33] In the early 1920s, until a sharp turning away from the maximato in 1928, the party advanced a "united front" strategy that successfully reached out to labor and peasant organizations, making common cause with anarchists and socialists whom the PCM generally found politically unreliable and ideologically distasteful.[34] Although the PCM would not begin organizing women in earnest until April 1931, when it created its Women's Department, through the 1920s the party established a presence in many regions, exposing women to the party and its ideas.

Meanwhile, women activists pursued less controversial strategies to affect public policies. As with the U.S. progressive movement and the prerevolutionary *científicos* (technocrats), widespread concerns about alcohol consumption created opportunities for women, pushing a household issue onto the policymaking agenda and creating forums for those with political concerns only obliquely related to alcohol consumption. As the presumed guardians of morality (despite persistent fears about women's moral frailty), women temperance activists found a receptive audience at the government's highest levels, offering ambitious organizers the opportunity for hands-on, professional experience, sometimes on the state or national rather than the community or municipal level where women activists operated most frequently. With the government struggling to break the Catholic church's near-monopoly on women's moralizing labors, temperance campaigns offered a convenient convergence of interests.

Ernestina Alvarado, for example, appealed to the Secretariat of Public Education (SEP) in 1923 to support her temperance efforts in Mexico City. After submitting a detailed description of her plans for "scientific instruction," she received a letter of introduction signed by José Vasconcelos, the SEP's indefatigable director. In 1928, having expanded her project to a national network, she negotiated directly with Undersecretary Moisés Sáenz to secure financial backing. By 1930, the endeavor had burgeoned into a more expansive effort, not only promoting temperance but also offering instruction in child rearing, dressmaking, conference organizing, and "all that knowledge that gives mothers and women in general a complete preparation to be model housewives and society members useful to the Patria." In return for SEP support, the leagues committed their members to "help[ing] the school morally or materially, whenever necessity requires or the director requests."[35] Such formulations followed the grammar of revolutionary citizenship, engaging in the quid pro quo of reciprocal obligation and seeking to render women "useful to the Patria."

Temperance did not offer women the only means to filter into the political realm, however. Local political parties and organizations — primarily state-level entities that would later constitute the ruling PNR — created mechanisms for "ideologically correct" women to participate in their activities. Tamaulipas's Socialist Border Party, for example, included in the first article of its 1924 program a commitment to the "social, economic, and political liberation of woman, in whom it recognizes all the necessary faculties for the proper dispensation of public functions."[36] The founding document went on to explain that the women who joined the party, "while being in full possession of their rights, must be of advanced ideas, profess principles of morality, and accept in all parts the present statutes." This caveat captured the ambivalence among self-styled socialists toward women's political rights. While revolutionary leaders — particularly those who aligned themselves with the radical faction — exhorted women to embrace "advanced ideas," they had anticlericalism and public education in mind, not birth control and the redistribution of unpaid domestic labor.

Nonetheless, these openings, however narrow, heightened women's presence in public debate. The 1920s witnessed several national and international women's congresses in Mexico City, vindicating Palavicini's concern about the imminence of a suffragist movement.[37] In 1923, 180 women from throughout the Americas converged on Mexico City for the Panamerican Women's Congress.[38] The Yucatecan delegation, building on its momentum from the 1916 congress, played a pivotal role in the 1923 Panamerican Congress.[39] Led by the prominent radical feminist Elvia Carrillo Puerto, the group scandalized the congress by advocating sexual education, free love, and readily available contraception. Followed two years later by the Congress of Women of La Raza, also in Mexico City, these two congresses continued the progressive impulses of the feminist and constitutional congresses, centering their agendas on upper- and middle-class women's roles in shaping Mexico's future.

Questions of contraception and racial improvement sparked heated discussions about the centrality of motherhood to the identity of modern, postrevolutionary Mexican women. Carrillo Puerto and her allies advocated unrestricted access to birth control, allowing poor women to control their family size, but most attendees viewed contraception as violating natural laws; one congresista referred to it as an "inversion," and another referred to it as a "crime against nature and humanity."[40] The tone of both congresses, however, centered on how privileged women — even those with relatively modest backgrounds had more security and opportunity than the vast majority of Mexicans — would guide their less fortunate sisters to raise healthier children and build a stronger Mexican "race." Beneath these disputes lay a fundamental disagreement over whether women activists should concentrate on elevating motherhood or creating more extra-domestic opportunities for women. These differences would become more pronounced during the congresses of the 1930s, as more nonelite women participated.

If the 1920s congresses created a small opening for debating alternative femininities — such as the sexually liberated and economically independent chica moderna and the scientifically informed, fiscally prudent mother — that opening seemed to vanish in 1926. Behind debates over contraception and eugenics lay considerations of secularism and piety. The outbreak of the Cristero Rebellion sharpened this divide considerably, forcing progressive activists to situate themselves as anticlerical. Courageous and risky discussions challenging the conventional elision of womanhood and motherhood receded as secular activists struggled to contain church influences and became leery of alienating potential allies. Given the political leadership's opposition to upending traditional sexual mores and gendered divisions of labor, women activists may also have weighed the futility of prioritizing these. However, the Cristero Rebellion put the nail in the coffin for women's inchoate sexual liberation, heightening the culture wars over who could claim postrevolutionary morality; by the 1930s, sexual politics all but vanished from women activists' agendas.

*Containing Catholicism: The Cristero Rebellion and
the Birth of the Ruling Party*

The bloody and costly Cristero Rebellion exploded on 31 July 1926, when Catholic bishops suspended services in response to government anticlericalism. A popular revolt took hold in the center-west, including the highlands of Michoacán and Jalisco, and spread rapidly, counting as many as 50,000 combatants at the conflict's June 1929 apogee.[41] While the rebellion remained regionally centered, it found sympathizers throughout the republic, threatening to ignite a wildfire of religious insurgency. Religious and political leaders expressed dismay that the uprising grew beyond the control of both church and state officials, inciting violence and subversion that threatened the stability of both entities. By 1928, when Lázaro Cárdenas took office as Michoacán's governor, the Cristero Rebellion had overwhelmed the region, and confrontations between *cristeros* (Catholic rebels) and *agraristas* defined the political and social climate. In late June 1929, the church hierarchy and federal government secured a fragile peace, agreeing to mutual conciliation and the restoration of Catholic services. Church leaders discouraged lay radicalism by refusing to recognize organizations that had led the revolt and counseling church leaders not to interfere in political matters but, rather, to "reinforce the principle of authority."[42] Tensions mounted, however, between the centralizing Calles regime, still pursuing a conciliatory line toward the church, and state-level officials who, anxious to protect their authority, limited the number of practicing clergy. Although Callistas won key political battles, those victories did not necessarily garner support among locals suspicious of government incursions into their communities.

The Cristero Rebellion transformed the context of women's activism and the contingent terms of revolutionary citizenship, recasting women's piety from antimodern to potentially violent and disruptive. Cristero women's participation in armed combat, intelligence gathering, and provisioning brigades — the same roles women had taken up during the revolution itself — exacerbated the movement's disruption of social order and reinforced widespread assumptions about feminine fanaticism.[43] Combined with their longstanding role as guardians of family piety, women's involvement reinforced political leaders' determination to target women for state-sponsored education and organizing efforts.[44] Regime-supporting women activists still had to convince policymakers to trust women as agents of political change, but fears of Catholic militarism also helped their cause by creating an imperative to address the "woman problem" and prevent women from becoming "tools of the reaction."

Partly to consolidate its victory over the Cristero Rebellion, the governing elite united a loose confederation of pro-regime parties and organizations to form the PNR.[45] The new party met with resistance from local caciques concerned about retaining autonomy; from clergy and lay radicals wary that centralization presaged intensified anticlericalism; and from community members wary of policies emanating from Mexico City and imposed uniformly throughout Mexico's diverse regions. When Cárdenas assumed the presidency in 1934, he proved savvier than his predecessors about securing local support and controlling local opposition, but the party structure bolstered his centralizing and modernizing agendas.

To be sure, the PNR's program revealed its leaders' reticence to include women, pledging in its constitution "gradually to encourage Mexican women's access to the activities of civic life." To "prepare" women for political rights, the party promoted schools for light industry and "domestic arts," with "the goal of introducing [women] to productive activities." Peasant women would be "incorporated into the economic life, liberating them from the miserable tasks that they perform today . . . and distributing propaganda to develop a consciousness, so that the woman begins to be a *compañera* (partner) and leaves off being a slave."[46] Distinguishing women's unpaid labor from "productive" or "economic" activity, political leaders highlighted a contradiction in women's civic status. Before women could become citizens, they had to "leave off being slaves" but without, as party leaders made clear, abandoning the domestic labors that "nature" assigned to them.

Despite the tensions within the PNR's answer to the "woman question," the creation of the ruling party simplified the political landscape in which women's activism developed. In September 1928, the liberal feminist María Ríos Cárdenas, who went on to a career as a leading suffragist and PNR activist, felt obliged to assure state governors that her new magazine, *Mujer*, sought the "moral and intellectual elevation of women" and remained "completely apart from politics and religion."[47] By November 1929, the PNR's daily newspaper touted the Mexican Federation of Feminist Centers "to control all the women's groups who have been working in isolation." Claiming that women would have secured suffrage rights had they formed such a confederation before the 1917 Constitutional Congress, the article explained that the ruling party would unite women's organizing into a single front to establish job-placement centers, cooperatives, and mutual-aid societies. These opportunities for women to take on public posts would constitute "the first step to announce that in the Mexican Republic there exist members of the feminine sex trained in all orders of human knowledge."[48] Such statements exemplified a standard strategy of postrevolutionary policymakers. Although regional, national, and international women's congresses had brought together women from a range of professions and demonstrated their capacity for organization and mobilization, the PNR claimed for itself the accomplishment of enabling the "first step" to make women's abilities visible. Still, the claims also indicated a shift toward celebrating women in nondomestic roles.

In a way, the party's boasts hit the mark. By simply recognizing women's reproductive labor and political organizing, the party leadership rendered them more substantial. Furthermore, the 1929 PNR organization made visible the infrastructure through which women activists could access the state apparatus. Party leaders, more out of fear than a commitment to justice, made tentative overtures toward women activists to draw them into the Callista fold. In September 1930, the Ministry of Government asked all state governments to submit lists of organizations whose membership included women.[49] Apparently intended to take the measure of women's activism, the request prompted a list dominated by Catholic and temperance organizations and a smattering of labor unions. No PCM organizations appeared on these lists.

The "Flowering of Authentic Femininity": The Ejército de Mujeres Campesinas

The PNR leadership, steeped in theories linking revolutionary consciousness with wage labor, remained locked in an ambivalent embrace with both women and campesinos, who seemed at once to pose the greatest "reactionary" threat and to embody Mexico's cultural authenticity.[50] Within a materialist ideology, it seemed overdetermined that rural women would support conservative opposition movements, and the visibility of women and peasants in the Cristero Rebellion overshadowed their participation in the revolution. To create a socializing institution for rural women, therefore, the PNR sponsored the Ejército de Mujeres Campesinas (Army of Rural Women) under the leadership of Professor Jovita Boone de Cortina and with the endorsement of three influential state governors, Adalberto Tejeda, Leonides Andreu Almazán, and Saturnino Cedillo, who declared that "the new social tendencies necessarily require women's cooperation to emerge triumphant."[51]

The imprimatur of these agrarista governors, who would lead the anti–Callista charge a few years later, indicated a shift among some key radicals toward a more favorable view of women's political rights. The international climate made women's suffrage seem inevitable: by 1931, women had gained voting rights (albeit in some cases with limitations) not only in most of Europe and the English-speaking world but also in Ecuador and Chile. By 1934, Cuba and Brazil would join the list of Latin American countries allowing women to vote. Given this momentum, left-leaning political leaders likely hoped to secure women's loyalties. These changing convictions also had personal underpinnings. By 1931, the pro-suffrage radical Múgica, for example, had developed a close friendship with Mathilde Rodríguez Cabo, the radical feminist who would later become his wife. Moreover, the Cristero Rebellion and continued feminist agitation impressed on PNR leaders that engagement rather than containment offered the best strategy for putting women activists at the service of the postrevolutionary regime rather than its opponents.

The Ejército promised to bring together peasant women to work land donated through government-sponsored land reform, not only incorporating women into "economic life," but also increasing Mexico's agricultural production. Setting the program up as an "army," organizers underscored the continued importance of military leadership in postrevolutionary politics as well as the link between citizenship and military service, hoping to construct a foundation for claims to citizenship rights. Much like the PNR's platform and the survey following the 1916 Feminist Congress, the project rested on a fiction that rural women did not already participate in agricultural production; however, it created a structure that recognized women's labors.[52] Opposition newspapers suggested a more sinister motive behind the "formation of a large army of campesinas to the end of mixing them in politics and obtaining their votes to make certain agrarista candidates triumph."[53] Indicating that the revolutionary regime needed to "rebuild all that the revolution destroyed: credit, capital, national production, tranquility, and collective well-being," opponents residing in Havana asserted that it remained "unnecessary to mix peasant women in our electoral movements, if one bears in mind that the revolutionary family is in no danger of allowing power to escape its hands."[54] Nor did opposition to the Ejército come only from opponents on the right. The Communist Party described it as the PNR's effort to turn campesinas into fascists.[55]

The ruling party, however, depicted the Ejército as an affirmation of its role in guiding Mexico's transition to modernity, hailing the project as the political manifestation of a natural, truly Mexican feminism that neither challenged traditional femininity nor facilitated the imperialism of urban or foreign ideas. The feminism that arose during the revolution, the PNR newspaper explained, failed to attract support because it drew on external ideas to "address the most intimate problems of Mexican society."[56] Pointing to the Cristero Rebellion as "the only occasion in which women appeared in organized acts," the editorial once again effaced women's participation in the revolution and in postrevolutionary political organizing, reducing their public presence to "an undertaking of confused diagnosis and complex psychology." Based on the idea that "feminist organization depends upon the clever exploration of each pueblo's special domestic idiosyncrasies," the Ejército would foster a Mexican feminism that superceded both foreign and local movements and identities.

This project squared with the party's larger agenda of cultivating a nationalist culture to occlude both regional identities and internationalist (especially communist and anarcho-syndicalist) influences. The Ejército—mimetic of a quintessentially nationalist institution—would provide a "serious and transcendental impulse to Mexican feminism" by cultivating a distinctly Mexican motherhood. Describing the Mexican woman as the "soul of the home," the party newspaper explained, "that is the root of legitimate feminism, the flowering of authentic femininity. Through this, Mexican feminism will be born in the countryside, among the multitudes of *ejidatarios*, redeemed children of the Revolution. . . . Mexican feminism will come from the field to the cities."[57] This "legitimate feminism" and "authentic femininity" rejected urban-centered British or North American feminism as embodied by the radical suffragists but admired the Soviet Union and Scandinavian women who worked "shoulder-to-shoulder" with men to achieve economic liberation.

This distinction between Soviet/Scandinavian women laborers and British/North American suffragists mapped onto an emerging divide within the Mexican women's movement between those favoring mixed-sex organizations emphasizing social issues and those advocating women-only organizations stressing political rights. The Ejército, while women-only, would distract attention from women activists' emphasis on political rights. "In Mexico," the party newspaper proclaimed, "we have invoked too much 'citizenship [*ciudadanismo*]' running up against the civic coldness of the citizen head of household [*ciudadano jefe del hogar*]."[58] Despite widespread discussions of citizenship, the anonymous author rhetorically distanced the "civic coldness" of citizenship from an authentically Mexican political culture—at least, when it came to women. This stance highlighted central characteristics of the maximato: selectively anti-imperialist nationalism, modernization within the bounds of tradition, and "revolution" without radicalism.

The notion of an "authentic femininity" and a "Mexican feminism" exposed a growing anxiety among governing elites. At a time when revolution, civil war, and incipient industrialization drew women out of the home and unsettled prescribed gender roles, concern emerged across social classes about threats to traditional femininity.[59] Men and women alike elevated Mexican femininity—characterized by self-sacrifice, modesty, piety, and domesticity—as something that had value unto itself and inspired other countries' envy, a national treasure not to be squandered thoughtlessly by young women following European and North American fads of short hair and flapper skirts.[60] Thus, the Ejército became a battleground for emerging culture wars over acceptable feminine identities: communists and radicals celebrated the arrival of the overall-clad obrera as the harbinger of more profoundly revolutionary change, while more conservative observers praised the *rebozo*- (shawl) draped mujer abnegada as the icon of Mexican femininity.

The Ejército's organizers offered a third perspective, distancing themselves from both the ruling party and its opponents. The organizing committee shared the PNR's language of economic determinism but viewed its effects differently. In an interview with the party newspaper, Boone disagreed with its editorialist, insisting that the Ejército did not follow the Soviet model at all. Describing it as "not an armed institution but rather an organism capable of instructing itself, producing wealth, and elevating the rural standard of living," she protested that, "in Russia, the woman soldier is a machine, and her children from birth belong to the state and not to the family. On the contrary, the Mexican campesina of this Organization should be a thinking being and enjoy the facilities to nurture and raise their offspring in a way suitable for life's struggles."[61] While the PNR leadership understood changes in production systems as transforming gender identities by involving women in the consciousness-inducing activity of wage labor, the Ejército's organizers viewed the "prevailing social economy" as a hardship that precipitated a "sexual problem," resulting in prostitution, adultery, infanticide, and abortion. The organizers' "first step" was to study the sexual problem, publicly scrutinizing the effects of the intense economic and political changes on the most intimate realms of Mexican life.

Despite their consistent PNR boosterism, the organizers fumed at revolutionary leaders' failure to recognize their own complicity in maintaining sex-based hierarchies. "We consider ineffective," the organizing committee explained, "the revolutionary efforts of men who now fight to transform a social environment that maintains archaic Roman norms while they keep women, children, and above all the home within the absolute, oppressive, and absurd regime of archaic Roman laws stuck thousands of years in the past."[62] Organizers contended that ignoring women's domestic subjugation not only ran counter to the regime's egalitarian claims but also, more concretely, undermined the party's highest priorities. Even the most radical man turned a blind eye to conservatism in his own home, since "he always prefers peace within the family, even if it is reactionary and opposed to his radical convictions but allows him the compensation of rest after exhausting himself in the rough labor for existence." In the post-Cristero environment, women activists credibly wielded the threat of religious fanaticism as the price of ignoring their demands. Men's failure to uphold revolutionary principles at home, the Ejército's leaders implied, transformed it into an incubator for reactionary ideas.

Although the Ejército petered out after November 1931, its objectives and tactics did not fade from view. A 1931 national women's congress and the subsequent Cardenista program to organize rural women bore its distinct imprint, with an emphasis on agricultural labor for "non-working" women to cultivate their revolutionary consciousness.[63] However, if the Ejército strove to fashion a shared notion of Mexican womanhood—an "authentic femininity"—that illusory image shattered during the acrimonious 1931 congress, where disagreements over the meanings of femininity and womanhood persisted during the contentious deliberations.

Fractured Feminism: First National Congress of Women Workers and Peasants

The First National Congress of Women Workers and Peasants (Primer Congreso Nacional de Obreras y Campesinas), the first of three national congresses that occurred between 1931 and 1934, began with a hopeful spirit produced by momentum gained since the PNR's founding. By 1931, a handful of party leaders had expressed support for women's political rights and announced intentions to amend the electoral laws accordingly. Meeting in Mexico City's Alvaro Obregón Civic Center, congress participants followed an agenda designed to capitalize on this official support by showcasing their capacity for civic engagement. The proceedings also revealed the extent to which the PNR leadership had succeeded in defining the terms of political engagement. While participants disagreed about the practical implications of such abstractions, they understood that both political expediency and ideological allegiances required a discursive bow to the trinity of class, modernization, and nationalism when seeking state support for their initiatives.

Questions about women's citizenship and the most effective modes of collective representation — through women's organizations or through mixed-sex mass organizations — took center stage during the October 1931 congress. The divisions belied the imaginary of a unified "Mexican" feminism. PNR supporters, or *penerristas*, favored a "separate spheres" approach, arguing that women's demands always received short shrift within male-dominated organizations. Communists, who had turned sharply away from the Callistas in 1928 and intensified their women's organizing earlier in 1931, vociferously attacked the PNR and advocated women's participation in labor and peasant organizations, maintaining that separate women's organizations would foster intraclass divisions and ghettoize women's issues. This rift, which has characterized many women's movements and other identity-based projects, assumed the form in postrevolutionary Mexico of a debate over the revolution's legacy.

Specifying who assumed the mantle of revolutionary legitimacy required more than identifying who occupied the president's residence at Los Pinos and which faction controlled the legislature. While the PNR activist and congress organizer Florinda Lazo León defended party leaders, claiming they had spilled their blood for revolutionary principles, the Communist María del Refugio ("Cuca") García responded that they had, in fact, "been dragged into struggle by a pueblo starving for spiritual liberties and economic subsistence."[64] To García and her comrades, the maximato had squandered the revolution's potential, and sincere revolutionary commitment called for a challenge to the present regime. She decried the government's collusion with Mexico's continued semicolonial status, and the PCM newspaper celebrated her "unmasking" of the congress as the tool of "petty-bourgeois women seeking to build the PNR's political base."[65]

Much like the radical PNR leadership, the PCM viewed women's entrance into the wage-labor force as critical to reshaping their roles and centered their organizing strategies on effacing gender difference, highlighting the ways in which women's exploitation resembled men's. Invoking the Marxist idiom that permeated contemporary political discourse, García described women as "a very important factor in production." Arguing that employers exploited female labor at lower wages to return higher profits, she explained, "Women have swelled the ranks of the army of workers. Slaves yesterday only in the home and of the feudal State, today they are slaves of the factories and the workshops, of the capitalist system."[66] Rather than invoking the madre abnegada, PCM militants pointed to the hardships of women wage earners.

The penerrista and mainstream press expressed greater concern about gender identities as women raised their voices in the political arena. One speaker disparaged foreign influences, pleading that the congress avoid becoming "an incubator for . . . agitators of Mrs. Pankhurst's suffragist style." She continued, "What the workingwomen hope for is to take positions, positions appropriate to their sex, within the social upheaval that Mexico is experiencing, and to contribute to improving the female proletariat, which until today finds itself on the margin of the Mexican Revolution."[67] Such assertions willfully obscured persistent differences over what constituted suitable roles. Participants' engagement with issues such as suffrage, labor laws, and health care revealed efforts to find strategies "appropriate to their sex," allowing women to intervene in revolutionary politics while preserving the images of the demure, deferential señorita and the self-sacrificing, long-suffering mother. Nonetheless, the very act of convening, issuing demands, and tackling issues that, according to press reports, "even men avoid addressing in public" deviated from "appropriate" femininity.[68] One editorialist recoiled at women acting "in the same sphere of action as man," which would only serve "to *neutralize her* or to retire her from being a woman . . . to make of her a phenomenon."[69] Although particularly stark in its language, this sentiment permeated the press coverage of the congress.

Ideological divisions between Communists and penerristas — and their conflicts over whether to form separate women's organizations — dominated the congress even before it started. "We must be alert, compañeras!" advised a PCM flyer that circulated before the event's opening. "The PNR and other bourgeois organizations only want to use us. We should expect nothing from them. They are the petite bourgeoisie who joined the revolution and today ally with the great bourgeoisie, enriching themselves while we live in misery and die of hunger."[70] This admonition pushed beyond strategic questions about mixed-sex or women-only organizations and challenged the revolutionary legitimacy of PNR-linked feminism. Describing the current administration as "fascist," the Communists pointed out that, "in twenty years of struggle, the workers and peasants have received only promises from the government."

The PNR feminists, unsurprisingly, refused to cede this ground, responding with their own accusations of betrayal; they argued that the PCM, rather than the PNR, used women as political pawns. María Ríos Cárdenas, touting the Mexican Women's Confederation, of which she would become president, argued, "Only woman knows her problems, and therefore only she is capable of resolving them. Syndicalism, having conquered many benefits for workers, does not resolve women's problems."[71] Other detractors went further, describing Communists as "malinches, exploited by the concupiscence of the foreigners, especially the Russians, who have catechized them to satisfy their own sexual appetites."[72] Invoking La Malinche's betrayal, the penerristas not only challenged the Communists' patriotism but also branded them with a decidedly disparaging conception of femininity, that of the betrayer of dubious moral character, "catechized" by foreigners even more nefarious than the Catholic church.

This wrangling over revolutionary authenticity occurred amid ongoing conflicts over the revolution's animating principles. While the penerristas tapped into nationalist impulses, the Communists invoked egalitarian objectives; each side struggled to present itself as representing the majority opinion. The PNR's official daily gently mocked the Communists' position as naive idealism. Describing the Communists as "partisans of radical extremism, while others, perhaps the majority, adopted the party of moderation," the newspaper chided that "it is clearly understood that even the most erudite err; it is a blind step taken by women in search of collective betterment. The [Communist] tendency should not be taken as recognized and accepted doctrine by all Mexican women."[73] Unlike Russian women, who purportedly sought to "destroy the home" in their misguided search for a collective utopia, the Mexican woman "does not try to destroy anything but rather to reconstruct the devastated Patria."[74]

When such cultural and patriotic arguments failed to persuade, however, the ruling party could always resort to the state's coercive power. When President Pascual Ortiz Rubio attended the congress, Communist women shouted epithets, accusing him and other officials of fascism. Public-security agents arrested fifteen Communists, including the prominent activists Cuca García, Benita Galeana, and Concha Michel, for shouting "subversive" slogans. According to the Communist newspaper, the women, forced to walk from the auditorium to the police headquarters, marched arm in arm, singing revolutionary hymns and shouting, "*Vivas*" for the Communist Party and the Soviet Union to the cheers of supporting workers and "poor people in general."[75] The incident amounted to elaborate street theater on both sides, since Ortiz Rubio ordered the Communists' release upon their arrival at the police station.

The Communists' behavior scandalized the more conventional penerristas, intent on demonstrating women's decorum and civic responsibility. In the context of the maximato, where groups manifest their "preparation" for public life by expressing unwavering support for the regime, the Communists' dissent conveyed that women lacked the discipline to vote responsibly. Congress organizers hastened to distance themselves from the Communists, issuing a statement that, "conscientious of their duty," they supported "the men of the Revolution," particularly Ortiz Rubio and Calles, "who form the vanguard of Mexico's vindicating movement."[76]

By the congress's closing, however, two things had become clear. First, a national women's movement, however contested and fragmented in practice, had emerged on the scene and demanded official attention. Unlike the congresses of the 1920s, the 1931 congress focused on accessing political power and public resources to address social problems. Following the congress, a group of penerristas, under the leadership of Edelmira Rojas de Escudero, formed the PNR-affiliated Feminist Revolutionary Party with the goals of winning the vote and gaining "a more direct role in the life of the State."[77] As international momentum grew behind women's political rights, and as a national movement consolidated behind political aims, PNR leaders seemed as eager to co-opt feminists' efforts as feminists were to establish political legitimacy.

Second, the 1931 congress established the Communist Party's defining role in 1930s women's organizing. Following the congress, PCM leaders engaged in the customary "self-criticism," appraising the Communist women's performance. The assessment reveals the party's contemporary hostility toward any form of cooperation, lambasting participants for not insisting on diplomatic recognition of the Soviet Union, not rejecting resolutely enough the penerrista's Mexican Women's Confederation, and, in the case of one compañera, dining with a Catholic conferee in hopes of "convincing" her. In language echoing their PNR counterparts, PCM leaders blamed themselves for providing inadequate guidance and called for "an intense labor of organization and mobilization of workingwomen throughout the country, with the aim of incorporating them into the revolutionary movement under our Party's direction."[78]

The PNR-Communist divide persisted during two national congresses that followed, in 1933 and 1934, with each side claiming control over the organizing committee. Although penerristas accused the Communists of hijacking the events and preventing consensus formation, this discord also forestalled the movement's co-optation and in many ways strengthened it. So long as profound ideological and strategic differences persisted, a national debate — albeit at the level of urban activists — continued; the consolidation of women's activism during the mid-1930s necessarily simplified the identity of "woman" and crafted a movement more vulnerable to incorporation by the regime. By the late 1930s, this ostensibly unified movement would relinquish the weapons of subversion and dissent in favor of standing as good citizens and loyal allies. The deliberations over suffrage at the 1917 Constitutional Congress, however, should have demonstrated that the specter of resistance — particularly of armed rebellion — swayed policymakers more than promises of loyalty.

Citizen Shoppers and Citizen Workers:
Suffrage, Nationalism, and the "Public Realm"

The 1931 congress occurred amid discussions that increasingly recognized women as having a growing public presence and interests apart from their families. In addition to the Ejército, various government branches addressed women's civil and labor rights. In February, the Secretariat of Foreign Relations stated that Mexican women who married foreign nationals would no longer lose their nationality.[79] The 1931 Federal Labor Law reiterated constitutional protections for workingwomen and children, barring them from jobs and shifts considered unsafe and supporting maternity-leave and nursing provisions. The PNR newspaper ran sympathetic stories about women's efforts to amend provisions of the Civil Code that barred them from joining labor unions and political organizations without their husbands' consent.[80] The same year also witnessed two oddly linked campaigns to shape women's public roles: the first sustained consideration of women's suffrage and a buy-national campaign that targeted women consumers. These two episodes set in relief the interplay between gender ideologies and policymaking, underscoring the fluidity of gendered identities and revealing lawmakers' anxious efforts to pin down meaningful definitions of "femininity" and "masculinity."

Communist and PNR women's dominance of secular women's activism strengthened prevailing assumptions that women's political consciousness — and claims to revolutionary citizenship — derived from participation in wage labor or in political organizations. Communists linked demands to wage labor, and penerristas focused on civic engagement, but neither camp depicted these avenues to political consciousness as mutually exclusive. At pains to highlight women's activities apart from the everyday work of grinding corn, rearing children, nursing the ill, and feeding families, both Communists and penerristas obscured issues of reproductive labor that occupied most women's lives. For middle-class or elite activists, this obfuscation perhaps derived from the fact that they performed very little of this labor themselves, instead paying poorer (and generally darker) women to fulfill their households' reproductive needs. However, this tendency also reflects the expectation that reproductive labor, far from offering a path to revolutionary consciousness, instead bolstered women's reactionary "false consciousness" (as measured by their failure to support the PNR or PCM) and "enslavement."

In January 1931, a handful of PNR leaders proposed permitting women to vote for and hold municipal offices, allowing them to get their political feet wet without unduly disturbing complicated political arrangements. After all, women were accustomed to household administrative duties, and municipal posts would not require the ideological discipline that women presumably lacked. Further, by sheer force of their femininity, party leaders argued, women would infuse order and morality into notoriously corrupt local political contests. "The *ayuntamiento* [town council] is where the Mexican women can take their first steps in civic life," opined one Mexico City daily, "by virtue of the fact that the municipal function is essentially administrative, permitting them to develop their initiative and capacities to benefit the residents [*vecinos*] of a place. Furthermore, their participation in municipal functions will make [the municipalities] refine themselves, reflecting the elevated moral level of our country's women."[81]

Editorialists and policymakers expressed deep ambivalence about the onslaught of flapper skirts and bobbed haircuts from abroad and depicted suffrage as yet another undesirable foreign import whose consumption they should discourage. As a PNR editorial chided, feminists challenged Schopenhauer's aphorism depicting women as "animals, with long hair and short ideas, that one must beat frequently and caress from time to time" by adopting the fashion of having "ideas and hair that are equally short."[82] Those favoring women's political rights would have to counter these charges with their own nationalist posture.

The federal government had already developed a program to encourage consumption of Mexican-produced articles but did not yet aggressively cultivate women's participation. Nonetheless, in early January, a women's group in the northern town of Agujita, Coahuila, wrote to express its support, closing the correspondence with, "We will consume national articles to save Mexico."[83] The elite Mexican Women's Action Front, claiming 3,000 members in Mexico City, discouraged women from buying from "adventurers" arriving from abroad and "itinerant salesmen [*ambulantes*] who claim to enter the country to perform field labor but then congest the city's streets."[84] A group of Mexico City market women proposed "moralizing" efforts to expel Jews who had recently "invaded" the markets and to close down foreign-owned workshops that "mercilessly exploit our obreras."[85]

Perhaps inspired by women's apparent enthusiasm for the project, the PNR decided to target women's participation, linking one aspect of reproductive labor to women's entrance into public affairs.[86] In a national radio address, the campaign's director, Rafael Sánchez Lira, appealed for women's cooperation to secure Mexico's "economic salvation."[87] Sánchez Lira structured his appeal by class, which he defined by the occupation of a family's primary breadwinner, and offered specific advice to the "women of" peasants, laborers, employees, professionals, industrialists, and merchants. Elite women would make the greatest sacrifice, he maintained, since they not only consumed more foreign luxuries but also often derived family wealth from foreign commerce. Thus, his exhortation to elite women appealed to their patriotism, while pleas to peasants, laborers, and employees emphasized their own families' material stake in nationalist economic policies. The tone and emphases of the interventions underscored the campaign's cross-class pull. The Labor Department's decision to investigate sweatshops owned by "Armenians, Lithuanians, Russians, Poles, and other foreigners" held populist attraction for the urban working class without antagonizing Mexico's own industrialists or petite bourgeoisie.[88] Indeed, Mexican producers encouraged the Labor Department's muckraking attentions to their foreign competitors.[89] This broad appeal meshed well with the PNR feminists' efforts to muffle class antagonisms and stress civic engagement.

The Communist Party, meanwhile, lambasted the campaign as deceptive and xenophobic. Arguing that Mexico had no truly "national" industries, given the extent of foreign ownership of factories and extractive enterprises, the PCM newspaper maintained that "nationalist campaigns have always had the simple object of distracting the exploited masses during moments of crisis to divert their discontent toward noisy and vacuous patriotic demonstrations and toward a struggle against so-called inferior races or 'undesirable foreigners.'"[90] Pointing out that the nationalist campaign targeted not neo-imperialist foreign factory owners but, rather, Chinese laborers and Arab shopkeepers, the PCM dismissed labor unions that participated in government efforts to divide the working class. Anxious to reinforce the link between labor and political rights, Communists ignored the campaign's implications for women's organizing.

Keeping its focus on labor rather than consumption issues, the Communist Party stepped up its organizing efforts among women in the 1930s. In early 1930, the PCM circulated the recommendations of a European-based affiliate recommending workingwomen's inclusion in all party and union leadership and on all committees formulating labor demands. In any workplace where women composed the majority of workers, the proposal continued, women should form the majority of strike committees, and all strike activities should welcome female family members.[91] Honoring International Women's Day (8 March) in 1931, the PCM implemented these suggestions, acknowledging, "The proletariat cannot launch the definitive battles for its emancipation while workingwomen remain at the struggle's margins. We must confess that almost nothing has been done to organize women, and we must put an end to this criminal abandon."[92]

In April, the PCM established a Women's Department, and the party newspaper expanded to include greater coverage of women's participation in land and labor struggles.[93] In June, Francisca Guzmán, the head of the new Women's Department, issued a call from the party's Central Committee for increased attention to the women's sector. Describing the work so far as "plenty slack [*flojo*]," she asked, "What have we done for workingwomen so that they do not play the ridiculous role that they play these days, when there should be class battles, struggle without mercy and without quarter against the bourgeoisie that exploits us? . . . We cannot be communists if we do not work to organize her, defend her against her exploiters, and attract her to our ranks."[94] Six months later, at the party's national congress, the PCM leadership continued to lament its performance in recruiting women. "One of the Party's weaknesses and one of the recruitment campaign's flaws," the resolution on organizing explained, "consists in the scarce number of women and particularly workingwomen joining the Party." Demanding "special attention" to the effort, the party resolved to create women's organizing committees, "training them in leadership and organization, having them participate in the work of mass organizing, with the aim of forming a team of women leaders in the shortest time possible."[95]

The PCM continued to focus solely on women's rights as wage laborers, occasionally also pointing to the need for equal land rights; reproductive-labor issues remained outside the PCM's organizing program. Nonetheless, Communist Party proposals for attracting obreras encouraged unconventional mobilizing strategies. While the penerristas shied away from the confrontational tactics of "agitators" like Mrs. Pankhurst, the Communists regularly celebrated aggressive women. In addition to extolling women's participation in marches, hunger strikes, and political campaigns, the party spread news about their labor struggles. *El Machete* ran a glowing story when the Rosa Luxemburg Women's Center confronted Adalberto Tejada's armed forces in Jalapa, Veracruz. "We must say," the article exclaimed, "that this proletarian battle's triumph is due largely to the compañeras of the Centro 'Rosa Luxemburgo,' who valiantly demonstrated how workingwomen struggle when they have class-consciousness. Their example should be imitated by revolutionary workingwomen throughout the country."[96] The newspaper also reported that the municipal president of Sabinas Hidalgo, Nuevo León, summoned the officers of the Alexandra Kollontai Women's Center to his office, warning them to cease organizing or "who knows where this will end?" But "the compañeras know their role perfectly well, and they bravely answered the authority," *El Machete* reported. "They did not defect but rather prepared themselves to work, understanding that while there were 800 or 1,000 families there without bread, and this number [was] growing every day, they were obliged to struggle." In Tampico, Tamaulipas, a group of ten campesinas, accompanied by their twenty-five children, protested the enclosure of nearby land by eating in three different local restaurants and then refusing to pay the bills until the enclosure decree was repealed.[97]

These episodes were, of course, newsworthy for being exceptional. But the PCM's tone in reporting and editorializing about women's mobilizations remained — in contrast to the PNR's newspaper and mainstream nonpartisan papers such as *El Universal* and *Excélsior* — unequivocally enthusiastic when women adopted militant strategies. Given the party's limited success in recruiting women members, these tributes to a more assertive, radicalized Mexican femininity might have found a tiny audience. By the early 1930s, however, the Communist presence in cultural organizations such as the Revolutionary Artists and Writers League (LEAR) and the National Graphics Workshop, as well as in public education, meant that the party's cultural impact well exceeded the reach of its membership. Prominent artists such as the photographer Tina Modotti and the muralists Diego Rivera and David Alfaro Siqueiros maintained close ties with the PCM leadership and produced art intended for widespread public consumption. The National Graphics Workshop produced striking woodcuts and drawings that illustrated the covers of government-published pamphlets, and the covers of newspapers such as *Frente a Frente* and *Izquierdas* often featured dramatic socialist-realist images depicting the battle-ready women that the PCM lauded in *El Machete*. These images celebrated an alternative femininity to the madre abnegada, offering another model of how women might inhabit revolutionary citizenship.

The PCM fought strenuously for women's land and labor rights and, later, for suffrage. *El Machete* railed against a proposal to reduce male unemployment by firing women workers, and it argued assertively for women's rights to land and water claims.[98] The party struggled for maternity leave and women's social security and lambasted the 1931 Federal Labor Law for failing to provide adequate protections. Maternity leave of eight days before and one month after delivery, the party newspaper argued, meant that "the children of obreras will practically be born on the machinery."[99] Praising the bravery of communist tortilla vendors who faced police beatings and incarceration, *El Machete* reported with disgust that these women were subjected to—indeed, charged for—health inspections performed by a veterinarian.[100] However, the PCM waged these crusades not in the name of aggrieved and downtrodden mothers but, rather, on behalf of embattled, revolutionary workingwomen.

Thus, the gender ideology underpinning the Communist Party's organizing program differed markedly from more conventional efforts. If the feminine ideal of the penerrista feminists was the fashionable, cultured, and responsible citizen, and the ideal of the mainstream press was the rebozo-shrouded, self-sacrificing mother, the PCM's ideal woman wore overalls, earned a wage, and raised her voice against employers and politicians. The party favored strategies in which women acted in ways that were culturally coded as manly, confronting armed forces and defying municipal authorities. It focused on class-linked issues while ignoring women's concerns about reproductive-labor burdens and civil inequities. The party left little room for negotiation on this position. Michel—then the compañera of the PCM's secretary-general, Hernán Laborde—returned from the Soviet Union in late 1933 having decided that she fundamentally disagreed with the party's approach to women's organizing, arguing instead for a strategy that emphasized sexual difference and gender complementarity. After she threatened to publish her views, the party expelled her.[101]

While the PCM disparaged the nationalist campaign and honored the workingwoman, Congressional Deputy Faustino Roel viewed women's enthusiastic participation in the nationalist campaign as evidence of their civic preparation. He began his proposal to grant women full political rights by stating, "When the honorable House of Deputies solicited the women's cooperation for the nationalist campaign, undertaken to promote articles produced in the country, it fully recognized the enormous importance that woman has in the life of the nation."[102] This recognition, he continued, "simply did justice to our abnegated compañeras, who have contributed effectively in forming the Mexican nation, participating in our struggles, sharing our sufferings and miseries, and contributing within their sphere of action to the development of our country." In his defense against the editorial criticism that predictably followed, Roel again pointed to the nationalist campaign — not to the recent national women's congress or to the Ejército de Mujeres Campesinas — as evidence of women's political engagement.

The PNR leadership, divided on the suffrage issue as on many other political matters, questioned Roel's logic, reiterating the tautology of opposition to women's citizenship. True women, the argument held, remained homebound and therefore outside the civic realm. Conceding that "of course the feminine vote is a conquest of contemporary revolutions and forms part of the Mexican revolutionary program," a PNR editorial nonetheless responded to Roel's proposal by arguing, "The Mexican woman is too domestic [*hogareña*], and establishing feminine political rights requires a family organization that remains far off. Beyond some small groups that remain in downtown cafés until seven at night, women barely show up in the street. There is not even nightlife in Mexico City, and in the States of the Republic, the women live perpetually enclosed."[103] Some *diputados* (congressional deputies) stated their opposition even more starkly, pointing to women's presumed loyalty to the pope and innate conservatism, which made them "a menace to the revolution." As one congressman confided to a *New York Times* reporter, "If the men of Mexico often fail to understand politics, what can we expect from the women?"[104]

In the two decades following the 1916 First Feminist Congress in Mérida, Yucatán, progressive women activists struggled to shape postrevolutionary policies to include their most pressing concerns, precipitating open conflict among leading activists regarding the definition of "women's interests" and, by extension, womanhood itself. Communists and penerristas confronted each other with overt hostility and disdain. Thorny issues of church-state relations sparked tense debates. Suffragists held that formal political rights should form the centerpiece of the women's movement, while others argued that political rights remained meaningless without mobilization and strong, legitimated organizations. However, this plurality and complexity gave women's organizing tremendous dynamism as activists cultivated a sense of possibility that any of these ideas might take root and capture the imaginations of policymakers and ordinary women alike. Women activists seized the opportunity to define the significance for women of the revolution and revolutionary citizenship.

Activists and policymakers approached the "woman question" within this framework. On the one hand, women's political rights seemed both the logical position of a government claiming to be democratic and revolutionary and the inevitable result of international momentum toward expanding women's rights and opportunities. On the other, women's presence in Mexican political life seemed incongruous and even unfathomable. "Will the sensitive character of the Mexican woman," asked one editorial, "be able to influence, vary, and modify the electoral corruption to which we have become accustomed since time immemorial?"[105] Communists and radical penerristas argued that women's labor-force participation would cultivate revolutionary consciousness, while feminists and liberal penerristas viewed political activities as the route to civic "preparation." Both these strategies sought to banish domesticity, widely seen as antithetical to citizenship. However, to most women, including many who identified themselves as feminists, the whole point of securing political rights was to span this divide, forcing "domestic" concerns onto policy agendas.

TWO

Laboratory of Cardenismo:

Constructing Michoacán's

Postrevolutionary

Edifice

In 1920, when the agrarian radicals Primo Tapia and Pedro López returned from the United States, where they had organized among anarchosyndicalists and communists, they immediately established a women's league. Likening a peasant woman to a "slave of a slave," Tapia encouraged women's unions (*sindicatos femeniles*) wherever he organized agrarista leagues.[1] "The organization of woman is indispensable now," he wrote to his comrade Apolinar Martínez Múgica, "because she is joining the world proletariat, and without organizing her we will fail miserably. . . . The women's union is stronger than the compañeros' and has more spirit; we've never had such uniform organization. We can now speak of woman as we would of any other fighter; she is no longer duped by the man in the cassock."[2] Tapia's remarks reflected the growing conviction that organization offered a panacea to the antirevolutionary ills plaguing Mexico.

Michoacán's political culture exhibited the influence of both Catholic radicalism and Communist organizational strategies, and women's organizing bore the imprint of the often violent rivalry between cristeros and agraristas.[3] In women's organizing, as in political strategies and popular organizing more generally, Michoacán served as Cardenismo's first laboratory, experimenting with programs and tactics that reappeared on the national scene, often modified as a result of lessons learned in Michoacán.[4] State-sponsored temperance and public-assistance leagues created an infrastructure for secular women's organizing, appropriating activities normally associated with Catholic charities and co-opting crucial aspects of the Communists' program. These leagues also gave women an entrée into political life, creating the organizational structures of revolutionary citizenship. Particularly as they gained official recognition and duties, they offered women activists the experiences and the leverage to make demands on the state government, albeit within limits.

The trajectory of Michoacán women's organizing—increasing centralization culminating in the incorporation of women's organizations into national confederations—foreshadowed the difficult choice women would face at the national level later in the decade. As the state's political climate shifted with changing administrations, women found that their popular organizations fell victim to political retaliation even more quickly than those run by men. Knowing the pitfalls of close political ties—particularly the loss of autonomy and the vulnerability to changes in administration—how close should women stay to a particular political faction? In Michoacán, at least, loyalty seemed the access road to political success, but uncertainties about loyalty to whom and on what terms underscored the contingent and gendered practice of revolutionary citizenship.

Articles of Faith: Agraristas, Cristeros, and Women's Leagues

In Naranja in December 1922, Tapia formed the Liga de Comunidades Agrarias (League of Agrarian Communities and Agrarista Unions) of Michoacán, establishing many of the agrarian-reform strategies Cárdenas would elaborate as governor and then president.[5] During Francisco Múgica's brief gubernatorial stint (1920–22), he provided crucial support to the agraristas, including arms and military protection, thus formalizing the state-agrarista alliance.[6] The league engaged in far-reaching rural social reform, advocating temperance and anti-fanaticism campaigns along with land distribution. Setting itself up as the counterpoint to the National Catholic Labor Confederation, the league directed its efforts at combating religious "fanaticism" and concerned itself as much with the popular Catholicism that governed quotidian rural life as with the formal church hierarchy.[7] Both Múgica and Tapia vocally and unapologetically railed against Catholicism. As

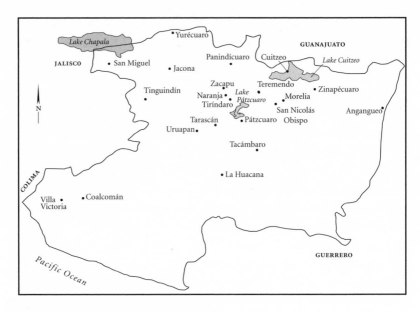

Map 2. "Michoacán." By Natalie Hanemann.

Múgica declared during the 1917 Constitutional Congress, "I am an enemy of the clergy because I consider it the most dangerous and perverse enemy of our Patria."[8] Meanwhile, Alfonso Soria, Tapia's comrade and a leader in Michoacán's Communist Party, countered that their anticlerical emphasis reduced their effectiveness by driving a wedge between agrarista leaders and the predominantly Catholic peasants whom they sought to organize.[9]

In defining the central conflict as between agrarian radicals and Catholic faithful, agraristas gave women a significant role in this struggle, viewing them as critical to any campaign to limit church influence in rural communities. Women, after all, had traditionally served as guardians of the faith, and piety was considered an obligatory aspect of traditional femininity. Recounting that he had just organized women's unions in ten different pueblos around Uruapan, Tapia wrote to a friend in 1923, "I spoke with the Indian compañeros of that pueblo [in Uruapan] to convince them that women's organization is indispensable . . . because while women remain under the priest's influence, he would drag even the last secret from our women. As long as she is not made independent in this sense, we will not have gained anything."[10] Gesturing toward malinchismo, Tapia predicted that women, as presumably naive political actors, would betray the revolutionary struggle at the hands of conniving priests.

Because of its strong ties to the state government, Tapia's Liga de Comunidades Agrarias became an arena for internal patronage struggles, long-standing personal rivalries, and more ideologically inflected political disputes.[11] As control over state politics swung away from the radical Múgica-Cárdenas faction during the years between their terms as governor (1922–28) and again during the tenure of Benigno Serrato (1932–35), agrarista leaders came under attack. Even during sympathetic administrations, the state government tried to contain peasant mobilizations, forcing organizations to traverse a complicated and unstable political terrain. Organizers like Primo Tapia played a critical role in cultivating this double-edged practice of simultaneously mobilizing and disciplining agraristas.

The anthropologist Paul Friedrich has documented the development of *caciquismo* (boss rule) among Michoacán's popular organizers, who often possessed experience outside their communities, above-average levels of education, and the ability — linguistically and culturally — to move among cultures.[12] Tapia, a Naranja native who could "pass" as either Tarascan or mestizo, frequently socialized with campesinos and learned to play and sing Tarascan folk songs. However, he also attended seminary in the United States, where he organized for the anarcho-syndicalist Industrial Workers of the World. While few agrarian leaders — and even fewer women's activists — boasted such a breadth of experience, many organizers had similar cultural, linguistic, or educational advantages that favored them as intermediaries between popular groups and state bureaucracies. Their power — their *cacicazgo* — depended on their ability to understand their constituencies, effectively represent their issues, and structure those issues in line with their own interests as local political leaders.

For women organizers, this position entailed representing women's needs to male-dominated parent organizations, such as the Liga de Comunidades Agrarias and the Communist Party, adding another layer of mediation. Furthermore, the conditions that made these women viable intermediaries — education, experience outside their communities, freedom from domestic obligations, contacts with public figures, participation in public events — often removed them further from their constituencies than these same conditions would for their male counterparts. Nonetheless, in Michoacán and elsewhere, women leaders did gain recognition and prestige through their roles as activists, occasionally securing government positions or moving up the ranks of organizations and parties. Activists like Dolores Núñez and Cuca García started out in Michoacán's popular-organizing network and by the 1930s and '40s had become prominent national and even international figures. Women, in short, learned to navigate the terrain between activism and clientelism just as men did. Although the league reduced its activities after Tapia's 1926 assassination, it left a legacy in women's organizing.[13] Throughout the 1930s, the vast majority of women's leagues clustered around agrarista strongholds, nestled among the lakes Chapala, Cuitzeo, and Pátzcuaro and amassed along the border with Jalisco and Guanajuato, as a bulwark against the nefarious influences of the state's conservative northern neighbors.

The Cradle of Cardenismo

The hallmark of Cardenismo, the alliances between mass organizations and the state, solidified with the 1929 establishment of the Revolutionary Labor Confederation of Michoacán (CRMDT).[14] Having orchestrated its creation, Cárdenas served as honorary president and promoted its leaders as labor, agricultural, and education inspectors. (By comparison, the Liga de Comunidades Agrarias, founded partly in response to Múgica's removal from the governor's office, had cultivated a more ambivalent relationship with the state government.) The CRMDT's founders included several leaders of Michoacán's Communist Party, which Tapia and other radical Liga de Comunidades Agrarias members had established in Morelia in 1923.[15] Under the symbol of the hammer and sickle and the slogan "Union, Land and Labor," the new confederation tied the agrarista movement more closely to state structures, broadened its agenda to include industrial labor organizing, and elaborated its program of organizing women. To be sure, the CRMDT's integration with the state bureaucracy, combined with the increasing orthodoxy of the Mexican Communist Party (PCM) during the 1929–35 period, heightened suspicion between the two groups. Nonetheless, many Communists remained active in the CRMDT, creating a network of connections among leaders of Michoacán's organized left.

The CRMDT constitution pledged to work for improvements for all workers, "without neglecting the same goals for women."[16] True to these principles, CRMDT organizers, including many wives and sisters of agrarista leaders, mounted an extensive campaign to organize workingwomen into unions and campesinas into temperance and anticlerical leagues. The promise not to "neglect" women's interests, however, bespeaks their continued marginalization, and they waxed and waned in their importance within the confederation's overall agenda, garnering more attention during Cárdenas's favorable tenure but fading to obscurity during the precarious years of the conservative Serrato government. Nonetheless, the CRMDT, like the Liga de Comunidades Agrarias, devoted resources and created infrastructures to promote women's organizing and eventually incorporated women activists into its leadership. Furthermore, it often served as advocate or trouble-shooter for women's leagues — particularly temperance leagues — established through the state or municipal governments.

The CRMDT faced limitations in industrial organizing. Michoacán had very little industrial development in 1929, and most nonagricultural work took place in small workshops more closely resembling households than large factories.[17] By late 1932, the largest workplace in the capital city of Morelia was a timber mill employing thirty-five people, followed by an apparel work-shop of twenty-two workers. Furthermore, the CRMDT leadership had signed an agreement not to organize where the Callista labor confederation, the Confederación Regional de Obreros Mexicanos (CROM), had already orga-nized, including the American-owned mining company in the eastern town of Angangueo, which employed some 1,100 workers in 1929.[18] The relatively small number of women performing paid labor most often worked in family-owned workshops or performed seasonal agricultural labor.[19]

In keeping with contemporary ideas about social change, wage labor fig-ured just as prominently into Cárdenas's modernizing vision for women as temperance and anticlerical campaigns. When he assumed office, he quickly established a women's vocational school in Morelia, the Josefa Ortiz de Domínguez Industrial School for Women. The school, named after an independence-era heroine, promised to transform "women's labor" into "skilled labor." A companion to the Alvaro Obregón Technical–Industrial School in Morelia and the Indigenous Industrial School in Pátzcuaro, the women's vocational school invited girls between 12 and 18, "orphaned at least by the father," and members of Michoacán's proletariat to study "do-mestic arts and small industries."[20] The school gained immediate popularity, with one mother even requesting special dispensation for her 7-year-old daughter to attend.[21] Women and girls thronged to opportunities for train-ing and certification for labor — "domestic arts and small industries" — they often performed anyway.

Meanwhile, the CRMDT made headway organizing workingwomen, par-ticularly in Morelia and Uruapan, both of which had well-established PCM organizing committees. One of the confederation's earliest campaigns targeted roughly fifty women sock and stocking makers in Morelia's El Globo factory.[22] The El Globo case illuminates not only strategies for women's organizing, but also the relationships among women's unions, the CRMDT, and state politics. The factory's workers formed the union in January 1930 in the CRMDT meeting hall, seeking "our collective and individual improvement, morally and materially speaking, as well as the emancipation of and respect for woman, elevating her economically and socially." Two weeks later, El Globo fired two workers for joining the union. Antonio Mayés Navarro, the state labor inspector and founder of the CRMDT, elicited a confession from the factory foreman that the women's dismissal resulted from their union activity. The union's officers appealed to Morelia's municipal president for support, but he responded that the union still lacked official recognition, requiring the aggrieved workers to plead their cases individually.

If the factory's owner, José Jury, intended to intimidate the women and discourage union organizing, his plan backfired: his actions apparently only strengthened their resolve to secure effective representation and protection. Two weeks after the workers' dismissal, the union combined forces with Morelia's all-women hatters union and formed the Sole Front of Women Workers. In March 1931, the union filed a class-action suit on behalf of seven of its members, charging Jury with reducing their pay and failing to pay the promised 10–15 percent commission on their work, and of falsely blaming them for "losing or stealing" bolts of cloth.[23] Several women accused Jury of "poor treatment," with one worker losing her job for "refusing to submit to such exploitation." Jury implored the state's labor-arbitration board to allow him to close his factory, arguing the unfeasibility of operating with unionized workers. The CRMDT petitioned both the labor board and Municipal President Carlos García León (the de jure president of the city labor board) to order Jury not to remove any machinery, which constituted the only guarantee that he would pay back wages. García León, surely wanting to duck the crossfire, begged off, saying that such an action fell beyond his authority. The state labor board then voted against the union, with the workers' representative inexplicably supporting Jury.[24]

Perhaps seeing their own interests threatened, other CRMDT unions took strong stances on the El Globo conflict, writing to Cárdenas and García León in solidarity with the El Globo workers.[25] The secretary-general of the bricklayers' union wrote that his "compañeras in struggle" had been mistreated by Jury "for the sole crime of organizing within the ranks of the revolutionary element and seeking the emancipation of the working class." The El Globo women, he maintained, "very much in spite of the obstacles placed before them, have remained firmly within the ranks of revolutionary workers." He then called on Cárdenas to support "our sisters of class." Several unions went even further and called on Cárdenas to expropriate the factory's machinery and turn it over to the union.

Their pleas failed, however, producing an ambiguous defeat that offered important lessons about the limits of institutional alliances. On the one hand, CRMDT support helped union members develop a strong sense of their rights and of collective action's benefits. The CRMDT provided the requisite impetus, physical space, patronage links, and incidental resources, and the CRMDT's leader, Luis Mora Tovar, intervened to transform a brewing inter-union dispute into the strengthened Sole Front of Women Workers. The official support enjoyed by the CRMDT placed leaders such as Mayés Navarro within the state bureaucracy, enabling them to advocate more effectively than outsiders. Finally, the solidarity of other CRMDT unions and the secretary-general strengthened the El Globo workers' resolve and legitimacy. In short, the CRMDT's support made a critical difference, a fact that the union organizers involved clearly understood. While the confederation had its own motivations for cultivating women's support, it took seriously the task of organizing and backing women workers.

On the other hand, by the conflict's end, some fifty women had lost their jobs. While the CRMDT dedicated resources to organizing and backing the union, it could only write letters and file legal petitions; support did not run deep enough to threaten labor actions or demonstrations to champion the beleaguered union. Although CRMDT leaders must have despaired at the idea that the high cost of union labor justified closing a factory, the fact that the case involved a women's union and women's work made it exceptional and less threatening to organized labor as a whole, which still viewed women's income as supplementary rather than as a family wage.

The El Globo case was unusual in many ways, since most wage-earning women worked in education or the service sector rather than in manufacturing, and the vast majority of women performed nonwage labor in the countryside, where the CRMDT concentrated its organizing energy on obtaining and defending plots of land through agrarian reform, with clear gender divisions.[26] Most women could not benefit directly from the land reform, and the CRMDT did not call on women to participate in agrarian communities' armed defense.[27] Like the 1930s Cardenista agrarian-reform program, the CRMDT understood land reform as structured around male heads of household and patriarchal families. Nonetheless, while the CRMDT neither explicitly mentioned women in its agrarian-reform agenda nor originally included any women among its officers, the organization bore the stamp of Primo Tapia's commitment to organizing women. A founder of the Liga de Comunidades Agrarias wrote to Múgica in October 1931 that several women's leagues bearing either Múgica's or Tapia's name existed in the agrarista region near Zacapu, and the CRMDT women's leagues became the models for women's organizing during the Cárdenas presidency.[28]

The CRMDT emerged as a central political force and offered a novel and ultimately prototypical strategy for organizing workers and peasants into a government-supported confederation, consolidating the pro-regime organizing efforts and offering the paradigm for Cardenista corporatism. The creation of the Mexican Labor Confederation (CTM) in 1936 and the National Peasant Confederation (CNC) in 1938 would obviate the CRMDT, but by then it had demonstrated that vertically structured organizations not only facilitated state control over mass participation but also allowed the government to play the part of the benevolent patron, settling land claims and labor disputes while keeping potential agitators invested in political stability. Further, the CRMDT's mounting radicalism, power, and violence convinced Cárdenas of the wisdom of maintaining separate labor and peasant organizations—a stance that labor leaders such as Vicente Lombardo Toledano would challenge during his presidency.

Cultural Violence and Violent Cultures: Organizing in Cristero Territory

The rhetoric of cristeros and agraristas so permeated the political discourse of 1920s and '30s Michoacán that it remains difficult to distinguish when these labels referred to identifiable sets of beliefs and when they were simply epithets used to discredit political enemies. State representatives expressed genuine concern over Catholic influences, particularly on girls and women. Education Inspector Celso Flores Zamora complained in November 1929 that girls in the town of Tacámbaro refused to attend school because the priest threatened them with damnation.[29] Other anticlerical conflicts, however, reveal more about local power struggles than about genuine concerns that the Catholic church posed a danger to the revolutionary regime. Particularly in the region surrounding Zacapu, which boasted a high concentration of women's leagues by the 1930s, agrarista-cristero conflicts defined political camps. As the political scientist Jennie Purnell has shown, local Purépecha elites exploited the Cárdenas–Múgica faction's state-building efforts to regain land and power they had lost to an alliance of mestizo elites and clergy. "These identities of Catholic and agrarista," she explains, "forged in the conflicts of agrarian reform in the 1920s, continued to dominate factional conflict well into the 1930s."[30]

In the Zacapu municipality, Tiríndaro's Severo Espinosa offers the most notorious case of agrarista abuses. A one-time Tapia comrade, Espinosa made suppressing Catholicism a centerpiece of his political activities. The anthropologist Paul Friedrich recounts that, one night in 1923, Espinosa and several fellow agraristas raided Tiríndaro's church, killing five parishioners and ransacking the building.[31] As the town's self-anointed agrarista representative, Espinosa controlled the distribution of *ejido* (collective) lands, making renunciation of Catholicism a prerequisite for inclusion in the land reform. Thus excluding nearly three-quarters of the area's families left larger parcels for residents who complied with Espinosa's demands, exacerbating hostilities between the two camps.

In January 1930, Espinosa, supposedly in prison for his atrocities, continued acting as president of Zacapu's CRMDT-affiliated anticlerical league.[32] By March, a group of 140 women protested Espinosa's mounting hostility. Concerned about his proclivity for violence, they explained, "We were threatened again by a group of men and women from the agrarista party, who, with harassment and words unworthy of repetition, insulted us and mistreated us with impunity . . . and announced that they would exterminate all the Catholics."[33] Espinosa would find, however, that he had tied his fortunes too closely to those of the Cárdenas government. While the Cardenistas turned a blind eye to his abuses and a deaf ear to the complaints about him, Cárdenas's political rivals proved all too willing to act against him.

Like the Zacapu women, women's leagues often censured renewed violence. In March 1930, when the peace accords still seemed fragile and perhaps not quite real, cristeros attempted to reopen Zurumútaro's churches. "We oppose this," the women's league informed Cárdenas. "We have had a more or less peaceful life around here, and if they return, all the blood that has been spilled to emancipate us from those so harmful to the Republic and to the entire world will have been for nothing."[34] Although playing to Cardenistas' anticlerical commitments, their concerns were hardly spurious. In April 1930, the municipal authorities of Coalcomán — a predominantly small-holding, mestizo region that had come under cristero control in April 1927 and briefly declared itself an autonomous republic—complained that a widow distributed antigovernment religious propaganda, potentially rekindling old conflicts. Three weeks later, the town's priest reportedly had been "killed in struggle" after exhorting his flock to take up arms against the government.[35] While church-related organizing in other regions provoked concern among government officials, in Michoacán, with its recent experience of bloody religious conflict, the threat of renewed violence sparked terror.

Even without urging their followers to commit violence, church leaders controlled important religious rites. In April 1930, the priest in the northeastern town of Zinapécuaro posted a notice on the church doors stating, "Catholics of any condition or sex, who for any reason—sectarianism, employment, comradeship, or egotism—mixed with subversive elements at the Masonic and Revolutionary meeting in the Teatro Hidalgo . . . do not have the right to receive sacramental absolution. They must first address the Minister of Government, either individually or together, and describe the outrages committed by the Bolshevik Mafia against the Catholics of a country that prides itself on being civilized. . . . They should demand an investigation into the origins and results of this trouble, so that those responsible are punished to the full extent of the law."[36] Such statements resonated with Catholics who had endured agrarista abuses and systematic exclusion from agrarian reforms. Furthermore, the threat of denying sacraments particularly concerned women, who often viewed religious observance as a core family duty and the church as the centerpiece of their community.[37]

As government and church officials each tried to secure popular support, many Michoacanos sought to extricate themselves from the polarized political situation. "The indigenous People, obeying old traditions," Jacinto Espinoza petitioned in August 1930, seeking to tap into Cárdenas's respect for indigenous cultures, "respectfully request special permission to take an image into the field to end the scarcity of water that causes us to forsake the labors that sustain our children. This in no way will harm the institutions of your supreme Government, which we pledge to obey."[38] Perhaps because the church in Espinoza's town of Jacona had flown a cristero flag beside its altar only four months earlier, state authorities denied the request, explaining that "such religious demonstrations are prohibited by law." In the same month in the town of La Huacana, some 90 miles southeast of Jacona, a group of "principally señoras" paraded through the streets with saints and sacred images to "implore God to bring rain to the cornfields [*milpas*]." A federal agent who happened to be passing through the town informed the gathering that its activities violated the constitution and promptly arrested the local authority who had allowed it.[39]

Concerns about clerical influences extended to prohibitions against ringing church bells, which cristeros had used as a call to arms. Church bells had demarcated the rhythms of daily life in most towns, but in December 1931, the state congress decreed that, to announce religious acts, one bell could be rung no more than ten times and only with the permission of appropriate authorities.[40] The attempted extirpation of such deep-rooted cultural practices, such as the sounding of church bells and public prayer to ward off natural disasters, sparked popular resistance. The town council in the Tarascan village of Tingüindín informed the state government that the town's priest continued to tell time "astronomically" and to ask for tithes from pedestrians and ambulatory vendors. A local official, Juan Picazo, had stopped him. "For this reason," the council's president explained, "the women are indignant . . . and have committed endless inanities in the place occupied by the municipal presidency. There is no reason for the fanatical women to treat me in this way. Several of the most fanatical women congregate and create disturbances in this office."[41] If the state government acceded to the women's demand to remove him from office, he concluded, it would constitute a grave injustice.

Such incidents underscore the extent to which the agrarista-cristero conflict was woven into the quotidian political culture. Popular, customary activities — formerly unassociated with political meaning — looked like direct attacks on the governing regime when viewed through the lens of the violent conflicts of the 1920s. However, outlawing such activities amounted to banning the cultural practices surrounding the tragic and joyful events that punctuated Michoacanos' everyday lives, many of which placed women at their center. Although men participated in greater numbers in armed cristero violence, it was women's participation — and even leadership — that most alarmed Cardenistas. Reports of cristero violence or of violations of laws governing religious activities frequently mentioned women's roles. Clandestine services might take place in the homes of pious spinsters or widows.[42] Particularly galling to anticlerical authorities, women came out into the streets and demonstrated publicly, as they had in Tingüindín. The idea of "fanatical women" entering a government building to "congregate and create disturbances" seemed especially distressing and disorderly to authorities, who remained uncertain how to discipline these women. Furthermore, women spilling into the public, masculinized space of the *palacio municipal* and demanding the removal of the municipal president jarred local officials. Assuming that women would not engage in such disruptions on their own, these incidents almost invariably resulted in actions taken against men — the arrest of a supposed leader, the removal of a permissive municipal authority, or the expulsion of the local priest.

Guardians of Public Order: The Politics of Temperance and Welfare

Cárdenas and his supporters sought to attract Michoacanas' allegiance away from the church by carving out public roles for them, establishing all-women temperance and public-assistance committees — sites for the practice of revolutionary citizenship — in every municipality.[43] Seeing women as imbued with natural morality, Cárdenas enlisted their support in rooting out vice and corruption, but these committees sparked considerable controversy. Antialcohol leagues, after all, sanctioned women's interference in the manly world of cantinas and the traffic in "intoxicating beverages," which often rendered profits to local caciques. Even when municipal presidents did not profit from the alcohol trade themselves, they regularly protected those who did. Efforts to shutter cantinas on payday or near schools, factories, and ejidos frequently met with violent resistance or simple noncompliance.

The Michoacán government had struggled with the temperance question at least since 1907, when it debated temperance legislation. Decrying the difficulties of legislating alcohol consumption, temperance advocates complained, "The monster lives, grows, advances menacingly, and will end by strangling us in its steel claws."[44] Nearly twenty years later, with the revolution intervening and the Cristero Rebellion on the horizon, the state legislature once again tried to control alcohol consumption, this time with a clear concern about productivity. In March 1926, the state congress banned sales of alcohol near factories, labor centers, rancherías, agrarian communities, or haciendas, explaining that, for lack of vigilance, there were "scandals, brawls, and homicides provoked by drunkenness." Citing similar concerns expressed by the American Federation of Labor's leadership at its convention in Denver, lawmakers sought to combat the deleterious practice of honoring "Saint Monday" by suspending alcohol sales between Sunday afternoon and Monday morning. Regulatory violations brought hefty fines, jail terms, and the revocation of one's liquor license. Even possessing alcohol in the home or workplace above amounts allowed for "medicinal purposes" constituted a violation that carried a 100 peso fine. Finally, the 1926 law declared that "intemperance" justified removal from public office.[45]

These far-reaching efforts attest to persistent concerns among lawmakers and postrevolutionary leaders about modernizing Mexico, hoping to destroy the image (and practice) of the swaggering, gun-toting, pulque-guzzling political boss. By involving women, temperance leagues gave them a role in the project of creating a modern, reliable labor force.[46] The extent of these regulations — even monitoring whether someone had an excessive amount of alcohol in the privacy of her own home — becomes even more striking given that, by 1930, the state government empowered women's leagues to monitor regulatory compliance.

The idea of charging women with policing such matters unsettled local authorities. One mayor reported that "the fathers of the señoritas cannot allow the mentioned señoritas to watch over the town in the antialcohol question."[47] League supporters argued that women would participate only in propaganda and education campaigns, but in practice, the committees generally took responsibility for reporting infractions. This tension continued through the 1930s as a national temperance campaign emerged using women's committees as intermediaries between local authorities and state and national governments. In May 1930, Cárdenas imposed a new alcohol tax and called on all municipal presidents to form temperance committees to ensure the laws' enforcement.[48] When several municipalities submitted committees composed of men, Secretary of Government Agustín Leñero promptly notified them that the "temperance committees should consist exclusively of women."[49] Santiaguito residents, however, "refused to allow their wives to form the committee." Leñero assured local authorities that "said subcommittee, formed by señoras or señoritas, is in no way obliged to perform the role of guardian of public order nor, for that reason, to hold nocturnal vigils." Instead, he explained, the women would "form clubs, organizations, etc." to "develop a campaign of persuasion and goodwill around their husbands, sons, brothers, or relatives, affectionately calling them home, making them see alcoholism's disastrous consequences, organizing honest festivals to distract men from vices, etc., etc."[50] Despite Leñero's soft-pedaling of women's involvement, Santiaguito's men perceived these committees as a threat. Intended as community, and even household, watchdog groups, they disrupted traditional gender relations by placing women in a position of power—or, at least, of state-sanctioned vigilance—over their communities' men. Indeed, women would come to use their leverage within temperance committees to influence local politics.

In February 1931, the state legislature further restricted alcohol sales and granted the temperance committees explicit power to monitor enforcement.[51] The 1931 legislation reinforced class- and ethnicity-defined concerns about alcohol abuse, banning the sales in union halls and cultural centers near agricultural and industrial workplaces, and communities with a majority indigenous population. The law limited the hours of alcohol sales and prohibited such sales between Saturday afternoon and Monday morning as well as on sixteen different patriotic holidays. The law further banned the sale or consumption of alcohol in spaces associated with poor women, including brothels, "any public place where women or children may be found," and public markets.

While municipal authorities determined who would receive sales permits and the severity of punishments for temperance violations, state law granted legal status to the women's temperance committees, "recognized by the Government and by popular action to watch over and denounce to the appropriate municipal authorities those establishments that disobey this law, with the aim of applying the sanctions that it outlines." Persistent concerns about alcohol undercutting productivity led state officials to instruct municipal presidents "to report immediately the women's temperance-committee members in that municipality, so that they may undertake the task of combating, to whatever extent possible, the vice of drunkenness so pervasive in our laboring classes."[52] The repetition of these circulars, like the periodic passage of new temperance legislation, indicates that compliance fell short of official expectations.

The CRMDT formed women's temperance leagues that often doubled as anticlerical leagues. In Teremendo, CRMDT organizers simultaneously established the Isaac Arriaga Women's Anticlerical League and the Primo Tapia Women's Antialcohol League, naming both after well-known agrarista leaders. "We gave them ample explanation about the dangers wrought as a consequence of 'religious fanaticism,'" the CRMDT organizers recounted. "They then were asked to express their opinion about whether or not they agreed to organize and constitute the Anticlerical League. . . . They agreed to form said Anticlerical League to muzzle . . . the henchmen of the Vatican, represented by the Pseudo God of fanaticism or an image of the All Powerful."[53] The tone of the minutes indicates the limited space available for dissent.

Although the temperance league was formed at the same meeting, its founding document switches the authorial voice to the women themselves. "Our institution has as its object the complete extermination of alcoholic beverages of which we have been the constant victims," it explains, "as much through the misery that invades our homes as through the difficulties among our fathers, husbands, and sons, who in an inebriated state commit acts of which they would normally be incapable. We have also noticed that this results in dangers to our children and to humanity in general, for which reason we are firmly decided in achieving complete extermination."[54] These two descriptions reveal members' relative investment in these two projects. To be sure, many agrarista family members demonstrated genuine commitment to anticlericalism, and many women produced, sold, and consumed alcohol themselves. Nevertheless, most ordinary Michoacanas remained far more concerned about alcoholism — which could have immediate, concrete, and even violent effects on their lives, as well as disastrous effects on household budgets — than about the local clergy's misdeeds.

For many women, anticlericalism's Manichaean terms obscured the nuances of their relationship to their faith. Esperanza Quintero Castellanos, the wife of agrarista Salvador Cervantes Vargas, began organizing in the temperance leagues in 1923. In a 1998 interview, she proudly described her temperance work, and, given her association with agraristas and her description of the agrarista baptisms in which she participated, she likely also participated in anticlerical organizing. However, she recalled none of that, explaining only, "I am a believer."[55] For Quintero and other activist women, the anticlerical campaign may simply have served as a form of dues — paying to gain indispensable institutional support for more pressing temperance concerns. The temperance campaign, in turn, became an avenue to access decision-making structures more generally.

In cases where local authorities remained unresponsive to the leagues' complaints, the CRMDT often stepped in to help the league negotiate matters. Following a scandal in which the local school inspector became so brazenly drunk during Independence Day festivities that he started a brawl with other local authorities, the women's temperance league in San Miguel del Monte contacted the CRMDT, which reported the incident directly to state officials. They, in turn, ordered the director of primary-school education to intervene.[56] While this circuitous route may seem inefficient, it offered the league several advantages. First, the men who participated in the brawl were likely to have been friends, relatives, or rivals of the women who filed the complaint; in any case, they were unlikely to have been anonymous strangers. Second, the league capitalized on the CRMDT's legitimacy within state and municipal governments, using temperance organizers' moral authority to intervene in formal politics. Finally, having the legal advantage, the women benefited by drawing more public figures into the matter and getting them invested in its outcome. Had the conflict remained internal to their community, the women would have simply gone toe-to-toe with local political authorities and almost surely would have been rebuffed.

However, women's own roles in producing, selling, and consuming alcohol complicated their temperance efforts. Although generally banned from the cantinas, either by law or by tradition, women frequently supplemented household budgets by making and selling liquor, particularly home-brewed elixirs such as pulque and *aguardiente* (moonshine). Furthermore, women — although not nearly so frequently as men — appeared in police blotters for disrupting public order or fighting while intoxicated. Nonetheless, they took temperance efforts seriously, largely because men's drinking habits reflected family power structures, including men's control over wages. State-sponsored temperance campaigns offered women recourse for contesting patriarchal control, albeit in a limited fashion, and an entry into formal politics by challenging local authorities' temperance violations.

Much like the temperance campaign, Michoacán's public-assistance committees defined women's emerging political roles.[57] Cárdenas described the committees as a means of securing the "cooperation of . . . the feminine element, whose feelings are recognized and justly praised by all." The committees included women "of recognized probity and altruism," related to neither public functionaries nor military officers. Further, the positions remained unpaid to avoid diverting funds from welfare projects and to guarantee that those who held the positions would be "truly enabled by their altruism."[58] In other words, committees consisted of wealthy women who remained completely outside politics and therefore protected from its corrupting influences; their very status as private actors made entrance into public life possible. In effect, male union members, professionals, merchants, and property owners elected women to represent them on commissions monitoring public assistance in prisons, hospitals, and asylums.

Like temperance leagues, public-assistance committees served multiple objectives, including modernization, displacing the Catholic church, more equitably distributing resources, and gradually incorporating women into public affairs. Legislators designed them to fulfill revolutionary obligations to "take care of the dispossessed classes who, for reasons of age, lack of health, or special conditions, are prevented from earning their subsistence or improving themselves through their own efforts."[59] Charity and welfare fell within the traditional bounds of "feminine" duty, and the committees' tasks, such as overseeing prison nutrition and hygiene and attending to children in hospices, meshed with women's reproductive-labor obligations. These efforts would induce upper-class women to perform for the state the type of charitable work that they had traditionally done through the church.

The official public-assistance committees retained a complexion similar to a private charity. The legislation establishing them included no prohibitions against church affiliation or even promoting Catholicism, which traditionally would have accompanied many of the committees' activities, such as visiting prisons, hospitals, and invalids' homes; providing food and clothing to destitute mothers; and establishing vocational training centers to teach girls skills "appropriate to their sex." The less controllable, less predictable "fanaticism" of lower-class women concerned the government far more than upper-class women's charitable "piety." Also, the official committees could tap into state and municipal budgets and levy a tax on public performances of up to 5 percent. The CRMDT women's leagues had an explicitly anticlerical agenda, could only petition for funds on a case-by-case basis, and existed primarily to support CRMDT efforts within their communities. As part of a popular movement, albeit one choreographed from above, the CRMDT leagues agitated and organized on their own behalf rather than as a charity and increasingly challenged the idea that only women of "recognized probity and altruism" who had the luxury of donating their time and labor should shape welfare policies.

State-sponsored welfare committees, like the temperance leagues, also provided women with leverage within the state government and, even allowing for their exclusivity, created a venue in which women voted and were elected to influence public policy. Such structures enabled women to inhabit revolutionary citizenship, providing crucial political and material support. This inchoate form of citizenship practice attained greater significance during the Cárdenas presidency, as the question of women's formal political rights gained currency and activists translated their political experience into a sense of entitlement to a recognized political voice.

Seeds of Discontent: Serrato and the Attack on the CRMDT

Even as the CRMDT advocated for grassroots-level issues, close observers expressed concern that the organization had become too involved in state politics, leading to its professionalization and bureaucratization. "It surprised me to hear that the [CRMDT] had changed its tactics, resolving to enter into politics," Múgica wrote in 1932 to his fellow radical, the federal deputy and state PNR leader Ernesto Soto Reyes, "since its directing bodies are not exactly managed by workers and peasants, and some of their members are prowlers seeking to take advantage. I fear that the campesinos and obreros will be dragged into unclean commitments that could disorganize them, or even worse, divide them. Furthermore, *liderismo* could become entrenched among them, and they would see the social struggle only through politics."[60] A memo to the CRMDT leadership insisting that the central and political action committees consist entirely of people whom Cárdenas held in complete confidence would only have heightened Múgica's concerns.[61] This tension between formal politics and popular mobilization — or "social struggle" — persisted through the 1930s, remaining an important concern within women's organizing as well. Múgica, having witnessed firsthand how quickly tides could turn, understandably cautioned against political entanglements.

Severing the CRMDT's political commitments, however, would have appeared neither feasible nor desirable to its leaders. Cárdenas's support meant organizational jobs for loyal men and women as well as positions in the state and municipal governments. Cárdenas had his own concerns regarding the group's influence over its honorary president. "He did not want us to be his sheep," Soto Reyes wrote to Múgica, "but nor did he want to be ours, merely approving things that we had discussed earlier without consulting him."[62] As the gubernatorial election drew closer and leading activists expressed doubts about the candidates, Soto Reyes encouraged Múgica to toss his hat in the ring.[63] Apolinar Martínez Múgica lamented to his "friend and *correligionario* [fellow traveller]" Francisco Múgica, "They have already given the names of the candidates, and they have nothing in common with the proletarian interests. Benigno Serrato and Francisco Ortiz Rubio. One praetorian and the other bourgeois." He urged Múgica to consider making a bid as "the Michoacano who has most entered the hearts of the masses and is trained to assume the [governorship]."[64]

These concerns proved to be well founded; anti-CRMDT harassment commenced almost immediately after the change in administration. Cárdenas's gubernatorial term had created Cardenistas and anti-Cardenistas in Michoacán before they existed in the rest of the republic. When Serrato succeeded Cárdenas in September 1932, he promptly replaced all the Cardenista municipal authorities, functionaries, and CRMDT leaders with his own supporters. With endorsements from both the Knights of Columbus and Calles, the Serrato government marked not simply a leadership change but a pendulum swing away from Cárdenas's policies, particularly agrarian-reform and anticlerical campaigns. The military commander Rafael Sánchez Tapia informed Múgica that "fanatics" governed the municipalities of Suhuayo, Huarachita, Zamora, and Chavinda, causing endless problems.[65] In December, a CRMDT affiliate in Zamora reported that the new local authorities had threatened opposition groups and jailed several CRMDT members.[66] One CRMDT leader recounted more than forty political assassinations in the first eight months of Serrato's administration.[67]

Just as Catholic women had endured attacks under the Cárdenas government, agrarista women suffered under Serrato. A 1933 congressional report on political violence in Michoacán described nine cases that included women among those attacked or jailed by either local Serratista authorities or private guardias blancas.[68] Cristina Verduzco, a prominent CRMDT activist, was fined and briefly jailed for opposing Serrato's efforts to replace the CRMDT leadership. María Corona, the president of the Revolutionary Anticlerical Central Committee in the volatile Hacienda Nueva Italia, requested federal protection, explaining that she had received threats and that people threw stones at her house while the police watched.[69]

As they had a decade earlier, women protested against the mounting violence. In Naranja, the cradle of *agrarismo* (agrarian radicalism), the Primo Tapia Women's Union denounced assaults on their compañeros, who were harassed and arrested without cause and denied basic services such as water.[70] "We, the undersigned ladies of the society of Yurécuaro," wrote a group from a town bordering the state of Jalisco, "representing all social classes, request a change in the municipal authorities, who are responsible for the current state of things and for the crimes committed against defenseless campesinos, as the press has stated. We want authorities that offer social guarantees so that our pueblo enjoys tranquillity and everyone can dedicate themselves to the sacred mission of work."[71]

In March 1933, Serrato's supporters convened a CRMDT congress and replaced the Cardenista officers with Serratistas. As several scholars have pointed out, Serrato's assumption of the governor's office rekindled not only dormant agrarista-cristero hostilities but also divisions within agrarista movements, which served as a cover for Serratista violence.[72] When municipal police opened fire on a CRMDT meeting, killing three people and wounding ten others, Serrato maintained that the incident resulted from internal CRMDT divisions and not anti-Cardenista hostilities.[73]

With two camps claiming to represent the "authentic" CRMDT, women's organizing on gender-specific issues slowed considerably. Very few new CRMDT women's organizations appeared, and existing ones concentrated on fending off Serratista attacks. Nurses and midwives organized a union in Morelia but without any CRMDT association, avoiding the language of class struggle and emphasizing that it was "a society of a professional character to defend the interests of the guild." Unlike the CRMDT's calls for "Union, Land and Labor," the nurses and midwives demanded "social and moral elevation."[74] Moreover, men replaced women on temperance committees, eliminating an important structure of women's organizing.[75]

The tide turned with Cárdenas's unveiling as the PNR's likely presidential candidate. The label Cardenista, which had become a magnet for Serratista abuse, now ensured the protection of one of the republic's most powerful men. In July 1933, expelled CRMDT leaders, with Pedro López at the helm, created the Radical Socialist Federation of Michoacán and appealed to Cárdenas, Múgica, and several other well-placed sympathizers for support.[76] Focused on gaining greater political representation for working-class and peasant Michoacanos, the federation cited women's leagues among the revolutionary organizations requiring protection from "reactionary" hostilities but did not mention any gender-specific demands. Women's political rights had already entered the national discussion about political freedoms but remained absent from the federation's lengthy letter about democratic processes, a striking omission given that López's wife, Matilde Anguiano, had become a prominent political activist. Confronting a well-organized, well-supported reaction to Cardenista anticlericalism, the federation's leadership may have harbored its own concerns that women would defend the church. The federation instead focused its political energies on promoting Cárdenas's presidential candidacy.[77]

Women activists also appealed to their patrons. Dolores Núñez, the only woman up to that point to have served on any CRMDT standing committee, informed Múgica that "358 revolutionary members who support [his] teachings" had held a women's convention in Pátzcuaro.[78] "I want you to tackle enormous problems and choose practical means of action," Múgica responded. "Our state needs to organize itself, and I believe that women will accomplish everything that until now has failed in the hands of men."[79] Although such correspondence showcased Múgica's political skills as much as his conviction, throughout the 1930s he remained — among politicians of national stature — the staunchest advocate of women's rights, a fact not lost on women's organizations when he made his 1939 presidential bid.[80]

"The Strong Arm of Labor": Women and the Cardenista Renaissance

With Cárdenas's presidential nomination secured and the CRMDT's Cardenista faction regrouping, women's organizing gained momentum with renewed vigor. Women's CRMDT involvement began paying dividends as women emerged as prominent organizers. In 1931, Elvira Chávez had organized twenty-seven women into the CRMDT-affiliated Lázaro Cárdenas Women's Union in Jesús del Monte.[81] After a period of inactivity, Chávez reorganized the group in 1934 as a CRMDT-associated temperance league. The CRMDT's leader, Pedro López, took a personal interest in the organization, perhaps identifying Chávez as a promising leader.[82] The following year, Chávez became the vice president of the CRMDT's newly established women's branch, the Michoacán Socialist Women's Federation (FFSM).[83] The CRMDT, much like the Communist Party and the Secretariat of Public Education during the same years, had become a training ground for women activists.

Among those involved in the FFSM's July 1934 founding, several had some PCM association. Most either earned their living as teachers, bringing them into contact with the PCM through teachers' unions, or had family associations with the CRMDT. By 1934, the PCM had gained strength in Michoacán and had aggressively recruited women for several years.[84] The FFSM's founders, several of whom went on to achieve greater prominence at the state or national level, came not from a middle-class, reformist background but, rather, from the more radical, class-based activism influenced by communist and agrarista ideals. The FFSM constitution began on a note of confidence, explaining that "Michoacán's revolutionary woman, brimming with enthusiasm and optimism for the emancipation of the oppressed, understanding her obligation to struggle alongside her compañero in suffering, and emerging from the humiliating life of the pariah," would organize to "confront the capitalists' selfishness and the arcane social systems that relegate workers to the miserable condition of defenseless serfs."[85]

The FFSM hit its stride just as state politics turned in the CRMDT's favor. Cárdenas's ascent had shifted the organization's mood from that of a beleaguered, divided, and imperiled organization to that of a movement that had survived the most brutal attacks and now saw a light at the end of the tunnel, "emerging from the humiliating life of the pariah."[86] Persecution had strengthened bonds among Cardenistas, inducing activists to put aside personal differences, if only temporarily, for the sake of organizational solidarity. Cárdenas's July 1934 presidential victory meant that his supporters saw not only an end to their hardships but also vindication in the not-too-distant future.

Weaving together strands of Cardenismo with elements of Mexican communism, ideas set forward by teachers' unions, and an unusually high dose of pacifism, the FFSM pledged to organize proletarian woman "along the lines demarcated by the postulates of the Mexican revolution" and "to struggle against all phenomena that exploit human energies and restrain the will and spiritual liberty." Declaring that "woman is not the weaker sex, but rather the strong arm of labor [*bracero de trabajo*] that fights to attain her own emancipation and that of workingmen of the fields and the city," the organization promoted socialist education and the CRMDT. The program of action included five sections — labor union, peasant, temperance, anticlerical, and antiwar — and justified women's legitimacy in the public realm as "integral members of society and workers in the *campo* [field] and the workshop." The antiwar sentiments coincided with the PCM's agenda; only a month before the FFSM was founded, a delegation of PCM women had attended the Paris peace conference.[87] However, this pacifist emphasis also suggested the anxieties about Michoacán's persistent violence, no doubt fueled by continued attacks against public-school teachers, a major FFSM constituency.

The assertions and silences in the FFSM's constitution reveal an ambivalence regarding gendered activism. Pacifism, temperance, and education campaigns all squared well with a nurturing, protecting, maternal femininity inflected by local experiences and political culture. Similarly, the anticlerical tenet reiterated fears about feminine piety — fears heightened in the homeland of the Cristero Rebellion. However, although suffragists had already pushed their way onto the national stage, questions about women's political rights remained conspicuously absent from the FFSM's program. In November 1934, the federation held the second Women's Socialist Congress, following the example Dolores Núñez had set the previous year, to cultivate state- and local-level women's leadership within the CRMDT.[88] Organizers lined up their usual patrons, including Múgica, Cárdenas, and Gabino Vázquez (then a federal deputy), requesting endorsements and financial assistance to defray expenses. The congress produced modest demands, such as transforming a church into a workingwomen's cultural center, but generated excitement among women activists that their movement had achieved a critical mass, an institutional framework, and much needed momentum.

Shortly after the FFSM's founding, Benigno Serrato died in a plane crash, transforming Michoacán's political complexion. Cárdenas appointed an ally and revolutionary veteran, Rafael Sánchez Tapia, interim governor. With Cárdenas in the presidency and a sympathetic governor, the CRMDT and its affiliates breathed more easily. Persecution at the hands of Serratistas, however, had left Cardenistas with limited tolerance for dissent and division. Even as the CRMDT's opposition lost strength, its leadership remained wary of threats to its fragile unity.

The CRMDT and FFSM thus collaborated in settling disputes within and among member organizations. When Natividad Cupa lodged a complaint against Zacapu's Lázaro Cárdenas Women's Socialist League regarding the organization's finances and election officers, Cristina Verduzco, the league's president and the FFSM officer who had been jailed in 1933 for opposing the Serratistas, called a meeting to discuss Cupa's accusations.[89] That Cupa had circumvented the organization's leadership in lodging her initial complaint no doubt exacerbated its leaders' animosity toward her. Although the meeting took place in Verduzco's home, several leading agrarista men directed it, and active participation by high-level CRMDT leaders — in lieu of the FFSM officers Matilde Anguiano and Dolores Núñez — marked the episode as exceptional. Verduzco, with a clear record of leadership and commitment, undoubtedly could have run the meeting without their assistance. The CRMDT's intervention indicates a masculinization of political discipline — reflected also in the 1917 and 1931 discussions about women's suffrage — that placed the FFSM under CRMDT trusteeship to ensure that affiliated women's organizations did not stray too far afield.

The discussion centered on enduring conflicts between individual and collective interests, with league members arguing that collective improvements would be "ideological and not material" and Cupa stating that she had joined the league "for personal improvement, not so that the members of the league could benefit from her." The membership rejected Cupa's charges of fiscal impropriety and maintained that the league had amply compensated her for any support by helping her secure land. The membership then expelled Cupa "as a traitor and intriguer," and Cupa left the meeting "in an irate manner." Although the CRMDT's and FFSM's leadership apparently took Cupa's complaints seriously enough to involve prominent leaders in their resolution, the organizations also moved quickly to quash a brewing personalist conflict.

If dissent had its costs, however, loyalty brought benefits. With renewed support, the FFSM intensified the anticlerical and temperance campaigns that had served as women's most important vehicles for activism. Under Anguiano's leadership, the FFSM provided organizational guidance, ran interference with state and local authorities, and educated activists about legal rights and protections. "Our compañeras have complained for more than two years about abuses they have suffered," she explained to the state's minister of government, "leaving them insulted and embittered, without securing justice when they informed the authorities of these cases. For that reason, in the name of these compañeras, we ask for justice, since the current Governor offers his goodwill."[90]

Signing the letter, "Yours as the Noble Mujer Organizada [Noble Organized Woman]," Anguiano both expected and received the respect that accompanied her status as "organized." With allies in the state government, the FFSM and its constituent leagues capitalized on this legitimacy, cultivating an understanding that membership in an organized, recognized entity entailed certain political powers normally tied to citizenship rights. "Since the day is coming soon when the civil authorities will change in this community," the members of Tzintzimacato Grande's Women's Temperance and Anticlerical League wrote to Morelia's Municipal President José Molina in 1935, "and since we do not support the above-mentioned authorities, we ask that you grant us your strongest guarantees. We are absolutely certain that if you accept this demand, tranquillity will be restored in our town, and everyone will have the same security and guarantees."[91] Molina responded by asking the league for short lists of men they would support as candidates for various civil offices, giving its members access to political influence through collective action. Shortly thereafter, Tzintzimacato Grande's authorities changed to coincide with the league's demands.[92]

The Tzintzimacato Grande case was unusual but hardly unique. That same month, the FFSM-affiliated league in Teremendo entered into pro-tracted disputes with the local authorities. Indicating that these leftover Serratista officials "exercised reprisals against the league and the confederated compañeros, instead supporting those we dubbed *clericales* [clericals, i.e., Cristeros]," the league informed Michoacán's minister of government that the municipal government undermined his authority.[93] Appealing to both paternalist nation-building efforts and an ethical code of state obligation, league members indicated that they had done the government's bidding by petitioning for the secular use of the churches, only to find that the state could not protect them against the violent response their request provoked. "We will not give more details, because they would only enrage you," they continued cryptically. "Suffice it to say that we were driven from our homes and now hope that you can provide us safe-conduct to return, so that we and our husbands can develop the efforts initiated by the current President of the Republic and supported by you as a sympathizer. We believe that with some indication from you, the town authorities will give us the guarantees we require." The league copied the letter to the FFSM, which contacted officials who, in turn, called on Teremendo's jefe municipal, Luis Huape, to offer the league all appropriate guarantees.

However, these instances demonstrate not only the opportunities created by organizational infrastructure and institutional loyalty but also the limitations and frustrations of informal citizenship. Despite state intervention, Huape, a powerful cacique and the CRMDT's Teremendo liaison, felt little compulsion to tolerate the league's interference in local politics.[94] He allowed protection for the league's president, Calixtra Rodríguez, but continued to obstruct her efforts, bluntly telling her that she had no authority regarding alcohol sales, since anyone he permitted could legally sell alcohol. Baffled regarding the league's role, Rodríguez enlisted the support of the FFSM's Morelia office. Anguiano then reminded Molina that Interim Governor Sánchez Tapia had prohibited alcohol sales, particularly near workplaces and indigenous communities, the "places where alcoholism is most entrenched."[95] Rodríguez thus transformed a conflict between the women's league and the town authorities into one between township and state authorities.

A month later, the Teremendo league lodged another complaint with the FFSM, this time regarding a cantina belonging to Ramón Vargas, having discovered that another town had expelled him. "This señor was surely thrown out of his community for trying to intoxicate the campesinos," the league wrote, "only to come here and put his cantina in our town, to continue his exploitative way of life." Demanding "justice," league members threatened "consequences for this one individual, since we have been working to harmonize with those who are not sympathetic with [the CRMDT] and do not want outsiders coming in to foment more division." Leaning on the twin pillars of temperance and anticlericalism to support their efforts, they also demanded the removal of the Catholic and Presbyterian curates as "enemies of the current government."[96] By mid-August 1935, Anguiano had apparently tired of Molina's foot-dragging regarding the Teremendo situation and once again turned to higher authorities, reminding government ministries in Mexico City, as well as Cárdenas, Sánchez Tapia, and Molina, of her ability to mobilize women behind the government's agenda. Amid renewed religious violence, the involvement of church leaders exacerbated the conflict, and Anguiano underscored the danger their presence posed. The Teremendo and Tzintzimacato Grande conflicts intertwined when women in the latter town, which fell within the Teremendo's district, charged Huape with selling illicit liquor licenses for 4 pesos each.[97] Molina again asked local authorities to investigate and mete out the appropriate punishments.

The women's leagues became increasingly aware that they were fighting a losing battle without reinforcements, underscoring the uncertainty surrounding women's citizenship. Sales of temporary liquor licenses significantly enriched local political leaders such as Huape, raising the stakes of temperance disputes. The Tiripetío league repeatedly told CRMDT officers and local officials that military and civil authorities protected the alcohol trade.[98] Growing impatient with officials' unresponsiveness, the league accused Governor Gildardo Magaña of turning a blind eye to alcohol sales. Describing themselves as "organized members with an interest in improving our country according to the ideals of the Revolution," they demanded recognition of women's leagues as "official entities." Citing repeated temperance violations, the letter reveals a profound sense of indignation and betrayal at the hands of the state government. "If we have been organized simply for the sake of mocking the leagues," they wrote, "we want to be told, once and for all, that you desire alcohol sales to bring in money. The vendors themselves say that both you and the municipal president facilitate their sales without any concern for the workers, who are the lifeblood of the country." Demanding an end to alcohol sales and the removal of the local priest, they urged Magaña to "declare whether the ideals of the Social Revolution will be followed, or whether they are simply formalisms. You issued a call for organization, exposing us to danger, and now you leave us alone."[99] Pointing to the revolutionary principles for which Magaña had fought as a Zapatista military commander, the women hoped to hold the government accountable to its promises.

To the Tiripetío activists, the temperance and anticlerical campaigns were of a piece. They consistently tied alcohol abuse to religious festivals and the presence of priests and maintained that converting religious sanctuaries into secular cultural centers would combat both fanaticism and alcoholism.[100] Although CRMDT leaders and government officials also linked these two issues in their organizing efforts, they addressed them as distinct policy matters. In contrast with their temperance efforts, when the Tiripetío women's league requested the expulsion of local priests, its requests met with prompt compliance.[101] This disparity was not lost on women activists, who recognized that they provoked more response when they mentioned the presence of a priest.

Particularly as the religious violence intensified during the mid-1930s, responding to the 1934 educational reforms promoting "socialist" pedagogy, the government sought to quell religious unrest before it could ignite another Cristero Rebellion. The CRMDT demanded that Molina send protection for the señorita profesora in San Nicolás Obispo, where women identified as "possibly members of the fanatics guild" stood outside the school, a building that formerly housed the parish priest, and threatened the teacher.[102] Julia Mayés Navarro, sister of the CMRDT leader Antonio Mayés Navarro and a teacher and activist herself, reported that Virginia Ponce offered catechism and Sunday school classes and kept children from attending the public school, leading Molina to threaten Ponce with the full legal sanctions.[103] Another teacher reported that school attendance had fallen from one hundred students to thirty-three since the local priest had instructed his parishioners to withdraw their children from public schools.[104]

The temperance and anticlerical campaigns also served as proxies for other political disputes as recognized leagues used their status to draw attention to concerns beyond alcoholism and fanaticism. Organized women advanced community land claims, especially in the homeland of agrarismo, near Naranja and Zacapu. The Coeneo Women's Antireligious Group wrote to Cárdenas twice in 1935 to secure definitive ejidal grants.[105] On the estate that had sparked the agrarista movement, the Noriega brothers' Hacienda Cantabria, the women's temperance league petitioned to resolve ongoing land conflicts.[106]

Other women's organizations dispensed with any pretext of other objectives in their efforts to secure land rights. Tarejero's Lázaro Cárdenas Women's League turned to Anguiano and the FFSM to procure definitive land grants.[107] Several leagues sought lands for the collective use by women themselves, rather than their spouses. In June 1935, the Women's Socialist League in Villa Jiménez claimed lands that the Serrato government had granted to another women's group. The affronted Serratista group appealed to Cárdenas, invoking both justice and patriarchy: "bearing in mind that the majority of the members of the [socialist league] are wives of ejidatarios in possession of a parcel, we beg of you to intervene so that our lands are returned to us."[108] The league responded that its members had a legitimate claim because they had cultivated that territory since 1924, submitting an agrarian census as proof. By August the situation looked dire, as the municipal president tried to expropriate lands that they had already sown. In late December, the league renewed requests to secure its title but lost its claim and would receive a considerably smaller, 1.5 hectare parcel in January 1937.[109]

Women's efforts to secure land precipitated violence just as men's did. The CRMDT-affiliated women's league in the nearby community of San Antonio Tariácuri also petitioned for lands, hoping to acquire a plot as part of the August 1935 resolution with the hacienda owner Antonio Carranza, but encountered multiple layers of patriarchal prerogative. Not having received a response after two months' time, Petra Constantino, the league's president, explained to Cárdenas that "fanatics" controlled all the public offices and reserved the best land for their allies. Meanwhile, former President Pascual Ortiz Rubio requested Cárdenas's support to assist his "good friend" Carranza. The situation escalated, and by June 1936 the CRMDT reported that the Carranza brothers had provoked riots, resulting in several injuries, deaths, and more riots. By October 1937, the women's league still had not secured a parcel, although the ejidatarios had succeeded in wresting land from the Carranza brothers. The league appealed to Cárdenas for an unoccupied parcel of land. "The Ejidal Commission president roundly denies us," they explained, "instead giving everyone who has a parcel two or three extra furrows, with a preference for the 'free element' that is not organized, rather than delivering to this Liga Femenil the parcel to which we have a right. [He] is an enemy of this women's organization, trying to destroy it at any cost, to break up its activities by spreading reactionary propaganda among nonmembers and trying to find a way to tear this group to pieces."[110]

The ejidatarios' opposition to the league's land claims exposed a crack in the CRMDT's façade. While the CRMDT leadership and the Cárdenas government rhetorically supported organized women's rights to land parcels for collective cultivation—much as they in principle supported temperance—they remained reluctant to challenge the patriarchal claims of the local agrarian leaders, undermining their allies' legitimacy for the sake of secondary objectives. When confronted with the decision between backing a loyal cacique and making good on promises to organized women, the Cardenistas nearly always chose the former for the sake of political peace.

The Federalization of Cardenismo

By 1936, the national Cardenista project had eclipsed its Michoacán antecedent. National mass organizations overshadowed and eventually obviated their state-level counterparts, such as the CRMDT and FFSM, and the men and women who had populated Michoacán's Cardenista infrastructure accepted positions within Cárdenas's presidential administration or national-level mass organizations. Antonio Mayés Navarro—the native of Cárdenas's hometown who had intervened on behalf of the El Globo factory workers—became the PNR's secretary of agrarian action. Gabino Vázquez, who had served as the secretary of state government under Cárdenas and as interim governor during his leave, became the head of the Agrarian Department. Their presence in the agrarian sector of the state/party bureaucracy perhaps explains why the Cardenista women's organizing program grew out of that division despite the administration's lukewarm support for women's land claims. Both Vázquez and Mayés Navarro understood their tasks not simply as adjusting land distribution but as restructuring and modernizing rural society. Their experiences with the Liga de Comunidades Agrarias and the CRMDT had taught them that women's organizations would have to figure into that agenda.

The Cardenista transition also catapulted women activists onto the national stage, often working with state chapters of national organizations. Agustina Oliva, who had worked her way up to the executive committee of the CRMDT-affiliated teachers' union, also served on the executive committee of Michoacán's chapter of the Mexican Popular Front, became the secretary-general of the state's Sole Front for Women's Rights (Frente Unico Pro-Derechos de la Mujer, or FUPDM), the Popular Front women's organization, and served on state and local labor commissions. Julia Mayés Navarro worked as a schoolteacher in Morelia and then served with Oliva on a Popular Front price-controls commission and as an FUPDM officer. Cuca García, the national secretary-general of the FUPDM, ran for congress in Michoacán with the support — albeit uneven — of PCM and CRMDT activists. Dolores Núñez, the first woman involved at the CRMDT's highest levels, became more involved with national and international women's organizing through the FUPDM, although she returned to Michoacán to support Cuca García's 1937 congressional bid. María Guadalupe Granados served as the secretary-treasurer of the Mexican Popular Front's state committee and then held the analogous office for the Michoacán United Teachers' Front and served as the labor secretary for the Michoacán FUPDM. María Guadalupe Sánchez de Rangel, vice president of the the FFSM at its founding in 1934 and representative of a member league from La Angostura in 1935, was by 1939 the ruling party's secretary-general of the Michoacán women's coordinating committee.

If the creation of temperance, welfare, and anticlerical leagues had created new local and state-level opportunities for women, the elaboration of the Cardenista agenda at the national level multiplied and magnified women's public presence. In Morelia, where state and national mass organizations often shared offices, these transitional years of 1936–37 offered immense possibilities for growth and diversification. With activists moving among militant teachers' unions, Popular Front campaigns, the CRMDT, and various party-affiliated entities, women organizers were buoyed by the exponential increase in attention and resources dedicated to women's issues. Meeting with particular success in the service sector, labor activists organized women ranging from tortilla and food vendors to hospital workers, hotel and restaurant workers, and public employees.[111] Activists appealed to Cárdenas's conviction that supporting women's organizations marked his regime as authentically revolutionary. "We have in mind your revolutionary ideology," Augustina Oliva explained, "and our eagerness to secure moral and economic support from individuals who see in women's organization not a threat of revolutionary failure but rather a complement to the work they courageously pursue."[112]

As the Popular Front's FUPDM overshadowed Michoacán's FFSM, even community activists tapped into the opportunities created by the emerging national political climate. Women in the northern town of Panindícuaro, "wanting our organization to prosper under the auspices of your Revolutionary Government," secured through Cárdenas financing to establish a poultry cooperative and then requested, perhaps partly in jest, that he send them "a few good roosters [*sementales*]."[113] Similarly, a group of laundresses appealed directly to Cárdenas, rather than to the local labor board, to complain that their salaries remained below the minimum wage.[114] Women even routed through national organization petitions regarding matters that fell inescapably under the jurisdiction of municipal governance, such as public utilities and scholarships to the Josefa Ortiz de Domínguez Industrial School for Women.[115]

Although the focal point of mass organizing did not shift suddenly from state to national organizations, the change alienated many longtime local organizers and disrupted patronage networks that had developed over more than a decade. The expulsion of leading dissidents at the CRMDT's August 1936 congress sparked an outcry from dozens of member organizations, including many women's leagues, who objected that the new leadership emerged not from the battle-hardened ranks of agraristas but instead from educational and political bureaucracies. "We protest energetically, and although we are women, we are flush with rights attendant to us," one women's league remonstrated to Cárdenas. "If you do not intervene, we ourselves, with our own forces and on our own behalf, will work in a manner appropriate to our collective interests, which have been trampled and ridiculed by teachers who, too inept and unprepared to fulfill their mission in the school, today engage in a divisive effort among Michoacán's peasants and workers."[116] Teachers themselves remained divided over the question of federalizing public education, with Oliva and the union organizer Esther Sosa among those leading the charge for federalization.[117]

The changing national political climate moved the center of women's activism in Michoacán from temperance and anticlerical leagues to mass organizations and labor unions, but the earlier leagues had helped build the infrastructure of revolutionary citizenship. Temperance and anticlerical leagues provided women with a recognized civic identity, including membership cards, internal elections, and contact with public officials. Women gained skills in community organizing, leadership training, and experience negotiating with and around local authorities. In short, despite the Cardenistas' linking these activities with an essentialized femininity, the leagues drew women into the masculinized realm of political praxis. All of these experiences — electing officers, organizing meetings, confronting intransigent authorities — cultivated among league members a sense of revolutionary citizenship, drawing on both liberal ideals and experiences of mobilization.

These leagues highlighted both the emancipatory and disciplinary aspects of popular organizing and demonstrate that they operated in tandem. In other words, organizations did not start out emancipatory and become co-opted for disciplinary purposes; nor did they progress from disciplinary objectives to emancipatory ones. Following the recognition of women as a critical component of mass organizing, the leagues served both purposes. They clearly promoted the Cardenistas' goals of advocating "modern" labor and domestic practices and discouraging religious loyalties, but they also provided the avenues by which members made land claims, established cooperatives, and embarked on labor struggles.

The Michoacán experience also underscores a point that often gets lost in studies of popular mobilizations: it really did matter who held political office. During the anti-Cardenista backlash under the Serrato administration, the CRMDT (or, at least, its left wing) struggled to survive, and women's organizing took a backseat to efforts to fend off Serratista attacks. With the return of a more progressive state government, women's organizing flourished, rekindled by the allocation of human and material resources and the conviction that their efforts would find sympathetic audiences among policymakers. Even in cases where women activists did not enjoy official support, the Cardenistas cultivated a political climate — marked by populist policies and rhetoric — that facilitated organizers' appeals both to officials and to their constituent publics. With the creation of the political and bureaucratic infrastructure of revolutionary citizenship, teachers and activists from throughout the republic and from a wide range of ideological orientations began to populate these organizations and define their objectives.

THREE

Educators and Organizers:

Populating the National Women's

Movement

In late 1933, Concha Michel returned from the Soviet Union committed to promoting grassroots mobilizations by encouraging rural Mexicans, particularly campesinas, to demand that the revolutionary government intervene on their behalf. Having formerly worked for the Secretariat of Public Education (SEP) collecting indigenous folk songs, Michel signed up as a "rural organizer" with the SEP's Cultural Missions program—a mobile branch of the public-education corps established in 1923—in La Huerta, Michoacán. In a March 1934 report, she described her plans to help women solicit land independently from their husbands and fathers.[1] Particularly in places where definitive land grants had been delayed, Michel argued that collectively cultivated parcels for women would allow their families to subsist. As she had in the standoff on Calles's Hacienda Santa Bárbara, she became involved in conflicts among agraristas as well as between communities and guardias blancas, struggling to protect customary rights such as gleaning forest products and cultivating fallow land. Poorly planned land distributions, she explained, had led some agraristas to employ others as sharecroppers, a situation clearly contrary to the spirit of agrarian reform.

Michel focused on extricating campesinas from the conflicts and rivalries pervasive in Michoacán to better their lives "without waiting for the situation of their husbands, fathers, or brothers to improve." She also advocated a revolutionary policy that would become central to rural women's organizing: the allocation of land for women's collective cultivation. Explaining her work in Undameo, a town of some 2,000 inhabitants outside Morelia, she reported success in enlisting men's support to abate "existing prejudices." Men's collaboration remained indispensable to women's organizing, and Michel, despite her emphasis on promoting independent women's groups, understood the importance of securing the consent or even endorsement of community patriarchs. "In all the communities visited," she concluded, "I intensified (in agreement with the agronomist and using the women's organization) the struggle for land as the economic base for all the families of the campo." Michel, like many secular women activists, drew on her Mexican Communist Party (PCM) organizing experience and utilized the SEP infrastructure to pursue aims only obliquely connected to education policy. As the national Cardenista project blossomed during the heyday of Mexico's Popular Front, the SEP became a hotbed of women's activism. Given the PCM's growing presence within the SEP and federal teachers' unions by the mid-1930s, these two institutions' influences dovetailed, blurring the lines between education and consciousness-raising and largely defining the terms and practices of women's activism across ideologies.

By the time of Cárdenas's 1934 presidential election, popular organizing had taken root in Mexico. The National Revolutionary Party (PNR) certainly did its best to stifle dissent, but its very existence created clearer avenues for popular groups to gain access to government officials. In the early 1930s, endeavors such as the Ejército de Mujeres Campesinas, the national women's congresses, and the federalization of Michoacán's women's organizations cultivated a national women's movement intent on exploiting these new political opportunities. Through these activities, women activists had developed leadership skills, planned meetings and agendas, conducted house visits, and established organizing committees. Government agencies such as the SEP and the Agrarian Department provided meeting spaces, office equipment, housing for cooperatives, and other material aid. Taken together, all these factors contributed to a praxis of revolutionary citizenship, creating a framework, a quotidian practice, and a grammar for articulating grievances within the postrevolutionary political system.

Mexico's political climate shifted significantly in mid-1935 as the international crisis of capitalism generated questions about the surest road to economic stability and development. Cárdenas surprised the nation by breaking with Calles, ending the maximato and leading the country down a leftward path. The Communist Party, following the Popular Front line, sought a reconciliation with and radicalization of the ruling party. Progressive women activists across a range of ideologies identified a chance to make dramatic gains in women's rights and opportunities, but exploiting this opening required them to make common cause, developing not only shared priorities and strategies but also a common notion of femininity. The emergence of Cardenista corporatism heightened the importance of forming an identifiable interest group, a bloc—like "peasants" or "workers"—that the state-party could incorporate integrally into its apparatus. To unify a national women's movement and gain a seat at the corporatist bargaining table, leading activists needed first to agree on who women were and what they wanted.

The vitality of local women's organizing, the progressive turn in the postrevolutionary regime, and an international climate favoring women's suffrage made gains in women's rights seem inexorable and escalated the conflicts about their specific objectives and about who deserved credit for their achievement. Meanwhile, women's heightened political activism and party leaders' increased attention to "women's interests" reinforced one another; every indication of support for the regime encouraged stepped-up activism, which, in turn, underscored the importance of drafting women activists as party supporters. Activists accrued political capital through their contact with officials, on the one hand, and, on the other, through their capacity to mobilize rank-and-file members. Factions within organizing circles not only competed with each other but also navigated patronage protocols, striving to maintain legitimacy while according adequate deference to powerful local and national political figures.

As the Revolutionary Labor Confederation of Michoacán (CRMDT) and temperance leagues had in Michoacán, the national organizing campaigns generated an infrastructure that both promoted and disciplined an emergent national women's movement. As teachers, mothers, and social workers, women would bring the revolutionary government's modernizing message into households and communities, rendering them more productive and less devout. These women would play crucial roles in remaking Mexican bodies: instilling habits of hygiene, temperance, and athleticism while promoting sanitation and vaccinations. Women activists, in short, positioned themselves as the critical link between what the postrevolutionary government was (a loose collection of like-minded political enclaves) and what it aspired to be (a centralized, modernizing, national structure shaping lives in the furthest reaches of the republic). To instrumentalize women's energies, political leaders in Mexico City needed to integrate women into their state-building project. Far from serving as handmaidens of state formation, however, activists like Concha Michel articulated a gendered revolutionary program, one that — albeit in multivalent and plurivocal ways — took advantage of the regime's commitment to refashioning the social realm through state apparatuses. Women activists ultimately confronted the limits of postrevolutionary tolerance for social transformation, but the Cardenistas' radical reformist agenda created unprecedented opportunities to implement their projects.

Teaching Revolutionary Citizenship

During the 1920s and '30s, the SEP served as the locus for mediating between state and household, as the school and programs under its purview adopted an expansive role in Mexican society. "Whereas the prerevolutionary school had etched itself into a restricted place in daily life," explains the historian May Kay Vaughan, "the revolutionary school presumed to overflow customary boundaries in order to transform community life."[2] The teacher's position now encompassed the roles of social worker and community organizer as well as educator. "We were everything," recalls Ana María Flores Sánchez, a teacher in the Comarca Lagunera. "We were the town's teachers, lawyers, counselors, midwives, organizers. . . . We did everything; we knew everyone."[3] As the federal government aggressively promoted public education through rural federal schools, normal schools, and the Cultural Missions programs, the number of people in regular contact not only with the SEP but also with other federal-government agencies increased exponentially.

SEP employees, especially rural teachers and organizers like Michel, embodied both the enabling and disciplinary guises of organizing, helping popular groups navigate arcane bureaucracies and communicate with government officials. They taught ejidatarios and women's groups how to apply for government loans and to craft petitions and grievances, using typewriters and following epistolary protocols. But they also shaped the contents of those entreaties, framing petitions to coincide with the federal government's own objectives for rural communities, mediating popular appeals but also rendering them more efficacious. Not surprisingly, these petitions often included special requests for school improvements.

The SEP played a particularly important role for women activists, offering a dynamic base from which to promote women's organizing. Teaching had long provided women with a gateway to professional identities and public engagement, and teachers' central role in women's congresses dating from the 1916 Feminist Congress indicates the link between teaching and activism.[4] The swelling ranks of the ministry's administrative and teaching staff generated unprecedented opportunities for women to gain professional status and practical training. Women constituted the majority of rural federal schoolteachers, and their prominence in the SEP shaped its institutional culture.[5] Within communities, teachers organized the regime-sanctioned women's leagues and championed women's rights. SEP publications consistently included articles by and about women, covering topics ranging from stretching household budgets to maximizing women's participation in "revolutionary" activities. Whereas many government agencies' doors remained closed to women, the SEP — as temperance organizations had in the 1920s — offered determined women material support, legitimacy, and access to powerful men who could facilitate their ambitions, even those only tenuously connected with education.

In 1923, the SEP adopted John Dewey's vision of "action pedagogy," bolstering its commitment to socialization and popular organizing. The normal-school curriculum tested novice teachers' ability to establish unions and cooperatives and to teach women about "appropriate" marriage practices, offering recommendations about the suitable ages for men and women to marry, counsel about which marriage partners to avoid, advice for newlyweds, and warnings about syphilis. Reflecting policymakers' desire for both a comprehensive portrait of everyday life and a means of shaping the most intimate realms of social practice, the SEP instructed Mexicans not only on how to read and write but also on how to defend their rights, how to provision their families, and even how to (and more pointedly, how not to) copulate. As one rural-education director explained, in addition to the standard curriculum of arithmetic and Spanish, rural teachers "oblige children to action" and encourage "habits of work and order," rendering them "channelers and directors of energies within the broadest social service."[6] Steeped in historical-materialist theories and structural explanations of inequality, SEP employees formed the link between the new regime's reformist vision and its intended beneficiaries.

The SEP's commitment to action pedagogy grew under the leadership of Narciso Bassols (1931–34), officially incorporating activism into teachers' duties and deepening teacher-community relations.[7] To mitigate suspicions about their objectives, many teachers first cultivated ties with community members, since even in the unusual instance that a teacher taught in her home district, she had inevitably left for some time to attend normal school, setting her apart in most rural villages. "Social work should be performed not only within the school," advised one SEP memo, "but also outside of it, visiting homes on Saturdays and Sundays, as much to build closer friendships with parents as to advise them about improvements to their homes. It would also be appropriate to have the señoritas of humble backgrounds join the societies [for domestic economy]."[8] Through the proactive and pragmatic tactics of action pedagogy, teachers reached out even to those parents who remained suspicious of the government's education agenda.

The 1934 educational reforms, promoted by Bassols and authored by the Michoacano and staunch Cardenista Alberto Bremauntz, codified the direction in which Bassols had pushed education, banning religious education and advocating action pedagogy. While some on the left criticized these measures as superstructural, cosmetic changes that fell far short of transforming the material conditions of the Mexican proletariat and peasantry, Bassols's vision inspired many others to pursue social change through practical education. However, the reforms also antagonized community members already suspicious of the new regime's objectives. Calles's July 1934 "Grito de Guadalajara" in defense of the federal government's agenda for "socialist" education only exacerbated tensions. "With complete guile, the reactionaries say that the child belongs to the home and the youth to the family," Calles proclaimed. "This is a selfish doctrine, because the child and the youth belong to the collectivity. The Revolution has the indisputable duty to take charge of consciences, to unearth prejudices, and to form a new national soul . . . because the children and youth should belong to the Revolution."[9] Unsurprisingly, this attitude vexed parents, particularly those already wary of state intrusions, and required SEP teachers to expend considerable energy rebuilding local confidence.

SEP administrators fashioned many of the action-pedagogy strategies through its Cultural Missions program.[10] With the exceptions of two "permanent missions" established in the center-west to combat religious fervor and to prevent further violence, the Cultural Missions inhabited areas for several weeks, trained teachers, organized committees, established cooperatives, and then left town. As Ezequiel Padilla, Vasconcelos's successor at the SEP's helm, explained to a group of *misioneros* (missionaries) heading into the provinces, "After four weeks of fertile action, you will be withdrawn to install other institutes in other regions, and the rural teachers will return, like the disciples of Zarathustra, carrying honey to their communities."[11] In some cases, mission members spread out into neighboring communities, rendering their impact more diffuse. Not surprisingly, when they revisited these locales the following year they often found that their efforts had all been for naught or the results had changed beyond recognition. As the SEP program evolved, administrators developed methods to render these teacher-organizers' accomplishments more permanent.

The Cultural Missions' redemptive, evangelical overtones, derived from the SEP's Jacobin ideology, animated its efforts to have schools replace churches as centerpieces of local social and cultural life. In most communities, the Catholic church served as a touchstone of community cohesion, and the church itself offered a venue for social interaction and spiritual reflection as well as the enactment of hierarchies, feminine piety, and rites of passage. "In the past, the church has been the only unifying influence and today's cultural and psychological unity results from that inheritance," the misionera Catarina Vesta Sturges explained to a U.S. education specialist in the 1930s. "The missions work with adults and with the community as a whole, especially directing popular arts, music, and drama to help the community feel the school as a cultural and social influence and to see the teacher as a leader in many aspects of community life."[12] Thus, the Cultural Missions set out to "organize the community, establish recreational activities, and bring together resources . . . with the goal of 'dignifying' the life of the peasant population."[13]

Drawing on the emerging field of social work in the United States and Europe, the Cultural Missions included two organizers — one for men and another for women.[14] The women's organizers served as master social workers, visiting homes, suggesting changes in hygiene and nutrition, and training teachers in the methods and benefits of social work and collective organizing.[15] "The Mexican woman should put all her energies and goodwill to the service of the current social movement," wrote one teacher, "since falling behind or watching events develop without directly intervening is a crime against the Patria for which future generations will be unable to pardon her."[16] One rural organizer described her "program of orientation and instruction" to Eliseo Silva Garza, the head of the SEP's Institute for Social Action, as having "the great purpose of transforming each teacher into a true Social Organizer within his own community."[17] Silva Garza responded by spelling out the formula for "preparing the terrain," beginning with a session to "explain the concept of 'cooperation' " to interest women in "an organization of this nature."[18] Silva Garza indicated that organizers should divide women into three committees—Domestic Education, Domestic Production, and Civic Education—each with specified tasks, rules, and meeting times. Like the mandate to "instill habits of work and order," Silva Garza echoed scientific management's rationalizing rhetoric, instructing, "Work plans are given to each of the committees mentioned and time allotted to each plan." Once the women were well-trained, he explained, the committees "should work for themselves."[19]

The tenor of the "programs of action" that misioneras developed in training often contrasted starkly with the reports they sent from the field, where teachers frequently balked at the conditions they encountered in rural communities. Most of them came from "the modest middle class" and brought with them a tremendous enthusiasm for their mission and a passionate belief in its ability to realize the revolution's most progressive ideals.[20] In addition to difficult living conditions and frequently suspended salaries, teachers often faced opposition or even violence from community members who opposed the state-sponsored educational project. Even those who supported public schools frequently viewed the teacher as an interloper and a government agent over whom the community had to exert control.[21] Misioneras became involved in the most intimate aspects of women's lives, fostering an awkward, forced familiarity that resulted from close contact through home visits and long meetings with a near stranger who would leave within a few days or weeks.

Sara Valero de Marines, for example, ran a discussion with the women of Tlaltetelco, Morelos, entitled, "Methods for Keeping a Man at Home and in Love with His Compañera," sparking a lively conversation and "innumerable questions."[22] Valero recounted the warm relationship she had developed. After her departure, she said, the women fetched her from her next assignment and, despite her debilitating fever, took her back to Tlaltetelco for a *comida* (afternoon meal) to celebrate her efforts. Valero had not always been so sanguine, however. From an earlier mission in nearby Atlatlahucan, she had candidly reported to SEP higher-ups, "It requires a great deal of effort to make these [women's clubs]. First, because the campesina woman's ignorance makes her resist civilization; second, because the men do not allow the women to leave home; and third, because the campesinas are tied by multiple and heavy duties of home and field."[23] Valero, like many other organizers, discovered that initiatives that eased domestic labor burdens drew women's interest.[24] Communal kitchens, sewing classes, and instruction in "light industries" such as candy making and fruit preservation attracted plenty of takers. However, when women became absorbed in Holy Week preparations, Valero found that even the popular sewing classes remained empty.

Along with their missionary enthusiasm, SEP employees often harbored race- and class-based prejudices toward the communities where they worked. This distance between social worker and subject—between organizer and organized—belied the notion of a shared womanhood. One SEP-employed social worker in Yucatán, Julia Moreno de Medina, described the signs of a "degenerate race" resulting from disease-propagating filth.[25] "The campesina woman's condition is very sad," she reported to her superior.[26] Alarmed by what she viewed as "rough and rude" language, Moreno described the campesinas—in this case, quite likely Maya-speakers—as "dazed as if affected by idiocy" and "spiritually impoverished and physically infirm." More appalling still, these women remained "ignorant of female modesty; it matters little to them who sees them dirty, disheveled, full of parasites, and they do not give a whit if other people know about their menstrual periods." Describing the campesinas as "anomalous living bodies," Moreno marked them as both deviant and inscrutable. To Moreno, these women, with their incomprehensible and "rough" language and their shameful habits, were alien, "anomalous" creatures, only distantly akin to anything she deemed feminine.

In Moreno's description of "anomalous living bodies," she highlighted sexual and marriage practices as evidence of "impoverished spiritual psyches and corporal infirmity."[27] Teachers' own sexuality remained closely guarded, particularly amid the furor over the 1933 proposals to integrate sex education into the curriculum. The SEP required pregnant teachers to take leave by their sixth month and charged normal schools with instructing aspiring female teachers in morals and "the formation of character, particularly from the sexual perspective."[28] As part of a "Hispanicization [*castellanización*]" campaign, the Cultural Mission in the Maya-dominated region of Dzitbalché, Campeche, included plans to improve family relations and discourage "premature marriages."[29] These efforts, rather than resting on a shared "biological" experience of womanhood and female sexuality, set in relief the cultural differences between predominantly urban, middle-class SEP employees and the rural women among whom they worked.

Catholic Women's Organizing and Renewed Religious Violence

The SEP's stepped-up activism, frank discussions of sexuality, and explicitly materialist curriculum antagonized lay Catholics, making schoolteachers frequent targets of both secular and religious violence. Tensions increased exponentially with the 1934 education reforms and Calles's "Grito de Guadalajara." Notably, women often spearheaded this violence against schoolteachers, who frequently were also women, unleashing a battle to control the realm where women held sway—that of child rearing. The response of mothers in Presidio, Durango, was not uncommon. As the head of the Cultural Mission there tried to justify the government's policy, "the shouts of the feminine element would allow no explanations." One woman, he reported, "in a voice shaking with emotion, hurled insults at the Government, teachers in general, the school, and the undersigned, using obscene language."[30]

Violent encounters often took on a spectacular quality involving community members as both witnesses and participants. The 19-year-old rural teacher María Mora, for example, was brutally murdered in the hacienda San Nicolás, Nayarit, and her body was left out in the open "because everyone was too afraid of the *hacendado* to move it."[31] In Contepec, Michoacán, the ringing of the church bells brought a group of three hundred people— "predominantly women"—to the home of the schoolteacher and CRMDT activist Trinidad Ramírez, whom they proceeded to murder. Ramírez, described in a local newspaper as a "consummate anticlerical" and an officer of the anticlerical league, had orchestrated the expulsion of the town's priest, who was to leave that very day.[32] Narratives of Ramírez's assassination vary, but all emphasize women's uncontrolled savagery, implying that their roles most troubled observers. According to the municipal president, "hoards of the *hijas de María* [daughters of Mary]" dragged Ramírez outside to lynch him, "and afterwards the fanatical women, in the height of their mystical hysteria, dragged him through the streets of the town amid applause and exclamations of 'Long Live Christ the King!'" Another version related that women threw stones at Ramírez's face, battering it to pieces.[33] Yet another version claimed that the crowd had fractured Ramírez's arm before one man put a machete to his skull and several women hog-tied him. An unnamed hija de María then urinated on his face before the crowd dragged him through the street.[34]

Such episodes forced communities to reestablish their credibility with secular authorities. "It can be assumed that the motives for the deeds related above had their origins in the confusion surrounding the socialist teachings and the religious practices entrenched in our humble classes," Contepec residents explained in a letter to the Michoacán government, "who, without meditating on the act or foreseeing its consequences, and driven only by their own fanaticism, committed the bloody act that we, the majority of the entire pueblo, now lament."[35] The town's explanation and apology reinforced the Cardenistas' commitment not only to softening its anticlerical stance to forestall further violence but also to stepping up its campaign to eliminate "fanaticism" among the "humble classes," especially women.

Women involved with on-the-ground organizing during the 1930s recognized the difficulty of luring women away from church-sponsored organizations because of the strength of their faith as well as more tangible incentives, such as church-based charities, support networks, and vocational classes. "It is completely absurd," Concha Michel argued, "to arrive in places that have been subject to a religious education for centuries and offer a socialist orientation or a socialist education saying that 'God is a phantasm and the saints are the products of the fantasies of unscrupulous artists.'"[36] Rather, she contended, organizers needed to provide practical lessons about how to fight for land rights, better wages, and potable water. Further, they should respond to spiritual needs with an autochthonous cosmogony to attenuate the cultural hold of the Catholic church.[37] Dolores Heduán de Rueda, an agrarista lawyer, echoed Michel's sentiments, explaining that if women remained more "fanatical" than men, it was only because "nobody . . . admitted the complete collaboration of the feminine sex as much as the propagators of religious dogma; no door was opened as wide to woman as the door of the religious temples."[38]

Much like the SEP, both clerical and lay leadership within the Catholic church recognized the importance of keeping women within the fold. As one church scholar wrote, "Woman is the best pedagogue; thus, by educating her well, the whole society will also be educated."[39] In the battle over women's allegiance, the church enjoyed tremendous success in propagating women's lay organizations. In 1930, the Union of Catholic Mexican Ladies changed its name to the Mexican Catholic Women's Union (UFCM) and joined the national organization of Mexican Catholic Action.[40] The UFCM and its parent organization maintained very specific lines of authority mirroring those of the church hierarchy and, unlike the PCM or the SEP's women's clubs, did not aspire to building a mass membership. The historian

Kristina Boylan has argued that the UFCM maintained "a fairly clear divide between the 'helpers' and the 'helped,'" as its upper-class-dominated membership "looked to the campesinas primarily as women to be helped back into the Catholic fold, rather than future collaborators in the work of the UFCM."[41]

Nonetheless, the UFCM's tactics — albeit oriented toward training women in Catholic rites and child rearing rather than toward building membership — bore a striking resemblance to those of PCM activists and the Cultural Missions' rural organizers, indicating widely shared beliefs about popular organizing. Mexican Catholic Action and its branches divided organizing tasks into "sections" that covered geographic areas and reported to the central committee.[42] As one UFCM member recounted, "The means used in this section's efforts consist in going from house to house, through all the paths within its jurisdiction, instructing families about [specific rites]."[43] The UFCM offered support for the most indigent as well as classes in sewing, cooking, and other "domestic arts" designed to attract working-class and peasant women.

Like their counterparts in the Cultural Missions, UFCM activists often expressed frustration with the women they sought to influence. María Guadalupe Sandoval, a UFCM leader from Cuernavaca, Morelos, described the particular difficulties of mustering support in the cradle of Zapatismo. Complaining of "paganism and indifference" as well as a "lack of comprehension" and "apathy" toward the UFCM's mission, Sandoval railed against the menace of secular influences. "Just as Morelos advances rapidly toward economic and social resurgence and progress," she decried, "it also advances rapidly toward moral ruin. The enemies of the Church and of Christ have taken Morelos, above all Cuernavaca, as a center for their perverse actions. With the pretext of modernism, they have brought women vain demands, making them forget their Christian duties and burying them in an abyss of immorality."[44]

These laments highlighted concerns common among UFCM organizers that "modernity" drove women out of churches and homes and into factories and brothels. Despite their general rejection of "modernism," materialist language and analysis so permeated Mexican political discussion that Catholic organizers apparently shared the widespread belief that women's labor-force participation would draw them into unions and communist cells. Women, after all, provided the first line of defense against "socialist" education and other anticlerical measures such as church closings and cultural

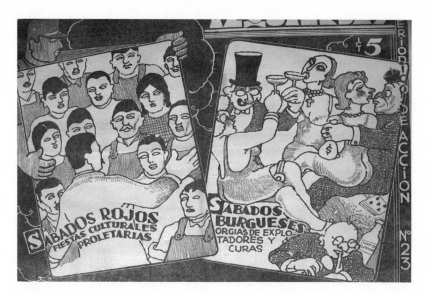

Figure 1. "Red Saturdays, Bourgeois Saturdays." *Izquierdas*, 15 October 1934.

prohibitions. If women neglected to perform Catholic rites and "Christian duties" in the home and ceded education to the "socialist" teachers, church officials feared, the next generation of Mexicans would be lost.

The newspaper *Izquierdas*, edited by progressive PNR leaders, responded in kind to the UFCM's moralizing criticisms. Depicting priests as corrupt and lascivious, the newspaper frequently portrayed monstrous-looking clerics drooling over attractive young women and even appearing to abuse them sexually.[45] The paper also published a response to an anti-SEP leaflet that Catholic clerics had distributed. "Socialist education," the unsigned response explained, "will make men abandon vice, drive misery from homes, and allow wives to have an independent spiritual life, without the 'advice' of the priests, which always shatters husbands' confidence in their wives, even when it does not end in surreptitious adultery between prayers and prudishness, realizing, in this case, *the destruction of the family and the moral and physical ruin of wives*."[46] Public schoolteachers, in this characterization, stood as beacons of morality and wisdom. The front cover of the tabloid-format newspaper depicted the lecherous "Bourgeois Saturdays: Orgies of Exploiters and Priests" and the wholesome "Red Saturdays: Proletarian Cultural Festivals," with the schoolteacher instructing a crowd of working-class mestizos.[47]

Despite the tensions between church and state hierarchies, teachers and Catholics often found a modus vivendi that allowed them to coexist. The misionera Sara Valero seemed unsurprised, if a bit disappointed, that her students vanished during Holy Week preparations. A former student from a Galeana, Nuevo León, rural school recalled widespread resistance to socialist education and remembered the parish priest railing against the dangers of the "atheist and communist" school. Nonetheless, most people remained "believers but not fanatics," and teachers and students occasionally attended Mass together. When townspeople discovered the church's Christ figure knocked down and demolished, they initially blamed the students but quickly established the culpability of a group of drunken men.[48] While the incident might have sparked a riot amid Michoacán's fraught church-state relations, in Galeana it passed much like any other community scandal. By the mid-1930s, many progressive groups had abandoned antagonistic attitudes in favor of a more conciliatory posture toward popular religiosity, reaching out to those not yet incorporated into mass organizations. If the Catholic church provided the institutional backing for conservative women's activism, the organizational discipline and influence of Mexico's Communist Party did the same for radical women; postrevolutionary officials labored to attenuate both institutions' power to influence the state's hegemonic project.

Communists and Counterrevolutionaries: Defining the Cardenista Political Climate

The PCM's strength among teachers magnified the SEP's emphasis on action pedagogy. "The teachers were all Communists," explains a former teacher from the party's stronghold of the Comarca Lagunera, "pure Communists. We wore uniforms and medals; everyone knew we were Communists."[49] Many prominent militants — women such as Cuca García, Concha Michel, Elena Torres, and Adelina Zendejas — cut their activist teeth in the PCM and worked for the SEP. Teachers who did not join the party would still have had regular contact with its ideas, organizers, and approaches to popular mobilization. Michel, even after her 1933 expulsion from the PCM, called meetings among fellow Cultural Mission members to criticize SEP administrators for not adequately instilling "scientific Marxist socialism."[50] The mission leader Tomás Cuervo defended the government, arguing that Cárdenas had come from the "ranks of the exploited class." Pointing to Calles, who still held political sway in late 1934, Michel quipped that he might be proletarian compared with *mister Roquefeler* but, relative to the "true proletariat," the revolutionary leaders well understood the position they occupied. Class struggle resolved, she maintained, not by having "two, three or ten individuals emerge from the working class and become millionaires." Declaring Michel "antigovernment," Cuervo rejected her criticism, and the school's director, Tito Huereca, defused the controversy by simply declaring vacation a day early.

The PCM left a deep imprint on Cardenista political practice, and its influence grew considerably amid the economic uncertainty of the mid-1930s, when it emphasized an expansive approach to organizing, building coalitions, celebrating popular cultures, and attacking fascism and imperialism. As Barry Carr has shown, party membership peaked during the Cárdenas presidency.[51] Having endured severe persecution since 1929, the party reasserted itself as a political force following Cárdenas's election and, throughout the late 1930s, boosted its membership and distribution of periodicals.[52] Even at its height in 1939, the party claimed an uneven membership of about 35,000, but membership cards signed or elections won does not offer an accurate measure of the PCM's influence.[53] The party's strong showing in teachers' and railroad workers' unions, for example, yielded a presence beyond its membership.

The PCM shaped popular organizing and mobilization rooted in the party's organizing structure of cells, committees, and sections and increased the weight given to turning people out for demonstrations and actions. Although the mobilizational aspects of organizing predated the Popular Front and even the revolution itself, these disciplinary aspects — building membership, forming committees, and adhering to a well-delineated program — intensified with increased communist influence. While the PCM presence in places such as Mexico City, Michoacán, and Veracruz dated back to the 1920s, by the mid-'30s its mode of organizing even informed organizing practices in counterrevolutionary organizations such as Mexican Catholic Action and the emerging fascist tendencies, the Camisas Doradas (Gold Shirts) in the north and the *sinarquistas* in the center-west.

The Dorados generated urgency among Communists and Cardenistas to close ranks against a shared threat. Among the earliest targets of the Dorados' hostilities, the PCM sounded the first warning signal, describing them as disaffected revolutionary generals supported by foreign investors. Operating under the name Mexican Revolutionary Action, the Dorados called for the expulsion of "undesirable" foreigners — apparently including Jews, Arabs, and Chinese but excluding Brits and North Americans. "It is one of the first outbreaks of a fascist mass movement," cautioned the Communists, "which the bourgeois and landowning Mexicans will support and use to accelerate the onset of fascism [*fachización*] in the country in the same way the movements have been utilized in Italy, Germany, etc., and are being fomented in France, England, Spain, the United States, and some South American countries."[54] By November 1935, when Dorados and Communists clashed violently in Mexico City's main plaza, concerns about fascism had taken hold among Cardenistas as well as Communists.

These concerns mounted as the sinarquistas, whom the historian Jean Meyer dubs the "counterrevolutionary response of the postrevolutionary generation," built a following in Michoacán, the homeland of Cardenismo.[55] Coined in 1914 as a term to connote the opposite of anarchism, sinarquismo signified "with authority, power, and order" and emphasized nationalism, the primacy of the family, and the protection of private property, bearing a striking resemblance to Franco-style fascism.[56] The National Sinarquista Union (UNS), the "popular muscle of the Catholic right," descended from a leading organizational force behind the Cristero Rebellion a decade earlier and tapped into widely held fears about Cardenista policies.[57] Officially established in May 1937 as a branch of the conservative Catholic organization El Base, the UNS developed into a stronger, more national movement than its parent organization but maintained strong roots in the region where revolutionary and counterrevolutionary forces had battled one another since the early 1920s.

Meyer has shown that Michoacán had a larger number of active sinarquistas than any other state (85,000) and among the highest levels of per capita participation (7.3 percent), claiming more members in Michoacán alone than the PCM did nationally.[58] The UNS established organizing committees in 73 of Michoacán's 102 municipalities, with hundreds of rural subcommittees. The Puruándiro municipality, in the agrarista region's northern reaches, claimed 54 rural organizing committees.[59] Women apparently accounted for at least a quarter of every UNS organizing committee and 60 percent of the committee in Zinapécuaro, Michoacán.[60] Their participation in public events remained exceptional enough, however, to attract notice from observers. "We all entered in the best order that we could," described one report from eastern Michoacán, "and what most captured our attention were the señoras who entered marching gallantly, with the valor of true sinarquistas."[61] Women's strong showing among Michoacán's sinarquistas reflected the state's significant UFCM presence. Morelia alone claimed 29,274 UFCM members, with Zamora reporting another 17,372 and Tacámbaro,

3,696.[62] While Mexican Catholic Action and the UNS were distinct entities, those areas with strong Catholic Action membership also tended to have larger numbers of sinarquistas, with considerable overlap between the two organizations.

In addition to its ballooning membership, the UNS's appropriation of nationalist and patriotic rhetoric and symbols unsettled Cardenistas. The sinarquistas held that the regime had exchanged one form of imperialism for another, given its purported communist sympathies. The group even managed to stake a claim to land reform, substituting the slogan "Todos Propietarios [Everyone Property Owners]" for the Communists' "Todos Proletarios [Everyone Proletarian]," eroding the agrarista base and tapping into longstanding peasant demands for titles to small subsistence plots. Furthermore, Michoacán's history of Catholic radicalism made sinarquismo even more menacing than the north's Camisas Doradas.

Amid this rising national and international tide of counterrevolutionary mobilization, fueled everywhere, like the left's growing appeal, by the deepening economic depression, the PCM abandoned its hostility toward the postrevolutionary regime. At the August 1935 Comintern congress, the Mexican delegation supported the strategy of forging a Popular Front to unite the country's mass organizations against fascism. While it would oversimplify the relationship between the PCM and the Soviet Party leadership to say that the PCM took direct orders from Moscow, concerns about maintaining international solidarity and legitimacy with the Communist International coincided with domestic concerns about conservative organizing. The PCM's secretary-general Hernán Laborde — Cárdenas's opponent in the 1934 presidential election and Concha Michel's longtime compañero — confessed that the party had erred by initially opposing Cárdenas. The president's response to Calles's aggressive attacks on organized labor convinced the PCM leadership that he crafted a different agenda from that of his predecessor. "Cárdenas vacillates, hesitates, alters his national-reformist measures and his concessions to the masses with very serious concessions to imperialism," Laborde explained, "but Cárdenas's policies, taken all together, are something new and something very different from what Calles wanted."[63] Cárdenas had proved so formidable an opponent, Laborde continued, that the Communists must instead make of him an ally.

Laborde urged the PCM to reverse course and build alliances with Cardenista mass organizations "to facilitate the struggle for proletarian hegemony within the movement, to transform the Communist party into a strong party linked with the great masses and trained to organize and direct the revolution, and to utilize to the greatest measure possible the temporary national-reformist allies."[64] Thus, Communist activists abandoned their hostile stance toward the ruling party and adopted instead a strategy of constructive engagement, building alliances across party and class lines. With the advent of the Popular Front, trained and committed organizers extended their reach while moderating their rhetoric, weaving together the contradictory impulses of nationalism and internationalism, integration and separatism, and reform and revolution.

"Her Dignity as Woman and Her Sovereignty as Citizen": Women on the Popular Front

In keeping with Comintern recommendations, Laborde pointed to the need to "give special attention to women, who will be more sensitive to certain aspects of the struggle against imperialism."[65] The strategy for organizing women consisted of uniting all "non-reactionary" and working women into one organization and having the party "take a definite and categorical position in support of women's suffrage, demanding that women's right to vote become a reality."[66] His suggestions for incorporating women focused on reducing electricity rates and food prices, issues that, like suffrage, appealed to the middle and poorer classes more generally and avoided marking women's issues in gendered terms.[67] The PCM program did rhetorically link women with concerns about reactionary groups; Laborde followed his statement regarding women's importance to the party with one about needing to differentiate between the popular Catholic masses and the reactionary church hierarchy.[68] Upon returning from the congress, the Mexican delegation proposed a platform whose third plank read, "Ample democratic liberties; women's suffrage; dissolution of the 'Dorados' and guardias blancas."[69]

This gesture of linking women and conservatism appeared more as a conceit to the liberal left than a concern of the PCM itself, although linking the "woman question" with antifascism created an imperative for women's organizing that squared well with the party's agenda. The PCM and its more progressive allies continued to celebrate women's radical interventions and avoided the language so prevalent in mainstream newspapers and political discussions that characterized women as essentially and unalterably domestic, self-sacrificing, passive, or conservative. According to the party's guiding ideology, all antirevolutionary factions could arrive at revolutionary consciousness through a combination of political education and labor-force participation. Throughout the 1930s, the PCM remained committed to women's voting rights, even as ruling-party support flagged, indicating that the PCM leadership did not share the fear that women's political rights would bring about a counterrevolutionary government.

The Popular Front required party activists to shift gears quickly. Miguel Angel Velasco, a PCM leader who ardently defended the need for autonomy from the postrevolutionary regime, nonetheless endorsed the program of building broad alliances. He proudly pointed to Communist women's success in "conquering" the 1933 Second National Congress of Women Workers and Peasants and in leading the workingwomen's movement.[70] In fact, PCM militants had adopted an increasingly adversarial stance toward the PNR during the second and third national congresses as well as at a June 1934 conference on prostitution, which coincided with the PCM's "Neither with Calles nor with Cárdenas" campaign proclaiming Laborde's presidential candidacy. The Communists attacked the penerristas for holding a rival congress, supporting the "farce" of socialist education, and backing a "bachelor tax" on single men over 30 years of age.[71]

Then, in a striking reversal just over a month after the opening of the 1935 Comintern congress, PNR and PCM women came together to form the Sole Front for Women's Rights (FUPDM).[72] A small group of mostly Communist women, including Cuca García, Esther Chapa, Matilde Rodríguez Cabo, Consuelo Uranga, and Luz Encina — names that, as the renowned columnist Salvador Novo explained, "little by little would become familiar to newspaper readers."[73] Meeting regularly in Mexico City's garment district, the group confronted differences early. The prominent Yucatecan feminist Elvia Carrillo Puerto, for example, renounced the group in favor of promoting "the vote for its own sake" rather than a more expansive agenda.[74]

The FUPDM adopted the PCM's organizational structures and the PNR's emphasis on building a cross-class, women-only membership, pursuing a two-pronged strategy of fighting for both immediate gains, such as mechanized corn mills and land reform, and long-term political aims of securing suffrage and combating fascism.[75] The leadership remained dominated by Communist militants, with García, long the instigator of anti-PNR attacks, at the helm. This combination of Communist organizational discipline and the ruling party's big-tent politics brought a broad array of women's groups under the FUPDM's umbrella.

The shift in the Communist women's attitude toward the penerristas

Figure 2. FUPDM demonstrators on the Zócalo. AGN, Archivo fotográfico "Enrique Díaz."

must have come as something of a surprise. Women like Cuca García and Ana María Hernández, who had spent the first half of the decade exchanging barbs, found themselves collaborating on the FUPDM's original executive committee. Indeed, even the FUPDM's cultural aspect marked a significant departure for Communists, whose meetings often included popular folk songs, revolutionary ballads, and the "International" rather than the European violin and vocal compositions that accompanied the FUPDM's inaugural plenary.[76] A poster beckoning women to the organization's founding meeting highlighted its efforts to close the divides that had stymied earlier efforts to forge a unified women's movement. Offering attendees a "fraternal welcome," the flyer promised "gains in favor of organized women, without distinction of political or religious creed, since our objectives focus on economic improvement, cultural evolution, and the acquisition of political rights."[77]

Much like that of the PCM during these years, the FUPDM's leadership struggled with its ambivalent relationship to the ruling party, trying to maintain autonomy while enjoying the legitimacy that accompanied cooperation and a more mainstream presence in Mexican politics. At its founding, the FUPDM remained technically independent of both the PNR and the PCM, bringing together women from all strains of women's activism, particularly those seeking a "third way" between penerristas and Communists. In Puebla, for example, a group of forty-six women met in the barbers union's assembly hall to form the Women's Defense League.[78] The FUPDM organizer and Michoacana Dolores Núñez ran the meeting along with Dolores Nájera de Chargoy, and the agenda reflected a strong PCM-PNR collaboration. They stressed the importance of remaining "within the lines of the government and the PNR" and concentrated their efforts on the "emancipation of the proletarian woman," with Nájera promoting a women's organization "free from all male leadership." Using pamphlets, meetings, demonstrations, and boycotts to advance its objectives, the league pledged "to inculcate in woman a profound class consciousness, standing in struggle against anything that attacks her rights, her dignity as woman, and her sovereignty as citizen." Despite insisting on women-only leadership, the league expressed "frank and decided" solidarity with the "masses of workers."

In this way, the FUPDM paralleled the model of left/center-left cooperation between the PCM and the labor leader Vicente Lombardo Toledano, a model that defined Cardenista labor policies—and, to a certain extent, the Mexican left in general—through the creation and maneuverings of the Mexican Labor Confederation (CTM), the left-leaning labor union that rivaled the Callista CROM. Similarly, the FUPDM anchored the women's movement during the Cárdenas presidency by uniting rival factions of women's organizing. Like the CTM-PCM alliance, the FUPDM at times exposed the strained collaboration among activists with closely held but occasionally divergent views. And, also like the CTM-PCM partnership, the FUPDM's creation marked a distinct radicalization of women's organizing, tipping the balance toward its mobilizational objectives over its disciplinary efforts to inculcate the values of modernity, nationalism, and regime loyalty.

The FUPDM's tactical and strategic aims—centered on women's suffrage and opposition to fascism—hewed closely to those of the PCM and the PNR's left wing, now self-constituted as Cardenistas. To these ends, the FUPDM self-consciously emulated PCM organizing structures by establishing organizing committees, cultivating leadership and solidarity ties, and formulating agendas for mobilization. The headquarters remained in Mexico City and dispatched organizers to establish FUPDM locals throughout the country while maintaining transnational associations and cultivating alliances abroad among other Communist and Popular Front organizations, feminist groups, and multilateral organizations such as the League of Nations and the Pan-

American Union. By emphasizing women's suffrage and antifascism, FUPDM leaders participated in linking women and antirevolutionary movements but inverted the argument to contend that only through state incorporation could women effectively fend off fascism.[79]

The FUPDM's success in building a mass-based, influential confederation stemmed from its effort to combine these more abstract objectives with concrete, practical gains such as potable water, consumption and production cooperatives, and protections against domestic and community violence, distilling elements of the SEP and suffragist projects to attract a broad constituency. Like temperance leagues and the SEP mothers' clubs, the FUPDM offered its affiliates the political contacts, the organizational infrastructure, and the language to pursue their objectives. Given the extensive overlap among the PCM, the FUPDM, and the SEP, it is unsurprising that their organizing strategies converged. In keeping with penerrista preferences, the FUPDM was run by and for women but maintained close associations with male-dominated labor unions and peasant organizations. It claimed a membership of 35,000 in 1936 and 50,000 by 1939.[80] These figures doubtless exaggerated its size, but much like the ruling party's estimates, they represent an expansive accounting that included members of all affiliated organizations.

These membership claims — even bracketing the question of their credibility — masked wide regional variations in the meanings of Front membership. Some chapters maintained closer ties to the PCM and others to the ruling party. Local economies and political climates defined both the feasibility of FUPDM programs and the meanings of political affiliations. Industrial settings, port cities, agricultural collectives, and rural villages all had different objectives in establishing chapters. The Front remained sensitive to local contexts and needs by having local leaders mediate between rank-and-file membership and national entities. As the organization's magazine explained, "In every place where the FUPDM is installed, we must struggle for the local demands of particular interest to women . . . always linking these demands with those contained in the general program."[81] Thus, the FUPDM developed not as a monolithic organization but, rather, as a loose confederation and as an institution constantly in formation. Adelina Zendejas, a Communist militant and FUPDM founder, described the Front as "not an organization but, rather, a movement struggling for women's rights."[82] This description is not entirely accurate, since the FUPDM had offices and a clear organizational structure and program, but its complexion as a national confederation reflected local politics and cultures as much as the leadership's agenda.

Local members and activists fashioned a wide variety of goals, defining the FUPDM's character and demonstrating a burgeoning sense of entitlement cultivated through popular organizing. Organizers appropriated the Communists' and penerristas' advocacy of temperance, education, and labor rights but often added demands that exposed the lacunae in programs formulated in Mexico City office buildings. Rank-and-file members repeatedly proclaimed that the FUPDM brought the revolution to women, and, although these petitions' authorship necessarily remains in the realm of conjecture, this formulation allowed organizers to tap into the Cardenistas' renewed commitment to the postrevolutionary government's populist promises. The tactical aspects of this discourse, however, should not overshadow the fact that it allowed and inspired ordinary women to claim significantly expanded rights that reflected their own conceptions of the revolution's legacy. Organizers' insistence that the revolution — both as an experience and as institutionalized within the governing regime — remained indebted to women fostered what the literary critic Raymond Williams has famously dubbed "structures of feeling," or a set of beliefs (in this instance, about justice and revolutionary rewards) shaped not by "more formal concepts of 'world-view' or 'ideology'" but instead by a more dynamic and amorphous interplay of cultural practices, affective relationships, and lived experiences.[83]

The workings of the Lucrecia Toriz Women's Union in Villa Azueta, Veracruz, exemplified how this political climate encouraged women's revolutionary citizenship. The Lucrecia Toriz women formed an FUPDM chapter in June 1936, choosing a name to honor a martyr of the 1907 Río Blanco textile strike that presaged the revolution. The officers registered the group with local and federal officials, requesting "every form of guarantee from the civil and military authorities in order to meet our economic and social demands, to which every woman has a right as head of the household [*jefa de casa*] as well as a duty before the social movement of working-class and peasant women."[84] Like many popular organizations, the Villa Azueta union wove together liberal rhetoric of rights and responsibilities with revolutionary language of mobilization. Referring to women as jefa de casa simultaneously subverted and reinforced the prevailing gender ideology of feminine domesticity, locating women in the home but making them the *jefas*, or masters, of that space with attendant rights (contradicting the civil code and widely held concerns about men's status as household heads). The Villa

Azueta women also linked their rights as jefas de casa with their responsibilities as revolutionaries, or participants in the "social movement of working-class and peasant women," underscoring an argument advanced by many women activists that their reproductive-labor obligations deepened rather than attenuated their revolutionary convictions.

Using the FUPDM's political network, the Lucrecia Toriz union wrote to Cárdenas via the Mexican Popular Front, perhaps to ensure a more attentive reading.[85] Outlining the union's objectives, the letter began by asserting that the Cárdenas government had opened "a new stage of social struggle" and indicated that the union's founding marked its members' coming to political consciousness. "The Mexican woman has been exploited in an unconscionable manner since time immemorial," the letter explained, "and until this moment . . . has remained silent, without understanding the enormity of conquering her civic and economic rights." The union allowed women to "understand their decisive role and assert their rights." Emboldened by the legitimacy of institutional recognition, the union requested economic support to establish a sewing, washing, and ironing cooperative as well as the enforcement of minimum-wage laws for women working as household cooks. Pointing out that these *cocineras* generally labored from six in the morning until ten at night for a paltry eight to ten pesos per month, the union warned that they would inevitably succumb to prostitution, making them carriers of infectious diseases. The union asked not only that the cocineras receive higher wages but also that price controls be imposed on basic necessities.

This petition highlights the complex nature of mass organizing during this period and reflects multiple layers of mediation and appeal. Although specifying local concerns about inflation and household economies, the entreaties conform to government programs promoting cooperatives and public-health initiatives. Its authors assumed an audience within the FUPDM and Popular Front headquarters as well as within government bureaucracies and, both as a collectivity and as individual activists establishing their credentials, sought to impress potential patrons with their revolutionary commitment. Even as the authors claimed revolutionary entitlements, they deferentially attributed a redemptive power to organizers and policymakers, indicating that "until this moment" the Villa Azueta women had "remained silent, without understanding." Drawing on the vocabulary of the Popular Front and postrevolutionary populism, the union appealed to Cárdenas (and indirectly to the Popular Front) as a "progressive government" and a "model before the world, which is preoccupied by the position that women should take in the current moment of struggle" and offered a vision of revolutionary gains that centered on improving the conditions of both paid and unpaid reproductive labor.

FUPDM chapters did not focus exclusively on reproductive labor. The FUPDM local in the port city of Salina Cruz, Oaxaca, for example, worked closely with the CTM's longshoremen's and petroleum workers' unions, which supported its protests against rampant inflation and efforts to secure better working-class housing.[86] However, when sixty FUPDM members, many unable to sign their names, demanded, among other things, employment in the traditionally male spaces of the docks and salt mines, they met with CTM resistance. "There are jobs in the offices in the loading docks," they wrote to President Cárdenas, "that women could fill with greater efficiency, such as the positions of wholesaler, time keeper, and squad leader." They argued that they should not be denied these jobs "for the sole fact of not being recognized as a union."[87] Subsequently, the organization's officers insisted "that the unions, employers, and workers in general understand that women have the right to work" and "that women workers not be the object of harassment and evasions."[88]

Similar experiences played out in a variety of contexts, despite PCM and government backing for wage-earning women. FUPDM activists generally garnered more local support from male allies when they remained within the realm of home-front concerns such as food prices and housing standards. When they transgressed these boundaries, they often encountered "harassment and evasions." The Salina Cruz organizers also highlighted the importance of official recognition. Although FUPDM members viewed themselves as meriting the attendant benefits of an organized group, CTM members clearly saw them as encroaching on their territory and threatening to undermine union control. By securing Cárdenas's endorsement, FUPDM organizers hoped to quell opposition and legitimate their objectives. The case of Acapulco offers an example of how the FUPDM wove together innovative strategies and well-established political conventions, highlighting the stakes of competing bids for legitimacy.

"To Struggle for Their Demands": Acapulco and the Popular Front

The PCM's embrace of more collaborative, nationalist efforts and the Cardenistas' commitment to mass organizing converged in Acapulco, where the most successful, enduring campaigns utilized established patronage and organizing networks, created opportunities for women without challenging male privilege, and linked local issues within national and international concerns. Acapulco, Mexico's largest Pacific-coast port, had incubated radicalism — particularly anarcho-socialist and, later, communist organizations — since before the revolution, and the atmosphere informed popular political interpretations.[89] Communist militant Benita Galeana, for example, recalled that her experiences in 1920s Acapulco shaped her political consciousness and her decision to join the PCM once she arrived in Mexico City.[90]

In 1935, under the leadership of the tireless Communist activist María de la O, the ninety-six founding members of the Revolutionary Women's Union of Acapulco allied with the port's male-dominated stevedores' and day laborers' union as well as other women's labor unions, such as the Union of Red Women.[91] Like other women's organizations, the Revolutionary Women's Union gained strength through alliances with like-minded groups, pursuing land rights, medical facilities, and schools. Its leaders explicitly modeled their efforts after the women's leagues in neighboring Michoacán, hoping to achieve similar gains and to build connections with them. At the union's inaugural meeting, the head of the local ejidal zone (and husband of a SEP employee and union officer) explained that the time was ripe for women's unification and exhorted its members to become a "bastion of rights in this port." The women's union maintained offices in the stevedores' union hall, where union leaders occasionally attended the women's meetings to offer advice and words of support.

Endorsements from prominent men legitimated the project in the eyes of male community members, emphasizing that the women struggled "at the side of the ejidatarios" for community needs such as schools and medical facilities. These were no feminist agitators imported from Mexico City to insist on women's political rights but, rather, class-conscious revolutionaries reinforcing men's efforts. While men's involvement likely constrained women from speaking openly about their concerns, it remained indispensable to the organizations' viability; the consent of the husbands, fathers, and brothers of the community's women made membership in these organizations practicable.

Radical women's organizing, with all its attendant conflicts, spilled into the surrounding region. In the coffee-growing area of Atoyac, the local ejidal delegate "authorized" the creation of a women's group to "contribute its grain of sand" to support the labor federation.[92] Claiming two hundred members and enjoying the backing of the Liga de Comunidades Agrarias, this group organized a regional congress that itself became a site of conflict, prompting de la O to demand guarantees against anticipated attacks by state-government supporters against conference attendees.[93] Meanwhile, 118 campesinas in nearby Petatlán met in the "customary place for organized elements" to form a union with the same affiliations as their Atoyac compañeras.[94] In the capital city of Chilpancingo, widows and orphans of Zapatistas agitated for medical dispensaries, cooperatives, and workshops where they could support themselves, while a seamstresses' union requested 1,500 pesos "so that we will not have to continue suffering the exploitations and injuries of the foreign owners of the El Traje del Obrero clothing factory."[95] When the El Traje del Obrero seamstresses struck two months later to protest persistent labor-law violations, the head of the state PNR committee requested federal troops to protect the women from strikebreakers and bosses.[96] In short, the Acapulco-centered mobilization, bolstered by the institutional infrastructure of male-dominated, PNR-affiliated labor and peasant unions, encouraged women's organizing in outlying areas.

These opportunities also bred conflicts, however. In 1934, only days after delivering campaign speeches lambasting "voracious capitalism" and endorsing the arming of Guerrero's agraristas, Cárdenas established an Acapulco chapter of the National Women's League.[97] By March 1936, leadership divisions precipitated an organizational split, with several officers calling for the removal of secretary-general María de Jesús Véjar.[98] In addition to hoarding the league's files in her home and failing to hold regular meetings, Véjar had expressed uncertainty about the league's future under the Cárdenas presidency, marking her as anti-Cardenista. She had made expenditures without the board's approval and had threatened to expel anyone who failed to attend meetings in the place of her choosing, "a declaration that offended the dignity of threatened members." Further, the affronted officers informed Cárdenas, Véjar came from a family known for mental illness, making her ill-suited to her duties.

The dissenters included nearly all of the officers, with the notable exception of the local teacher María Valencia. They copied the letter to the league's national president at its Mexico City headquarters, who, in December, became the target of an ouster herself. By May, this rebellious group had formed the rival First Acapulco Red National Women's League (hereafter, Liga Roja), which fashioned itself a "leftist" women's organization.[99] According to attendance lists, 455 women attended this founding meeting, witnessed by several prominent men, including Senator Román Campos

Viveros, who volunteered to register the new organization with the appropriate authorities. Valencia then reconstituted the original league.

Two months after the Liga Roja's creation, two FUPDM organizers arrived from Mexico City to bring peace among Acapulco's estranged women's organizations. Ofelia Domínguez Navarro, a Communist and Cuban national organizing for the FUPDM, relied on local teachers and activists to "call on women without distinctions of political or religious creeds, [to] unify on the basis of this pact of solidarity, which will enable them to struggle for their demands."[100] To promote unity, the governing body included delegates from all member organizations, which pledged, on penalty of expulsion, to uphold the solidarity pact and organize FUPDM locals throughout the state. "The organizations commit themselves to maintaining the broadest spirit of fraternity," the confederation's constitution began, "lending mutual support with the aim of constituting a true Frente Único, without this signifying an intervention in internal affairs or a violation of autonomy."

The organizers enumerated a wide-ranging program that included issues as varied as combating inflation and discounted women's wages; agitating for maternity clinics, labor laws compatible with childbearing, and indigenous women's incorporation into political and social movements; and opposing "imperialist war," "humiliating treaties," and the payment of the national debt. Finally, it included a call for women's suffrage. Using an arsenal of press campaigns, demonstrations, solidarity networks, and "any act that will procure the mobilization of the greatest number of women," the chapter echoed the PCM's priorities of combating fascism and "capitalist imperialism."[101] Legislative and structural changes, they assumed, would follow the momentum of mass organizing. The officers of the estranged National Women's League and the renegade Liga Roja signed the pact. To cement the peace, the new confederation agreed to hold a *comida de fraternidad* (solidarity meal) the following Sunday afternoon.

This strategy of integrating campaigns for local, tangible gains with international objectives such as combating imperialism was the FUPDM's hallmark. For Domínguez, one newspaper explained, "as for any good socialist, borders and nationalities do not exist."[102] Not only did expatriate activists like Domínguez organize in Mexico, but FUPDM leaders also attended international women's congresses, and the FUPDM maintained an international network of contacts with like-minded women's organizations that supported its efforts. This web of connections, from neighborhood meetings to ruling-party conferences to transcontinental congresses, reinforced the organizers' roles as intermediaries among these different levels, giving them legitimacy as negotiators of women's rights.

However, the détente between the rival leagues faltered over the crucial issue of legitimacy and the material benefits it entailed. The Liga Roja found itself under attack from two directions. In January 1937, the National Women's League wrote to Cárdenas insisting on the Liga Roja's subordination "as an act of discipline and respect for your superior accord."[103] The Liga Roja, the National Women's League pointed out, affronted Cárdenas himself, since he had founded the original league. "Submitting this issue to our sentiments of patriotism and justice," the National Women's League wrote, "we will never permit the Liga Roja nor anybody else to lack obedience and respect for your acts." The following month, the corn-mill owners' union complained that the Liga Roja's milling cooperative violated a 1932 presidential decree controlling competition among corn millers.[104] If Cárdenas delivered to the Liga Roja the mills he had promised them a few weeks earlier, the owners' union explained, "it would take the bread from our mouths and throw us back to the disastrous situation of a previous era, with days when we earned enough to get by and days when we did not."[105]

Undaunted by these attacks, the Liga Roja continued to press for corn mills and formed a second chapter of a hundred women in the town of Tixtlancingo, "also submitting itself to fulfill faithfully and patriotically not only the statutes that govern this Liga Roja but also those of the [FUPDM] in Mexico City."[106] This new delegation received endorsements from the transport workers' union, the port's labor center, and the secretary of "agrarian action," as well as from a widow who identified herself only as a "revolutionary." The organization also secured Cárdenas's commitment to donate several corn mills and sewing machines to establish a cooperative.

Despite Senator Campos's intervention, however, the Liga Roja agitated for several years for its milling cooperative, complaining that it had been the object of mockery and attacks by guardias blancas "constituted by the capitalists."[107] It finally secured a locale and one mill but soon found it was in such disrepair that it failed to meet sanitation codes. The National Women's League, meanwhile, seemingly effortlessly received 7,000 pesos to purchase two corn mills and a van, apparently provoking no response from the mill owners' union. By 1940, the shifting political winds had turned against the Liga Roja, with its self-proclaimed "leftism," and favored the more moderate National Women's League. The Liga Roja protested that abuses committed by local reservists went unchecked by military authorities.[108] Perhaps in an effort to recast itself as less stridently revolutionary, the Liga Roja renamed itself the "New Woman" cooperative and sought support from local CTM offices. Explaining that the port's head of public works had taken over the building intended to house its cooperative, that it had lost its official recognition, and that it still had only one barely operative mill, the organization asked the labor federation to intervene on its behalf.[109] The documentary trail runs cold on the Liga Roja at this point, but four months later, the National Women's League secured a promise for another 10,000 pesos for a school-restoration project.[110]

The developments in Acapulco followed the general arc of Cardenismo and highlighted one of the Popular Front's pitfalls. Schoolteachers and PCM militants played central roles in secular women's organizing, although one scholar of the region has argued that the PCM had a moderating effect on radical politics, pulling agitators like María de la O into line with official priorities even while advocating progressive policies.[111] Concerned about organized counterrevolutionary threats, progressive organizations put aside their differences to fight for common goals. With official support, however, came conflicts over legitimacy and access to public resources. As the feud between the National Women's League and the breakaway Liga Roja demonstrated, even support from well-placed patrons did not guarantee results. The changing political climate of the late 1930s left organizations such as the Liga Roja out of sync with Cardenistas' efforts to consolidate the administration's achievements. In the Comarca Lagunera — arguably the region where the Mexican Popular Front staged its most successful campaign outside Mexico City — the effects of this cooperation emerge more starkly but in the context of a more disciplined and focused movement that foregrounded labor issues.

FOUR

"All the Benefits of the Revolution":

Labor and Citizenship in the

Comarca Lagunera

On 19 August 1936, some 20,000 agricultural wage laborers walked off the job in the middle of the Comarca Lagunera's cotton harvest. Strikers flew the red and black flags of the Communist-supported labor unions over their houses as entire families abandoned the vast plantations, demanding union recognition, land for subsistence cultivation, and improved working conditions. More than 45,000 industrial and manufacturing workers had signed solidarity pacts, pledging economic support and threatening sympathy strikes to support agricultural workers on 154 haciendas.[1] Regional production stalled as observers and participants held their breath, anxiously anticipating a resolution to long-standing grievances over labor and living conditions. The strike officially ended on 3 September, after Cárdenas committed to break up the huge haciendas and distribute them among the 15,000 eligible resident laborers (*peones acasillados*). By the time he declared the agrarian reform on 6 October, that number had ballooned to include 10,000 casual workers and another 15,000 seasonal workers, many of whom had been imported as strikebreakers. However, reform brought more than a massive redistribution of land. It included a dramatic collectivization and modernization of government, production systems, and social structures. The Cárdenas regime saw the Laguna reforms as an opportunity not only to

resolve a volatile labor situation but also to model its vision for postrevolutionary Mexico.[2]

The strike's success fostered a regionally defined conception of revolutionary citizenship that informed political structures and popular organizations. By the time the conflicts exploded into a general strike, widespread upheaval had drawn in men and women alike, including peasants, agricultural wage laborers, and industrial workers. Although interunion disputes had plagued early organizing efforts, the strike exemplified the Popular Front's unity. When government officials finally stepped in, the mobilization's breadth and strength required the regime to make significant concessions. Cardenista tolerance of the PCM and of mass mobilizations afforded communist and anarchist organizers greater legitimacy than they had enjoyed during the maximato, and activists pressed the government to implement progressive policies. Forced to choose between repression and co-optation, Cárdenas chose the latter, but co-optation came dearly in the context of a well-organized, highly mobilized population. During the Cárdenas administration, the federal government laid out an estimated 100 million pesos ($360 million), antagonized powerful northern landowners, and required local and national bureaucracies to commit significant human and material resources to ensure the agrarian reform's success.

As exceptional as the 1936 strike was, its resolution and legacy resembled other postrevolutionary experiences. Much in the way that agrarismo and the Cristero Rebellion defined the contours of popular organizing in Michoacán, the PCM and the strike did the same in the Comarca Lagunera, refracting politics through the prism of this massive upheaval. Also, in a pattern that postrevolutionary statesmen repeated time and again, the government claimed credit for the hard-earned gains of a dramatic popular mobilization. Just as Francisco Múgica separated the creation of the campesinas' vocational school from Concha Michel's Santa Bárbara invasion (attributing the inspiration instead to Cárdenas's intervention in the Comarca Lagunera), or lawmakers severed the 1953 women's suffrage amendment from the dynamic 1930s suffrage movement, the Cárdenas government claimed credit for the progressive changes that resulted from the Laguna strike, ignoring the years of organization that preceded it.

As in other aspects of the Laguna reforms, the government had a strong but not deciding hand in shaping women's organizing through the state-sponsored Ligas Femeniles de Lucha Social (Women's Leagues for Social Struggle). Implemented by local activists, the leagues translated policy from

Mexico City into the local political vernacular, creating a movement that was, on the one hand, place-bound and specific and, on the other, meant to serve as a model to the republic. The ensuing consolidation of regional women's organizing strengthened the movement but also professionalized and bureaucratized it, tying it more closely to official priorities. While women activists hardly parroted the party line, they did learn to operate effectively within the political parameters that governed popular organizing while still fashioning their own conception of revolutionary citizenship. Within limits, the official organizing program of the Ligas Femeniles allowed them the space to render their labor — both wage labor and unpaid reproductive labor — visible and their mobilizations efficacious.

A Land without History? The Roots of the Laguna Conflict

The commonly accepted narrative of Laguna history describes it as wasted space until investors with vision and capital created irrigation systems that rendered it viable for cultivation. Local historians propagate this youthful image of a region unburdened by its colonial past, maintaining a progressive teleology centered on the pursuit of ever more efficient machines and modes of production.[3] One such account asserted that the region remained "deserted other than a few errant Chichimecan tribes that were wiped out in the last century."[4] Another begins, "La Laguna, 'like an honorable woman, has no history,' or like a girl who begins the hard but attractive ascent in life but hardly seeks to understand her historical origins."[5]

An arid region of about 6,000 hectares (14,826 acres), the Comarca Lagunera straddles the border between the northern states of Coahuila and Durango. This liminal positioning affected popular organizing and created legal complexities. The Comarca Lagunera lacked a state-based popular organizing structure akin to Michoacán's Revolutionary Labor Confederation (CRMDT) or Yucatán's Socialist Party of the Southeast (PSS), allowing for more pluralism and greater influence from supraregional mass organizations. In labor disputes, union leaders argued that only the federal labor board, rather than the more compromised state labor boards, could rule on strikes involving workplaces from both states. In short, regional popular organizations developed stronger ties to national and international entities than to local or state political structures.

Two major rivers, the Nazas and the Aguanaval, crisscross the region. They remained uncontrolled until the mid–nineteenth century, when two

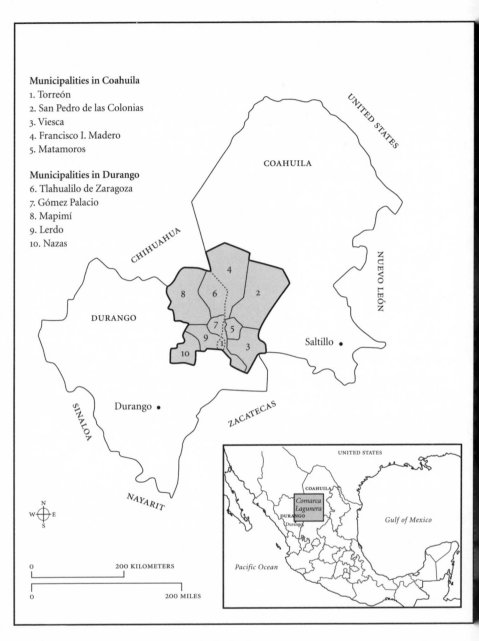

Municipalities in Coahuila
1. Torreón
2. San Pedro de las Colonias
3. Viesca
4. Francisco I. Madero
5. Matamoros

Municipalities in Durango
6. Tlahualilo de Zaragoza
7. Gómez Palacio
8. Mapimí
9. Lerdo
10. Nazas

Map 3. "Comarca Lagunera." By Natalie Hanemann.

families purchased most of the land from the indebted descendants of a Spanish marquis and began the construction of a vast irrigation network, creating a fertile area suited to cotton and wheat cultivation. The families subsequently sold parts of their estates, and the Juárez government rewarded veterans of the French intervention with other parcels, resulting in a patchwork of plantations that depended on concentrated capital and a large supply of low-paid laborers. In 1890, the Anglo-American–owned Tlahualilo Land Company began the most ambitious irrigation project.[6] In 1895, seeking a more stable workforce, the company imported some six hundred African Americans, many of whom died of smallpox soon after their arrival, compelling the rest to return to Alabama.[7]

During the Porfiriato, the region flourished amid rising demand for cotton, encouraging concentrated property holdings and capitalist production systems. Agricultural wage labor, however, coexisted with a lesser but nonetheless important tradition of peasant smallholding that offered an escape for rural proletarians.[8] Access to cultivable land promised rural workers not only a buffer against the seasonal nature of cotton cultivation but also access to subsistence other than through the company-run stores (*tiendas de raya*), which provoked countless worker grievances during the Porfiriato and into the 1930s. This practice particularly victimized peones acasillados, since scrip payments and the absence of other vendors often left them with few options. A study comparing prices and wages on the Tlahualilo hacienda in 1935 found that the average laborer earned 355.84 pesos annually and spent 292 pesos to provide a family of five with a modest diet, leaving fewer than 64 pesos to pay for clothes, medicines, and other expenses.[9]

Agricultural labor primarily occupied men. During most of the year, they labored long hours for wages ranging between half a peso and 1 peso daily and could not count on steady employment. Meanwhile, campesinas dedicated themselves to reproductive labor, rising before dawn to fetch water, start kitchen fires, and grind corn for tortillas, and they supplemented men's wages by growing subsistence products for household consumption or sale at markets. Women and girls living in or near Torreón, the region's urban center, often performed wage labor in the service or manufacturing sectors, particularly the textile mills and incipient garment industry. Only during the summer harvest would women and children join the men in the fields.[10] During this period, landowners paid workers by weight rather than by day, generally offering between 3 and 6 centavos per kilogram, with individual male laborers earning as much as 3 pesos for a twelve-hour day and entire families earning up to 40 pesos in a week.[11] This opportunity attracted *bonanceros*, seasonal workers who arrived from throughout the country for the "bonanza" of the cotton pick.

In addition to the more predictable seasonal changes, agricultural labor demand fluctuated wildly depending on rainfall, global markets, and blights. The Depression decimated cotton production as commodity prices plummeted, shrinking cotton production from 132,000 hectares (326,172 acres) in 1926 to 43,231 hectares (106,824 acres) by 1932, leaving an estimated 13,000 laborers unemployed.[12] Such uncertainty for male breadwinners unsettled household gender dynamics and tightened already Spartan household budgets. Grueling working conditions — ten- or eleven-hour workdays, abusive labor bosses, and complete dependence on the hacienda owner's goodwill — compounded this insecurity.[13] Peones acasillados, although enjoying greater security than seasonal or temporary workers, found that if they fell out of favor with the owner or foreman, they could lose access to medical facilities, credit at the tienda de raya, or even their jobs. This insecurity and instability, as much as the material conditions of agricultural labor, contributed to agricultural workers' receptiveness to labor organizers.

Despite the strong Villista presence during the revolution, Laguna landowners survived the postrevolutionary land reform relatively unscathed.[14] The new regime remained reluctant to subject the region to land reform since its value as a commodities-producing region required concentrated capital to maintain economies of scale; control the Nazas and Aguanaval rivers; and survive plagues of boll weevil and bollworm, droughts, and floods. Workers themselves, many of them either peones acasillados or migrant workers who flocked to the region for the cotton-picking season, did not demand wholesale land redistribution. Most Laguna labor agitation during the 1920s and early '30s, much like in Yucatán, centered on wages, labor conditions, prices in the tiendas de raya, and the provision of education and health services. To the extent that agricultural laborers wanted land, they mostly demanded subsistence plots to cultivate corn, beans, and occasionally fruit.

By the end of the 1890s, the region had a burgeoning working class. In addition to factories related to cotton production — including gins, textile mills, and cottonseed-oil presses — the region also boasted a significant mining industry. By 1887, Torreón had become the crossroad of two major railroad lines, one running north–south from Ciudad Juárez, Chihuahua, to Mexico City, and the other running east–west from Durango City to Monterrey, Nuevo León. In the 1930s, the federal government constructed highways connecting Torreón to other major cities. In May 1935, a modern highway between Torreón and San Pedro facilitated transportation through the heart of the cotton-growing region at a cost of 630,000 pesos ($2.268 million).[15]

Regionalizing the Popular Front

Given the prevalence of peones acasillados and the relatively fluid migrant-labor population, the Comarca Lagunera may have seemed an unlikely setting for Popular Front organizing. In addition to facing widespread repression by police and guardias blancas, progressive organizations fought bitterly among themselves. In Torreón, the Socialist League and the PCM sparred constantly, with the former enjoying the support of local authorities. Former Municipal President Francisco Ortiz Garza asked the governor to intervene on Communists' behalf, "given that the guarantees that citizens deserve are founded in the law and not in the sympathies of the authorities," but PNR stalwarts dubbed PCM organizers "anti-patriotic" defenders of communism who celebrated the Bolshevik Revolution and disturbed pro-government demonstrations.[16]

Despite these conflicts, certain economic and political factors made the region fertile ground for Popular Front ideas. Railroads and highways transported people and ideas as well as cotton and wheat. Much as they did in the radical port cities of Veracruz, Acapulco, Tampico, and Progreso, anarchist and communist sympathizers arrived in Torreón in growing numbers after the revolution.[17] In addition to a large seasonal workforce, the region attracted railroad and highway-construction workers — sectors that, along with the mining and textile industries, bred radical labor politics and strong PCM membership. By 1934, the Torreón police department estimated that about 200–250 Communists met regularly in cells throughout the municipality, and the historian María Vargas-Lobsinger identifies the PCM as the most active and successful of the many entities that organized Laguna workers and peasants during this period.[18]

Furthermore, unemployment and poverty skyrocketed in the early 1930s. The PNR newspaper asserted that only the "innate goodness of our people and the principle of discipline in social organization" kept Laguneros from "resorting to direct action to eat a crust of bread."[19] The Mexico City paper *El Universal*, reporting that in San Pedro alone 30,000 campesinos lacked work, chided that "innate goodness" and "discipline" would not prevent Communists from "organizing and mobilizing tens of thousands of unemployed peones."[20] The PCM paper reported that a woman working at Torreón's La Fe textile factory died of starvation.[21] Across the state border, in Gómez Palacios, a committee of unemployed workers agitated for secure seeds and rent forgiveness.[22] The Socialist League, the Liga de Comunidades Agrarias, and the anarchist General Labor Confederation (CGT) disavowed state and local governments that reneged on promises to protect workers' rights, leading them tentatively to join forces with the PCM. By May 1935, the PCM backed the Socialist League in a struggle with Coahuila's Governor Jesús Valdez Sánchez, who continued to support landowners in the Comarca Lagunera and the wheat-growing region of Arteaga, where "the campesino classes . . . have been brutally harassed by the *latifundistas* (plantation owners) and the guardias blancas."[23]

Although the revolution left plantations intact, it created both the legal framework and the expectation for more equitable land and labor policies. The 1920s had commenced with a monthlong strike involving roughly 10,000 agricultural laborers on thirty-five haciendas and calling for a daily minimum wage of 3 pesos, shorter workdays, and union recognition. The decade brought repeated land invasions and union-organizing campaigns by the PCM and the Callista CROM.[24] Campesino discontent deepened in November 1934, when President Abelardo Rodríguez pronounced an end to land reform in the Comarca Lagunera. Local landowners, eager to quell growing labor agitation, spent 2.5 million pesos ($9 million) to create two ejidal zones on the region's outskirts, one in Coahuila and the other in Durango. They distributed land to qualifying communities and declared land reform complete, arguing that landowners would not invest in improvements so long as they feared expropriation. Even given the exclusion of peones acasillados and communities too small to form viable ejidos, however, the measure precipitated 1,405 new land petitions and could only accommodate 365, leaving the remaining petitioners frustrated by the elusive opportunity.[25]

Other abuses compounded this sense of betrayal. While the U.S. consulate portrayed Governor Valdez Sánchez as "intellectual" and upright, labor leaders said he undermined workers' rights to organize.[26] One agricultural workers' union informed Cárdenas that a hacienda owner had fired its organizers "for the only 'crime' of having organized ourselves into a front of resistance."[27] The PCM newspaper reported that hacendados fined peasants a full day's pay if their burros strayed onto plantation land, "without doing any damage."[28] Hacendados evicted the teacher Andrés López and his family for organizing workers into a "revolutionary union instead of a company union," forcing López, his wife, and their six children to "live exposed to the elements because they would not bow to the desires of a despotic *patrón* [boss]."[29]

From the outset, Laguna labor actions marked an exceptional organizing achievement, developing impressive levels of solidarity among industrial and agricultural unions. As Barry Carr has pointed out, this solidarity stemmed not only from the proletarianized nature of regional agricultural labor but also from the fact that workers moved seasonally between agricultural and industrial work.[30] On 11 June 1935, a strike erupted at the Hacienda Manila in Durango.[31] The principal strike demands reflected long-standing grievances: an eight-hour workday, a 1.5 peso minimum daily wage, and the presence of a union member during the cotton weighing. Waves of sympathy strikes targeted some of the region's most powerful landowners, and industrial workers expressed solidarity with the striking agricultural laborers.[32] The strike ended after 32 days, with a partial labor victory of a 1.5 peso minimum wage.

Despite its limited gains, the movement sparked organizing campaigns among agricultural workers throughout the region. Employers engaged in aggressive union-busting efforts and created company unions (*sindicatos blancos*), but some strikers came from sindicatos blancos that became radicalized. Threats against union organizers of dismissal, violence, and even assassinations precipitated protests and labor actions. The local labor board pronounced these strikes illegal, but striking workers responded that labor inspectors never ventured beyond the landowner's house, that municipal authorities disrupted meetings and interfered with their organizing rights, and that the local PNR encouraged sindicatos blancos and arranged for the dismissal of workers who spurned them.[33] The strikers' bottom-line demands called for the enforcement of federal labor laws, and a sympathetic district court repeatedly upheld their right to strike.[34]

Torreón municipal authorities tried to impose order, calling for crackdowns on unlicensed prostitutes and homeless people sleeping on benches in the city's Alameda Zaragoza.[35] A cerebrospinal-meningitis outbreak in the spring of 1936 increased insecurity among residents and officials, heightening concerns about rampant poverty and deteriorating sanitation as population growth exceeded infrastructural capacities.[36] The Coahuilan governor exploited this unease to shutter churches, theaters, and municipal schools, all regular meeting places for labor and community organizations.[37]

The most successful Communist organizing also mobilized women. The PCM stronghold of Matamoros, Coahuila, produced the Josefa Ortiz de Domínguez Women's Union, which played a critical role in regional women's organizing into the 1940s. Martina Derás, the union's founder and leader, became an icon of radical women's activism after local authorities killed her during a 1929 massacre of communist sympathizers.[38] Six months later, Matamoros elected the Communist Alejandro Adame as municipal president. "The women demonstrated great activity," the PCM newspaper proudly reported of the campaign. "Several of them spoke in meetings, organized festivals to raise campaign funds, and participated as magnificent militants in all efforts."[39] In 1934, the Matamoros women protested that local authorities had arrested thirteen of their compañeros — including two women — during a demonstration and incarcerated them in Torreón to prevent their participation in that year's elections.[40]

Women's participation in PCM activities unsettled authorities. When Torreón police arrested two women and their seven children among Communist demonstrators, they seemed uncertain what to do and released them after four hours without charging them but fined the men 50 pesos each, the equivalent of more than a month's wages.[41] A Matamoros police report describing a 1935 May Day demonstration remarked with alarm about children carrying a "Red Pioneers" banner and women shouting "*Mueras* [death to]" against the PNR, the federal government, and Lázaro Cárdenas, and "*Vivas* [long live]" for the Soviet Union.[42]

Women also entered the fray through labor and teachers' unions, temperance leagues, and neighborhood organizations. In San Pedro, an active center of labor agitation, hundreds of women protested the cost of prostitutes' new health-inspection requirements, generating a speedy official response that the government would lower the cost, per their specifications, and had never intended to impose an extra tax on them.[43] In Torreón, women millers and seamstresses agitated through labor unions for the enforcement of minimum-wage laws, accusing the labor board of consorting with factory owners and engaging in "disgusting manipulations" to workers' disadvantage.[44] Several garment workers' unions petitioned Cárdenas for sewing machines to establish a cooperative.[45] Other groups focused on community issues: the Working Women's Union of Colonia Ana joined several other renters' organizations in a fierce struggle to defend their neighborhood from an "urbanization" program and to expropriate the properties they rented.[46]

Women's activism, however, did not dissolve social conventions. Other than women's unions, labor unions maintained almost exclusively male leadership and elevated the ideal of an independent, family breadwinner, reinforcing patriarchal control over economic resources in an effort to rectify the dissonance between the image of the postrevolutionary citizen-peasant and the reality of dependence, subjugation, humiliation, and uncertainty that most agricultural laborers endured. One union of peones acasillados asked Cárdenas to enforce the federal labor laws and uphold the constitution, explaining, "We have concentrated so many of our hopes in it; we want you to make of us men of labor and of faith."[47] They went on to request schools, clean lodgings, and a living wage. Furthermore, labor disputes and even peaceful demonstrations often exploded into violent confrontations that retained a masculine tint, notwithstanding women's participation.

In February 1936, seeking to exert some control over the regional labor and political situation, the PNR and the Liga de Comunidades Agrarias sponsored an agrarian congress in Saltillo, Coahuila's capital, with more than 2,000 delegates from throughout the state. The government's concerns extended beyond the Laguna labor unrest; the counterrevolutionary Camisas Doradas had established a Saltillo headquarters and had begun organizing throughout the state, including in Torreón, appealing to landowners and employers who maintained that outside agitators stirred up labor troubles.[48] Notwithstanding its modest aims, the congress distressed Laguna landholders, who perceived it as a harbinger of further land reform, despite Rodríguez's 1934 decree. Thus, the Cárdenas government confronted a choice between jeopardizing the regime's legitimacy among the landowning elite or among organized peasants and workers.

Resistance and Accommodation: The 1936 General Strike

Labor disputes continued unabated during the off-season. When Deputy Minister of Government Agustín Arroyo arrived to meet with landowners, industrialists, and union leaders, he encountered demonstrations and counterdemonstrations, each bringing an estimated 1,500–2,000 men and women into the streets.[49] Communist-led groups protested against state mediation of the labor conflicts, while more moderate, PNR-affiliated organizations such as the Liga de Comunidades Agrarias invited more government intervention. Participants in the February agrarian congress complained that the government had fallen down on its promises to improve agricultural labor conditions and to create greater transparency and accountability in local government.[50]

By May 1936, the situation had become critical. The Dorados organized openly, with the complicity of landowners and a few local officials.[51] Communist labor unions, united under the umbrella of the Mexican Labor Confederation (CTM), added modest land reforms to their demands — requesting one hectare of land and simple tools for each laborer — and threatened a general strike of industrial and agricultural workers for 26 May. Employers showed no signs of capitulating, maintaining that "unscrupulous leaders upset the proletarian masses in this region, causing serious disturbances with fundamental and damaging repercussions for the regional economy."[52] Local authorities asked military forces to keep order.[53] Distressed at the specter of a worker-peasant alliance spiraling out of control and dismayed by the employers' intransigence, Cárdenas summoned leaders of employers' and laborers' unions to Mexico City to negotiate a settlement before the strike deadline. The employers committed to reinstating workers dismissed for union organizing, dismantling the sindicatos blancos, signing a collective contract complying with federal minimum-wage laws, and improving living conditions for peones acasillados. In return, the laborers' union agreed to postpone the strike for twenty days to allow employers to implement these changes.

Escalating violence in the Comarca Lagunera accompanied these tense negotiations in Mexico City. The foreman of the Spanish-owned Hacienda San Ignacio was killed on 11 May.[54] PCM-affiliated unions informed Cárdenas that union organizers had been unjustly arrested for the crime and then kicked and beaten by the Spanish hacendado while police and local authorities looked on. The women's union petitioned repeatedly for guarantees of physical safety and due process for their compañeros.[55]

On 2 June, as employers demonstrated little intention of fulfilling their commitments, the CTM and PCM orchestrated a brief work stoppage on 109 haciendas and in the major textile and metalwork factories.[56] The more moderate CGT unions pressed laborers to return to work and complained that the communist Nicolás Lenin Union had, in turn, threatened them with guns.[57] They asked Cárdenas to guarantee their safety but already enjoyed the sympathies of local landowners and civil and military authorities, who assured strikebreakers and employers that federal troops would prevent further disturbances.[58] The conflict's rapid escalation made it nearly impossible to remain aloof from the hostilities. A white-collar union supported a settlement without endorsing either side, calling for "harmony between capital and labor for the equilibrium of the national economy."[59] To most Laguneros, however, harmony between capital and labor seemed unattainable, and neutrality impossible.

When the second deadline arrived on 15 June, the labor unions once again deferred the strike. They ostensibly wanted to provide employers with another opportunity to comply with the collective contracts but also needed to solidify their support among organizations sympathetic to calls for labor peace. PCM organizers appealed directly to reluctant unions' membership; aggravated Liga de Comunidades Agrarias unionists complained that Communist organizers "egged on the workers, promising them on the one hand the sun and on the other the moon."[60] The CGT leadership explicitly favored government officials over militant, communist organizers to organize campesinos and resolve labor disputes.[61] Cárdenas, however, declared during a late July visit to the region that the government would not intervene but would allow employers and workers to settle matters among themselves.

Despite Cárdenas's purported neutrality, rumors about expropriation spread quickly among landowners when sixty engineers came to survey the territory. In turn, landowners sent a delegation to meet with Cárdenas in Mexico City and make their case against dividing the large estates.[62] Meanwhile, the CTM's chief, Vicente Lombardo Toledano made the reverse journey, from Mexico City to the Comarca Lagunera, to shore up support for the much anticipated strike. As the final deadline approached, the unions reiterated their principal demands: a daily minimum wage of 2.5 pesos, improved housing, one hectare for each peón acasillado, reinstatement of workers dismissed for union organizing, and the presence of a union member during the weighing of picked cotton. The employers' union responded that it was still "studying" the matter, maintaining that plantations could not remain solvent if they conceded the wage and housing improvements workers demanded. Meanwhile, hoping to reach an agreement before the midnight deadline on 18 August, the federal labor board reconvened the labor and employer representatives who had met in May.[63] Employers and government representatives hoped to convince the unions to defer the strike once again, pushing the deadline beyond the cotton-picking season. However, union leaders understood the opportunity at hand during the height of the harvest, and organized workers had grown weary of waiting for employers to finish "studying" their demands. The gap between the union leaders and the employers remained too great to close before the clock struck midnight on 18 August.

The strike brought panic and increased violence. The national textile manufacturers' organization asked Cárdenas to intervene to prevent a national cotton shortage.[64] Landowners' henchmen attacked striking workers as they blocked the hacienda gates, attempting to convince strikebreakers not to cross picket lines.[65] The labor leader Dionisio Encina, who later became the PCM's secretary-general, cabled Lombardo Toledano, "Federal forces arrested compañeros in an effort to break strike. Some haciendas, compañeros request economic aid. Situation desperate."[66] State labor boards declared the strike illegal, but union leaders immediately appealed to the Torreón federal district court, which upheld the appeal. Meanwhile, the PCM-affiliated legal-defense group International Red Aid protested that local police agents arbitrarily detained its members.[67] Lombardo Toledano accused landowners of offering strikebreakers the astronomical wage of 10 pesos per day to perform the same labor for which local, unionized workers earned 1.5 pesos.[68] The strike also sharpened conflicts among organized workers as strikers accused CGT unions, which initially opposed the strike, of being sindicatos blancos.[69] Three days into the strike, the CGT committed its sixty-nine unions to the effort, which continued to grow despite mandates for strikers to return to work.[70]

Although the conflict played out primarily as a struggle between male laborers and landowners, organized women participated as well. The Communist militant Ana María Flores Sánchez recalls women armed with rifles and machetes acting as lookouts during union meetings.[71] Women's unions outside the strike region wrote solidarity letters.[72] The local CTM leader Mario Pavón Flores told reporters that women and children threatened a hunger march to protest striking agricultural workers' starvation conditions.[73] Women provided food and support, struggling to stretch reduced provisions to meet their families' needs. With limited resources, the strikers could not afford to stay out indefinitely. The strike committee appealed to Mexico City for support, requesting "beans and corn to alleviate the strikers' most urgent needs" and asking that Cárdenas intervene "to end persecutions against strikers by federal guards who have become strikebreakers." The unidentified functionary receiving the telegram penned a note at the bottom querying, "How do we answer?"[74]

Circumstances saved Mexico City bureaucrats from having to settle that troubling question. By the time the telegram had wended its way through government offices, the strike neared resolution; neither landowners nor strikers could hold out much longer. The hacendados risked losing their entire crops, and strike leaders saw workers trickling back as hunger set in and the strike's dubious legal status instilled fears of losing their jobs for good. Continued violence accompanied the workers' return to the harvest, as more militant unionists tried to continue the strike until reaching a definitive settlement. However, union leaders had secured Cárdenas's commitment to bring the region in line with the federal agrarian code and labor laws. Given their trying situation, the promise of government intervention was sufficient to bring most strikers back to work. By 3 September, sixteen days after it had begun, the strike officially ended.

It remained unclear how the government would fulfill its commitments, but several of its objectives had become apparent. The Cárdenas regime wanted to transform the Comarca Lagunera into a modern, efficient producer of cotton and other agricultural commodities. It also wanted to maintain a division between industrial and agricultural labor organizations rather than encouraging a unified bloc that could upset the political balance of powers. Finally, the conflict's resolution tested the regime's ability to separate itself from the maximato and implement its agenda. By 6 October, when Cárdenas officially declared the region's dramatic agrarian reform, landowners had already begun selling off their machinery and dismantling their irrigation systems. Cárdenas decreed that each landowner could choose 150 hectares (370.65 acres) to keep. The government would redistribute the remainder and compensate landowners based on the land's value as declared for tax assessments, plus an additional 10 percent. The government expropriated 74 percent (114,814 hectares or 283,705 acres) of the region's irrigated land and less than 10 percent (127,272 hectares or 314,489 acres) of the unirrigated land.[75]

Sweeping changes made the region a showcase for Cárdenas's state-building objectives. In contrast to previous measures, the Laguna agrarian reforms mandated the collectivization of the cotton plantations. Ejidatarios would cultivate their own plots but would, with the support of the National Ejidal Credit Bank, share the expenses of seeds, machinery, fertilizer, and other inputs. Some former hacendados took advantage of the opportunity to sell off large animals and heavy machinery, but most refused to facilitate the reform in any way.[76] Like Yucatán's agrarian reform a year later, the Laguna reform transformed the haciendas into large, collectively owned and collectively run cooperatives. Ejidatarios periodically elected administrators and judges from among their number. Progressive U.S. observers saw in the Laguna collectivization a model for resolving similar problems in their cotton-growing regions.[77] The PNR published a pamphlet in English to demonstrate not only that agrarian reform did not constitute a wholesale challenge to private property but also that the Laguna reforms could offer a prototype for other countries confronting agrarian conflicts.[78]

"To Shape a Happy Home": Liga Femeniles and the Remaking of the Laguna

Given women's participation in the Laguna conflict and the increasingly unified and mobilized women's movement in Mexico City, policymakers spotted an opportunity to shape gender roles in this model society. In mid-October, at a speech marking the first definitive land grant, Agrarian Department Chief Gabino Vázquez urged an audience of new ejidatarios to include women in the project of social reforms. "Woman, who has always stood outside the transcendental acts of the social family, should abandon her role as slave," he explained. "You should intervene so that she does not continue being simply a beast of labor and pleasure but rather assumes her direct role as mother and as an element of social struggle who participates in the acts and assemblies discussing economic and social issues of the ejido." To fulfill these objectives, he counseled that women "be brought together to oversee the fulfillment of the [ejidal] principles, to combat alcoholism, to ensure that the profits you earn are used for better clothing for your children, to shape a happy home, to obtain a corn mill, to form a cooperative to satisfy all your needs and avoid diverting profits to middlemen."[79]

Women's activism remained seemingly illegible as politics; Vázquez's intervention acknowledged none of its vitality nationwide and, particularly, in the Comarca Lagunera. Instructing a group of men ("you should intervene") to remake women's roles and prevailing notions of femininity, to transform women from "beasts of burden and pleasure" to mothers and revolutionary citizens, Vázquez situated men as the redeemers, allowing women only limited agency in their own liberation.[80] Under men's guidance, women would "shape a happy home" and advance modernization by promoting temperance, hygiene, and labor-saving technologies. They would attend community meetings to learn, not to improve community governance. Although he portrayed women as vilified and abused, Vázquez failed to identify the agents of this treatment, implying that women created this role for themselves and that men would rescue them.

The government's program for organizing Laguna women had roots in the Cardenistas' experiences in Michoacán. In August 1935, the Agrarian Department created the Committee for Social and Cultural Action, pledging to "pursue an intense social effort to be more useful to society, to the campesinos whom we serve, and to ourselves."[81] Careful to avoid distracting from pressing land-reform issues, the committee orchestrated social programs supporting the regime's "modernization" of the campo, promoting literacy and hygiene as well as athletic competitions and fitness classes to build solidarity and purge vices among campesinos. This committee did not set out to organize women. Its original program did not mention women's leagues and included no officer for women's affairs; the committee's only woman served as the secretary of "artistic action." A March 1936 reorganization, however, introduced a secretary of women's affairs charged with promoting women's leagues and keeping track of their registrations. "Considering the campesina a decisive factor for improving the physical, moral, [and] intellectual state of Mexico's rural population," the committee reported in August 1936, "[we have] begun to organize in both provisional and definitive ejidos the 'Ligas Femeniles de Lucha Social.'"[82] However, the committee initially paid virtually no attention to organizing Laguna women, concentrating their energies instead in the center-west as a safeguard against mounting religious violence. Of the fifty-four leagues formed by July 1936, forty-four were in Jalisco and Michoacán, representing more than 80 percent of the total membership. Within six months, the Laguna project completely overshadowed efforts in the cristero region, and the women's leagues became more closely tied to agrarian reform than to anticlericalism.

In addition to responding to events in the Comarca Lagunera, the Agrarian Department's organizing project addressed national concerns. The region's dramatic events coincided with mounting suffragist agitation in Mexico City; government representatives arriving from the capital brought with them the ideas and experiences of the metropole. Antonio Luna Arroyo, a Mexico City-born educator and bureaucrat, assumed a connection between Laguna women's mobilizations and urban feminism. "Woman should collaborate with man, and for this purpose she must be educated, naturally without losing her femininity, without destroying her character as a domestic women [*mujer hogareña*]," Luna Arroyo assured the conferees at the

February 1936 agrarian congress. "She will not be transformed into a mannish voter [*electora marimacho*] but, rather, will continue being feminine, educated for the new life, for the new humanity."[83] Luna Arroyo thus articulated the regime's inchoate strategy on the "woman question," advancing the ideal of the domestic helpmate over the feminist firebrand. The leagues celebrated rather than subverted the traditional patriarchal household directing rural women to "dedicate all your attentions to your husband, who arrives from the field tired from work, looking for the tranquillity of your home, and with a good appetite. Serve him and be amiable with him, making sure to listen to him and never reveal a bad mood. Be an agreeable wife and a self-sacrificing mother [*madre abnegada*]."[84]

The Ligas Femeniles promised to become the ultimate hegemonic project, weaving postrevolutionary values into the social fabric by drafting women to fight alcoholism, rout out corruption, and ensure that men worked hard and brought home their wages. Soon after Cárdenas declared his far-reaching reform project, the entire gamut of popular organizations developed strategies for organizing women. The PCM had organized Laguna women since the 1920s. The Liga de Comunidades Agrarias registered two leagues in San Pedro, with a total of eighty-four members.[85] One Agrarian Department agent reported, "Simultaneous with the first land grant, the first Liga Femenil de Lucha Social was formed. This labor has continued, with forty-five leagues organized according to the statutes of the Head of the Department. . . . In addition to these leagues, no fewer than fifty more have been formed by the members themselves."[86]

If women's activism in Michoacán bore the imprint of enduring conflicts between agraristas and cristeros, its Laguna counterpart just as surely demonstrated the legacy of PCM organizing and intense labor conflicts. The major dividing line — between Communists, fellow travelers, and CTM organizers on one side and the CGT and the Liga de Comunidades Agrarias on the other — replicated itself within women's organizing as different factions established competing leagues. The FUPDM had virtually no regional presence, as PCM organizers focused instead on shaping the official Ligas Femeniles.[87] When Cárdenas returned to the region after implementing the land reform, he laid out his plan for creating the Ligas Femeniles as a national model for women's organizing.[88] "The Laguna woman is a hope for the future of Mexico," he explained in a national address. "Her consciousness is as awakened as any in the Republic: she is brave and self-sacrificing [*abnegada*]; prejudices have not left a deep mark on her; and she is exceptionally prepared to fulfill her lofty aims in the heart of the family and the collectivity."[89] As he did in Michoacán, Cárdenas assigned Laguneras a moralizing role within communities and a nurturing role within the home.

Situating the leagues as a productive resource to facilitate modernization efforts, the Agrarian Department's survey of ejidal resources asked about the number of mules, access to water, area of irrigated land, and whether the ejidos had a women's league.[90] Most responded that they did not, but several added that they were "already disposed to its organization." During Cárdenas's November tour, several communities specifically requested support to establish leagues, along with petitions for new wells, health clinics, and increased access to credit.[91] Cárdenas urged women and youths to "become elements of activity and advancement within the communities."[92]

Cárdenas's and Vázquez's emphasis on women's involvement opened the door for women's organizations to shape the Agrarian Department's emerging program, couching gender-specific claims within the prevailing framework of labor struggles.[93] The seasoned militants of Matamoros's Josefa Ortiz de Domínguez Women's Union spearheaded efforts to define women's issues for the regionwide reform program.[94] "We have a decided determination to cooperate by every means within our reach to change the system of production," the organization's officers told Vázquez enthusiastically. "Woman's work within the home is excessive, with the constant bustle of the kitchen, washing clothes, caring for children, making humble clothes, and performing an infinity of tasks: all this impedes her studying to improve her physical and moral well-being." The women demanded reduced prices for basic foodstuffs and potable water, a cooperative, child-care centers to allow them to perform field work alongside their compañeros, schools, a library, collective cooking and laundry facilities, a health clinic, a special tribunal for women's and children's court cases, and sporting equipment and facilities. In short, they sought control over the conditions of their own labor and opportunities for their self-improvement and independence.

Rather than demanding changes in electoral laws — the political structures governing their lives had, after all, just undergone a dramatic transformation — they sought the material conditions that enabled them to "elevate their physical and moral culture." The letter did not mention suffrage rights, even though the PCM actively promoted women's citizenship and, in March 1936, the PNR had granted women voting rights in party plebiscites. On 6 September, Torreón women participated in the PNR election for the municipal president. The Josefa Ortiz de Domínguez Women's Union, however, emphasized the government services they might have gained through voting rights. Having developed a consensus about women's needs within their community, its members established their legitimacy as "working women" who "always operated within the revolutionary framework" and made claims as a rightful collective. By improving women's access to education, child care, and legal appeals, these activists sought a more direct and participatory route to social change than they could have accomplished through the ballot box.

Cárdenas's final address ending his forty-day regional tour concentrated largely on the details of the new Ligas Femeniles, which figured prominently in government propaganda about the Laguna reforms.[95] Exhorting his audience that "we should fulfill our obligation to stimulate and strengthen all acts that advance her liberation," he again rhetorically distanced women from their own emancipation. "Women's intervention in the functioning of the communities," he explained, "will ensure that efforts are not lost or wasted, that saving and economizing benefit families, that the profits produced by working the land are poured into improving the quality of food, clothing, and housing, constantly elevating the standard of living." In the brief period between Cárdenas's 30 November national address, when he announced his government's intention to prioritize women's organizing, and his departure from the region on 9 December, the Agrarian Department constituted the first sixteen Ligas Femeniles de Lucha Social, with a total membership of 1,256 women. The Agrarian Department donated eighteen sewing machines to these leagues, and the PNR donated another twenty-five to leagues formed shortly after Cárdenas left the region.[96] By 1940, the Agrarian Department claimed 159 leagues with a total membership of 4,000 women, all pledging to support the department's program.[97]

In December 1936, the daily *El Siglo de Torreón* published a pamphlet with the text of Cárdenas's speech, the Ligas Femeniles' statutes and declaration of principles, and prototypes for registration, membership cards, and officers' credentials.[98] This pamphlet became the handbook for leagues throughout the country, and Gabino Vázquez touted it during a national radio address soon after its publication.[99] Intertwining the rhetoric of old-style patronage and revolutionary entitlement, it began, "We recognize the moral impulse and support that the señor President of the Republic, Division General Lázaro Cárdenas, and his respectable wife, the señora Amalia Solórzano de Cárdenas, give to all peasant women and especially those who live in the Comarca Lagunera so that the benefits of the Revolution not only reach the men but also belong directly to us."[100] The language underscored that the leagues would make women "worthy wives and mothers" and exist only with the support of their husbands and (male) heads of families.[101] "Far from keeping her from fulfilling her domestic obligations and her high moral goals in the heart of the family and of the collectivity," the pamphlet elaborated, "the time a woman spends on her preparation and organization makes her more dignified and respectable."[102] The Agrarian Department reassured its public that league meetings were "not political acts" but, rather, social events.[103] Although the department asserted that the leagues allowed women to gain "equality to men with respect to rights and duties," it continued, "The above does not mean to say that the woman has abandoned the place she has traditionally occupied in the home. Very much to the contrary; today more than ever she is owner and mistress of the domestic realm; today more than ever she is tender and loving with her man and sweet with her children."[104]

The program emphasized community improvements through official, bureaucratic channels such as the National Ejidal Credit Bank and the Department of Public Health. Those activities that did not involve government agencies relied instead on local support for projects such as constructing homes, planting fruit orchards and ornamental trees, establishing public washing facilities, and maintaining public sanitation. The program also promoted Cardenista modernization projects, such as public education, temperance campaigns, and sanitation — a priority following the meningitis epidemic — and instituted mechanisms through the ejidal credit system to establish consumer cooperatives and to acquire sewing machines and motorized corn mills.

In many ways, the pamphlet merely explicated practices in which women's leagues already engaged, such as temperance campaigns, as well as customary duties, such as domestic work and family health care. But women demonstrated enthusiasm for these leagues despite their seemingly limited objectives. The pamphlet's formality, much like the leagues themselves, not only legitimated their organizing efforts but also explicitly valued women's work within their households and communities. The language regulating membership — requiring members to be at least 14 and "living honestly in the village" — echoed the conditions for Mexican citizenship, linking revolutionary citizenship with women's reproductive labor. More important, Cárdenas's endorsement brought legitimacy and leverage, creating an organizing infrastructure with access to government agencies. Thus, the Ligas Femeniles accrued material benefits and official recognition within a long-standing Mexican political culture of patronage. By pledging their allegiance to Cardenismo, league members expected greater access to government services.

The program rested on two premises. First, Ligas Femeniles would remain distinct from feminist organizations. They would neither promote women's formal political rights nor advocate for women's interests as distinct from or in opposition to those of their husbands and families. A 1939 student thesis argued the leagues meant that "today, more than ever, a woman is a woman in the fullest and best sense of the word."[105] The Agrarian Department's consistent emphasis on this point revealed an effort to deflect perceived attacks against traditional, patriarchal family structures. Programs such as child-care cooperatives, a high priority for the PCM-affiliated women's leagues, remained conspicuously absent from its agenda. Second, the organizing program assumed that the Comarca Lagunera offered a tabula rasa on which the Agrarian Department could inscribe its vision. Public statements did not acknowledge that the first women's leagues took root in places like La Flor de Jimulco, Lequeitio, and Matamoros with active, PCM-sponsored women's organizations since the 1920s. To bolster the illusion that the agrarian reform resulted from a bestowal of the Cárdenas government rather than the hard-fought war between landowners and organized labor, the Agrarian Department hailed women's leagues as its own invention.

Theory into Praxis: Translating the Ligas Femeniles Program

Much as officials intended the Michoacán women's leagues to lure women away from the cristeros, they designed the Laguna Ligas Femeniles to attract women away from PCM organizations. The women who joined the leagues, however, spotted an opportunity to achieve tangible gains. Members of the Liga Femenil "Lic. Gabino Vázquez" wrote to Cárdenas on the very day that he departed the region to say that they had been promised a corn mill upon forming the league but had not yet received one. They explained that they had also read in the press that all women's leagues would receive corn mills.[106] Within a month of the campaign's inauguration, registration materials inundated the Mexico City bureaucracy, accompanied by requests for corn mills and sewing machines as well as medical assistance and school improvements.

Organized women took to heart Cárdenas's exhortation to act as the ejidos' moral conscience, and many leagues petitioned to close billiard halls and cantinas, where workers wasted "money that would be better spent buying things that we urgently need and must do without because the money does not go far enough."[107] Contemporary observers remarked on the leagues' critical temperance role. "The women's leagues and parcels are, I think, of urgent necessity to combat alcohol," the Spanish vice-consul in Torreón informed Cárdenas, "since these and sports will have a certain degree of efficacy in uprooting the vice of intoxication that causes so much harm to the peasant collectivity, leading to deaths and tragedies among those who should be morally united."[108] These efforts often encountered obstacles, as they had in Michoacán. Women frequently called on state and federal authorities to intervene in temperance conflicts, earning them the disapprobation of local authorities and, of course, cantina owners.[109] Even when the women's leagues enjoyed local support, they often found that they lacked the power to compel adherence to their temperance aims, exposing the limits of the government's commitment, but they occasionally demanded — and often secured — the removal of local officials who flouted temperance regulations.[110]

If the Ligas Femeniles' program emphasized the disciplinary aspects of organizing, it also created a favorable atmosphere for other organized women to demand official backing for their efforts. The Amalia Solórzano de Cárdenas Seamstresses' Union wrote to Cárdenas on Christmas day in 1936 to request his support for a garment-making cooperative. It wrote again four months later, this time asking him to prevent the bank from repossessing its sewing machines.[111] Similarly, the Liga Femenil de "La Fe" complained that the La Fe textile mill in Torreón, a PCM stronghold that had endured numerous strikes, resisted employing women. The league asked Cárdenas to intervene, arguing that women should enjoy the same labor rights and opportunities as men.[112] Torreón domestic workers petitioned in March 1938 for CTM union recognition so that they would "enjoy all the benefits of the revolution"; they had received it by November.[113]

Official recognition, however, hardly protected women activists from the manipulations of powerful caciques. One league sought to deport a local Spanish merchant, Vicente Arteaga, charging that he employed a henchman who "has never believed in the ideals of the revolution, was never a unionized campesino, and is not an ejidatario" and harassed the local schoolteacher who organized the league.[114] Arteaga retained many campesinos' allegiance by offering them work and occasionally lending out his truck.

Several women, torn by their husbands' loyalties and lured by Arteaga's proffering use of his corn mill and merchandise from his store, abandoned the league. "Since the women's league was organized," its officers wrote, "the members' husbands have suffered dangerous attacks and are currently labeled 'cuckolds.' When the league meets in the schoolhouse, it is the target of vulgar, trash-talking criticisms by its opponents, who stand at the windows and, wanting to provoke us, throw clods of dirt and lighted cigarettes at us." Arteaga's hostility reflected concerns that the league's members had violated class and gender protocols through their organizing activities and that its consumption and milling cooperatives would compete with his enterprises. Two weeks after filing this complaint, however, the league withdrew it, saying that Arteaga had always been a friend of the ejidatario. During an investigation, league members confessed that they recognized their signatures on the original letter but claimed that the complaints against Arteaga all resulted from "intrigues."[115] Although such episodes underscore the complexity of community power relationships, they also highlight the problems of pitting women's organizations, which promised future material improvements, against those who could offer tangible and immediate access to them.

Ligas Femeniles also intervened in political rivalries, indicating their assumptions about revolutionary citizenship. When ejidatarios in San Pedro objected to the defeat of Eladio Cerda — the Liga de Comunidades Agrarias candidate — for the municipal presidency, they walked out on strike.[116] They won a short-lived victory for Cerda as tensions mounted between CTM unions and the Liga de Comunidades Agrarias. A May Day riot culminating in four deaths forced the municipal authorities to resign, resulting in the appointment of a former police chief from the border town of Piedras Negras as municipal president.[117] One of the municipality's Ligas Femeniles objected, arguing that "enemies of the revolution" had instigated the riot, that the state government had illegally imposed an outsider, and that San Pedro had plenty of men qualified to govern the municipality.[118] The Ministry of Government in Mexico City responded that it would consider their appeal.

This exchange reveals not only that these women felt entitled to a say in formal politics — at least at the local level — but also that the Ministry of Government responded by acknowledging the letter and taking the matter under advisement. However disingenuous, this response legitimated organized women's voice and sustained the illusion that the women could intervene in electoral matters. With the CTM in disarray, and the Liga de Comunidades Agrarias ascendant in state politics, Cerda resumed the municipal presidency, supported by a sympathetic city council, following a common practice in Mexican political culture of giving precedence to preserving social peace over upholding election results.[119] In this way, organized women influenced local political struggles despite their lack of formal electoral rights; their importance to the regime's social programs — and, conversely, their potential for the disruption of social peace — gave organized women modest sway in political matters.

However, the practice of bowing to popular organizations raised thorny issues — as they did in Acapulco — about which organizations claimed a representative voice as leagues rivaled one another for legitimacy. The Liga Femenil "Consuelo Alfaro de Vázquez" (named after Gabino Vázquez's wife) complained that the ejido's current labor manager, Samuel López, had organized a sindicato blanco during the strike, continued to take orders from the former hacendado, and, as a carpenter, remained removed from agricultural matters. The fifty-six women who signed the letter said that López added insult to injury when he organized a dance to honor the former patrón, who proceeded to get drunk and exhibit "obscene and arrogant behavior . . . thus mocking our compañeros." Another league's officers reported that they had heard the complaints against López but that the protesting league lacked the imprimatur of the Agrarian Department. Thus, the charges went unheeded despite persistent objections.[120]

Although Agrarian Department organizers may have envisioned the Ligas Femeniles as pliant auxiliaries to the ejidal committees, the women met separately from the men, developed their own sets of goals and grievances, and formed distinct identities. They frequently issued separate endorsements for local political candidates, even if they coincided with the ejidal committee's.[121] Given the many concerns that men and women shared, it is unsurprising that the women's leagues and ejidal committees frequently worked in concert. However, the women's leagues increasingly established themselves as separate entities and pursued interests apart from — or even opposed to — those of the male ejidatarios.

The "Shameful Slavery" of the Metate and the Salvation of the Molinos de Nixtamal

Nothing sparked as much controversy as the coveted *molinos de nixtamal* (corn mills) promised by the Agrarian Department.[122] The discord stemmed from a host of symbolic and material factors. By the late 1930s, the labor-saving molinos had become the emblem of rural women's emancipation and a focus of women's organizing, with many organizers viewing them as a league entitlement. "Before even uttering the phrase 'feminine emancipation' in a town," one Agrarian Department pamphlet explained, "molinos must be sent to prevent women from having to prostrate themselves as slaves before the rough metate [stone grinding tablet]."[123] Hand grinding corn for the dough, or *masa*, for a family's daily tortilla ration was in many ways the physical act of abnegación. Rural women rose before dawn and spent exhausting and tedious hours on their knees, bent over the metate. According to the historian Arnold Bauer, corn tortillas made up 70–75 percent of ordinary people's daily caloric intake by the early twentieth century, giving them "a decreased range of food and, in the case of tortillas, the calories were purchased at the cost of massive inputs of female labor."[124]

Available since the late nineteenth century, molinos remained commercially owned and mostly urban until the 1930s. Although women occasionally requested molinos before the Ligas Femeniles, the Agrarian Department made them widely available through donations and credits. As the single most sought-after benefit of league membership, they symbolized women's embrace of the national modernization project; the Cárdenas government's promotion of milling cooperatives transformed rural women's labor burdens much as land and labor reforms changed men's. Between 1935 and 1940, the number of molinos de nixtamal in Mexico jumped from 927 to almost 6,000.[125] Rural teachers argued that corn mills and sewing machines reduced women's daily household labor duties from ten to twelve hours to two or three. "Once the [women's] leagues were constituted," proclaimed the Agrarian Department, "their first emancipatory step was directed at destroying the shameful slavery that the metate meant for women. 'Here are the mills! Away with the metates!' went the cry of salvation that was heard in all the ejidos once this liberating act took place."[126] Leagues often impatiently informed Cárdenas that they awaited promised mills or the credit to purchase one.[127] In petitions listing a community's needs, women often placed a mill above schools, health clinics, and water rights; in many cases, no other demands competed with the request for a molino. Thus, the molinos formed part of the Cardenista program to remake Laguna society through education and technology, providing women not only with relief from one of their most taxing domestic chores but also with a modest income.

Urban feminists have often overlooked or dismissed the momentousness of this technological innovation. "The Ligas Femeniles Campesinas," the activist intellectual Clementina Batalla de Bassols asserted in the 1950s, "did not incorporate rural women — as they should have been — into the general struggle for radical agrarian reform, for their integral rights as rural workers, but rather distracted them with small demands of daily life (such as obtaining a molino de nixtamal, sewing machines and at most a school) but that did not direct them to support our country's greater campesino struggles."[128] Situating the desire for corn mills apart from women's struggle for rural labor rights — branding them a form of payoff that distracted women from "greater campesino struggles" — ignores the extent to which women's daily experience of arduous reproductive-labor tasks shaped their priorities as activists and revolutionaries.

Given their obvious benefits, countless disputes erupted over the mills and the profits they yielded. Ejidal regulations granted the women's leagues exclusive rights to operate the mills and limited competition based on the local population. To "encourage women's organizing," competing corn mills required the municipal president's express permission, and a 1932 presidential decree regulating competition among molinos limited the number of mills per capita and their proximity to one another.[129] Thus, organized women in the ejidos gained access to monopoly, or near-monopoly, control over one of the communities' most basic services. Cooperatives unaffiliated with the Ligas Femeniles contended that the new mills violated the 1932 decree.[130] Commercial millers like the Spaniard Vicente Arteaga, meanwhile, often sidestepped legal avenues entirely, simply using their influence to undermine the leagues' cooperatives. Opposition to the molinos also came from another, less likely source. Some campesinos objected that the mechanized mills produced inferior masa and therefore inferior tortillas. Rural men complained that the molino — along with its labor-saving cousin, the sewing machine — would give women too much free time, and rural women looked askance at their neighbors who, failing in their femininity, relied on a molino.[131] The Francisco I. Madero Federation of Women's Leagues informed Cárdenas that ejidatarios expropriated mills from the women's leagues, and some even established competing mills to undermine the leagues' cooperatives.[132]

The characterization of the metate as enslaving women (and the molino as emancipatory) appears frequently both in official materials and in petitions from women's leagues pointedly linking government patronage and postrevolutionary citizenship.[133] Complaining that requests to the state government for a molino had only met with "interviews, evasions, reversals, waiting, and unfulfilled offers," a Durango Liga Femenil appealed to Cárdenas for support, noting his "ideology that has raised women from the lethargy in which, until now, she found herself submerged, without voice or vote."[134] The letter's tone and temporal location of this advance ("until now") not only depicted the Cardenista government as a more effective patron than its predecessors but also indicated that women, no longer "submerged," now enjoyed the rights of "voice and vote," the standard formulation of citizenship.

Government officials used the molino to attract league members, but this incentive depended on the discretion of local Agrarian Department administrators and PNR officials. The link between political allegiance and patronage rewards was both implicitly understood and openly acknowledged. A particularly fortunate league would receive a donated motorized mill, a building in which to house the cooperative, and access to the electricity necessary to power the mill. Other leagues acquired some or all of these components with credits from the National Ejidal Credit Bank. The head of the ruling party's Women's Coordinating Committee in Michoacán, for example, agreed with Cárdenas to reward molinos to a group of 140 Ligas Femeniles "that should be stimulated for their arduous revolutionary labor" and "as a reward for their revolutionary attitude and faith."[135] While it often remains murky why some leagues received mills and others did not, officials clearly denied some requests — often citing budgetary limitations — while granting seemingly identical petitions. Conversely, officials might reclaim molinos from leagues they felt had gone astray. The Liga Femenil "Amalia S. de Cárdenas" informed the president that an interim Agrarian Department engineer had taken control of its corn mill for two weeks "so that they could reorganize." However, the league's president explained, the league had installed new officers but still had not recovered its molino.[136]

Leagues that acquired mills often also fought to retain control over them as opposing factions, male community leaders, and competing milling enterprises challenged them. The Liga Femenil "Rosa Luxemburgo" protested that "reactionary elements," led by the president of La Flor de Jimulco's ejidal committee, had started a competing milling cooperative.[137] The women addressed their complaint to the Central Consultative Committee of Ejidatarios in Torreón, which conveyed to the municipal president that the league and the cooperative corresponded to Cárdenas's program. However, the committee explained, "many ejidatarios of ideological backwardness oppose

[the women] because according to them it is immoral that women be organized, and this constitutes one of the many obstructions to the women's
organizations."[138] The municipal president promptly ordered the competing mill's closure, since he only authorized the women's leagues to operate
milling cooperatives. This ability to garner official support constituted an
crucial gain for women activists, but the layers of mediation — through
the municipal president, the central ejidal committee, and the league leadership — informed their demands' manner and content. Torreón authorities
expected women's leagues to conform to the Cardenista agenda, but a
strongman still controlled local politics. Trumping his informal power required the league to find a more powerful patron, an act that would bring
only temporary change and might engender animosity between the women
activists and local caciques.

Confrontations over the mills occasionally turned bitter and even violent.
In one incident, new league officers accused the former officers of refusing to
surrender the mill's keys.[139] Claiming to represent 180 compañeras and another 280 ejidatarios, the new officers objected that the outgoing officers
brought politicians from the town of San Pedro to interfere with the league's
affairs. They called a general assembly to transfer power, but the meeting degenerated into chaos as men arrived from the Liga de Comunidades Agrarias
and the municipal labor board to intervene. With no clear authority in the
meeting, everyone spoke at once. Speakers arbitrarily took the podium while
opponents shouted obscenities from the audience. The new officers grew
frustrated and turned to leave the assembly but found that armed municipal
police had blocked the meeting hall's only exit. Their husbands arrived to
demand their release, but municipal police beat several women as they fled
the premises. The outgoing officers then instructed Coahuila's governor not
to deliver the mill to the new officers, whom they claimed represented a
minority faction.[140]

An Agrarian Department representative oversaw a new election, won by
the officers who had previously claimed victory. According to the new officers, they enjoyed greater legitimacy because their husbands "practice[d]
Cardenismo by working daily in the field," while their opponents' husbands
appeared on the census rolls but did not work the land. After taking control
of the league and its molino, as well as the sewing workshop, consumer
cooperative, and offices, the new officers applauded the Agrarian Department's intervention and carefully balanced claiming credit for their initiative

and paying homage to government patronage. The incident, they explained, "proved to us as well as to our husbands that we are right to defend ourselves against calumnies intended to make us the victims of those who would live at our expense, who have always flaunted their influence in the highest spheres, subjugating the majority. . . . But we are momentarily satisfied that by our small influence we have brought justice through an honorable employee of the Agrarian Department." The new officers had won the battle but not the war, however. Within a year, as the two factions continued feuding, federal forces intervened, confiscating the league's possessions to prevent further conflicts.[141]

Not all women's leagues expressed such enthusiasm about the Agrarian Department. The same functionary who settled matters for the women's league described above subsequently alienated another league. The Liga Femenil de Lucha Social "Leona Vicario" met with particular success in its milling enterprise, using the profits to pay off its loan and purchase another mill.[142] League members had turned a storage house into a meeting hall and established a consumer cooperative, a first-aid center, and a sewing workshop. They divided some profits among themselves using a system analogous to the one used to calculate shares of the ejidal profits (based on the amount of labor each member contributed) and resolved to pool other resources to build a henhouse and a stable and to purchase a film projector for the community. Any further income would fund home improvements for league members.

Perhaps the league's success made some ejidatarios uneasy. Or, perhaps, the women who had not joined the league simply became envious. At any rate, the ejidatarios and several town council members confiscated the mill's keys and fuses. The civil judge, also an ejidatario, proclaimed the creation of the women's leagues an error and vowed to eliminate this one. The beleaguered officers claimed that several women's husbands prevented them from joining the women's league, but these women now claimed the mills for the community rather than the league. Adding insult to injury, the civil judge who opposed the league turned its meeting hall, which also housed its cooperative, into a cantina and billiard hall. The women's league turned to local and state authorities for support, but to no avail. The Agrarian Department engineer whom the San Pedro women's league had so roundly praised dismissed the women's concerns and discouraged the local schoolteachers from involving themselves in the matter. Hoping to circumvent local opposition, the league's officers asked Cárdenas to rectify matters and restore

"Revolutionary Government." Eleven months later, the issue remained unresolved, and the league asked Cárdenas to donate a replacement mill but expressed concern that it would meet the same fate.[143]

Conflict, Consolidation, and Co-optation

The official party's March 1938 reorganization transformed the context of these quotidian political interactions by inaugurating women's committees in municipalities throughout the region and providing women activists with another pipeline to public officials.[144] However, women's growing participation in public matters generated rancor among more conservative Laguneros. "What would happen to Mexico if women were granted powers to govern us?" one representative of a Torreón veteran's organization queried Cárdenas. "Undoubtedly it would be a disaster because woman can be more criminal than man. . . . Woman is in this world for the man's home, not for politics or to mix with the affairs of men."[145] Such attitudes remained commonplace as the women's leagues met with greater success in their endeavors and departed from the Agrarian Department's scripted program.

Facing growing hostility from local officials, some leagues solicited books of legal code to understand their rights. A league representing several towns in Durango complained that the Welfare Ministry had recently prohibited league members from sending their sick to the public hospital, explaining that the policy change resulted from their league membership. The state education director informed the league's members that he "did not recognize any [women's] league." When they sent a delegation to investigate conflicts in the local schools, they reported being dubbed "country women and ignorant of the issues under consideration; so we returned to our villages quite offended and not wanting to participate in more commissions."[146] The Tlahualilo municipal president evicted a women's league from its meeting place, forcing its members to petition Cárdenas to intervene.[147] Even the Agrarian Department hedged its support; only a few months after the Ligas Femeniles' creation, one league objected that an Agrarian Department representative had arbitrarily imposed officers.[148] Another complained that the Agrarian Department revoked its water rights, diverting the water instead to a former hacendado.[149] Yet another submitted that the ejidal committee "refused to recognize [them] as organized women."[150]

To be sure, not all women's leagues garnered enough success to provoke such a backlash. Some never really got off the ground. One observer wrote in

May 1939 that in the two and a half years since the women's leagues had functioned in the Comarca Lagunera, many of them had already ceased to exist in any meaningful way. She commented that the teachers charged with organizing them often lacked commitment and simply raffled off the leagues' possessions when the membership lost interest. She cited one instance in which the woman in charge of temperance matters sold wine on the ejido, and observed that the increase in the number of billiards halls in the region underscored the leagues' inefficacy. "Things will go from bad to worse," she concluded, "unless [the Agrarian Department] improves the effort by putting matters in the hands of conscientious directors and better organizers."[151]

Despite conflicts and apathy, milling and garment-making cooperatives, along with other improvements, strengthened the leagues' memberships. By late 1937, confederations of women's leagues had developed in Coahuila and Durango, including a regional confederation and several municipal confederations in the Comarca Lagunera. These aggregations gave the leagues greater collective force but also created new layers of authority and bureaucracy that often generated tensions among organizers. As the leagues and confederations exercised control over material resources, power struggles developed within and around them, intensifying hostility and opposition within their communities.[152]

The PCM remained the motor force behind this organizing, and, as it tied its fortunes more closely to the PRM, its Laguna affiliates threw their support behind the Cardenista consolidation. During the 1938 May Day parade in Torreón, in sharp contrast to the violent 1935 confrontation in neighboring Matamoros, the women's leagues carried pro-Cárdenas banners and praised the postrevolutionary regime.[153] During the following year's May Day parade, amid the PCM's "Unity at Any Cost" campaign, women carrying signs memorializing the Haymarket massacre and bearing the slogan "Workers of the World Unite!" marched alongside women carrying signs supporting the candidacy of the PRM nominee Manuel Avila Camacho.[154]

The circumstances of regional agrarian reform induced women's leagues to cultivate connections with federal rather than local or state officials and to ally with ejidatarios, teachers, and labor organizers to ensure land, credit, and infrastructure for future generations.[155] They petitioned the Agrarian Department for improvements to canals and irrigation systems that landowners had formerly maintained.[156] In a case where the municipal president tried to prevent the construction of a federally mandated workers' colony, the women's league solicited Cárdenas's intervention.[157] They also secured federal aid in cases of natural disasters, such as the floods and droughts that plagued the region.[158]

As the leagues became more established, their leadership increasingly pursued aims beyond the Agrarian Department's prescriptions. In addition to the mills, women established garment workshops and sold ready-to-wear clothing at local markets.[159] Members and officers interpreted the directive to be "worthy wives and mothers" as a justification to agitate for publicly funded child-care centers and maternity clinics. Furthermore, women's leagues petitioned for land for their members to cultivate collectively—a measure unanticipated in agrarian reforms—and trucks to transport organizers into the farthest reaches of the region to organize women and instruct them about their rights vis-à-vis the postrevolutionary government.[160]

Following the Cárdenas administration's conservative turn, however, its commitment to allocating resources to women's organizing waned; by 1939, federal, state, and local authorities had all reduced their subsidies for the women's leagues.[161] As resources became scarcer, leagues fortified their confederations. In August 1939, the Coahuila women's leagues convened in Saltillo to consolidate their efforts and strengthen ties among leagues across the state.[162] Similarly, the Comarca Lagunera Confederation of Ligas Femeniles convened the following February to produce detailed regulations governing the region's corn mills and garment-making workshops.[163]

As jurisdictional disagreements exacerbated conflicts, the confederations became battlegrounds for broader disputes over popular organizing. Although the CTM claimed credit for the successful labor mobilizations, the 1938 creation of the National Peasant Confederation (CNC) fostered the expectation that the CTM would abandon organizing agricultural workers. Communists dominated the group that initiated the Laguna confederation and controlled it in early 1940, publishing *8th of March: An Organizing Newsletter*, named after the communist holiday to celebrate workingwomen's revolutionary activity.[164] The newsletter carried poems and articles proclaiming the virtues of union organizing and peasant land ownership. However, the confederation declared its intention to organize only rural women, excluding the compañeras obreras.[165] In June 1940, the confederation submitted a series of reports to an ejidatarios' convention and then convened its own congress to solidify its objectives for the coming year.[166] In both cases, the demands emphasized access to land, credit, education, and health care; enforcement of the leagues' exclusive control over corn mills; and provision of tools analogous to those granted the ejidatarios, including sewing machines, kitchen equipment, and spaces to establish cooperatives. In other words, organized women sought improvements in working and living conditions similar to those men had gained after the 1936 strike — "all the benefits of the revolution."

However, Liga de Comunidades Agrarias affiliates complained to Cárdenas that the Communists had denied them the floor at the 1939 state and regional congresses. Dubbed divisionists and Almazanistas (supporters of the opposition presidential candidate Juan Andreu Almazán) by the Communists, the dissenters finally abandoned the proceedings but demanded the confederation's reorganization, ousting the CTM organizers. Similar to CRMDT organizers in Michoacán, these women rejected the professionalization and bureaucratization of popular organizing through national mass organizations. They wanted campesinas to administer the confederation and its member leagues, their cooperatives, and their corn mills. "We are certain," they explained, "that these members [the CTM organizers] have never felt the sufferings of the campesina, and thus we consider them incapable of organizing the campesina. For this reason, we ask [Cárdenas] to order these women to dedicate themselves exclusively to organizing workingwomen in the city rather than misleading the rural women with false promises."[167] Other leagues switched their affiliation from the CTM to the Ligas de Comunidades Agrarias. One league from the Communist stronghold of Matamoros charged that CTM leaders had expelled their husbands "for not agreeing with their communist ideas" and that confederation leaders assaulted them with blows for demanding justice for rural women.[168]

These attacks, and the ensuing efforts to install competing women's leagues in the ejidos, sparked hostility from the existing leagues, many of which hoped to remain above the ideological fray. Remonstrating against the efforts of Cecilia Magallanes, a leader in the dissenting Ligas de Comunidades Agrarias faction, one league informed Cárdenas that Magallanes had undermined its hard-fought efforts. "The señora was expelled from the organization for being a type that is inappropriate for us due to her bad activities, and now she dedicates herself to sowing divisions among the ligas femeniles," the league explained. It added menacingly, "We ask that attention is paid to Sra. Cecilia's work, or else it will be us who will put a stop in some way to her efforts."[169] Ironically, Magallanes had been not only a staunch advocate of that league's interests but also a strong proponent of unity and solidarity among the region's women's leagues.[170]

When Avila Camacho assumed the presidency in 1940, support for the leagues—both moral and financial—evaporated.[171] Indeed, government backing for the entire Laguna project dwindled. "The peasant movement . . . was quickly stigmatized," the historian Tomás Martínez Saldaña explains. "It was declared communist, and subsidies and resources were withdrawn; laws changed to remove control of the [ejidal credit] bank; the army intervened to disorganize the movement; leaders were incarcerated. . . . [I]n little time, the bureaucrats from the Ejidal Bank took over everything that campesinos had formerly controlled."[172] Women's leagues protested the expropriation of their land, corn mills, and sewing machines. One PCM-linked league struggled for at least five years to maintain control of its vineyard.[173] However, the two strongest confederations—the Comarca Lagunera Confederation of Ligas Femeniles and the Leona Vicario Durango Women's Union—endured at least into the administration of Miguel Alemán in the early 1950s.[174] Women involved with these leagues often became lifelong activists well beyond the disappearance of state support. Although fraught with conflict and dissent during the later years of the Cárdenas administration, the discord rendered them stronger, forcing them to engage with their constituencies and organize more aggressively. As a result, the Comarca Lagunera had the most elaborate network of women's leagues in Mexico, and those leagues remained explicitly engaged with local issues.

The legacy of the PCM, as well as of the regime's efforts to contain the Laguna conflicts, forged a distinct concept of revolutionary citizenship that manifested itself in the Ligas Femeniles. Unlike their Michoacán counterparts, which remained heavily embedded in state-level political networks and invested in temperance and anticlerical struggles, or the Mexico City organizations that turned their attention almost exclusively to ballot-box politics, the Laguna women's leagues grew out of labor upheaval and the federal government's direct intervention. Their conception of citizenship rested on ideals of participation, mobilization, and labor-centered identities, and their patronage networks had a national rather than a local orientation. Laguna leagues concentrated on improving the conditions of their unpaid reproductive labor and access to petty industries through organizing and direct action. In many cases, even formal politics capitulated to this direct intervention by organized groups.

The Agrarian Department and the ruling party attempted to impose ideals of women's organizing that centered on domesticity and support for government programs of public education, hygiene, and public health. However, the legacy of the strikes, the strength of PCM networks, and the participatory concept of citizenship often led organized women to make demands beyond what the Cárdenas regime had intended and beyond what many ejidatarios would tolerate. Women who had endured arrests and beatings at the hands of local and federal authorities as well as rival factions within ejidos had steeled themselves against opposition and had invested a real stake in the process and goals of organizing. While still susceptible to factional disputes and petty politics, these women articulated a vision of social change in which women had their own cooperatives, collectively cultivated land, and subsidized child care and in which women's domestic labor assumed the status on par with agricultural and industrial production. Ironically, in trying to sidestep the suffrage issue, officials had facilitated another, more immediate experience of citizenship.

FIVE

"Her Dignity as Woman

and Her Sovereignty as Citizen":

Claiming Revolutionary

Citizenship

Late one afternoon in April 1937, some fifty leading suffragists marched en masse to the Mexico City headquarters of the National Revolutionary Party (PNR), demanding voting rights and decrying reported abuses against women attempting to exercise their recently gained right to participate in party plebiscites. On reaching the PNR's offices, however, they learned that party leader Silvano Barba González would not receive them. Undeterred, they proceeded to the presidential residence, Los Pinos, where one of the president's assistants informed the group that it should seek an appointment at Cárdenas's Palacio Nacional (National Palace) office. Sensing a bait and switch, the assembled activists refused to leave, declaring that they would remain until Cárdenas saw them. At ten o'clock, as darkness settled in and reporters left to file their stories, the women stood firm; some even threatened to stage a hunger strike in front of Los Pinos. Finally, after receiving word that Cárdenas would receive them the following morning, the group dispersed.[1]

The women who descended on the president's residence formed a motley crowd, including the patrician Margarita Robles de Mendoza, who split her time between Mexico City and the Union of American Women (UMA) offices in New York City, the Communist FUPDM leader Cuca García, and the middle-class members of several public employees' and teachers' unions. Much like its U.S. counterpart two decades earlier, the Mexican women's suffrage movement attracted activists of different ideological and class backgrounds and united them, temporarily, behind a common cause.[2] Just as women's pacifist activism had informed the tenor and strategies of the U.S. movement, the Popular Front encouraged Mexican Communists' interest in electoral politics and served as the critical backdrop for suffrage battles.

The changing rules of political engagement forced suffragists to struggle on a shifting terrain, rendering their task even more difficult, and the diversity within the suffrage movement meant that its leaders often adopted competing strategies. Although some tapped into the masculinized rhetoric linking citizenship rights to military service, paid labor, and civic engagement, others mobilized distinctly feminine assertions of citizenship rights based on unpaid reproductive labor, motherhood, and claims to morality. Some suffragists favored liberal, constitutionalist arguments, while others preferred the revolutionary tactics of mass mobilization.

Within the context of Cardenismo and the Popular Front, however, the distinctions among these camps faded as the suffrage movement developed hand in hand with the proliferation of women's organizations. Struggles for political rights, land grants, and social services became intertwined and mutually advanced one another. The looming possibility of suffrage increased the stakes for securing women's loyalty to the Cárdenas government, and stepped-up activism strengthened the suffragists' claim that women had sufficient "preparation" to exercise the vote responsibly. Furthermore, Popular Front efforts joined suffragists with other activists, encouraging them to borrow from one another's playbooks. The suffragists who threatened to pitch camp in front of Los Pinos deviated from their earlier commitment to officially recognized channels and parliamentary procedures, turning instead to the collective-action tactics of informal politics. By 1936, as success seemed imminent, a growing number of individuals and organizations devoted resources to the suffrage campaign, hoping to capitalize on the seemingly inexorable victory.

Unraveling the conundrum of why Mexico's dynamic and mobilized women's movement ultimately failed to secure the most basic liberal right of voting requires an examination of the relationship between competing notions of citizenship. Popular Front mobilizations, mounting concerns about national and international fascism, and the ruling party's corporatist reorganization all reshaped the contours of revolutionary citizenship, blurring the distinctions between liberal, individual rights and identity-based, collective rights, underscoring both the contingency of citizenship and the importance of political and bureaucratic structures in defining its terms. Suffragists' mounting frustration with Mexico's juridical and legislative processes contributed to the appeal of more informal avenues to change. While the suffrage cause energized women when the vote seemed close at hand, it increasingly seemed like a poor investment of activist energies as it constantly receded just beyond their reach.

The Gathering Storm: Momentum behind the Suffrage Movement

Although the women's movement lacked unity during the discordant 1931–35 period, somewhere between fear and opportunity it had created political openings. Building on the PNR's founding pledge to allow women "gradually to gain access to civic life," the feminist congresses and the repeated organization and reorganization of feminist parties and confederations capitalized on the party's apparent willingness to concede women full voting rights.[3] Despite opposition from antisuffragist politicians and public intellectuals, by the mid-1930s, several suffrage proposals gained traction by either feminizing political duties or requiring women to prove their manliness in order to exercise political rights. The former group often limited women's political rights to the municipal realm, where housewives might put their well-honed administrative skills to profitable use. The latter generally proposed limiting women's suffrage to union members, property owners, or those meeting educational or literacy requirements. The Feminist Revolutionary Party, for example, suggested amending electoral laws to allow women to vote if they were "21 years old, not a member of any religious congregation, not collaborating in any occult activities, and economically independent and autonomous."[4]

Centered primarily in Mexico City, the suffrage debate also took hold in other urban areas. The Secretariat of Public Education's Urban Cultural Mission in the border city of Ciudad Juárez, Chihuahua, for example, organized a forum on women's suffrage.[5] In Torreón, an elite woman responded to the suffragist argument by characterizing politics as "nothing but an infected quagmire" that was "incompatible with honor."[6] Women "should prepare themselves for the hard struggle of life and know how to confront every situation," she contended, "but I can never conceive of a woman standing before a chamber, gesticulating and haranguing the crowds against governors and politicians." Asking how women could "cross this threshold of ignominy," she insisted that true feminism called for women to be "indulgent and good, simple and amiable, and this effort will be, in the long run, far more useful and advantageous than the other." As if in unwitting response, the humor column on the same page included a cartoon of two men watching a woman walk by in a silk dress and comparing her to a butterfly's cocoon, "wrapped in silk on the outside, but within is a writhing worm and nothing more."

By late 1935, the PNR leadership appeared firmly behind the suffrage movement. In Cárdenas's annual congressional address, he endorsed women's organizing and pledged his support for women's efforts to participate in civic life, sending Palma Guillén to Colombia as the first woman in Mexico's diplomatic corps. The party leaders Ignacio García Tellez and Emilio Portes Gil invited the suffragist Margarita Robles de Mendoza to return to Mexico to assist in strategizing women's "preparation" to exercise citizenship rights.[7] In February 1936, Portes Gil described the argument of "women's inferiority" as "contrary to the postulates of the Revolution," since women faced social problems that they could resolve only through electoral participation and the exercise of political power.[8] The PNR allowed women to vote in party plebiscites but not to vote in national elections or to stand as candidates, a small advance that left many suffragists dissatisfied. Referred to as a "passive vote," it confirmed suffragists' suspicions that the party leadership distrusted women's political judgment. The Yucatecan feminist Elvia Carrillo Puerto referred to Portes Gil's announcement as "political sweet talk," maintaining that "women have completely different problems from those understood by men."[9]

Nonetheless, the PNR transformed the context of women's political organizing. If its constitution had offered a small opening to women activists and Cárdenas's presidency had widened that aperture somewhat, the PNR's plebiscites seemed further evidence of the momentum behind women's suffrage. Apparently chagrined by suffragists' "passive vote" criticisms, the party enlisted Robles de Mendoza as the secretary of women's affairs and announced in late February that women would "enjoy full citizenship rights within the party," allowing them to vote and be elected.[10] Not surprisingly, this announcement precipitated considerable confusion, since it indicated that women could seek the party's nomination and, presumably, hold office if they won their elections. Scores of new groups — along with more estab-

Figure 3. Suffragists at the National Palace. AGN, Archivo fotográfico "Enrique Díaz."

lished entities such as the FUPDM and the UMA — registered with the Ministry of Government. The National Civic Women's Party, for example, pledged to "work through all legal means within its reach to realize its desires: to obtain the vote for women in the same conditions and with the same rights as men."[11] In Querétaro, a nationalist organization calling itself Patrismo inverted antisuffragist language by proposing that, "in view of men's moral corruption," women assume all the organization's administrative and governing duties "until this produces capable and honest results, when said posts will pass gradually and partially into men's hands."[12]

Two weeks after the party's announcement, the FUPDM convened to celebrate the newly unified women's movement. Instead, however, the congress only highlighted activists' differences.[13] The Popular Front's big tent covered women with explicitly opposing ideologies, precipitating inevitable conflicts. The anticommunist Yucatecan Mercedes Betancourt de Albertos chaired sessions by Communists and fellow travelers such as Consuelo Uranga, Mathilde Rodríguez Cabo, and Otilia Zambrano. An early resolution denounced women who supported the fascist Camisas Doradas, whose concomitant confrontations with the Mexican Communist Party (PCM) infused the discussion with a heightened ideological sensitivity. During a discussion of Uranga's anti-imperialist presentation, for example, Blanca Lydia Trejo, who later broke with the FUPDM to campaign for the conservative 1940 presidential candidate Juan Andreu Almazán, argued in favor of admitting women Dorados.

Congress participants even disagreed about the advisability of women's political participation. Rodríguez Cabo cautioned about women's inadequate "preparation" for political rights. Hermila Garduño Castro, the National Democratic Party's secretary of women's affairs, argued that women should avoid politics and limit themselves to domestic matters, since these "constitute a true feminism, healthy, practical, and reasonable." She vowed — with no apparent sense of irony about her own political activities — to "crusade" against women's involvement in politics.[14] Other participants traded insults about the degree to which women were manipulated by political or religious influences.

Although the FUPDM tried to incorporate a broad array of members, its tactics reflected its predominantly communist leadership. The day of the March congress, the front released a suffragist pamphlet written by its political-action officer, the Communist physician Esther Chapa.[15] In contrast to those who pointed to motherhood to justify women's enfranchisement, Chapa stressed women's engagement in the same activities credited with bringing men to political consciousness. Describing the entrance of women into workplaces, universities, and "the most important social struggles of our time: against the war, against imperialism, against fascism," Chapa explained, "she is in offices and schools, continues at home and takes to the street for demonstrations, organizes meetings, acts in revolutions and, finally, favors the sanctioning of leftist governments to support the proletarian class that has the mission of destroying the capitalist regime under which we live. And this modern woman is denied the vote under the pretext that she is incapable of exercising it!" Rather than distinguishing women as more nurturing and maternal, Chapa described them as "by nature a bit more legalistic than men" and said that they would, given proper knowledge of electoral laws, avoid involvement in "electoral vices."

Despite persistent divisions among women activists, suffrage reforms proceeded apace, largely because government representatives expressed confidence that the party could adequately guide women in civic acts, steering them toward a more maternalist orientation than Chapa promoted.[16] "Women of my Patria, we have found the path!" exclaimed one PNR activist.

"The Government of the Revolution has ignited a brilliant blaze of hope in the gloom of our lives—the hope of an ascent to a better life of fullness and strength." Turning the expectation of feminine sentimentality on its head, she continued: "given that in the home's heart the mother-woman is the pivot around which the family revolves, we will agree that, on this basis alone, she will always be worthy to intervene in social problems when a brain is needed to think and a heart to feel."[17] Such assertions—that women would provide the heart and men the brains of postrevolutionary politics— bespoke a tenacious maternalism among women activists.

Suffragists also exploited the regime's self-identification as revolutionary, pressing policymakers to place Mexico at the vanguard of women's rights, since Uruguay, Cuba, and Brazil, along with the United States, Britain, and several European countries, had already granted women's suffrage. Chapa argued that Mexico should follow the example of the Soviet Union, where, she averred, women enjoyed parity with men "not out of charity or pity, or as a favor granted by men, but rather as a right enjoyed by workingwomen and as a means to achieve a better race and a more humane life."[18] The cosmopolitan UMA, which listed Robles de Mendoza as its founder and honorary president, lauded Cárdenas for his commitment to women's rights and, inverting the antisuffragist rhetoric, proclaimed its support for "magistrates like you who know how to put women in their proper place."[19]

The well-connected Robles de Mendoza invoked Mexico's duty as a regional leader. Urging Cárdenas to sign the Montevideo Treaty granting equal rights to men and women, she pleaded, "Surely Mexico must not continue the absurdity of not signing it. Mexico has great duties to fulfill as an advanced country. It is the example and the standard of the majority of American peoples, and it will certainly not be the international pressure that obliges [Mexico] to sign, but it will clearly do so by its own willingness."[20] Robles de Mendoza remained particularly bitter about the 1933 Montevideo conference, since the government had refused her a spot with the delegation because, as a woman, she was not a full citizen.[21] Explaining that Foreign Affairs Secretary Eduardo Hay had promised to send her as part of the delegation to the upcoming Pan-American Peace Conference in Buenos Aires, Robles de Mendoza urged Cárdenas to authorize her to sign the Montevideo Treaty there. Exposing the limits of the government's commitment to women's political rights, Hay responded that it remained "impossible" for Mexico to sign the treaty. Although he sent his "assurances of friendship and special appreciation," he explained that Robles de Mendoza must have "made a mistaken interpretation of our conversation" if she believed that he intended to include her in the Buenos Aires delegation.[22]

Undeterred by Hay's rebuff, Robles de Mendoza again raised the issue of Mexico's international stature. Deploying the language of manly honor, she argued that the Montevideo Treaty "addresses a transcendental step that our Fatherland must take for its prestige and honor. Sooner or later, Mexico will adhere to this treaty anyway, and, for its undying glory, it is better that it do so as soon as possible and by mutual accord rather than being obligated by international pressure." She further appealed to Cárdenas's efforts to distinguish his government from the maximato. "It is public and notorious," she explained, "that only the reactionary attitude of the Callista delegation impeded that signing of the Montevideo Treaty, but there is no reason for this attitude in the current moment of historic rectifications."[23] This cajoling, however, proved insufficient. By the following April, Robles de Mendoza found herself among those leading demonstrations in front of Los Pinos and the Palacio Nacional.

"Without Legal Force but with Moral Force": Women and the PNR

The momentum behind women's suffrage mounted as several states granted women the rights to vote for and be elected to state and local offices. Notably, two of the first states to create inroads for women's voting rights, Guanajuato and Puebla, remained centers of conservative Catholic organizing. In 1934, Guanajuato allowed women property owners to vote. In 1936, Puebla ceded women the vote on a par with men, subjecting both men and women to the stipulation that voters "have an honest way of life and not belong to any monastic orders or perform any office of a religious character."[24] Other states reinforced the PNR's policy by permitting women to participate in local and state plebiscites, allowing two women from Veracruz, María Tinoco and Enriqueta Limón de Pulgarón, to run for deputies' seats in the state legislature.[25] Directing their appeals to working and unsalaried women — linking rights claims to paid and unpaid labor — Tinoco and Limón de Pulgarón proclaimed themselves "completely apart from the filth in which the professional politicians wallow" and urged women to "demand your rights that have been trampled for so long by the pestilent bureaucracy."[26]

In May 1936, the PNR platform described the plebiscite vote as an important step toward women's full citizenship rights. The party, "always with its gaze turned upwards but with its feet firmly planted in realities," took women under its political tutelage. "Thus, without legal force but with moral force," the platform continued, "the women — the organized ones really — have been able, equal to men, their laboring comrades, to indicate their will regarding candidates designated for certain posts of national responsibility."[27] This conceit reinforced the notion that full citizenship rights would only accrue to women by establishing themselves as "organized" (by joining officially recognized entities) and as "laboring" (by either joining the wage-labor force or increasing the legitimacy and visibility of their unpaid labor). By June, the PNR's program for the upcoming year seemed to chart a clear trajectory toward women's enfranchisement. Under its program for the "feminine sector," the party called for "equality of civic rights for popularly elected posts, including those of the town council [*ayuntamiento*] as well as in the local chambers and the national Congress."[28]

The party bolstered its commitment by launching a national women's organizing campaign through its newly created Committee for Women's Social Action "to be more in consonance with the spirit of the time, courageous, attractive, and combative."[29] Acción Femenil, as the committee was called, emulated PCM tactics of establishing organizing committees in cities and towns throughout the republic to "support and defend the principles of its Central Committee" and to inculcate "the basic principle of the Revolution, Effective Suffrage and No Reelection, so that these principles will be respected, a concrete reality, and be effectively incorporated into the nascent civic ideology of Mexican women."[30] While the PNR's report on 1935–36 organizing activities emphasized that Acción Femenil put particular energy into organizing women wage earners, "who have been incorporated into the sufferings and privations of the unjust economic regime in which we live," it also acknowledged the need for greater attention to women in families. Even the most revolutionary men, the party conceded, "perhaps because their mentalities are, subconsciously, educated in an old-fashioned way," continued to view women as "beings destined for protection, incapable of seeing for themselves, useless in struggle, and, above all, not as beings apart, with their own individuality and aspirations, hopes and deserts, but rather as a complementary part of man, who alone is capable of fighting for his improvement and enjoying the advantages and conquests achieved."[31] On this basis, the party advocated repealing protective labor laws that excluded women from certain jobs and shifts.

The PNR's efforts stress the persistent tension between celebrating "beings apart" and the mobilization and discipline of collective organizing. Emphasizing that the party restricted plebiscite voting to "organized women," the report explained, "another new aspect of the Party's advanced doctrine is the following: woman is on the road to attain civic equality with man, that is a right; but, like him, she must form part of an organized collectivity, that is a duty. As an individual, woman can only serve, as until now, as wife and mother; but as a member of a collectivity, she is called to a mission that, without forgetting this aspect of her role within humanity, trains her to collaborate in the great crusade that has been undertaken for workers' social and economic improvement."[32] Despite all this rhetoric of rights and duties and of individuals and collectivities, in the end the party's official line returned to the question of women's civic preparation. "In Mexico," the party's report elaborated, "it is disquieting to grant women the vote without preparing her. The Mexican woman will vote; of course she will vote. Of course she will intervene with her intense cooperation in the country's problems. But this will be in the future, a future that the PNR's educational activities will strive to approach as quickly as possible."[33]

Thus, by mid-1936 the PNR's elaborate maneuvering set in relief the continued importance of both labor and organizing in defining citizenship rights. Feminist activists seized on this growing emphasis on labor. When the "colorless" PNR President Emilio Portes Gil promised in August 1935 that "working" women would vote in municipal elections, Robles de Mendoza pressed him to include teachers, store clerks, and housewives among those who "contribute to the country's development" and thus would enjoy these limited voting rights.[34] And although the party would take the definitive step toward corporatism with its 1938 reorganization, this "new aspect of the party's advanced doctrine" — making collective mobilization a "duty" of citizenship — moved the PNR considerably further in that direction. The report explaining this strategy focused, not coincidentally, almost entirely on activities aimed at women and campesinos, the two groups that provoked the most concern among postrevolutionary leaders who feared a popular backlash against their modernizing agenda. By limiting political rights to those who fell explicitly under the influence of regime-approved organizations, political leaders hoped to retain legitimacy and minimize the possibility of electoral defeat.

The ruling party could not, in the end, closely dictate the terms of this organizing, and the party's platform and program of action left plenty of room for interpretation. In Coahuila's capital city of Saltillo, for example, sixty women formed the Municipal Feminist Committee in response to the party's call. Although the organization cited the PNR's program of action, it mentioned only those elements most connected to education and political rights and pledged to "struggle for women without distinction of class, dogma, or religion, to emancipate themselves spiritually, economically, and morally, implementing the prerogatives that the revolutionary laws have created for their benefit."[35] Such language deviated considerably from the party leadership's more confining and regulating approach. Nonetheless, much as it did with the promises of motorized corn mills, by proffering the carrot of political rights the party succeeded in drawing more women — particularly urban women — into party structures.

Other women's organizations had responded more antagonistically to party interventions. Early in 1936, the women's section of the PNR state committee in Guadalajara, Jalisco, expressed outrage that the governor had replaced its elected leader with his own appointee.[36] While party leaders and government officials may have considered these positions meaningless political giveaways, the women took them quite seriously and immediately challenged the imposition. Having found the party and state authorities unresponsive to their objections, the section continued to recognize its elected representative and asked Cárdenas to intervene on its behalf. As one committee member, Guadalupe P. de Padilla, declaimed to her compañeras, the indignity lay not only in the governor's ignoring their express decision but also in his failure to consider any current member qualified to lead the section, instead appointing an outsider. In the nearly three years since the committee's founding, Padilla recounted, the women who formed the committee had struggled "step by step with the difficulties of organizing in the reactionary atmosphere of Guadalajara." To impose someone who had not endured those exertions insulted the group's solidarity, provoking cynicism among the affronted women. "We believe that the PNR called on us to organize ourselves so that after collaborating with its revolutionary campaign, it could abuse our hard-won rights," Padilla contended. "Instead of an example of high democracy, it gave us one of imposition. We are women, compañeras, but women forged in struggle. . . . To be servile, compañeras, we do not need to be within the PNR." Padilla's intervention demonstrates the quandary women political activists confronted. After all, if the committee capitulated to the governor's capricious imposition, perhaps it would yield even more readily under the priest's nefarious influence. Padilla exhorted the committee's members to distinguish themselves as "women forged in struggle" by standing up for their rights, even in the face of the revolutionary regime itself. By September, a third woman, who had not signed the letter of complaint, held the disputed position.

The anticommunist Women's Civic Action in Mexico City faced a similar dilemma while establishing an institute to train women in civics and to "unite all Mexican women, ending forever the hatred between classes."[37] Declaring itself "independent of any official organism, private or communist," the group nonetheless requested "the same rights and prerogatives as any other association of the same character that exists within the PNR." Although the group pledged to work "in consonance with the PNR," its leadership expressed concern that, "to conserve its independence and to avoid suspicion, it does not necessarily want to subject itself to [the party]." But this rejection came with a price. Although the group claimed several thousand members and had chapters outside Mexico City, its secretary-general repeatedly requested an audience with Cárdenas's private secretary, to no avail.

As the suffrage campaign picked up steam and appeared close to achieving its goal, the FUPDM leadership poured more of its energies into the effort. Several weeks after its divided congress, Front members demonstrated in favor of price controls and women's suffrage, linking strategic and practical issues in the organization's characteristic fashion. Starting out from the Juárez memorial in Mexico City's Alameda Central, an estimated two hundred women marched to the Palacio Nacional, stopping occasionally for speeches. Perhaps still smarting from the fractured congress, the organization's leadership refused to allow a speaker from the Mexican Popular Front to speak, citing concerns that he would "touch on political questions."[38] On arriving at the Palacio Nacional, the marchers petitioned Cárdenas to act immediately on their demands. "The [FUPDM] does not consider men its enemies; on the contrary, we count them among our collaborators," FUPDM Secretary-General Cuca García explained to a reporter after the rally. She vowed that front members remained "prepared to fight until we obtain our complete civil rights." But, she continued, "we do not fight for utopias that we know beforehand are unrealizable. We understand that before forming women citizens, a solid consciousness must be cultivated among them."[39]

Two weeks later, the FUPDM held another plenary, attracting roughly four hundred women to the Teatro Hidalgo to clarify its suffrage program.[40] The meeting precipitated a minor scandal when PNR President Portes Gil, always a thorn in the PCM's side, ordered all public employees to return to work, forcing some 250 women to abandon the meeting. Portes Gil claimed that Cárdenas had issued the order, but Cárdenas denied any involvement.[41] The following day, nearly 250 women appeared at Cárdenas's office, protesting the "sabotage" and declaring the act contrary to his "progressive revolutionary spirit in favor of women."[42] Taking advantage of the interview, they presented a host of demands, ranging from land parcels for peasant women to educational reforms, maternity clinics, and voting rights.[43] The incident had not resulted from a simple misunderstanding, however. When the FUPDM leadership rescheduled the event for the following week, word went out to public employees that the organization's leaders were "of a communist affiliation . . . and for the most part not public employees."[44]

Exposing the Popular Front's political limits, Portes Gil established a competing PNR women's committee to address women public employees' concerns independently of the FUPDM.[45] He took the situation seriously enough to preside over the founding meeting himself. Women public employees, who had a particular debt to the ruling party for its consistent defense of women's right to work in public offices, expressed concern about voting rights but placed greater emphasis on labor issues such as maternity leave and a civil-service law. The party leadership clearly intended to use this leverage to retain influence over a key sector of women's activism and to prevent the suffrage mobilizations from straying too far from the party's control.

If the PNR leadership had hoped to head off the FUPDM by co-opting one of its most prominent constituencies, the women employees had other plans, choosing instead to view Portes Gil's involvement as a sign of the party's commitment to women's issues. "We cannot remain at the margin of the struggles for the improvement and equality of women's rights," one employee explained. "Our organization will always fight to advance, struggling to achieve the prerogatives that the Revolution offers women. . . . It will be a serious group that will channel the feminist movement in Mexico."[46] With this sense of purpose, the public employees transformed Portes Gil's new organization into the one they had set out to create. Rather than simply addressing issues pertinent to public employees, they proposed a vast national organizing campaign to improve women's conditions across all sectors of the population and refused to capitulate to Portes Gil's efforts to exclude the FUPDM from their campaign, pointedly inviting Cuca García to attend their meetings.[47]

By the fall of 1936, the FUPDM had turned its attention almost exclusively to suffrage, subordinating all other objectives. In September, FUPDM chapters from Baja California to Yucatán sent Cárdenas letters and telegrams expressing their support for the front and demanding any constitutional reforms necessary to allow women to vote.[48] One group from the Comarca Lagunera urged Cárdenas not to allow Portes Gil to "become a nuisance" so that he could "carry out your Revolutionary Program on which all the proletariat have trained our attention."[49] Often named after international revolutionaries such as Rosa Luxemburg or Clara Zetkin or local heroines such as the martyred radicals Martina Derás and Lucrecia Toriz, these leagues marked themselves as "revolutionary" within the idiom of Cardenismo and progressive within the international currents of women's and labor's mobilizations. From the PCM's perspective, the suffrage movement offered an avenue into the mainstream of women's organizing. In December 1936, the Communist newspaper urged the front — somewhat unjustly — to shift from being the "sectarian group that it is today to a great movement of the united front, not just of workingwomen but of all women who defend their rights, putting forward the central demands such as the complete equalization of civil and political rights, and especially the right to the vote." This emphasis on electoral politics indicates a sharp reversal from the party's pre–Popular Front stance.[50] Reaching across long-standing divides to create a "great movement of the united front" required not only the relinquishing of old animosities but also patience with organizations and strategies the Communists previously had dismissed with disdain, embracing legalistic tactics over mass mobilization.

Grammar Lessons: Legislative and Constitutional Reform Efforts

In late summer of 1936, the UMA shifted tactics, submitting to the Senate a petition asserting that the denial of women's voting rights resulted from a grammatical misinterpretation of the constitution's relevant clause. When the constitution's authors granted to all *mexicanos* the right to elect officials and to hold public office, the petitioners argued, that stipulation included women, subsumed under the category of *mexicanos* rather than distinguished as *mexicanas*. Therefore, granting women's suffrage required only minor changes to federal electoral laws rather than a full-fledged constitutional amendment.[51] Other groups, including the FUPDM, the Organizing League of Women's Action (led by Elvia Carrillo Puerto), and the Mexican Women's Confederation (led by María Ríos Cárdenas), submitted similar letters to Cárdenas and to both houses of Congress.[52]

Opponents countered with an argument favoring "original intent" over textual analysis, and the transcripts of the 1917 constitutional convention revealed that the constitution's authors had not only explicitly rejected women's suffrage but also, in the main, found the idea unworthy of further debate. Nevertheless, the prominent convention participant and presidential hopeful Francisco Múgica, now married to one of Mexico's leading feminist activists, the psychologist Mathilde Rodríguez Cabo, and cultivating political support among women's organizations, publicly stated that the constitution's "not making any distinction between man and woman indicated the equality of rights for both."[53] Félix Palavicini, a more conservative delegate who had favored women's citizenship in 1917, declared that the participants "considered citizenship unrelated to sex."[54] Several days later, Luis Monzón, a vocal opponent of women's suffrage in 1917, held that they had intended citizenship equally for men and women.[55] As with many other issues, post-revolutionary statesmen wanted to revise the historical record to conform to the regime's current trajectory.[56]

Despite suffragists' efforts to line up legislative supporters, proposals to amend the federal electoral laws languished in Congress as antisuffragists held that women would support church-endorsed candidates, subverting the anticlerical regime.[57] Suffragists throughout the republic lambasted the hypocrisy of this position. In the eastern port city of Tampico, Tamaulipas, a stronghold of Communist women's organizing, the FUPDM chapter addressed the three leading concerns: that women lacked the intellectual capacity, the civic training, and the independence from the church required to exercise effective suffrage.[58] The chapter's leadership responded to allegations of women's intellectual inferiority by describing the notion as a "a medieval inheritance . . . banished by scientific studies as well as by the growing activity and social responsibility of women." To the argument that women lacked "civic preparation," they pointed to the "great majority of male voters" who also lacked formal preparation for electoral politics. "But the argument that the enemies of woman suffrage wield with the most energy," the Tampiqueñas continued, "is that woman is influenced by the most conservative and reactionary currents and will therefore be inclined to the political right of the country. However, this argument is countered by remembering that an enormous male population in fact is clerical and reactionary, conservative and cristero, which is not a reason to deny them the vote."[59] Thus, drawing on the logic of both liberalism and revolutionary mobilization, FUPDM suffragists insisted that policymakers should not deny women voting rights based on predicted voting patterns. The slogan "Effective Suffrage and No Reelection" implied, according to many suffragists, that democracy allowed even the government's opponents to vote.

By late November, rumors had spread that the thirty-sixth legislature would not grant women's suffrage before adjourning. Citing concerns that women's suffrage posed a "danger to the Revolution itself," lawmakers deferred the issue.[60] Suffragists once again took to the streets, this time setting up a rotating picket line in front of the Chamber of Deputies.[61] With the well-heeled Robles de Mendoza in the lead, women picketed the congressional chamber wearing sandwich boards and carrying signs calling on Congress to address the matter of women's suffrage. "We Want the Vote to Defend Our Children," declared one sign. Another exhorted, "Revolution, Fulfill Your Promise, Emancipating Woman and Conceding the Feminine Vote." Robles de Mendoza told reporters, "We will resume on Monday. Until when? Until justice has been done."[62]

Throughout the winter of 1936–37, the suffrage campaign intensified along with debates about the compatibility of Mexican womanhood and political rights. The legal scholar Elodia Cruz F. published her 1931 thesis on women's political rights, arguing that no contradiction existed between women's suffrage and their duties under Mexico's Civil Code. "Therefore," she explained, "there is no danger that [a woman] will fail to fulfill her obligations as spouse or mother by exercising her political rights, nor will she stop being prudent in the home guided by the demands of her functions as wife, mother, or daughter."[63] In Mexico City, the PNR Women's Executive Committee of the Federal District supported Cárdenas's policy of granting political rights to organized workingwomen, thus resolving the gender trouble by granting masculine rights to those women who transcended conventional gender boundaries by performing wage labor.[64]

Despite the legislative uncertainty, women activists proceeded as though they had won the suffrage battle. The FUPDM backed two candidates for federal deputy seats. Its own Secretary-General Cuca García ran in her home district of Uruapan, Michoacán, and the Mexican Popular Front's secretary of women's affairs, Soledad Orozco Avila, ran in León, Guanajuato. Campaigning in one of the republic's most conservative regions, the cradle of the Cristero Rebellion and the counterrevolutionary sinarquista movement, both women sought support from local labor and peasant organizations, and both claimed that they won the right to stand as PNR candidates in the 1937 congressional elections. "I launched my candidacy with the support of the [FUPDM] and the [Mexican Labor Confederation (CTM) of León]," Orozco recalled nearly half a century later. "This bravery, particularly in such a reactionary time and place, awakened such power in the citizenry that it resulted in my registration as the PNR municipal committee's candidate. To tell the truth, it was a very unusual case. The breach had been opened."[65]

PCM activists had already launched García's congressional campaign by the spring of 1936, soon after the FUPDM's Mexico City congress.[66] García attracted national attention for her role in the national women's congresses and as the FUPDM's secretary-general; by December 1935, the U.S. chargé d'affaires had identified her as a noteworthy figure in communist circles.[67] The following March, Gabino Alcaraz, a prominent Michoacán Communist, contacted supporters to instigate her campaign. "You should do everything possible to form Pro–Cuca García Committees in the most important places," he wrote to an organizer in La Huacana. "Do not judge importance by the size of the town but, rather, by the quantity of sympathizers that we have."[68] However, the local PCM did not fully unite behind García, seeing her as an imposition by party leaders in Mexico City. "There is true confusion among our compañeros," Alcaraz informed García within a month of the PNR plebiscite, "in that as Party members they support different candidates from that of the Party, always alleging that they have their reasons and casting blame on the [PCM] directors. I do not know to what extent they are correct, but the fact is that this happens."[69]

In a letter to Múgica, García referred to her opponents as "not only fools but crooks" and described her efforts to mobilize support among the region's highway and railroad workers.[70] The mixed reaction to García's campaign may have stemmed in part from the fact that, compared with the other candidates, she had little remaining connection to Michoacán politics. Although a native of Taretán, she had been active on the national political scene since 1913 and resided primarily in Mexico City.[71] Even during the campaign, her attention seemed trained more on international events such as the Paris peace conference than on local Uruapan social and political matters.[72] While running this historic campaign in Michoacán, she also managed a crisis at a Mexico City maternity clinic and intervened in an interunion dispute in Orizaba, Veracruz.[73] The day of the PNR plebiscite, however,

García wrote to Múgica to proclaim that their campaign had "roundly triumphed" in Uruapan and that she anticipated "no obstacles to recognizing the legality" of the vote.[74]

Ironically, on 8 March, International Women's Day, the Senate had released a report dubbing women "untrained for the exercise of political rights."[75] The FUPDM turned to the Socialist Lawyers Front for support, commissioning a study about the constitutional implications of women's suffrage.[76] However, when the party refused to allow García and Orozco to stand for office, the suffragists marched to the PNR offices, leading to the aforementioned demonstration before Los Pinos, the moment when their attention turned from the legislature to the executive, in hopes that Cárdenas would decree women's voting rights. As the secretary-general of the Morelos Women's Civic Union appealed to Cárdenas in her preamble to the organization's "Manifesto on Women's Citizenship": "I have infinite desires to serve my Fatherland, and I have spared no sacrifice to achieve my desire. If you do not help, I will have no choice but to put a veil over my ideas, since I understand that my efforts alone are not enough to undertake something, no matter how much they may benefit the People."[77]

The radicalization of suffragists like Robles de Mendoza resulted not only from her frustrations in Mexico but also from her contact with militant suffragists from outside Mexico. In May 1937, Anna Kelton Wiley, a member of the National Woman's Party in the United States and an activist in the equal rights amendment movement, traveled through central Mexico with Robles de Mendoza as her guide. At the 1936 Buenos Aires peace conference that Robles de Mendoza had lobbied to attend, Wiley had expressed a sentiment ascendant in Mexican suffragist circles. "Woman have always done the unpaid work of the world," she told the congress. "Remunerative work is not sacred to men. Economic warfare between men and women is as undesirable as it is unfortunate."[78] Asserting that Mexican women had "earned the right" to suffrage, Wiley linked enfranchisement with both political struggle and women's labor.

Speaking to an FUPDM meeting in Mexico City, Wiley exhorted her small audience of about twenty-five women to continue with the tactics demonstrated at Los Pinos. "The last eight years of our struggle were years full of drama and frightful effort," she explained. She described a "monster parade" in Washington, D.C., and eleven conferences with President Woodrow Wilson. When Wilson refused to meet with the suffragists any more, they, much like their Mexican counterparts twenty years later, began to picket the White

House in 1917. "The members of the Woman's Party picketed peacefully for five months, and the pickets at the White House gates became as great an object of interest to the tourists as the cherry blossoms are today," she continued. When a Russian delegation visited the White House, the picketers carried banners reading, "The President of the U.S. Is as Much of a Czar to the Women of the U.S. as the Czar of All the Russians," precipitating the arrest of 218 women "from all walks of life," who served sentences from two weeks to two months. "When the women were sent to prison they were treated with great brutality," Wiley explained. "They were thrown into punishment cells and onto hard floors. One of the leaders, because she called out to a comrade, was hung up by her thumbs. It hardly seems possible that such brutality could have been practiced on American women only twenty years ago. But every word I am staying is *true*."[79] Suffragists continued to picket the White House until 10 November, three days after the Bolshevik Revolution.

Cuca García, still bruised from her congressional campaign, chafed at Wiley's condescension, pointing out that although the U.S. suffragist movement served as an inspiration in Mexico, the FUPDM struggled in the context of a "semicolonial country." Rejecting the implication that Mexican suffragists needed only to demonstrate adequate valor to achieve their aims, she explained, "The gunpowder from the battlefields passed through our hair many times without making us turn back, but our country's Government, when the Revolution was ended and they had taken advantage of our services, sent us back home, saying that 'the woman's place is in her home.'" García's bitterness belied the Popular Front's language of unity that characterized most FUPDM interventions. "I was nominated for the Federal Congress by 10,000 votes, but was not allowed to take my seat," she explained. "I wish to make this promise as a fighter for my rights. I do not care for the National Revolutionary Party's decisions. The National Revolutionary Party does not represent the people's will. I will return to my District for the June elections because the people will back me. This shows that the people are with the women and, helped by them, we will open the doors of Congress to all the country's women."[80]

Despite García's bravado and invocation of popular will, it became increasingly clear that executive pressure offered the most promising route to women's enfranchisement, particularly after Alberto Bremauntz of the Socialist Lawyers Front published his opinion that women's suffrage required a constitutional amendment and recommended that only "revolutionary" women initially be allowed to vote.[81] The pamphlet remained noticeably vague about how the state would measure women's revolutionary commitment for the purposes of voter rolls but offered membership in a state-sanctioned organization as one suggestion. A dissenting opinion presented at the organization's convention accompanied Bremauntz's report. "Due to old and currently unsustainable prejudices," submitted Valetín Rincón, "we men have been afraid to resolve, once and for all, the problem of women's citizenship, to discover this keystone, to recognize the reality of her extreme importance in the production process and in all other aspects of life, and to accept as evident the justice that attends their demands for full respect of their rights."[82] Describing women's citizenship as "just and constitutional, in addition to being by nature socialist and revolutionary," Rincón proposed a resolution to accept a constitutional reading that extended full rights to men and women equally. However, while Rincón's argument rested on broad principles of justice, Bremauntz deployed seemingly indisputable documentary evidence. The defeat of the suffragists' strategy seemed overdetermined. Lawmakers wary of allowing women to vote could now muster arguments about constitutional liberalism and the rule of law; no grammatical or constitutional maneuvering would salvage the suffragists' efforts without Cárdenas's explicit endorsement.

"Why Condemn Her before She Has Acted?": The Asymptotic Approach to Suffrage

The suffragists' faith in Cárdenas seemed well founded. In late August in the eastern port of Veracruz, Cárdenas announced that he would call on Congress the following month to make "whatever legal reforms necessary" to grant women political equality with men.[83] "It is not just," he explained to the assembled women's confederation, "that we demand women's presence in social acts but have placed them on an inferior political plane."[84] He reiterated this commitment in his annual congressional address several days later.[85] Given Mexico's *presidencialismo* (strong presidency), advocates and opponents of women's political rights indicated that this proposal amounted to a presidential decree that would become law without any significant challenge.

Cárdenas's announcement precipitated a deluge of telegrams and letters from an array of suffrage supporters ranging from the national actors' union to revolutionary veterans' widows and from the Communist Party to Masonic lodges. The longtime suffragist Hermila Galindo de Topete, who had argued for women's suffrage at the 1917 Constitutional Congress, emerged from a long silence to heap praise on Cárdenas. "With such a noble and just act," she wrote to him, "you make yourself worthy not only of those monuments of Hellenic marble and Florentine bronze but also of those that neither time nor malice nor human ingratitude can destroy. That is: an altar in our souls."[86] The radical activist Mathilde Rodríguez Cabo informed the audience for her lecture to the Socialist Lawyers Front that she had to rewrite her address, which had been openly hostile to the administration's position on women's rights.[87]

While Mexico City remained the suffragist epicenter, the organizational reach of the FUPDM and the PNR and the influence of local schoolteachers carried the message into rural areas, albeit with considerably less force. By 1935, demands for suffrage came from other cities, particularly industrial cities, port cities, and state capitals, and by late 1936, smaller towns, villages, and ejidos often included political rights among laundry-list petitions to the federal government. FUPDM members in the village of Yahuapan, Veracruz, for example, wrote to Cárdenas in broken Spanish to demand suffrage without restrictions, calling for the campaign to be carried out "faithfully and principally" by chapters of the FUPDM.[88] Even in the thick of the suffrage battle, however, FUPDM chapters outside Mexico City often submitted petitions that made no mention of voting rights.

Cárdenas's announcement attracted international attention, apparently catching Mexico's diplomatic corps somewhat by surprise. Two weeks after the fact, Foreign Relations Minister Hay sent an urgent telegram requesting that its text be sent to Mexico's League of Nations delegate, Isidro Fabela.[89] In addition to the persistent communications from the UMA, the Inter-American Women's Commission, a branch of the Pan-American Union, offered Cárdenas "fervent congratulations" and delivered 1,000 copies of his congressional address to government and diplomatic offices throughout the Americas.[90] The Interamerican Education Conference, meeting in Mexico City's Palace of Fine Arts, approved a resolution from the Peruvian delegation lauding Cárdenas with a "warm vote of applause" for his action.[91] Even the World Affairs Study Club in Seattle added its two cents, commending Cárdenas after having learned of his position from the *Christian Science Monitor*.[92]

The suffrage debate shifted at this point from a discussion about whether to grant women voting rights to one about the conditions under which women would vote. Even suffragists remained divided between those who championed universal voting rights, putting women on a par with men, and those who favored limited rights based on literacy, organizational membership, or political affiliation.[93] This last consideration stemmed from the widely held conviction that, due to their lack of experience in civic affairs, women would easily be manipulated by counterrevolutionary elements. As one functionary commented, "If we granted women the right to vote, the Archbishop of Mexico would be the next President of the Republic."[94] Nonetheless, Puebla Senator Gonzalo Bautista supported unrestricted women's suffrage. "According to modern historical methods of interpretation," he argued, "the sophisms against the feminist ideal used routinely in Mexico and around the world are simply the same dogmatic arguments used against popular suffrage at the height of the era of oppression. Their true aim is to maintain a distance between the exploited majority and access to power."[95]

However, it was not only antifeminists who encouraged limiting women's franchise. Even as the FUPDM and PCM consistently endorsed unrestricted suffrage, radical leaders like Mathilde Rodríguez Cabo and Cuca García repeatedly expressed reservations about women outside the influence of progressive organizations. For women activists who had invested themselves in institution building — under the rubric of the FUPDM, the PNR, or some smaller, less well-established entity — the imperative of organizational membership created an incentive structure that redounded to their benefit. Members of the Atlixco, Puebla, FUPDM, asserted that "as [FUPDM] militants we know to rise to our duty and for no reason will we consent to having the fanatical women of our Republic take ownership of social or public posts without first having shed the religious fanaticism that currently weighs like an onerous burden on their shoulders."[96] Conceding women's "fanaticism," in other words, strengthened the role of organizations like the FUPDM in socializing and modernizing Mexican society. Similarly for schoolteachers, the insistence on literacy underscored the value of their labor and made education a gauge of civic preparedness. Progressive PNR leaders, concerned that women's political intervention threatened to disrupt the party's carefully balanced political arrangements, applauded efforts to limit suffrage to members of unions and recognized organizations.

Nonetheless, many women activists unsurprisingly bristled at the allegations of women's "natural" conservatism, rendering them "ideologically unprepared" to exercise political rights. The officers of the Women's Center for Proletarian Action in the Communist stronghold of Monterrey, Nuevo León, echoed other suffragists who argued that if men followed corrupt, misguided, and conservative political paths, then these attributes could hardly pertain exclusively to women. "Was it perhaps a group of women who made a special trip to deliver the Crown of Mexico to the Archduke of Austria Fernando Maximiliano?" they submitted sardonically. "The Santa Annas, the Huertas and other traitors who have torn apart our Fatherland, selling it or arranging shameful treaties (such as those of Bucarelli), and have committed the most horrendous crimes to keep themselves in power, were [these men] perhaps in fact women? Why fear woman so much when she has done nothing but refuse to endure her own slavery? Why condemn her before she has acted?"[97] Underscoring that they viewed the suffrage issue as more than a matter of principle, they emphasized the practical gains for wage-earning women, ranging from improved pension and maternity laws to the resolution of the "sexual problem" and a more pacifist foreign policy. Failure to include women in policymaking circles, the group emphasized, carried a greater risk than the uncertainties about how women might exercise their franchise.

Lawmakers and activists debated this matter through the fall of 1937, and in late November, Cárdenas proposed a constitutional amendment specifying that "men and women" enjoyed all rights attendant to citizenship. In December, he reinforced this proposal with statements about the ruling party's planned reorganization and described women's participation in social and political matters as "extremely important [*trascendentalísimo*]." Simultaneously invoking both equality and difference, he called on Congress "to eliminate for good the traditional injustice of relegating half of humanity to inferior positions, and with it the most noble and esteemed part of our society."[98] A week later, the Senate unanimously approved the women's suffrage amendment and sent it to the Chamber of Deputies for approval.

The deputies focused their debate on the conditions under which women would vote, with the committee report and majority of deputies endorsing unlimited suffrage rights. Pointing out that arguments about "preparation" had previously prevented men from voting, the committee asserted, "If Mexico truly aspires to strengthen its democratic system, one of the most suitable ways to achieve it is clearly through women's suffrage."[99] To applause from the sign-waving suffragists who packed the chamber galleries, legislators called for an end to the "prejudices of the Porfirian dictatorship" and exhorted their colleagues to become "standard-bearers of feminism in the Republic."[100] Finally, in July 1938, the lower house of Congress also unanimously approved the amendment. Now, with the approval of two-thirds of the states and the publication of the votes in the congressional record, the *Diario Oficial*, the amendment would become law.[101]

Congressional approval did not silence opponents of women's political rights, however. "Mending socks is humiliating to the marimachos," wrote one editorialist, "but it inspires such tenderness to see the little woman [*mujercita*] dedicated to this task! I compare, in my mind, this spectacle with that of a señora in the parliamentary chamber, and in spite of my vanguardism, I feel like laughing or become irritated."[102] In newspapers' "lightning surveys," men and women on the street regularly expressed mixed views. As one man explained, "Looking at how things have gone with men as deputies, with women it would only be worse, and God only knows what would become of us."[103] Women often argued that they were most naturally suited for the home and did not feel adequately prepared for political life. However, when asked what they might do if elected to Congress, women often said that they would work to eliminate injustices against women and children.[104]

Despite earlier opposition within state legislatures, one by one they approved the constitutional amendment. On 17 November 1938, the front page of the PNR newspaper anticipated the congressional declaration of women's suffrage. However, Congress did not make the long-anticipated declaration on that day or any day that year and recessed at the end of December without finalizing the amendment's passage. Although some sessions had particularly full agendas, other sessions simply met, heard minutes from the previous session, and adjourned. When Congress reconvened in January 1939, it again demurred. The legislators' reticence was not lost on women activists, who continued to insist that Congress fulfill its legal obligation to publish the amendment in the *Diario Oficial*, formally enacting it as law.[105] In May 1939, a leading national teachers' union coordinated a march from the Juárez monument on the Alameda Central to the Chamber of Deputies, where protesters called on Congress to publish the amendment. The demonstration included speeches by Robles de Mendoza and the ruling-party activist Thais García but apparently no FUPDM representative.[106] Following the recommendations of several women's organizations, the ruling-party leadership called for a special session to declare the amendment.[107] In July, however, Congress once again recessed without making the declaration. In several public speeches, including his annual report to Congress, Cárdenas urged lawmakers to publish the amendment, but to no avail.[108]

In late March 1940, Congress declared that it had tabled the suffrage question indefinitely. Newspaper reports expressed bafflement at the congressional refusal to finalize the amendment, publicly wondering why lawmakers would pass it unanimously and then refuse to publish it. The commonly accepted explanation that women would support conservative policies and candidates seems unconvincing, since the organized left, including the PCM, the CTM, and the CNC (National Peasant Confederation) openly endorsed women's suffrage, referring to it as unfinished business of the revolution.[109] One newspaper commented that the legislators' reasoning—that women would lose the "spiritual heritage of feminine virtues" or lacked the interest in or preparation for political rights—conspicuously echoed early-nineteenth-century arguments against universal male suffrage. However, the editors offered their own assessment of the legislators' behavior, asserting, "They continue building, in secret, the women's sanctuary within the patriarchal family, where women vegetate as the property of men."[110]

The documentary record remains eerily silent on the question of why Congress did not enact the women's suffrage amendment; most scholars have accepted Ward Morton's explanation that, with the 1940 election on the horizon, lawmakers denied women's suffrage out of concerns about women's Catholic piety.[111] A somewhat more complicated picture emerges from the scant evidence, however. To be sure, the conservative challenger, Juan Andreu Almazán, posed a credible threat to the Party of the Mexican Revolution (PRM) candidate, Manuel Avila Camacho, and the party leadership grew nervous that women would follow the Catholic church's lead in supporting Almazán, who appealed to women as both mothers and voters. "I offer woman, the heroic Mexican woman, the right to vote in the first election of my administration," he stated in a campaign speech, "because I know full well that she will defend the most noble and patriotic ideals required for the well-being and prosperity of the Republic." Offering the Mexican woman "tranquillity, respect for her home, freedom to educate her children as she sees fit," and the opportunity to work and "enjoy the fruits of her labor," Almazán promised "recognition of the important mission that she has in the family and in society."[112] Indeed, significant numbers of women—including prominent activists like Elena Torres and Blanca Lydia Trejo—campaigned for Almazán.[113]

However, the assumed connection between Almazán's candidacy and the scuttling of the suffrage amendment demands closer scrutiny. First, most political leaders and activists on the left—those who most strenuously opposed Almazán — actively continued to support women's suffrage. If the PCM, Cárdenas, and the left-leaning sectors of the ruling party wavered in their support for women's suffrage, their doubts remained fleeting and private. Indeed, when one deputy sought to establish his leftist credentials in a December 1938 congressional debate, he pointed out that he had, "with ardor and enthusiasm," thrown his support behind women's suffrage "another conquest of the left and another conquest of the Revolution."[114] Múgica, whose bid for the PRM nomination faltered over concerns that he pulled too far to the left and risked a conservative backlash, vocally advocated women's voting rights and garnered support for his campaign from women throughout the republic.[115] Meanwhile, conservative editorialists generally disparaged women's suffrage as a "Bolshevik" objective.[116]

Second, women's suffrage enjoyed the greatest support in Guanajuato, Michoacán, and Puebla — arguably the republic's three most ardently Catholic states — where women would presumably endorse openly Catholic candidates. However, the women who garnered support in these states, women like Cuca García and Soledad Orozco, had ties with the Popular Front rather than Catholic Action. Although these openings came about through complex and often shrouded negotiations between civil and religious leaders, policymakers would have observed Catholic women choosing to stay away from the polls rather than exploiting opportunities for political influence.

Finally, the ideological differences between the PRM candidate, Avila Camacho, and Almazán remained negligible; the latter had served as part of Cárdenas's inner circle of advisers. Almazán's breakaway party, the Revolutionary Party of National Unification (PRUN), enjoyed little support among the most viable conservative forces, the sinarquistas in the center-west and the National Action Party (PAN) of the Monterrey, Nuevo León, industrialists. The PRUN held few ideological convictions beyond protecting private property, a priority shared by Avila Camacho. As the historian Luis González has commented, "In general terms, the PRM and the PRUN agreed about nationalism, about the participation of the masses in political life, and, above all, about improving conditions for the poor without taking from the rich. Almazán could have been the candidate of the PRM, and Avila Camacho that of the PRUN."[117]

If the congressional refusal to declare women's suffrage resulted from Almazán's candidacy, it was not because a tectonic ideological shift seemed imminent. Rather, lawmakers and politicians throughout the country demonstrated greater concern that Almazán would replace the PRM's political machinery with his own. In other words, women voters might actually have helped to clean up Mexican electoral politics, not because of their inherently more developed sense of morality, but, rather, because they threatened the practice of *chambismo*, or securing work through the party apparatus. The denial of women's suffrage during the declining years of the Cárdenas administration appears less a blow to Almazán's conservatism than an integral part of the rightward drift of the postrevolutionary regime. The argument that women remained "less prepared" for civic life than the vast majority of men rang hollow to many contemporary observers, lawmakers included.

Larger structural and historical factors provide more compelling explanations than the Almazán campaign for the suffrage amendment's foundering. Most critically, the revolution's democratic promise increasingly played out beyond the realm of electoral politics, taking shape instead in union halls, ejidal committees, and community meetings, which participants understood as the enactment of revolutionary citizenship. In these settings, ordinary Mexicans fashioned their own understandings of rights and responsibilities, of belonging and exclusion, and of the border between revolutionary and nonrevolutionary. Thus, rhetorical commitments to democracy and even to "effective suffrage" often indicated an expectation to speak up and be heard in decision-making deliberations rather than an expectation to cast a ballot. Revolutionary citizenship seemed less a fixed status than a range of possibilities, with degrees of rights and responsibilities and gradations of political leverage.

"The Necessary and Immediate Task": Corporatism and the Transformation of Citizenship

Amid this legislative battle over suffrage rights, the meaning of voting underwent a critical change in Mexico. In March 1938, the very month that Cárdenas nationalized the petroleum industry, PNR leaders restructured the ruling party as the PRM, creating the political infrastructure that Cárdenas saw as his legacy to perpetuate his vision of the Mexican revolution. While the reorganization set out in part to resolve some of the internecine conflicts that plagued the party, the most important factor distinguishing the PRM from its predecessor was corporate party membership.[118] The PRM followed a model ascendant internationally, most notably in fascist Italy, Spain, and Germany but also in non-fascist countries such as Brazil that fashioned "pacts" between central governments and dominant labor federations.

With the PRM, the regime distilled interests into centralized, defined, legitimated representatives, clarifying and simplifying the political landscape. One joined the party not as an individual but, rather, as a member of an organized, recognized group, creating a tension in its very conception: it sought both to promote class-consciousness through class-based organizations and to strengthen cross-class commitments through corporatist negotiations and identity-based political strategies.

Although the boundaries of corporate entities and the meanings of political identities remained blurred and unstable, in the case of the "party of the workers, peasants and soldiers," they generally assumed a male political subject. The party's national executive committee included six male officers, and women activists struggled unsuccessfully to establish a secretary of women's affairs. Unsurprisingly, leading activists could not agree on a single woman to represent "women's interests," and support split among the FUPDM leader, Cuca García; the PNR women's committee chair, Thais García; and the lawyer Mercedes Martínez Montes, who served as secretary for women's action for Mexico City's PNR chapter.[119] Women's organizing assumed a line under the budget for the Secretariat of Popular and Cultural Action but received relatively modest funding of 1,000 pesos per month (while the parade commemorating the revolution, for example, received 15,000 pesos).[120] Meanwhile, local-level women activists complained that meetings to discuss the party's reorganization excluded them, often meeting in secret. One activist in Campeche indicated to Cárdenas that so long as the state and municipal PNR leadership excluded the FUPDM and the Ligas Femeniles, the "PNR's transformation will not really represent Campeche's popular forces but, rather, a select group of politicos who do not even apply the line of your government."[121]

The reorganization shifted the weight of popular organizing, placing greater emphasis on discipline and order than on mobilization. The PRM allowed no affiliate parties and forbade competing organizations within the party; dissenting members of party organizations could not expect to enjoy the legitimacy, political voice, and material benefits accorded to regime-sanctioned organizations. The PNR, as an initial attempt at regime consolidation, necessarily had allowed more plurality among its member organizations for the sake of preserving a tenuous political peace. In the PRM, with its corporatist representation, dissidence often meant structural exclusion from political negotiations. To be sure, official support had been critical before the

PRM, but the viability of dissent decreased over the course of the Cárdenas administration as the party's imprimatur gained consequence.

The PRM's creation and accompanying government support for organizing shaped how subaltern actors understood citizenship. The women's suffrage debate set in relief many of the contradictions and conflicts surrounding citizenship more broadly as ordinary Mexicans navigated between collective, identity-based and liberal, individualist conceptions, both adulterated by a patronage-based political culture. Membership in a recognized, collective organization implied party membership, and considerable discussion and voting about political issues occurred at the level of local organizations. For many people, citizenship became associated less with the experience of casting a ballot in a polling booth than with discussion, debate, and consensus achieved in organizational meetings. While individual voting rights remained important, as the tense deliberations over women's suffrage makes clear, the new party organization and the institutional support accorded to recognized collectives offered women another avenue toward effecting political change, one that seemed more promising and more rooted in existing political practices.

While Cárdenas kept his distance from the PCM and certainly antagonized its leadership by granting asylum to Leon Trotsky in 1937, the party reorganization bore the Popular Front's imprint, although more by appropriation than by capitulation. Still, the PRM adopted PCM-favored goals and structures and strengthened the political commitment to mass mobilization and organization. As Barry Carr has pointed out, Communists endorsed the reorganized ruling party "as the incarnation of the Popular Front" and actively promoted the cultural and political influence of the postrevolutionary state.[122] PCM Secretary-General Hernán Laborde called the new party an "iron wall" against the efforts of counterrevolutionaries, reactionaries, and fascists and pledged to Cárdenas that the PCM would "back [his] government and cooperate in any form available and under any circumstances," submit itself to PRM party discipline, and not run independent presidential candidates in 1940.[123] Despite the PCM's support, the ruling party's constituent organizations still entreated it to accept the PCM into the new "party of workers, campesinos, and soldiers."[124]

The FUPDM's incorporation into the PRM marked the definitive co-optation of the Communist women's movement. Although García warned in February that "the mockery of suffrage had corroded the PNR" and expressed concern about the continuity in party leadership, by late March she had assured Cárdenas that her organization would "cooperate completely" with the party's restructuring "to achieve our country's democracy and independence that you defend with such virility."[125] But already in January 1938, soon after Cárdenas announced the upcoming party reorganization, the PCM circulated a directive calling on Communists to organize women into groups that would "incorporate into the PNR or its organisms." The circular instructed rural organizers to use the Ligas Femeniles de Lucha Social pamphlets and statutes, and it encouraged all organizers to make demands on government welfare agencies.[126]

This approach reflected the PCM's new "Unity at Any Cost" campaign that emerged in response to both fascism's international threat and the auspicious opportunity created by the Cárdenas government.[127] Intensifying its "boring from within" strategy, PCM organizers encouraged popular groups to join the ruling party rather than the PCM. The decision to organize women into the ruling party's ranks coincided with several PCM objectives. Most obviously, Communists felt a pressing need to "orient" women before they could vote. "If each Communist, man or women, lends himself with enthusiasm to this work of women's organizing," the circular implored, "Mexico will be very quickly transformed, and above all we will have removed from the reaction one more weapon. Women's citizenship constitutes a serious danger for the revolutionary conquests if we do not succeed in fully incorporating her into the movement, into the struggle."[128] Despite the "transformation in all orders of life," women remained alienated by men "who call themselves revolutionary" and by "the slavery that even now is imposed upon her." Thus, if the matter of organizing women appeared pressing in 1931, when the PCM created its women's department, it seemed imperative now that women stood at the threshold of full citizenship. "Comrades," the instructions concluded, "women's organization is a necessary and immediate task not only for the Communists but for anyone who boasts of loving humanity, liberty, and democracy."

Second, by encouraging women to make demands on the Agrarian Department, the PNR, and the welfare agencies, the PCM used the emergent organizational infrastructure — one clearly mimetic of the PCM's own structures — both to bring women into contact with PCM ideals and to press the emerging bureaucracy toward the more expansive welfare policies the party endorsed. In other words, through Communists' efforts, the women populating the ranks of ruling-party affiliates would pull those organizations to the left. PCM organizers, generally more experienced and disciplined than their PRM counterparts, could thus attain influence disproportionate to their numbers. Finally, the PCM hoped the ruling party would become a genuine Popular Front coalition government and hastened to reinforce its credentials as a loyal ally. "The Party organizer or compañero who has the will to help organize Mexican women," the PCM advised, "should organize everyplace, whenever possible, discussions to orient women, carefully explicating the role and responsibility that the revolution assigns them at men's side as defenders of the revolutionary conquests and supporters of the government of General Cárdenas, who has made her a citizen so that she can participate broadly in the political and economic life of our fatherland."[129]

For its part, the Cárdenas government pointedly endeavored to incorporate women's organizations into the PRM, focusing on leaders and organizations with established constituencies. Prominent groups such as the FUPDM and the Ligas Femeniles de Lucha Social joined the party's popular sector and reached out to incorporate new organizations. The Eastern Women's Regional Committee in Cadereyta Jiménez, Nuevo León, organized an annual congress every 8 March to celebrate International Women's Day and renew organizing among the region's women's groups. In addition to presentations about temperance, inflation, schools, women's access to credit and political rights, and securing benefits due to "organized women," the 1939 agenda included a plan to "ratify or rectify" the appointment of one of their number to the PRM's municipal committee. The following year's congress specified that every Liga Femenil could send delegates whether or not it had registered with the PRM and the Agrarian Department. Those without PRM credentials needed proof that a recognized league had elected them as delegates, and any town without a recognized women's organization could send one delegate who would have speaking but not voting privileges during the sessions. The congress's agenda reflected the ruling party's priorities — defusing an "armed movement" in Mexico, combating inflation, and promoting women's organizing — and its outreach efforts demonstrated its aspiration to get new groups behind it.

The ruling party's reorganization encouraged heterodox conceptions of citizenship, weaving together notions of liberal rights and popular mobilization. Women from a broad array of organizations throughout the country exploited the changing political climate to assert themselves in civic matters without pursuing electoral channels. The Unifying Group of Women in Tampico, Tamaulipas, for example, tapped into both old and new political practices, bolstering its legitimacy not only by affirming its loyalty to the PRM but also by pledging to form a women's guard to protect Cárdenas during his travels.[130] Thus, the organization invoked the citizenship markers of armed service, party loyalty, and willingness to cooperate with emergent bureaucratic structures. Having established its credentials as a "revolutionary" organization, the group submitted a typical list of requests for sewing machines, potable water, first-aid kits, more teaching staff, and recreational equipment. The group's strategy apparently met with success; within two months, a member of Cárdenas's staff had attended to all its requests, forwarding them to the appropriate government agencies.

The women in the northern mining community of Sierra Mojada, Coahuila, took a more legalistic approach, citing their constitutional rights to form associations and to petition the government. Indicating that their male family members spent most of their time in the mines "searching for sustenance," the Women's Club convened in the miners' union hall to organize against a decree moving the seat of municipal government from Sierra Mojada to nearby Esmeralda. Explaining that the "disposition of the government was not made known to the Pueblo" and that "with this change the Pueblo loses its history, and its downfall will be definite," the members pledged that "complying with the sacred duty of insuring that a pueblo not be annihilated that has a right to live through its past, we will not rest until we have realized our desires."[131] Although local authorities had refused to recognize their organization, club members protested, "Our group is completely legal and nobody can discredit it without blatantly mocking Article 9 of the General Constitution." They requested a copy of the Ligas Femeniles organizing statutes "so that we can adopt those that pertain to our interests, which we would do well to defend in these moments of general evolution in our country."

Two years later, in the throes of the presidential campaign, the Sierra Mojada women renewed their constitutional appeals, now in the interest of political peace. Describing women as "apolitical as long as they have not been conceded the right to vote," club members protested the violence between partisans of the opposing presidential candidates Avila Camacho and Almazán.[132] "Is it not possible to guarantee human life and also the free and frank popular expression?" they inquired plaintively. "Will Mexico always debate in this horrendous chaos and will 'effective suffrage' be the mockery of those who fought for its implementation?" Though they acknowledged the impossibility of eliminating illegal and immoral "subterfuge" from politics, they maintained that Mexico could not become a constitutional republic so long as "blood spilled by one or another band has filled many homes in this country with grief, and that blood requests and demands justice."[133]

Other seasoned activists created organizations meant to pull the PRM in specific directions. Elvia Carrillo Puerto created the Women's Sector of the Mexican Revolutionary Front.[134] Indicating that "the government is in the hands of the appropriately prepared working classes," she advocated "the tactics of revolutionary syndicalism" including "public demonstrations, meetings, boycotts, strikes, etc." In addition to more commonplace advocacy of education, "de-fanaticization," and production cooperatives, the program also called for ending the "white slave trade," improving education about divorce laws as the "safeguard of dignity and honor," and establishing birth-control clinics to "avoid the procedure that puts a woman's life in danger to sacrifice the product of conception."[135]

While many saw advantages in joining the PRM, others resisted the party's advances. Carmen Aguilar, secretary-general of the Latin American Agrarista Women (which adopted the mischievous acronym MALA), concentrated her energies on securing land rights for peasants, especially campesinas, and maintained a cordial but distant relationship with government officials.[136] She often voiced disagreements with Agrarian Department policies, particularly the exclusion of unmarried women from the ejidal censuses. By October 1938, she had agreed to lead the Organizing Committee for Women's Unification, which established women's organizing leagues and nominated members to the PRM's secretariat of women's affairs. Although Aguilar's efforts ultimately bolstered the party's power, she remained wary of its intervention. When she communicated with Cárdenas about the project, she insisted "with all due respect" that the PRM not interfere in any way in the committee's formation or functioning.

The Ligas Femeniles de Lucha Social, using the organizing pamphlet produced in the Comarca Lagunera, already deployed this heterodox revolutionary citizenship.[137] Having expressed loyalty by forming a league, members demanded the promised "benefits of the revolution." A Querétaro league, for example, requested a sewing machine, a school, potable water, and a coveted corn mill. In exchange, the women promised to make their children attend school, keep their homes clean, prevent their compañeros from getting drunk, and fight against all vices in the region.[138] In short, they would implement the Cardenista social-reform agenda in exchange for labor-saving devices and community services.

A San Luis Potosí league underscored that Cárdenas's support distinguished his government as more revolutionary than its predecessors by "attending to the needs of all people." The league explained, "The past authorities never heard our complaints, and we found ourselves abandoned to a lethargy in which they never extended a compassionate gaze toward us but, rather, made us bear the heaviest yoke, which the other class could not support. The hardest task we embraced with affection."[139] Highlighting its sense of entitlement, the league requested a corn mill, a sewing machine, and four irons to establish a cooperative, asserting that it would serve "the collective benefit and future generation, who are our daughters. Thus we will honor your word that our race will be civilized through justice and not through charity. What we ask for is justice, Ciudadano Presidente, and we want the objects that we mentioned because we have a right to them, so long as we seek economic and social improvement." The Potosinas thus framed revolutionary citizenship as securing "justice" for the sake of "economic and social improvement" rather than political rights.

Women's efforts to assert influence in public matters often brought them into direct conflict with the men in their communities. A league on the outskirts of Saltillo, the Coahuilan capital, requested the removal of an auxiliary judge, whom the league described as obstructing school operations, fomenting vice, and neglecting his duties. The letter, signed by twenty-two ejidatarias, offered a list of three men they considered suitable for the position. Two weeks later, the same league wrote "in mass protest" because the ejido's governing committee had not followed proper electoral procedures and had ignored the league's recommendations. "Now, Señor Presidente," the league, clearly exasperated, addressed the municipal president, "the members who form the Liga Femenil here want to know if there are guarantees for organized women or not, because with great difficulty we have found ourselves obligated to protest against the judge for permitting so many scandals and for not giving guarantees. . . . The Ejidatarios tell us that we have neither voice nor vote and only they are entitled to add and remove candidates." Objecting that they found it "shameful and degrading" to have the "lowest and most poorly educated" as the judge, they described the ejidal committee's candidate as "not a person to whom this charge should be given for the simple fact of his not fulfilling his duties as father."[140] The members clearly expected full citizenship rights of "voice and vote" and the power to "add and remove candidates," deriving them not from a liberal conception of citizenship but, instead, from "guarantees for organized women."

In a poignant example of confusion over these ambiguous citizenship rights, a Sonoran league addressed both Cárdenas and his wife, requesting their endorsement with the local ejidal committee. "Because without [the committee's] support," the letter explained, "we cannot fulfill the role assigned to us, and we cannot arrange anything. . . . While you assigned us our duties in the statutes, we ask that you give us guarantees so that we can fulfill that obligation." On several occasions, the league's officers explained, they had arranged meetings with government agencies, but the ejidal commissioners went by themselves, "leaving us waiting and ready to attend; we do not know where these difficulties come from that they keep presenting to us."[141]

At other times, less direct conflicts centered on the leagues' organizing tactics or the demands they placed on their members. When a league was founded in Fraile, Guerrero, the ejidatario Aurelio Hernández commented that he had opposed it; when the Agrarian Department's representative established the league, Hernández said, he "did not offer an ample enough explanation of the league's aims but, rather, wanted to form it in a brusque, rapid, imperialist manner, using vulgar words despite the presence of families in the assembly." Others echoed Hernández's views, arguing that the Agrarian Department's agent had "disoriented and disorganized" the community members. Under the local schoolteacher's leadership, however, forty-two women enthusiastically joined the reestablished Liga Femenil.[142]

Despite assurances that the leagues reinforced women's domestic duties, men such as the Veracruz ejidatario José Herrera expressed concern that the size of his family created a great deal of work for his wife, and he asked to strike her name from the membership rolls, excusing her from attending meetings. Another ejidatario responded that most women shared similar circumstances, and exempting Herrera's wife from the meetings would open the way for many more requests for special dispensation. The assembled community members concluded that they would accept no renunciations and that women could obtain individual excuses to skip meetings.[143] Although the statutes stated that members must express a desire to belong to the league, this brief exchange indicates that membership became only nominally voluntary, as Agrarian Department agents apparently saw the leagues as a command performance, much like the official labor unions and peasant organizations. The documents do not reveal whether Herrera's wife (whose name never appears in the minutes) actually attended the meetings or even wanted to attend them. Strikingly, the minutes include no women's voices. The ejidal committee president, the only other person recorded, thanked the outgoing officers for demonstrating "sufficient calm in their proceedings" and offered the new governing board his help and guidance. In other words, this public transcript recorded only men debating how women should negotiate between the demands of the paternalist state and those of the patriarchal household.[144]

The Limits of the Popular Front

Lacking formal political rights, women activists leaned heavily on patronage connections and corporatist politics to achieve their aims. For Communist militants, patronage meant retaining legitimacy within the PCM as well as with state agencies and local political brokers. Falling in with the PCM's "Unity at Any Cost" strategy, the FUPDM's February 1938 congress issued a resolution declaring, "Unification is of the highest importance. . . . [It] is the solution to our needs."[145] With each step the suffrage bill took toward passage and each overture the Cárdenas administration made to give organized women a voice in decision making, FUPDM leaders increasingly shifted their strategy from militant demonstrations and hunger strikes to establishing themselves as responsible, reasonable political actors who worked within the official channels. They seemed certain that they needed only to prove their loyalty to gain their long-sought-after political rights. Much like the embarrassing reversal that had subordinated the PCM to the CTM leadership in June 1937, the FUPDM's decision to pursue unification within the PRM tied its hands, preventing it from posing the credible challenge to the regime that remained necessary to force the suffrage amendment's passage.

The Popular Front showed signs of strain as Communist women became frustrated by the alliance's limitations. In different settings throughout the republic, the PCM–PRM cooperation frayed around the edges as activists competed over resources, jurisdiction, and organizational control. Soon after its October 1936 founding, for example, the FUPDM proudly inaugurated the Maternidad Primero de Mayo (May Day Maternity Clinic) in Mexico City, offering working-class women services from prenatal care to pediatric clinics and nutritional counseling. Under the leadership of Cuca García and a fellow PCM militant, Dr. Concha Palacios, the clinic encountered obstacles almost immediately after opening its doors. A court order mandated that the clinic relinquish its building to the Catholic church — a practice that became increasingly common as the Cárdenas administration sought to preserve the church-state détente by restoring church land expropriated during the maximato.[146] Palacios, warning that the clinic would soon be unable to feed inpatients, repeatedly addressed Cárdenas and the secretaries of treasury and welfare to secure the promised 4,000 peso-per-month subsidy. The government's own inspector offered a generally positive report but expressed concern about the clinic's lack of resources.

In November 1938, the clinic shut down for lack of funds. It temporarily reopened the following January when Múgica, presidential hopeful and Cárdenas's secretary of communications and public works, provided funding from his own resources to pay the clinic's debts and back salaries. But at the end of the month García sent a terse telegram to Cárdenas saying, "The month is ending. Maternidad completely filled with the sick. Subsidy detained at Treasury. Economic situation desperate. We implore you to order immediate payment." Meanwhile, the FUPDM expelled three members from its Mexico City chapter because of "disloyalty" and "indiscipline" with regard to the clinic.[147] García mobilized support from groups as diverse as the predominantly communist railroad workers' union and the elite-oriented UMA.

Driven to desperation, she wrote to Cárdenas in early March threatening a hunger strike if he would not meet with Maternidad representatives. That same day, Cárdenas received a confidential report commissioned by his office enumerating the clinic's appalling conditions, concluding that "having retired several employees, suspended the ambulance services, cut off the phone, and turned down the heat, the situation of said establishment has worsened to the point that the budget covers only the barest necessities." The staff, facing imminent unemployment, pleaded with Cárdenas, apparently shifting the blame to García herself. "Deceiving and pressuring workers of the 'Maternidad Primero de Mayo,'" a group of nurses wrote to Cárdenas in early July, "Sra. Refugio García obliged us to resign from our jobs. Those who would not resign she dragged into the streets saying that the subsidy had been sent to buy military equipment for the army. We courteously beg you to tell us what you have done in this respect; hunger obliges us to take defensive measures." Palacios attempted to support the clinic out of pocket, receiving assurances that the Welfare Ministry would reimburse her. Palacios was never repaid, and at the end of 1940, as Avila

Camacho assumed the presidency, the Maternidad Primero de Mayo finally closed its doors for good.

The events surrounding the Maternidad Primero de Mayo reflect several larger trends during this period. García's mobilization of a broad range of supporters typified the Popular Front strategy. The roller-coaster ride of state support followed the general curve of Cardenista politics, with radicalism peaking in 1938 and then retreating through the end of his term, when he appointed Avila Camacho rather than his mentor, the radical elder statesman Múgica, as the PRM's candidate for the 1940 presidential elections. This anecdote also underscores the limitations of paternalist rather than entitlement-based welfare practices, with the clinic's founders pleading with various patriarchal figures, such as Múgica and Cárdenas, for relatively modest funds. Múgica's interest in subsidizing the clinic apparently faded once he had withdrawn his presidential candidacy. In the absence of both formal political rights and a sufficiently mobilized organization, the FUPDM retained little leverage. Finally, García's heated outburst and frustrated comment about diverting funds for social spending to "buy military equipment for the army" reveals the enduring strain between the PCM and the postrevolutionary regime.

In addition to competing for scarce resources, the FUPDM struggled with the PRM over jurisdictional issues. In August 1938, the Communist activist and FUPDM officer Esthela Jiménez Esponda wrote to Cárdenas that the front had "succeeded in controlling the majority of peasant women [in the western state of Nayarit], counting no fewer than 70 to 75 Ligas Femeniles in the state," including one in the village of Heriberto Casas.[148] That league had utilized all the appropriate channels to acquire a corn mill, but the Agrarian Department representative informed its members that neither the National Ejidal Credit Bank nor the Agrarian Department could help them unless their league changed its affiliation from the FUPDM to the Agrarian Department. Accordingly, league members set about establishing a new organization affiliated with the Agrarian Department. Outraged that a branch of the state party would undermine the FUPDM's efforts, Jiménez Esponda reminded Cárdenas that one of the PRM's guiding tenets specifically forbade competing party-affiliated organizations. She candidly informed the president that allowing such behavior would "remain a damaging precedent by the Department, which is on a higher level than us and, as an official dependency, counts on greater economic resources, while our organization relies only on the reduced dues of the unionists and the efforts and sacrifices of the same."[149]

Underscoring that the FUPDM had "always openly supported your frank and progressive policies and endeavored to avoid any conflicts with your government's dependencies," she reminded Cárdenas that he had promised that front members would remain "absolutely at liberty to affiliate with whomever they wanted" and that, "in order to avoid conflict with the Agrarian Department, the front should not organize where [the Agrarian Department] organized, understanding that the Agrarian Department remained subject to the same conditions. That is to say, not to organize where we were already organized. But this case demonstrates the reverse." The National Ejidal Credit Bank maintained that it never interfered with the Ligas Femeniles "except in special cases" and had no knowledge of the case. No new league registration exists for Heriberto Casas for the remainder of the Cárdenas presidency, implying that the FUPDM retained control. Indeed, the FUPDM remained relatively strong in Nayarit, and the state's women continued to form Ligas Femeniles Pro-Derechos de la Mujer even after the FUPDM had dissolved, implying that the front's influence endured in the region.[150]

This exchange illuminates more than territorial conflict between the two primary secular institutions organizing women during the Cárdenas period. First, it reveals that pragmatic gains such as corn mills justified changing allegiances. Given the choice between an organization that promised suffrage and one that promised a corn mill, the Heriberto Casas women opted for the corn mill. Second, the divvying up of organizing tasks and the pledge of noninterference indicates early FUPDM suspicion. Jiménez Esponda candidly pointed out the inequality of resources and called on Cárdenas and his party to intervene on behalf of the underdog. The PRM justified its existence, after all, by committing to even out conflicts between unequal parties — workers and employers, peasants and landowners, women and men. The FUPDM's complaints, however, raised the troubling question of how the party would act when it was one of the unequal parties. Jiménez Esponda invoked the PRM's own ethos, calling on Cárdenas to protect the front's right to organize and mobilize women, as well as the right of women themselves to affiliate with whomever they preferred without the state threatening to withdraw its support.

Finally, Jiménez Esponda's appeal demonstrates an enduring clientelism that characterized corporatist citizenship. She pointed out to Cárdenas that the FUPDM had always supported his regime and in exchange asked for the paternalist shelter of the PRM — ironically, in this case, from one of its own branches. As in all patron-client relationships, the association between the FUPDM and the Cárdenas regime remained one of uneven reciprocity. Having committed itself to affiliating with the ruling party and to the PCM's "Unity at Any Cost" campaign, an attack on the ruling party would undermine not only the project in which the FUPDM had so recently invested itself but also its legitimacy within the PCM. A few months after this conflict, Jímenez Esponda published a column in the ruling-party newspaper reiterating the importance of organizing within the PRM's ranks, insisting that "it is impossible to speak of the complete liberation of the Mexican people if that liberation does not reach the great masses of women, and we cannot imagine the Revolution's decisive triumph if it does not draw in the feminine masses."[151]

Conflicts such as those over the Maternidad Primero de Mayo and the Heriberto Casas women's league highlight a persistent tension over the FUPDM's role within the PRM. While some clearly continued to view it as a membership-driven organization, others understood it as more of a bureaucratic entity within the new party structure. Monterrey, Nuevo León, and its environs had a strong and diverse tradition of secular women's organizations, from those advocating feminine domesticity to liberal clubs, a women's meat-packing union, and the Women's Center for Proletarian Action.[152] In addition to active PCM affiliates, national organizations such as the National Women's League, Women's Civic Action, and the FUPDM all had Monterrey chapters, along with the Feminist Revolutionary Party, which doubled as the PNR state women's committee.[153] The Ligas Femeniles de Lucha Social existed in the rural areas outside the industrial city.[154] In his famous 1936 "Fourteen Points" speech marking his administration's leftward turn, Cárdenas particularly "applaud[ed] the attitude of Monterrey women who, like the teachers, mix with workers and peasants . . . because women should be ever attentive, as they already are, to back the laboring classes in their aspirations for social improvement."[155] Cárdenas's praise revealed the continued tension between the charitable and mobilizational strains of women's activism as well as his conviction that women and "laboring classes" remained separate categories.

In November 1938, seven Monterrey women started a new FUPDM chapter, explaining to Cárdenas and Cuca García that a chapter did not really exist there.[156] They admitted that García probably believed that one existed under the leadership of Severa L. de Canseco, a local organizer of the Feminist Revolutionary Party, formed after the combative 1931 national women's congress. However, they elaborated, the chapter never held meetings because it could not achieve a quorum. While the situation appeared not to trouble Canseco, who had participated in PNR organizing and charity work in Monterrey since at least 1934, a handful of FUPDM members saw a lost opportunity. Marina R. de Zapata, leading a breakaway group, envisioned a more participatory organization and recommended biweekly meetings, to which each member would bring seven compañeras until they formed a critical mass. With such an organization, the leadership argued, they could offer assistance and create opportunities for Monterrey's hundreds of unemployed women by establishing production cooperatives and lobbying functionaries and factory owners to hire more women.

Zapata's vision for the organization apparently won out, gaining accreditation from García and Cárdenas as an FUPDM-affiliated Liga Femenil de Lucha Social. Its projects focused on community organizing and helping women to navigate the bureaucracy of retirement, insurance, and veterans' benefits, but its members also committed themselves to "struggle diligently for the conquest of the economic, social, and political rights of woman," an objective that distinguished it from the Agrarian Department's Ligas Femeniles de Lucha Social but fell short of the more specific, aggressive agenda that the FUPDM had pursued a year earlier. Further, the group's official status hardly guaranteed support, as requests for pecuniary aid repeatedly met with elusive responses about budgetary constraints.

Questions about whether one accrued citizenship rights through status (e.g., sex, property ownership, or literacy), activities (e.g., labor, military service, or community activism), or affiliation (with a party, union, or official organization) remained in play throughout the postrevolutionary decades. Women's citizenship status remained ambiguous as policymakers deliberated the conditions under which they might claim the title of ciudadana. Jury duty and military service, common markers of citizenship, remained unavailable to women. Throughout the 1930s, discussions continued about not only suffrage but also women's nationality if they married foreigners and lived abroad. As late as 1944, a woman appealed to the Supreme Court to secure work as a notary, a public office that required citizenship. In a 3–2 vote, the court ruled that restrictions on women's citizenship applied only to her political rights and not to her "social, civic, or professional rights."[157]

For most Mexican women, however, these formal markers of citizenship had little bearing on the contingent, inhabited, and gendered ways in which they practiced revolutionary citizenship. While the urban suffrage movement created leverage for women's organizations, forcing political leaders to consider how to secure women's allegiance, most women—even activist women—practiced revolutionary citizenship far from the voting booth. Neither apathetic about political rights—expressing outrage when they were denied "voice and vote" in union or ejidal meetings—nor, by and large, ignorant of suffrage efforts, most women viewed the "benefits of the revolution" more as alleviated labor burdens and improved social services than as "Effective Suffrage and No Reelection." Women regularly insisted on this citizenship, however, transgressing both codified and customary boundaries to claim their revolutionary entitlements.

The PRM gave political rights new meaning by weaving together practices of traditional patronage, liberal citizenship, and revolutionary mobilization. While the party sought to discipline the practice of revolutionary citizenship, it also contributed to the expectation of entitlements. As PCM organizers urged women to join the ruling party and support the "Unity at Any Cost" strategy, official organizations took on increased importance as the loci for political engagement. At the same time, space for dissenting visions both within and outside these organizations all but vanished. With the approaching presidential elections and the mounting strength of the Almazán campaign, Cardenistas seemed to lose faith in the suffrage agenda. The decision—or inaction, in this case—appears more political than ideological, given the organized left's consistent support for women's suffrage. But by 1940, the political landscape looked less certain than it had in 1938, when Congress had first approved the amendment. Despite the suffragists' powerful patrons, they learned the lesson that the Yucatecan experience had driven home quite forcefully: the value of patronage remains contingent on which direction the political winds blow.

SIX

"All Are Avowed Socialists":

Political Conflict and Women's

Organizing in Yucatán

If women's organizing in Michoacán bore the marks of the Cristero Rebellion and in the Comarca Lagunera reflected the region's labor mobilizations,
their counterpart in the southeastern state of Yucatán just as surely reflected
its local political tumult. Yucatán had elements in common with the other two
cases. It displayed the ethnic pluralism and pronounced folk Catholicism of
Michoacán, although the former was more evident and the latter less so in
Yucatán than in contemporary Michoacán. It also shared with Michoacán the
legacy of a radical postrevolutionary political leadership during the 1920s,
which in both cases fostered strong ties between the state governments and
popular organizing structures. As it did in both Michoacán and the Comarca
Lagunera, the Mexican Communist Party (PCM) had a strong presence in
Yucatán. Much like the Comarca Lagunera, Yucatán's economy rested largely
on the production of a single agricultural commodity—in Yucatán's case,
henequen, a fibrous plant that yielded a strong binder twine. Not surprisingly, the two regions had similarly heated battles over agrarian reform.

However, the extent of political turmoil at the level of state politics during the 1930s set Yucatán apart. Cárdenas's six-year presidential administration overlapped with the terms of four different Yucatán governors.[1] When
Cárdenas assumed the presidency, César Alayola Barrera (February 1934–
October 1935) occupied the governor's mansion in Mérida. However, in

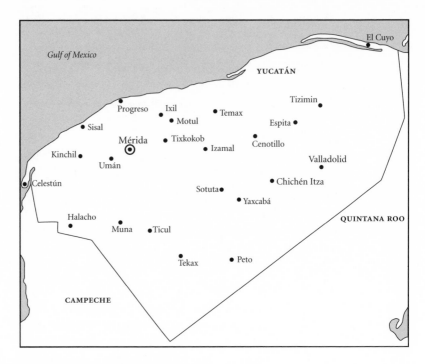

Map 4. "Yucatán." By Natalie Hanemann.

the wake of the Cárdenas–Calles confrontation, thousands of laborers protested in the streets of Mérida, purportedly in favor of Cardenismo and
against the local government, forcing Alayola Barrera into an indefinite leave
of absence and bringing Fernando López Cárdenas, Yucatán's secretary-
general, into the governor's office. One newspaper estimated that 20,000
workers and peasants filled the streets, and another described the protests as
a "soviet in Yucatán."[2] López Cárdenas (October 1935–June 1936), implemented Cardenista practices, building alliances with PCM leaders and Popular Front activists. Two Communist organizers in Yucatán assumed important positions in the López Cárdenas administration: Antonio Betancourt
Pérez became the director of public education, and the charismatic activist
Rogerio Chalé became the president of the state's Socialist Party of the
Southeast (PSS).

In July 1936, following another general strike and violent confrontation
before Mérida's palace of government, López Cárdenas took a leave of absence and was replaced by Florencio Palomo Valencia (July 1936–January
1938), who oversaw the August 1937 agrarian-reform project and presided

over the return to a more settled, party machine–based politics. He reached a compromise with the Cárdenas government that allowed for continued regional political autonomy in exchange for the implementation of Cárdenas's agrarian reform. Palomo Valencia's successor, Humberto Canto Echeverría (February 1938–January 1942), had not enjoyed Cárdenas's support during his campaign and assumed office amid a floundering agrarian-reform project. In March 1938, the same month as the creation of the Party of the Mexican Revolution (PRM) and the nationalization of the petroleum industry, Canto Echeverría convinced Cárdenas to return the administration of Yucatán's land reform to the state government, creating the "Great Ejido," run by a joint commission of old hacendados and new ejidatarios and paving the way for the reprivatization of henequen land and machinery.

Widespread labor unrest and popular mobilizations as well as shifts in political climate generally accompanied the turnover in gubernatorial administrations. Although often top-heavy and manipulative, the state's popular organizations cultivated a mobilizational infrastructure. Yucatecan political leaders and activists, like their counterparts elsewhere, often utilized worker and peasant organizations for political leverage but also had to make good on their promises or risk losing legitimacy, and popular groups could influence state and local politics by demonstrating their ability to organize and mobilize substantial portions of their communities. In this way, competing political factions nurtured a propitious environment for popular organizing. The Cuban Communist Ofelia Domínguez Navarro described warm support from Bartolomé García Correa and the Yucatecan left during her 1933 exile, participating in lively gatherings at Mérida's Casa del Pueblo.[3] And characterizing Yucatán's political leaders, the U.S. consul in Progreso explained, "Whether sincere or not, all are avowed socialists, and the appearance of maintaining the rights of the working man against the oppression of capitalism must be maintained at all costs."[4]

The Yucatán peninsula, of which the state makes up a wedge-shaped third, juts out into the Gulf of Mexico, stretching toward Cuba. From the latter part of the nineteenth century through the 1930s, Yucatán's economy depended largely on the cultivation and processing of henequen.[5] Mayan laborers, many of them bound to estates through debt peonage, performed the arduous seasonal labor of henequen production. As in the Comarca Lagunera, these highly exploitative, semifeudal labor relations remained intact until after the revolution, although they came under attack first during the gubernatorial administrations of Salvador Alvarado (1915–18) and

Felipe Carrillo Puerto (1922–24), and again during the presidency of Lázaro Cárdenas.[6]

The henequen plantation system had a complicated effect on regional ethnic identities. The isolation of Maya communities in the henequen zone bolstered their sense of community identity, but plantation owners, as the historians Allen Wells and Gilbert Joseph have argued, "effectively reinvented the prevailing terms of regional ethnicity."[7] They became known as mestizos, or hispanicized Indians, although plantation owners referred to them as "*indios*." Indeed, most whites and mestizos also spoke some Maya, and Yucatán effectively functioned as a bilingual state. Felipe Carrillo Puerto, for example, spoke fluent Maya. Much like the bilingual, cross-cultural activists in Michoacán, the most successful activists and organizers in Yucatán spoke both Spanish and Maya.[8] Yucatán's impressive cultural duality posed a challenge to Mexico City centralizers seeking to construct a national identity that bridged ethnic, class, and gender differences. The bloody 1847 Caste War left a legacy of ethnic separatism and fears of interethnic violence that persisted through the 1930s.[9] Even as Cárdenas celebrated indigenous cultures and folded indigenous identities into an all-encompassing mexicanidad, he brandished the threat of another Caste War to justify his hasty and ambitious agrarian-reform program.[10]

Yucatán had a historically conflicted relationship with Mexico City. Indeed, twice during the first half of the nineteenth century, regional political leaders threatened to secede from the young republic.[11] While disasters such as the Caste War and periodic henequen-price collapses generally convinced Yucatecan elites to stop short of demanding complete independence, their ambivalence about Mexico City's interference in local affairs persisted. Even as political leaders held aloft the Cardenista banner, they often played off local and federal rivalries, exploiting both Yucatecan separatism and Cardenista populism.[12]

Yucatán's volatile political climate, historically complex relationship with Mexico City, and history of feminist organizing shaped regional women's activism and conceptions of revolutionary citizenship. As in Michoacán, the strength of women's organizing fluctuated along with the continually disputed relationship between the Cárdenas administration and Yucatán's state government. As the federal government ceded more state autonomy, the legitimacy and leverage of nationally affiliated women's organizations flagged. Finally, when Cárdenas left office and support for the Popular Front gave way to widespread anticommunism, many women activists lost their patronage links to Mexico City. Those organizations that endured these transitions often boasted a broad membership base and a multigenerational leadership that allowed them to weather political change. But while the Yucatecan women's movement did not vanish after 1940, women emerged from the 1930s with fewer rights and less political leverage than they had enjoyed in the early 1920s.

"Without Painful Distinctions of Sex": Organizing in the Cradle of Mexican Feminism

Yucatán's 1916 feminist congresses established Mérida as a focal point for women's activism.[13] Organizing efforts intensified during the Carrillo Puerto administration, which revitalized the PSS and turned sharply left, including with regard to women's rights. Carrillo Puerto's approach to women's organizing reflected his larger political program of building local popular support. While Alvarado had enlisted Hermila Galindo to give the provocative and divisive keynote address at the 1916 First Feminist Congress, Carrillo Puerto cultivated leading activists within Yucatán. He proposed an amendment permitting women to hold state and municipal offices, allowing the feminist congress participant Rosa Torres to gain a seat on Mérida's ayuntamiento in 1923, becoming the first Mexican woman to hold elective office.[14] Furthermore, the PSS slate for state legislature included three women candidates and one woman alternate.

Several scholars have attributed Carrillo Puerto's progressive record on women's rights to the influence of his younger sister Elvia.[15] A "modern" woman, Elvia Carrillo Puerto had been married, widowed, remarried, and divorced. She worked as a schoolteacher and, in 1912, founded Yucatán's first Rural Feminist Women's League. During the Alvarado administration, she organized Feminist-Socialist Resistance Leagues, the precursors to the women's leagues organized during her brother's administration.[16] She and her brother apparently agreed in their support for contraception. The Feminist Leagues, the Resistance Leagues' women's cells during the Carrillo Puerto government, organized around common women's issues—public education, temperance, and hygiene—with the addition of advocating contraception and defending prostitutes' rights while seeking to eliminate the poverty that drove prostitution.[17] In February 1922, Felipe Carrillo Puerto ordered the publication and distribution of one of Margaret Sanger's pamphlets on birth control.[18] Elvia Carrillo Puerto's controversial appearance at the 1923 Panamerican Women's Congress brought her into contact with like-minded women, including militants of the recently founded PCM, Cuca García and Elena Torres, but also exposed her differences with fellow feminists. Although she abandoned Yucatán—and her elected position in the Mérida town council—after her brother's assassination at the hands of Delahuertista counterrevolutionaries in January 1924, she remained politically active.[19]

Felipe Carrillo Puerto's assassination signaled the rolling back of many progressive policies, including expanded political rights for and organizing efforts among women. The new state government promptly replaced the women who occupied state and municipal posts. Still, Carrillo Puerto's patronage and women's activism of the 1910s and '20s had left a legacy. When Governor García Correa (1930–33) took office, he quickly sought the Yucatecan medical community's opinion on regulating prostitution, an issue Elvia Carrillo Puerto and her allies had foregrounded.[20] Girls and young women also had a stronger presence in Yucatecan student organizations than they had in their counterparts elsewhere in the republic.[21] The PSS—now an affiliate of the National Revolutionary Party (PNR), operating as a state-level organizing structure analogous to the Revolutionary Labor Confederation of Michoacán (CRMDT)—revived the party's Mothers' Clubs, a more feminine and less disruptive version of the Feminist Leagues, and the party magazine published articles about infant health care alongside stories about Japanese women's struggle for political rights.[22] The Mothers' Clubs offered women a forum to air grievances, but they also provided the local and national governments with a means to communicate with local populations. When the secretary of industry in Mexico City decided to mobilize women behind a national temperance campaign encouraging worker productivity and reliability, the effort set off a chain of responses through state and federal agencies that, in Yucatán, led to the state government working through the PSS Mothers' Clubs.[23]

The PSS favored efforts targeting workingwomen and, like the PCM, emphasized gender equality rather than maternal abnegation and feminine morality. Its code included explicitly gender-inclusive language, a demand for wage parity, and a commitment to promote temperance and fight prostitution. The "Norms of Socialist Morality" pledged to "inculcate respect and consideration for women," adding that men should consider women their "collaborators in humane and just efforts for the good of the people in general, without painful distinctions of sex" rather than as "weak and incapable, as they were under the evil and selfish men who formerly led societies."[24]

The party's rhetorical commitment provided a foothold for women activists. In a case that bore a striking resemblance to that of Morelia's El Globo stocking factory, the women of the foreign-owned Liberty stocking factory in Progreso denounced their dismissal without indemnification. Invoking the "grandiose constitutional law that the revolution bequeathed us," the workers protested to García Correa about the PSS lawyers' unresponsiveness to their plight. Describing his government as "a socialist Government emerging from the people and for the people," they entreated him to intervene on their behalf, explaining that "workers' rights should never be neglected by foreign capitalists who, after exploiting the country's laborers, remove themselves from our native soil."[25]

Much as the CRMDT had in Michoacán, the PSS and its Resistance Leagues mediated matters related to welfare and social services. The party created child-welfare centers and maternity clinics — services of critical importance to workingwomen — and provided women (and men) with vocational training and primary education, support for cooperatives, and legal support to defend land and labor rights.[26] Unaffiliated organizations also turned to the state for welfare support, but those that did not seek government approval often encountered uncooperative bureaucrats who hindered their efforts.[27] For organizations with limited resources, obstruction or just the lack of an official endorsement generally meant the failure of the enterprise in question.

The García Correa government deployed myriad tactics to constrain women's revolutionary citizenship. Even matters that elsewhere had become women's province — issues such as community sanitation, education, public health, and patriotic festivals — in early 1930s Yucatán remained under the control of all-male town councils or Resistance Leagues.[28] Furthermore, the state government mediated women's representative efforts by appointing or approving nominations of delegations to local and national congresses. Citing budget constraints, the governor declined to send anyone to the 1934 PNR-sponsored Third National Congress of Women Workers and Peasants in Guadalajara.[29] In lobbying for different candidates, advocates pointed to a woman's service as a teacher or activist, often emphasizing participation in early organizing efforts under the Carrillo Puerto government, but under García Correa, women activists appeared to have exhausted Yucatán's feminist inheritance.[30]

"The Terrain of Revolutionary Conquests":
Cardenismo Comes to Yucatán

By the mid-1930s, the combined forces of Popular Front efforts and centralizing Cardenismo rekindled women's organizing in Yucatán. As elsewhere, socialist education played an important role as federally employed schoolteachers spread into the Yucatecan countryside with missionary zeal. Teachers, social workers, and organizers from the Secretariat of Public Education's Cultural Missions program implemented sanitation and nutrition programs in the hopes of Mexicanizing the region's Maya population.[31] Teachers had formed the backbone of women's organizing efforts in Yucatán (and elsewhere) since the Porfiriato, but the national education agenda increased resources and renewed legitimacy for their efforts. The state's public-education department asserted that socialist education formed the foundation of women's social and political emancipation, and teachers emphasized the importance of coeducation.[32] Women who encountered opposition from either community members or educational administrators could turn to the state and federal governments for reinforcement, arguing that they promoted the revolutionary principles of socialist education.[33]

Furthermore, teaching offered educated women administrative sinecures with job security and regular salaries, encouraging them to promote the priorities of the state government and Education Ministry.[34] Yucatán's most prominent and enduring women activists — women such as Elvia Carrillo Puerto, Mercedes Betancourt de Albertos, Concepción L. Sabido, and Ana Bravo Gómez — worked as teachers or education inspectors. Although these women proved as adept as any man in securing salaries through the state government, the PNR, or the PSS, this patronage occurred within gender-informed relationships. Bravo Gómez, for example, appealed to the governor's "recognized chivalrousness" to preserve her job directing a Mérida normal school.[35]

However, even those women activists who explicitly advocated socialist education could find themselves under fire from unexpected corners. As the Acapulco case demonstrated, competition over legitimacy and resources precipitated bitter disputes. Yucatán's Radical Revolutionary Women's Bloc, for example, proudly informed the governor of its November 1934 founding and enumerated its objectives, all of which seemed uncontroversial from the perspective of the postrevolutionary regime: a temperance campaign, "anti-fanaticism" efforts, the establishment of socialist education programs, and "women's emancipation." A subsequent letter explicitly endorsed the governor's administration, especially its temperance efforts. However, not two weeks later the group found itself accused in a Department of Public Education meeting of existing only to collect dues and of threatening those who refused to join the bloc. The accuser, the schools inspector Vicente Gamboa, encouraged all those present to join the Teachers' League and maintained that the Radical Revolutionary Women's Bloc should seek members who were not state teachers.[36]

In jockeying for patrons, however, the Radical Revolutionary Women's Bloc apparently won out. The following month, pss President José Baqueiro penned a personal note to the governor endorsing the bloc's efforts and requesting promotions for several officers, citing their "goodwill, enthusiasm, and struggle for the ideals of the Revolution."[37] Perhaps to shed the stigma of discord, its members reorganized in early 1936 under the name Women's Revolutionary Action of Yucatán, maintaining a PNR affiliation and offices in Mérida's pss-run Casa del Pueblo.[38] The group's balance of rights claims and missionary tone remained the same, calling anew for "the conquest of women's political and social rights, an anti-fanaticism effort, a temperance campaign, and the promotion of the peasantry's socialization."[39]

Women resisted anticlerical policies promoted by federally employed schoolteachers, much as they did in Michoacán (although without the backdrop of the Cristero Rebellion to make them seem quite so menacing). Literally thousands of women signed or put their thumbprints to letters and petitions to reopen churches.[40] Some protested that the state closed "spiritual centers" and "centers for psychic studies" that had been mistaken for churches (*templos*).[41] Others argued that closing the churches would cause damage due to the humidity.[42] Still others cited their constitutional rights to religious freedom. "Sir, return peace and tranquillity to the Catholic citizens," eighty-two women beseeched the governor, "delivering our Catholic temple, and if possible our priests, to our Parish. We respect the law that guarantees us the practice of our beliefs, which do not offend anyone."[43] Some faithful indicated that they grasped the postrevolutionary critique of the Catholic hierarchy, conceding that the revolution sought to cast off "the yoke of capitalism, which uses the clergy as its intermediary," but maintained that they only brought in a priest for special occasions.[44]

As in Michoacán, women's presumed fanaticism also bolstered the arguments of those advocating women's organizing. Teachers highlighted women's importance to integrating the regime's agenda into the social fabric. One schoolteacher, in an essay entitled "Women and Revolution," maintained that the clergy's focus on bringing women into the Catholic fold should serve as a model for revolutionary organizers.[45] "Since Religion looks to woman to enslave the man through her influence," he argued, "the Revolution must also go in search of her, to instruct her in its theories, to make her understand the great mission of the current moment, and to ask for her collaboration to eliminate that host of prejudices that ties man to antiquated and selfish patterns." The program he laid out reflects the assumptions and strategies not only of Cardenismo but also of many feminists. "Through woman," he asserted, "we should make the revolutionary doctrines reach the Mexican home. We should take advantage of her to transform the social structure based in capitalist and individualist principles, to make man understand his obligation to struggle for community, and that its well-being is his own well-being." He maintained that "the Revolution" should support feminist organizations so that "they can better contribute to forming a more just and less selfish humanity than we have now."

Another Yucatecan teacher submitted to the governor a poem entitled, "Do Not Kneel, Woman," exhorting Mexican women to defy the "manipulations" of the clergy.[46] His words echo the concerns that Primo Tapia had expressed to his comrades more than a decade earlier in Michoacán — that faithful women would unwittingly betray their agrarista husbands — as well as the belief among anticlerical policymakers that socialist education and "anti-fanaticism" campaigns would transform the way ordinary Mexicans, particularly women, viewed the church and its social role:

Si eres tú la fiel esposa	If you are the faithful spouse
de hombre Revolucionario,	Of a Revolutionary man,
nunca dejes tus secretos	Never leave your secrets
en ningún confesionario. . . .	In any confessional. . . .
Apoya en todos sus puntos	Support Socialist teaching
la enseñanza Socialista,	In every aspect.
que es la hermana salvadora	It is the redeeming sister
que a la lucha nos alista.	That prepares us for struggle.
Coopera con el Gobierno	Cooperate with the Government
de esta tierra soberana	Of this sovereign land,
y cumplirás la misión	And you will fulfill your mission
de la mujer mexicana. . . .	As a Mexican woman. . . .

Nunca tiembles al hablarle	Never tremble to speak
a ninguna autoridad,	Before any authority.
que es el siglo de las luces,	This is the century of lights
del amor y la lealtad.	Of love, and of loyalty.
Si tu patrón te maltrata	If your boss mistreats you
y llégase a herir tu pecho,	Or even wounds you deeply,
ve al Palacio de Gobierno	Go to the Palace of Government
a reclamar tu derecho. . . .	To demand your rights. . . .
¡Odiemos a los obispos!	We must hate the bishops!
A esos hombres de sotana,	Those men of the cassock
que ya no tienen cabida	Who now have no place
en la Nación Mexicana.	In the Mexican Nation.

Although both the poet and the essayist invoked a monolithic, gender-neutral "Revolution," they situated women simultaneously inside and outside of that construct by deploying manly images of the revolutionary husband and paternalist protector. They implored women to join the revolutionary ranks through interactions with the state — to "fulfill their mission" women should "cooperate with the Government" — and by turning their backs on the "men of the cassock." But they did not anticipate the "Revolution" changing as a result of women's participation. Women would come to the revolution, not the revolution to women.

Even more controversial than Cardenista anticlerical policies were its accelerated land-reform efforts.[47] As in the Comarca Lagunera, the production of a critical agricultural commodity in Yucatán — henequen — had deterred the postrevolutionary regime from engaging in significant agrarian reform. Also similar to the Laguna case, landowners and their government allies organized peones acasillados in opposition to agrarian-reform policies and conspired to institute preemptive but minimal land-reform measures to prevent more extensive expropriations. Reformers stressed that the ejido could impart independence, masculinity, and citizenship. "Now that you are breaking your chains, many cannot resign themselves to seeing you free and the owner of your own destiny," one ejido advocate cautioned, "because they understand that it brings to an end the riches they have amassed by your labor with the slavery that they had in past years. . . . [T]hey will feign to be your friends, advise you not to exercise the rights the agrarian laws grant you, because they want to prevent you from being free, from being a citizen, and from being a man with ambitions and with a future."[48] Thus, the agrarian-reform program appealed to an ideal of manly independence and an exclusive notion of citizenship.[49]

A clear divide between independent, masculine breadwinners and dependent, feminine protégées remained an imagined distinction in Yucatán, as it did elsewhere. Women worked as domestic servants and seamstresses, produced henequen crafts, ran small businesses, and performed other income-producing jobs that constituted a critical portion of their household budget. The popularity of vocational training for women and girls testifies to the importance of women's wages. When one night school opened in Mérida in 1935, offering classes in seamstressing, cooking, commercial mathematics, and applied geometry, it immediately enrolled one hundred students, "mostly señoras or señoritas of the working or laboring class."[50] Women organized separate, PSS-affiliated labor unions, claiming a revolutionary space for women and driving a wedge into the small opening that had developed for women's organizing. The Union of Women Workers and Peasants of Yucatán, for example, sought "the defense of women's interests and rights in [Yucatán], within the prerogatives conceded by law, seeking always to elevate women's moral and material level, placing her in the terrain of Revolutionary conquests."[51]

However, Yucatecan political leaders distinguished between the 1930s organizing efforts — of women's labor unions and PSS supporters — and the feminist campaigns of the 1910s and '20s. PSS President Baqueiro wrote to Governor Alayola Barrera about Elia María Abán, an elderly spinster who required state support, describing her as "an old fighter in the Socialist Party" who had formed a union "not of feminists but of campesinas and obreras."[52] While he viewed the latter as a crucial reinforcement of the post-revolutionary regime's national and state objectives, the former challenged its priorities and the most basic unit of social organization, the family. Such statements destabilize the standard assertion that concerns about women's political participation centered wholly on women's "fanaticism." While Baqueiro might have compared Abán's activities to any number of Catholic women's groups, he instead distinguished them from feminism, a movement with strong roots in Yucatán that consistently upheld anticlerical positions. Likewise, one Communist teacher underscored the distinction between Communist women's organizations of working-class and peasant women and "bourgeois" feminist organizations. "The former is just and the latter is not," he explained. "Man and woman are comrades rather than enemies in the social struggle."[53] Even in Yucatán—perhaps especially in Yucatán, with its feminist tradition—women activists struggled against the assumption that they pitted women and men against one another, subverting the class-defined structures of postrevolutionary political institutions.

The Kaleidoscope of Yucatecan Women's Organizing

Yucatán's political instability hampered the creation of a unified state women's movement. While both Michoacán and the Comarca Lagunera had heady conflicts over who controlled the political agenda, in both cases one popular organization—albeit often fragmented and self-destructive—succeeded in defining the terms of political engagement. In Michoacán, the organization had been the CRMDT (including its precursor, the Liga de Comunidades Agrarias, and its successor, the Mexican Labor Confederation [CTM]–National Peasant Confederation [CNC]), and in the Comarca Lagunera, the dominant institution for popular organizing had been the allied PCM-CTM. While both of these institutions excluded certain groups and distorted the aims of others, they also described a common political idiom. Women seeking political allies—whether comrades, patrons, or protectors—could more readily discern the political landscape.

In Yucatán, particularly in the years just prior to the August 1937 agrarian reform, the local political scene became exceedingly complicated. The PSS, while technically subordinated to the PNR, exerted independent political influence, and control over its agencies changed along with gubernatorial administrations, increasing the sense of political chaos. The PCM maintained a significant Yucatecan presence but with more uneven results than in the Comarca Lagunera; interunion struggles proliferated as PSS unions resisted joining the CTM. Agrarian reforms proceeded haphazardly, often leaving peasants worse off than before. Since the National Ejidal Credit Bank was a creditor rather than an employer (although the distinction would have seemed semantic to those who worked under the bank's regulations), it was exempt from federal labor laws mandating a daily minimum wage, advances, and one paid day off per week. Furthermore, agrarian reform excluded peones acasillados until 1937. Indeed, most hacendados and quite a few peasants agreed that the latter enjoyed more security, if considerably less autonomy, as employees of the henequen plantations. Dissatisfaction with agrarian reform, economic insecurity from the shaky henequen market, and continued uncertainty about the relationship between the state and federal governments fostered considerable political instability.

The regional political situation framed the tremendous diversity in women's activism — in terms of class, ethnic, and ideological identification — to create a kaleidoscopic effect in women's organizing. As the revolving door of the statehouse turned, women activists reoriented themselves, adapting to the political climate. Amid national debate and dissent about women's roles, Yucatán's constantly shifting political winds compounded the anxiety. The "woman question" remained prominent in the minds of Yucatán's policymakers and organic intellectuals but isolated from pressing questions of land and labor reform. Yucatán's major dailies relegated women's activism and political rights to the social pages.[54] Still, articles appearing alongside wedding and *quinceañera* announcements included items such as a speech delivered by Lenin's widow, Nadezhda Krupskaya, about women's difficult double role fulfilling both domestic and public duties in postrevolutionary societies.[55] Without a strong regional feminist legacy, women activists might have faced an insurmountable challenge in Yucatán, but organizers from the Alvarado and Carrillo Puerto eras continued mobilizing during the 1930s.

As Popular Front efforts gathered steam, Communist and fellow-traveler organizations gained a higher profile in popular organizing.[56] As the historian Ben Fallaw has documented, the PCM had particular success among teachers. The U.S. vice-consul in Mérida reported in horror that Yucatán's new public-education director, Antonio Betancourt Pérez, professed communism, had spent eighteen months in the Soviet Union, and required students to sing the "International" and "other songs of an exotic nature."[57] In January 1936, a group of Mérida schoolteachers launched an FUPDM chapter. Teachers and other activists assembled women in school- or PSS-sponsored temperance organizations. Groups such as the FUPDM and Women's Revolutionary Action consistently pointed to their temperance campaigns as evidence of their truly revolutionary spirit and unflagging support for the Cárdenas government. Furthermore, much as they had in Michoacán and the Comarca Lagunera, temperance campaigns offered women an opportunity not only to challenge a physical space of masculine domination — the cantina — but also to insert themselves into local political conflicts through charges of temperance-law violations.[58]

Moral strictures could work against women, as well. When Carlota Baeza Aldana requested a police detachment to come to the village of Ixil and defend the school against those who would "distort" the school's contributions, the governor demanded the municipal president's cooperation. The municipal president responded by questioning Baeza Aldana's moral standing, saying that she had political meetings nearly every night at the schoolhouse, "where she stays with several other people until very advanced hours." No decent woman, he implied, would stay out so late, much less hold political meetings. He admitted that most Ixileños considered her a personal enemy but maintained that she had "never been threatened or injured in [his] presence" and had filed no formal complaints; he saw no reason to have to guarantee her safety.[59]

Nonetheless, women regularly intervened in matters broadly understood as "political," although generally within a gendered framework, appealing to political leaders' patronage and protection and invoking obligations to home and family. "We beg of you to consider our petition," the Mérida FUPDM beseeched Cárdenas, "given that we are women in need and that all our small state's working and peasant women are anxious to see their dreams fulfilled."[60] They went on to request a maternity clinic for every major town (*cabecera*) and "a school to instruct our own and for their progress and wellbeing."[61]

Despite their deferential tone, organized women expected local officials to take their demands seriously, expressing a sense of entitlement tantamount to citizenship rights. A group of middle-class Progreso women, for example, sent an irate letter to the governor, the state congress, and the state attorney general decrying the behavior of the city's municipal president.[62] When presented with the women's petition, the *alcalde* (mayor) rebuffed them, saying that he feared neither the governor nor congress and even less "a few poor women," but the group's indignation indicated that such a dismissal was neither expected nor commonplace.

Women's political involvement, however, often posed an unwelcome intrusion. Felipa Poot, a peasant woman from the village of Kinchil, became radicalized by a Communist teacher, joined the PCM, and became an important intermediary between Kinchil and Mérida.[63] However, when she became a leader in a local political dispute stemming from a contested race for one of Yucatán's senate seats, an opposing faction gunned her down from the rooftops of the town's main intersection. Poot's faction, predominantly communist, had orchestrated the ouster of Gualberto Carrillo Puerto's supporters from the municipal government several months before her assassination. Ironically, Carrillo Puerto—whose brother suffered a similar fate and whose sister had inspired the Feminist League Poot organized — probably bears intellectual responsibility for the assassination, carried out in support of Kinchil's powerful merchants and ranchers who supported his political machinery.[64]

Although violent incidents remained distressingly commonplace in 1930s Yucatán, a woman's involvement not only in leading a faction but also in a deadly encounter fueled animosities. However, if Poot's opponents thought they would prevent women's involvement in the town's political struggles, they had miscalculated. Just as Martina Derás's assassination had animated women's organizing in the Comarca Lagunera, Poot's death apparently stimulated rather than dampened her comrades' convictions. Six months later, a group of her female comrades, now identifying themselves as an FUPDM chapter, expressed outrage when her assassins threatened, with yet another turn of the political wheel, to regain the municipal government. The offending group wanted "to sow disorder and unrest again in the town, using calumnies before the military authorities," the group asserted. "We demand punishment for these individuals or their prompt expulsion as undesirable influences and enemies of work, order, and morality."[65] Notably, their appeal invoked not notions of justice or revenge but, rather, three fundamental elements of revolutionary citizenship: work, order, and morality. Indeed, women's traditional role as guardians of morality in their communities lent legitimacy to the FUPDM's complaint.

While the Kinchil incident certainly offers glimpses of the possibilities and limitations of women's political interventions, Poot's experiences — including her demise — remained exceptional. Most women activists neither achieved such prominence nor met with such an unfortunate end. However, a closer examination of more typical experiences illuminates not only the different modes of women's organizing in 1930s Yucatán but also the changing terms of political engagement following the August 1937 reforms.

Mercedes Betancourt de Albertos's career demonstrated the pitfalls of women's frequent reliance on local authorities' patronage, particularly in a volatile political climate. A staunch anticommunist, Betancourt participated vocally at the 1916 First Feminist Congress and later found employment through the state Department of Public Education.[66] She campaigned for Alayola Barrera during his pre-candidacy for the PSS nomination and had achieved enough prominence by November 1934 that she was a featured speaker at the PSS civic festival commemorating the outbreak of the Mexican revolution.[67] In return for her loyalty, she secured employment not only for herself but also for her husband, an art teacher who had been unemployed for several years. In her communications with the governor, Betancourt carefully reminded him of her political support, occasionally taking a respectfully conspiratorial tone. She confided in one letter, "Some Senators should arrive soon. Watch out and be careful of the enemy. You will always triumph because you have reason and law on your side. You understand perfectly. One must remain ever alert and not trust everyone."[68]

When (despite her warning) Alayola Barrera became a casualty of the Cárdenas–Calles conflict, Betancourt shifted tactics from the patronage style of the maximato to the party-centered style of Cardenismo. López Cárdenas's interim gubernatorial administration marked a sharp turn to the left, openly supporting communists within the state bureaucracy. While Betancourt retained a position running the PNR state women's committee, she became embroiled in confrontations with Popular Front organizations early in 1936, and her position on the federal education promotions committee brought her into direct conflict with many Communists and fellow travelers.[69] As other PNR-affiliated women's groups, such as Women's Revolutionary Action, set up offices alongside Betancourt's in the Casa del Pueblo, she must have felt her prestige slipping within the party bureaucracy. Indeed, with Communists Antonio Betancourt Pérez and Rogerio Chalé as the state public-education director and PSS president, respectively, Betancourt de Albertos lost purchase on the two entities that had afforded her livelihood and status.[70]

Although she adopted a Cardenista-style approach to outreach, traveling throughout the state to work "in defense of working and peasant women," she clearly understood her task more as charity than as organization and mobilization. She promoted a nutritional program for "proletarian children" and a women's vocational school "to prevent them from turning to prostitution." When the PNR allowed women to vote in party plebiscites, Betancourt called on the governor to order the police to uphold this right, protesting reported abuses in the western coastal town of Celestún.[71] Indeed, Betancourt may have been the feminist counterexample that PSS President José Baqueiro had in mind when he described a party member who organized "not feminists, but obreras and campesinas." As ideological tempers flared in the second half of 1936, Betancourt, seemingly in spite of herself, joined a series of political controversies. She and her son, Arturo Albertos Betancourt, also vocally anticommunist, sparred with the Popular Front–linked Revolutionary Teachers' Union (UMR).[72]

In early November, Betancourt received a telegram from the PNR women's organizer in the remote eastern town of Dzitás complaining that the compañeras Manuela Chuc and Alejandra Ku—the wives of the men accused in the September assassination of the charismatic Communist and PSS President Rogerio Chalé—had been "dragged from their homes, robbed, and ridiculed" by the local authorities. "We understand that [these women] are innocent," Betancourt informed the governor, "and for no reason should they be reviled in this age when we should have done away with those *caciquiscos* [*sic*] that denigrate the good name of the Revolution and of our worthy leaders, Lázaro Cárdenas and Ing. Florencio Palomo V."[73] The state attorney general offered assurances that the proper authorities would guarantee justice and the women's safety.[74]

Betancourt contended that the left-leaning municipal president "believes that his job is to threaten defenseless women and that we are still in the age of barbarism."[75] Indeed, the violence against Chuc and Ku almost certainly had ideological roots. While the women had been obliquely implicated in Chalé's murder, the local authorities' response bore more resemblance to vigilante justice than to the rule of law.[76] "It is awful to say that those who should protect guarantees trample on them, abusing them and ridiculing them," Betancourt added, perhaps to preempt accusations of disloyalty. "In the name of the PNR women's committee, I ask you for justice and equity. The politics and the people are of no interest to me. My creed is collective: for the liberation of Woman and most especially for the campesinas." A local official offered a somewhat different version of events, saying that Betancourt had come to Dzitás to organize a sindicato blanco (company union) and had provoked widespread protests. "Although it did not reach the degree portrayed in [Betancourt's] letter," the official wrote, "in political meetings and assemblies, speakers have used strong words against the sindicato in formation, without mentioning specific people."[77]

Such conflicts drew Betancourt further into the political fray. The state PNR committee ignored her petitions for financial support for her organizing efforts, perhaps in response to her controversial role in the Dzitás conflict or perhaps as a result of her increasingly public confrontation with the UMR. Betancourt appealed directly to the governor, emphasizing that her principal objective was "to orient the campesinas of the pueblos, giving them lectures so that they benefit their children and husbands."[78] Describing the campesinas as "constant victims of their ignorance, since unfortunately 90 percent of the rural population does not even know how to read," she explained, "I make no politics in the pueblos, nor in any place, since I understand my mission is feminine in the sense of procuring the collective improvement, and not the work of intrigues and gossip that sully any activity."[79] Underscoring her endeavor's femininity, she perhaps hoped to make herself seem less threatening to Cardenista officials.

By January 1937, Betancourt, stripped of her position directing the PNR's state women's committee, appealed again for a state sinecure.[80] She also requested the reinstatement of all her compañeros who had lost teaching positions as a result of the UMR conflict. Reminding the governor that she had spent twenty-eight years as a teacher, she asserted that she had fallen victim to Antonio Betancourt Pérez's manipulations. "We truly believe," she explained, "that you will not be convinced by our enemies' mafia."[81] Following this communication, Betancourt de Albertos kept a low profile. Unable to adapt from the Callista political practices of elite and party networking to the Cardenista style of mobilizing a popular constituency, she found herself embroiled in political disputes without the popular base to shore up her position. Although expectations of patronage persisted, the changing culture of organizing—from feminist congresses that excluded the illiterate to populist organizing that depended on their support—had left Betancourt behind.

The story of Teófila González picks up where Mercedes Betancourt's leaves off and follows the opposite trajectory, illustrating the dangers of remaining aloof from state institutions. González emerged as a leading Progreso activist during Cárdenas's August 1937 state tour, when she came forward as the secretary-general of the Women's Committee for Social Improvement.[82] The organization's demands indicated a working-class orientation, emphasizing concerns about unemployment, inflation, and elevated rents and specifically requesting "a union with a registration number and a juridical status. The union will consist of unsalaried women, ironers, laundresses, cooks, tortilla makers, and petty saleswomen." González renewed her request for union recognition a month later, lamenting that the women's employers had fired them because they lacked union protection.[83] She did not, however, seek an affiliation with any officially recognized union or with the PSS.

In October 1937, González again contacted Cárdenas, explaining that the women had constituted themselves as the Women's Union of Wage Workers and General Laborers to fight for their rights and material improvements and to seek Cárdenas's endorsement for official recognition.[84] Two weeks later, the group changed its name again, this time to Women Domestic-Service Workers' Union.[85] The new union boasted a modest letterhead that included slogans celebrating women's contributions as workers and as mothers, indicating the continuity that most women experienced between their wage and nonwage labor. These constant name changes and constitutional revisions stemmed from the group's ongoing effort to obtain legal status. In February 1938, González and another officer expressed their frustration with the bureaucratic and legal obstacles they had encountered. "After eight months of sterile struggle," they implored Cárdenas, "no authority grants us the support to which we have the right, as obreras and campesinas who cement the Revolution that you brought. . . . Equality of rights is not denied us today but neither is it given to us."[86] Explaining that the labor authorities informed the women that "there is no law that supports our rights as woman workers," they requested support for ironing and washing workshops "to liberate ourselves from the patronas who have done us so much harm in the past months, aided by some teachers who, forgetting their mission, have been the first to dismiss our comrades illegally, for the serious crime of belonging to this union." Without "effective aid," they explained, "we, the officers, will have to emigrate because of the campaign they've waged against the union, . . . carrying in our souls, as always, the pain of once again not having attention paid to us."[87]

That letter apparently signaled the end of González's union-organizing efforts. It seems that she either did not seek or did not secure protection from any national or state labor organizations that might have facilitated her efforts. Even the city's schoolteachers, normally at the vanguard of supporting women's activism, apparently undermined González's union, perhaps indicating class tensions between organized domestic workers and middle-class professionals. Furthermore, her campaign occurred just as the Cárdenas administration and the state government turned away from mass mobilization in favor of more disciplined, institutional means of securing popular support and legitimacy. In other words, González fell victim to the opposite trend from the one that had befallen Betancourt. She attempted a popular mobilization divorced from party support and patronage connections at a moment when both the state and national governments reasserted the importance of institutional affiliations.

The final example — that of Gumercinda Pérez — demonstrates a more successful alternative to the earlier two cases. Much like Teófila González, Pérez believed that the new regime would represent the needs of peasants and workers, "the cement of the Revolution." She lived in the town of Tixméuac, in the southern municipality of Tekax, and, through the local Society of Friends of the School, became involved with the UMR during its confrontation with Betancourt de Albertos. She signed a letter to the governor from Tixméuac's Popular Front organization, the Yucatecan Popular Alliance, whose members described themselves as "humble in our backgrounds but strong in our feelings."[88]

By early 1938, Pérez served as the secretary of "agitation, press, and propaganda" for Tixméuac's FUPDM chapter, established in October 1936. The chapter's membership had repeatedly solicited the help of the state FUPDM office in Mérida but to no avail. "Perhaps because of their many preoccupations," she explained to Cárdenas, "or because of our humble condition, they have taken no notice."[89] Deploying a mixture of revolutionary radicalism and patriotic fervor common in letters to the president, Pérez articulated a vision not only of revolutionary promise but also of women's centrality to the process of social transformation. "We peasant women know and understand the sufferings of our proletarian class" she explained, "and struggle for the complete emancipation of the workers of the campo, who with their labor have made our beloved Mexico great." The letter went on to imagine a world that celebrated new "profiles of a feminine ideal" and in which peasants "govern and exploit the earth and workers own the machines, the tools, and the systems of transportation." Furthermore, Pérez explicitly linked this vision to the government of "our model compañero, Lázaro Cárdenas, who . . . fights so that organized workers, the majority, are those who definitively decide all political, social, and economic matters of the nation." Committing itself to corporatism and the political culture of organizing, the FUPDM and the Society of the Friends of the School requested Cárdenas's help to build a new schoolhouse and asked that he put them in contact with the FUPDM in Mexico City "to have relations with the women of the interior and to keep up with the progress that the Mexican Revolution is making under your able guidance."[90]

In December 1938, the Tixméuac FUPDM took the unusual step of submitting a complete membership list, including ages, civil status, nationality, birthplace, occupation, and literacy levels.[91] This evidence offers a glimpse of the group's composition and allows for speculations about what made Tixméuac's chapter outlive the frequent political shifts in Yucatán during this period. The group boasted ninety-six members at the end of 1938, up from thirty-six at its founding more than two years earlier. In many ways, the group's membership mirrored rural Yucatecan society, and even Mexican demographics more broadly. The average age of the members was 26.2, reflecting Mexico's relatively young population. The oldest member, the 58-year-old widow Liberata Cetina, identified herself as a schoolteacher, while all the others, including Pérez, stated their occupation as "domestic labors." This chapter also counted twelve 15 year olds, the minimum age for FUPDM membership. Married women constituted 43 percent of the group, with unmarried women making up another 49 percent and widows accounting for the remainder. Nearly a third of the women (thirty out of ninety-six) had indigenous names.[92] Two-thirds (not, however, the same two-thirds with Hispanic surnames) said that they could both read and write. While high for rural Mexico, this figure reflects the strong showing of young women (thirty-eight were 25 or younger), who would have enjoyed greater access to public education and literacy programs. Furthermore, the clear association between the FUPDM and the Society of the Friends of the School meant that the group most likely self-selected those with some commitment to promoting education.

The membership rolls reveal other important facts about Tixméuac's FUPDM. For example, the organization successfully reproduced its leadership. While women such as Pérez, 33, and Serafina Heredia, 30, had started the chapter in 1936, by late 1938, Victoria Reyes and Olga Peralta, both only 18, held the two top offices. While Pérez and Heredia, as well as the widowed teacher Cetina, continued to hold offices, they had transferred leadership to younger activists. Furthermore, the officers submitted the membership list apparently with no other purpose than to demonstrate their growing numbers and to reiterate their support for Cárdenas's government, underscoring the importance of both organizational strength and political reliability to secure government support.

The Tixméuac FUPDM had a mixed record in achieving its objectives. In 1943 it still lobbied for a new schoolhouse, although the issue seemed to be approaching resolution. However, it is also clear that in mid-1943, the group remained active, albeit under the rubric of the PSS-affiliated Women's Sub-committee of the Syndical League of Workers and Peasants.[93] Many of the same women, including Pérez, occupied officers' posts, and in 1941 she consulted with Rosa Pasos, a former officer of the statewide FUPDM in Mérida, about creating a new regional organization, Socialist Women of the Southeast.[94] Compared with similar groups, the Tixméuac women's group proved unusually enduring through a period of significant political uncertainty.

This durability stemmed from several factors. First, although some women, including Pérez, occupied leadership positions, the officers changed often enough to avoid making the organization the province of one woman or a small clique. Similarly, the FUPDM emphasized building a broad membership, giving it legitimacy not only before state and national governments but also within the communities themselves. Third, the direct clash between Popular Front–connected and anticommunist teachers provided a focal point and a framework for women's organizing as well as a natural alliance among left-leaning groups. As in the Comarca Lagunera, in Yucatán the divide provided a boundary marker for who fell inside and outside the parameters of revolutionary citizenship. Finally, the FUPDM leaders cultivated not only connections with state political leaders and women activists but also patronage ties to Mexico City. When they requested support from the Cárdenas government, it responded, if only by endorsing the group's efforts within the relevant bureaucratic agencies. When they complained to the governor about violence committed by a military officer in Tixméuac, the governor ordered an investigation, and when PSS officials came to town, they made a point of meeting with Gumercinda Pérez and other leading women activists.[95] In short, this combination of popular mobilization, working within state-sanctioned institutions, and the existence of a politically and ideologically defined conflict within their community (between communists and anticommunists) provided the FUPDM leadership with legitimacy, allies, and relatively clear terms of political engagement.

Land Reform, Political Compromise, and Women's Organizing

As in the Comarca Lagunera, nothing defined the terms of political engagement so much as the August 1937 land-reform decree and concomitant "Crusade of the Mayab." Cárdenas arrived in Yucatán envisioning an ethnically informed version of the Laguna project, combining loyalty to the federal government with a populist celebration of Mayan history and culture.[96] His plan met with limited success. The stronger and better-established Yucatecan political machine did not yield willingly to intervention from Mexico City. Furthermore, the constantly shifting alliances among the PNR, the PSS, and the Communist Party created confusion in both popular organizing and electoral politics. Several years of political tug-of-war between regionalist political leaders in Mérida and the centralizing postrevolutionary regime finally ended in a détente in which Cárdenas conceded considerable regional political autonomy in exchange for promises of party loyalty and support for his agrarian-reform program.[97]

Even by the most charitable accounts, the Yucatecan agrarian reform met with uneven success and offered women a mixed bag. Like similar efforts elsewhere in Mexico, the Yucatán reform encountered difficulties with allocating credit and land. Henequen production required costly equipment to process the fiber, and the acquisition of or access to this machinery by campesinos often proved difficult. The predictable corruption and politicking that often accompanies such reforms put in an appearance in Yucatán as well. Even before government's modernization effort, some ejidatarios complained that they wanted to use their plots for subsistence production of corn and beans, but officials from the National Ejidal Credit Bank pressed them to cultivate henequen.[98] Agrarian reform also, as indicated in the pamphlet calling on campesinos to make themselves men and citizens through the ejido, reinforced patriarchal control over family resources by basing land distribution on male heads of households.[99] Although women activists did not make ejidal plots a principal demand, it did not escape their notice that women's de facto exclusion from land-reform measures largely defined their access to material resources. During Cárdenas's August 1937 visit, Mérida's FUPDM chapter requested land for any widowed or single women who demonstrated need.[100] Women's occasional — albeit infrequent — appearance on the ejidal censuses lent credibility to their petition.[101]

Cárdenas's Yucatán tour and agrarian-reform decree informed the regional political climate beyond questions of land tenure, inviting popular groups, including women's organizations, to deal directly with the federal government. Hoping to weaken regional caciques, Cárdenas encouraged more direct contact between federal agencies and local popular organizations. The tour coincided with growing suffragist radicalism in Mexico City, increasing his incentive to cultivate relations with women's organizations, and the introduction of an "Open Door" policy in Yucatán meant that women who joined recognized organizations could vote in the 1937 gubernatorial election.[102] Thus, women's organizing assumed a higher profile during Cárdenas's visit, offering activists the opportunity to gain greater legitimacy and to make their appeals directly to federal officials, who often manifest more sympathy to their claims than local and state officials. Impressed by the vitality of Yucatecan women's activism, Cárdenas wrote to his friend and mentor Francisco Múgica after visiting Kinchil that the "women are brave and fanatically animated about the plan for Yucatán's economic transformation."[103]

The FUPDM and the Agrarian Department's Ligas Femeniles de Lucha Social, both headquartered in Mexico City, offered the most common vehicles for Yucatecan women's organizing. The FUPDM particularly succeeded in the state's outlying regions, such as the eastern cities of Valladolid and Espita and the southern town of Tixméuac. The Ligas Femeniles maintained a less conspicuous presence—a surprising fact given the extent to which Cárdenas and the Agrarian Department hoped to model the Yucatán reforms after the Comarca Lagunera. The FUPDM's strength in Yucatán may well have discouraged Cardenistas from promoting a competing organizing structure. None of the explicit discussion about women's organizing and ceremonial inaugurations of women's leagues that had occurred in the Comarca Lagunera accompanied the Yucatán land reform.

Operating since January 1936, the FUPDM gained momentum during the pro–Popular Front López Cárdenas administration and cultivated solidarity ties with Socialist Youth groups, prominent leftist labor unions, and teachers' organizations. FUPDM affiliates regularly signed letters backing beleaguered labor unions, and standard FUPDM issues—improved health care and maternity clinics, increased school funding, and lower prices for basic goods and services—enjoyed support among a broad coalition of Yucatecan popular organizations.[104] When the Sole Union of Education Workers of Yucatán (SUTEY) formed in May 1937, incorporating the UMR and other Popular Front teachers' organizations, it specified that every female teacher (*maestra*) should consider herself an FUPDM organizer.[105]

When Cárdenas arrived in Yucatán, FUPDM chapters submitted petitions as he passed through their communities.[106] Still others had sent petitions in advance of his arrival, anticipating that he might resolve pressing questions during his stay. A chapter in Espita, for example, requested forgiveness of the debt it had incurred with the National Ejidal Credit Bank to buy a corn mill and to use a public building to house the mill.[107] Other appeals centered on standard demands for improved health care, lower prices, increased funding for education, and support for women's cooperatives. After Cárdenas's departure, the state FUPDM headquarters submitted a summary petition, including local chapters' "bread and butter" demands as well as a request for a pension for the mother of the assassinated Communist Rogerio Chalé and, on the heels of Cárdenas's Veracruz announcement supporting women's political rights, an endorsement of women's suffrage.[108] The response this petition generated in Mexico City indicated that the administration took the FUPDM's concerns seriously. Cárdenas's private secretary, Raúl Castellanos, personally delivered it to Cárdenas, who informed the officers three days later that he had forwarded their demands to the appropriate agencies and that Castellanos would oversee their implementation.[109]

Though less of a presence than the FUPDM, several Ligas Femeniles petitioned Cárdenas during his stay in Yucatán. In the central town of Tekantó, in the henequen zone's eastern reaches, league members submitted a desperate entreaty for firewood for cooking and milk for their children, as well as some basic materials to establish a cooperative.[110] The Liga Femenil "Nicte-ha" in Cuncunu appealed to Cárdenas's paternalism in its request for a grain mill and a sewing machine. Like its counterparts in the Comarca Lagunera, the league focused on reproductive labor issues and labor-based rights. "Since time immemorial, the campesina has performed most domestic work, and the man has cared very little about her improvement and well-being," the league explained, "keeping her enslaved all her life in domestic duties and forgetting that she, too, should be emancipated through her honorable work. This has inspired us to organize ourselves into a Liga Femenil to procure our improvement and to facilitate our daily tasks in our homes, keeping in mind the interest that you have taken in helping the Mexican woman and in her improvement throughout the Republic."[111] Forty-five women, including many with indigenous surnames, signed the letter, telling Cárdenas they had been "animated by the extensive revolutionary labor that you have developed through the federal executive branch." Although it remains impossible to judge the sincerity of such appeals to paternalism, the league's insistence on recognition for women's work and that women, "too, be emancipated through [their] labors" exploited the possibilities the regime created for a gendered revolutionary citizenship.

The "Great Ejido" and the Return to Regionalism

The failure of the Cardenista agrarian-reform measures was, and remains, a hotly contested issue among Yucatecans and scholars examining the region.[112] Charges abounded of shoddy planning, corrupt and inept administration, and inadequate provision of credit and technical expertise. Not surprisingly, most hacendados held that the agrarian reform amounted to an irresponsible and ill-advised experiment in communism. Regardless of the explanations, within six months of the measure's implementation, complaints from ejidatarios flooded the offices of federal and state agencies, and the newly inaugurated governor, Humberto Canto Echeverría, pushed through his "Great Ejido" plan, devolving responsibility for agrarian reform to the state government and replacing the National Ejidal Credit Bank with the hacendado-ejidatario joint endeavor, Henequeneros de Yucatán.

Coinciding with the FUPDM's absorption into the PRM, the Great Ejido meant a step backward for women's organizing. State and local officials offered considerably less support for women's activism, and the reduced presence of federal officials meant that women's groups struggled to maintain patronage connections with Mexico City. They did benefit some from the transitional fallout; the Abalá FUPDM, for example, received a grain mill and all its accoutrements from the retreating Agrarian Department.[113] Overall, however, the Great Ejido abandoned popular organizations, including women's groups.[114] The teacher and activist Concepción L. Sabido, for example, filed a grievance in Mexico City about police violence against her organization, the Central of Agrarian Communities and Women's Unions of the Mexican Republic. However, local officials denied any record of her complaints, assuring federal lawmakers that they had always given Sabido "support and justice."[115]

Within this inhospitable climate, women appealed to state authorities regarding less controversial issues or couched long-standing demands in less radical language. The FUPDM state offices sought emergency relief for members of its Valladolid chapter recently victimized by a cyclone. They appealed for meager amounts, ranging between 12 and 20 pesos, for "abandoned women, widows and women in general with no help of any kind."[116] Mothers' Clubs avoided the Popular Front's language of class struggle, instead citing domestic obligations. The Mérida Mothers' Club implored the governor not to close the Center for Social Assistance, which provided breakfasts, health care, and support for some 730 children. The CTM's electrical workers' union wrote a letter supporting the Mothers' Club and called on the governor to expand his programs to attend to needy children.[117] In many such requests, the language of charity overshadowed the language of entitlement.

Women's organizing received a boost in March 1939, when the PRM's regional office exhorted its local organizing committees to devote more resources to organizing the "popular sector," which included the FUPDM and most other women's groups. The renewed interest may have stemmed in part from the fact that the prominent women's activist Ana María Bravo had served as the committee's secretary of popular and cultural activities since early January.[118] Yucatecan women activists called for stronger support from their Mexico City allies, and their delegation to the PRM's presidential nominating convention published a hard-hitting pamphlet exhorting workers everywhere to support their demands for equal civil, political, and labor rights; improved women's educational opportunities; allocations of land and credit for women's organizations; and the "complete liberation of the campesina."[119]

The pamphlet's preamble revealed activists' frustration that Yucatecan women's long-standing struggle had failed to yield more significant gains. "Women, who for some time have fought for political, social, and economic emancipation," the authors asserted, "have served a struggle that appears to prolong itself indefinitely with no variation in the results." Highlighting the efforts of previous generations who "contributed their share and sacrificed the better part of their lives to conquer their future well-being," The authors reassured their audience that "we are not pessimists, believing that all efforts have been useless. We cannot say that all our work has been sterile. Despite everything, however, a much greater task remains. We need the efforts of all Mexican women and the disinterested support of all the men to achieve a complete victory."[120] This strained optimism reflected a widespread disappointment on the Mexican left that the PRM had not fulfilled its promise to become the political incarnation of the Popular Front.

Still, pressing for women's expanded political and social rights, the Yucatecan women took advantage of the corporatist restructuring, linking citizenship to women's work by blurring the divide between waged and unwaged labor, the line that so often demarcated the boundary between inside and outside of revolutionary citizenship. "Who has not seen the campesina throughout our Republic, with the child on her back, laboring under the inclemencies of snowfall or the asphyxiating heat?" they retorted to those who contended that motherhood made women unsuited for agricultural cultivation. "Whoever knows the henequen plantations of our beautiful Yucatán, the lovely land of the Mayab, will have seen countless times our legendary Indian woman with her head down and the glowing *huipil* [indigenous dress], with a child on her hip, taking the thorns from the [henequen leaves] that her husband has cut." They continued to mobilize not only an alternative feminine ideal but also the Cardenistas' romanticized indigenismo. "On many occasions, she grabs the sharp-edged leaf when her husband has given in to fatigue. If she performs all these labors, we do not see why she should not also be given a parcel of land. Women must come together and stand united."[121] Thus, to those who maintained that "feminism" threatened the treasured national patrimony of Mexican femininity, the Yucatecan women activists countered that the Maya women who balanced motherhood and labor embodied an authentic ideal of Mexican feminism.

The ardor of this entreaty points to the simultaneous hope and frustration that Yucatecan activists harbored as they struggled for survival by the end of the decade. After a long lull in activity, the FUPDM and the Ligas Femeniles revived their efforts during Cárdenas's late-1939 visit to promote Avila Camacho's presidential candidacy. The FUPDM state offices reiterated persistent requests for health and maternity clinics, educational opportunities, wells, and corn mills but notably eliminated women's political rights from its stated demands.[122] The Agrarian Department founded two new Ligas Femeniles, and a third took advantage of the opportunity to petition directly for a corn mill, a sewing machine, and a radio.[123] Shortly after Cárdenas's departure, the FUPDM's Ticul chapter informed him that the recent economic travails had hit it especially hard, since the chapter's members lived off corn production and all the economic aid went to the henequen zone. The chapter pleaded for a women's production cooperative, a medical dispensary, a public dining hall, and five dozen sweaters for the area's poorest children.[124] These appeals elicited at least a modest response. The minister of public health notified Cárdenas six weeks later of his efforts to establish a location for Ticul's health clinic.[125]

However, once Cárdenas had left the region, support for the FUPDM apparently vanished. In February 1940, an officer of the FUPDM's state headquarters telegraphed Cárdenas saying that government *pistoleros* (gunmen) and police forces had blockaded its offices.[126] While the conflict's causes remain murky, apparently Cárdenas failed to intervene. A year later, the organization wrote to the recently inaugurated Avila Camacho to request office space in a federal building, explaining that the state government had evicted it from its former offices.[127]

The strength of the Communist Party and its fellow-traveler organizations had bolstered the well-rooted Yucatecan women's movement. Women activists developed solidarity ties with labor unions, teachers' organizations, and peasant groups, placing them squarely within the realm of revolutionary citizenship — "not feminists, but obreras and campesinas." However, in the tussle between Mexico City and Mérida for control over state politics, ongoing political conflicts often overshadowed women's organizing efforts. In this climate, women activists turned to the Cárdenas government to fulfill revolutionary promises and incorporate women's demands into its agenda. When Cárdenas arrived in Yucatán in August 1937 to promulgate his agrarian-reform decree, he raised hopes among FUPDM organizers and the state's handful of women's leagues that the regime would intervene in Yucatán as it had in the Comarca Lagunera.

The Cárdenas administration understood quite well, however, that the two regions' political cultures differed considerably. While Cardenistas may have misjudged the Comarca Lagunera as a tabula rasa awaiting the inscription of the regime's blueprint, they correctly identified the critical difference in the strength of the two regions' local political machinery. While the Communist Party and its allies were the most influential, best-organized political players in the Comarca Lagunera, Yucatán had a complex network based on the PSS; competing *camarillas*, or political factions; and emerging popular organizations. Yucatán's political culture, then, bore a stronger resemblance to Michoacán's established state organizing structures and dramatically shifting political climates than to the more autonomous and pluralist Comarca Lagunera. The Cárdenas government harbored no illusions that it could step into the state in 1937 and declare a complete social, political, and economic overhaul as it had in the Comarca Lagunera. Yucatecan agrarian reform would require a more nuanced approach and a complicated negotiation with local political leaders.

The agrarian reform's failure, the need for political stability to ensure the PRM's success, and the nationalization of the petroleum industry combined to create an opportunity for state political leaders to regain control over agrarian policy in Yucatán. The shifting of the balance of power back to the state government bode ill for local women's organizations, which had largely switched their alliances to nationally affiliated organizations. The PSS's Radical Revolutionary Women's Bloc, for example, changed its affiliation during the López Cárdenas administration and repackaged itself as the PNR's Women's Revolutionary Action. This change may have seemed inconsequential at the time, an obvious adjustment to the national trend toward increased centralization or the natural result of the strong presence of federally trained schoolteachers in their ranks. However, the decision would have deleterious effects on the organization's efficacy when the locus of political power migrated from Mexico City back to Mérida.

Following the political chaos of the Alayola Barrera and López Cárdenas administrations, the intervention of the Cárdenas government in 1937 promised to instill the political stability that would facilitate women's organizing efforts. Many women activists would have welcomed the hegemonic Cardenista project and its support for women's organizing. However, as the Cárdenas regime withdrew from local political matters following the creation of the Great Ejido and leading up to the tense 1940 presidential election, even the most organized women's groups found themselves without support. By late 1939, Yucatecan women lamented the "struggle that appears to prolong itself indefinitely with no variation in the results."[128] Indeed, the Cardenista chapter in Yucatecan history would close with regrettably little progress on the frontier of women's rights.

CONCLUSIONS AND EPILOGUE

The Death of Cardenismo

Cardenismo was, in the end, a Janus-faced enterprise. "Revolutionary" yet traditional and paternalist, Cárdenas at once promoted and circumscribed his radical agenda of social programs, land redistribution, and labor reforms. He advocated collective organizing, providing historically disenfranchised actors a legitimated base from which to challenge landowners and capitalists, but he also sought to contain the potential radicalism of these "mass" organizations by consolidating them under the centralizing state's tutelage and control. He supported more inclusive, transparent, democratic processes, but only so long as their outcomes could be predicted and controlled. In the Cardenista utopia, informed as much by concerns about renegade radicalism as by aspirations to fulfill the promise of Mexico's "interrupted" revolution, state-sponsored organizations of educated workers and peasants received guidance from a strong but benevolent central government that mediated among conflicting interests, intervening to protect the weaker party in any dispute.[1]

By the time Manuel Avila Camacho assumed the presidency, the Mexican women's movement had retreated. The suffrage campaign's failure deflated Mexico City–based feminists and FUPDM organizers, and the state's withdrawal of support for popular mobilizations undermined efforts to utilize informal politics. The corporatist Party of the Mexican Revolution (PRM) gave women a nominal voice but in practice relegated women's activities and organizing efforts to the margins of Mexican politics. "Everything changed then," recalled activist Ana María Flores Sánchez. "Cardenismo died when he left office."[2] The Avila Camacho administration turned sharply rightward, closing down opportunities for significant change and beginning anticommunist purges that exposed the limits of Mexico's Popular Front. What looked in 1937 like a massive popular mobilization by 1940 had become state co-optation of popular organizing.

Following the defeat of women's suffrage, urban feminists who had constituted the FUPDM attempted to regroup in 1941 under the banner of the National Feminist Council and again in 1944 as the National Women's Alliance, but the opportunities created during the dynamic postrevolutionary period had evaporated. In 1946, the newly elected president, Miguel Alemán, proposed an amendment to allow women to vote in municipal elections. The proposal sailed through Congress, with the only dissenting vote coming from a conservative National Action Party (PAN) deputy, who expressed concerns about women encroaching on masculine prerogatives and destroying Mexican homes.[3] Then, in 1951, Adolfo Ruiz Cortines, the Institutional Revolutionary Party (PRI) candidate for the upcoming presidential election, declared his support for a constitutional amendment granting women full suffrage.[4]

Ruiz Cortines's proposed amendment varied only cosmetically from the 1937 amendment—substituting the word *varones* (males) for its synonym *hombres* (men)—and drew on traditional gender ideologies, referring to women as "an example of abnegación, labor, and morality."[5] In the months that followed, battle-hardened suffragists must have wondered if they heard the next verse of the same old song as the proposed amendment immediately became a pretext for political maneuvering. The PAN proposed ratifying the 1937 amendment, hoping to force PRI representatives to vote against either Cárdenas's proposal or Ruiz Cortines's.[6]

In December 1952, Communist and former FUPDM organizer Esther Chapa testified on the chamber floor in favor of publishing Cárdenas's proposed amendment rather than ratifying Ruiz Cortines's. She cast her testimony as homage to Cárdenas but also paid tribute to the thousands of women who had struggled for the original amendment. Chapa insisted on the genealogical connection from the militancy of the 1930s to the voting rights of the 1950s. She had witnessed too often—in instances as small as Concha Michel's Hacienda Santa Bárbara invasion and as massive as the 1936 general strike in the Comarca Lagunera—how the postrevolutionary regime appropriated popular mobilizations, circumscribing and transforming their social and political effects.

Despite Chapas's pleas, Congress approved Ruiz Cortines's proposal,

Figure 4. Congressional galleries during the 1952 suffrage debate. AGN, Archivo fotográfico "Hermanos Mayo."

which was nearly identical to Cárdenas's in content but very different in context. Suffragists no doubt held their breath as the amendment wended its way through Congress and then to state legislatures and once again awaited publication in the *Diario Oficial*. They just as surely breathed a sigh of relief followed by a shout of victory when, at last, on 6 October 1953 Congress officially declared the amendment to the constitution's Articles 34 and 115, granting women the rights to vote and hold office at every level of government. In July 1958, twenty years after Congress had passed the original amendment, women finally voted in a presidential election.

However, severing the suffrage victory from popular mobilization and linking it instead to state patronage transformed its meaning, honoring women as political housekeepers rather than revolutionary citizens. Vicente Lombardo Toledano's Popular Party published a *corrido* (ballad) urging women to use their "civic broom" to sweep out the PRI and the PAN by voting for those who would "serve the Patria with manliness and truth."[7] The historian Gabriela Cano has written, "If, for Lázaro Cárdenas, the establishment of women's suffrage was a question of democracy, for Adolfo Ruiz Cortines it was an act of chivalry."[8] By the time women actually won voting rights, it seemed a common — if somewhat empty — courtesy. With the "Mexican

Figure 5. Women voting for federal deputies in 1955. AGN, Archivo fotográfico "Hermanos Mayo."

Miracle" underway, the country entered a period of rapid economic growth and political stability but witnessed growing disregard for democratic process. Although Cano's characterization may appear unduly generous regarding Cárdenas's motives for endorsing women's suffrage, it remains crucial to avoid understanding Cardenismo with a teleological eye to the PRI. Suffragists demonstrating in front of Los Pinos expressed the sincere belief that voting rights would make a difference. Women activists envisioned not the consolidation of one-party rule but, rather, the opening of democratic participation and political pluralism.

Students of U.S. history will likely identify familiar patterns. The aborted Mexican women's suffrage movement certainly bears a striking resemblance to the failed U.S. equal rights amendment.[9] One Torreón woman, however, retrospectively likened postrevolutionary women's organizing efforts to the U.S. civil-rights movement.[10] While the analogy has limitations, the civil-rights scholarship offers useful insights for a comparative perspective.[11] As segregation supporters and Jim Crow lawmakers understood the importance of controlling the meanings of race, Mexican statesmen and public intellectuals recognized the need to define gendered meanings. Also like Jim Crow laws, Mexican suffrage laws explicitly excluded women because, "unprepared" for citizenship, they seemed politically unreliable. Like the civil-rights movement, Mexican women's organizing confronted internal divisions and external opposition, relied heavily on federal support to mitigate local hostilities, faced co-optation by a government seeking social peace and national unity, and achieved mixed long-term results. In both movements, the emphasis on identities raised important questions about their meanings, and communities often bristled against the interventions of outsiders endeavoring to describe them. Perhaps most important, the 1930s Mexican women's movement no more eliminated sexism in Mexico than the civil-rights movement eliminated racism in the United States, although in both cases they made progress down long roads of social and political change.

In Mexico, even as the postrevolutionary regime increasingly tried to dictate the terms of democracy, women insisted on the "benefits of the revolution," seeking "voice and vote" at every level, from the household to the Palacio Nacional. Activists navigated an array of tensions—between nationalism and internationalism, tradition and modernity, maternalism and materialism, consciousness and loyalty, mobilization and discipline, and, not least, gendered equality and difference—by adapting to the contingent, inhabited, and gendered aspects of revolutionary citizenship. As the experiences in Michoacán, the Comarca Lagunera, and Yucatán demonstrate, the line between malinchismo and mexicanidad, between traitorous disloyalty and revolutionary mobilization, followed locally specific contours. Factions competed for the power to define who enjoyed the legitimating cloak of citizenship within particular experiences of religious violence, labor conflicts, and political machinations as well as more generalized influences of revolutionary nationalism, modernization efforts, and class-centered politics.

In the end, it really did make a difference who held positions of power. Many historians, particularly revisionists, have depicted the postrevolutionary regime as a seamless trajectory from Calles to Cárdenas to Avila Camacho, and on to Gustavo Díaz Ordaz, who presided over the 1968 student massacre in the Plaza de Tlatelolco. However, women activists' postrevolutionary experience demonstrates that it mattered not only who held the presidency but also who held state and local offices. As Giorgio Agamben reminds us, the power to define and suspend exception—and women remained exceptional in the realm of citizenship—defines sovereignty as the "point of indistinction between violence and law."[12] Postrevolutionary Mexican politics laid bare that aspect of sovereignty. The cases under consideration here reveal how the intense struggle for legal claims to violence often drew activists' attention away from gender-specific concerns and toward more pressing matters of resolving local disputes. Lacking full citizenship status, women could not bring electoral pressure to bear on public officials and therefore depended on patronage networks and clientelist relationships. Under these conditions, in particular—with women's concerns not only marginalized but also reliant on informal politics—a sympathetic mayor, governor, or president made a significant difference in women's abilities to secure concrete gains in land rights, labor protections, public utilities, and social services.

By the 1940s, the contingencies of citizenship had changed in critical ways. The Popular Front gave way to the Cold War as liberals inscribed a boundary between communism and democracy. Obscuring the Communist Party's leadership in combating not only fascism but also racist and sexist political practices both in Mexico and beyond, Mexico's political leadership turned away from its radical allies. Anticommunism also exacerbated conflicts within the Mexican Communist Party (PCM), further destabilizing one of the most important institutions for training women like Concha Michel, Cuca García, and Esther Chapa, who continued as committed activists even if they left or were expelled from the PCM. The Laguna militant Ana María Flores Sánchez worked as a teacher on a hacienda before the region's agrarian reform and joined International Red Aid at 14. She organized through the PCM and, after the agrarian reform, organized Ligas Femeniles de Lucha Social, giving them a strong communist flavor. Continuing as an activist throughout her life, at 80 she organized a peace march in Torreón, bringing in speakers from as far away as Mexico City.[13] For Flores Sánchez, the PCM provided not only a political education and organizational support but also a sense of community, much in the way that parish churches did for Catholic women. With the party's decline, its role in training women activists dropped off precipitously, and women like Flores Sánchez became the exception rather than the rule within Mexico's teaching corps.

The ruling party's restructuring produced another critical context for revolutionary citizenship as leading women activists decided to compromise their autonomy for the sake of a voice within the PRM. This decision, while understandable and perhaps even advisable in the context of Cardenismo and the Popular Front, proved disastrous in retrospect, making the FUPDM seem like simply another "unhappy marriage of Marxism and feminism." In her oft-quoted essay, Heidi Hartmann quips, "The 'marriage' of Marxism and feminism has been like the marriage of husband and wife depicted in

English common law: Marxism and feminism are one, and that one is Marxism."[14] The PCM's gender ideology amounted to demonstrating that women militants could behave in conventionally manly ways, working in factories and participating in violent confrontations. Moreover, its decision to support the ruling party obliged the FUPDM to follow suit. Once incorporated, women found the party neither as Marxist nor as feminist as they had hoped. As the PCM came under fire during the Avila Camacho administration and afterward, women once again found themselves pushed to the margins of the Mexican left.

Although the PRM foreclosed democratic possibilities through its efforts to fix political meanings, Cardenista co-optation appealed to women activists on several fronts. First, official interest validated their activism as a political rather than a social practice, offering women a seat at the political bargaining table and including their concerns in the calculation of interests made by the corporatist regime. As Raymond Williams reminds us, "Much incorporation looks like recognition, acknowledgement, and thus a form of *acceptance*."[15] Second, incorporation promised access to public resources as the ruling party and almost every mass organization created offices for women's affairs. This trade-off of political loyalty for material security has deep roots in Mexico's political tradition of patronage, but it now assumed the more bureaucratic guise of clientelism. For communities that survived by a very close margin, staying in the party's good graces provided a buffer in cases of natural disaster or personal tragedy. For most men and women, revolutionary citizenship secured the ability to provide for their families at such moments, and the expectations of the local party boss often seemed an improvement over those of the local hacendado.

Finally, in the wake of nearly three decades of bloodshed and uncertainty, the ruling party offered Mexicans relief from the rigors of revolutionary agitation, a political stopping-off point outside the fray of antagonisms that, in Ernesto Laclau's and Chantal Mouffe's formulation, constitute the substance of democratic politics. Feminist theorists have observed that political systems that require constant deliberation and engagement often exclude women, particularly those women with the heaviest domestic-labor obligations.[16] Although many women embraced the opportunity for political involvement — and many who did not still insisted that it remain a possibility — others no doubt welcomed relief from the triple shift of domestic, nondomestic, and political labors. If they could secure a corn mill or a maternity clinic or a vote on the community board by joining a ruling-party affiliate, that may have seemed a more sensible option than insisting on political antagonisms that remained unlikely to yield any tangible benefits.

Co-optation carried a price, to be sure. During the second half of the Cárdenas presidency, the administration took a sharp rightward turn on most social, political, and economic matters. Following the March 1938 nationalization of the petroleum industry and reorganization of the ruling party, the Cárdenas government consolidated its gains, discouraging the popular mobilizations that had legitimated it. Just as the regime's labor and agrarian policies became more conservative, so, too, did its policies on women's rights. Gains that seemed imminent in 1937 had become unattainable by 1939, when the regime favored stability over militancy. While the government tolerated and even implicitly condoned the 1936 Santa Bárbara invasion, for example, it most likely would have crushed it in 1939. And the vibrant and contentious movement that had pushed women's issues prominently onto the regime's agenda in the 1920s and early '30s became so complicit with the ruling party that by 1939 it lacked the autonomy to force the suffrage question. Unified and incorporated, the women's movement had compromised its ability to mobilize women against regime policies.

These local, national, and transnational contingencies often demarcated the distinction between those inside and outside sovereign law, but they also created opportunities for new political actors to inhabit revolutionary citizenship. Temperance leagues, mass organizations, labor unions, the PCM, and the Secretariat of Public Education (SEP) all created infrastructures that facilitated both formal and informal citizenship practices. The more successful organizations — measuring success by, for example, a group's longevity, membership, and ability to secure goods, services, or rights — did not cohere around a single issue, agitate for it, and break apart. Instead, they developed organizational structures, cultures, and bonds of solidarity within the organization and with like-minded groups.

These organizations were often mimetic of formal citizenship practices, deploying rhetoric that emulated Mexico's Constitution and Civil Code. Women — many of them for the first time — signed membership cards, agreed to bylaws and objectives, and convened meetings to design and execute programs. This formality did not imply stasis, as the most successful organizations demonstrated flexibility in their strategies and aims and became more ambitious as their strength allowed. The Ligas Femeniles, for example, adapted their programs to shifting political climates as well as to their memberships' changing needs and capacities. As they grew, they redefined their objectives, adding demands such as land, legal protections, and welfare services to earlier petitions for official recognition, health clinics, and motorized corn mills. Their formality as membership organizations made them exclusive, either implicitly or explicitly, but also gave them clear mandates and well-defined representative capacities. Delineating their constituencies lent specificity to their demands — linking them to a membership rather than to a more elusive and ill-defined group such as "women," "campesinas," or "Laguneras" — and afforded them greater legitimacy and leverage both within their communities and with federal officials.

In becoming "organized" in both the mobilizational and disciplinary senses women understood themselves as joining the polity, donning the garb of revolutionary citizenship. They developed a sense of entitlement to everything from corn mills to health clinics and from state patronage to "voice and vote." The regime's elasticity — its sovereign power to allow exceptions — determined its co-optive success as state agencies and party-loyal popular organizations selectively accommodated new constituencies. Depending on their strength and importance to the regime's priorities, co-opted organizations required the state party to expand or reorient to incorporate their priorities. While they retained limited leverage in defining this process, these groups hardly remained passive vessels of state indoctrination. Rather, they exercised citizenship by forcing some degree of political change.

In Agamben's articulation, the "bare life" — the "no-man's-land between the home and the city" — constitutes the "originary political element" and the "most intimate relationship with sovereignty."[17] By practicing revolutionary citizenship, women activists inhabited this space of political intimacy between the *oikos* and the *polis*, structuring sovereignty through their unavoidable exception. What made women exceptional before the law and before sovereignty, of course, was their sex. Prevailing gender codes of both formal and informal politics assumed a male political subject. During the postrevolutionary decades, women activists' questioning of these gender practices precipitated a public debate that rendered them more visible and more self-consciously rationalized.

This debate played out in complicated ways. Supporters and opponents of women's political rights did not fall neatly on one side or the other of a clear divide. Both suffragists and antisuffragists, for example, pointed to women's purported morality or abnegación to bolster their arguments about women's suitability for political involvement. While advocates of women's rights might stress their gender transgressions through participation in wage labor or political organizations, their opponents held these activities up as evidence of the social and cultural instability introduced by feminism, often depicted as a foreign influence that threatened Mexican femininity and families. Secular women activists also reinscribed dominant gender ideologies by exploiting them. In the absence of clear entitlements, women often appealed to state paternalism by highlighting their vulnerability as women, mothers, or widows. Even an epithet as derogatory as "malinchismo" opened political space; activists at times indicated that the inadequate or incomplete attention to their concerns would push women to the disloyalty of assisting cristeros, undermining socialist education, or backing an opposition candidate. In other words, assumptions about women's potential for betrayal empowered them in a limited fashion.

The PCM and its fellow-traveler organizations took the opposite tack, insisting on women's loyalty by nearly effacing gender difference in favor of class identities and often failing to appreciate the extent to which women's labor — their quotidian, unpaid, reproductive labor — defined their identities and allegiances much as the labor experiences of railroad workers and peones acasillados defined theirs. While the terms and content of these labor obligations varied by context, they cultivated a gendered identity that simple indoctrination or "orientation" would not readily alter. The Ligas Femeniles de Lucha Social attracted a popular following not only because they enjoyed official support but also because they created physical and political space for ordinary women to organize around the concerns most immediate to them and their communities. Experiences, more than identities, galvanized their participation in collective mobilizations.

By the 1940s, the fortification of traditional gender roles and patriarchal family structures overshadowed alternative visions for women's activism. "The study of this last [postrevolutionary] stage is fundamental to avoid misunderstanding women's struggle as an isolated movement," observes María Antonieta Rascón, a historian of women's participation in the revolution. "It transcends established economic and political frameworks and explains how women's traditional role is vitally important to the survival of a class-based society. If the woman that emerges from the revolutionary stage tried to break with this role, the new, postrevolutionary ideology tried to reimpose it."[18] This reimposition, like all hegemonic endeavors, encountered roadblocks. Many women engaged in activities the regime deemed inappropriate, and the meanings of womanhood and the "traditional role of women" remained unstable and readily manipulated. Perhaps most important, programs designed in Mexico City could only be implemented unevenly and imperfectly in the towns and villages outside the nation's capital. In the context of postrevolutionary regime consolidation, the tug-of-war between resistance and reimposition pulled at the meanings and expectations of revolutionary citizenship.

Despite women's marginalization from formal politics and persistent anxieties about unstable gender roles, however, the masculinity of Mexican politics began to erode in both subtle and conspicuous ways. Avila Camacho became the first postrevolutionary president to declare himself a practicing Catholic — signaling the end of the state's aggressively anticlerical position — and the last president to have served in the revolutionary army. In 1940, the PRM eliminated its military sector, leaving only the worker, peasant, and popular sectors, and Avila Camacho's appointment of a civilian successor marked a definitive turn away from a political masculinity centered on military service and toward one centered on the professional bureaucracy.[19] Catholic piety and military service had served as two important gender identifiers during the postrevolutionary period — albeit imperfect ones, as men were often pious and women occasionally took up arms. Although Avila Camacho's choices hardly signaled the wholesale feminization of Mexican politics, they did indicate the possibilities for altering prevailing gender codes.

The evolving state bureaucracy also blurred the gender lines within Mexican politics. The welfare legislation that passed in 1941 and took effect in 1943 bore the imprint of women's activism, although continuing to provide for women principally within the patriarchal framework of the male breadwinner.[20] Growing professionalization and bureaucratization within popular organizations, particularly following the ruling party's 1938 reorganization, created new opportunities for women in the public sector but left many women with only a tenuous connection to the groups that claimed to represent them. As the National Peasant Confederation (CNC) bureaucracy incorporated the Ligas Femeniles de Lucha Social, their administration increasingly fell to women who earned their living as party functionaries, and full-time mothers, workers, or peasants rarely worked as paid employees in mass organizations or government bureaucracies. The women who occupied the posts of secretary of women's affairs for the Mexican Labor Confederation (CTM) or the CNC, in other words, had less connection than most women with the traditional markers of femininity, such as motherhood, domestic labor, and abnegación. The bureaucratization of popular organizing did not affect only women. Those who became intermediaries between indigenous groups and the state, for example, similarly compromised the cultural, linguistic, and material ties that linked them with the communities they represented.[21]

Despite the regime's growing authoritarianism and the bureaucratization of popular organizing, it remains critical to distinguish this postrevolutionary period from what ensued. Women's activism waxed and waned during the Cold War era, burgeoning during and after the 1975 United Nations Year of the Woman congress in Mexico City and again following Mexico City's devastating 1985 earthquake.[22] In both instances, women were galvanized in part by the state's failure to respond to crises. The periods before and after the Cold War resembled one another in their heightened emphasis on industrialization and democratization but within critically different contexts. The democratization of the 1930s occurred in the spirit of anti-imperialist nationalism; the wave of the 1990s took place within a national sovereignty closely circumscribed by corporations and international lending agencies that make voting rights seem nearly irrelevant. Similarly, the nongovernmental organizations (NGOs) that now structure and populate Mexico's — and Latin America's — "civil society" differ markedly from Cardenista popular organizations. While the latter emphasized class-oriented and state-centered organizing, NGOs and "new social movements" have eschewed class identities and drawn their support largely from private foundations, mostly based in the United States and Europe.

This transformed context yields countless practical changes with regard to popular organizations. Today, in San Pedro de las Colonias, Coahuila, in the heart of the Comarca Lagunera, the CNC still facilitates the establishment of women's "cooperatives," but they are no more cooperative than the PRI is revolutionary. Rather than collectively operated ventures designed to give women greater control over their labor power, these privately capitalized, foreign-owned assembly plants set up shop among clusters of ejidos to attract women to work near home rather than heading to the border region to work in one of the thousands of foreign-owned maquiladoras.[23] CNC organizers intend these "cooperatives," like the Ligas Femeniles de Lucha Social, to prevent modernization and industrialization from upending conventional gender roles. The maquiladoras undeniably exploit women's labor and have notoriously deleterious working conditions, and their growing presence coincides with an explosion in rapes and murders of female laborers in the border cities where they concentrate. However, these assembly plants have also disrupted gender roles by giving women greater access to income and therefore more influence in household decision making. The CNC "coopera-tives" would offer women only the exploitative labor conditions without the opportunity to escape traditional patriarchal households, although they likely would have material benefits for the CNC. As industrial parks of these foreign-owned factories become a growing presence throughout the region, however, the new "cooperatives" seem inevitable and, to some, perhaps, a lesser evil. Women could perform low-wage, nonunion labor without aban-doning the family home, resulting, it would seem, in an unhappy marriage of capitalism and patriarchy.

When Concha Michel invaded the Hacienda Santa Bárbara in 1935, she wielded a carefully fashioned critique of the marriage between capitalism and patriarchy. Her controversial 1934 pamphlet, *Marxistas y "marxistas"* (Marxists and "Marxists"), had precipitated her expulsion from the Com-munist Party, which she insisted did not go far enough in confronting capi-talism's particular toll on women outside the wage-labor force. Michel, and many other women activists, struggled to push women's issues — and the "woman question" — out into the daylight, subject to public scrutiny and debate. After all, if the new regime transformed the feudal relationships of agricultural labor, it might do the same for the arduous, unequal, paternalis-tic, often abusive, conditions of women's household labor. Efforts such as Michel's — making visible women's labor and community involvement — formed the core of women's revolutionary citizenship, rendering their activ-ism both revolutionary and civic. If the peasant approaching the landlord with his head bowed and hat in hand seemed an icon of Mexico's prerevolu-tionary past, perhaps the rebozo-shrouded madre abnegada stooped over the grinding stone might similarly give way to the ciudadana revolucionaria.

NOTES

Introduction

1 Paz, *Labyrinth of Solitude and Other Writings*, 66.
2 Alegría, *Emancipación Femenina*; *Novedades*, 15 August 1977.
3 Michel, *Marxistas y "marxistas."*
4 Daniels to Secretary of State, 28 January 1936, NARA, 812.00/30334.
5 Michel, *Casa-escuela de la mujer trabajadora.*
6 *El Nacional*, 17 November 1937, 1. Women's suffrage appeared so certain that a contemporary observer erroneously commented in a work published in 1939 that Cárdenas had granted women's suffrage, and another historian recently repeated the mistaken assertion: Plenn, *Mexico Marches*, 322; Cockcroft, *Mexico's Hope*, 129.
7 Ashby, *Organized Labor and the Mexican Revolution under Lázaro Cárdenas*; Gilly, *Cartas a Cuauhtémoc Cárdenas*, *El cardenismo*, and *La revolución interrumpida*; Tannenbaum, *Mexico*; Townsend, *Lázaro Cárdenas*. Revisionist scholars, responding to the post-1968 crisis of confidence in a regime still clinging desperately and hypocritically to the label "revolutionary," often viewed the Cárdenas period as the moment when regime consolidation foreclosed the possibility of a truly popular revolutionary movement: Córdova, *La ideología de la revolución mexicana*, *La política de masas del cardenismo*, and *La revolución y el estado en México*; Hamilton, *The Limits of State Autonomy*; Medin, *Ideología y praxis política de Lázaro Cárdenas*. Postrevisionists, particularly in light of the democratic challenge by Cárdenas's son Cuauhtémoc, have softened this characterization, dispensing with the hero-or-villain debate that painted Cárdenas as "redeemer or tarnished messiah" or surrounded him with "mythology and black legend," and taking seriously the actions and aspirations of popular actors rather than seeing them as hapless pawns of the political elite: Bantjes, *As If Jesus Walked on Earth*, xiv; Becker, *Setting the Virgin on Fire*, 4; see also Boyer, *Becoming Campesinos*; Cortés Zavala, *Lázaro Cárdenas y su proyecto cultural en Michoacán*; Fallaw, *Cárdenas Compromised*; Joseph and Nugent, *Everyday Forms of State Formation*; Knight, "Cardenismo: Juggernaut or Jalopy?" "Popular Culture and the Revolutionary State in Mexico, 1910–1940," and "Populism and

Neo-populism in Latin America"; Nugent, *Rural Revolt in Mexico*; Purnell, *Popular Movements and State Formation in Revolutionary Mexico*; Rubin, *Decentering the Regime*; Vaughan, *Cultural Politics in Revolution*. For a review of these debates, see Spenser and Levinson "Linking State and Society in Discourse and Action."

8 Bourdieu, *Outline of a Theory of Practice*.

9 Habermas, *The Structural Transformation of the Public Sphere*; Pateman, *The Sexual Contract*.

10 Although much work remains to be done on conservative movements, see Boylan, "Mexican Catholic Women's Activism, 1929–1940"; Meyer, *La Cristiada*, *El sinarquismo, un fascismo mexicano*, and *El Sinarquismo, el Cardenismo y la Iglesia, 1937–1947*; Reich, *Mexico's Hidden Revolution*; Schell, "Training Loving Hands"; Servín, *Ruptura y oposición*.

11 Hufton, *Women and the Limits of Citizenship in the French Revolution*; Judt, *Past Imperfect*, 234–35; Mayer, *The Furies*; Waldinger et al., *The French Revolution and the Meaning of Citizenship*.

12 *El Nacional*, 15 November 1931, 8.

13 Lister, *Citizenship*; Pateman *The Sexual Contract* and *The Disorder of Women*; Phillips, *Engendering Democracy* and *Democracy and Difference*.

14 Arendt, *Eichmann in Jerusalem*, 135–50.

15 Wolin, "Fugitive Democracy," 38.

16 Agamben, *Homo Sacer*, 16.

17 *El Nacional*, 27 January 1936.

18 Wolin, "Fugitive Democracy," 38.

19 Joseph and Nugent, *Everyday Forms of State Formation*.

20 Knight, "Popular Culture and the Revolutionary State in Mexico, 1910–1940," 396.

21 On regional fragmentation, see Simpson, *Many Mexicos*. On the usefulness of a regional framework, see Benjamin and McNellie, *Other Mexicos*; Benjamin and Wasserman, *Provinces of the Revolution*; González, *San José de Gracia*, and "Microhistory, *Terruño*, and the Social Sciences"; Van Young, *Mexico's Regions*. Luis González's call for attention to local specificity generated countless studies that have borne out the importance of regional perspectives.

22 Dienstag, *"Dancing in Chains"*; Benhabib, "Sexual Difference and Collective Identities," 347.

23 Benhabib, "Sexual Difference and Collective Identities," 344.

24 On popular appeals to the rule of law, see Thompson, *Whigs and Hunters*, esp. 258ff. On the class differentiation in relationships between citizens and states in Latin American, see Reis, "Nationalism and Citizenship."

25 Davis, *The Problem of Slavery in the Age of Revolution*, 308.

26 Cott, "Marriage and Women's Citizenship in the United States," 1440. Kathleen Canning has similarly argued for understanding the "process by which historical actors assigned meanings to the prescriptions and delineations of citizenship and

hence became subjects in their encounters with citizenship laws, rhetorics, and practices": Canning, "Class versus Citizenship."

27 Constitución de los Estados Unidos Mexicanos 1917, art. 34.

28 Knight, "The Rise and Fall of Cardenismo," 274.

29 Wolin, "Fugitive Democracy," 39.

30 Ashby, *Organized Labor and the Mexican Revolution under Lázaro Cárdenas*.

31 Vaughan, *Cultural Politics in Revolution*.

32 Paz, *The Labyrinth of Solitude and Other Writings*, 86. See also Bartra, *The Cage of Melancholy*, 147–62; Cypess, *La Malinche in Mexican Literature*; Franco, *Plotting Women*, 129–46. La Malinche arguably embodies Agamben's notion of the *homo sacer* — sold into slavery and then given to Cortés as a gift, she remained both literally and metaphorically "banned," simultaneously sacred and profane, subject to being killed but not sacrificed.

33 For a feminist analysis comparing schoolchildren's perceptions of La Malinche and the Virgin of Guadalupe, see *Fem* 242 (May 2003): 4–9.

34 The anthropologist Guillermo de la Peña observes that "a populist project requires intermediaries who can translate it favorably": de la Peña, "Populism, Regional Power, and Political Mediation," 194.

35 *Izquierdas*, 17 December 1934; Tuñón Pablos, *Mujeres que se organizan*, 37.

36 *El Nacional*, 8 June 1930, 8. On the elastic meaning of the term "feminist," see Cano, "Feminismo."

37 *Orientaciones para las Ligas Femeniles de Lucha Social en los Ejidos*.

38 Circular 1 to Comités Regionales (CRs), Comités Secionales (CSs), y células from Secretario, Comité Central (CC) Comisión de Organización, 24 May 1934, Condumex, AGRA, Fondo MXLVI, carpeta 4, legajo 288.

39 FUPDM, Córdoba, Veracruz, to Cárdenas, 16 January 1938, AGN, RP, LCR, exp. 136.3/388; Sección feminista, Partido "Leones de la Revolución," 28 April 1936, AGN, RP, LCR, exp. 544/1.

40 UFCM, caja 2, folder 15.

41 *El Maestro Rural*, vol. 5, no. 7, 1934, 6–7.

42 *El Universal*, 13 November 1931, 11.

43 Cano, "La íntima felicidad del Coronel Robles"; O'Malley, *The Myth of the Revolution*; Reséndez, "Battleground Women"; Rubenstein, *Bad Language, Naked Ladies, and Other Threats to the Nation*; Salas, *Soldaderas in the Mexican Military*.

44 *Excélsior*, 20 October 1933, 10.

45 Guerrero, "Por la madre y el niño," 7.

46 Butler and Scott, "Contingent Foundations: Feminism and the Question of the 'Postmodern,'" 16.

47 For Gayatri Spivak's subsequently disavowed discussion of "strategic essentialism," see Grosz, "Criticism, Feminism, and the Institution."

48 Alonso, *Thread of Blood*.

49 Pallares, *Ley Sobre Relaciones Familiares*, 16–17.

50 The legal scholar Luis Muñoz argues, "The feminist movement, without a doubt, influences our legislators" in crafting such egalitarian languange: Muñoz and Castro Zavaleta, *Comentarios al Código Civil*, 98.

51 On indigenous women as the bearers of an ethnic national identity, see Nelson, *Finger in the Wound*.

52 Luna Arroyo, *La mujer mexicana en la lucha social*, 19.

53 Applewhite and Levy, *Women and Politics*, 97. Dominique Godineau similarly refers to women who engaged in a practice of citizenship as "*citoyennes* without citizenship" in Godineau, "Masculine and Feminine in the Political Practice," 68.

54 On women's participation in the revolution, see Reséndez, "Battleground Women"; Turner, "Los efectos de la participación femenina en la Revolución de 1910."

55 Liga Femenil de Resistencia, Naranja, Michoacán, to Félix Ireta, Governor of Michoacán, 25 September 1940, AGN, RP, LCR, exp. 542.1/20.

56 Confederación de Mujeres Revolucionarias, Mexico City, to Cárdenas, 20 June 1940, AGN, RP, LCR, exp. 544/1. See also correspondence of the Legión Femenil Militar in AGN, RP, MAC, exp. 111/1399.

57 Petition from the Sección Femenil del Militar del PRM, 27 September 1939, AGN, RP, LCR, exp. 151.3/1301.

58 Flores Sánchez, interview.

59 *El Nacional*, 7 June 1931, 8.

60 Ibid., 15 October 1932, 8; *El Maestro Rural*, vol. 3, no. 5, 1 August 1933, 5–6.

61 *El Maestro Rural*, vol. 8, no. 4, 15 February 1936, 33.

62 Laclau and Mouffe, *Hegemony and Socialist Strategy*, 13.

63 Arno Mayer distinguishes between counterrevolutionary movements coming from above "to institutionalize their own revolt at the expense of crushing all others in their drive to establish or impose their monopoly of centralized state power" and antirevolutionary movements coming from below "to curb the centralizing, modernizing, and secularizing reach of the revolution rather than restore the *ancién régime* of feudal or seignorial servitude": Mayer, *The Furies*, 30, 59.

64 Civera Cerecedo, *Entre surcos y letras*, 122.

65 Cárdenas, *Palabras y documentos*, 233.

66 For a concise account, see Knight, "The Rise and Fall of Cardenismo."

67 On the concept of state efforts to impose "legibility" on popular movements and practices, see Scott, *Seeing Like a State*.

68 Múgica to Cárdenas, 9 July 1937, CERM, FJM, vol. 179, no. 60.

Chapter One "A Right to Struggle"

1 Turner, "Los efectos de la participación femenina en la Revolución de 1910," 611.

2 García Quintanilla, *Los tiempos en Yucatán*; Macías, *Against All Odds*; Pérez, "Feminism-in-Nationalism"; Soto, *The Emergence of the Modern Mexican Woman*.

3 Although the Mérida congress is referred to as the First Feminist Congress in Mexico, Julia Tuñón Pablos points out that Francisco Múgica organized a feminist congress in 1915 while serving as governor of Tabasco. Unfortunately, scant evidence survives from this early congress: Tuñón Pablos, *Mujeres en México*, 94.

4 According to Gabriela Cano, the term "feminist" had been used at least since 1903, when Justo Sierra used it to dismiss ideas of women's inferiority. Cano underscores the term's plurality of meanings, but it gained currency among women activists in the 1910s and '20s, particularly among those distinguishing themselves from communists and socialists, on the one hand, and antiregime Catholics, on the other: Cano, "Feminismo."

5 Joseph, *Revolution from Without*; Pérez, "Feminism-in-Nationalism."

6 *La Voz de la Revolución*, 11–19 February 1916. I thank Alejandra García Quintanilla for providing me with this source.

7 Cited in Macías, *Against All Odds*, 73.

8 Orellana Trinidad, "'La mujer del porvenir.'" For the text of the speech, see *El primer congreso feminista de Yucatán*, 195ff.

9 Cited in Orellana Trinidad, "'La mujer del porvenir,'" 117. See also Cano, "Revolución, femenismo y ciudadanía en México (1915–1940)," 306–307.

10 *El primer congreso feminista de Yucatán*, 197–98.

11 Ibid., 53, 56.

12 Ibid., 133.

13 For a striking example of the revolution enabling unconventional gender identities, see Cano, "La íntima felicidad del Coronel Robles."

14 *El primer congreso feminista de Yucatán*, 79, 145.

15 Ibid., 79.

16 Picatto, *El discurso sobre el alcoholismo en el Congreso Constituyente de 1916–1917*.

17 *Diario de los debates del Congreso constituyente de 1916–1917*, 1:517, 1:528.

18 Ibid., 1:679.

19 For a comparison, see Bredbenner, *A Nationality of Her Own*, on the United States' 1907 Expatriation Act.

20 *Diario de los debates del Congreso constituyente de 1916–1917*, 2:133.

21 Ibid., 2:482.

22 Ibid., 2:395, 2:494, 2:601ff. See also Cano, "Hermila Galindo"; Tuñón, *¡Por fin . . . ya podemos elegir y ser electas!* 34.

23 *Diario de los debates del Congreso constituyente de 1916–1917*, 2:601.

24 Ibid., 2:714.

25 Ibid., 2:711. A 1918 amendment to the electoral laws specified that only men could vote and be elected: Cano, "Revolución, femenismo y ciudadanía en México (1915–1940)," 311.

26 A teacher and school administrator, Monzón described himself as hailing from "the most virile region of the virile state of Sonora," which selected him as a representative to the congress because he was "the most savage and intransigent

revolutionary with regard to radical convictions": *Diario de los debates del Congreso constituyente de 1916–191*, 1:166.

27 Cott, *The Grounding of Modern Feminism*; Dubois, *Feminism and Suffrage* and *Woman Suffrage and Women's Rights*; Kraditor, *The Ideas of the Woman Suffrage Movement*.

28 For similar postrevolutionary phenomena, see Chatterjee, *Celebrating Women*; Hufton, *Women and the Limits of Citizenship in the French Revolution*; Rowbotham, *Women, Resistance and Revolution*. See also Knight, "Popular Culture and the Revolutionary State in Mexico, 1910–1940."

29 Ward Morton argues that "at the very moment when victories for woman suffrage elsewhere gave impetus to Mexican sentiment in its favor, the Mexican Constitutional Congress bypassed the problem largely on the basis of . . . Monzón's somewhat confused assertion that the Committee did not take it into consideration": Morton, *Woman Suffrage in Mexico*, 8.

30 *Diario de los debates de la Cámara de Diputados del Congreso de los Estados Unidos Mexicanos*, no. 48, 2 June 1917, 10.

31 *Diario de debates del Congreso constituyente de 1916–1917*, 2:678; Picatto, *El discurso sobre el alcoholismo en el Congreso Constituyente de 1916–1917*.

32 On the changing posterevolutionary understandings of race, see Knight, "Racism, Revolution, and *Indigenismo*"; Stern, "From Mestizophilia to Biotypology."

33 Carr, *Marxism and Communism in Twentieth-Century Mexico*, 39.

34 Ibid., chap. 1; *The Strategy of the Communists*, 11–13.

35 SEP, IOS, caja 3952/3091/3, exp. 4.

36 "Programa y Estatutos del Partido Socialista Fronterizo," 15 May 1924, AGN, DGG, vol. 2.312(24)4, caja 16, exp. 18.

37 Buck, "El control de la natalidad y el día de la madre"; Cano, "México, 1923"; Macías, *Against All Odds*; Soto, *The Emergence of the Modern Mexican Woman*.

38 For proceedings of the congress, see *Primer congreso feminista de la Liga Pan-Americana de Mujeres*. For a comparison with the 1916 congress in Yucatán and the contentious 1931 congress in Mexico City, see Cano, "Congresos Feministas en la Historia de México," 24–27.

39 Buck, "El control de la natalidad y el día de la madre" and "Activists and Mothers."

40 Cited in Buck, "Activists and Mothers," 104.

41 Bailey, *¡Viva Cristo Rey!*; Meyer, *La Cristiada* and "Revolution and Reconstruction in the 1920s," 206; and Miller, "The Role of Women in the Mexican Cristero Rebellion."

42 Cited in Reich, *Mexico's Hidden Revolution*, 24.

43 During the 1917 Constitutional Congress, for example, Modesto González Galindo sought to eliminate Catholic confession, which made women "an instrument of the clergy . . . to serve the political aims of the Church": *Diario de los debates del Congreso constituyente de 1916–1917*, 1:756.

44 The presumed link between women and counterrevolutionary organizations demands more investigation. In leftist publications, women never appear — in articles, photographs, or caricatures — among the fascist and reactionary organizations, except when depicted as elite or religious women. More commonly, the
leftist press celebrated working-class and peasant women's participation in revolutionary and antifascist struggles both in Mexico and abroad.

45 Garrido, *El partido de la revolución institucionalizada*; Nava Nava, *La ideología del
Partido de la Revolución Mexicana*. On partisan realignment and democratic transi-
tions creating opportunities for women's organizations, see Baldez, *Why Women
Protest*; Friedman, *Unfinished Transitions*.

46 National Revolutionary Party (PNR), "Constitución del Partido Nacional Revolucionario," 3, 8–9, 15.

47 Ríos Cárdenas to Governor of Yucatán, 11 September 1928, AGEY, PE, Gob., caja
924.

48 *El Nacional*, 29 November 1929, 8.

49 AGN, DGG, vol. 2.331.9(29)101, caja 79, exps. 19–20.

50 Despite inchoate industrialization, Mexico remained a predominantly rural nation. James Wilkie has found that the economically active population employed in
agriculture was still 67.7 percent in 1930, 63.4 percent in 1940, and 58.3 percent by
1950: Wilkie, *The Mexican Revolution*, 193. On indigenous women as a prosthesis
for embattled cultural groups, see Nelson, *Finger in the Wound*.

51 *Excélsior*, 9 March 1931, 10.

52 For studies of women's agricultural labor, see Fowler-Salamini and Vaughan, *Creating Spaces, Shaping Transitions*.

53 *La Prensa* (San Antonio ed.), 10 February 1931, 2.

54 *Heraldo de Cuba*, 10 February 1931, 4.

55 *El Machete*, 30 June 1931, 2.

56 *El Nacional*, 10 March 1931, 8.

57 Ibid. *Ejidatarios* are members of an agricultural cooperative.

58 Ibid.

59 Partha Chatterjee explores this ambivalence within nationalist projects between
the masculinized, materialist, Westernized aspect of culture and its feminized,
spiritual, authentic counterpart: Chatterjee, *A Nation and Its Fragments*, 116ff. See
also Nelson, *A Finger in the Wound*, 245ff. On its manifestations in Mexican popular culture, see Rubenstein, *Bad Language, Naked Ladies, and Other Threats to the
Nation*.

60 Rubenstein, *Bad Language, Naked Ladies, and Other Threats to the Nation*. On similar concerns in contemporary Europe, see de Grazia, *How Fascism Ruled Women*;
Roberts, *Civilization without Sexes*. A *New York Times* article described Mexican girls
shopping at the "Thieves Market" for "military breeches and engineers' boots":
New York Times, 21 December 1930, 76.

61 *El Nacional*, 21 June 1931, 8.

62 Memorandum Comité Organizador del Ejército de la Mujer Campesina, 20 November 1931, LTAE, carpeta voto femenino.

63 *Excélsior*, 1 October 1931, 10; *New York Times*, 6 October 1931, 26.

64 *El Nacional*, 6 October 1931, 8.

65 *El Machete*, 10 October 1931, 1.

66 *Excélsior*, 3 October 1931, 1.

67 Ibid.; *La Prensa*, 9 October 1931, 11.

68 *El Nacional*, 7 October 1931, 8.

69 *Excélsior*, 7 October 1931, 10; emphasis in the original.

70 Departamento Femenino del Partido Comunista, "¡A las obreras, campesinas y mujeres indígenas en general!" 1 October 1931, Hoover, REM, box 16, folder 7.

71 *El Universal*, 4 October 1931, 9.

72 *El Universal Gráfico*, 5 October 1931, as cited in Tuñón Pablos, *Mujeres que se organizan*, 37.

73 *El Nacional*, 7 October 1931, 8.

74 Ibid.

75 *El Machete*, 10 October 1931, 1; *Excélsior*, 6 October 1931, sec. 2, 1.

76 *El Universal*, 8 October 1931, 9.

77 Ibid., 6 October 1931, 9; *El Nacional*, 12 November 1931, 8.

78 *El Machete*, 30 October 1931, 3.

79 *El Heraldo de Cuba*, 20 February 1931, 4.

80 *El Nacional*, 7 June 1931, 8.

81 *Excélsior*, 20 January 1931, 10.

82 *El Nacional*, 15 November 1931, 8.

83 Comité Nacionalista de Damas adherido a la Unión Nacional Mexicana "Pro-Raza y Salud Pública" to Secretario de Gobernación, 4 January 1931, AGN, DGG, vol. 2.331.9(3)15, caja 55-A, exp. 21.

84 *Excélsior*, 27 March 1931, 10.

85 *La Prensa*, 5 May 1931, 11; *El Nacional*, 6 May 1931, 8.

86 On consumption as women's work, see Frank, *Purchasing Power*.

87 *El Nacional*, 24 June 1931, 8.

88 *La Prensa*, 1 June 1931, 11.

89 Olcott, "Miracle Workers."

90 *El Machete*, 30 September 1931, 2.

91 "Boletín de la Internacional Sindical Roja," 7 February 1930, Condumex, AGRA, Fondo MXLVI, carpeta 2, legajo 92.

92 *El Machete*, 15 February 1931, 1.

93 Ibid., 15 April 1931, 5.

94 "A todas las locales del Partido," 11 June 1931, Condumex, AGRA, Fondo MXLVI, carpeta 2, legajo 131.

95 "Séptima Conferencia Nacional del Partido Comunista de México: Resolución de

Organización," January 1932, Condumex, AGRA, Fondo MXLVI, carpeta 3, legajo 185.

96 *El Machete*, 10 July 1931, 2.

97 Ibid., 1 May 1933, 2.

98 Ibid., 30 June 1931, 2; Ibid., 20 July 1931, 2.

99 Ibid., 15 March 1931, 1.

100 Ibid., 20 March 1934, 1.

101 Ibid., 10 November 1933, 2; Michel, *Marxistas y "marxistas"*; Olcott, "'Sing What the People Sing.'"

102 *El Nacional*, 12 November 1931, 8.

103 Ibid., 13 November 1931, 8.

104 *New York Times*, 15 November 1931, 20.

105 *La Prensa*, 13 November 1931, 11.

Chapter Two   Laboratory of Cardenismo

1 Martínez Múgica, *Primo Tapia*, 92.

2 Ibid., 195.

3 Boyer, *Becoming Campesinos*, and Purnell, *Popular Movements and State Formation in Revolutionary Mexico*, both characterize the cristero-agrarista divide as local and relational, providing a political shorthand for distinguishing among rivals rather than a clear-cut, static ideological identity. See also Becker, *Setting the Virgin on Fire*.

4 On Michoacán as a regional "laboratory" of Mexican state formation, see Benjamin, "Laboratories of the New State, 1920–1929."

5 Friedrich, *Agrarian Revolt in a Mexican Village*; Martínez Múgica, *Primo Tapia*.

6 Purnell, *Popular Movements and State Formation in Revolutionary Mexico*, 62–63; Tobler, "Peasants and the Shaping of the Revolutionary State, 1910–1940," 502.

7 On the Confederación Nacional Católica del Trabajo (CNCT), see Meyer, *La Cristiada*, 2:215–16.

8 *Diario de los debates del Congreso constituyente*, 1:642.

9 Cited in Castellanos Guerrero and López y Rivas, *Primo Tapia de la Cruz*, 39.

10 Primo Tapia to Apolinar Martínez Múgica, September 1923, cited in Hernández, *La Confederación Revolucionaria Michoacana del Trabajo*, 15.

11 Friedrich, *The Princes of Naranja*.

12 Ibid.; Friedrich, *Agrarian Revolt in a Mexican Village*.

13 Múgica Mártinez maintains that the Liga de Comunidades Agrarias "was not paralyzed by the physical death of Primo Tapia," since his comrades continued to organize around Tapia's ideas: Múgica Mártinez, *La Confederación Revolucionaria Michoacana del Trabajo*, 90. For an opposing view, see Friedrich, *Agrarian Revolt in a Mexican Village*, epilogue.

14 Hernández, *La Confederación Revolucionaria Michoacana del Trabajo*; Múgica Mártinez, *La Confederación Revolucionaria Michoacana del Trabajo*.

15 Embriz Osorio, *La Liga de Comunidades y Sindicatos Agraristas del Estado de Michoacán*, 121–48; Embriz Osorio and León García, *Documentos para la historia del agrarismo en Michoacán*.

16 Múgica Martínez, *La Confederación Revolucionaria Michoacana del Trabajo*, 99.

17 The 1930 industrial census showed that fewer than 1 percent of all Michoacán firms employed more than fifty people, with 40 percent claiming no employees at all. More than three-quarters of those who identified themselves as workers labored in settings with one hundred workers or fewer: Dirección General de Estadística, *Primer censo industrial de 1930*, 96.

18 Hernández, *La Confederación Revolucionaria Michoacana del Trabajo*, 35; Múgica Martínez, *La Confederación Revolucionaria Michoacana del Trabajo*, 107–109.

19 The 1930 industrial and population censuses both give relatively small figures, estimating that women made up about 3 percent of Michoacán's economically active population and 9 percent of its paid labor force. Even given the high probability of undercounting women's labor, it is unlikely that more than 20 percent received a wage for their labor. Much of women's "economic activity" (occasional vending of foodstuffs or crafts, marketing, occasional seamstress or domestic work) remained invisible to census takers: see Dirección General de Estadística, *Primer censo industrial de 1930* and *Quinto censo de población de 1930*.

20 Flyer dated December 1929, AHMM, caja 104, exp. 2.

21 María Ponce to Carlos García León, Presidente Municipal, Morelia, 28 December 1929, AHMM, caja 104, exp. 2.

22 AHMM, caja 102, exp. 5.

23 AHMM, caja 110, exp. 15.

24 Hernández maintains that Jury bribed the workers' representative: Hernández, *La Confederación Revolucionaria Michoacana del Trabajo*, 39.

25 AHMM, caja 106, exp. 93.

26 Múgica Martínez, *La Confederación Revolucionaria Michoacana del Trabajo*, 103–105.

27 According to agrarian-reform law, female heads of household enjoyed the same ejidal rights as their male counterparts. In practice, however, women rarely received ejido plots. By the mid-1930s, rural women's leagues had agitated for greater access to land, either as heads of households or as collectivities. On the gendered effects of agrarian-reform policies during this period, see Velázquez, *Políticas sociales, transformación agraria y participación de las mujeres en el campo*. For a helpful analysis of the role of agrarian reform in reinforcing patriarchal gender ideologies, see Deere and León de Leal, *Empowering Women*; Tinsman, *Partners in Conflict*.

28 Múgica Martínez, *La Confederación Revolucionaria Michoacana del Trabajo*, 95–109.

29 Report from Flores Zamora, 27 November 1929, AHPEM, Gobierno, Religión, caja 8, exp 29. On Michoacán's church-state conflict over public education, see Becker, *Setting the Virgin on Fire*; Romero Flores, *La historia de la educación en Michoacán*.

30 Purnell, *Popular Movements and State Formation in Revolutionary Mexico*, 133.

31 Friedrich, *Agrarian Revolt in a Mexican Village*, 121.

32 Espinosa to Cárdenas, 20 January 1930, AHPEM, Gobierno, Religión, caja 8, exp. 31.

33 Cira Ponce and Modesta Rangel to Cárdenas, 22 March 1930, AHPEM, Gobierno, Religión, caja 8, exp. 31.

34 Pascuala Talavera to Cárdenas, 31 March 1930, AHPEM, Gobierno, Religión, caja 8, exp. 30.

35 Purnell, *Popular Movements and State Formation in Revolutionary Mexico*, 83; AHPEM, Gobierno, Religión, caja 8, exp. 11.

36 "Aviso," 21 April 1930, AHPEM, Gobierno, Religión, caja 8, exp. 23.

37 Bantjes, *As If Jesus Walked on Earth*; Becker, *Setting the Virgin on Fire*; Boylan, "Mexican Catholic Women's Activism, 1929–1940."

38 Espinoza to Cárdenas, 26 August 1930, AHPEM, Gobierno, Religión, caja 8, exp. 24.

39 Report from Pedro Pablo, Encargado General, Orden de la Hacienda, August 1930, AHPEM, Gobierno, Religión, caja 8, exp. 27.

40 ACEM, Legis. XLIII, Decretos 16 September 1930–16 September 1932, carpeta 7, caja 3.

41 Secretaría del Ayuntamiento, Tingüindín, to Cárdenas, 17 July 1930, AHPEM, Gobierno, Religión, caja 9, exp. 24.

42 AHPEM, Gobierno, Religión, caja 9, exp. 34.

43 See 1930 correspondence between Agustín Leñero, Secretary of Government, and Municipal Presidents, AHMM, caja 101, exp. 4.

44 ACEM, Legis. XXXII, Decreto, carpeta 10, caja 4.

45 Ibid., Legis. XLIII, Decretos 16 September 1924–16 September 1926, carpeta 4, caja 4.

46 In 1930, Mexico's national temperance campaign operated through the Department of Industry, Commerce, and Labor. In the mid-'30s it would move to the Department of Public Health. Throughout, the SEP actively promoted temperance organizations.

47 Juan Molina, Jefe Municipal, Santiago Undameo, to Presidente Municipal, Morelia, 23 October 1930, AHMM, caja 101, exp. 5.

48 Circular from Agustín Leñero, 22 May 1930, AHMM, caja 101, exp. 4.

49 Leñero to Presidente Municipal, Morelia, 10 June 1930, AHMM, caja 101, exp. 4.

50 Leñero to the Presidente Municipal, Morelia, 25 July 1930, AHMM, caja 101, exp. 4.

51 ACEM, Legis. XLIII, Decretos 16 September 1930–16, September 1932, carpeta 9, caja 2.

52 Circular from Manuel Cárdenas, 28 July 1931, AHMM, caja 106, exp. 2.

53 Federación Agraria y Forestal to Presidente Municipal, Morelia, 15 March 1931, AHMM, caja 106, exp. 10.

54 Liga Femenil Anti-alcohólica Femenil "Primo Tapia" to Presidente Municipal, Morelia, 15 March 1931, AHMM, caja 106, exp. 11.

55 Quintero Castellanos, interview.

56 Manuel Cárdenas to Director, Educación Primaria en el Estado, 15 October 1931, AHMM, caja 106, exp. 2.

57 ACEM, Legis. XLII, Decretos 16 September 1928–16 September 1930, carpeta 3, caja 5; AHMM, caja 101, exp. 7.

58 "Ley de asistencia social," ACEM, Legis. XLII, Decretos 16 September 1928–16 September 1930, carpeta 3, caja 5.

59 Ibid.

60 Múgica to Soto Reyes, 26 September 1931, CERM, FJM, Volúmenes, vol. 16, doc. 439.

61 Unsigned, undated memo [probably September 1931], CERM, FJM, Volúmenes, vol. 16, doc. 445.

62 Soto Reyes to Múgica, 28 September 1931, CERM, FJM, Volúmenes, vol. 16, doc. 446.

63 Ibid.

64 Martínez Múgica to Múgica, 3 January 1932, CERM, FJM, Volúmenes, vol. 19, doc. 280.

65 Sánchez Tapia to Múgica, 6 July 1933, CERM, FJM, Volúmenes, vol. 24, doc. 187.

66 Report from the Federación Distrital, Agraria, y Sindicalista de Zamora, 10 December 1932, AHPEM, Gobierno, Conflictos, caja 2, exp. 4.

67 Múgica Martínez, La Confederación Revolucionaria Michoacana del Trabajo, 146–49.

68 Report to the Congreso de la Unión, 26 December 1933, CERM, FJM, Documentos, caja 15, carpeta 364, doc. 4796.

69 Corona to Secretaría de Gobernación, 29 September 1934, AGN, DGG, vol. 2.340(13)54.

70 Sindicato Femenil "Primo Tapia" to Abelardo Rodríguez, 26 May 1933, CERM, FJM, Volúmenes, vol. 24, doc. 225.

71 Report to the Congreso de la Unión, 26 December 1933, CERM, FJM, Documentos, caja 15, carpeta 364, doc. 4796.

72 Becker, Setting the Virgin on Fire; Friedrich, The Princes of Naranja; Gledhill, Casi Nada.

73 Report from 14 June 1933, AHPEM, Gobierno, Conflictos, caja 2, exp. 3.

74 Registration, Sociedad de Enfermeras y Parteras Tituladas, Estado de Michoacán, 25 April 1933, AHMM, caja 138, exp. 15.

75 Circular no. 33, 13 December 1933, AHMM, caja 137, exp. 2.

76 López et al. to Diputado Primitivo Juárez, 12 July 1933, CERM, FJM, Volúmenes, vol. 24, doc. 230.

77 Bulletin of the Federación Política Radical Socialista de Michoacán, 21 August 1933, CERM, FJM, Volúmenes, vol. 24, doc. 32.

78 Núñez to Múgica, 14 August 1933, CERM, FJM, Volúmenes, vol. 24, doc. 27.

79 Múgica to Núñez, 15 August 1933, CERM, FJM, Volúmenes, vol. 24, doc. 28.

80 CERM, FJM, Volúmenes, vol. 205; CERM, FJM, Tomos, cajas 7, 8.

81 *Acta constitutiva* (founding document) of the Sindicato Femenil "Lázaro Cárdenas," 9 August 1931, AHMM, caja 106, exp. 89.

82 López to José Barriga Závala, Presidente Municipal, Morelia, 19 April 1934, AHMM, caja 150, exp. 42.

83 Federación Femenil Socialista Michoacana, CRMDT, to Lázaro Cárdenas, 16 August 1935, AGN, DGG, vol. 2.340(13)54.

84 The CRMDT activists Alfonso Soria and Pánfilo Saldaña campaigned on the same slate with PCM President Hernán Laborde in 1934. Laborde, Soria, Saldaña, and two other PCM leaders, Gabino Alcaraz and Salvador Pintor, campaigned on the slate of the Bloque de Obreros y Campesinos de Morelia, the PCM's political arm during the intense anticommunist persecution of 1929–34.

85 Múgica Martínez, *La Confederación Revolucionaria Michoacana del Trabajo*, 172–73.

86 Ibid., 172.

87 *El Machete*, 20 June 1934, 1.

88 AGN, RP, LCR, exp. 404.4/64; AGN, DGG, vol. 2.340(13)5411; CERM, FJM, Volúmenes, vol. 49, doc. 136.

89 Minutes of meeting of the Liga Femenil Socialista "Lázaro Cárdenas," 15 December 1934, AGN, RP, LCR, exp. 437/99.

90 Anguiano to Alfaro Pérez, 8 January 1935, AHMM, caja 168, exp. 3.

91 Liga Femenil Anti-alcohólica y Anti-clerical de Zinzimacato Grande to Molina, 10 March 1935, AHMM, caja 168, exp. 3.

92 Molina to Alfaro Pérez, 3 May 1935, AHMM, caja 168, exp. 3.

93 Alfaro Pérez to Molina, 4 May 1935, AHMM, caja 168, exps. 3, 36.

94 Múgica Martínez, *La Confederación Revolucionaria Michoacana del Trabajo*, 170.

95 Anguiano to Molina, 22 June 1935, AHMM, caja 168, exp. 3.

96 Liga Femenil, Teremendo, Mich., to FFSM, 13 August 1935 AHMM, caja 168, exp. 3.

97 Anguiano to Molina, 19 January 1936, AHMM, caja 174, exp. 49.

98 Justino Chávez to Molina, 8 June 1936; Chávez to Secretary-General, CRMDT, 21 June 1936; Comisariado Ejidal, Federación Agraria, and Sindicato Femenil to Jefe, Operaciones Militares del Estado, 30 August 1936; all in AHMM, caja 174, exp. 18.

99 Sindicato Femenil de Tiripetío to Magaña, 22 February 1937, AHMM, caja 190, exp. 35.

100 Sindicato Femenil, Tiripetío, Mich., to Cárdenas, 13 March 1937, AGN, RP, LCR, exp. 547.3/146; Sindicato Femenil, Tiripetío, Mich., to Cárdenas, 11 May, and 5 December 1937, AGN, RP, LCR, exp. 562.4/21; 1938 correspondence in AHMM, caja 213, exp. 15.

101 See, for example, two 1936 cases in AHMM, caja 174, exp. 51.

102 Elías Miranda and J. Jesús Múgica to Molina, 9 February 1935, AHMM, caja 168, exp. 17.

103 See correspondence in AHMM, caja 170, exp. 28.

104 Josefina González R., Director, Escuela Oficial Mixta de Río de Parras, Municipio Queréndaro, to Secretario del Gobierno, 4 May 1935, AGN, DGG, vol. 2.340(13)54.

105 Gómez to Cárdenas, 9 February and 15 March 1935, AGN, RP, LCR, exp. 404.1/1238.

106 Liga Femenil Anti-alcohólica, Cantabria, to Cárdenas, 28 March 1935, AGN, RP, LCR, exp. 404.1/57. See also Liga Femenil Anti-alcohólica y Anti-clerical, Santiago Azajo, to Cárdenas, 13 April 1935, AGN, RP, LCR, exp. 404.1/1704.

107 Liga Femenil "Lázaro Cárdenas" to Cárdenas, 10 April 1935; Anguiano to Cárdenas, 9 June 1935, both in AGN, RP, LCR, exp. 404.1/57. See also Liga Femenil Socialista Michoacana, Santa Isabel, Estación Ajuno, to Cárdenas, 21 April 1935, AGN, RP, LCR, exp. 404.1/2742.

108 Comité Particular Ejecutivo Agrario de la Colonia "Lázaro Cárdenas," Villa Jiménez to Cárdenas, 28 June 1935, AGN, RP, LCR, exp. 404.1/2747.

109 AGN, RP, LCR, exp. 404.1/3351; *Periódico Oficial de Michoacán*, 4 January 1937.

110 All correspondence in AGN, RP, LCR, exp. 404.1/3422.

111 AHMM, caja 168, exp. 4; AHPEM, Laboral, Sindicatos, caja 4, exps. 8, 21, caja 9, exps. 7, 15, 17, 28.

112 Agustina Oliva, María del Carmen Zavala, María Guadalupe Granados, and Julia Mayés Navarro to Cárdenas, 17 May 1937, AGN, RP, LCR, exp. 136.3/564.

113 Liga Femenil Anti-clerical, Panindícuaro, to Cárdenas, 19 July and 7 October 1937, AGN, RP, LCR, exp. 521.7/223.

114 María Concepción Padilla viuda de Rosales et al. to Cárdenas, 4 October 1937, AGN, RP, LCR, exp. 432/986.

115 Correspondence between FUPDM and Molina, AHMM, caja 190, exp. 36, caja 226, exp. 6. The school now fell under the careful watch of the prominent revolutionary feminist Juana Belén Gutiérrez de Mendoza.

116 Liga Femenil de Cofradía to Cárdenas, 4 September 1936, AGN, DGG, vol. 2.331.8(13)20424, caja 30-A, exp. 51.

117 CERM, Fondo CERM, caja 14, carpeta 8, doc. 1.

Chapter Three   Educators and Organizers

1 Michel to Director, Departamento de Enseñanza Agrícola y Normal Rural, 3 March 1934, SEP, DEANR, caja 3252/363, exp. 10.

2 Vaughan, *Cultural Politics in Revolution*, 65.

3 Flores Sánchez, interview.

4 Vaughan, *The State, Education, and Social Class in Mexico, 1880–1928*.

5 Vaughan, *Cultural Politics in Revolution*, 59.

6 Cárdenas, *Organización del Circuito Rural*, n.p.

7 Vaughan, *Cultural Politics in Revolution*, 31.

8 "Recomendaciones que se hacen a los maestros de la Escuela de San José de Gracia, Durango," 8 November 1934, SEP, DEANR, caja 3251/363, exp. 6.

9 Cited in Monroy Huitrón, *Política educativa de la revolución, 1910–1940*, 92–93.

10 Civera Cerecedo, *Entre surcos y letras*; Cook, *La Casa del Pueblo*; Departamento de Misiones Culturales, *Bases de organización y funcionamiento de las misiones culturales*; Sierra, *Las Misiones Culturales, 1923–1973*; Tostado Gutiérrez, *El intento de liberar a un pueblo*; and Vaughan, *Cultural Politics in Revolution*.

11 Padilla, "La cruzada de los maestros misioneros," 2.

12 Cook, *La Casa del Pueblo*, 62–63.

13 Valero Chávez, *El trabajo social en México*.

14 On the history of social work in Mexico and its ties to European and U.S. models, see Evangelista Ramírez, *Historia del Trabajo Social en México*; Valero Chávez, *El trabajo social en México*.

15 Sierra, *Las Misiones Culturales, 1923–1973*, 30.

16 *Magisterio Revolucionario*, vol. 2, no. 2, 8 December 1934.

17 Clelia de la F. de Jiménez, Agente, Organización Rural, Instituto de Acción Social, Zacatecas, to Silva Garza, 30 April 1934, SEP, DEANR, caja 3262/373, exp. 12.

18 Silva Garza to Jiménez, 31 July 1934, SEP, DEANR, caja 3262/373, exp. 12.

19 Ibid.

20 Vaughan, *Cultural Politics in Revolution*, 12.

21 Ibid.; Rockwell, "Schools of the Revolution."

22 Valero de Marines to Manuel Mesa, 31 March 1934, SEP, DEANR, caja 3252/364, exp. 364/8.

23 Valero to Mesa, 30 January 1934, SEP. DEANR, caja 3259/370, exp. 995/3.

24 Civera Cerecedo, *Entre surcos y letras*; Schell, "Training Loving Hands"; Vaughan, "Modernizing Patriarchy."

25 Moreno de Medina to Mesa, 18 November 1934, SEP, DEANR, caja 3233/365, exp. 8.

26 Ibid., report for 16 November–25 December 1934, SEP, DEANR, caja 3233/365, exp. 8.

27 Ibid., 18 November 1934, SEP, DEANR, caja 3233/365, exp. 8.

28 Circular no. I-6–42 to Directores, Educación Federal en los Estados, from Rafael Padilla Nervo, Jefe, Departamento Administrativo, 2 March 1934, SEP, DEANR, caja 3242/353, exp. 14; "Informe que rinde el jefe de la Sección Técnica de Enseñanza Normal Rural, al C. Jefe del Dpto. acerca de la visita practicada a la Escuela Normal Rural de Rioverde, SLP," 19 March 1934, DEANR, caja 3248/360, exp. 2.

29 Gustavo Jarquín, Jefe, Misión Cultural, Dzitbalché, Camp. to Mesa, 22 January 1934, SEP, DEANR, caja 3259/370, exp. 995/1.

30 Adolfo Reyes, Jefe, Misión Cultural, Presidio, Durango, to Mesa, 30 October 1934, SEP, DEANR, caja 3251/363, exp. 6.

31 *El Maestro Rural*, vol. 3, no. 14, 15 December 1933, 33.

32 Cited in Múgica Martínez, *La Confederación Revolucionaria Michoacana del Trabajo*, 207.

33 Report from Presidente Municipal, Contepec, to Secretario del Gobierno, Michoacán, 4 May 1935, AHPEM, Gobierno, Conflictos, caja 2, exp. 5. Becker describes the hijas de María as a church-initiated campaign to enlist women in efforts to stem the "loss of modesty among women," "lack of respect for private property," and attacks on "conjugal bonds and domestic authority": Becker, *Setting the Virgin on Fire*, 27.

34 Cited in Múgica Martínez, *La Confederación Revolucionaria Michoacana del Trabajo*, 207.

35 Letter from residents of Contepec, Michoacán, 21 May 1935, AHPEM, Gobierno, Conflictos, caja 2, exp. 5.

36 Michel, *Marxistas y "marxistas,"* 8; see also report from Michel, Organizadora Rural, La Huerta, Michoacán, 3 March 1934, SEP, DEANR, caja 3252/363, exp. 10.

37 Michel, *Dios nuestra Señora* and *Dios-principio es la pareja*.

38 Heduán de Rueda, *A la mujer mexicana digo*, in AGN, RP, LCR, exp. 437.2/738.

39 Castillo y Piña, *Cuestiones sociales*, 190.

40 UFCM circular, 7 March 1930, UFCM, caja 2, folder 15, doc. 976; Boylan, "Mexican Catholic Women's Activism, 1929–1940"; Juventud Católica Femenina de México, *Orientaciones a las dirigentes*.

41 Boylan, " 'They Were Always Doing Something,' " 26.

42 UFCM, caja 7, folder 38.

43 Juana Pitman de Labarthe, Comité Diocesano, UFCM, to María Luisa Hernández, Comité Central, UFCM, 4 August 1934, UFCM, caja 2, folder 15.

44 Sandoval, Comité Diocesano, Morelos, Cuernavaca, UFCM, to Comité Central, UFCM, 24 October 1935, UFCM, caja 7, folder 39.

45 See, in particular, *Izquierdas*, 22 October 1934, 17 December 1934.

46 Ibid., 15 October 1934; emphasis in the original.

47 Ibid., 17 December 1934.

48 Fabre Baños, *Normal rural de Galeana*, 31.

49 Flores Sánchez, interview.

50 Tito Huereca, Director, Escuela Regional Campesina de Ayotzinapa, Guerrero, to Jefe, Departamento de Enseñanza Agrícola y Normal Rural, 27 December 1934, SEP, DEANR, caja 3242/353, exp. 2.

51 Carr, *Marxism and Communism in Twentieth-Century Mexico*, chap. 2.

52 On the treatment of communists during the early 1930s, see ibid. See also Campa, *Memorias de Valentín Campa*; Galeana, *Benita*.

53 This figure constitutes about 3 percent of Mexico's adult population and about 10 percent of industrial workers: Dirección General de Estadística, *Tercer censo industrial de 1940*. For membership estimates, see Carr, *Marxism and Communism in Twentieth-Century Mexico*, 10; Weyl and Weyl, *The Reconquest of Mexico*, 350.

54 *El Machete*, 30 April 1934, 1.

55 Meyer, *El Sinarquismo, el Cardenismo y la Iglesia, 1937–1947*, 45.

56 Abascal, *Mis recuerdos*; Gill, *El sinarquismo*; Meyer, *El sinarquismo, un fascismo mexi-*

cano, 113; Padilla, *Sinarquismo*; Zermeño and Aguilar, *Hacia una reinterpretación del sinarquismo actual*.

57 Knight, "The Rise and Fall of Cardenismo, c. 1930–c. 1946," 298.

58 Meyer, *El sinarquismo, un fascismo mexicano*, 47.

59 Ibid., 62–63.

60 Ibid., 50–51.

61 Ibid., 67.

62 Cited in Zermeño and Aguilar, *Hacia una reinterpretación del sinarquismo actual*, 26.

63 Cited in Alemán, *Fascismo, democracia y frente popular*, 429.

64 Ibid., 433.

65 Ibid., 435–36.

66 Ibid., 55–56.

67 Laborde, *La política de Unidad a Toda Costa*, 48–49.

68 Alemán, *Fascismo, democracia y frente popular*, 435–36.

69 Laborde, *La política de Unidad a Toda Costa*, 48.

70 Alemán, *Fascismo, democracia y frente popular*, 406–408.

71 *El Machete*, 10 October 1934, 3.

72 The most complete account to date of the FUPDM is Tuñón Pablos, *Mujeres que se organizan*.

73 From *Hoy*, 16 July 1938; reprinted in Novo, *La vida en México en el periodo presidencial de Lázaro Cárdenas*, 327–28.

74 Ibid.

75 See the discussion of practical and strategic gender interests in Molyneux, "Mobilization without Emancipation?"

76 List, interview; program of the FUPDM's inaugural meeting, 6 November 1935, AGN, RP, LCR, exp. 544/1.

77 AGN, RP, LCR, exp. 544/1.

78 Liga de Defensa Femenina to Cárdenas, 8 July 1936, AGN, RP, LCR, exp. 437.1/17.

79 See, for example, García's statements at the congress of the Frente Popular Antiimperialista, 27–28 February 1936, AGN, RP, LCR, exp. 433/121.

80 FUPDM, Tampico, Tamaulipas, 6 September 1936, AGN, RP, LCR, exp. 544/1; Millan, *Mexico Reborn*, 165.

81 Cited in Tuñón Pablos, *Mujeres que se organizan*, 70–71.

82 Ibid., 67.

83 Williams, *Marxism and Literature*, 128–35.

84 Unión Femenina "Lucrecia Toriz," Villa Azueta, Veracruz, to Cárdenas, 21 June 1936, AGN, RP, LCR, exp. 437.1/531.

85 Frente Popular Mexicano to Cárdenas, 23 July 1936, AGN, RP, LCR, exp. 437.1/531.

86 Liga Acción Femenina to Cárdenas, 8 January 1936, AGN, RP, LCR, exp. 521.8/24; Liga de Acción Femenina Pro-Derechos de la Mujer, CTM, and FUPDM to Cárdenas, 15 March 1940, and CTM to Cárdenas, 10 May 1940, AGN, RP, LCR, exp. 151.3/879.

87 FUPDM, Salina Cruz, Oaxaca, to Cárdenas, 29 December 1937, AGN, RP, LCR, exp. 151.3/879.

88 Liga de Acción Femenina Pro-Derechos de la Mujer, CTM, and FUPDM, Salina Cruz, Oaxaca, to Cárdenas, 15 March 1940, AGN, RP, LCR, exp. 151.3/879.

89 Gill, *El movimiento Escuderista de Acapulco*; Vizcaíno and Taibo, *Socialismo en un solo puerto*.

90 Galeana, *Benita*, 65–66; Ojeda Rivera, *Benita Galeana*, 13.

91 Unión de Mujeres Revolucionarias de Acapulco, 16 February 1935, AGN, RP, LCR, exps. 437.1/147, 534.3/45, 433/481. According to Nélida Flores Arellano and América Wences Román, de la O had a hand in establishing at least sixteen other women's organizations in southern Guerrero: Arellano and Wences Román, *Doña María de la O, una mujer ejemplar*. Francisco Gomezjara describes de la O as one of the Costa Grande's two most important activists during the Cárdenas period: Gomezjara, *Bonapartismo y Lucha Campesina en la Costa Grande de Guerrero*, 119–35.

92 AGN, RP, LCR, exps. 437.1/292, 437.3/116.

93 Ibid., exp. 404.4/90.

94 Ibid., exp. 437.1/469.

95 Comité de Viudas y Huérfanas del los Defensores del Plan de Ayala, 30 September 1936, AGN, RP, LCR, exp. 210.5/33; Unión de Costureras de Chilpancingo to Cárdenas, 30 December 1936, AGN, RP, LCR, exp. 521.7/319.

96 Jesús Salazar Romero, Secretary-General, Comité Estatal, PNR, to Cárdenas, 19 February 1936, AGN, RP, LCR, exp. 432.2/156.

97 On the Liga Nacional Femenina, see AGN, RP, LCR, exps. 437/112, 136.3/20. For Cárdenas's Guerrero campaign speeches, see Cárdenas, *Palabras y documentos*, 127–29.

98 Juana M. de Guadarrama et al. to Cárdenas, 19 March 1936, AGN, RP, LCR, exp. 437/112.

99 Demetria G. de Ortiz et al. to Cárdenas, 7 May 1936, AGN, RP, LCR, exp. 437/112.

100 FUPDM, Acapulco, Guerrero, 27 June 1936, AGN, DGG, vol. 2.312(9)21, caja 6, exp. 37.

101 Ibid.

102 *Redención*, 7 March 1936, 1. See also Domínguez Navarro, *50 años de una vida*.

103 AGN, RP, LCR, exp. 437/112.

104 Unión de Propietarios de Molinos de Nixtamal to Cárdenas, 16 February 1937, AGN, RP, LCR, exp. 604.11/95.

105 Ibid.

106 Liga Roja to Cárdenas, 14 June 1937, AGN RP, LCR, exp. 437/112.

107 Ibid., 22 February 1938, AGN, RP, LCR, exp. 542.1/735.

108 Ibid., 12 April 1940, AGN, RP, LCR, exp. 542.1/735.

109 Federación de Trabajadores (CTM), Acapulco, Guerrero, to Cárdenas, 1 June 1940, AGN, RP, LCR, exp. 136.3/20.

110 Liga Nacional Femenina to Cárdenas, 29 September 1940, AGN, RP, LCR, exp. 534.3/45.

111 Gomezjara, *Bonapartismo y Lucha Campesina en la Costa Grande de Guerrero*, 130.

Chapter Four "Benefits of the Revolution"

1 *El Universal*, 19 August 1936, 1. Narratives of the Laguna strike and land reform mirror the historiography of postrevolutionary Mexico. Studies produced immediately after the land reform lauded the benevolent government intervention. To the extent that these studies mention popular mobilization, they generally attribute it to a spontaneous effervescence inspired by the revolution, to opportunities created by the postrevolutionary regime, or to Cárdenas's personal courage: Ashby, *Organized Labor and the Mexican Revolution under Lázaro Cárdenas*; Flores Múñoz, *Revolución versus imperialismo* and *The Solution of the Social, Economic and Agrarian Problem of the "Laguna" Region*; Millan, *Mexico Reborn*; Reyes Pimentel, *La cosecha*; Townsend, *Lázaro Cárdenas*. Revisionist scholarship underscores the land reform's co-optative objectives: Hewitt and Landsberger, "Peasant Organizations in the Laguna, Mexico"; Martínez Saldaña, *El costo de un éxito político*. Postrevisionists have differentiated between ideologically based and clientelist modes of incorporation, reassessing the episode's popular aspects and seeing the state as neither benevolent patriarch nor malevolent juggernaut: Carr, "The Mexican Communist Party and Agrarian Mobilization in the Laguna, 1920–1940" and *Marxism and Communism in Twentieth-Century Mexico*; Hellman, "Capitalist Agriculture and Rural Protest," "The Role of Ideology in Peasant Politics," and *Mexico in Crisis*.

2 Carr, "The Mexican Communist Party and Agrarian Mobilization in the Laguna, 1920–1940"; Hernández, *¿La explotación colectiva en la Comarca Lagunera es un fracaso?*; Liga de Agrónomos Socialistas, *El colectivismo agrario en México*.

3 De la Mora, *Tierra de hombres*; Moreno, *Torreón*; Reyes Pimentel, *La cosecha*; Tamayo, *Transformación de la Comarca Lagunera*.

4 Tamayo, *Transformación de la Comarca Lagunera*, 7.

5 Moreno, *Torreón*, 228.

6 Meyers, *Forge of Progress, Crucible of Revolt*.

7 Jacoby, "Between North and South."

8 Carr, *Marxism and Communism in Twentieth-Century Mexico*, 83–84.

9 Liga de Agrónomos Socialistas, *El colectivismo agrario en México*, 270–71.

10 Flores Sánchez, interview.

11 Liga de Agrónomos Socialistas, *El colectivismo agrario en México*, 38.

12 Carr, *Marxism and Communism in Twentieth-Century Mexico*, 85.

13 Liga de Agrónomos Socialistas, *El colectivismo agrario en México*; Senior, *Democracy Comes to a Cotton Kingdom*.

14 Katz, *The Life and Times of Pancho Villa*.

15 Nelson R. Park, American Consul General, "Monthly Political Report, Torreón Consular District," 31 May 1931, NARA, 812.00 Coahuila/166.

16 Cámara de Diputados, Saltillo, to Governor of Coahuila, 17 October 1934, AGN, DGG, vol. 2.331.8(3), caja 16-A, exp. 20. Comité Municipal, PNR, to Cárdenas, 9 November 1934, AGN, DGG, vol. 2.331.8(3), caja 16-A, exp. 20. On Ortiz Garza's municipal administration, see Moreno, *Torreón a través de sus presidentes municipales*, 91–92.

17 Meyers, *Forge of Progress, Crucible of Revolt*; Rivera Castro, "Organización y conflictos laborales en La Laguna."

18 Inspector General de Policía, Torreón, to Gobernador del Estado, Saltillo, 7 April 1934, AGN, DGG, vol. 2.331.8(3), caja 16-A, exp. 9; Vargas-Lobsinger, *La Comarca Lagunera*, 122–23.

19 *El Nacional*, 24 March 1932.

20 *El Universal*, 25 March 1932.

21 *El Machete*, 10 May 1932, 2.

22 Ibid., 20 January 1932, 2.

23 Cámara Nacional del Trabajo de la República Mexicana to Secretario de Gobernación, 7 May 1935, AGN, DGG, vol. 2.331.8(3)703, caja 16-A, exp. 32.

24 Carr, "The Mexican Communist Party and Agrarian Mobilization in the Laguna, 1920–1940," 381–85; Rivera Castro, "Organización y conflictos laborales en La Laguna." The PCM newspaper *El Machete* and the U.S. consulate in Torreón also recounted the PCM's activities: NARA, 812.00 Coahuila.

25 A. P. Hernández, *¿La explotación colectiva en la Comarca Lagunera es un fracaso?* 85–86; *Periódico Oficial: Organo del Gobierno del Estado Independiente, Libre y Soberano de Coahuila de Zaragoza*, vol. 41, no. 96, 1 December 1934, 5–17.

26 H. C. Moses, American Vice-Consul, "Saltillo Political Review for December 1934," 5 January 1935, NARA, 812.00 Coahuila/189.

27 Sindicato de Obreros y Campesinos "Francisco I. Madero," Hacienda Buenavista de Arriba, Est. Porvenir to Cárdenas, 7 January 1935 and 25 November 1935, AGN, DGG, vol. 2.331.8(3)5941, caja 16-A, exp. 72. Many more examples of abuses against groups of campesinos attempting to organize unions can be found in AGN, DGG, vol. 2.331(8), cajas 16-A, 17-A.

28 *El Machete*, 10 October 1933, 2.

29 Centro Femenil "Josefa Ortiz de Domínguez," Torreón, to Cárdenas, 21 October 1935, AGN, DGG, vol. 2.331.8(3)1088, caja 16-A, exp. 40.

30 Carr, *Marxism and Communism in Twentieth-Century Mexico*, 86–87.

31 AGN, DGG, vol. 2.331.8(7)2772, caja 23-A, exp. 16.

32 Liga de Agrónomos Socialistas, *El colectivismo agrario en México: La Comarca Lagunera*, 39.

33 AGN, DGG, vol. 2.331.8(3)1244, caja 16-A, exps. 42, 48, 58.

34 The district court judge was moved to Mexico City after the 1936 strike. The U.S.

consular office reported that he "left a record locally of having consistently acted in favor of the laboring classes, having frequently granted injunctions against decisions of local Conciliation and Arbitration Boards declaring strikes illegal": Park to Secretary of State, 31 December 1936, NARA, 812.00 Coahuila/265.

35 Armin S. Valdes, Presidente Municipal, to Inspector General de Policía, 26 July 1935 and 26 April 1935, IMDT, Presidencia, caja 24, exp. 6.

36 José Siurob, Jefe, Departamento de Salubridad Pública, to Valdes, 6 August 1936, IMDT, Presidencia, caja 30, exp. 9.

37 On the meningitis outbreak, see IMDT, Presidencia, caja 31, exps. 3–5.

38 Hernández, *¿La explotación colectiva en la Comarca Lagunera es un fracaso?* 72–76; Olcott, "*Mueras y Matanzas.*"

39 *El Machete*, 20 December 1930, 3.

40 Sindicato Femenista "Josefa Ortiz de Domínguez" to Secretario de Gobernación, 28 May 1934, AGN, DGG, vol. 2.312(3)28, caja 2, exp. 12; Park to Secretary of State, "Monthly Political Report, Torreón Consular District," 31 May 1934, NARA, 812.00 Coahuila/166.

41 Comisión Permanente del Congreso Nacional de Mujeres Obreras y Campesinas to Cárdenas, 11 April 1935, AGN, RP, LCR, exp. 542.2/289.

42 José María Rodríguez de la Fuente, Municipal President, and Jesús Aguilera, Municipal Secretary, Matamoros, to Cárdenas, 2 May 1935, AGN, DGG, vol. 2.331.8(3), caja 16-A, exp. 34.

43 IEDC, 1935, caja 3.2.45, legajo 36, exp. 2–19.

44 Liga Socialista de Torreón to Cárdenas, 24 September 1935, AGN, RP, LCR, exp. 432.1/91; Sindicato de Costureras y Similares de Torreón to Cárdenas, 15 January 1936, AGN, DGG, vol. 2.331.8(3)12166, caja 17-A, exp. 27.

45 Sindicatos Femeniles "Josefa Ortiz de Domínguez," "Vicente Guerrero," and "Heroínas Mexicanas" to Cárdenas, 7 March 1936, AGN, RP, LCR, exp. 136.3/455.

46 Sindicato Femenil de Obreras de Colonia Ana, Federación de Trabajadores de Torreón, to Cárdenas, 11 August 1935, AGN, RP, LCR, exp. 437/131; Sindicato Femenil de Obreras de Colonia Ana, Federación de Trabajadores de Torreón, to José Siurob, Jefe, Departamento de Salubridad Pública, 30 January 1937, AGN, DGG, vol. 2.331.8(3)7748, caja 17-A, exp. 18. On renters' unions, see IMDT, Presidencia, caja 30, exp. 10, caja 32, exp. 28, caja 33, exp. 17.

47 Sindicato Agrario "Aquiles Serdán," Lequitio, Coahuila, to Cárdenas, 28 November 1935, AGN, DGG, vol. 2.331.8(3), caja 17-A, exp. 23.

48 Park to Secretary of State, 31 December 1935, NARA, 812.00 Coahuila/226; H. Claremont Moses, Vice-Consul General, to Secretary of State, 29 February 1936, NARA, 812.00 Coahuila/232.

49 Park to Secretary of State, 31 March 1936, NARA, 812.00 Coahuila/231.

50 Sindicato de Obreros y Campesinos "Melquiades Contreras Lerma," San Pedro, Coahuila, to Cárdenas, 23 April 1936, AGN, DGG, vol. 2.331.8(3), caja 18-A, exp. 21.

51 Asociación Revolucionaria Mexicanista to Presidente Municipal, 2, 4, and 8 July 1936, IMDT, Presidencia, caja 32, exp. 27.

52 *El Universal*, 8 May 1936, 1.

53 Presidente Municipal to Jefe, 6 Zona Militar, 25 May, 1936, IMDT, Presidencia, caja 31, exp. 5.

54 Pierre de L. Boal, Chargé d'Affaires ad interum, to Secretary of State, 16 June 1936, NARA, 812.00/30379.

55 Sindicato de Obreros y Campesinos "Melchor Ocampo" and Sindicato Revolucionario Femenil "Martina Derás," Hacienda San Ignacio, Est. Concordia, Coahuila, to Cárdenas, 22 May 1936, AGN, DGG, vol. 2.331.8(3), caja 18-A, exp. 31. See also correspondence among Secretaría de Gobernación, Procurador General de Justicia, Governor of Coahuila, and Cárdenas's office regarding letters from the Sindicato Revolucionario Femenil "Martina Derás," IEDC, 1936, caja 3.1.1.8, legajo 25, exp. 2–205.

56 *El Universal*, 3 June 1936, 1.

57 Sindicato de Obreros y Campesinos "Ignacio Zaragoza," Hacienda El Consuelo, Municipio Matamoros, to Cárdenas, 4 June 1936, AGN, DGG, vol. 2.331.8(3), caja 18-A, exp. 22.

58 *El Universal*, 3 June 1936, 8.

59 Unión Sindical de Empleados de la Laguna to Cárdenas, 10 June 1936, AGN, DGG, vol. 2.331.9(3)18343.

60 Sindicato de Campesinos "José María Morelos" to Cárdenas, 20 June 1936, AGN, DGG, vol. 2.331.8(3)2856, caja 16-A, exp. 53.

61 Secretary of Organization and Propaganda, Confederación General del Trabajo, Coahuila, to Cárdenas, 28 July 1936, AGN, RP, LCR, exp. 437.1/696.

62 *El Universal*, 5 August 1936, 1.

63 Ibid., 12 August 1936, 1.

64 Unión Textil de la República Mexicana to Cárdenas, 21 August 1936, as published in ibid., 22 August 1936, 1.

65 AGN, DGG, vol. 2.331.8(3), caja 18-A, exp. 49; *El Universal*, 22 August 1936, 1.

66 Dionisio Encina to Vicente Lombardo Toledano, 22 August 1936, CERM, FJM, caja 3, vol. 32, doc. 129.

67 Socorro Rojo Internacional, Comité Regional de la Laguna, to Cárdenas, 19 August 1936, AGN, DGG, vol. 2.331.8(3)10838, caja 17-A, exp. 20.

68 *El Universal*, 22 August 1936, 11.

69 See letters to Cárdenas from the Sindicato de Obreros Agrícola "Alvaro Obregón" and the Sindicato de Obreros y Campesinos "Alvaro Obregón," 24 August 1936, AGN, DGG, vol. 2.331.8(3), caja 18-A, exp. 48.

70 *El Universal*, 23 August 1936, 1.

71 Flores Sánchez, interview.

72 Sindicato de Empleadas de Molinos y Similares, Durango, to Cárdenas, 20 August 1936, AGN, DGG, vol. 2.331.8(3)10838, caja 17-A, exp. 20.

73 *El Universal*, 25 August 1936, 1.

74 Genaro S. Cervantes, Comité de Huelga, to Secretaría de Gobernación, 27 August 1936, AGN, DGG, vol. 2.331.8(3)10838, caja 17-A, exp. 20.

75 Senior, *Democracy Comes to a Cotton Kingdom*, 15.

76 Guerra Cepeda, "El Ejido Colectivizado en la Comarca Lagunera," 48–49.

77 Bretton and Mitchell, *Land and Liberty for Mexican Farmers*; Senior, *Democracy Comes to a Cotton Kingdom*; Simpson, *The Ejido*.

78 Flores Múñoz, *The Solution of the Social, Economic and Agrarian Problem of the "Laguna" Region*.

79 Vázquez, "La resolución del problema agrario en la Comarca Lagunera," 37–38.

80 On the "modernization" of Mexican patriarchy in the service of national development, see Vaughan, "Modernizing Patriarchy."

81 Manuel Fabila, Comité de Acción Social y Cultural del Personal, Departamento Agrario, et al., to Gabino Vázquez, 10 August 1936, AGN, RP, LCR, exp. 606.3/158; José Luis Guerrero and Jorge A. Sagahún to Cárdenas, 19 August 1935, AGN, RP, LCR, exp. 437.1/282.

82 Comité de Acción Social y Cultural del Personal, Departamento Agrario, to Vázquez, 10 August 1936, AGN, RP, LCR, exp. 606.3/158.

83 Luna Arroyo, *La mujer mexicana en la lucha social*, 17.

84 *Orientaciones para las Ligas Femeniles de Lucha Social en los Ejidos*, n.p.

85 Liga Femenil de Ejidatarios, población El Estribo, Municipio San Pedro, to Cárdenas, 18 November 1936, AGN, RP, LCR, exp. 437.1/829; Sociedad Femenil, Liga de Comunidades Agrarias, población Alvio, Municipio San Pedro, to Governor of Coahuila, IEDC, 1936, caja 3.2.41, legajo 41, exp. 3–3.

86 Reprinted in Rosales and Ramos González, "Informe del primer delegado agrario en La Laguna, 1937," 75.

87 Flores Sánchez, a Communist active in the Ligas Femeniles, could not recall ever hearing of the FUPDM. Communist Cristina Ibarra appears to have tried to start a chapter but quickly abandoned the effort.

88 Cárdenas, *Palabras y documentos*, 233–34.

89 Ibid., 232.

90 AGN, RP, LCR, exp. 404.1/706–1.

91 "Gira afectuada por el C. Presidente de la República el día 27 de noviembre de 1936," 28 November 1936, AGN, RP, LCR, exp. 404.1/706.

92 Cárdenas, *Palabras y documentos*, 230.

93 For discussions about interpreting "gender-specific" demands, see especially Alvarez, *Engendering Democracy in Brazil*; Kaplan, "Female Consciousness and Collective Action", Molyneux, "Mobilization without Emancipation?"

94 Comité Femenil "Josefa Ortiz de Domínguez" to Cárdenas, 29 October 1936, AGN, RP, LCR, exp. 151.3/1334.

95 Cited in *El ejido en la Comarca Lagunera*; Flores Múñoz, *Revolución versus imperi-*

alismo and *The Solution of the Social, Economic and Agrarian Problem of the "Laguna" Region*; Vázquez, "La resolución del problema agrario en la Comarca Lagunera."

96 "Las Ligas Femeniles en la Laguna," 61–65.

97 Senior, *Democracy Comes to a Cotton Kingdom*, 65. A 1939 thesis put the number at 386 leagues: Guerra Cepeda, "El Ejido Colectivizado en la Comarca Lagunera," 137.

98 "Las Ligas Femeniles en la Laguna."

99 G. Vázquez, "La resolución del problema agrario en la Comarca Lagunera," 13–20.

100 "Las Ligas Femeniles en la Laguna," 25.

101 Ibid., 26.

102 Ibid., 29.

103 *¡Despertar Lagunero!* 137.

104 Ibid., 220.

105 Guerra Cepeda, "El Ejido Colectivizado en la Comarca Lagunera,"137.

106 Liga Femenil "Lic. Gabino Vázquez," Estación Noe, población Manila, Durango, to Cárdenas, 9 December 1936, AGN, RP, LCR, exp. 604.11/91.

107 Liga Femenil "Leona Vicario," Ejido 5 de Febrero, Municipio Francisco I. Madero, Coahuila, to Cárdenas, 16 January 1937, IEDC, 1937, caja 3.2.48, legajo 24, exp. 2–20–9.

108 Máximo Alvarez y Alvarez to Cárdenas, 27 October 1937, AGN, RP, LCR, exp. 404.1/706–1.

109 IEDC, 1937, caja 3.2.48, legajo 24, exp. 2–20–17.

110 See correspondence in IEDC, 1937, caja 3.2.48, legajo 24, exps. 2–20–4, 2–20–8, 2–20–9, 2–20–14, caja 3.2.38, legajo 24, exp. 2–20; AGN, RP, LCR, exp. 553/22.

111 Sindicato de Costureras "Amalia Solórzano de Cárdenas," Gómez Palacio, Durango, to Cárdenas, 25 December and 2 April 1937, AGN, RP, LCR, exp. 521.7/317.

112 Liga Femenil de "La Fe" to Cárdenas, 8 January 1938, AGN, RP, LCR, exp. 702.2/8804.

113 *El Machete*, 5 March 1938, 2; registration for Gremial de Obreras de Servicios Domésticos, Torreón, Coahuila, 16 November 1938, IEDC, 1938, caja 3.2.19, legajo 7, exp. 2–1.

114 Secretaría de Gobernación in Torreón to Governor of Coahuila, 1 March 1937, IEDC, 1937, caja 3.2.48, legajo 24, exp. 2–20–9.

115 See correspondence in IEDC, 1939, caja 3.2.48, legajo 22, exp. 2–20–9.

116 *El Universal*, 22 February 1937, 1; Park to Secretary of State, 27 February 1937, NARA, 812.00 Coahuila/270.

117 Park to Secretary of State, 3 May 1937, NARA, 812.00B International Red Day/167; ibid., 7 May 1937, NARA, 812.00 Coahuila/282.

118 Liga Femenil de Lucha Social, Ejido San Francisco de Arriba, Municipio San Pedro, Coahuila, to Cárdenas, 18 May 1937, AGN, DGG, vol. 2.331.8(3), caja 18-A, exp. 72.

119 Park to Secretary of State, 25 May 1937, NARA, 812.00 Coahuila/283.

120 See August 1937 correspondence in AGN, DGG, vol. 2.331.8(3), caja 18-A, exp. 82.

121 Liga Femenil "Caridad Mercader" to Manuel Mijares V., Presidente Municipal, Torreón, 16 March 1938, IMDT, 2.1.4.31, caja 4, folder 5.

122 "Nixtamal" refers to maize soaked in lime-treated water that is ground into a damp meal (*masa*) for corn tortillas. In some instances, women requested gas or electric motors for these mills, and in other cases they seemed to expect manually powered mechanized mills. On women's labor and the molino de nixtamal, see Bauer, "Millers and Grinders"; Keremitsis, "Del metate al molino"; Pilcher, *¡Qué vivan los tamales!* All draw heavily on the 1920s ethnographies of Redfield and Lewis.

123 *¡Despertar Lagunero!* 136.

124 Bauer, "Millers and Grinders," 9–10.

125 Ibid., 16.

126 *¡Despertar Lagunero!*, 220.

127 AGN, RP, LCR, exps. 604.11/91, 136.3/1223.

128 AGN, Colección Clementina Batalla de Bassols, vol. 2, exps. 4, 74–83.

129 Comité Consultivo Central de Ejidatarios, Torreón, to Francisco Rivera, Presidente Municipal, Torreón, 11 April 1939, IMDT, 2.1.5.8, caja 3, folder 20.

130 See correspondence in IEDC, 1936, caja 3.2.51, legajo 40, exp. 2–23.

131 This characterization appears in ethnographic accounts from the 1920s to the 1940s. See Bauer, "Millers and Grinders," 13–17. The anthropologist Diane Nelson has found a similar dynamic in contemporary Guatemala. Indicating that "there are many men who claim that the only authentic tortilla is made of corn ground by hand," she cites one Mayan cultural activist as insisting, "A woman is not a woman unless she makes tortillas": Nelson, *A Finger in the Wound*, 165. I have not found this concern articulated in the 1930s, but this absence may reflect the nature of my sources.

132 Federación de Liga Femeniles del Municipio Francisco I. Madero, Coahuila, to Cárdenas, 19 March 1938; Liga Femenil "Petra Herrera" to Cárdenas, 12 April 1938, both in AGN, RP, LCR, exp. 604.11/122.

133 AGN, RP, LCR, exps. 136.3/69, 136.3/1391, 136.3/2314, 136.3/2402, 136.3/2571, 136.3/2639.

134 Liga Femenil "Leona Vicario," San Rafael, Durango, to Cárdenas, 7 July 1938, AGN, RP, LCR, exp. 604.11/133.

135 Comité Coordinador Femenil, PRM, Morelia, Michoacán, to Cárdenas, 5 October 1939, AGN, RP, LCR, exp. 604.11/121.

136 Liga Femenil "Amalia S. de Cárdenas," Ejido Florida, Coahuila, to Cárdenas, 30 May 1938, AGN, RP, LCR, exp. 604.11/130.

137 *El Machete*, 19 March 1938, 11; Liga Femenil "Rosa Luxemburgo" to Cárdenas, 8 April 1939, AGN, RP, LCR, exp. 432.3/178; correspondence between Comité Consultativo Central de Ejidatarios, Torreón, and Diputado Francisco Rivera, Presidente Municipal, Torreón, 11 April 1939, IMDT, 2.1.5.8, caja 3, folder 20.

138 Comité Consultativo Central de Ejidatarios, Torreón, to Rivera, 11 April 1939, IMDT, 2.1.5.8, caja 3, folder 20.

139 Liga Femenil "Amalia S. de Cárdenas," Ejido Luchana, Municipio San Pedro, Coahuila, to Cárdenas, 16 April 1938, AGN, RP, LCR, exp. 437.1/641.

140 Oficial Mayor to the Comisión Técnico-Consultativa, Estado de Coahuila, 15 April 1938, IEDC, 1938, caja 3.2.41, legajo 44.

141 Liga Femenil de Lucha Social "Amalia S. de Cárdenas" to Cárdenas, 26 April 1939 and 4 May 1939, AGN, RP, LCR, exp. 404.1/2326.

142 Liga Femenil de Lucha Social "Leona Vicario," Ejido Seis de Octubre, Municipio Francisco I. Madero, Coahuila, to Cárdenas, 1 June 1938, AGN, RP, LCR, exp. 604.11/125.

143 Liga Femenil de Lucha Social "Leona Vicario" to Cárdenas, 30 April 1939, AGN, RP, LCR, exp. 604.11/154.

144 See the reports from May and June 1938 by the Popular Sector of the PRM municipal committees, IEDC, 1938, caja 3.2.46, legajo 40, exp. 3–13.

145 Crescencio Treviño Adame to Cárdenas, 14 August 1938, AGN, RP, LCR, exp. 544/1.

146 Liga Femenil de Lucha Social "Leona Vicario," San Rafael, Canatlán, and El Carmen, Durango, to Cárdenas, 30 September 1938, AGN, RP, LCR, exp. 151.3/1130.

147 Liga Femenil de Lucha Social, población Zaragoza, Municipio Tlahualillo, Durango, to Cárdenas, 16 January 1939, AGN, RP, LCR, exp. 437.1/829, 2 February 1939, AGN, RP, LCR, exp. 562.4/486.

148 Liga Femenil Hormiguero, Municipio Torreón, to Cárdenas, 29 January 1937, AGN, RP, LCR, exp. 437.3/196.

149 Liga Femenil "20 de Noviembre," Ejido de Guatimapé, Municipio Canatlán, Durango, to Cárdenas, 7 March 1939, AGN, RP, LCR, exp. 404.2/501.

150 Liga Femenil de Lucha Social, Ejido Animas, Est. Gregorio I. García, Durango, n.d. [April 1940], AGN, DGG, vol. 2.331.9(7)/1, caja 58-A, exp. 100, and 18 April 1940, AGN, RP, LCR, exp. 437.1/829.

151 Emilia Guzmán to Banco Nacional de Crédito Ejidal, Torreón, 10 May 1939, CERM, FJM, caja 8, vol. 67, doc. 118.

152 *¡Despertar Lagunero!*; Senior, *Democracy Comes to a Cotton Kingdom*.

153 George R. Hukill to Secretary of State, 3 May 1938, NARA, 812.00 Coahuila/320.

154 Flyer describing 1939 May Day demonstration in Estación Concordia, Coahuila, IEDC, 1939, caja 3.2.53, legajo 38 (Festividades Públicas), exp. 3–11.

155 Frente Unico de Campesinos, Obreros, Ligas Femeniles y Maestros del Perímetro de Tlahualilo to Cárdenas, 9 August 1938, AGN, RP, LCR, exp. 508.1/393.

156 Liga Femenil de Lucha Social, Tlahualilo, Durango, to Cárdenas, 8 May 1938, AGN, RP, LCR, exp. 508.2/3.

157 Liga Femenil de Ejido de Las Vegas, Francisco I. Madero, Coahuila, to Cárdenas, 10 February 1939, AGN, RP, LCR, exp. 418.2/169.

158 Correspondence with Cárdenas in AGN, RP, LCR, exp. 561.3/4.

159 Cámara Nacional de Comercio e Industria, San Pedro, to Cámara Nacional de Comercio e Industria, Saltillo, 21 September 1938, IEDC, 1938, caja 3.2.46, legajo 40, exp. 3–14.

160 Flores Sánchez, interview; Unión Femenil Duranguense "Leona Vicario" to Cárdenas, 30 September 1938, 5 January 1939, AGN, RP, LCR, exps. 151.3/1130, 151.3/1132; Federación Regional de Ligas Femeniles de Lucha Social, Torreón, to Vázquez, 18 April 1939, AGN, RP, LCR, exp. 565.4/2005. The Laguna confederation demanded that the controversial Agrarian Department representative Samuel Azuela return the tires for the truck that Cárdenas had donated: Confederación de las Ligas Femeniles de la Región Lagunera to Cárdenas, 24 September 1940, AGN, RP, LCR, exp. 604.11/12.

161 Francisco Rivera to Confederación de Ligas Femeniles de la Comarca Lagunera, 7 March 1940; Rivera to Liga Femenil de Lucha Social, pob. de Compuertas, Municipio Matamoros, Coahuila, 8 March 1940, both in IMDT, 2.1.5.8, caja 9, folder 10.

162 Pedro V. Rodríguez Triana to Cárdenas, 22 August 1939, AGN, DGG, vol. 2.331.8(3)40559, caja 18-A, exp. 1.

163 "Reglamento de cooperativas de molinos de nixtamal," 4 February 1940, AGN, RP, LCR, exp. 604.11/12; acta constitutiva for Ligas Femeniles affiliated with the Confederación Ligas Femeniles de la Comarca Lagunera, 4 February 1940, AGN, RP, LCR, exp. 437.1/641.

164 AGN, RP, LCR, exp. 437.1/641; Flores Sánchez, interview.

165 Confederación de las Ligas Femeniles de la Región Lagunera to Cárdenas, 16 March 1940, AGN, RP, LCR, exp. 604.11/12.

166 AGN, RP, LCR, exp. 604.11/12.

167 Guadalupe Ríos, Isabel Santillán, and Cecilia Magallanes to Cárdenas, 1 July 1940, AGN, RP, LCR, exp. 604.11/12.

168 Liga Femenil "Amalia Solórzano de Cárdenas" to Cárdenas, 1 July 1940, AGN, RP, LCR, exp. 432.3/217.

169 Liga Femenil "Petra Herrera" to Cárdenas, 10 July 1940, AGN, RP, LCR, exp. 609/1292.

170 Magallanes to Cárdenas, 25 October 1938, AGN, RP, LCR, exp. 604.11/122; Federación Regional de Ligas Femeniles de Lucha Social, Torreón, to Gabino Vázquez, 17 April and 18 April 1939, AGN, RP, LCR, exp. 565.4/2005.

171 See, for example, AGN, RP, MAC, exps. 568.3/45, 565.4/53.

172 Martínez Saldaña, El costo de un éxito político, 35–36.

173 See dispute over the vineyard of the Liga Femenil de Lucha Social "Lázaro Cárdenas," Ejido El Coyote, Municipio Matamoros, Coahuila, AGN, RP, LCR, exp. 404.1/984.

174 Unión Femenil Durangueña "Leona Vicario" to Alemán, undated [March 1948], AGN, DGG, vol. 2.331.9(7)21, caja 59-A, exp. 127; Confederación de Ligas Feme-

niles de la Comarca Lagunera to Alemán, 22 July 1950, AGN, DGG, Agrupaciones Sindicatos, vol. 2.331.5 (3–34)/1, caja 12-A, exp. 7.

Chapter Five "Her Dignity as Woman"

1 *Excélsior*, 29 April 1937, 10; *La Prensa*, 29 April 1937, 11; *El Universal*, 9 April 1937, 9, 30 April 1937, 9.

2 Cott, *The Grounding of Modern Feminism*; DuBois, *Feminism and Suffrage*; Kraditor, *The Ideas of the Woman Suffrage Movement, 1890–1920*.

3 National Revolutionary Party, "Constitución del Partido Nacional Revolucionario," 3; AGN, RP, LCR, exp. 544/1. Morton's account—for decades the only substantive investigation of Mexican women's struggle for suffrage—rests on strikingly antifeminist assumptions, but subsequent studies, even by feminist scholars, have cited it fairly uncritically. Morton, a political scientist, details the movement from the perspective of male lawmakers and throughout his discussion remains alternately patronizing toward and disdainful of the women suffragists: Morton, *Woman Suffrage in Mexico*. For a more feminist account drawing on similar sources and the addition of oral testimony and personal archives, see Enriqueta Tuñón, *¡Por fin . . . ya podemos elegir y ser electas!*

4 *Excélsior*, 3 November 1933, 10.

5 *El Mexicano del Norte*, 15 June 1934.

6 *El Siglo de Torreón*, 12 August 1934, 4.

7 Robles de Mendoza to Cárdenas, 2 September 1935, AGN, RP, LCR, exp. 544/1.

8 *El Universal*, 7 February 1936, 9; *El Nacional*, 7 February 1936, 8. See also the editorial by the sociologist Lucío Mendieta y Núñez in the journal of the PNR's Institute for Social Science, *Política Social* (January–February 1936): 1–2.

9 *La Prensa*, 14 February 1936, 11.

10 *Excélsior*, 28 February 1936, 10; *El Universal*, 28 February 1936, 9.

11 Partido Nacional Cívico Femenino registration, 3 March 1936, AGN, DGG, caja 27, exp. 19.

12 María Consuelo Montes to Cárdenas, 3 March 1936, AGN, RP, LCR, exp. 544/1.

13 *Excélsior*, 11 March 1936, 10; *La Prensa*, 11 March 1936, 11.

14 *Excélsior*, 11 March 1936, 10.

15 Chapa, *El derecho de voto para la mujer*. While it is impossible to know the circulation of Chapa's pamphlet, language taken directly from it appears in subsequent FUPDM petitions from throughout Mexico: see pamphlets in AGN, RP, LCR, exp. 544/1.

16 *El Nacional*, 13 March 1936, 8.

17 Ibid.

18 Chapa, *El derecho de voto para la mujer*, n.p.

19 Ana Esther de Trujillo, Union of American Women (UMA), to Cárdenas, 19 March 1936, AGN, RP, LCR, exp. 544/1.

20 Robles de Mendoza to Cárdenas, 19 March 1936, AGN, RP, LCR, exp. 544/1.

21 *New York Times*, 8 September 1935, N7.

22 Hay to Luis I. Rodríguez, 9 April 1936, AGN, RP, LCR, exp. 544/1.

23 Robles de Mendoza to Rodríguez, 5 May 1936, AGN, RP, LCR, exp. 544/1.

24 *Excélsior*, 31 March 1936, 10.

25 *El Universal Gráfico*, 17 February 1936, 81.

26 Poster signed by the Veracruz Comité Femenil, PNR, 30 March 1936, AGN, RP, LCR, exp. 544/1.

27 PNR platform on "La Participación de la mujer en las actividades pre-electorales del Partido," AGN, RP, LCR, exp. 544.61/86.

28 National Revolutionary Party, *Programa de Acción del Partido Nacional Revolucionario*, 24.

29 *El Nacional*, 9 May 1936, 8; National Revolutionary Party, *Un año de gestión del Comité Ejecutivo Nacional*, 63.

30 National Revolutionary Party, Ibid., 64.

31 Ibid.

32 Ibid., 66.

33 Ibid., 67.

34 *New York Times*, 8 September 1935, N7. For the characterization of Portes Gil, see Novo, *La vida en México en el periodo presidencial de Lázaro Cárdenas*, 328.

35 Celia C. de Fraustro and María Luisa Rotunno, Comité Municipal Feminista del PNR, Saltillo, Coahuila, to Jesús Valdes Sánchez, Governor of Coahuila, 3 August 1936, IEDC, 1936, caja 3.2.41, legajo 41, exp. 3–3; and de Fraustro and Rotunno to Cárdenas, 26 July 1936, AGN, RP, LCR, exp. 544/1.

36 Carmen Loyo et al. to Cárdenas, 7 February 1936; Guadalupe P. de Padilla, "A las compañeras de la sección femenil del PNR," 27 January 1936, both in AGN, DGG, vol. 544.61/78, caja 7, legajo 46, exp. 544.61/78.

37 Esperanza F. G. de Santibáñez to Cárdenas, 24 April 1936, AGN, RP, LCR, exp. 111/1568.

38 *El Universal*, 3 April 1936, 9.

39 *La Prensa*, 6 April 1936, 11.

40 *El Universal*, 21 April 1936, 9.

41 *La Prensa*, 24 April 1936, 11; *Excélsior*, 24 April 1936, 10.

42 Esther Chapa et al. to Cárdenas, 23 April 1936, AGN, RP, LCR, exp. 544/1.

43 *El Universal*, 25 April 1936, 9.

44 *Excélsior*, 30 April 1936, 10; *El Universal*, 30 April 1936, 9.

45 *Excélsior*, 1 May 1936, 10; *El Nacional*, 1 May 1936, 8.

46 *El Nacional*, 9 May 1936, 9.

47 Ibid., 8.

48 See correspondence in AGN, RP, LCR, exp. 544/1.

49 Agrupación Femenil "Martina Derás," Santa Ana del Pilar, Coahuila, 12 September 1936, AGN, RP, LCR, exp. 544/1.

50 *El Machete*, 26 December 1936, 2.

51 *El Universal*, 30 August 1936, 9; *El Nacional*, 31 August 1936, 8.

52 *Excélsior*, 8 September 1936, 10; *El Nacional*, 10 September 1936, 8; *El Universal*, 24 September 1936, 9.

53 *Excélsior*, 24 September 1936, 10.

54 *El Nacional*, 25 September 1936, 8.

55 *Excélsior*, 28 September 1936, 10.

56 Contemporary observers pointed out the discrepancy between the statements and the *Diario de los debates del Congreso constituyente de 1916–1917*: *Excélsior*, 2 October 1936, 10; *Universal*, 2 October 1936, 3.

57 Novo, *La vida en México en el periodo presidencial de Lázaro Cárdenas*, 328–29.

58 FUPDM, Tampico, Tamaulipas, to Cárdenas, 6 September 1936, AGN, RP, LCR, exp. 544/1.

59 Ibid.

60 *Excélsior*, 22 November 1936, 10.

61 Novo, *La vida en México en el periodo presidencial de Lázaro Cárdenas*, 328–29.

62 *Excélsior*, 20 December 1936, 10.

63 Cruz, "Los derechos políticos de la mujer en México," 22–23.

64 Comité Ejecutivo Femenil, PNR, Mexico City, 17 March 1937, AGN, RP, LCR, exp. 544/1.

65 *Fem* 8, vol. 3 (October–November 1983): 25.

66 AGN, DGG, vol. 2.331.8(13)20424, caja 30-A, exp. 51; AGN, RP, LCR, exp. 544.4/15.

67 R. Henry Norweb to Secretary of State, 31 December 1935, NARA, 812.00/30325.

68 Gabino Alcaraz to Luis Rojas, 22 March 1935, Condumex, AGRA, Fondo MXLVI, Partido Comunista, 1935/1964, carpeta 4, legajo 462.

69 Alcaraz to García, 6 March 1937, Condumex, AGRA, Fondo MXLVI, carpeta 4, legajo 524. See also Abel Cabrera to Alcaraz, 13 March 1937, Condumex, AGRA, Fondo MXLVI, carpeta 4, legajo 530.

70 García to Múgica, 27 March 1937, CERM, FJM, Volúmenes, vol. 150, doc. 60.

71 Millan, *Mexico Reborn*, 159.

72 García et al. to Cárdenas, 6 August 1936, AGN, RP, LCR, exp. 433/142.

73 García to Cárdenas, 21 April 1937, AGN, RP, LCR, exp. 432/115.

74 García to Múgica, 4 April 1937, CERM, FJM, Volúmenes, vol. 150, doc. 62.

75 *El Universal*, 9 March 1937, 9; *Excélsior*, 9 March 1937, 10.

76 *El Universal*, 17 March 1937, 9; ibid., 22 March 1937, 9.

77 María Leonia Ortiz de la Peña, Unión Cívica Femenina Morelense, to Cárdenas, 29 May 1937, AGN, RP, LCR, exp. 544/1.

78 Wiley to Cárdenas, 30 September 1937, AGN, RP, LCR, exp. 544/1.

79 Speech to FUPDM, reprinted in *Equal Rights*, 15 July 1937, 102–104.

80 Ibid., 102.

81 Bremauntz, "El sufragio femenino desde el punto de vista constitucional"; Bremauntz to Cárdenas, 14 May 1937, AGN, RP, LCR, exp. 544/1.

82 Bremauntz, "El sufragio femenino desde el punto de vista constitucional," 47.

83 For Cárdenas's 1 September 1937 statement to Congress, see *Diario de los debates de la Cámara de diputados del Congreso de los Estados Unidos Mexicanos*, 37th Legis., 1:1, no. 7, 9.

84 *El Universal*, 28 August 1937, 9. Morton states that Cárdenas declared women's suffrage in response to a hunger strike on 15–26 August in front of Los Pinos and "thus deprived the fanatical feminists of the delicious pleasure of starving to death in the public streets of the capital before large and sympathetic crowds": Morton, *Woman Suffrage in Mexico*, 29. Subsequent scholars more disposed to the would-be hunger strikers have repeated this information: Cano, "Un episodio en la lucha por la ciudadanía," 10–11; Macías, *Against All Odds*, 143. Morton's citations, however, lead back to a *New York Times* blurb stating that Mexican women "finally forced the issue some months ago by staging a hunger strike in front of General Cárdenas' home. The President promised suffrage": *New York Times*, 12 September 1937, sec. 6, 7. The blurb probably refers to the April demonstration that opens this chapter, which one Mexico City newspaper dubbed a hunger strike: *La Prensa*, 29 April 1937, 11. No major Mexico City newspaper mentioned a hunger strike in August 1937. Morton's assertion, however, is critical to his explanation for the long delay of women's suffrage. He argues, first, that Cárdenas and other public officials (including the participants in the 1917 Constitutional Congress) were "very busy" and had many more important issues to address. Second, he asserts that the "doughty feminine warriors" of the FUPDM and the "fanatical feminists," too strident in their tactics, misunderstood the mechanisms of politics, thus proving their lack of preparation for political life: Morton, *Woman Suffrage in Mexico*, 29. I argue, by contrast, that women activists' efforts to cooperate and prove themselves to be "good citizens" restrained them from being forceful enough to propel women's suffrage to the top of the Cárdenas administration's agenda.

85 *El Universal*, 2 September 1937, 1.

86 Galindo de Topete to Cárdenas, 30 August 1937, AGN, RP, LCR, exp. 544/1.

87 Rodríguez Cabo, *La mujer y la revolución*, 7.

88 FUPDM, Yahuapan, Veracruz, to Cárdenas, 24 August 1938, AGN, RP, LCR, exp. 544/1.

89 Hay to García Tellez, 13 September 1937, AGN, RP, LCR, exp. 544/1.

90 Doris Stevens to Cárdenas, 16 September 1937, AGN, RP, LCR, exp. 544/1.

91 Manuel R. Palacios and Enrique Arregún to Cárdenas, n.d. [most likely 28 August 1937], AGN, RP, LCR, exp. 544/1; *La Prensa*, 29 August 1937, 11; *El Universal*, 30 August 1937, 9.

92 Anne Marie Brueggerhoff to Cárdenas, 27 September 1937, AGN, RP, LCR, exp. 544/1.

93 *Excélsior*, 14 September 1937, 10; *El Universal*, 14 September 1937, 9; *El Machete*, 9 October 1937, 13. See also Rodríguez Cabo, *La mujer y la revolución*.

94 *La Prensa*, 15 September 1937, 11.

95 *El Universal*, 20 September 1937, 9.

96 FUPDM, Atlixco, Puebla, to Cárdenas, 27 August 1937, AGN, RP, LCR, exp. 544/1.

97 "Manifiesto a la nación," Centro Femenil de Acción Proletaria, April 1938, AGN, RP, LCR, exp. 544/1.

98 Cárdenas, *Palabras y documentos*, 272.

99 *Diario de los Debates de la H. Cámara de Diputados*, 37th Legis., Año Legis. 1, no. 16, 17.

100 Ibid., 20, 26.

101 For an overview of this process, see Serna de la Garza, *Derecho Parlamentario*.

102 *Universal Gráfico*, 6 July 1938, 12.

103 *La Prensa*, 2 July 1938, 12.

104 *La Prensa*, 8 July 1938, 11.

105 *Excélsior*, 31 December 1938, 10; *El Nacional*, 1 April 1939, 8.

106 *El Nacional*, 19 May 1939, 8; *Excélsior*, 20 May 1939, 10.

107 *El Universal*, 18 May 1939, 9; *El Nacional*, 18 May 1939, 8.

108 Cárdenas, "Informe que rinde al H. Congreso de la unión el C. Presidente de la República," 37.

109 *Excélsior*, 8 March 1940, 10.

110 *El Universal*, 28 and 29 March 1940, 9.

111 Macías, *Against All Odds*; Morton, *Woman Suffrage in Mexico*. Cano, "Las feministas en campaña," expresses some skepticism about this conclusion.

112 *El Laborista*, 15 November 1939, 1.

113 Fisher, "The Influence of the Present Mexican Revolution upon the Status of Women"; Prewett, *Reportage on Mexico*, 212, 228.

114 *Diario de los Debates*, 37th Legis. 2, no. 27, 17.

115 CERM, FJM, Volúmenes, vol. 205; CERM, FJM, Tomos, cajas 7, 8. See also Moctezuma Barragán, *Francisco J. Múgica*, 530, 560; Ribera Carbó, *La patria ha podido ser flor*, 159–60.

116 *La Prensa*, 31 May 1939, 11. The conservative Mexico City dailies *La Prensa* and *Excélsior* consistently opposed women's suffrage. The liberal *El Universal* generally supported it, as did the ruling party's *El Nacional*.

117 L. González, *Historia de la Revolución Mexicana, 1934–1940*, 259.

118 Cano, "Una ciudadanía igualitaria"; Córdova, *La política de masas del cardenismo*; Garrido, *El partido de la revolución institucionalizada*; Hamilton, *The Limits of State Autonomy*; Nava Nava, *La ideología del Partido de la Revolución Mexicana*.

119 On efforts to create a Secretaría de Acción Femenil within the PRM's executive committee as well as debates over who would fill such a position, see AGN, RP, LCR, exp. 544.61/103.

120 Report of the Comité Ejecutivo Nacional, PRM, 15 August 1938, AGN, RP, LCR, exp. 544.61/103.

121 Elsie E. Mepina to Cárdenas, 10 March 1938, AGN RP, LCR, exp. 544.61/103.

122 Carr, "The Fate of the Vanguard under a Revolutionary State," 329–30.

123 Laborde to Cárdenas, 1 April 1938, AGN, RP, LCR, exp. 544.61/103.

124 See correspondence in AGN, RP, LCR, exp. 544.61/103.

125 García et al. to Cárdenas, 21 February 1938, and García to Cárdenas, 31 March 1938, AGN, RP, LCR, exp. 544.61/103.

126 "Instructivo para el trabajo femenil, que servirá de orientación a los organizadores del Partido que salgan a los Estados," 12 January 1938, CEMOS, doc. 000128.

127 Laborde, *La política de Unidad a Toda Costa*; Mexican Communist Party, *Contra el Peligro Fachista*.

128 "Instructivo para el trabajo femenil, que servirá de orientación a los organizadores del Partido que salgan a los Estados," 12 January 1938, CEMOS, doc. 000128.

129 Ibid.

130 See correspondence of the Grupo Unificador de la Mujer, Tampico, Tamaulipas, AGN, RP, LCR, exp. 544/1. Although rare, other women's petitions for weapons and military training are in the archives. See, for example, FUPDM, Pánuco, Veracruz, AGN, RP, LCR, exp. 437.1/1100; Confederación de Mujeres Revolucionarias, Mexico City, AGN, RP, LCR, exp. 544/1; Legión Femenil Militar, Mexico City, AGN, RP, MAC, exp. 111/1399; Liga Femenil de Lucha Social, Colonia Unión Roja, Chiapas, AGN, RP, LCR, exp. 503.11/283.

131 Club Femenil Pro-Sierra Mojada to Secretario de Gobernación, 12 August 1938, AGN, DGG, Agrupaciones Sindicales, vol. 2.331.9(3) 33715, caja 56-A, exp. 90. The term "pueblo" in this case most likely refers to the village itself, but it carries a popular connotation as well, indicating "the people."

132 Club Femenil Pro-Sierra Mojada to Cárdenas, 15 July 1940, AGN, DGG, Agrupaciones Sindicales, vol. 2.331.9(3) 33715, caja 56-A, exp. 90.

133 Ibid.

134 "Programa de acción, estatutos y reglamentos del Sector Femenino del Frente Revolucionario Mexicano," 9 April 1938, AGN, RP, LCR, exp. 544/1.

135 Ibid.

136 AGN, RP, LCR, exps. 702.2/4662, 404.1/1889, 534.6/1061, 545.3/320, 437.1/973.

137 Hundreds of Ligas Femeniles de Lucha Social submitted registrations explicitly referring to the Agrarian Department's statutes. Other groups organized leagues and then requested the pamphlet for more specific guidelines. It testifies to the limits of this legibility project that it remains exceedingly difficult to measure overall membership and even more elusive to gauge its meaning. Counting only the years when the Agrarian Department registered the official Ligas Femeniles de Lucha Social, I have found a total of 279 registrations or evidence of registrations, most of which do not specify membership size, although the statutes specified a minimum of fifteen women. Of those that did include membership rolls or numbers, sizes ranged from the fifteen-member minimum to a 455 member league in Acapulco. In addition to these registrations, I have found considerable correspondence from leagues and references to leagues for which I did not find

registrations in the archive. The 279 leagues should have yielded a minimum of 4,185 members, but the available data do not allow a more definite count.

138 Liga Femenil de Acción Social, El Colorado, Querétaro, to Cárdenas, 14 July 1937, AGN, RP, LCR, exp. 136.3/1391.

139 Liga Femenil de Lucha Social, La Purísima, San Luis Potosí, to Cárdenas, 14 March 1939, AGN, RP, LCR, exp. 136.3/2204.

140 Liga Femenil de Lucha Social, Ejido de Derramadero, Coahuila, to Pedro Cerdo, Municipal President, Saltillo, 23 January 1939, AMS, 1939, caja 182/2, legajo 15, exp. 50.

141 Liga Femenil de Lucha Social, Quecheheca, Sonora, to Cárdenas, 21 April 1939, AGN, RP, LCR, exp. 136.3/2267.

142 Founding meeting of the Liga Femenil de Lucha Social, población de Fraile, Municipio de Taxco, Guerrero, 27 October 1938, AGN, RP, LCR, exp. 437.1/209.

143 Meeting of the Liga Femenil de Lucha Social, Vega de Paso, Veracruz, 18 June 1938, AGN, RP, LCR, exp. 531.2/357.

144 On public and private transcripts, see Scott, *Domination and the Arts of Resistance*.

145 *El Machete*, 19 February 1938.

146 On the Maternidad Primero de Mayo, see AGN, RP, LCR, exp. 425.1/20.

147 *El Nacional*, 26 January 1939, 8.

148 See correspondence in AGN, RP, LCR, exp. 437.1/726. Jiménez Esponda succeeded Cuca García as the head of the PCM women's department after García left the party in 1940.

149 Esthela Jiménez Esponda to Secretaria de Educación, FUPDM, 12 August 1938, AGN, RP, LCR, exp. 437.1/726.

150 AGN, RP, MAC, exps. 151.3/230, 556.63/143, 546.2/70, 136.3/1057.

151 *El Nacional*, 28 February 1939, 8.

152 AMM, 1934, legajo "Sindicatos y Comités," carpeta 1; ibid., 1934, legajo 1, carpeta 5, exp. 12; ibid., 1934, legajo "Asociaciones y Uniones," carpeta 2; AGN, RP, LCR, exp. 704.11/31; *El Machete*, 20 July 1932, 3.

153 AGN, RP, LCR, exps. 437.1/29, 562.4/18, 533/4, 433/491, 544/1, 433/401, 702.1/111, 433/491, 606.3/20.

154 AGN, RP, LCR, exps. 437.1/687, 562.4/438, 425.1/34.

155 National Revolutionary Party, "Los Catorce Puntos de la Política Obrera Presidencial," 24.

156 AGN, RP, LCR, exp. 437.1/687.

157 *El Nacional*, 7 March 1944, 8.

Chapter Six "All Are Avowed Socialists"

1 The following political narrative draws heavily on Fallaw, "Peasants, Caciques, and Camarillas," and *Cárdenas Compromised*.

2 R. Henry Norweb, U.S. Consul in Mérida, to Secretary of State, 10 October 1935, NARA, 812.00/30289.

3 Domínguez Navarro, *50 años de una vida*, 272–75.

4 Rufus N. Lane, U.S. Consul in Progreso, "Monthly Report on Political Conditions, September 1930," 10 October 1930, NARA, 812.00 Yucatán/3.

5 Joseph, *Revolution from Without*; Wells, *Yucatán's Gilded Age*; Wells and Joseph, *Summer of Discontent, Seasons of Upheaval*.

6 For a comparison between Yucatecan henequen plantations and other coercive labor systems, see Joseph, *Rediscovering the Past at Mexico's Periphery*, 59–72.

7 Wells and Joseph, *Summer of Discontent, Seasons of Upheaval*, 153.

8 On the "invention" of Maya tradition and the limitations of ethnicity-based organizing during the 1930s, see Fallaw, "Cárdenas and the Caste War That Wasn't." On bilingual community leaders as power brokers, see Friedrich, *Agrarian Revolt in a Mexican Village* and *The Princes of Naranja*; Rus, "The 'Comunidad Revolucionaria Institucional.'"

9 For accounts of the Caste War, see Dumond, *The Machete and the Cross*; Reed, *The Caste War of Yucatán*; Rugeley, *Yucatán's Maya Peasantry and the Origins of the Caste War, 1800–1847*.

10 Fallaw, "Cárdenas and the Caste War That Wasn't," 569–77.

11 Wells and Joseph, "Modernizing Visions, *Chilango* Blueprints, and Provincial Growing Pains," caution against overstating the case of Yucatecan separatism and exceptionalism, however, demonstrating how local elites took advantage of Mexico City's centralizing campaigns.

12 For a detailed analysis of the relationship between Yucatán and the federal government during this period, see Fallaw, "Peasants, Caciques, and Camarillas."

13 See chapter 1.

14 Bustillos Carrillo, *Yucatán al servicio de la patria y de la revolución*, 180, 273.

15 Macías, *Against All Odds*; Ramos Escandón, "Women and Power in Mexico"; Soto, *The Emergence of the Modern Mexican Woman*. To date, the most exhaustive biography of Elvia Carrillo Puerto is Lemaître, *Elvia Carrillo Puerto*.

16 Lemaître, *Elvia Carrillo Puerto*, 43.

17 See ibid., chap. 4.

18 Buck, "El control de la natalidad y el día de la madre"; Macías, *Against All Odds*, 92–93.

19 In January 1924, local leaders of the counterrevolutionary de la Huerta uprising assassinated Felipe Carrillo Puerto. His death has attracted considerable speculation among both professional and amateur historians.

20 Circular from García Correa and César Alayola Barrera, 7 February 1930, AGEY, PE, Bene., caja 915.

21 Círculo de Estudiantes Secundarios "Adolfo Cisneros Cámara" to Oficial Mayor, Secretario de Gobierno, Yucatán, 2 June 1930, AGEY, PE, Gob., caja 921. Despite

girls' participation, officials continued to implement discriminatory programs. During the schools' Civics Day, for example, the schools sent boys, all of whom participated in the manly and militarized Yucatán Explorers' Corps, to accompany public servants ranging from the governor on down. Girls remained excluded from such public-minded activities: Subcommittee of the Día del Civismo, Comité Organizador de la Semana del Niño, to García Correa, 27 April 1932, AGEY, PE, Gob., caja 941.

22　See 1930 correspondence in AGEY, PE, Gob., caja 897; *Tierra*, September 1930.

23　Oficial Mayor, Yucatán, to Comités de Madres de Familia, 28 May 1930, AGEY, PE, Gob., caja 911.

24　García Correa, *Código del Partido Socialista del Sureste estudiado y decretado por el Tercer Congreso Obrero*.

25　Dolores Aldana B. et al. to García Correa, 16 August 1930, AGEY, PE, Gob., caja 924.

26　Report to the assembly of the Liga Central de Resistencia (PSS), 30 April 1931, AGEY, PE, Gob., caja 931, legajo 1.

27　Petition from Liga Obrera Feminista "Aurora Abán," AGEY, PE, Gob., caja 931, legajo 2.

28　Minutes of the Ayuntamiento of Akil, Yucatán, 1 May 1932, AGEY, PE, Gob., caja 943, legajo 1; Liga de Resistencia "Manuel Berzunza," Mérida, to García Correa, 26 September 1932, AGEY, PE, Gob., caja 952, legajo 2.

29　See August 1934 correspondence between Alayola Barrera and María Ríos Cárdenas, AGEY, PE, Gob., caja 998, legajo 2, caja 997, legajo 2.

30　See correspondence with García Correa in AGEY, PE, Gob., caja 933, legajo 2,caja 917.

31　Julia Moreno de Medina, Trabajadora Social, Misión Cultural de Tepich, Municipio Tixcalcupul, Yucatán, to Manuel Mesa, Jefe, Departamento de Enseñanza Agrícola y Normal Rural, SEP, DEANR, caja 3233/365, exp. 8.

32　Patrón, *La educación socialista*, 19; Unión Magisterial Revolucionaria to Florencio Palomo Valencia, 10 October 1936, AGEY, PE, Gob., caja 1013.

33　Concepción L. Sabido to Alayola Barrera, 19 December 1934, AGEY, PE, Gob., caja 997, legajo 2.

34　José C. Baqueiro to Alayola Barrera, 27 December 1934, AGEY, PE, Gob., caja 1004, legajo 1.

35　Bravo Gómez to Alayola Barrera, 8 January 1935, AGEY, PE, Gob., caja 1003.

36　Bloque Radical Revolucionario Femenino to Alayola Barrera, 10 November 1934, 11 November 1934, AGEY, PE, Gob., caja 1002, legajo 1; ibid., 23 November 1934, caja 998, legajo 1. At least one teacher, Salvador Ocampo of the Círculo Orientador de Profesores Socialistas, weighed in on the bloc's behalf.

37　Baqueiro to Alayola Barrera, 27 December 1934, AGEY, PE, Gob., caja 1004, legajo 1.

38　Bloque Radical Revolucionario Femenino to López Cárdenas, 17 February 1936, AGEY, PE, Gob., caja 1022. Domínguez Navarro recalled the Casa del Pueblo as a particularly critical space for leftist organizing: Domínguez Navarro, *50 años de una vida*, 273.

39 Acción Revolucionaria Femenina de Yucatán to López Cárdenas, 17 February 1936, AGEY, PE, Gob., caja 1022.

40 See esp. AGEY, PE, Gob., caja 1004, legajo 2, caja 1006, legajo 1.

41 See correspondence about the Centros de Espíritu in AGEY, PE, Gob., caja 1006, legajo 2.

42 Letter from *vecinas* (residents), n.p., n.d. [1935], to Alayola Barrera, and Cothilde Chan D. et al., Ixil, Yucatán, to Alayola Barrera, 7 February 1935, AGEY, PE, Gob., caja 1006, legajo 1; Paz Ibarra viuda de F. to Alayola Barrera, 27 March 1937, AGEY, PE, Gob., caja 998, legajo 1.

43 Madres de familia de Ticul to Alayola Barrera, 4 February 1935, AGEY, PE, Gob., caja 1006, legajo 1.

44 Petition from residents of Celestún to the ayuntamiento, 8 November 1935, AGEY, PE, Gob., caja 1006, legajo 1.

45 Eladio Novelo Gil, "La mujer y la Revolución," n.d. [c. 1935], AGEY, PE, Gob., caja 998, legajo 1.

46 Ernesto Baqueiro G., "No te arrodilles mujer," 6 March 1935, AGEY, PE, Gob., caja 998, legajo 2.

47 Fallaw, *Cárdenas Compromised*.

48 "El problema agrario de Yucatán: Visita del cuerpo diplomático al Centro Ejidal 'Xcanatun,'" 16 March 1935, CAIHY, CXXIV, 1936, 1/2, 08.

49 On linking masculinity and land reform, see oral testimony in Villanueva Mukul, *Así tomamos las tierras.* Male union organizers and party activists also often described their activities in explicitly masculine terms, equating "virility" with nobility of purpose: "A todos los trabajadores organizados de la República," 19 March 1935, AGEY, PE, Gob., caja 1004, legajo 1; Confederación de Ligas Gremiales de Obreros y Campesinos to Alayola Barrera, 11 September 1935, AGEY, PE, Gob., caja 1005; manifesto of the Unión Magisterial Revolucionaria, 25 November 1936, AGEY, PE, Gob., caja 1018.

50 Sociedad de Padres de Famila y Amigos de la Escuela "Santiago Meneses" to Alayola Barrera, 12 June 1935, AGEY, PE, Gob., caja 1003. Vocational schools had the added appeal of exemption from the socialist-education laws governing private secondary schools.

51 Circular no. 1 of the Sindicato de Obreras y Campesinas de Yucatán, 4 July 1935, AGEY, PE, Gob., caja 1003. The union did not explicitly state its affiliation with the PSS, but the language of the document, the union's offices in the PSS-run Casa del Pueblo, and the apparent expectation that Alayola Barrera would attend the inaugural ceremony for the union's officers indicate a close relationship with the party.

52 Baqueiro to Alayola Barrera, 28 July 1935, AGEY, PE, Gob., caja 1003.

53 Alvarez Barret, *Lecturas para trabajadoras*, 32. Fallaw identifies Alvarez as a Communist: Fallaw, "The Southeast Was Red."

54 The two major newspapers surveyed here are *Diario del Sureste* and *Diario de Yucatán*.

55 *Diario de Yucatán*, 23 September 1935.

56 Fallaw, "The Southeast Was Red" and *Cárdenas Compromised*.

57 Charles H. Taliaferro to Secretary of State, 19 January 1936, NARA, 812.00 Yucatán/67.

58 On the political uses of temperance regulations, see Fallaw, "Dry Law, Wet Politics."

59 See correspondence in AGEY, PE, Gob., caja 1018, legajo 2.

60 María Salomé Espinosa and Francisca Jesús Hoyos, FUPDM, Mérida, to Cárdenas, 3 August 1937, AGN, RP, LCR, exp. 462.1/58.

61 Ibid.

62 Vecinas Progreso de Sociedad Coreográfica "Maruja" to Canto Echeverría, 11 March 1938, AGEY, PE, Gob., caja 1037.

63 Fallaw, "The Life and Deaths of Felipa Poot"; Martín, "Gender and Maya Activism in Early 20th Century Yucatán"; AGEY, PE, Gob., caja 1013. The anthropologist Kathleen Martín argues, based on interviews with Poot's relatives, that Poot's radicalization occurred prior to the arrival of the teacher Bartolomé Cervera Alcocer and resulted from her experiences of rape and patriarchal subordination. As Martín demonstrates, organizations such as Elvia Carrillo Puerto's Ligas Feministas and, later, the FUPDM did not necessarily bring women to consciousness. Rather, they created the organizational infrastructure that enabled the activism of women galvanized by prior experiences.

64 Martín, "Gender and Maya Activism in Early 20th Century Yucatán."

65 FUPDM, Kinchil, to Palomo Valencia, 25 July 1936, AGEY, PE, Gob., caja 1013.

66 *El primer congreso feminista de Yucatán*.

67 Baqueiro and Alfonso Pérez Berzunza, PSS, to Alayola Barrera, 16 November 1934, AGEY, PE, Gob., caja 1002, legajo 1; Betancourt de Albertos to Alayola Barrera, 20 December 1934, AGEY, PE, Gob., caja 997, legajo 1.

68 Betancourt de Albertos to Alayola Barrera, 28 March 1935, AGEY, PE, Gob., caja 998, legajo 1.

69 Betancourt de Albertos to López Cárdenas 11 January 1936, AGEY, PE, Gob., caja 1018. I thank Ben Fallaw for providing this information about Betancourt's position on the federal education promotions committee.

70 There is no clear family relationship between Mercedes Betancourt de Albertos and Antonio Betancourt Pérez. Fallaw (personal communication, 27 January 2000) speculates that they were, perhaps, distantly related, and Betancourt Albertos referred to Betancourt Pérez simply as "Antonio" in some letters, indicating that the two had more than passing contact, but they remained committed ideological enemies.

71 Betancourt de Albertos to Palomo Valencia, 16 July 1936, 4 August 1936, 18 September 1936, AGEY, PE, Gob., caja 1022.

72 See correspondence in AGEY, PE, Gob., caja 1018.

73 Transcribed in Enrique Moguel Ruz, Oficial Mayor, to Presidente Municipal, Dzitás, 14 November 1936, AGEY, PE, Gob., caja 1022.

74 Victor C. Pérez, Procurador General de Justicia, to Palomo Valencia, 18 November 1936, AGEY, PE, Gob., caja 1022.

75 Betancourt de Albertos to Palomo Valencia, 11 November 1936, AGEY, PE, Gob., caja 1022. Héctor Erosa, the official named in Betancourt's complaint, organized for the Popular Front–connected — and staunchly Cardenista — Mexican Peasant Confederation.

76 The archives record other examples of women family members getting drawn into violent political disputes. In the town of Ucú, just west of Mérida, the municipal president went on a drunken rampage, assaulting his political enemies' female family members. The report's tone marks this behavior as extraordinary and as evidence of his inability to govern. Although it links the incident to political rivalries, the report leaves ambiguous whether the municipal president considered these women personal political enemies or merely enemies by association: Sindicato de Obreros, Campesinos–Agraristas y Cortadores de Pencas del Pueblo de Ucú to Jefe, Departamento Autónomo del Trabajo, 6 October 1936, AGEY, PE, Gob., caja 1013.

77 Letter transcribed in Víctor C. Pérez, Procurador General de Justicia, to Palomo Valencia, 21 November 1936, AGEY, PE, Gob., caja 1022. The "sindicato" in question most likely referred to the Sindicato de Profesores (Teachers' Union) that Betancourt and her son promoted to combat the PCM-supported UMR.

78 Betancourt de Albertos to Palomo Valencia, 18 November 1936, AGEY, PE, Gob., caja 1022.

79 Ibid.

80 Betancourt de Albertos to Palomo Valencia, 1 January 1937, AGEY, PE, Gob., caja 1027.

81 Betancourt de Albertos to Palomo Valencia, 8 January 1937, AGEY, PE, Gob., caja 1027.

82 González to Cárdenas, 17 August 1937, AGN, RP, LCR, exp. 437.1/730. González had some experience with organizing, serving as an officer of Progreso's Comité Femenil de Orientación Revolucionaria in 1934: Comité Femenil de Orientación Revolucionaria to Alayola Barrera, 17 November 1934, AGEY, PE, Gob., caja 1002, legajo 1.

83 González to Cárdenas, 13 September 1937, AGN, RP, LCR, exp. 437.1/730.

84 González to Cárdenas, 15 October 1937, AGN, RP, LCR, exp. 437.1/738; González to Secretario de Gobernación, 19 October 1937, AGN, DGG, vol. 2.331/8(27)28481, caja 49-A, exp. 52.

85 González to Cárdenas, 1 November 1937, AGN, RP, LCR, exp. 437.1/738.

86 González and Gertrudis Aguilar, Sindicato de Trabajadoras al Servicio Doméstico, to Cárdenas, 20 February 1938, AGN, DGG, vol. 2.331/8(27)31138, caja 49-A, exp. 61.

87 Ibid.

88 Alianza Popular Yucateca to Palomo Valencia, 9 November 1936, AGEY, PE, Gob., caja 1013.

89 Gumercinda Pérez and Saturnina Medina to Cárdenas, 6 February 1938, AGN, RP, LCR, exp. 437.1/733.

90 Ibid.

91 FUPDM, Tixméuac to Cárdenas, 3 December 1938, AGN, RP, LCR, exp. 707/11.

92 While it is difficult to assess ethnicity (much less the meanings of ethnic self-identification) through names, the significant number of indigenous names gives some indication of the group's ethnic makeup. Tekax had been a site of violent conflict during the 1847 Caste War, which would have imbued ethnic identification with specific, historically informed markers.

93 See correspondence in AGEY, PE, Gob., caja 1029.

94 Adriano Solís Quintal to Jefe del Trabajo, Confederación de Ligas Gremiales de Obreros y Campesinos de Yucatán, 17 March 1941, AGEY, PE, Gob., caja 1029.

95 Rafael Lugo Gruintal, Oficial Mayor, to Jefe, Departamento de Seguridad Pública, 4 May 1939; Solís Quintal to Jefe del Trabajo, 17 March 1941, both in AGEY, PE, Gob., caja 1029.

96 On the limitations of the "Crusade of the Mayab," see Fallaw, "Cárdenas and the Caste War That Wasn't."

97 See Fallaw, "Peasants, Caciques, and Camarillas," chap. 8.

98 Jefe de la Zona, Ticul, 3 December 1935, transcribed in Banco Nacional de Crédito Agrícola to López Cárdenas, 6 December 1935; Carlos R. Castellanos, Procurador General de Justicia, to López Cárdenas, 6 February 1936, both in AGEY, PE, Gob., caja 1022.

99 See "El problema agrario de Yucatán: Visita del cuerpo diplomático al Centro Ejidal 'Xcanatun,'" 16 March 1935, CAIHY, CXXIV, 1936, 1/2, 08. For similar phenomena with other agrarian-reform efforts in Latin America, see Deere and León de Leal, *Empowering Women*; Tinsman, *Partners in Conflict*.

100 FUPDM, Mérida, to Cárdenas, 3 August 1937, AGN, RP, LCR, exp. 462.1/58.

101 In the reparto of Homún, for example, one census shows 2 women out of 368 ejido recipients, while another shows 4 women out of 161 recipients. Yaxkukul had four women out of 251 recipients: see AGEY, PE, Gob., caja 1030, legajos 1, 2.

102 *El Universal*, 18 September 1937, 9. The "Open Door" policy prefigured the voting structure that the PRM adopted six months later: Fallaw, *Cárdenas Compromised*.

103 Cárdenas to Múgica, 14 August 1937, CERM, FJM, Volúmenes, vol. 179, doc. 88.

104 See, for example, the 4 December 1936 letter to Palomo Valencia from eleven popular organizations in Valladolid, AGEY, PE, Gob., caja 1018; the poster "Los trabajadores se unen en defensa de los cordoleros," in which the FUPDM, the PCM, and the UMR joined other organizations in supporting the Progreso cordage workers' union, 11 February 1937, AGEY, PE, Gob., caja 1019, legajo 2.

105 "Estatutos del Sindicato Unico de Trabajadores de la Enseñanza en Yucatán," 23–24.

106 FUPDM, Mérida, to Cárdenas, 3 August 1937, AGN, RP, LCR, exp. 462.1/58; FUPDM, Ticul, to Cárdenas, and FUPDM, Valladolid, to Cárdenas, both 6 August 1937, AGN, RP, LCR, exp. 151.3/1380; FUPDM, Chichimilá, to Cárdenas, 15 August 1937, AGN, RP, LCR, exp. 609/152.

107 FUPDM, Espita, to Cárdenas, 30 July 1937, AGN, RP, LCR, exp. 136.3/2530.

108 Comité Estatal, FUPDM, Yucatán, to Cárdenas, 19 October 1937, AGN, RP, LCR, exp. 462.1/58.

109 Coronel J. M. Núñez to Cárdenas, 19 October 1937; Cárdenas to FUPDM, Yucatán, 20 October 1937, both in AGN, RP, LCR, exp. 462.1/58.

110 Liga Femenil de Lucha Social, Tekantó, to Cárdenas, n.d. [August 1937], AGN, RP, LCR, exp. 163.3/2517.

111 Liga Femenil "Nicte-ha" to Cárdenas, 10 August 1937, AGN, RP, LCR, exp. 136.3/2571.

112 On the "Gran Ejido," see Benítez, *Ki*; Canto Echeverría and Durán Rosado, *Cárdenas y el Gran Ejido Henequenero de Yucatán*; Fallaw, *Cárdenas Compromised*; Sierra Villarreal and Paoli Bolio, *Cárdenas y el reparto de los henequenales*.

113 Report of the 19 April 1938 meeting of the executive committee of the Abalá FUPDM, AGEY, PE, Gob., caja 1037.

114 The U.S. consular office reported that when a group of 500 ejidatarios threatened a demonstration in Mérida to protest their working conditions, Canto Echeverría offered them all "a room in the state penitentiary." The group apparently called off its demonstration: Taliaferro to Secretary of State, 30 April 1938, NARA, 812.00 Yucatán/96.

115 Oficial Mayor, Yucatán, to Jefe, Policia Judicial del Estado, 2 May 1939; Oficial Mayor, Yucatán, to Presidente, Comité Central del Grupo de Acción Política de Diputados y Senadores, Distrito Federal 16 May 1939, AGEY, PE, Gob., caja 1049.

116 Comité Estatal, FUPDM, to Canto Echeverría, 26 September 1938, AGEY, PE, Gob., caja 1043.

117 Letter from the Mérida Club de Madres transcribed in General de Brígida Comandante de la Zona to Canto Echeverría, 7 July 1939; Feliciano Cocom and Antonio Hoil, Sindicato de Obreros y Empleados de la Industria Eléctrica de Yucatán, CTM, 8 July 1939, both in AGEY, PE, Gob., caja 1041.

118 Circulars no. 5 and no. 7 of the Comité Regional, PRM, 27 and 30 March 1939, AGEY, PE, Gob., caja 1049.

119 Bravo Gómez and Mendoza, "La mujer," 8.

120 Ibid., 3.

121 Ibid., 6–7.

122 Sección Yucateca del FUPDM to Cárdenas, 23 November 1939, AGN, RP, LCR, exp. 462.1/58.

123 Registrations for the Ligas Femeniles de Lucha Social of Muxupip and Temozón de Mena y Sosa, both 14 December 1939, AGN, RP, LCR, exp. 473.1/733; Liga

Femenil de Lucha Social, Ejido Sotuta, Municipio de Tecoh, to Cárdenas, 16 December 1939, AGN, RP, LCR, exp. 136.3/2502.

124 FUPDM, Ticul, to Cárdenas, 3 January 1940, AGN, RP, LCR, exp. 151.3/1380.

125 José Siurob, Jefe, Departamento de Salubridad Pública, to Cárdenas, 14 February 1940, AGN, RP, LCR, exp. 151.3/1380.

126 Sección Yucateca del FUPDM to Cárdenas, 29 February 1940, AGN, RP, LCR, exp. 433/474.

127 Sección Yucateca del FUPDM to Avila Camacho, 11 February 1941, AGN, RP, MAC, exp. 562.4/28.

128 Bravo Gómez and Mendoza, "La mujer," 3.

Conclusions and Epilogue

1 Gilly, *La revolución interrumpida*.

2 Flores Sánchez, interview.

3 *Diario de los debates de la Cámara de diputados del Congreso de los Estados Unidos Mexicanos*, 40th Legis., 1:1, no. 40, 11–22.

4 For a complete account of the debates, see Tuñón, *¡Por fin . . . ya podemos elegir y ser electas!*

5 Cited in Ponce Lagos, *Historia de las reformas a los artículos 34 y 115 constitucionales*, 35.

6 Ibid., 37, 65, 79–83.

7 Partido Popular, "Corrido del voto de la mujer."

8 Cano, "Una ciudadanía igualitaria," 73.

9 Cott, *The Grounding of Modern Feminism*; Mansbridge, *Why We Lost the ERA*.

10 González de Montemayor, interview.

11 See, for example, the discussion of co-optation and demoralization in Payne, *I've Got the Light of Freedom*.

12 Agamben, *Homo Sacer*, 32.

13 *El Siglo de Torreón*, 9 July 2003, 2C.

14 Hartmann, "The Unhappy Marriage of Marxism and Feminism," 1.

15 Williams, *Marxism and Literature*, 125; emphasis in original.

16 Phillips, *Engendering Democracy*.

17 Agamben, *Homo Sacer*, 67, 90.

18 Rascón, "La mujer y la lucha social," 141.

19 Centeno, *Democracy within Reason*; Connell, *Masculinities*; Hoganson, *Fighting for American Manhood*.

20 Nava Nava, "El Lic. Ignacio García Tellez y los inicios del Instituto Mexicano de Seguro Social."

21 Rus, "The 'Comunidad Revolucionaria Institucional.'"

22 For a summary of these movements, see Espinosa, "Ciudadanía y femenismo popular."

23 Cano, interview.

BIBLIOGRAPHY

Archives Consulted

Mexico City

AGN	Archivo General de la Nación
RP	Ramo Presidencial
LCR	Grupo Lázaro Cárdenas del Río
MAC	Grupo Manuel Avila Camacho
DGG	Dirección General del Gobierno
CP	Colecciones Particulares
CEMOS	Centro de Estudios del Movimiento Obrero y Socialista
Condumex	Centro de Estudios Históricos Mexicanos Condumex
AGRA	Archivo Gabino R. Alcaraz
HN	Hemeroteca Nacional
INAH	Instituto Nacional de Antopología e Historia
LTAE	Biblioteca Miguel Lerdo de Tejada, Archivos Económicos
SEP	Secretaría de Educación Pública, Archivo Histórico
DEANR	Departamento de Enseñanza Agrícola y Normal Rural
IOS	Instituto de Orientación Socialista
UFCM	Unión Femenina Católica Mexicana, Universidad Iberoamericana, Archivo Histórico

Michoacán

ACEM	Archivo del Congreso del Estado de Michoacán (Morelia)
AHMM	Archivo Histórico Municipal de Morelia
AHPEM	Archivo Histórico del Poder Ejecutivo de Michoacán (Morelia)

Gobierno	Fondo Gobierno
Conflictos	Ramo Conflictos Políticos
Educación	Ramo Educación
Elecciones	Ramo Elecciones
Partidos	Ramo Partidos Políticos
Religión	Ramo Religión
Laboral	Fondo Laboral
Sindicatos	Ramo Sindicatos
Leyes	Fondo Leyes y Decretos
CERM	Centro de Estudios de la Revolución Mexicana "Lázaro Cárdenas" (Jiquilpan)
FJM	Fondo Francisco J. Múgica
Documentos	Sección Documentos Sueltos
Tomos	Sección Tomos
Volúmenes	Sección Volúmenes
Fondo CERM	Fondo Centro de Estudios de la Revolución Mexicana
Michel Coll.	Personal papers of Concha Michel (Morelia)

Coahuila, Comarca Lagunera, and Durango

AMS	Archivo Municipal de Saltillo (Coahuila), Fondo Presidencia Municipal
IEDC	Instituto Estatal de Documentación, Coahuila
IMDT	Instituto Municipal de Documentación, Torreón (Coahuila)
Presidencia	Fondo Presidencia
Cabildo	Actos de Cabildo
UIPL	Universidad Iberoamericana, Plantel Laguna

Yucatán

AGEY	Archivo General del Estado de Yucatán
PE	Fondo Poder Ejecutivo
Gob.	Sección Gobernación
Bene.	Sección Beneficencia
CAIHY	Centro de Apoyo de Investigaciones Históricos de Yucatán

Other Regional Mexican Archives

AEV	Archivo del Estado de Veracruz (Jalapa)
AMM	Archivo Municipal de Monterrey, Nuevo León
PAA	Puebla, Archivo del Ayuntamiento

United States

Hoover	Hoover Institution Archives, Stanford University (Stanford, Calif.)
REM	Rodolfo Echeverría Martínez Collection
JF	Joseph Freeman Collection
NARA	National Archives and Record Administration, Record Group 59 (Washington, D.C.)

Interviews

Cano, María Natividad. San Pedro de las Colonias, Coahuila, 28 March 1998.

Escudero de Múgica, Carolina. Pátzcuaro, Michoacán, 15 November 1998. (Interview with the author and Stephanie Bryant.)

Flores Sánchez, Ana María. Torreón, Coahuila, 11 July 2003.

González de Montemayor, Beatriz. Torreón, Coahuila, 26 March 1998.

List, Germán. Mexico City, 20 June 1996.

Quintero Castellanos, Esperanza. Morelia, Michoacán, 22 November 1998. (Interview with the author and Stephanie Bryant.)

Periodicals

Asistencia

Diario de los debates de la Cámara de Diputados del Congreso de los Estados Unidos Mexicanos

Excélsior (Mexico City)

Frente a Frente (Mexico City)

El Machete (Mexico City)

Magisterio Revolucionario (Mexico City)

Memoria de la Secretaría de Educación Pública

El Mexicano del Norte (Ciudad Juárez, Chihuahua)

El Nacional (Mexico City)

La Palabra (Mexico City)

Política Social

La Prensa (Mexico City)

New York Times

Redención (Villahermosa, Tabasco)

Revista Mexicana del Trabajo

El Siglo de Torreón (Torreón, Coahuila)

El Universal (Mexico City)

El Universal Gráfico (Mexico City)

La Voz de la Revolución (Mérida, Yucatán)

Books, Theses, and Articles

Abascal, Salvador. *Mis recuerdos: Sinarquismo y colonia María Auxiliadora, 1935–1944*. Mexico City: Tradición, 1980.

Aboites, Luis. *La Revolución Mexicana en Espita, Yucatán (1910–1940): Microhistoria de la formación de Estado de la Revolución*. Mérida: Maldonado Editores, 1985.

Acosta Proudinat, Rodrigo. *Ixtacametl: Vida y obra del maestro rural mexicano*. Quito: Talleres Gráficos de Educación, 1938.

Agamben, Giorgio. *Homo Sacer: Sovereign Power and Bare Life*. Stanford, Calif.: Stanford University Press, 1998.

Aguila M., Marcos Tonatiuh, and Alberto Enríquez Perea, eds. *Perspectivas sobre el cardenismo: Ensayos sobre economía, trabajo, política y cultura en los años treinta*. Azcapotzalco: Universidad Autónoma Metropolitana, 1996.

Aguilar Camín, Hector, and Lorenzo Meyer. *In the Shadow of the Mexican Revolution: Contemporary Mexican History, 1910–1989*. Austin: University of Texas Press, 1993.

Aguilar Mora, Manuel. *La crisis de la izquierda en México: Orígenes y desarrollo*. Mexico City: Juan Pablos Editor, 1978.

Alegría, Juana Armanda. *Emancipación femenina en el subdesarrollo*. Mexico City: Editorial Diana, 1982.

Alemán, Homero, ed. *Fascismo, democracia y frente popular: VII Congreso de la Internacional Comunista, Moscú, 25 de julio–20 agosto de 1935*. Mexico City: Siglo Veintiuno Editores, 1984.

Alonso, Ana María. *Thread of Blood: Colonialism, Revolution, and Gender on Mexico's Northern Frontier*. Tucson: University of Arizona Press, 1995.

Alonso, Jorge, ed. *Lucha urbana y la acumulación de capital*. Mexico City: Centro de Investigaciones Superiores del Instituto Nacional de Antropología e Historia, 1980.

Alvarez Barret, Luis. *Lecturas para trabajadoras: Folleto no. 1 para ser utilizado en las escuelas nocturnas, en la campaña analfabetizante y en las organizaciones sindicales*. Mérida: Dirección de la Educación Federal del Estado de Yucatán, 1937.

Alvarez, Sonia E. *Engendering Democracy in Brazil: Women's Movements in Transition Politics*. Princeton, N.J.: Princeton University Press, 1990.

Alvarez, Sonia E., Evelina Dagnino, and Arturo Escobar, eds. *Cultures of Politics, Politics of Cultures: Re-visioning Latin American Social Movements*. Boulder: Westview Press, 1998.

Anguiano, Arturo. *El estado y la política obrera del cardenismo*. Mexico City: Editorial Era, 1975.

Anguiano, Arturo, Guadalupe Pacheco, and Rogelio Vizcaíno. *Cárdenas y la izquierda mexicana*. Mexico City: Juan Pablos Editor, 1975.

Applewhite, Harriet B., and Darline G. Levy, eds. *Women and Politics in the Age of the Democratic Revolution*. Ann Arbor, Mich.: University of Michigan Press, 1990.

Arendt, Hannah. *Eichmann in Jerusalem: A Report on the Banality of Evil*. New York: Penguin Books, 1964.

Arias Navarro, Santiago. "Las Misiones Culturales: Reflexiones de un misionero." Mexico City, 1934.

Arizpe, Lourdes. *La mujer en el desarrollo de México y de América Latina*. Mexico City: Universidad Nacional Autónoma de México, 1989.

Ashby, Joe C. *Organized Labor and the Mexican Revolution under Lázaro Cárdenas*. Chapel Hill: University of North Carolina Press, 1963.

Bailey, David. *¡Viva Cristo Rey! The Cristero Rebellion and the Church–State Conflict in Mexico*. Austin: University of Texas Press, 1974.

Baldez, Lisa. *Why Women Protest: Women's Movements in Chile*. Cambridge: Cambridge University Press, 2002.

Baños Ramírez, Othón, ed. *Sociedad, estructura agraria y estado en Yucatán*. Mérida: Universidad Autónoma de Yucatán, 1990.

Bantjes, Adrian A. *As If Jesus Walked on Earth: Cardenismo, Sonora and the Mexican Revolution*. Wilmington, Del.: Scholarly Resources, 1998.

Barrera Bassols, Dalia. *Mujeres, ciudadanía y poder*. Mexico City: El Colegio de México Press, 2000.

Bartra, Roger. *The Cage of Melancholy: Identity and Metamorphosis in the Mexican Character*. Trans. Christopher J. Hall. New Brunswick, N.J.: Rutgers University Press, 1992.

Bassols, Narciso. "The General Programme of Education in Mexico: An Address Delivered by His Excellency the Minister of Education, Señor Licenciado Narciso Bassols, before the Seminar in Mexico, on July 19, 1932." Mexico City, 1932.

Basurto, Jorge. *Cárdenas y el poder sindical*. Mexico City: Ediciones Era, 1983.

Bauer, Arnold J. "Millers and Grinders: Technology and Household Economy in Meso-America." *Agricultural History* 64, no. 1 (1990): 1–17.

Becker, Marjorie. *Setting the Virgin on Fire: Lázaro Cárdenas, Michoacán Campesinos and the Redemption of the Mexican Revolution*. Berkeley: University of California Press, 1995.

Beezley, William H., Cheryl English Martin, and William E. French. *Rituals of Rule, Rituals of Resistance: Public Celebrations and Popular Culture in Mexico*. Wilmington, Del.: Scholarly Resources, 1994.

Benhabib, Seyla. "Sexual Difference and Collective Identities: The New Global Constellation." *Signs* 24, no. 2 (1999): 335–61.

Benítez, Fernando. *Ki: El drama de un pueblo y de una planta*. 2d ed. Mexico City: Fondo de Cultura Económica, 1962.

Benjamin, Thomas. "Laboratories of the New State, 1920–1929: Regional Social Reform and Experiments in Mass Politics." Pp. 71–90 in *Provinces of the Revolution: Essays on Regional Mexican History, 1920–1929*, ed. Thomas Benjamin and Mark Wasserman. Albuquerque: University of New Mexico Press, 1990.

Benjamin, Thomas, and William Mc Nellie, eds. *Other Mexicos: Essays on Regional Mexican History, 1876–1911*. Norman: University of Oklahoma Press, 1984.

Benjamin, Thomas, and Mark Wasserman, eds. *Provinces of the Revolution: Essays on Regional Mexican History, 1920–1929*. Albuquerque: University of New Mexico Press, 1990.

Besse, Susan K. *Restructuring Patriarchy: The Modernization of Gender Inequality in Brazil, 1914–1940*. Chapel Hill: University of North Carolina Press, 1996.

Bethell, Leslie, ed. *Mexico since Independence*. Cambridge: Cambridge University Press, 1991.

Blanco Macías, Gonzalo, ed. *La Laguna y su desarrollo bajo el sistema colectivo de trabajo*. Torreón, 1940.

Bliss, Katherine Elaine. *Compromised Positions: Prostitution, Public Health, and Gender Politics in Revolutionary Mexico City*. University Park.: Pennsylvania State University Press, 2001.

Bloque Nacional de Mujeres Revolucionarias. "¿Qué puede esperar la mujer del gobierno del Gral. L. Cárdenas?" Mexico City, 1935.

Blum, Ann S. "Public Welfare and Child Circulation in Mexico City, 1877 to 1925." *Journal of Family History* 23, no. 3 (1998): 240–71.

Boils, Guillermo. *Los militares y la política en México, 1915–1974*. Mexico City: Ediciones El Caballito, 1975.

Bonifaz de Novelo, María Eugenia. *La mujer mexicana: Análisis histórico*, Mexico City, 1978.

Booth, George C. *Mexico's School-Made Society*. Stanford, Calif.: Stanford University Press, 1941.

Bosques, Gilberto. *The National Revolutionary Party and the Six-Year Plan*. Mexico City: Partido Nacional Revolucionario, 1937.

Bourdieu, Pierre. *Outline of a Theory of Practice*. Trans. Richard Nice. New York: Cambridge University Press, 1977.

Boyer, Christopher R. "The Cultural Politics of *Agrarismo*: Agrarian Revolt, Village Revolutionaries, and State-Formation in Michoacán, Mexico." Ph.D. diss., University of Chicago, 1997.

———. "Old Loves, New Loyalties: Agrarismo in Michoacán, 1920–1928." *Hispanic American Historical Review* 78, no. 3 (1999): 418–55.

———. *Becoming Campesinos: Politics, Identity, and Agrarian Struggle in Postrevolutionary Michoacán, 1920–1935*. Stanford, Calif.: Stanford University Press, 2003.

Boylan, Kristina. "'They Were Always Doing Something?': Catholic Women's Activism and Activity in Jalisco, Mexico, in the 1930s." Paper presented at the 21st Annual Meeting of the Latin American Studies Association, Chicago, 24–26 September 1998.

———. "Mexican Catholic Women's Activism, 1929–1940." Ph.D. diss., St. Cross College, Oxford University, 2001.

Brading, David. *Caudillo and Peasant in the Mexican Revolution*. Cambridge: Cambridge University Press, 1980.

Brandes, Stanley. *Power and Persuasion: Fiestas and Social Control in Rural Mexico*. Philadelphia: University of Pennsylvania Press, 1988.

Brannon, Jeffery T., and Gilbert M. Joseph. *Land, Labor, and Capital in Modern Yucatán: Essays in Regional History and Political Economy*. Tuscaloosa: University of Alabama Press, 1991.

Bravo Gómez, Anita, and Candelaria Mendoza de F. "La mujer: Su emancipación social y política — El voto sin restricciones." Mérida, 1939.

Bravo Gómez, José. *Historia sucinta de Michoacán: Estado y departamento (1821–1962)*. Mexico City: Editorial Jus, 1964.

Bredbenner, Candace Lewis. *A Nationality of Her Own: Women, Marriage, and the Law of Citizenship*. Berkeley: University of California Press, 1998.

Bremauntz, Alberto. "El sufragio femenino desde el punto de vista constitucional." Mexico City: Frente Socialista de Abogados, 1937.

Bretton, F. R., and H. L. Mitchell. *Land and Liberty for Mexican Farmers: Report of the STFU Delegation to Laguna Conference, Torreón, Coahuila, Mexico*. Southern Tenant Farmers' Union, 1939.

Brown, Lyle C. "General Lázaro Cárdenas and Mexican Presidential Politics, 1933–1940: A Study in the Acquisition and Manipulation of Political Power." Ph.D. diss., University of Texas, Austin, 1964.

Buck, Sarah. "El control de la natalidad y el día de la madre: Política feminista y reaccionaria de México, 1922–1923." *Signos Históricos* 5 (2001): 9–53.

———. "Activists and Mothers: Feminists and Maternalist Politics in Mexico, 1923–1953." Ph.D. diss., Rutgers University, New Brunswick, N.J., 2002.

Bustillos Carrillo, Antonio. *Yucatán al servicio de la patria y de la revolución*. Mexico City: Casa Ramírez Editores, 1959.

Butler, Judith. *Gender Trouble: Feminism and the Subversion of Identity*. New York: Routledge, 1990.

———. "Contingent Foundations: Feminism and the Question of the 'Postmodern.'" In Butler and Scott, eds. *Feminists Theorize the Political*.

Butler, Judith, and Joan Scott, eds. *Feminists Theorize the Political*. New York: Routledge, 1992.

Calderón R., Miguel Ángel. *El impacto de la crisis de 1929 en México*. Mexico City: Secretaría de Educación Pública, 1982.

Camp, Roderic Ai. *Mexican Political Biographies, 1935–1993*. 3d ed. Austin: University of Texas Press, 1995.

Campa, Valentín. *Memorias de Valentín Campa: 50 años con el movimiento obrero y revolucionario*. Monterrey, Nuevo León: Facultad de Filosofía y Letras de la Universidad Autónoma de Nuevo León, 1978.

Canning, Kathleen. "Class versus Citizenship: Keywords in Gender History." *Central European History* 37, no. 2 (2004): 225–44.

Cano, Gabriela. "Un episodio en la lucha por la ciudadanía." *Fem* 57 (September 1987): 10–11.

———. "Congresos feministas en la historia de México." *Fem* 58 (October 1987): 24–27.

———. "Hermila Galindo." *Fem* 72 (December 1988): 19–21.

———. "México, 1923: El Primer Congreso Feminista Panamericano." *Debate feminista* (1990): 303–307.

———. "Las feministas en campaña: La primera mitad del siglo XX." *Debate Feminista* 2, no. 4 (1991): 269–92.

———. "Revolución, femenismo y ciudadanía en México (1915–1940)." Pp. 301–12 in *Historia de la mujeres en Occidente*, ed. Georges Duby and Michelle Perrot. Madrid: Taurus, 1993.

———. "Una ciudadanía igualitaria: El presidente Lázaro Cárdenas y el sufragio femenino." *Desdeldiez* (1995): 69–116.

———. "La íntima felicidad del Coronel Robles." *Equis: Cultura y Sociedad* (June 1999): 25–35.

———. "Feminismo." Pp. 242–47 in *Léxico de la política*, ed. Laura Baca Olamendi, Judit Bokser de Liwerant, Fernando Castañeda, Isidro H. Cisneros, and Germán Pérez Fernández del Castillo. Mexico City: Facultad Latinoamericana de Ciencias Sociales, Consejo Nacional de Ciencia y Tecnología, Fundación Heinrich Böll, Fondo de Cultura Económica, 2000.

Canto Echeverría, Humberto, and Estebán Durán Rosado. *Cárdenas y el Gran Ejido Henequenero de Yucatán*. Mexico City: Costa-Amic, 1963.

Cárdenas, Enrique. *La industrialización mexicana durante la Gran Depresión*. Mexico City: El Colegio de México, 1987.

Cárdenas, Lázaro. "Informe que rinde al H. Congreso de la unión el C. Presidente de la República, general Lázaro Cárdenas, por su gestión de gobierno realizada del 1 de septiembre de 1938 al 31 de agosto de 1939." Mexico City, 1939.

———. *Ideario político*. Mexico City: Ediciones Era, 1972.

———. *Obras: I—Apuntes, 1913–1940*. Vol. 1. Mexico City: Universidad Nacional Autónoma de México, 1972.

———. *Palabras y documentos: Mensajes, discursos, declaraciones, entrevistas y otros documentos, 1928–1940*. Vol. 1. Mexico City: Siglo Veintiuno Editores, 1978.

Cárdenas, Magdalena. *Organización del Circuito Rural*. Mexico City: Secretaría de Educación Pública, 1929.

Carr, Barry. "The Mexican Communist Party and Agrarian Mobilization in the Laguna, 1920–1940: A Worker–Peasant Alliance?" *Hispanic American Historical Review* 67, no. 3 (1987): 372–404.

———. *Marxism and Communism in Twentieth-Century Mexico*. Lincoln: University of Nebraska Press, 1992.

———. "The Fate of the Vanguard under a Revolutionary State: Marxism's Contribution to the Construction of the Great Arch." Pp. 326–52 in *Everyday Forms of State Formation: Revolution and the Negotiation of Rule in Modern Mexico*, ed. Gilbert M. Joseph and Daniel Nugent. Durham: Duke University Press, 1994.

Casales, Rafaela, Paz Vaquera, Guadalupe Pérez, Bernarda García, and Salomé Bernal. "Colonia Cerro de la Cruz." *El Puente* 2, no. 12 (1992): 12–25.

Castellanos Guerrero, Alicia, and Gilberto López y Rivas. *Primo Tapia de la Cruz, un hijo del pueblo*. Mexico City: Centro de Estudios Históricos del Agrarismo en México, 1991.

Castillo y Piña, José. *Cuestiones sociales*. Mexico City: Impresores, 1934.

Caulfield, Sueann. "The History of Gender in the Historiography of Latin America." *Hispanic American Historical Review* 81, nos. 3–4 (2001): 449–92.

Centeno, Miguel Angel. *Democracy within Reason: Technocratic Revolution in Mexico*. 2d ed. University Park: Pennsylvania State University Press, 1997.

Chapa, Esther. *El derecho de voto para la mujer*. Mexico City: Frente Unico Pro-Derechos de la Mujer, 1936.

Chatterjee, Choi. *Celebrating Women: Gender, Festival Culture, and Bolshevik Ideology, 1910–1939*. Pittsburgh: University of Pittsburgh Press, 2002.

Chatterjee, Partha. *A Nation and Its Fragments*. Princeton, N.J.: Princeton University Press, 1993.

Civera Cerecedo, Alicia. *Entre surcos y letras: Educación para campesinos en los años treinta*. Zinacantepec: El Colegio Mexiquense, Instituto Nacional de Estudios Históricos de la Revolución Mexicana, 1997.

Clark, Marjorie Ruth. *Organized Labor in Mexico*. Chapel Hill: University of North Carolina Press, 1934.

Cockcroft, James D. *Mexico: Class Formation, Capital Accumulation, and the State*. New York: Monthly Review Press, 1983.

———. *Mexico's Hope: An Encounter with Politics and History*. New York: Monthly Review Press, 1998.

Collier, Ruth Berins. "Popular Sector Incorporation and Political Supremacy: Regime Evolution in Brazil and Mexico." Pp. 57–109 in *Brazil and Mexico: Patterns in Late Development*, ed. Sylvia Ann Hewlett and Richard S. Weinert. Philadelphia: Institute for the Study of Human Issues, 1982.

Collier, Ruth Berins, and David Collier. *Shaping the Political Arena: Critical Junctures, the Labor Movement and Regimes Dynamics in Latin America*. Princeton, N.J.: Princeton University Press, 1991.

Comisión de Estudios Económicos y Sociales. "Problemas sociales y económicos de México." Mexico City: Secretaría del Trabajo y Previsión Social, 1945.

Comisión Investigadora de la Situación de la Mujer y de los Menores Trabajadores. "Informe sobre las labores de la Comisión Investigadora de la Situación de la Mujer y de los Menores Trabajadores." Mexico City: Departamento del Trabajo, 1936.

————. "Informe sobre las Labores de la Comisión Investigadora de la Situación de la Mujer y los Menores Trabajadores." Mexico City: Departamento del Trabajo, 1938.

Connell, R. W. *Masculinities*. Berkeley: University of California Press, 1995.

Conniff, Michael L., ed. *Latin American Populism in Comparative Perspective*. Albuquerque: University of New Mexico Press, 1982.

————. *Populism in Latin America*, Tuscaloosa: University of Alabama Press, 1999.

Cook, Katherine M. *La Casa del Pueblo: Un relato acerca de las escuelas nuevas de acción de México*. Trans. Rafael Ramírez. Mexico City, 1936.

Córdova, Arnaldo. *La ideología de la revolución mexicana: La formación del nuevo régimen*. Mexico City: Ediciones Era, 1973.

————. *La política de masas del cardenismo*. Mexico City: Ediciones Era, 1974.

————. *La revolución y el estado en México*. Mexico City: Ediciones Era, 1989.

Cortés Zavala, María Teresa. *Lázaro Cárdenas y su proyecto cultural en Michoacán*. Morelia: Universidad Michoacana de San Nicolás de Hidalgo, Instituto de Investigaciones Históricas, 1995.

Cosío Villegas, Daniel. *Historia moderna de México*. Mexico City: Editorial Hermes, 1956.

Cott, Nancy F. *The Grounding of Modern Feminism*. New Haven, Conn.: Yale University Press, 1987.

————. "Marriage and Women's Citizenship in the United States, 1830–1934." *American Historical Review* 103, no. 5 (1998): 1440–74.

————. *Public Vows: A History of Marriage and the Nation*. Cambridge, Mass.: Harvard University Press, 2000.

Craig, Ann L. *The First Agraristas: An Oral History of a Mexican Agrarian Reform Movement*. Berkeley: University of California Press, 1983.

Cruz F., Elodia. "Los derechos políticos de la mujer en México." Mexico City, 1937.

Cypess, Sandra Messinger. *La Malinche in Mexican Literature: From History to Myth*. Austin: University of Texas Press, 1991.

Davis, David Brion. *The Problem of Slavery in the Age of Revolution*. Ithaca, N.Y.: Cornell University Press, 1975.

de Anda, Gustavo. *¡Yucatán! Los grandes fracasos de los gobiernos de la revolución*. Mexico City, 1978.

Deere, Carmen Diana, and Magdalena León de Leal. *Empowering Women: Land and Property Rights in Latin America*. Pittsburgh: University of Pittsburgh Press, 2001.

de Gómez Mayorga, Ana. *Tres Ensayos*. Mexico City: Talleres Gráficos de la Nación, 1941.

de Grazia, Victoria. *How Fascism Ruled Women: Italy, 1922–1945*. Berkeley: University of California Press, 1992.

de la Garza López, Hesiquio. "El problema agrario de la Comarca Lagunera." Licenciatura, Universidad Nacional Autónoma de México, Mexico City, 1952.

de la Mora, Elvira. *Tierra de hombres (Comarca Lagunera)*. Mexico City: Información Aduanero de México.

de la Peña, Guillermo. "Populism, Regional Power, and Political Mediation: Southern Jalisco, 1900–1980." Pp. 191–223 in *Mexico's Regions: Comparative History and Development*, ed. Eric Van Young. San Diego: Center for U.S.–Mexican Studies, 1992.

Delpar, Helen. *The Enormous Vogue of All Things Mexican: Cultural Relations between the United States and Mexico, 1920–1935*. Tuscaloosa: University of Alabama Press, 1992.

Departamento de Misiones Culturales. *Bases de organización y funcionamiento de las misiones culturales*. Mexico City: Secretaría de Educación Pública, Dirección General de Alfabetización y Educación Extraescolar, 1961.

¡Despertar Lagunero! Libro que relata la lucha y triunfo de la revolución en la Comarca Lagunera. Pamphlet. Sindicato y el Consejo Técnico de los Trabajadores de los Talleres Gráficos de la Nación, Mexico City, September 1937.

Diario de los debates del Congreso constituyente de 1916–1917. 2 vols. Mexico City: Cámara de Diputados, 1922.

Díaz Méndez, Alberto. *Lázaro Cárdenas: Ideas políticos y acción antimperialista*. Havana: Editorial de Ciencias Sociales, 1984.

Dienstag, Joshua Foa. *"Dancing in Chains": Narrative and Memory in Political Theory*. Stanford, Calif.: Stanford University Press, 1997.

Dietz, Mary. "Citizenship with a Feminist Face: The Problem with Maternal Thinking." *Political Theory* 13, no. 1 (1985): 19–37.

———. "Context Is All: Feminism and Theories of Citizenship." *Daedalus* 116, no. 4 (1987): 1–24.

Dirección de Acción Cívica, de Reforma y Cultural del Departamento del Distrito Federal. *Prontuario Cívico y Socia: Guía explicativa de las instituciones al servicio de los habitantes del Distrito Federal*. Mexico City, 1928.

Dirección de Estudios. *Desarrollo de la economía nacional, 1939–1947*. Mexico City: Secretaría de la Economía Nacional, 1947.

Dirección General de Estadística. *Primer censo industrial de 1930*. Mexico City: Secretaría de la Economía de la Nación, 1934.

———. *Quinto censo de población de 1930*. Mexico City: Estados Unidos Mexicanos, 1934.

———. *Segundo censo industrial de 1935*. Mexico City: Secretaría de la Economía de la Nación, 1941.

———. *Tercer censo industrial de 1940*. Mexico City: Secretaría de la Economía de la Nación, 1944.

Domínguez Navarro, Ofelia. *50 años de una vida*. Havana: Instituto Cubano del Libro, 1971.

Dorantes González, Alma, María Gracia Castillo Ramírez, and Julia Tuñón Pablos. *Irene Robledo García*. Guadalajara: Universidad de Guadalajara, Instituto Nacional de Antropología e Historia, 1995.

Dore, Elizabeth, ed. *Gender Politics in Latin America: Debates in Theory and Practice.* New York: Monthly Review Press, 1997.

Dore, Elizabeth, and Maxine Molyneux, eds. *Hidden Histories of Gender and the State in Latin America.* Durham: Duke University Press, 2000.

DuBois, Ellen. *Feminism and Suffrage.* Ithaca, N.Y.: Cornell University Press, 1978.

——. *Woman Suffrage and Women's Rights.* New York: New York University Press, 1998.

Dumond, Don E. *The Machete and the Cross: Campesino Rebellion in Yucatán.* Lincoln: University of Nebraska Press, 1997.

Eckstein, Susan, ed. *Power and Popular Protest: Latin American Social Movements.* Berkeley: University of California Press, 1989.

El Ejido en la Comarca Lagunera. Pamphlet. Torreón: El Siglo de Torreón, 1936.

Elshtain, Jean Bethke. *Public Man, Private Woman.* Oxford: Martin Robertson Press, 1981.

——."Antigone's Daughters." *Democracy* 2, no. 2 (1982): 46–59.

Elu de Leñero, María del Carmen. *El trabajo de la mujer en México: Alternativa para el cambio.* Mexico City: Instituto Mexicano de Estudios Sociales, 1975.

Embriz Osorio, Arnulfo. *La Liga de Comunidades y Sindicatos Agraristas del Estado de Michoacán.* Mexico City: Práctica Político-Sindical, Centro de Estudios Históricos del Agrarismo en México, 1984.

Embriz Osorio, Arnulfo, and Ricardo León García. *Documentos para la historia del agrarismo en Michoacán.* Mexico City: Centro de Estudios Históricos del Agrarismo en México, 1982.

Escarcega López, Everardo, ed. *Historia de la cuestión agraria: El cardenismo, un parteaguas histórico en el proceso agrario nacional 1934–1940.* 2 vols. Mexico City: Siglo Veintiuno Editores, 1990.

Escobar, Arturo, and Sonia E. Alvarez, eds. *The Making of Social Movements in Latin America: Identity, Strategy, and Democracy.* Boulder: Westview Press, 1992.

Espinosa, Gisela. "Ciudadanía y femenismo popular." In *Democracia y luchas de género: La construcción de un nuevo campo teorico y politico.* Ed. Griselda Gutiérrez Castaneda.

"Estatutos del Sindicato Unico de Trabajadores de la Enseñanza en Yucatán." Mérida: Sindicato Unico de Trabajadores de la Enseñanza en Yucatán, 1937.

Evangelista Ramírez, Elí. *Historia del Trabajo Social en México.* Mexico City: Universidad Nacional Autónoma de México, Escuela Nacional de Trabajo Social, 1998.

Fabre Baños, José Angel. *Normal rural de Galeana.* Vol. 38. Monterrey: Archivo General del Estado de Nuevo León, 1989.

Falcón, Romana. "El surgimiento del agrarismo cardenista: Una revisión de las tesis populistas." *Historia Mexicana* 27, no. 3 (1978): 333–86.

——. *Revolución y caciquismo: San Luis Potosí, 1910–1938.* Mexico City: El Colegio de México, 1984.

Falcón, Romana, and Soledad García, eds. *La semilla en el surco: Adalberto Tejada y el radicalismo en Veracruz, 1883–1960*. Mexico City: El Colegio de México, 1986.

Fallaw, Ben. "Peasants, Caciques, and Camarillas: Rural Politics and State Formation in Yucatán, 1924–1940." Ph.D. diss., University of Chicago, 1995.

———. "Cárdenas and the Caste War That Wasn't: State Power and Indigenismo in Post-Revolutionary Yucatán." *The Americas* 53, no. 4 (1997): 551–77.

———. "The Southeast Was Red: Left–State Alliances and Popular Mobilizations in Yucatán, 1930–1940." *Social Science History* 23, no. 2 (1999): 241–68.

———. *Cárdenas Compromised: The Failure of Reform in Postrevolutionary Yucatán*. Durham: Duke University Press, 2001.

———. "Dry Law, Wet Politics: Drinking and Prohibition in Post-Revolutionary Yucatán, 1915–1935." *Latin American Research Review* 37, no. 2 (Spring 2002): 37–64.

———. "The Life and Deaths of Felipa Poot: Gender, Violence, and Fiction in Post-Revolutionary Yucatán." *Hispanic American Historical Review* 82, no. 4 (November 2002): 645–83.

Fascismo, democracia y frente popular: VII Congreso de la Internacional Comunista. Mexico City: Siglo Veintiuno Editores, 1984.

Fisher, Lillian Estelle. "The Influence of the Present Mexican Revolution upon the Status of Women." *Hispanic American Historical Review* 22, no. 1 (1942): 211–28.

Flores Arellano, Nélida, and América Wences Román. *Doña María de la O, una mujer ejemplar*. Chilpancingo: Universidad Autónoma de Guerrero, Centro de Estudios Históricos del Agrarismo en México, 1992.

Flores Múñoz, Gilberto. *Revolución versus imperialismo (en la Comarca Lagunera)*. Mexico City: S. Turanzas del Valle, 1936.

———. *The Solution of the Social, Economic and Agrarian Problem of the "Laguna" Region*. Mexico City: Secretaría de Acción Educativa del PNR, 1937.

Flores Villaseñor, Alicia. "Escuela 'Casa Amiga de la Obrera No. 5.'" Licenciatura, Universidad Nacional Autónoma de México, Mexico City, 1962.

Formoso de Obregón Santacilia, Adela. *La Mujer Mexicana en la organización social del país*. Mexico City: Departmento Autónomo de Prensa y Própaganda (DAPP), 1939.

Foweraker, Joe, and Ann L. Craig, eds. *Popular Movements and Political Change in Mexico*. Boulder: Lynne Rienner Publishers, 1990.

Fowler-Salamini, Heather. *Agrarian Radicalism in Veracruz, 1920–38*. Lincoln: University of Nebraska Press, 1978.

Fowler-Salamini, Heather, and Mary Kay Vaughan, eds. *Creating Spaces, Shaping Transitions: Women of the Mexican Countryside, 1850–1990*. Tucson: University of Arizona Press, 1994.

Franco, Jean. *Plotting Women: Gender and Representation in Mexico*. New York: Columbia University Press, 1989.

Frank, Dana. *Purchasing Power: Consumer Organizing, Gender, and the Seattle Labor Movement, 1919–1929*. Cambridge: Cambridge University Press, 1994.

French, John D., and Daniel James. *The Gendered Worlds of Latin American Women Workers: From Household and Factory to the Union Hall and Ballot Box*. Durham: Duke University Press, 1997.

Friedman, Elisabeth J. *Unfinished Transitions: Women and the Gendered Development of Democracy in Venezuela, 1936–1996*. University Park: Pennsylvania State University Press, 2000.

Friedrich, Paul. *Agrarian Revolt in a Mexican Village*. Englewood Cliffs, N.J.: Prentice-Hall, 1970.

———. *The Princes of Naranja: An Essay in Anthrohistorical Method*. Austin: University of Texas Press, 1986.

Frost, Elsa Cecilia, ed. *El trabajo y los trabajadores en la historia de México*. Mexico City: Colegio de México, 1977.

Fuentes, Mario Luis. *La asistencia social en México: Historia y perspectivas*. Mexico City: Ediciones del Milenio, 1998.

Gabara, Esther. "Engendering Nation: *Las Bellas Artes Públicas* and the Mexican Photoessay, 1920–1940." *Yearbook of Comparative and General Literature* 49 (2001): 139–54.

Galeana, Benita. *Benita*. Trans. Amy Diane Prince. Pittsburgh: Latin American Literary Review Press, 1994.

Galván de Terrazas, Luz Elena. *El proyecto de educación publica de José Vasconcelos : Una larga labor de intentos reformadores*. Mexico City: Centro de Investigaciones y Estudios Superiores en Antropología Social, 1982.

———. *La educación superior de la mujer en México, 1876–1940*. [Mexico City]: Secretaría de Educación Pública Cultura, 1985.

Gamboa, Ignacio. *La Mujer Moderna*. Mérida: Imprenta Gamboa Guzmán, 1906.

García Canclini, Néstor. *Hybrid Cultures: Strategies for Entering and Leaving Modernity*. Minneapolis: University of Minnesota Press, 1995.

García Correa, Bartolomé. *Código del Partido Socialista del Sureste estudiado y decretado por el Tercer Congreso Obrero*. Mérida: Pluma y Lapiz, 1930.

García Guerrero, Gladys María Cristina. "De la patria potestad y de la emancipación." Licenciatura, Universidad Nacional Autónoma de México, Mexico City, 1963.

García, Max, José Rodríguez, Francisco Vázquez, and José Leonardo Calderón. "Los sastres de Torreón." *El Puente* 2, no. 12 (1992): 27–39.

García Quintanilla, Alejandra. *Los tiempos en Yucatán: Los hombres, las mujeres y la naturaleza (siglo XIX)*. Mérida: Claves Latinoamericano, 1986.

Garrido, Luis Javier. *El partido de la revolución institucionalizada (medio siglo de poder político en México): La formación del nuevo estado, 1928–1945*. Mexico City: Siglo Veintiuno Editores, 1982.

Gill, Mario. *El sinarquismo: Su origen, su esencia, su misión*. 2d ed. Mexico City: Comité de Defensa de la Revolución, 1944.

———. *El movimiento Escuderista de Acapulco*. Mexico City: Editores México Libre, 1956.

Gilly, Adolfo. *Cartas a Cuauhtémoc Cárdenas*. Mexico City: Ediciones Era, 1989.

———. *El cardenismo, una utopía mexicana*. Mexico City: Cal y Arena, 1994.

———. *La revolución interrumpida: México 1910–1920*. 2d ed. Mexico City: Ediciones Era, 1994.

Gledhill, John. *Casi Nada: A Study of Agrarian Reform in the Homeland of Cardenismo*. Austin: University of Texas Press, 1991.

Godineau, Dominique. "Masculine and Feminine Political Practice during the French Revolution, 1783–Year III." 61–80 in Applewhite and Levy, eds., *Women and Politics*.

Goldfrank, Walter L. "Theories of Revolution and Revolution without Theory: The Case of Mexico." *Theory and Society* 7 (1979): 135–65.

Gomezjara, Francisco A. *Bonapartismo y Lucha Campesina en la Costa Grande de Guerrero*. Mexico City: Editorial Posada, 1979.

González, Luis. *San José de Gracia*. Austin: University of Texas Press, 1974.

———. *Historia de la Revolución Mexicana, 1934–1940: Los artífices del cardenismo*. Mexico City: El Colegio de México, 1979.

———. *Historia de la Revolución Mexicana, 1934–1940: Los días del presidente Cárdenas*. Mexico City: El Colegio de México, 1981.

———. *Invitación a la microhistoria*. Mexico City: Clío, 1997 (Mexico City: Secretaría de Educación Pública, 1973).

González, Victoria, and Karen Kampwirth, eds. *Radical Women in Latin America: Left and Right*. University Park: Pennsylvania State University Press, 2001.

González Gamio, Angeles, and Lourdes Herrasti, eds. *Ser y hacer de la mujer*. Mexico City: El Día en Libros, 1989.

Gordon, Linda. "Social Insurance and Public Assistance: The Influence of Gender in Welfare Thought in the United States, 1890–1935." *American Historical Review* 97, no. 6 (1992): 19–54.

Gordon, Linda, ed. *Women, the State, and Welfare*. Madison: University of Wisconsin Press, 1990.

Gramsci, Antonio. *Selections from the Prison Notebooks*, ed. Quentin Hoare and Geoffrey Nowell Smith. New York: International Publishers, 1971.

Grosz, Elizabeth. "Criticism, Feminism, and the Institution." Pp. 175–87 in *The Post-Colonial Critic. Interviews, Strategies, Dialogues: Gayatri Chakravorty Spivak*, ed. Sarah Harasym. New York: Routledge, 1990.

Guerra Cepeda, Roberto. "El ejido colectivizado en la comarca lagunera." Thesis, Universidad Nacional Autónoma de Méxco, Mexico City, 1939.

Guerrero, Silvestre. "Por la madre y el niño (llamamiento a la nación)." Pamphlet. Mexico City: Departamento Autónomo de Prensa y Própaganda (DAPP), 1939.

Guha, Ranajit. "The Prose of Counter-Insurgency." Pp. 45–86 in *Subaltern Studies II: Writings on South Asian History and Society*, ed. Ranajit Guha. Delhi: Oxford University Press, 1983.

Gutiérrez de Mendoza, Juana B. "Las mujeres sin patria." *Alma mexicana: Por la tierra y por la raza* (15 November 1935). Pamphlet. 7–8.

———. *República femenina*. Mexico City: n.p., 1936.

Haber, Stephen H. *Industry and Underdevelopment: The Industrialization of Mexico, 1890–1940*. Stanford, Calif.: Stanford University Press, 1989.

Habermas, Jürgen. *The Structural Transformation of the Public Sphere: An Inquiry into a Category of Bourgeois Society*. 6th ed. Cambridge, Mass.: MIT Press, 1996.

Hamilton, Nora. *The Limits of State Autonomy: Post-Revolutionary Mexico*. Princeton, N.J.: Princeton University Press, 1982.

Haney, Lynne A. "Engendering the Welfare State: A Review Article." *Comparative Studies in Society and History* 40, no. 4 (1998): 748–67.

Hansen, Roger D. *The Politics of Mexican Development*. Baltimore: Johns Hopkins University Press, 1971.

Hartmann, Heidi. "The Unhappy Marriage of Marxism and Feminism: Towards a More Progressive Union." *Capital and Class* 8 (1979): 1–33.

Hartsock, Nancy C. M. *Money, Sex, and Power: Toward a Feminist Historical Materialism*. Boston: Northeastern University Press, 1988.

Heduán de Rueda, Dolores. *A la mujer mexicana digo*. Pamphlet (18 March 1938). Mexico City: Unión de Revolucionarios Agraristas del Sur, 1938.

Hellman, Judith Adler. *Mexico in Crisis*. New York: Holmes and Meier Publishers, 1978.

———. "Capitalist Agriculture and Rural Protest: The Case of the Laguna Region, Mexico." *Labour, Capital and Society* 14, no. 2 (1981): 30–46.

———. "The Role of Ideology in Peasant Politics: Peasant Mobilization and Demobilization in the Laguna Region." *Journal of Interamerican Studies and World Affairs* 25, no. 1 (1983): 3–29.

Herman, Donald L. *The Comintern in Mexico*. Washington, D.C.: Public Affairs Press, 1974.

Hernández, Alfonso Porfirio. ¿*La explotación colectiva en la Comarca Lagunera es un fracaso?* Mexico City: B. Costa-Amic Editores, 1975.

Hernández, Ana María. *Libro social y familiar para la mujer obrera y campesina mexicana*. 5th ed. Mexico City, 1938.

———. *La mujer mexicana en la industria textil*. Mexico City: n.p., 1940.

Hernández, Manuel Diego. *La Confederación Revolucionaria Michoacana del Trabajo*. Jiquilpan: Centro de Estudios de la Revolución Mexicana "Lázaro Cárdenas," 1982.

Hernández Chávez, Alicia. *Historia de la Revolución Mexicana, 1934–40: La mecánica cardenista*. Mexico City: El Colegio de México, 1979.

Hernández Madrid, Miguel J. *La comunidad autoritaria: Estudio de las estrategios de vida en un ejido de Ixtlán de los Hervores, Michoacán*. Zamora: El Colegio de Michoacán, 1990.

Hewitt, Cynthia, and Henry Landsberger. "Peasant Organizations in La Laguna, Mexico: History, Structure, Member Participation, Effectiveness." Comité Interamericano de Desarrollo Agrario (CIDA) Research Paper no. 17, Washington, D.C., November 1970.

Hidalgo, Berta. *El Movimiento Femenino en México*. Mexico City: Editores Asociados Mexicanos, 1980.

Hoganson, Kristin L. *Fighting for American Manhood: How Gender Politics Provoked the Spanish–American and Philippine–American Wars*. New Haven, Conn.: Yale University Press, 1998.

Hufton, Olwen H. *Women and the Limits of Citizenship in the French Revolution*. Toronto: University of Toronto Press, 1992.

Hutchison, Elizabeth Quay. *Labors Appropriate to Their Sex: Gender, Labor, and Politics in Urban Chile, 1900–1930*. Durham: Duke University Press, 2001.

Iglesias, Severo. *Sindicalismo y socialismo en México*. Mexico City: Editorial Grijalbo, 1970.

Instituto de Capacitación Política. *Participación de la mujer en México*. Siglo Veinte. Mexico City: Partido Revolucionario Institucional, 1984.

Irurozqui, Marta. "Ebrios, vagos y analfabetos: El sufragio restringido en Bolivia, 1826–1952." *Revista de Indias* (1996): 697–742.

Jacoby, Karl. "Between North and South: The Alternative Borderlands of William H. Ellis and the African-American Colony of 1895." In *Continental Crossroads: New Directions in Borderlands History*, ed. Elliott Young and Samuel Truett. Durham. N.C.: Duke University Press, 2004.

James, Daniel. *Resistance and Integration: Peronism and the Argentine Working Class, 1946–1976*. Cambridge: Cambridge University Press, 1988.

Jelin, Elizabeth, ed. *Women and Social Change in Latin America*. London: Zed Books, 1990.

———. *Family, Household and Gender Relations in Latin America*. London: Kegan Paul International/UNESCO, 1991.

Joseph, Gilbert. *Rediscovering the Past at Mexico's Periphery: Essays on the History of Modern Yucatán*. Tuscaloosa: University of Alabama Press, 1986.

———. *Revolution from Without: Yucatán, Mexico, and the United States, 1880–1924*. Rev. ed. Durham: Duke University Press, 1989.

Joseph, Gilbert M., and Jeffery T. Brannon, eds. *Land, Labor and Capital in Modern Yucatán: Essays in Regional History and Political Economy*. Tuscaloosa: University of Alabama Press, 1991.

Joseph, Gilbert M., and Daniel Nugent, eds. *Everyday Forms of State Formation: Revolution and the Negotiation of Rule in Modern Mexico*. Durham: Duke University Press, 1994.

Joseph, Gilbert M., Anne Rubenstein, and Eric Zolov, eds. *Fragments of a Golden Age: The Politics of Culture in Mexico since 1940*. Durham: Duke University Press, 2001.

Judt, Tony. *Past Imperfect: French Intellectuals, 1944–1956*. Berkeley: University of California Press, 1992.

Juventud Católica Femenina de México. *Orientaciones a las dirigentes*. 2d ed. Puebla: n.p., 1934.

Kaplan, Temma. "Female Consciousness and Collective Action: The Case of Barcelona, 1910–1918." *Signs* 7, no. 3 (1982): 545–66.

———. *Crazy for Democracy: Women in Grassroots Movements*. New York: Routledge, 1997.

Katz, Friedrich. *The Life and Times of Pancho Villa*. Stanford, Calif.: Stanford University Press, 1998.

Katz, Friedrich, ed. *Riot, Rebellion and Revolution: Rural Social Conflict in Mexico*. Princeton, N.J.: Princeton University Press, 1988.

Keesing, Donald B. "Structural Change Early in Development: Mexico's Changing Industrial and Occupational Structure from 1895 to 1950." *Journal of Economic History* 29, no. 4 (1969): 716–38.

Kelly, Isabel Truesdale. "Notes on the Culture of the Laguna Zone." Mexico City, Institute of Inter-American Affairs, 1954.

Keremitsis, Dawn. "Del metate al molino: La mujer mexicana de 1910 a 1940." *Historia Mexicana* 130, no. 2 (1983): 285–302.

Kirk, Betty. *Covering the Mexican Front: The Battle of Europe versus America*. Norman: University of Oklahoma Press, 1942.

Klubock, Thomas Miller. *Contested Communities: Class, Gender, and Politics in Chile's El Teniente Copper Mine, 1904–1951*. Durham: Duke University Press, 1998.

Knight, Alan. "The Mexican Revolution? Bourgeois? Nationalist? or Just a 'Great Rebellion'?" *Bulletin of Latin American Research* 4, no. 2 (1985): 1–37.

———. *The Mexican Revolution*. 2 vols. Lincoln: University of Nebraska Press, 1986.

———. "Racism, Revolution, and *Indigenismo*: Mexico, 1910–1940." Pp. 71–113 in *The Idea of Race in Latin America, 1870–1940*, ed. Richard Graham. Austin: University of Texas Press, 1990.

———. "The Rise and Fall of Cardenismo, c. 1930–c. 1946." Pp. 241–320 in *Mexico since Independence*, ed. Leslie Bethell. Cambridge: Cambridge University Press, 1991.

———. "Cardenismo: Juggernaut or Jalopy?" *Journal of Latin American Studies* 26 (1994): 73–107.

———. "Popular Culture and the Revolutionary State in Mexico, 1910–1940." *Hispanic American Historical Review* 74, no. 3 (1994): 393–444.

———. "Populism and Neo-Populism in Latin America, especially Mexico." *Journal of Latin American Studies* 30, no. 2 (1998): 223–48.

Koven, Seth, and Sonya Michel. *Mothers of a New World: Maternalist Politics and the Origins of Welfare States*. New York: Routledge, 1993.

Kraditor, Aileen. *The Ideas of the Woman Suffrage Movement, 1890–1920*. Reprint ed. Garden City, N.Y.: Anchor, 1981 (1965).

Krauze, Enrique. *Mexico: Biography of Power*. New York: HarperCollins, 1997.

"La Quinta Columna Roja." Volume 31. Mexico City: Frente Popular Anti-Comunista de México, 1954.

Laborde, Hernán. *La política de Unidad a Toda Costa: Informe al Pleno del Comité Central del Partido Comunista de México celebrado del 26 al 30 de junio de 1937.* Mexico City: Acere, 1980.

Laborde, Hernán, José Revueltas, and Miguel A. Velasco. *La nueva política del Partido Comunista de México 1935.* Mexico City: Acere, 1980.

Laclau, Ernesto, and Chantal Mouffe. *Hegemony and Socialist Strategy: Towards a Radical Democratic Politics.* 2d ed. London: Verso, 2001.

"Las Ligas Femeniles en la Laguna." *El Siglo de Torreón*, December 1936.

Leal, Juan Felipe. *México: Estado, burocracia y sindicatos.* Mexico City: Ediciones El Caballito, 1975.

Lemaître, Monique J. *Elvia Carrillo Puerto: La monja roja del mayab.* Monterrey: Ediciones Castillo, 1998.

León, Samuel, and Ignacio Marván. *En el Cardenismo (1934–1940).* Mexico City: Siglo Veintiuno Editores, 1985.

Lerner, Victoria. *Historia de la Revolución Mexicana: La educación socialista.* Mexico City: El Colegio de México, 1979.

Levy, Darline Gay, and Harriet B. Applewhite. "Women and Militant Citizenship in Revolutionary Paris." Pp. 79–101 in *Rebel Daughters: Women and the French Revolution*, ed. Sara E. Melzer and Leslie W. Rabine. New York: Oxford University Press, 1992.

Lewis, Oscar. *Five Families: Mexican Case Studies in the Culture of Poverty.* New York: Basic Books, 1959.

Liga de Agrónomos Socialistas. *El colectivismo agrario en México: La Comarca Lagunera.* Mexico City: Industrial Gráfica, 1940.

Lister, Ruth. *Citizenship: Feminist Perspectives.* New York: New York University Press, 1997.

Lombardo Toledano, Vicente. "The Labor Movement." *Annals of the American Academy of Political and Social Science* (March 1940): 48–54.

———. *El llanto del sureste.* Mexico City: Centro de Estudios Históricos del Movimiento Obrero Mexicano, 1977.

———. *Sin mujeres no hay democracia.* Mexico City: Partido Popular Socialista, n.d.

López Pardo, Gustavo. *La administración obrera de los ferrocarriles nacionales de México.* Mexico City: Ediciones El Caballito, 1997.

Loyo Bravo, Engracia. *La Casa del Pueblo y el maestro rural mexicano.* Mexico City: Consejo Nacional de Fomento Educativo, Secretaría, El Caballito, 1985.

Luna Arroyo, Antonio. *La mujer mexicana en la lucha social.* Mexico City: Partido Nacional Revolucionario, 1936.

Macías, Anna. *Against All Odds: The Feminist Movement in Mexico to 1940.* Westport, Conn.: Greenwood Press, 1982.

Macías, Pablo G. *Aula Nobilis: Monografía del colegio primitivo y nacional de San Nicolás de Hidalgo*. Morelia: Ediciones Vanguardia Nicolaita, 1940.

Madden, Marie R. *Communism in Mexico*. New York: America Press, 1936.

Mallon, Florencia. *Peasant and Nation: The Making of Postcolonial Mexico and Peru*. Berkeley: University of California Press, 1995.

Mansbridge, Jane J. *Why We Lost the ERA*. Chicago: University of Chicago Press, 1986.

Marshall, T. H. *Citizenship and Social Class*. Cambridge: Cambridge University Press, 1950.

——. *Class, Citizenship and Social Development*. Garden City, N.Y.: Doubleday, 1964.

Martín, Kathleen R. "Gender and Maya Activism in Early 20th Century Yucatán." *Secolas Annals*. 36: 31–47.

Martínez Assad, Carlos. *El laboratorio de la revolución*. Mexico City: Siglo Veintiuno Editores, 1979.

——. *Balance y perspectias de los estudios regionales en México*. Mexico City: Universidad Nacional Autónoma de México, 1990.

Martínez García, Roberto. *La visión agrarista del general Pedro V. Rodríguez Triana*. Torreón: Editorial del Norte Mexicano, 1997.

Martínez Múgica, Apolinar. *Primo Tapia: Semblanza de un revolucionario*. Morelia: Ediciones del Gobierno de Michoacán, 1976.

Martínez Saldaña, Tomás. *El costo de un éxito político: La política expansionista del estado mexicano en el agro lagunero*. Chapingo: Rama de Divulgación Agrícola, Colegio de Posgrados, 1980.

Martínez Saldaña, Tomás, Judith Adler, and Ricardo Estrada. *La Comarca Lagunera: Parte III: Análisis de su problemática*. Mexico City: Cuadernos de la Casa Chata, 1979.

Martinez Verdugo, Arnoldo, ed. *Historia del Comunismo en México*. Mexico City: Grijalbo, 1983.

Massolo, Alejandra, ed. *Mujeres y ciudades: Participación social, vivienda y vida cotidiana*. Mexico City: El Colegio de México, 1992.

——. *Los medios y los modos: Participación política y acción colectiva de las mujeres*. Mexico City: El Colegio de México, 1994.

Matute, Alvaro. "Salud, familia y moral social (1917–1920)." *Históricas* 31 (1991): 25–34.

Mayer, Arno J. *The Furies: Violence and Terror in the French and Russian Revolutions*. Princeton, N.J.: Princeton University Press, 2000.

Medin, Tzvi. *Ideología y praxis política de Lázaro Cárdenas*. Mexico City: Siglo Veintiuno Editores, 1972.

Medina, Luis. *Del cardenismo al avilacamachismo*. Mexico City: El Colegio de México, 1978.

——. *Civilismo y modernización del autoritarismo*. Mexico City: El Colegio de México, 1979.

Melzer, Sara E., and Leslie W. Rabine, eds. *Rebel Daughters: Women and the French Revolution*. New York: Oxford University Press, 1992.

Mendieta Alatorre, Angeles. *La mujer en la revolución mexicana*. Mexico City: Insituto Nacional de Estudios Históricos de la Revolución Mexicana, 1961.

Mendieta y Núñez, Lucio. *La administración pública en México*. Mexico: Universidad Nacional, 1942.

——. *Las clases sociales*. Mexico City: Instituto de Investigaciones Sociales, Universidad Nacional, 1947.

Mendívil, José Abraham. *Batalla Anti-comunista*. Hermosillo: Impresora del Noroeste, 1966.

——. "El Día del Trabajo en México: Debe ser una fecha nacional." Hermosillo, 1968.

Mendizabal, Othón de. "The Agrarian Problem of La Laguna." *Annals of Collective Economy* 15, no. 1 (1939): 163–208.

Mendoza Vázquez, Anacleto. *Páginas de las luchas sociales en Michoacán*, Uruápan: Amigos del autor, 1989.

Mexican Communist Party (PCM). *Contra el Peligro Fachista: Resolución adoptada por el pleno del Comité Central del Partido Comunista de México, sobre el informe del Compañero Hernán Laborde en el primer punto de la orden del día. 4 al 7 de Diciembre de 1937*. Mexico City: Editorial Popular, 1937.

Mexico, Secretaría de Fomento. *Reciprocidad comercial entre Mexico y los Estados Unidos*, 1890.

Meyer, Jean. *La Cristiada*. 3 vols. Mexico City: Siglo Veintiuno Editores, 1974.

——. *El sinarquismo: ¿un fascismo mexicano?* Mexico City: Editorial Joaquín Mortiz, 1979.

——. "Revolution and Reconstruction in the 1920s." In *Mexico since Independence*, ed. Leslie Bethell. New York: Cambridge University Press, 1991.

——. *El Sinarquismo, el Cardenismo y la Iglesia, 1937–1947*. Mexico City: Tusquets Editores, 2003.

Meyer, Lorenzo, Rafael Segovia, and Lejandra Lajous. *Historia de la Revolución Mexicana, 1928–1934: Los inicios de la institucionalización. La política del maximato*. Mexico City: El Colegio de México, 1978

Meyers, William K. *Forge of Progress, Crucible of Revolt: The Origins of the Mexican Revolution in La Comarca Lagunera, 1880–1911*. Albuquerque: University of New Mexico Press, 1994.

Michaels, Albert L. "The Crisis of Cardenismo." *Journal of Latin American Studies* 2, no. 1 (1970): 51–79.

Michel, Concha. *Marxistas y "marxistas."* Mexico City: n.p., 1934.

——. *Casa-escuela de la mujer trabajadora: Proyecto de organización*. Mexico City: n.p., 1936.

——. *Obras cortas de teatro revolucionario y popular*. Mexico City: n.p., 1936.

——. *Dos antagonismos fundamentales*, Mexico City: Ediciones de la Izquierda de la Cámara de Diputados, 1938.

Michel, Concha. *Dios nuestra Señora*. Mexico City: n.p., 1966.

——. *Dios-principio es la pareja*. Mexico City: B. Costa-Amic, 1974.

Middlebrook, Kevin. *The Paradox of Revolution: Labor, the State and Authoritarianism in Mexico*. Baltimore: Johns Hopkins University Press, 1995.

Millan, Virginia Carleton. *Mexico Reborn*. Boston: Houghton Mifflin, 1939.

Miller, Barbara. "The Role of Women in the Mexican Cristero Rebellion: *Las Señoras y Las Religiosas*." *The Americas* 40, no. 3 (January 1984): 303–23.

Miller, Francesca. *Latin American Women and the Search for Social Justice*. Hanover, N.H.: University Press of New England, 1991.

Ministerio de Gobernación. *Seis años de gobierno al servicio de México (1934–1940)*. Mexico City: Secretaría de Educación Pública, 1940.

Miranda, Alfredo Jaime, María Martínez Guel, and Gabriel Garcia de la Rosa. "El Torreón Viejo." *El Puente* 2, no. 12 (1992): 41–59.

Mitchell, Stephanie Bryant. "La Noble Mujer Organizada: The Women's Movement in Mexico 1930–1940." Ph.D. diss., St. Antony's College, Oxford University, 2002.

Moctezuma Barragán, Javier, ed. *Francisco J. Múgica: Un romántico rebelde*. Mexico City: Fondo de Cultura Económica, 2001.

Mohanty, Chandra Talpade, Ann Russo, and Lourdes Torres, eds. *Third World Women and the Politics of Feminism*. Bloomington: Indiana University Press, 1991.

Molyneux, Maxine. "Mobilization without Emancipation? Women's Interests, the State, and Revolution in Nicaragua." *Feminist Studies* 11, no. 2 (1985): 227–53.

Monroy Huitrón, Guadalupe. *Política educativa de la revolución, 1910–1940*. Repr. ed. Mexico: Cien de México, 1985 (Mexico City: Secretaría de Educación Pública, 1975).

Monsiváis, Carlos. *Entrada Libre: Crónicas de una sociedad que se organiza*. Mexico City: Ediciones Era, 1987.

——. *Aires de familia: Cultura y sociedad en América Latina*. Barcelona: Editorial Anagrama, 2000.

Montecino, Sonia. "Understanding Gender in Latin America." Pp. 273–80 in *Gender's Place: Feminist Anthropologies of Latin America*, ed. Rosario Montoya, Lessie Jo Frazier, and Janice Hurtig. New York: Palgrave Macmillan, 2002.

Moreno, Pablo C. *Torreón: Biografía de la más joven de las ciudades mexicanas*. Saltillo: Talleres Gráficas Coahuila, 1951.

——. *Torreón a través de sus presidentes municipales*. Mexico City: Editorial Patria, 1955.

Morton, Ward M. *Woman Suffrage in Mexico*. Gainesville: University of Florida Press, 1962.

Múgica Martínez, Jesús. *La Confederación Revolucionaria Michoacana del Trabajo: Apuntes acerca de la evolución social y política en Michoacán*. Mexico City: EDDISA, 1982.

La mujer y el trabajo en México (antología). Mexico City: Secretaría del Trabajo y Previsión Social, 1986.

Muñoz, Luis, and Salvador Carlos Zavaleta. *Comentarios al código civil*. Mexico City: Cárdenas, 1974.

Nacional Financiera, S.A. *Nacional Financiera, S.A., and the Economic Development of Mexico*. Mexico City: Nacional Financiera, 1964.

———. *Statistics on the Mexican Economy*. Mexico City: Nacional Financiera, 1974.

Nash, June. "Latin American Women in the World Capitalist Crisis." *Gender and Society* 4, no. 3 (1990): 338–53.

Nash, June, and Helen Safa, eds. *Women and Change in Latin America*. New York: Bergin and Garvey, 1985.

National Revolutionary Party (PNR). "Constitución del Partido Nacional Revolucionario." Mexico City, 1932.

———. *Un año de gestión del Comité Ejecutivo Nacional, 1935–1936*. Mexico City: S. Turanzas del Valle, 1936.

———. "Los Catorce Puntos de la Política Obrera Presidencial." Biblioteca de Cultura Social y Politica, Mexico City, February 1936.

———. *Programa de Acción del Partido Nacional Revolucionacio para el periodo 1936–1937*. Mexico City: Partido Nacional Revolucionario, 1936.

Nava Nava, Carmen. *La ideología del Partido de la Revolución Mexicana*. Jiquilpan, Mich.: Centro de Estudios de la Revolución Mexicana Lázaro Cárdenas, 1984.

———. "El Lic. Ignacio García Tellez y los inicios del Instituto Mexicano de Seguro Social." *Desdeldiez* (1986): 3–19.

———. "La democracia interna del Partido de la Revolución Mexicana (PRM)." *Revista Mexicana de Sociología* 50, no. 3 (1988): 157–66.

Nava Nava, Carmen, ed. *Los abajo firmantes: Cartas a los presidentes, 1934–1946*. Mexico City: Secretaría de Educación Pública, Archivo General de la Nación, Editorial Patria, 1994.

Nelson, Barbara J. "The Origins of the Two-Channel Welfare State: Workmen's Compensation and Mother's Aid." Pp. 123–51 in *Women, the State, and Welfare*, ed. Linda Gordon. Madison: University of Wisconsin Press, 1990.

Nelson, Diane M. *A Finger in the Wound: Body Politics in Quincentennial Guatemala*. Berkeley: University of California Press, 1999.

Newhall, Beatrice. "Woman Suffrage in the Americas." *Bulletin of the Pan American Union*, May 1936, 424.

Noriega, Carlos. "La fruticultura como una transformación racional de la agricultura mexicana." *Los Problemas Agrícolas de México* 1, no. 2 (1934): 585–616.

Novo, Salvador. *La vida en México en el periodo presidencial de Lázaro Cárdenas*. Mexico City: Consejo Nacional para la Cultura y las Artes, 1994.

Nugent, Daniel, ed. *Rural Revolt in Mexico: U.S. Intervention and the Domain of Subaltern Politics*. Durham: Duke University Press, 1998.

Oficina de Barómetros Económicos. *El desarrollo de la economía nacional bajo la influencia de la guerra, 1939–1946*. Mexico City: Secretaría de la Economía Nacional, 1946.

Oikión Solano, Verónica. *Michoacán en la vía de la unidad nacional, 1940–1944*. Mexico City: Instituto Nacional de Estudios Históricos de la Revolución Mexicana, 1995.

Ojeda Rivera, Rosa Icela. *Benita Galeana: Mujer indómita*. Mexico City: Quadrivium Editores, 1998.

Olcott, Jocelyn. "Las Hijas de la Malinche: Women's Organizing and State Formation in Postrevolutionary Mexico, 1934–1940." Ph.D. diss., Yale University, New Haven, Conn., 2000.

———. "'Worthy Wives and Mothers': State-Sponsored Women's Organizing in Postrevolutionary Mexico." *Journal of Women's History* 13, no. 4 (2002): 106–31.

———. "Miracle Workers: Gender and State Mediation among Textile and Garment Workers in Mexico's Transition to Industrial Development." *International Labor and Working-Class History* 63 (2003): 45–62.

———. "Mueras y Matanzas: Spectacles of Terror and Violence in Postrevolutionary Mexico." Paper presented to the conference "Rethinking Latin America's Century of Revolutionary Violence." Yale University, 15–17 May 2003.

———. "'Sing What the People Sing': Concha Michel and the Gender of Cultural Revolution." In *Forjando Matrias*, ed. David Sweet. Lincoln: University of Nebraska Press, forthcoming.

O'Malley, Ilene V. *The Myth of the Revolution: Hero Cults and the Institutionalization of the Mexican State*. Westport, Conn.: Greenwood Press, 1986.

Orellana Trinidad, Laura. "'La mujer del porvenir': Raíces intelectuales y alcanes del pensamiento feminista de Hermila Galindo, 1915–1919." *Signos Históricos* 5 (2001): 109–35.

Orfila Rosello, Jaime. *Mujer moderna*. Chihuahua: Imprenta Palmore, 1936.

Orientaciones para las Ligas Femeniles de Lucha Social en los Ejidos. Mexico City: Sindicato de Trabajadores del Departamento Agrario, Comisión de Asuntos Femeninos, 1938.

Osorio Marban, Miguel. *El Partido de la Revolución Mexicana*. Mexico City: Impresora del Centro, 1970.

Padgett, L. Vincent. *The Mexican Political System*. Boston: Houghton Mifflin, 1965.

Padilla, Ezequiel. "La cruzada de los maestros misioneros." Mexico City: Publicaciones de la Secretaría de Educación Pública, 1929.

Padilla, Juan Ignacio. *Sinarquismo: Contrarrevolución*. Mexico City: Editorial Polis, 1948.

Pallares, Eduardo. *Ley sobre relaciones familiares*. 2d ed. Mexico: Librería de la vda. de Ch. Bouret, 1923.

Party of the Mexican Revolution (PRM). *Seis años de gobierno al servicio de México: 1934–1940*. Mexico City: La Nacional Impresora, S.A., 1940.

Pateman, Carole. *The Sexual Contract*. Cambridge: Polity Press, 1988.

———. *The Disorder of Women*. Stanford, Calif.: Stanford University Press, 1989.

Patrón P., Prudencio. *La educación socialista*. Mérida: Departamento de Educación Pública, Relaciones y Publicidad, Gobierno Socialista de Yucatán, 1935.

Payne, Charles M. *I've Got the Light of Freedom: The Organizing Tradition and the Mississippi Freedom Struggle*. Berkeley: University of California Press, 1995.

Paz., Octavio. *The Labyrinth of Solitude and Other Writings.* Trans. Lysander Kemp. New York: Grove Press, 1985.

Pérez, Emma. "'She Has Served Others in More Intimate Ways': The Domestic Servant Reform in Yucatán, 1915–1918." *Aztlán* 20, nos. 1–2 (1991): 11–37.

———. "Feminism-in-Nationalism: The Gendered Subaltern at the Yucatán Feminist Congress of 1916." Pp. 219–39 in *Between Woman and Nation: Nationalisms, Transnational Feminism, and the State*, ed. Caren Kaplen, Norma Alarcón, and Minoo Moallem. Durham: Duke University Press, 1999.

Pérez Escutia, Ramon Alonso. "Historia del Partido de la Revolución en Michoacán, 1928–1946." Unpublished ms., Fundación Michoacán Cambio 21, Partido Revolucionario Institucional, Morelia, Mich.

Perló Cohen, Manuel. *Estado, vivienda y estructura urbana en el cardenismo: El caso de la ciudad de México.* Vol. 3. Mexico City: Universidad Nacional Autónoma de México, Instituto de Investigaciones Sociales, 1981.

Petras, James F. *Politics and Social Structures in Latin America.* New York: Monthly Review Press, 1970.

Phillips, Anne. *Engendering Democracy.* University Park: Pennsylvania State University Press, 1991.

———. *Democracy and Difference.* Cambridge: Polity Press, 1993.

Picatto, Pablo. *El discurso sobre el alcoholismo en el Congreso Constituyente de 1916–1917.* Mexico City: Honorable Cámara de Diputados, Secretaría de Gobernación, 1992.

Pilcher, Jeffrey M. *¡Qué vivan los tamales! Food and the Making of Mexican Identity.* Albuquerque: University of New Mexico Press, 1998.

Plenn, J. H. *Mexico Marches.* Indianapolis: Bobbs-Merrill, 1939.

The Policies of the Present Administration of Mexico. Mexico City: Departamento del Trabajo, 1936.

Ponce Lagos, Antonio. *Historia de las reformas a los artículos 34 y 115 constitucionales, que conceden la ciudadanía a la mujer mexicana.* Mexico City, 1954.

Popular Party. *Corrido del voto de la mujer.* Mexico City: Taller de Gráfica Popular, 1955.

Porter, Susie S. *Working Women in Mexico City: Public Discourses and Material Conditions, 1879–1931.* Tucson: University of Arizona Press, 2003.

Presencia de la Mujer Revolucionaria en la Vida de México. Memoria del ciclo de conferencias del Consejo Nacional para la Participación de la Mujer, 27–30 de enero de 1986. Mexico City: Partido Revolucionario Institucional, 1987.

Prewett, Virginia. *Reportage on Mexico.* New York: E. P. Dutton, 1941.

Primer congreso feminista de la Liga Pan-Americana de Mujeres. Mexico City: El Modelo, 1923.

El primer congreso feminista de Yucatán: Anales de esa memorable asamblea. Mérida: Talleres Atenzo Popular, 1916.

Purnell, Jennie. *Popular Movements and State Formation in Revolutionary Mexico: The Agraristas and Cristeros of Michoacán.* Durham: Duke University Press, 1999.

Raby, David L. *Educación y revolución social en México.* Mexico City: SepSetentas, 1974.

Ramírez Sainz, Juan Manuel. "Aportaciones políticas del Movimiento Urbano Popular." *Revista Mexicana de Sociología* 56, no. 3 (July–September 1994): 89–112.

Ramos, Samuel. *El perfil del hombre y la cultura en México*. Buenos Aires: n.p., 1951.

Ramos Escandón, Carmen. "Women and Power in Mexico: The Forgotten Heritage, 1800–1954." In Victoria E. Rodríguez, ed. *Women's Participation in Mexican Political Life*. Boulder: Westview Press, 1998.

Ramos Escandón, Carmen, ed. *Género e historia: La historiografía sobre la mujer*. Mexico City: Instituto Mora, Universidad Autónoma Metropolitana, 1992.

Ramos Escandón, Carmen, et al., eds. *Presencia y transparencia: La mujer en la historia de México*. Mexico City: El Colegio de México, 1987.

Rascón, María Antonieta. "La mujer mexicana como hecho político: La precursora, la militante." *La Cultura de México* no. 569 (3 January 1973): 9–12.

———. "La mujer y la lucha social." Pp. 139–74 in *Imagen y realidad de la mujer*, ed. Elena Urrutia. Mexico City: Secretaría de Educación Pública Diana, 1979.

Redfield, Robert. *Tepoztlán: A Mexican Village*. Chicago: University of Chicago Press, 1930.

Reed, Nelson. *The Caste War of Yucatán*. Stanford, Calif.: Stanford University Press, 1964.

Reich, Peter L. *Mexico's Hidden Revolution: The Catholic Church in Law and Politics since 1929*. Notre Dame, Ind.: University of Notre Dame Press, 1995.

Reis, Elisa P. "Nationalism and Citizenship: The Crisis of Authority and Solidarity in Latin America (Brazil)." Pp. 261–80 in *Citizenship and National Identity: From Colonialism to Globalism*, ed. T. K. Oommen. New Delhi: Sage, 1997.

Reséndez Fuentes, Andrés. "Battleground Women: 'Soldaderas' and the Female Soldiers in the Mexican Revolution." *The Americas* 51, no. 4 (1995): 525–33.

Restrepo, Ivan, and Salomon Eckstein. *La agricultura colectiva en México: La experiencia de la Laguna*. Mexico City: Siglo Veintiuno Editores, 1975.

Reyes Pimentel, José. *La cosecha*. Mexico City: Departamento Autónomo de Prensa y Propaganda, 1939.

Ribera Carbó, Anna. *La patria ha podido ser flor: Francisco J. Múgica, una biografía política*. Mexico City: Instituto Nacional de Antropología e Historia, 1999.

Riley, Denise. *"Am I That Name?": Feminism and the Category of "Women" in History*. Minneapolis: University of Minnesota Press, 1988.

Ríos Cárdenas, María. *La mujer mexicana es ciudadana: Historia con fisonomía de una novela de costumbres, 1930–1940*. Mexico City: n.p., n.d.

Rivera Castro, José. "Organización y conflictos laborales en La Laguna." Pp. 165–84 in *Anarquismo, socialismo y sindicalismo en las regiones*, ed. Jaime Tamayo and Patricia Valles. Guadalajara: Universidad de Guadalajara, 1993.

Rivera Garza, Cristina. "The Criminalization of the Syphilitic Body: Prostitutes, Health Crimes, and Society in Mexico City, 1867–1930." Pp. 147–180 in *Crime and Punishment in Latin America: Law and Society since Late Colonial Times*, ed.

Ricardo D. Salvatore, Carlos Aguirre, and Gilbert M. Joseph. Durham: Duke University Press, 2001.

Roberts, Mary Louise. *Civilization without Sexes: Reconstructing Gender in Postwar France, 1917–1927*. Chicago: University of Chicago Press, 1994.

Robles, Jorge, and Luís Angel Gómez. *De la autonomía al corporativismo: Memoria cronológica del movimiento obrero en México, 1900–1980*. Mexico City: El Atajo Ediciones, 1995.

Robles de Mendoza, Margarita. *La evolución de la mujer en México*. Mexico City: n.p., 1931.

——. *Silabario de la ciudadanía de la mujer mexicana*. Jalapa: Talleres Gráficos del Gobierno, 1932.

Rocha, Martha Eva. *El álbum de la mujer: Antología ilustrada de las mexicanas*. Vol. 4. Mexico City: Instituto Nacional de Antropología e Historia, 1991.

Rockwell, Elsie. "Schools of the Revolution: Enacting and Contesting State Forms in Tlaxcala, 1910–1930." Pp. 170–208 in *Everyday Forms of State Formation: Revolution and the Negotiation of Rule in Modern Mexico*, ed. Gilbert Joseph and Daniel Nugent. Durham: Duke University Press, 1994.

Rodríguez Chihuahua, Matías. "Matamoros: Sudor y sangre." *El Puente* 1, no. 6 (1991): 25–31.

Rodríguez, Victoria E., *Women in Contemporary Mexican Politics*. Austin: University of Texas Press, 2003.

Rodríguez, Victoria E., ed. *Women's Participation in Mexican Political Life*. Boulder: Westview Press, 1998.

Rodríguez Cabo, Mathilde. *La mujer y la revolución: Conferencia dictada por la Dra. Mathilde Rodríguez Cabo en el Frente Socialista de Abogados*. Mexico City: Frente Socialista de Abogados, 1937.

Romero Flores, Jesús. *La historia de la educación en Michoacán*. Mexico City: Talleres Gráficos de la Nación, 1948.

Rosales, Rafael R., and Heriberto Ramos González. "Informe del primer delegado agrario en La Laguna, 1937." *El Puente* 2, no. 12 (1992): 73–76.

Rosas, Javier, ed. *50 años de oposición en México*. Mexico City: Universidad Nacional Autónoma de México, 1979.

Roseberry, William. "Hegemony and the Language of Contention." Pp. 355–66 in *Everyday Forms of State Formation: Revolution and the Negotiation of Rule in Modern Mexico*, ed. Gilbert Joseph and Daniel Nugent. Durham: Duke University Press, 1994.

Rosemblatt, Karin A. *Gendered Compromises: Political Cultures and the State in Chile, 1920–1950*. Chapel Hill: University of North Carolina Press, 2000.

Rosenthal, Noami, and Michael Schwartz. "Spontaneity and Democracy in Social Movements." *International Social Movement Research* 2 (1989): 33–59.

Rowbotham, Sheila. *Women, Resistance and Revolution: A History of Women and Revolution in the Modern World*. New York: Pantheon Books, 1972.

Rubenstein, Anne. *Bad Language, Naked Ladies, and Other Threats to the Nation: A Political History of Comic Books in Mexico*. Durham: Duke University Press, 1998.

Rubin, Jeffrey W. *Decentering the Regime: Ethnicity, Radicalism, and Democracy in Juchitán, Mexico*. Durham: Duke University Press, 1997.

Ruddick, Sarah. "Maternal Thinking." *Feminist Studies* 6, no. 2 (1980): 342–67.

Rugeley, Terry. *Yucatán's Maya Peasantry and the Origins of the Caste War, 1800–1847*. Austin: University of Texas Press, 1996.

Rus, Jan. "The 'Comunidad Revolucionaria Institucional': The Subversion of Native Government in Highland Chiapas, 1936–1968." In *Everyday Forms of State Formation: Revolution and the Negotiation of Rule in Modern Mexico*, ed. Gilbert Joseph and Daniel Nugent. Durham: Duke University Press, 1994.

Salas, Elizabeth. *Soldaderas in the Mexican Military: Myth and History*. Austin: University of Texas Press, 1990.

Sánchez, Martín. *Grupos de poder y centralización política en México: El caso Michoacán, 1920–1924*. Mexico City: Instituto Nacional de Estudios Históricos de la Revolución Mexicana, 1994.

Sanderson, Steven. *Agrarian Populism and the Mexican State: The Struggle for Land in Sonora*. Berkeley: University of California Press, 1981.

Santa Cruz Ossa, Elvira. "Latin American Women as Industrial Workers." *Pan American Union Bulletin*, March 1927, 259–63.

Santiago Sierra, Augusto. *Las Misiones Culturales (1923–1973)*. Mexico City: Secretaría de Educación Pública, 1973.

Santibáñez García, Ernesto. *La Comarca Lagunera: Ensayo monográfico*. Torreón: Tipográfica Reza, 1992.

Sargent, Lydia, ed. *Women and Revolution: A Discussion of the Unhappy Marriage of Marxism and Feminism*. Boston: South End Press, 1981.

Sarkisyanz, Manuel. *Felipe Carrillo Puerto, Mr. Gilbert Joseph, y la Asociación Norteamericana de Historiadores: Una demistificación de un "demisitificador."* Mérida: Talleres Gráficos del Sudeste, 1996.

Schell, Patience. "Training Loving Hands: Women's Vocational Education in 1920s Mexico City." *Journal of Women's History* 10, no. 2 (1999): 78–103.

——. *Church and State Education in Revolutionary Mexico City*. Tucson: University of Arizona Press, 2003.

Schryer, Frans J. *The Rancheros of Pisaflores: The History of a Peasant Bourgeoisie in Twentieth-Century Mexico*. Toronto: University of Toronto Press, 1980.

Scott, James C. *The Moral Economy of the Peasant: Rebellion and Subsistence in Southeast Asia*. New Haven, Conn.: Yale University Press, 1976.

——. *Domination and the Arts of Resistance: Hidden Transcripts*. New Haven, Conn.: Yale University Press, 1990.

——. *Seeing Like a State: How Certain Schemes to Improve the Human Condition Have Failed*. New Haven, Conn.: Yale University Press, 1998.

Scott, Joan Wallach. *Gender and the Politics of History*. New York: Columbia University Press, 1988.

Secretaría de Acción Agraria. *Tierras libres para todos los mexicanos: Cartilla explicativa para los campesinos*. Mexico City: Partido Nacional Revolucionario, 1937.

Senior, Clarence. *Democracy Comes to a Cotton Kingdom: The Story of Mexico's La Laguna*. Mexico City: Centro de Estudios Pedagógicos e Hispanoamericanos, 1940.

Serna de la Garza, José María. *Derecho Parlamentario*. Mexico City: UNAM/McGraw-Hill, 1997.

Servín, Elisa. *Ruptura y oposición: El movimiento henriquista, 1945–1954*. Mexico City: Cal y Arena, 2001.

Sherman, John. *The Mexican Right: The End of Revolutionary Reform, 1929–1940*. Westport, Conn.: Praeger, 1997.

Siegel, Reva B. "Valuing Housework: 19th-Century Anxieties about the Commodification of Domestic Labor." *American Behavioral Scientist* 41, no. 10 (1998): 1437–51.

Sierra, Augusto Santiago. *Las Misiones Culturales, 1923–1973*. Mexico City: Secretaría de Educación Pública, 1973.

Sierra Villarreal, José Luis, and José Antonio Paoli Bolio. *Cárdenas y el reparto de los henequenales*. Mérida: Consejo Editorial de Yucatán, 1986.

Silva Herzog, Jesús. *Lázaro Cárdenas: Su pensamiento económico, social, y político*. Mexico City: Editorial Nuestro Tiempo, 1975.

Simpson, Eyler. *The Ejido: Mexico's Way Out*. Chapel Hill: University of North Carolina Press, 1937.

Simpson, Lesley Bird. *Many Mexicos*. Berkeley: University of California Press, 1966.

Sindicato Nacional de Trabajadores de la Educación. *SNTE Seccion XVIII Michoacán*. Morelia: Sindicato Nacional de Trabajadores de la Educación, 1987.

Sinha, Mrinalini, Donna J. Guy, and Angela Woollacott. *Feminisms and Internationalism*. Oxford: Blackwell, 1999.

Slater, David, ed. *New Social Movements and the State in Latin America*. Amsterdam: Center for Latin American Research and Documentation, 1985.

——. "Rethinking the Spatialities of Social Movements: Questions of (B)orders, Culture, and Politics in Global Times." Pp. 380–401 in *Cultures of Politics, Politics of Cultures: Re-visioning Latin American Social Movements*, ed. Sonia E. Alvarez, Evelina Dagnino, and Arturo Escobar. Boulder: Westview Press, 1998.

Snodgrass, Michael David. "The Birth and Consequences of Industrial Paternalism in Monterrey, Mexico, 1890–1940." *International Labor and Working-Class History* 53 (1998): 113–36.

Sosa Elízaga, Raquel. *Los códigos ocultos del cardenismo: Un estudio de la violencia política, el cambio social y la continuidad institucional*. Mexico City: Plaza y Valdés Editores, 1996.

Soto, Shirlene. *The Emergence of the Modern Mexican Woman: Her Participation in Revolution and Struggle for Equality, 1910–1940*. Denver: Arden Press, 1990.

Sotomayor Garza, Jesús G. *Anales laguneros*. Torreón: Editorial del Norte Mexicano, 1992.

Spenser, Daniela. *The Impossible Triangle: Mexico, Soviet Russia, and the United States in the 1920s*. Durham: Duke University Press, 1999.

Spenser, Daniela, and Bradley A. Levinson. "Linking State and Society in Discourse and Action: Political and Cultural Studies of the Cardenas Era." *Latin American Research Review* 34, no. 2 (1999): 227–45.

Stern, Alexandra Minna. "Responsible Mothers and Normal Children: Eugenics, Nationalism, and Welfare in Post-revolutionary Mexico, 1920–1940." *Journal of Historical Sociology* 12, no. 4 (1999): 369–97.

———."From Mestizophilia to Biotypology: Racialization and Science in Mexico, 1920–1960." Pp. 187–210 in *Race and Nation in Modern Latin America*, ed. Nancy P. Appelbaum, Anne S. Macpherson, and Karin A. Rosemblatt. Chapel Hill: University of North Carolina Press, 2003.

Sternbach, Nancy Saporta, Marysa Navarro-Aranguren, Patricia Chuchryk, and Sonia E. Alvarez. "Feminisms in Latin America: From Bogotá to San Bernardo." *Signs* 17, no. 2 (1992): 393–434.

The Strategy of the Communists: A Letter from the Communist International to the Mexican Communist Party. Chicago: Workers Party of America, 1923.

Taibo, Paco Ignacio, II. *Los Bolshevikis*. Mexico City: Joaquín Mortiz, 1986.

Tamayo, Jorge. *Transformación de la Comarca Lagunera, sus perspectivas y problemas*. Mexico City: Academia Nacional de Ciencias Antonio Alzate, 1941.

Tannenbaum, Frank. *Mexico: The Struggle for Peace and Bread*. New York: Alfred A. Knopf, 1950.

Thompson, E. P. *Whigs and Hunters: The Origins of the Black Act*. New York: Pantheon Books, 1975.

Tinsman, Heidi. *Partners in Conflict: The Politics of Gender, Sexuality, and Labor in the Chilean Agrarian Reform, 1950–1973*. Durham: Duke University Press, 2002.

Tobler, Hans Werner. "Peasants and the Shaping of the Revolutionary State, 1910–1940." Pp. 487–518 in *Riot, Rebellion, and Revolution: Rural Social Conflict in Mexico*, ed. Friedrich Katz. Princeton, N.J.: Princeton University Press, 1988.

Tostado Gutiérrez, Marcela. *El intento de liberar a un pueblo: Educación y magisterio tabasqueño con Garrido Canabal: 1924–1935*. Mexico City: Instituto Nacional de Antropología e Historia, 1991.

Townsend, William Cameron. *Lázaro Cárdenas: Mexican Democrat*. Ann Arbor, Mich.: George Wahr Publishing, 1952.

Tuñón, Enriqueta. *¡Por fin... ya podemos elegir y ser electas! El sufragio femenino en México, 1935–1953*. Mexico City: Instituto Nacional de Antropología e Historia, 2002.

Tuñón Pablos, Esperanza. *Mujeres que se organizan: El Frente Unico Pro Derechos de la Mujer, 1935–1938*. Mexico City: Grupo Editorial Miguel Angel Porrúa, 1992.

Tuñón Pablos, Julia. *Mujeres en México: Una historia olvidada*. Mexico City: Planeta, 1987.

Tuñón Pablos, Julia. "Las mujeres y su historia: Balance, problemas y perspectivas." Pp. 375–412 in *Estudios sobre las mujeres y las relaciones de género en México: Aportes desde diversas disciplinas*, ed. Elena Urrutia. Mexico City: El Colegio de México, 2002.

Turner, Frederick C. "Los efectos de la participación femenina en la Revolución de 1910." *Historia Mexicana* 16, no. 4 (April–June 1967): 603–20.

Urrutia, Elena, ed. *Imagen y realidad de la mujer*. Mexico City: Secretaría de Educación Pública, Diana, 1979.

Valadés, José C. *Sobre los orígenes del movimiento obrero en México*. Mexico City: Centro de Estudios Históricos del Movimiento Obrero Mexicano, 1979.

Valdivia Pueyo, Francisco. *La Beneficencia Pública del Distrito Federal, precursora y co-adyuvante de la asistencia social en México*. Mexico City: Universidad Autónoma de Guadalajara, 1988.

Valero Chávez, Aída. *El trabajo social en México: Desarrollo y perspectivas*. Mexico City: Universidad Nacional Autónoma de México, Escuela Nacional de Trabajo Social, 1994.

Van Young, Eric, ed. *Mexico's Regions: Comparative History and Development*. San Diego: Center for U.S.–Mexican Studies, 1992.

Vargas-Lobsinger, María. *La Comarca Lagunera: De la revolución a la expropiación de las haciendas, 1910–1940*. Mexico City: Universidad Nacional Autónoma de México, Instituto Nacional de Estudios Históricos de la Revolución Mexicana, 1999.

Vasconcelos, José. *La raza cósmica: Misión de la raza iberoamericana*. Paris: Agencia Mundial de Librería, 1944 (1921).

Vaughan, Mary Kay. *The State, Education, and Social Class in Mexico, 1880–1928*. DeKalb: Northern Illinois Press, 1982.

———. *Cultural Politics in Revolution: Teachers, Peasants, and Schools in Mexico, 1930–1940*. Tucson: University of Arizona Press, 1997.

———. "Modernizing Patriarchy: State Policies, Rural Households, and Women in Mexico, 1930–1940." Pp. 194–214 in *Hidden Histories of Gender and the State in Latin America*, ed. Elizabeth Dore and Maxine Molyneux. Durham: Duke University Press, 2000.

Vázquez, Gabino. *La resolución del problema agrario en la Comarca Lagunera*. Mexico City, 1937.

Vázquez, Josefina Zoraida. *Nacionalismo y educación en México*. Mexico City: El Colegio de México, 1970.

Velarde, C. J. *Under the Mexican Flag*. Los Angeles: Southland Publishing House, 1926.

Velasco Ceballos, Rómulo. *El niño mexicano ante la caridad y el estado: Apuntes históricos que comprenden desde la época precortesiana hasta nuestros días*. Mexico City: Beneficencia Pública en el D.F., 1935.

Velasco, Miguel Angel. *La lucha contra el Trotskismo en los años 30*. Mexico City: Acere, 1980.

Velázquez, Margarita. *Políticas sociales, transformación agraria y participación de las mu-*

jeres en el campo: 1920–1988. Cuernavaca: Universidad Nacional Autónoma de México, Centro Regional de Investigaciones Multidisciplinarias, 1992.

Villanueva Mukul, Eric. *Así tomamos las tierras*. Mérida: Maldonado Editores, 1984.

Villarreal Méndez, Norma. "Género y clase: La participación política de la mujer de los sectores populares en Colombia, 1930–1991." *Jornadas de Investigación Interdisciplinaria sobre la Mujer, 9th, Madrid, 1992: La mujer latinoamericana ante el reto del siglo XXI* (1992): 127–61.

Vitale, Luís. *La mitad invisible de la historia latinoamericana: El protagonismo social de la mujer*. Buenos Aires: Sudamérica/Planeta, 1987.

Vizcaíno, Rogelio, and Paco Ignacio Taibo II. *Socialismo en un solo puerto: Acapulco 1919–1923*. Mexico City: Editoriales Extemporáneos, 1983.

Waldinger, Renee, Philip Dawson, and Isser Woloch, eds. *The French Revolution and the Meaning of Citizenship*. Westport, Conn.: Greenwood Press, 1993.

Weber, Eugen. *Peasants into Frenchmen: The Modernization of Rural France*. Stanford, Calif.: Stanford University Press, 1976.

Wells, Allen. *Yucatán's Gilded Age: Haciendas, Henequen, and International Harvester, 1860–1915*. Albuquerque: University of New Mexico Press, 1985.

Wells, Allen, and Gilbert M. Joseph. "Modernizing Visions, *Chilango* Blueprints, and Provincial Growing Pains: Mérida at the Turn of the Century." *Mexican Studies/Estudios Mexicanos* 8, no. 2 (1982): 167–215.

——. *Summer of Discontent, Seasons of Upheaval: Elite Politics and Rural Insurgency in Yucatán, 1876–1915*. Stanford, Calif.: Stanford University Press, 1996.

Weyl, Nathaniel, and Sylvia Weyl. *The Reconquest of Mexico: The Years of Lázaro Cárdenas*. London: Oxford University Press, 1939.

Wilkie, James W. *The Mexican Revolution: Federal Expenditure and Social Change since 1910*. Berkeley: University of California Press, 1967.

Wilkie, James W., ed. *Society and Economy in Mexico*. Los Angeles: University of California, Los Angeles, Latin American Center Publications, 1990.

Wilkie, James W., and Stephen Haber, eds. *Statistical Abstract of Latin America*. Los Angeles: University of California, Los Angeles, Latin American Center Publications, 1981.

Wilkinson, Patrick. "The Selfless and the Helpless: Maternalist Origins of the U.S. Welfare State." *Feminist Studies* 25, no. 3 (1999): 571–97.

Williams, Raymond. *Marxism and Literature*. Oxford: Oxford University Press, 1977.

——. *Keywords: A Vocabulary of Culture and Society*. Rev. ed. New York: Oxford University Press, 1983.

Wolin, Sheldon. "Fugitive Democracy." Pp. 31–45 in *Democracy and Difference: Contesting Boundaries of the Political*, ed. Seyla Benhabib. Princeton, N.J.: Princeton University Press, 1996.

Wood, Andrew Grant. *Revolution in the Street: Women, Workers, and Urban Protest in Veracruz, 1870–1927*. Wilmington, Del.: Scholarly Resources, 2001.

Young, Iris Marion. "Polity and Group Difference: A Critique of the Ideal of Universal Citizenship." *Ethics* 9 (1989): 250–74.

Zaragoza, Alex. *Monterrey Elite and the Mexican State, 1880–1940*. Austin: University of Texas Press, 1988.

Zepeda Patterson, Jorge. *Michoacán: Sociedad, economía, política y cultura*. Mexico City: Universidad Nacional Autónoma de México, 1990.

Zermeño P., Guillermo, and Rubén Aguilar V. *Hacia una reinterpretación del sinarquismo actual*. Mexico City: Universidad Iberoamericana, Departamento de Historia, 1988.

Index

26, 233–35; visits Comarca Lagunera, 140–41; visits Yucatán 219, 224–26, 229–30

Cardenismo, 24, 122, 160, 172, 232, 235, 237; agrarian reform agenda of, 67; anticlericalism of, 80, 103, 108, 139, 195; antifascism of, 107–8; as arrival of authentic revolution, 90–91, 116, 150, 192, 220, 226, 230; conservative turn of, 122, 155, 185, 196, 220, 239; labor policies of, 68, 113, 134, 137; mass organizing as characteristic of, 3, 12, 64, 68, 109, 124, 217, 219, 239; in Michoacán, 60–61, 63–64, 69, 71, 79–80, 82, 89, 91–92; populism of, 10, 20, 92, 107, 115, 116, 197, 204, 232; program of, for organizing women, 47, 140–42, 144; radical reformism of, 95, 124, 196, 232; in Yucatán, 202, 208, 217

Carr, Barry, 107, 131, 187

Carranza, Antonio, 88

Carranza, Venustiano, 30, 32

Carrillo Puerto, Elvia, 39–40, 111, 162, 172, 191, 205–6, 208, 282 n.63

Carrillo Puerto, Felipe, 204–7, 214, 279 n.19

Carrillo Puerto, Gualberto, 215–16

Castellanos, Raúl, 226

Caste War (1847), 204

Castro, Agustín, 36

Catholic Church, 14, 38, 76, 195; as community center, 72, 99, 237; efforts to displace, 72, 76, 99, 237; El Base as conservative wing of, 108; as foreign influence, 8, 50; intimidation by, 68, 70; Mexican Catholic Action, 103–4, 107, 109, 184; National Catholic Labor Confederation, 61; sinarquismo emerges from, 108; women's activism supporting, 3, 43, 70–71, 102–3, 209, 246 n.10, 260 n.33. See also Unión Femenina Católica Mexicana (UFCM)

Cedillo, Saturnino, 43

Central Consultative Committee of Ejidatarios (Torreón, Coah.), 150

Centralization, political, 10, 42, 61, 208, 224, 232, 242–43

Cerda, Eladio, 146

Cervantes Vargas, Salvador, 75

Cetina, Liberata, 222

Chalé, Rogelio, 202, 217–18, 225

Chapa, Esther, 111, 164–65, 233, 237

Chatterjee, Partha, 250 n.59

Chávez, Elvira, 81

Chuc, Manuela, 218

Citizenship, 3–4, 11, 45, 199–200; limitations of informal, 85, 215. See also Revolutionary citizenship; Suffrage (women's)

Ciudad Juárez (Chihuahua), 128, 161

Civera Cerecedo, Alicia, 24

Civil Code (1928), 19, 52, 174, 239

Class: consciousness, efforts to raise, 113, 186; postrevolutionary politics structured by: 8, 22, 54, 198, 213, 236, 241, 243; protocols of, 146; as source of political legitimacy, 106–7, 115–16, 198; tensions between classes, 130, 170, 220; of women, 33; women's activism informed by, 53, 76, 81–82

Coahuila; Agujita, 53; Arteaga, 130; Esmeralda, 190; Piedras Negras, 146; Saltillo, 133, 155, 169, 192–93; Sierra Mojada, 190–91

Cold War, 237, 243

Comarca Lagunera, 123–58 passim.; compared with Yucatán 203, 211, 213, 214, 216, 223, 226; effect of geography on popular organizing and, 125; general strike in, 9, 25, 123–24, 133–138, 201, 233, 263 n.1; Hacienda Manila (Dgo.), 131; Hacienda San Ignacio (Coah.), 134; infrastructure, 125–129; La Flor de Jimulco (Coah.), 144, 150;

Feminism, 29–30, 144, 162, 204, 209, 212–13, 247 n.36, 249 n.4; as foreign influence, 17, 19, 24, 31, 44–45, 49, 53, 184, 229, 241; nationalist, 45, 229; urban, 44, 139, 148, 232–33

Feminist Revolutionary Party, 51, 198–99

First Acapulco Red National Women's League (Liga Roja), 119–22

Flores Sánchez, Ana María, 96, 136, 232, 237

Flores Zamora, Celso, 68

French Intervention, 127

Frente Socialista de Abogados, 176–79

Frente Unico Pro–Derechos de la Mujer (FUPDM), 16, 116, 117, 186, 267 n.87; in Acapulco, Guerrero, 120–21; anti-fascism of, 111, 114, 120; campaign for women's suffrage, 111, 113–14, 120, 160, 163, 170–77, 179–80, 182, 194, 232–33; in Comarca Lagunera, 140; conflicts within, 113, 195; creation of, 111; gender discourses within, 16; internationalism of, 113, 120, 172; labor organizing in, 117; in Monterrey, Nuevo León, 198–99; PCM and, 111, 114, 164, 238; programmatic goals of, 111, 113–14, 120; regional diversity within, 114–15; ruling party (PNR/PRM) and, 112, 113, 187, 189, 194, 196, 198, 227; as training ground for leading activists, 89–90; in Yucatán, 214–16, 221–27, 229–30, 282 n.63

Friedrich, Paul, 69

Galeana, Benita, 50, 118

Galindo de Topete, Hermila, 30–31, 32, 33, 178–79, 205

Gamboa, Vicente, 209

García, María del Refugio ("Cuca"), 63, 106, 278 n.148; candidacy of, for federal deputy, 174–77, 184; as FUDPM secretary-general, 90, 111–12, 160,

170–71, 175, 180, 186, 187–88, 194–96, 198–99; as PCM militant, 48, 50, 206, 237

García, Thais, 182, 186

García Correa, Bartolomé, 203, 206–7

García León, Carlos, 66

García Tellez, Ignacio, 162

Garduño Castro, Hermila, 164

Gender, 52, 128, 138, 241; conventions of, disruptions of, 2, 17, 22, 46, 49, 140, 146, 240, 243, 249 n.13; domesticity and femininity, 3, 36, 39, 45, 58, 139–41, 143, 149, 164, 168, 177, 182, 183, 215, 220; femininity debate and, 15–20, 32, 40, 49, 57, 95, 101, 115, 221, 228, 233, 242; foreign influences on, 45–46, 53; language as describing, 15–17; masculinity and, 2, 18–19, 35–37, 133, 160, 166, 192, 211–12, 233–34, 242, 249 n.26, 281 n.49; maternalism and, 17, 32, 160, 165, 174, 228, 241, 242; military service and, 21, 242; morality and femininity, 4, 20, 53, 72, 139–41, 143, 151, 160, 163, 164, 166, 183, 185, 215, 216, 240; nationalism and, 45–46, 59, 251 n.59; organizing and, 82, 96; piety and femininity, 41, 58, 62, 70–71, 82, 99, 173, 180, 183, 209–11, 242, 250 n.43; political practice and, 83, 91, 161, 182, 186, 206–7, 215, 219, 238, 240, 242; public space and, 14, 71–72, 74; womanhood and, 4–5, 18, 28, 33–34, 36, 40, 47, 52, 59, 101, 144, 169, 174, 186, 241

General Labor Confederation (CGT), 130, 134–36

Gold Shirts. See Camisas Doradas

González, Luis, 184

González, Teófila, 219–20, 283 n.82

González Torres, S., 33

Granados, María Guadalupe, 90

Grupo Unificador de la Mujer, 189–90

and, 38; political culture of, 45–46, 51, 217, 219

May Day celebrations, 132, 146, 154

Mayer, Arno, 248 n.63

Mayés Navarro, Antonio, 66, 67, 87, 89

Mayés Navarro, Julia, 87, 90

Metate, 147–49, 244. *See also* Corn mills

Mexican Catholic Women's Union. *See* Unión Femenina Católica Mexicana (UFCM). *See also* Catholic Church

Mexican Communist Party (PCM). *See* Partido Comunista de México (PCM)

Mexican Federation of Feminist Centers, 42

Mexican Labor Confederation. *See* Confederación de Trabajadores de México (CTM)

Mexican Miracle, 234–35

Mexican Peasant Confederation (CCM), 26

Mexican Revolutionary Action. *See* Camisas Doradas

Mexican Revolutionary Front: Women's Sector of, 191

Mexican Women's Action Front, 54

Mexican Women's Confederation, 50, 172–73

Mexico City: as center for women's organizing, 39, 54, 58, 111, 113, 161, 179, 243; PCM in, 107, 118; PNR in, 174; women's leagues in, 157, 170

Meyer, Jean, 108

Michel, Concha: as activist, 9, 93–94, 103; leads invasion of Hacienda Santa Bárbara, 1–3, 7, 25–26, 93, 124, 233, 244; PCM affiliation of, 50, 57–58, 106, 109, 237, 244; as SEP employee, 93–94, 96, 106–7

Michoacán, 25, 60–92 passim., 106; Angangueo, 65; Chavinda, 79; Coalcomán, 69; Coeneo, 87; compared to the Comarca Lagunera, 140, 141, 157; compared to Yucatán, 204, 209, 213, 214, 230; Contepec, 102–3; Hacienda Cantabria, 87; Hacienda Nueva Italia, 79; Huarachita, 79; Jacona, 70; Jesús del Monte, 81; La Angostura, 90; La Huacana, 70, 175; La Huerta, 93; Morelia, 64–67, 84, 90, 108; Naranja, 61, 63, 79, 87; Panindícuaro, 90; Pátzcuaro, 65, 80; Puruándiro, 108; San Antonio Tariácuri, 88; San Nicolás Obispo, 87; Santiaguito, 73; Suhuayo, 79; Tacámbaro, 68, 108; Tarajero, 88; Taretán, 175; Teremendo, 74, 84–86; Tingüindín, 71; Tiríndaro, 69; Tiripetío, 86–87; Tzintzimacato Grande, 84, 86; Undameo, 94; Uruapan, 62, 65. 174–76; Villa Jiménez, 88; Yurécuaro, 79; Zacapu, 68–69, 83, 87; Zamora, 79, 108; Zinapécuaro, 70, 108; Zurumútaro, 69

Michoacán Socialist Women's Federation. *See* Federación Femenil Socialista Michoacana (FFSM)

Michoacán United Teachers' Front, 90

Michoacán Women's Coordinating Committee (PRM), 150

Michoacán Women's Resistance League, 21

Modernization: Catholic Church and, 104; Comarca Lagunera as model for, 124, 137–38, 144, 148; commodity production as aspect of, 22, 125, 137, 224; education and, 143, 209; embodiment and, 95; gender ideologies of, 19, 29, 39–40; labor and, 65; political, 21; as postrevolutionary project, 9, 12, 23, 37, 42, 44, 92, 143, 148, 168, 180, 236; public welfare and, 76, 99, 116, 131, 143, 205, 208, 217; rural, 89, 139, 209, 218; scientific management and, 100. *See also* Temperance

Modotti, Tina, 57

Molina, José, 84–87

Molinos de nixtamal. *See* Corn mills

Montevideo Treaty (1933), 165–66

Monzón, Luis G., 34–35, 173, 249 n.26

Mora, María, 102

Mora Tovar, Luis, 67

Morelos: Atlatlahucan, 100; Cuernavaca, 104; Tlatetelco, 100

Morelos Women's Civic Union, 176

Moreno de Medina, Julia, 101

Morton, Ward, 183, 250 n.29, 272 n.3, 275 n.84

Mouffe, Chantal, 23, 238

Múgica, Francisco, 78, 79, 124, 225, 249 n.3; anticlericalism of, 61–62; as governor of Michoacán, 61, 63, 64, 68, 69; as patron, 26, 80, 83, 195–96; as presidential hopeful, 196; supports women's suffrage, 33, 44, 81, 173, 175–76, 184

Mujeres Agraristas Latinoamericanas (MALA), 191

Municipal Feminist Committee (Saltillo, Coah.), 196

Nájera de Chargoy, Dolores, 113

National Action Party. *See* Partido de Acción Nacional (PAN)

National Catholic Labor Confederation, 61

National Civic Women's Party, 163

National Democratic Party, 164

National Ejidal Credit Bank. *See* Banco Nacional de Crédito Ejidal

National Feminist Council, 233

National Graphics Workshop, 56–57

Nationalism: citizenship and, 8, 20, 99, 110, 181, 189; consumption and, 52–55, 58; counterrevolutionary, 107, 109; feminism and, 24, 30, 45, 48, 163, 165, 181, 229; hemispheric leadership as form of, 165; labor and, 54–55;

patriotism and, 15; revolutionary, 221, 236, 243; xenophobia and, 54, 107

National Peasant Confederation. *See* Confederación Nacional Campesino (CNC)

National Revolutionary Party. *See* Partido Nacional Revolucionario (PNR)

National Sinarquista Union (UNS). *See* Sinarquistas

National Woman's Party (U.S.), 176–77

National Women's Alliance, 233

National Women's Civic Party, 163

National Women's League, 119–22, 198

Nayarit; Heriberto Casas, 196–97; San Nicolás, 102

Nelson, Diane, 269 n.131

Newspapers: *Excélsior*, 56; *Frente a Frente*, 57; *Izquierdas*, 57, 105; *Machete, El*, 56–7; positions of, on women's suffrage, 276 n.116; *Siglo de Torreón, El*, 142; *Universal, El*, 56, 129

Nicolás Lenin Union (Matamoros, Coah.), 134;

Novo, Salvador, 111

Nuevo León; Cadereyta Jiménez, 189; Galeana, 106; Monterrey, 129, 180, 184, 198–99; Sabinas Hidalgo, 56; Women's Center for Proletarian Action, 180

Núñez, Dolores, 63, 80, 83, 90, 113

Oliva, Agustina, 89–91

Organizers: as cultural mediators, 63, 204; as labor brokers, 242–43; as navigators of bureaucracy, 114, 143, 207; as political mediators, 62, 84, 85, 92, 95–96, 116, 120–21, 215

Organizing: as disciplinary project, 13–14, 29, 60, 92, 95, 122, 168, 186, 200, 232, 240; encouragement of, by SEP, 96, 106; fostering of, by ruling party (PNR/PRM), 94, 119; infrastructure

Primo Tapia Women's Union (Teremendo, Mich.), 79
Prostitution, 28, 31, 33, 46, 116, 131, 132, 191, 205–6, 217
Puebla, 113, 184; Atlixco, 180
Purnell, Jennie, 69

Querétaro, 32, 163, 191
Quintero Castellanos, Esperanza, 75

Race, 101, 107, 120, 165, 192, 235, 250 n.32; eugenics and, 36–37, 39–40; raza cósmica, 15
Radical Revolutionary Women's Bloc (Yucatán), 208–9, 230
Radical Socialist Federation of Michoacán, 80
Ramírez, Trinidad, 102
Rascón, María Antonieta, 241
Recognition, bureaucratic: conflicts over, 117, 121–22; corporatism and, 187, 240; labor unions and, 116, 130, 145–47, 219–20; women's organizations and, 84, 143, 153, 189, 190, 199, 208, 223
Regionalism, 9–10, 24, 246 n.21; in Yucatán, 204, 224, 229, 279 n.11
Repression, 130–31, 132, 134, 136, 158, 236, 285 n.114
Reproductive labor, 29–30, 57, 127, 136, 222, 241; as basis for rights claims, 160; childcare, 141–44, 155, 158; citizenship and, 20–22, 42, 53–54, 143, 176, 228; efforts to improve conditions of, 100, 117, 148–49, 157, 200, 226; efforts to make visible, 125, 141–42, 158, 244; gendered, 16, 252 n.86; Ligas Femeniles de Lucha Social as effort to modernize, 140–44; silence regarding, 53, 55–56, 59; women's political opportunities shaped by, 77, 116, 238, 242
Revolution (Mexican, 1910–17), 27;

anthropomorphized, 10, 36, 210–11; defining legacies of, 15, 50, 98, 100, 115, 230; as foundation for political legitimacy, 10, 13, 29, 37, 48, 86, 172, 177, 218, 189; women's claims to benefits of, 59, 96, 171, 198, 212, 220–21, 236; women's suffrage as dividend of, 174, 178, 184
Revolutionary Anticlerical Central Committee (Michoacán), 79
Revolutionary Artists and Writers League (LEAR), 56
Revolutionary citizenship, 6–7, 25–26, 236; ambiguities regarding women's, 86, 174, 192–93, 199; civic engagement as element of, 11, 21, 53, 160, 164, 244; collective identities and, 92, 115, 160–61, 174, 187, 215, 240; contesting parameters of, 59, 149–50, 192, 200, 216, 236–37, 240, 242; contingent, 7–10, 61, 124–25, 161, 204, 223; gendered, 5, 11, 15–22, 28, 53, 61, 160, 164, 182, 212, 234–36; inhabited, 10–15; labor and, 11–12, 21–22, 28, 29, 143, 160, 167–68, 174, 176, 220, 226, 228, 244; liberal elements of, 92, 115, 160–61, 174, 187, 189–190, 200; military service and, 11, 20, 28, 35, 44, 160, 190, 242, 277 n.130; organizational recognition and, 61, 77, 84, 86, 88, 91, 115, 146–47, 167–68, 187, 189–90, 207, 240; political loyalty as marker of, 15, 61, 160, 190, 194, 240; practice of, 94, 185, 187, 200, 239–40, 246 n.26; public space as marker of, 14, 94, 156, 185, 229, 241; women's leagues as vehicles for exercising, 72, 141–43, 145, 157–58, 191–93
Revolutionary Feminist Party, 161
Revolutionary Labor Confederation of Michoacán. *See* Confederación Revolucionaria Michoacana del Trabajo (CRMDT)

Soria, Alfonso, 62, 257 n.84
Sosa, Esther, 91
Soto Reyes, Ernesto, 78
Soviet Union, 50, 51, 57, 93, 109, 132, 165, 214; influence in Mexico, 129, 184, 202; Bolshevik Revolution in, 176
Stalin, Joseph, 2
Suffrage (women's): campaigns for, 2, 6, 51, 171, 172, 174–75, 177, 200; Catholic Church and, 166, 173, 180, 183–84; changes in meaning of, 186–87; "civic preparation" for, 164, 168 170, 174, 180–82, 185, 188, 235–36; Communist Party and, 110–11, 172; constitutional amendment regarding, 2, 25, 124, 172–74, 176–78, 181–83, 194, 200, 233–34, 245 n.6; debates over, 4, 28, 32, 33–37, 52–53, 58, 240, 250 n.29; demonstrations supporting, 159, 170, 171, 176, 182; electoral laws regarding, 33, 172–73, 249 n.25; failure to secure, 183–85, 232, 235, 239; in Guanajuato (state), 166; internationally, 43–44, 51, 95, 165–66, 179; limited, 33–35, 53, 161, 166–67, 168, 174, 177–78, 180, 183, 224, 233; in Michoacán, 184; opposition to, 53, 58, 161–62, 174, 176, 182, 240; "passive vote," 162; PNR support for, 162–63, 166–68; Puebla (state), 166; silence regarding, 80, 82, 118, 139, 141, 144, 179, 229; supported by Cárdenas, 2, 162, 178–79, 181, 184, 200, 225–26, 233–35, 275 n.84; unifies political rivals, 160–61, 163–64; urban-centered, 139, 161, 169, 179, 200, 224; in Veracruz (state), 166; in Yucatán, 205–6, 208–9, 224–26, 228

Talleres Gráficos de la Nación, 56–57
Tampico (Tamaulipas), 56, 129, 173, 189
Tapia, Primo, 60–64, 68, 69, 210, 253 n.13

Teachers: harassment of, 87; as organizers, 13–14, 25, 93–94, 96–97, 122, 154, 193, 214, 225, 237; PCM influence among, 106, 202, 214; as social workers, 96–101; violence against, 82, 102; women's professional opportunity, 208. See also Education; Secretaría de Educación Pública (SEP)
Tejada, Adalberto, 43, 56
Temperance: in Comarca Lagunera, 132, 138, 143, 145, 154; Constitutional Congress (1917) and, 36–37; encouragement of productivity through, 72, 74; in Michoacán, 61, 64, 72–76, 80, 84–87, 95, 144; modernization and, 36–37, 73; national campaign for, 206, 255 n.46; Primo Tapia Women's Anti-alcohol League, 74–75; women's activism for, 38–39, 43, 80, 84, 97, 189, 192, 239; in Yucatán, 205–6, 208–9, 214
Tiendas de raya, 127–28
Tinoco, María, 166
Tlahualilo Land Company (Durango), 127
Toriz, Lucrecia, 172
Torres, Elena, 16, 106, 183, 206
Torres, Rosa, 205
Trejo, Blanca Lydia, 164, 183
Trotsky, Leon, 187

Unifying Group of Women (Tampico, Tamps.), 189–90
Unión de Mujeres Americanas (UMA), 159, 163, 165, 172, 179, 195
Unión Femenina Católica Mexicana (UFCM), 16, 103–5
Union of American Women. See Unión de Mujeres Americanas (UMA)
Union of Catholic Mexican Ladies (Unión de Damas Católicas Mexicanas), 103

Yucatán, 101, 201–31 passim.; Abalá, 227; Casa del Pueblo (Mérida) as center for popular organizing, 203, 209, 217, 280 n.38, 281 n.51; Celestún, 217; compared with Comarca Lagunera, 128; "Crusade of the Mayab" in, 223; Cuncunu, 226; Dzitás, 218; Espita, 225; feminism's legacy in, 204–7, 212–14, 228; Feminist Leagues in, 205–6; First Feminist Congress (1916) in, 28–32; "Great Ejido" in, 203, 226–27, 231; Ixil, 214–15; Kinchil, 215–16, 225; Mérida, 28, 202–3, 214–15, 227; Mothers' Clubs in, 206, 227; "Open Door" policy of, 224, 284 n.102; polit ical instability in, 9, 25, 201–3, 213–14, 221, 223, 229–30; Progreso, 129, 203, 207, 215, 219–20; Resistance Leagues in, 205, 207; separatism in, 204; Tekantó, 226; Tekax, 221; Ticul, 229; Tixméuac, 221–23, 225; Valladolid, 225, 227

Zambrano, Otilia, 163
Zapata, Marina R. de, 199
Zapatistas, 27, 87, 104, 119
Zavala, Consuelo, 30
Zendejas, Adelina, 106, 114
Zetkin, Clara, 172

JOCELYN OLCOTT is an assistant professor
in the Department of History, Duke University.

LIBRARY OF CONGRESS CATALOGING-IN-PUBLICATION DATA

Olcott, Jocelyn.

Revolutionary women

in postrevolutionary Mexico / Jocelyn Olcott.

p. cm. — (Next wave)   Includes bibliographical references and index.

ISBN 0-8223-3653-7 (cloth : alk. paper) — ISBN 0-8223-3665-0 (pbk. : alk. paper)

1. Women revolutionaries — Mexico — History — 20th century. 2. Women political

activists — Mexico — History — 20th century. 3. Mexico — Politics and government —

1910–1946. 4. Political participation — Mexico — History — 20th century.

5. Feminism — Mexico — History — 20th century. 6. Mexico — History —

Revolution, 1910–1920 — Participation, Female. I. Title. II. Series.

HQ1236.5.M6043 2005   320'.082'0972 — dc22

2005021134

Rock
Paper
Scissors

Rock
Paper
Scissors

Winning Battles
Against the Unrelenting
Foe of Multiple Myeloma

Bruce Moffatt

Dedication

THERE IS A MULTITUDE OF people to whom I am deeply indebted for supporting me as I fight my battles against Multiple Myeloma. My minister father, Fred Moffatt, before his death, contacted every church he pastored and asked the current pastor to put me on the prayer list of his congregation. As a result, hundreds, if not thousands of people whom I don't even know have prayed for my healing. If she was still living, my mother, Jane Moffatt, would have continued to give me the unconditional love and support my sister and I received from both our parents. My sister, Mary Jane Yates, has been an ardent supporter at every twist and turn of my journey. MJ would take my illness on herself if that were possible.

As you will read, there are over fifty friends and family I kept apprised of my treatments and progress (or lack thereof) through emails for the past 6 years. Their replies to my communications have been overwhelmingly supportive and have helped me keep a positive attitude which is critical to fighting this illness. Mike and Anne Pace, along with my Uncle Miles Kanne, have ardently persisted I assemble my emails and experiences into the book you now have before you. Without their assistance, this book would never have happened. The amazing doctors and nurses that have directed and administered my care deserve my undying appreciation for making their contributions to extending my life. And our two Labrador Retrievers, Choco and Latte, have provided their example of unconditional love, bringing us joy and laughter daily.

But one person stands above all others for a debt I cannot repay. That is my wife, Sandra. She has been at my side every step of the way. Sandra has attended meetings with doctors, taking notes and helping the flow of information remain accurate and on schedule. And there is a lot of information to track. As my disease progressed, the time came when I had to retire from working. Sandra continued to work full time, allowing us to meet our financial obligations without sacrificing our standard of living.

During much of this time, she even continued to bring home the groceries and prepare our meals as I had no experience in cooking nor any interest in doing so. One day before Covid, she pointed out that since I was no longer working, it was time for me to take over grocery shopping and dinner preparation. I could not argue with the fairness of her request and felt sure once she ate dinners prepared by me, she would immediately return to preparing our meals. I googled "simple dinners", "meals with no more than five ingredients" and "crock pot dinners". The result? She was thrilled with the meals and labeled me "Chef Bruce". Clearly an exaggeration but eliminating food shopping and meal prep was a tremendous weight off her daily routine. Had I known how happy this would make her, I would have retired from work years ago, without complaint, to take over the shopping and cooking. (Take a lesson here boys.)

My current level of unchecked disease and compromised immune system during Covid and the Delta Variant has interrupted my ability to do the shopping and cooking. Sandra has resumed these responsibilities without complaint, but I hope the next treatment I receive will greatly reduce my cancer, improve my physical stamina and allow me to take over all kitchen duties again. It would be an answer to prayer for me.

If you have Multiple Myeloma or any other incurable, chronic disease, it is my wish you have a spouse at least half as loving and supportive as Sandra. She has made all the difference in my life both pre and post Myeloma. Thank you, Sandra.

I love you to the moon and back!

Foreword

I'VE HAD THE PRIVILEGE OF being Bruce's oncologist since early 2019, when he came to Penn in search of clinical trial options as his myeloma became resistant to standard therapies. Since his initial diagnosis in 2015, Bruce has received numerous standard multiple myeloma therapies, enrolled on three phase-one clinical trials, and is now recovering from his second course of high-dose melphalan and autologous stem cell transplant. His honest reflections in this book of his rollercoaster course, captured in the updates he sent to family and friends throughout his illness, would be helpful to any multiple myeloma patient or caregiver of a multiple myeloma patient.

Bruce's course with multiple myeloma reflects both the successes and shortcomings of modern cancer therapy. The success is undeniable. Prior to the early 2000s, when the first modern multiple myeloma therapies became widely available, it was rare for multiple myeloma patients to survive as long as Bruce has. Bruce has ridden a wave of new myeloma therapies that were not available when he was first diagnosed, and we hope to make yet more options available for him soon. For multiple myeloma patients, however, this success can feel more like purgatory because our shortcoming has been an inability to cure the disease. Even when the disease is well controlled and quality-of-life is good, there is always the continuous background worry about relapse. While many are fortunate enough to enjoy years of good disease control with minimal therapy, others, like Bruce, have a much rockier course. Bruce has been extraordinarily resilient and optimistic throughout his illness. Even as an oncologist who spends much time with patients in this predicament, I cannot describe the experience nearly as well as Bruce's honest and compelling first-person account. We are indebted to him for his willingness to share these most personal reflections.

Dr. Alfred L. Garfall, MD
University of Pennsylvania Medical Center
Philadelphia, Pennsylvania

Acknowledgements

My good friend, Bruce Moffatt, asked me to write an acknowledgement for this book. While acknowledgements are usually written by the author, I was honored to oblige in this case.

Over the last twenty-five years, Bruce and Sandy and Michael and I have traveled, golfed and dined our way around a wonderful and trusted friendship. We probably owe Bruce a big bag of money for all of the golf lessons he has generously given us over the years while he was a Golf Pro. There have been many times since his diagnosis that I wish Bruce was with me to 'fix' my swing. I know Michael feels the same.

I'll never forget the day after Bruce received the news that he had Multiple Myeloma. Bruce, Sandy, Kris and Don Jewell, and Michael and I had tickets to the Lady Gaga and Tony Bennett concert in Washington, DC. It's always fun to get together with our favorite couples but the heightened concern for Bruce definitely thickened the air.

Multiple Myeloma was new to me. And I believe it was new to Sandy and Bruce. Kris and Don have medical backgrounds so they probably had a better grasp of what was coming. And to make things a bit heavier, a friend of Sandy's had recently passed, very quickly, from MM. She was full of life, a great gal and way too young to die.

Here we are, six years later, and Bruce is still fighting the fight. As you will read in this book, he continues to keep his 'friends and family' up to date through an email chain on all aspects of living with MM. It's been extremely educational and informative for those of us who did not know much about the disease. But two things loomed large to me in the words journaled by Bruce. The first happy surprise was his ability to write and write well. I always knew he was a good communicator (he was a great golf instructor). But through his writing, he would sometimes use humor or spiritual encouragement to keep us up to date with his day-to-day health situation, including the advances and trials happening in the world of Multiple Myeloma treatments. We all wish we didn't have to read the emails but in a weird way, seeing an email from Bruce to the group meant something was happening. Happening could be good!

The second happy surprise was the way he shared his joy for life and his commitment to God and his family through his writing. Getting a difficult diagnosis might send someone falling down a dark hole, screaming 'why me'? But not Bruce! I'm sure he's had some soul searching moments but outwardly, his positive outlook and commitment to fight this evil disease has been amazing and awesome. I mean who starts an email with "Howdy Pardners"?

Bruce sheds a beautiful light on the world around him. His uplifting attitude and concern for his fellow man (or woman) is contagious. I pray the light will shine for many, many more years to come!

Shine bright my friend.
Love, Anne Pace

Oh . . . and he loves dogs! Pure joy!

The weather was excellent.

Eighty degrees, sun shining, a perfect top-down motoring day and the first time we enjoyed this together.

We avoided I-95 North and headed over the Chesapeake Bay Bridge for a more scenic and less trafficked route. Once we were in the flat open country of the Eastern Shore, we seemed to be the only car on the road. Tunes were blasting and Sandra even commented that the sound was amazing. The Love Theme from Dances with Wolves queues up from my Spotify list. It's a beautiful and somewhat haunting melody.

As I listen, a calm overcomes me. I'm happy, content. Life has been so good to me and continues to do so through times of struggle. I could have allowed a few tears to roll out, but I resisted. My soul was full of good feelings. I told this to Sandra later and choked up a bit. She squeezed my hand. We can remember the past and guess at the future, but we can only live in the present.

This was one of those special moments in my life.

Table of Contents

Why This Book and Who Is It For?

WELCOME TO MY LIFE WITH Multiple Myeloma ("MM"). For the last six years, I have been tested, tested and tested again, in ways most of you will hopefully never experience. Tested mentally, tested physically and tested spiritually. This book is for all those who have contracted MM, as well as those friends and family members who are undertaking the journey to recovery with them. The book would not have been possible without the encouragement, and sometimes insistence, from people I trust and love.

Six years ago, I started sending health updates to about fifty Friends and Family. The purpose of the emails was to keep everyone in my circle apprised of my current state of health and the ever-changing challenges of this chronic disease. Much to my surprise, the feedback was very flattering for both my writing and communication skills. Chief among those pushing me to complete this writing task have been my sister, Mary Jane Yates, Mike and Anne Pace, and my uncle, Miles Kanne (pronounced Connie). Many others echoed their appreciation for what they called my "writing skills" and suggested publishing my experiences. They felt doing so could benefit others facing similar challenges with MM, other cancers, or other serious illnesses. The compliments seemed overly effusive at times. Maybe they were just trying to be nice. But I finally realized their sincerity so here, on these pages, is the fruit of their influence.

This is not an authoritative medical journal, nor is it an outline for expectations regarding your personal course of treatment. We are all unique and the way cancer affects similar individuals can be dramatically different. It is simply an opportunity to share my experiences with the hope you can gain some encouragement and insights on dealing with the physical, emotional, and medical journey that lies ahead.

As you will see, my attitude to life is highly shaped by my faith in God and belief that Jesus Christ was His Son, sent to redeem us from our fall from grace. After all, I was raised in a Christian home by a mother and father who dedicated their lives to God by serving others and spreading the Good News of the Gospels. This has been the foundation of my life even though I have been far from a good example of a dedicated Christian. If given the chance, I'd change a lot of things I've said and done over the years, hopefully with the result of leading a better life with greater emphasis on others and less on my unimportant self-desires.

Please accept my undying thanks to everyone who has supported me with their thoughts, prayers and encouragement. You are an amazing group of accomplished and successful people, and I am so fortunate to have you in my life. Knowing you are loved and appreciated is so valuable and I count each of the people listed in this book as a blessing in my life. I can only hope what follows might help a reader struggling with MM or other serious illness find peace, calm, and assurance.

No matter your faith (or even if you have no religious faith) you might find these words from Matthew (6: 25-34) helpful whether you're personally dealing with cancer or accompanying a loved one on that journey. They continue to give me great comfort and express my own personal attitude toward life in general.

Therefore, I tell you, do not worry about your life, what
you will eat or drink; or about your body, what you will

wear. Is not life more than food, and the body more than clothes? Look at the birds of the air; they do not sow or reap or store away in barns, and yet your heavenly Father feeds them. Are you not much more valuable than they?

Can any one of you by worrying add a single house to your life? And why do you worry about clothes? See how the flowers of the field grow. They do not labor or spin. Yet I tell you that not even Solomon in all his splendor was dressed like one of these. If that is how God clothes the grass of the field, which is here today and tomorrow is thrown into the fire, will he not much more clothe you-you of little faith?

So do not worry, saying, 'What shall we eat?' or 'What shall we drink?' or 'What shall we wear?' For the pagans run after all these things, and your heavenly Father knows that you need them. But seek first his kingdom and his righteousness, and all these things will be given to you as well.

Therefore, do not worry about tomorrow, for tomorrow will worry about itself. Each day has enough trouble of its own.

One day at a time with faith, courage, and optimism. That's my attitude.

May it be so with you.

That's me holding my baby girl, Choco, 2011.
Boy I wish I was still that thin.

What's the Rock, Paper, Scissors reference about?

I'M SURE YOU'RE FAMILIAR WITH this game. Rock smashes scissors, scissors cut paper, paper covers rock. Managing cancer is like that game. The doctor and nurses direct your care and treatments. They are the ROCKS! The medications offer relief and containment of disease: the PAPER. The Insurance companies have the last word whether you get your medications or not: The SCISSORS. To win the battles, good choices must be made with each of these critical components. More about these critical segments that manage your disease and treatment options later.

What Is Multiple Myeloma

THE FOLLOWING INFORMATION CAN BE found on the Multiple Myeloma Research Foundation website: (themmrf.org)

MM is a type of blood cancer that affects plasma cells. In MM, malignant plasma cells accumulate in bone marrow—the soft, spongy tissue at the center of your bones—crowding out the normal plasma cells that help fight infection. These malignant plasma cells then produce an abnormal antibody called M protein, which offers no benefit to the body and may cause tumors, kidney damage, bone destruction and impaired immune function. The hallmark characteristic of multiple myeloma is a high level of M protein in the blood.

How does multiple myeloma start?

In healthy bone marrow, there are normal plasma cells that make antibodies to protect your body from infection. In MM, plasma cells are transformed into cancerous MM cells, which grow out of control and produce large amounts of a single abnormal antibody called M protein. As the cancerous cells multiply, there is less space in the bone marrow for normal blood cells, resulting in decreased numbers of red blood cells, white blood cells and platelets. The myeloma cells may activate other cells in the marrow that can damage your bones.

How does this affect the body?

Decreased blood cell numbers can cause anemia, excessive bleeding and decreased ability to fight infection. The buildup of M protein in the blood and urine can damage the kidneys and other organs.

Bone damage can cause bone pain and osteolytic lesions, which are weakened spots on bones. This bone destruction increases the risk of fractures and can also lead to a serious condition called hypercalcemia (increased levels of calcium in the blood).

Causes and increased risk factors

Researchers have made advancements in understanding how multiple myeloma develops, but the exact cause has not yet been identified. Like all cancers, MM is heterogeneous, meaning each case is unique. The genetic mutations that cause MM are different from person to person. There are some specific mutations that have been identified as genetic risk factors, but MM is not thought to be a hereditary disease. Increased incidence of MM has been found in males, African Americans, and people over the age of 45. Keep in mind these factors have not been proven to cause MM, and new studies regularly demonstrate new findings that help us identify risk factors and work towards a cure.

Google your disease for drug explanations and current therapy trends. Keeping up with new disease management therapies will help you see the positive forces at work on Myeloma and remove some mystery from your disease. There are a lot of good things happening in controlling Myeloma and you need to know what's evolving. Here's an example:

From the International Myeloma Foundation
(myeloma.org)

We read, hear, and see so much negative news that it is important to remember that good things are happening too. That includes getting closer to finding a cure for myeloma.

But what does "a cure" really mean?

The outlook on response, remission and survival is already very bright for many patients diagnosed in 2019 and beyond. Over 90 percent of patients will respond well with initial therapy. First remission will be in the four-year range. And overall survival for good responding patients (VGPR or better) is more than eight years. Then there is the impact of new immunotherapy and additional novel approaches.

When does remission become cure?

Achieving minimal residual disease (MRD) negative is the subject of much discussion. Bone marrow samples that show zero out of a million myeloma cells remaining are predictive of long remission and very good survival. But what about cure? This is the next step in the research: If MRD negative persists at one year, this is excellent. If it persists at three and five years, even better. But this is not an absolute guarantee of permanent success, or the fabled cure.

It is important to take a step back and understand what we know about long survival in myeloma patients:

1. Excellent response, including MRD-negative status, is a definite indicator of best outcomes.

2. A study from the University of Heidelberg showed that half of patients who had survived 20 years and beyond had residual disease. But these patients were still in remission and doing well. They had achieved a new equilibrium. Their immune system could control residual myeloma and, thus, prevent relapse. This immune status is now the focus of intense study.

3. Some MRD-negative patients become MRD-positive with relapsing disease. This resistant disease pattern is the subject of intense study.

4. Long survival can occur with and without negative MRD status, and negative MRD status may not be permanent.

What is a useful definition of cure today?

A good way to define cure right now is when patients live with a good quality of life and succumb to something other than myeloma—such as old age, vascular disease, or other common illnesses of the elderly. By this definition we are well on the way to curing many myeloma patients, with the prospect of curing many more in the future.

It is worth noting that even with older therapies, long-term follow-up showed survival at 20 years as 14.36 percent, not zero. So, with our new Cure trials we are not starting at rock bottom.

Learning from HIV and hepatitis C treatments

As in MM, AIDS researchers have long sought a cure. Fortunately, ongoing triple therapy for AIDS has achieved long-term disease control. Without maintenance treatment, researchers found, HIV rapidly rebounds, the result of reservoirs of infection. These reservoirs are primarily found in macrophages, where the virus hides.

A key advance in HIV treatment came from understanding that without triple therapy, infection came roaring back. Triple therapy can overcome the many mutants that emerge given the chance. Mathematical modeling showed that single or double therapy was not enough to prevent emergence of mutant virus. Triple therapy provides long-term disease control and, essentially, cure status for most patients.

If this is starting to sound familiar, it is because this is exactly what we face with myeloma therapy. The questions that arise in myeloma are therefore parallel to those in HIV:

- Is there a hidden reservoir, despite apparent MRD negativity?

- Is the mutation rate so low in some cases that new clones emerge very slowly over months to years?

All this certainly supports the current strategy to recommend ongoing maintenance. The advantage we have with myeloma is that relapse tends to emerge after months to years versus days to weeks if HIV treatment is stopped.

FIRST LINE TREATMENT FOR NEWLY DIAGNOSED MYELOMA PATIENTS (Again, from the International Myeloma Foundation)

What Are Your First-Line Treatment Options for Active Myeloma?

In the past decade, many new agents in various drug classes have become available and effective in the treatment of multiple myeloma. Ideally, your frontline therapy (also called "induction" or "first-line therapy") should

1. effectively control the disease
2. reverse myeloma-related complications
3. decrease the risk of early mortality
4. be well-tolerated with minimal or manageable toxicity
5. and not interfere with the need for stem cell collection.

Some of the top recommendations for initial therapy include the following:

1. Many studies have demonstrated the superiority of three-drug combination therapies over two-drug combinations for fit, newly diagnosed patients.

2. In the U.S., the most used induction therapy for fit, transplant-eligible patients is the combination of Velcade® (bortezomib), Revlimid® (lenalidomide), and low-dose dexamethasone (VRd).

Other induction therapies include the following:

Velcade (bortezomib), Cytoxan® (cyclophosphamide), and dexamethasone (VCD or CyBorD)

Velcade (bortezomib), Thalomid® (thalidomide), and dexamethasone (VTD)

Revlimid (lenalidomide) and dexamethasone (Rd)
Velcade (bortezomib) and dexamethasone (Vd)

VRd Lite (reduced dose and schedule of Velcade, Revlimid, and dexamethasone)

After maximum response to induction therapy has been achieved, your physician may recommend an autologous stem cell transplant (ASCT) followed by maintenance therapy. If you are not a candidate for ASCT or decline the transplant for other reasons, your health-care team may discuss continuous therapy with you. The benefit of continuous therapy until disease progression has been amply demonstrated to improve survival but is not necessary or appropriate for every patient. The financial, physical, and emotional implications of continuous therapy must be taken into consideration along with the characteristics of each patient's MM.

The Latest Standard of Care for Newly Diagnosed Multiple Myeloma Patients

The combination of a proteasome inhibitor and an immunomodulatory agent plus the steroid dexamethasone is the standard of care for newly diagnosed patients.

Autologous stem cell transplant should be considered early in all transplant-eligible patients.

Maintenance therapy after transplant, or continuous therapy after initial treatment, has shown progression-free survival and overall survival rate.

My take on all of this…

As you can see there are a lot of drug options for treating our disease. It gets complicated and the names and purposes of the drugs are not easy to recall and comprehend (much less pronounce). But the more you know, the more you know.

I do not recommend you Google every drug in the MM universe and start second-guessing your doctor on the combinations he or she suggests. This is a fast way to alienate your doctor. I can, however, predict your path forward as a newly diagnosed patient.

After determining your level of disease, you will start on some combination of two, three or four medications to begin lowering your cancer markers. The goal will be to lower your disease to a level safe enough to perform an Autologous Stem Cell Transplant. This uses your own stem cells, previously harvested, to be returned to you, following the complete destruction of your bone marrow. The regrowth of new marrow can take two to three months and will require you to avoid all possible sources of infection during this time. With such a new and weak immune system, infections are dangerous and could lead to death. Once completed, you will most likely enjoy some level of remission, perhaps a complete remission. In my case, I enjoyed 17 months of a good partial remission before the disease returned full force. At this time, you will be referred to as having Relapsed Refractory Myeloma. You will also become the candidate pharmaceutical companies are looking for to participate in clinical trials and your journey to finding new therapies and medication to control this disease begins.

As I hope you gleaned from the reporting above by the International Myeloma Foundation, there is much to be hopeful about.

My Doctors

Flavio W. Kruter, MD
Carroll Hospital
Westminster, Maryland

Alfred L. Garfall, MD
University of Pennsylvania Medical Center
Philadelphia, Pennsylvania

Arun Bhandari, MD
Chesapeake Oncology Hematology
Annapolis, Maryland

Peter A. Reyes, MD (Cardiologist)
Mercy Hospital Heart Center
Baltimore, Maryland

Ashraf Z. Badros, MD
University of Maryland Oncology Associates, PA
Baltimore, Maryland

Terms You Should Know

YOU'RE GOING TO HAVE A lot of blood draws to analyze and track your disease. Here's a list of key indicators your doctor will be looking at.

Plasma: Plasma is the clear, straw-colored liquid portion of blood that remains after red blood cells, white blood cells, platelets and other cellular components are removed. It is the single largest component of human blood, comprising about 55 percent, and contains water, salts, enzymes, antibodies and other proteins.

Composed of 90% water, plasma is a transporting medium for cells and a variety of substances vital to the human body. Plasma carries out a variety of functions in the body, including clotting blood, fighting diseases and other critical functions. Plasma cells are born in the marrow, mature and die. New cells are constantly being generated to replace those that have ended their life cycle. With Multiple Myeloma, your plasma cells turn cancerous instead of dying and can form lesions or tumors on bones as well as attacking your internal organs such as the kidneys in advanced stages of disease.

CBC: Complete Blood Count. This test measures the number of red blood cells, white blood cells and platelets in your blood. These are all produced in your bone marrow and the excess of plasma cells can crowd out these normal cells leading to low counts.

WBC: White Blood Cells. These cells fight infections, and a low count inhibits your body's ability to fight infections. Normal range is 3.5-10.5 x 10(9th)/ Liter

Neutrophils: These are a type of White Blood Cells that provide the highest levels of protection against infection. Normal range is 1.7-7.0 x 10(9th)/ Liter

RBC: Red Blood Cells carry oxygen to body tissues. Low counts lead to anemia, creating shortness of breath and a lack of energy. Normal levels for men: 4.32-5.72 x 10(12th)/Liter. For women: 3.9-5.03 x 10(12th)/Liter.

Note: As of August 4, 2021, shortness of breath and a lack of energy have been my constant companion for many years. This improves with periods of partial remission but it is currently at its worst level as we search for the next treatment to reduce my level of disease.

HgB (Hemoglobin): This is a protein in your Red Blood Cells which carries oxygen to all parts of your body. Low levels indicate an abundance of myeloma cells that crowd out space necessary for normal marrow cells that produce red blood cells. Normal for men: 13.5-17.5 grams/deciliter. Women: 12.0-15.5 g/dL.

Platelets: These blood cells help blood to clot. Too low and there is a risk for serious bleeding. Too high opens the risk for blood clots. Normal: 150-450 x 10(9th)/L. Clinical trials will require at least a level of 50 x 10(9th)/L

BUN (Blood Urea Nitrogen): Urea Nitrogen in the blood occurs when protein breaks down. Too much of this can lead to a risk of kidney disease. Caught early, renal function can be restored, but later stages require dialysis. Normal: 7-20 milligrams/deciliter. (mg/dL)

Calcium: All cells require calcium to function. High levels may indicate kidney or bone damage. Normal: 8.9-10.1 mg/dL

B2M (Beta 2 Microglobulin): A protein produced by malignant cells, B2M does not cause problems, but high levels indicate more advanced disease and a potentially worse prognosis. Normal: 1.21-2.7 micrograms/milliliter. (mcg/mL)

Ig: Ig is the prefix abbreviation for antibody proteins produced by normal plasma cells. In MM, plasma cells produce abnormal proteins called Monoclonal Proteins abbreviated as M Proteins. Each type of plasma cell produces only one type of Ig's. They are:

IgG: Antibodies used to fight bacterial and viral infections. This is the most common type of monoclonal protein in MM.

IgA: These antibodies are present in the mucous membranes of the gastrointestinal and respiratory tract as well as in saliva and tears.

IgM: These are the first Ig's produced when exposed to an antigen (toxin or foreign substance). They fight blood infections.

IgE: Fight allergic reactions in the lungs, skin and mucous membranes.

IgD: Normally found in very small quantities, this antibody protein is not completely understood.

SPEP: Serum Protein Electrophoresis is the test used to separate and identify the levels of M Proteins (monoclonal) in the blood. That is, the Ig's listed above.

M Spike: In multiple myeloma, one plasma cell goes bad and makes multiple copies of itself (clones). Each copy makes the same antibody protein or M spike. SPEP is used to separate and identify the presence and levels of M protein in the blood. Patients with a higher M spike (greater than 1.5 g/dL) are at a higher risk of disease progression.

Note: I have experienced levels of 2.5 g/dL for extended periods of time and thus higher levels of disease progression)

Serum free light chain assay: Smaller units called heavy chains and light chains make up Igs. Produced within the plasma cells, these heavy and light chains bind together to form whole Igs. Typically producing more light chains than required, the cancerous plasma cells then enter the blood as free light chains. The presence of an M protein is consistent with the excess production of 1 type of light chain (kappa or lambda).

Note: Kappa Free Light Chains can lead to kidney failure. Although my levels of KFLC's have been extremely high, my kidneys continue to function normally. Lucky me.)

Remission: Remission simply means that there has been a decrease in the amount of myeloma as a result of your treatment. In myeloma, there are many kinds of remission. For those patients with a measurable "M spike," a partial remission means that the M spike has decreased anywhere from 50% to 90% of the level it was immediately prior to treatment. A very good partial remission refers to a 90% or greater decrease in the M spike. A complete remission means that the M spike is no longer detectable and there are less than 5% plasma cells on a repeat bone marrow biopsy. A stringent complete remission meets all measures of a standard complete remission, but also includes a normal serum free light chain ratio and the plasma cells on the bone marrow biopsy must be polyclonal.

Note: Chemotherapy treatments reduced my M Spike from 2.5 g/dL to 1.3 g/dL prior to my Autologous Stem Cell Transplant in Jan of 2017. Post-transplant, my M Spike was .6 g/dL. Compared to the 1.3 level, I had a partial remission for which I received 17 months of greatly reduced myeloma and a return to much better health and activity levels.)

My Life Before Myeloma

I Am Special

Special in the way everyone is special.

We all have gifts and talents, and we generally think our level of uniqueness is small and unimportant when compared to others. Our names will not live on through the ages like Beethoven, Lincoln, Aristotle, Babe Ruth or the person I believe did more to change the world than any other, Jesus Christ. You probably wish you had more money, were taller, thinner, more athletic, smarter or better at your job, or could drive a golf ball 300 yards. But if you have ever given $1.00 to a homeless person, offered a sincere compliment to a stranger or performed any of a thousand other acts of kindness, your contribution to this world is great.

As with any deadly illness, one can see life closer to its end rather than at its beginning. Naturally, this may cause you to take stock of your life more seriously than ever. I certainly have. And I find myself wanting more in so many ways. And if you're lucky, you have time to make changes and create something positive out of an undesired turn in your life. For example, I have not been as giving with my financial support for my faith and for charitable organizations. In fact, I've been quite selfish with my blessed financial situation. That has changed. We are now giving financial support regularly to a church or charitable organization. And it feels really good to do for others no matter how large or small that level of sharing.

Think about it. Do it. Make your changes as guided by your conscience. Just be sure to dwell on the positive and your contribution will be enormous.

Oh My! More About Me!

A Fighter's Blood

I was born on March 14, 1954, in Louisville, Kentucky to Fred and Jane Moffatt. My sister, Mary Jane, arrived 13 months earlier.

I'm a baby boomer. The 60's and 70's seem to have been a more idyllic time despite serious social upheaval during those years: civil rights, Vietnam, Watergate, the energy crisis. But each generation no doubt looks back upon their youth with rose-colored glasses.

We never locked our doors. My Dad left his keys in the ignition when he parked the car around town. We actually played outdoors, often 'till dark with no fear of harm or great injury. Everyone's parents kept an eye out for everyone's children. It was a good time to be a kid.

Does your family tree affect your disease and outcomes? I think my family history and bloodline is what keeps me going when others may suffer less fortunate outcomes.

Forgive my inclusion of family members whom you will never meet or may not have any interest in. But I believe the bloodlines we inherit can give insight and encouragement to managing our disease. Let me briefly introduce them.

Fred T. Moffatt, Sr.

Born and raised in Dundee, Scotland, we called him Granda. He lied about his age to enlist in the Black Watch during WWI. He served four years, escaped a concentration camp, and recovered from injuries at Buckingham Palace. We have the handwritten letter King George V penned congratulating him for his service to his country. Granda was a successful and well-known Minister and Preacher at the First Baptist Church of Frankfort, Kentucky for twenty-four years. He always appeared to me to be a very meek and mild personality. I think he was one tough cookie. His Scott blood runs in my veins and has helped me survive a high degree of disease.

Fred Moffatt, Sr. (Paternal Grandfather)

Mary Martin Moffatt

Born and raised on a farm in Pickens, South Carolina., we called her Gaga, long before there was a Lady Gaga. She met Granda at Carson Neuman College at a time when few women attended college. She double majored in Chemistry and Home Economics earning all A's and only one B. She excelled at everything she set her mind to. Gardening, sewing, needlepoint, crocheting, quilting, knitting; her hands were always busy. She was a Bible Scholar equal to or even greater than her husband. And the best cook to ever set food before me. A brilliant woman.

Mary Martin Moffatt

Patrick C. Morrison

Our Maternal Grandfather was an Irishman and a notorious defense attorney in Mobridge, South Dakota. We called him Grampa. Mother took us by train every year to visit Grampa and her brother Pat. I was in cowboy country and the adventure of train travel and the wide-open western landscape is forever etched in my mind. Grampa purchased a summer cabin on Rapid Creek in Hisega, South Dakota. Twenty-five minutes from Rapid City, Hisega is firmly planted in the Black Hills. If I could turn back the clock, that simple summer cabin would be my first destination. The Hisega Lodge is still operating as a B&B and if you're traveling to the Black Hills, you should spend a few days there. It's beautiful. As you can see, there's a good supply of Irish blood in my veins. Scot and Irish! MM has a fight on its hands.

Me, Grampa, and Mary Jane

Me and MJ at Hisega, SD

Hisega Lodge

We never knew our grandmother, Mary Morrison. She died of a brain tumor when our Mother was only 17. I hope to meet her in the next life.

The First Generation of Moffatts: Fred Sr., Fred Jr.,
Jimmy, Don, and Mary

Fred T. Moffatt, Jr. and Jane Morrison Moffatt

Mary Jane and I hit the jackpot with our parents. My Dad felt God's call and followed in his father's footsteps as a Minister and Preacher. My Dad was my best friend, pastor, preacher and confidant. We could talk about anything with nothing but love and support being the outcome. Dad was intelligent and the hardest working man I have ever known. He passed along his love of cars and motorcycles to me, and we spent hours together in deep motor head conversation. His two largest pastorates were the First Baptist Church of Shelbyville, Kentucky and Heritage Baptist Church in Annapolis, Maryland. He was a moderate theologically which some church members would take issue with, but I can't recall anyone who disliked or spoke ill of my Dad. I'm so proud of all he accomplished and his unrelenting service to others.

Fred T. Moffatt, Jr. and Jane Morrison Moffatt

Mother was the consummate Preacher's wife. She had a beautiful Soprano voice, excelled at the piano and was always ready to work alongside Dad whenever needed. She majored in Speech and Communication in College and was equal to Dad in her ability with public speaking. She gave Mary Jane and me such a great childhood. Always available and ready for something fun and interesting, we shared so many great times of joy and laughter together. Mother died from Alzheimer's at the age of 80. How I wish she could have been spared such an awful fate. But her bloodline was strong too. She never complained and I never saw her feel sorry for herself even with the diagnosis of Macular Degeneration and later, the onset of Alzheimer's. She was one tough cookie.

Mary Jane Yates

My sister, Mary Jane Yates (MJ) has been so supportive and helpful to me. She has beaten breast cancer and suffered the loss of the love of her life, Joe Yates. Joe became ill suddenly and required a double lung transplant and open-heart surgery at the Cleveland Clinic. He was in ICU for 9 months and MJ lived by herself in a nearby hotel to be near him every day. He was moved to a step-down clinic in Louisville closer to

Mary Jane (Moffatt)

their home but his time there was short lived, and he was returned to the Cleveland Clinic. Joe was ready to be freed from his confinement and taken off life support. He died on December 16, 2019. Such a tragedy. This has been gut wrenching for my sister, and I don't have to look outside of my immediate family to see someone who has and is enduring terrible loss. I love you MJ and continue to pray for the peace you need and deserve.

Family time: Fred and Jane Moffatt and Mary Jane and me

Beyond the bloodline, other external factors have been an influence on me as well and shaped my resolve to fight and never give up. I learned to resist and fight back against bullies and unfair treatments early in life. I remember at a young age, stopping at a gas station with my father for some directions. The three men behind the counter were using foul language. In a loud and "I'm not messing around voice", dad told the men he did not appreciate that language in front of his young son. Quiet descended, heads were turned away and directions came forth without incident. Scared me a bit, but my dad was fearless. Dad also had an encounter at a basketball game with a drunk and disruptive obnoxious fan. He turned to the man a few rows up and asked him to stop shouting obscenities and spilling his beer on other people. The man did not cooperate, and my father got him removed from the game. He had his limits for bad behavior no matter where, when or who was involved.

Driving home from church one night, my sister, mother, and I started singing a hymn at the top of our lungs and laughing like crazy. A cop pulled us over, for what reason I can't recall. My mother was pleasant and polite. The officer was rude, and she quickly changed her demeanor. Ever seen by me as a soft spoken and courteous woman, I saw a new side to mom. She got right in the officer's grill, expressing her disappointment at the treatment she was receiving. She told him this would not end at this confrontation. She went to court, got the ticket dismissed, and the Judge expressed his disappointment in the officer. Go mom!

As with most people, there were other major influences in my life. I loved TV shows and movies. I had the Internet before there was an Internet. When watching a show of any kind, if something piqued my interest, I pulled down the World Book Encyclopedia and read about the subject. You can pick up a lot of useless, trivial information watching Gilligan's Island, Under Dog, Leave It to Beaver and Get Smart. Alternately, I learned a lot of good life lessons from cowboy movies and shows. Roy Rogers was my early favorite and at the ripe old age of 5, my Father convinced me he taught Roy how to ride, rope and shoot. No wonder my Dad is my hero! Shane is my favorite cowboy movie. The Lone Ranger became my favorite lawman. I don't think he ever killed anyone on his show. He shot the enemy's gun from his hand or pummeled him with his fists. He stood for Law and Order and always let the courts supply justice. I liked the Rifleman too, but he killed someone every week. It was always as a last resort and done in defense of others or himself with a moral accounting to his son Mark at the end.

We have lost something in our society today with the absence of the cowboy and right and wrong.

MJ, her son, Chip, Mom and Dad, and me

Me, MJ, Dad, and brother-in-law Joe

Me, Mom and Dad at the Jefferson Hotel in Richmond, VA

Jobs, Jobs, Jobs

My first big sales job came at 16 years of age with a target market of one — my mother. My Father, who loved everything with a motor, purchased a Harley Davidson motorcycle much to the objection of his wife. Early on, I showed Mother brochures of motorcycles with beautiful paint jobs, designed for the beginner rider. I gained approval and purchased a Honda 350 motorcycle in Candy Apple Red. After an accident with no major injuries to myself and only a sprained ankle to Roger Drury, I got Mother to agree to buy a Triumph 650. My sales career had peaked early.

The people I worked for in my youth were also great role models: Bruce Wells (Home Builder/Contractor) Briggs and Bobby Lawson (Men's Clothing Store), Bill Borders and Shug Hickman (Smith-McKenney Drug Store), Harold Burge (The Convenience Store) and Roland Thompson (Plumber). I think I could have dropped out of College, worked for Roland and been very happy and successful as a plumber. All these men treated me with patience and respect and took a personal interest in me. How I wish a few of the employers I worked for as an adult were as fine and wise as these businessmen.

While I did not become a plumber, I have had a wide and checkered work career. I'm one of the millions of ordinary people that never felt a calling or all-consuming passion to any one life's work. Maybe I should re-evaluate that a bit. I grew up with the cowboy on TV. Loved their sense of justice and the underdog triumphing over the oppressors. Combine that with the Bible teachings I was exposed to, and I wound up with a B.A. in Law Enforcement/Criminology from the University of Maryland. Truth, Justice, the American Way was alive in me. But in 1976, there was a hiring freeze on all government positions. I did get to the end of the application and testing process for the Fairfax County

Virginia Police Department. They could hire three new officers. I came in fourth. Preferring investigate work with the FBI, I contacted them. A four-year waiting list of applicants with CPA or Law degrees was ahead of me. If I had to go to Law School, I'd be a lawyer most likely. Thus, ended that career path and maybe for the best.

The most passionate activity for me has been golf. I played for a couple of years at ages 13 and 14 but became frustrated shooting 83 one day and 96 the next. I wish I had stuck with it. But the bug for golf captured my attention again at age 29. I was working at Frito-Lay in sales and management and had started to climb the corporate ladder. Although we sold fun food, the business was intense. Frito-Lay gave me the best sales training I ever experienced, and they expected results. Golf became a great release from the pressure of long hours and stress at work. By May of 1988, I was smoking two packs of cigarettes a day and totally frustrated with my Regional Manager position. I cashed in my chips, (pun intended) and quit without another job. Man did that feel good. Quit the butts, too!

I played golf every day the next week at Eisenhower Golf Course in Annapolis. Bob Fretwell was the Head Golf Pro, and he was surprised to see me playing so much. It occurred to me to ask Bob for some contacts in the golf club and clothing industry as that would keep me in touch with my passion for golf and make use of my sales background. But Bob had a different idea. He wanted to hire me as an Assistant Pro and get started on a path to be a PGA member. Who me? I had only broken 80 twice and while that's far better scoring than most who play the game it did not sound like the term Pro should apply. But I said yes, and the course of my life was forever changed. I left a $45,000 salary, bonuses, a company car and expense account for entertaining clients for a $15,000 Assistant Golf Pro position at a municipal golf course. Smart, yes?

Bob moved on to a Private Club and the other Assistant Pro I worked with got the Head Pro position. He was Billy Molloy. And man could Billy play golf. He was also a very quiet and shy person and even though I could not hold a candle to his proficiency with golf, we became great friends. I learned so much from him just by watching and observing his play. We took winter trips to Florida with other players for endless days of competition and fun. Billy was killed in a car crash many years ago and I lost one of my all-time best friends. How I miss him.

Eventually I secured a Head Pro job at a Semiprivate, 27-hole facility in Westminster, MD. I came into my own there by dealing with every possible duty a Club Pro could encounter. Running member events, local PGA sponsored competitions, buying for the Pro Shop and organizing large groups of players using the course for all day charitable fundraisers. Unfortunately, what should have been a truly great experience was instead a sizzling pressure cooker with a very toxic environment behind the scenes. I left there in 2006 and my good friend Phil Lande gave me a sales job in the stone countertop business. A very big change but a good one. More money, fewer hours and lower stress. Thank you, Phil!

Looking back, the ten years I spent at Eisenhower Golf Course were some of the best years of my life. After all, I met my wife Sandra there and that has proven to be the greatest thing that ever happened to me. Let me explain . . ..

Myeloma takes things away. I've had to quit working. My shortness of breath is chronic, my energy levels are low, and I have a very elevated heart rate. Physical activity is difficult. I wanted to replace some fun in my life, and I turned back the clock for a motorcycle. Well, three to be exact. Like Goldilocks I had a hard time finding just the right one. First, a Big Dog Chopper. I took a U-Haul to

Georgia to buy it from the owner. It was a work of art, but the foot pegs vibrated so wildly I could not enjoy the ride. Next, a Triumph. Smooth as silk but no wind protection and I wanted something bigger. Finally, a Harley Davidson Street Glide. Perfect. However, my disease was increasing and while I can drive a car safely when I'm tired, not so with a motorcycle. So, Sandra made me an offer. Sell the Harley and get a fun sports car, preferably convertible, that we could both enjoy. I asked her what she thought I should get. She said, "anything you want". Wow. Hey guys, would your wife let you buy and sell 3 motorcycles in eighteen months without complaint and then suggest you spend even more money for something more practical but fun? I'm the luckiest man alive in the wife department. More about Sandra later!

My family history of standing up to steep odds influenced me before Myeloma came to visit. For example, as a District Manager for Frito Lay, three of my route salesmen failed to show for work one tumultuous Monday morning. We only had two swingmen to cover for sick salesmen and they were already spoken for. I farmed out as many accounts as I could to other drivers, loaded a truck and set out to service what customers I could. A particular large volume Deli in a government building in D.C. did not get its delivery and had no chips to sell. He called HQ in Dallas and got the President of Frito Lay on the phone. Not good! My Division Manager was waiting for me when I got back to the office. He was furious and blamed me for not doing my job. The ire in me quickly spilled out. I told Jim it was a joke that a wealthy company like Frito Lay would not hire enough extra swing men/women to cover these issues. I did not apologize or back down. Jim thought I would probably quit and seek work elsewhere. He was wrong and I wanted to shove this down his throat. Months later, Jim was leaving the company and he invited me to dinner along with a couple other employees. The dinner was to award me a promotion to Trade Development Manager. He liked that I stood up to him and did not give up. Thanks Jim. It would have been easier to quit and take a sales job with a major manufacturer of golf equipment. But I could not back down. Not with that resilient flow of family history flowing through my veins.

As an assistant golf pro, I was not naturally gifted as much as I would have liked in ball striking, but I fashioned a good short game, chipping and putting. Part of the Apprentice Program was to pass a 36-hole, one day, playing ability test hitting a target score of no more than 12-14 shots over the course rating for the day. These large events were held four or five times a year, and the pressure to perform was intense. I failed so many times I can't remember the exact number. Then, my home course was invited to host this event. Talk about pressure! Many of the golfing regulars wanted to see me play. My first eighteen holes were a dream come true. I shot 73, only two over par.

On the third nine I did not play as well, and I shot 39 as I recall. I started leaking oil on the last nine, tired from the heat and nervous about keeping my scores in check. I bogeyed 15 and 16. Double bogey on 17. I did not want to count the strokes, but I believed I was still able to pass with a good score on my last hole. An uphill Par four, I pulled my drive left but had a decent lie in the rough. I hit a 7 iron over the top of the pin and faced a twenty-five foot, downhill, left to right putt that would break four or five feet. I could easily three putt— not the way I wanted to finish. So, I holed the putt for birdie and passed my test with a few strokes to spare. I got sprayed with champagne and was relieved to have accomplished the goal required. I've considered myself a good putter ever since that intensely pressured birdie putt dropped.

Dr. Alfred Garfall recently referred to me as "living on the razor's edge with Myeloma". My marrow is 95% myeloma cells, leaving little room for any healthy blood cells of any type and has been at that level for a long time. This month marks six years since my diagnosis and I'm still standing. No infections, no fevers, no organ failure, and I don't look the least bit ill. Something in my constitution is not giving my disease total free reign over me. I believe at least part of that something can be traced to my family roots and their strong constitution, as well as the influence of great people in my work history.

Stand up to bullies! MM is the biggest bully yet. Never give up!

The Love of My Life

Her maiden name is Sandra Kerr (another great Scot!). We met through golf at Eisenhower Golf Course. Her friend Judy wanted her to give up sailboat racing and take up golf. She suggested me for some lessons, **but** she signed up for lessons with someone else. **For** the first time in his teaching career, the guy forgot about the appointment. So, Sandra came and took a few lessons from me.

Being divorced for the past three years and hardly shy, I inquired to see if she might be available for a date. She was quite attractive, and I wanted to find out more about her. But ... she was married. So sad, so bad. But a year later, she separated from her husband and headed toward divorce. *Bada boom bada bing.* We played golf together for the first date and she seemed relatively uninterested in me until the first tee shot. Was my swing really that impressive? By the third hole I could tell there was mutual interest. The rest is history. What a lucky man I am.

Sandra drove a Mercedes Benz 2 door convertible roadster. She had this awesome Chocolate Lab named Tally. She learned the construction business from working with her ex-husband and could run her own design/build business. It appeared she had good taste in everything except men, and I hoped to be the exception to that rule. Another date, early in our relationship on a cool fall day, we drove out of her community in the Benz with the top down and Tally perched in the bench seat behind us. Her soon to be ex-husband passed us and her car phone immediately rang. Who's that young guy driving you and Tally. (I'm 5 years junior to my wife). We had a big laugh. Jealousy came a little too late. Gun shy from my first marriage; I took too long to propose and will never live that down. Deservedly so.

We married on February 21, 2003, and it's the best thing that ever happened to me. She brought her immediate family with her. Sister Cheryl, her husband Cliffe, and their children Alex and Emily. Jackpot again. Who could ask for better family relatives? Sandra had a long list of fabulous friends that immediately became my friends too. My parents were so happy with her. Mom and Dad lived in Richmond, VA at the time, and we joined them for Thanksgiving brunch at the Famous Jefferson Hotel in Richmond. Friends of my parents, Waddy & Zena Jesse, were also present as they would all leave the next day for a trip to Williamsburg, VA. Sandra and I shared plates of food together and made no effort to conceal our attraction. The next day, on route to Williamsburg, my dad announced to Waddy, Zena and my mother that if we shared one more bite of food he would vomit. So glad to make a good impression.

Sandra and Bruce Moffatt

My world has been full of happiness and joy since Sandra came into
my life. I don't think we've had more than three or four arguments in
the past 25 years together. She rises early, ready to face the day and work,
work, work. She cannot sit still. She is so like my father in this respect as
well as in the success she brings as the Construction Manager for McHale
Landscaping Design/Build Company. She deserves a better husband, one
capable of providing for her as he works while she enjoys retiring to a less
demanding and stressful job. How I wish I could give her that.

It's scary to think what my life would be without her. The fabulous home we have is a product of her design and remodeling skills.
Our pool and patio would have cost so much more without her expertise. I could not have indulged myself in cars and motorcycles
without her willingness for me to search for some largely unnecessary
distractions due to cancer. And would I have our precious children
Choco & Latte? These two Labrador Retrievers give us joy and laugh-

ter every day and add so much to our lives. Dogs are the best and two dogs are one hundred times better than one dog. She has been my medical advocate, attending doctor appointments, taking notes and making sure we are all communicating effectively. This is so important, especially early on in dealing with the overwhelming amount of information about treatment and schedules.

> *Thank you, Sandra, for choosing me and loving me. Having you in my corner, knowing I can trust you in all things, without hesitation or reservation has given me the best years of my life. I love you so much.*

Can you tell I'm blessed beyond what I deserve? I can. I hope you are too. As you may recall from several pages ago, I expressed how we all have gifts and judging yourself by the accomplishments of others is a false equivalency. But I think you can see this would be a very easy trap for me to fall into. I am surrounded by family and friends who have led amazing lives and achieved so much. I believe a large amount of historical family DNA has passed to me and has helped me face this chapter of my life with courage and optimism as well as physical resistance to my disease. I pray you also have strong family DNA and role models in your life that uplift you along your personal journey with MM or any other serious illness you are facing.

Sandra and Dad at an Orioles game

Rock Paper Scissors: Multiple Myeloma And Cancer

Discovering My Myeloma

I've enjoyed good health for the first sixty years of my life. Heart disease runs in my father's side of the family, so attention has been paid to have regular visits with my cardiologist and do what's necessary to avoid having my chest cracked open to install new plumbing. Mission accomplished to date.

Around 2013, I noticed I was starting to get short of breath bounding up a flight of stairs or even simply walking up a few flights. Not terrible. Different. Labored. Well, I was 59 years old, working a job with an hour and a half commute, with longer hours and a lot more stress. My diet was not optimal, I was not exercising, and I needed to lose about 20 pounds. Seems reasonable I was not in cardiovascular splendor. I did not take medical action.

In September of 2014, my nephew, Alex Cheston, was getting married to his lovely fiancée Sophie in San Francisco. This was a great opportunity for a weeks' vacation and escape the stress and rigors of work. Sandra and I jumped at the chance. Alex's parents, Cheryl and Cliffe, rented a house for our accommodations, and we looked forward to a great week and a very special family affair.

As if the cake needed more icing, Cliffe is very well connected in the golfing world; he's a member at two great courses in the Philadelphia area. Cliffe secured a tee time for us at the San Francisco

Golf Club. This is a renowned private course complete with caddies. If you have never played golf with a caddy, you're missing a great experience. Walking the course without having to carry your clubs and have someone familiar with the nuances of the layout advise you before you hit a shot, creates the optimal way to play. At least I was walking!

I can't recall the exact hole I was playing, but my shot to the green was only about 100 yards. I hit a good shot and started walking the gentle uphill slope to the green. When I arrived at my golf ball, I was breathing heavily. I told Cliffe I thought I had a problem, and something may be wrong.

Still not taking quick action (stupid me), I finally saw my cardiologist around June of 2015. A stress test showed some concerning changes, and a heart catheterization was scheduled. I probably had a blockage in an artery and maybe a stent or two would resolve the problem. But there was only one small constriction in a blood vessel and a stent was installed which made no difference in my lung capacity. What did show up was an elevated protein level in my blood. For this, I was directed to see Dr. Flavio Kruter, an oncologist at Carroll Hospital Center in Westminster, MD, where we were living at the time.

More blood tests were ordered and while a diagnosis was not yet confirmed, I knew there was a problem. Dr. Kruter performed a bone marrow biopsy, and the results took about a week to come back. We met in his office on July 23, 2015, and he gently informed me I had Multiple Myeloma.

Dr. Kruter was very positive about managing this disease. While no cure existed, therapies were allowing many people to beat the odds and have a good quality of life for many years to come. As I stood to leave, Dr. Kruter gave me a hug. I will never forget this kindness and his willingness to share his humanity with me. I imagine most doctors try to keep their emotional distance from patients for their own self-protection. Dr. Kruter's kindness sets him apart and above his calling as a healer. My spirit was uplifted despite the news that my health was diminished.

I left his office and got in my car. It was a beautiful day. Warm and sunny with a blue sky and a few large white clouds. A rather perfect weather day. I sat still waiting for a reaction. Would I start to cry? Would I feel I didn't deserve this; so unfair? What will the future hold? I had no real reaction to any of this. No tears. No self-pity. Myeloma was a fact and facts had to be faced and dealt with.

I called Sandra from the car and gave her the news. When she got home from work, we hugged but did not cry. We opened a bottle of wine and decompressed from the news. I emailed my father who lived in Kentucky and shared my news. His hearing had become so bad it was very difficult to carry on a phone conversation. He reacted as expected; encouraging and positive while expressing his sorrow at the diagnosis. If he could take this on in my place he would do so without hesitation. I also emailed my sister, Mary Jane. I knew if I called her, she would start to cry and that might domino back on me. I was not ready for tears and mourning.

September 22, 2015, I was home in bed with cold chills and a fever from my medication. As I surfed the TV channels, I landed on a Billy Graham sermon. I don't remember his words, but the tears finally came, and I mourned the loss of my health. The tears came in three waves. After the third round, I felt cleansed. Time to move on and take each day in stride and do whatever necessary to ride the ups and downs of managing this disease that were sure to become a driving force in my life.

As you will read in the coming pages, this journey has had many twists and turns, ups and downs. As of the date of publication, I'm still standing (August 2021), beating the odds, awaiting the next new treatment that holds great promise for beating back my disease, and giving myself more time with better health and the ability to enjoy life with less limitations.

I'm so lucky, so blessed in so many ways.

Doctors and Nurses
(The Rocks of Your Care)

I HAVE BEEN TRULY BLESSED with the Doctors who manage my care. The first oncologist who worked with me was Dr. Flavio Kruter in Westminster, MD. He diagnosed my illness and oversaw my treatment for about ten months prior to introducing me to Dr. Ashraf Badros, a Multiple Myeloma Specialist at the University of MD Hospital in Baltimore. Dr. Badros is a nationally and internationally known specialist in MM. Having him on my team was another stroke of luck, knowing I was under the care of one of the best of the best.

Dr. Kruter worked to get my cancer markers as low as possible in order to prepare me for an Autologous Bone Marrow Transplant. Initially, I was put on the drug Revlimid (Lenalidomide). It is highly regulated due to its similarity to Thalidomide which causes birth defects in unborn children. The normal dose is a 25 mg pill taken once a day. Everyone can react to medications differently, and Revlimid gave me daily cold chills and fevers. Dr. Kruter reduced the strength to 10 mg and increased the dose by 5 mg each month, until I was able to tolerate the 25 mg formula.

Get to Know Dex for Pain

Dexamethasone (Decadron) was combined with Revlimid. "Dex" is a powerful steroid that reduces inflammation and was at one time the only medication used to treat this disease. I have a real love/hate relationship with Dex. On the negative side, it prevents sleep for about 24 hours or more depending on the dose and creates weight gain.

For me, I gained about 40 pounds due to constant hunger leading to eating too much. As of today, I've lost 25 pounds thanks to Weight Watchers and less use of Dex for my ongoing treatment.

On the positive side, it gives a boost of energy for several days and helps reduce my excessively high heart rate, a side effect myeloma has inflicted me with. It is also the ONLY drug that eliminates bone pain. The cancerous plasma cells in the bone marrow bore little holes in bones to escape the marrow and attack internal organs. They can also form lesions or tumors on your bones and can be extremely painful. This has happened to me on two occasions. Oxycontin, Morphine, Dilaudid and other opioids will not relive this type of pain, but Dexamethasone will. Keep this in mind if you're ever in the ER with bone pain from a myeloma lesion or tumor pressing on your spine or other bone in your body. When the attending physician starts treating you with opioids, do whatever necessary to get him or her to prescribe Dexamethasone. You'll thank me when the relief kicks in.

Autologous Bone Marrow Transplant

Dr. Badros did a masterful job of guiding me and his team through this potentially dangerous but life renewing procedure. This is a process of using your own stem cells to rebuild a healthier marrow after it is destroyed by a powerful drug like Melphalan (Alkeran). The process uses drugs like Revlimid, Dex, or in my case Kyprolis (Carfilzomib) or other chemotherapy drugs to reduce your cancer as much as possible. At that point, a process called 'aphaeresis" is used to extract stem cells from your blood. An IV pulls blood from one arm and runs it through a machine where the heavier stem cells are separated from the blood. An IV in your other arm returns the filtered blood to your body. Collection can take 5-8 hours or may even require two sessions. In my case, more than a billion stem cells were captured over a six to seven hour period. They are frozen in liquid nitrogen until it's time to give them back.

The next step is admittance to the hospital and the introduction of Melphalan or other powerful chemo drugs, to wipe out your bone marrow. This leaves you as "clean" as a newborn baby, but totally void of the ability to fight infections. This is not the time to go swimming in the river near your home or hang out with a friend who has a cold or a case of the flu. You could die without the ability to fight these infections. But a day or two later, a smoking canister of liquid nitrogen will arrive at your bedside. Several small bags of your stem cells will be thawed in a few minutes and given to you via a port that was previously installed in your chest. All done!

Now, the Miracle of the Human Body

After getting their marching orders, your stem cells will migrate to your bones and build new marrow. Some stem cells will become white blood cells, some red ones, some plasma cells until you have a new and healthier marrow operating without myeloma cells or at least a very low level of them. Two to three weeks in the hospital are required to manage any side effects and avoid infections. Then, two to three months at home, largely in quarantine, until your white count, red count, platelet count and other important markers achieve a "normal" level. This procedure was performed on me in January of 2017. I achieved a good partial remission that lasted for about seventeen months, which allowed me to return to work and enjoy a better lifestyle.

A Word About Medication Names

You may have noticed I listed two names for the medications above. This represents the "chemistry name" of the drug and the retail name of the drug. Isn't that special? As if this flood of information is not complicated enough, each drug has two names. Do you need to know both names? Probably not, but I try to learn both. Your doctor may prefer the word Decadron and your name choice is Dexamethasone. Knowing both prevents misunderstanding and shows your doctor the seriousness with which you are involved with your treatment. Involve yourself as much as possible in your treatments!

Dr. Arun Bhandari became my third highly qualified and outstanding caregiver. We moved from Westminster, MD in April of 2016 to Annapolis. The hour plus drive to see Dr. Kruter was inconvenient, so Dr. Badros referred me to Dr. Bhandari. While not the primary doctor treating my disease, Dr. Bhandari has remained very involved in following my treatment and progress. There have been times when I received infusions in his practice and avoided trips to Baltimore or Philadelphia. I have also been admitted to our local hospital or in the ER for emergency treatment on occasion. Since Dr. Bhandari has kept up with my treatments and progress, he has proven to be a valuable resource during these events.

As previously mentioned, my bone marrow transplant (BMT) gave me seventeen months of a good partial remission. Then I relapsed, with the myeloma overcoming the effects of the BMT. Time to move on to new drugs and possible clinical trials. In addition to the relapse, my myeloma is refractory, meaning "does not respond well to treatment". I've had several potent medications and therapies that had no effect on my cancer levels. At those times my disease can get quite high, but fortunately my body has tolerated these high levels, avoiding infections, illness, organ damage or even the outward appearance of being ill. On the opposite side of the spectrum is the famous journalist, Tom Brokaw. He was diagnosed with MM in 2013 and his treatments have contained his cancer successfully for many years. I don't think he has even had a BMT, and I believe his level of disease is currently extremely low or maybe even in complete remission. I hope you will share his experience over mine.

A Turning Point

During a visit with Dr. Badros in November of 2018, his previous hopes of enrolling me in one of his clinical trials or one at Johns Hopkins Hospital evaporated. My options for treatment were becoming limited and clinical trials were not in my future. This was a gut punch and caught Sandra and me off guard. Little information was offered how this change of prognosis came about. It was even suggested I might have only 6 months to live unless one of the few treatments open to me successfully intervened. Mention was made of a drug called Venclexta (Venetoclax) which showed success for patients that had a T (11-14) Gene Translocation. Whatever that was.

We drove home, numb from this news and shared some wine while sitting on our sun porch. Sandra is my rock and she remained supportive and encouraging despite this news. No tears. No panic. We needed to absorb the information and prepare ourselves that this may be a new reality in our lives. We all know we won't live forever, but my impeding death seemed much closer than anticipated. I was prepared to accept this fate, but not quite ready to retreat into a space of gloom and doom. I decided to email the 50+ friends and family I have kept apprised of my journey with this news.

Cheryl Donnelly emailed me back that she would like to put me in touch with Daniela Hoehn. Daniela is a MD, PhD and brilliant Physician in the blood cancer research field. Daniela set up interviews for me with two Doctors in New York City and with Dr. Alfred Garfall at the University of Pennsylvania Medical Center in Philadelphia. Dr. Chari at Mount Sinai in NY and Dr. Garfall each reviewed my history extensively and gave us in depth options for treatment. Clinical trials were back on the table and hope once again filled us with promise.

Why the difference in prognosis? My lengthy history of cancer medications wreaked havoc on my platelets that enable blood to clot properly. A normal platelet count ranges from 150,000 to 450,000 platelets per microliter of blood. Clinical trials often require a platelet count minimum of 50 -75 thousand platelets per microliter of blood and my count was consistently below 50,000. This alone could exempt me from experimental trials. Dr. Badros was correct in the bad news he delivered. It turned out however, that two to three weeks off chemo infusions and my count would rise to the 75,000 units required and the door that closed turned into an open window.

Dr. Garfall has treated me at University of Pennsylvania since that time. We are on the same wavelength and agree to throw everything including the kitchen sink at this disease. He is constantly looking for the next treatment, keeping me apprised of all available options. On our visits, Al is never in a hurry and answers my questions with the obvious authority of someone well versed in his knowledge and ability to make the complicated understandable. I believe he's as good as they come, and I look forward to every visit we have together. Al has placed me in several clinical trials. One trial failed and was later judged to have not been dosed at a sufficiently high level. Another trial did not give a great response but did contain the growth of cancer well enough to continue with its treatment. The best result came from Venclexta (Venetoclax) giving me seven to eight months of a good partial remission. I'm getting ready for my first Car-T therapy which you will read about later. This is a new cutting-edge therapy that holds great promised for remission of this disease.

As I write this, I remain astounded at my good fortune with these turn of events from almost three years ago. Luck? Providence?

Is there an unfilled purpose left for me? Perhaps it's this book. Maybe you will find encouragement or renewed hope from my experiences. If that happens, I will be forever grateful for the opportunity to have my story impact you in a positive way. Never give up. Maybe there's a Cheryl Donnelly or Daniela Hoehn or Alfred Garfall waiting to change your life and give you the gift of living longer. I pray it may be so for you as it has for me.

Nurses, the Rocks of Administering Your Care

Your doctors will direct your care, but the Nurses will deliver it. These men and women cannot be praised enough in my experience for their commitment to their profession and the interest and dedication they will give you. Throughout my journey, I have yet to meet a single nurse that was not eager to help, pleasant in disposition and willing to accommodate my requests for help or assistance.

So, don't be difficult. You may feel bad and be in pain but do not annoy your nurses. Keep them on your side by not directing your frustration toward them. If they can't do something you want, it's not their fault, it will be because the protocol for your treatment prohibits it. In fact, do something better. Get to know them. Ask about their family. How did you get into nursing? Are you married with children? What does your spouse do? Hobbies? Become friends and above all try to interject your sense of humor if you have one. You'll be surprised how your day will get better when you try to make their day better.

A side benefit to my time at the University of Pennsylvania Hospital, is that most of the nurses are young and from all walks of life; gals I would have been happy to date were I forty years younger. And at age 67, happily married and no threat to anyone, a little flirting can be good for both parties.

Medications, the Paper

If you are recently diagnosed, you no doubt have feelings of anxiety and concern. If your doctor hasn't told you, let me deliver this news. Medical science is making great strides in managing and controlling Multiple Myeloma. Powerful drugs in pill or infusion form are becoming approved by the FDA with great frequency and efficacy. If a series of drugs you are currently taking lose their effectiveness, many other options stand ready to take up the fight and bend this disease to their will.

The latest cutting-edge tool for attacking Multiple Myeloma is Chimeric Antigen Receptor T Cell Therapy or more simply, Car-T Therapy. I was due to enter a clinical trial in February of 2019, but Covid 19 closed the door. Celgene Pharmaceuticals recently achieved FDA approval for their version of the therapy named Abecma (Ah beck ma) and I'm in one of the first groups of people to receive this treatment since its approval for use with this disease. Here's the skinny.

This past June 10th, I completed aphaeresis where my killer T-cells that fight infection and disease were extracted from my blood. These cells have been sent to a lab where they will have a re-engineered HIV molecule, incapable of infecting me with HIV, attached to the T-cells. These cells will be replicated over a 4-week period until a sufficient quantity is ready to be given back to me. The new T-cells will target the B Cells, which are present on the surface of the myeloma cells. When they embrace, death of the myeloma cell occurs. Way cool and amazing.

There are risks involved with all therapies. Cytokine Release Syndrome and Neurotoxicity are dangerous side effects. Left unchecked they can lead to death. Fortunately, Dexamethasone and Tocilizumab can quickly reverse these potentially dangerous outcomes. I have experienced both CRS and Neurotoxicity from previous treatments, and they were successfully shut down. A fever of 100.4 or greater is the first sign of trouble. My bout with neurotoxicity was the worst, causing high fever, delirium, a fall, and I couldn't get up. Not pleasant. To closely monitor these events, I will remain in the hospital for seven to ten days after receiving my new T-cells. I will also have to stay within a one hour drive to the hospital for twenty-eight days which requires me to stay in Philly with my Brother and Sister-In-law. Fortunately, we get along famously, and Sandra will be able to drive up on weekends with our dogs for a visit. There is one other major difficulty. I'm not supposed to drive a car for eight weeks. The cruelest cut of all.

In trials, seventy-two out of one hundred people received some level of remission for eleven months on average. Twenty-eight out of one hundred achieved a complete remission, which lasted on average for nineteen months. A repeat of the Abecma therapy is possible though not yet tested for efficacy. Achieving the duration of either eleven or nineteen months of a good response gives me great hope for returning to a more normal lifestyle. The treatments I have received over the past eight to nine months have not been effective other than to stabilize my already high level of disease. The next two months will be challenging, but a good outcome will have me gleefully skipping along, able to play golf and perform other physical activities I cannot currently tolerate. Lowering my elevated heart rate and acquiring more energy for activity would be the best present I could possibly receive.

Janssen Pharmaceuticals has their version of Car-T nicknamed Cartitude; Car-T with an attitude. In trials, 100% of patients achieved a positive response. If success with Abecma declines, perhaps Cartitude will become FDA approved and that will give me another option for remission and life extending therapy.

Are you encouraged? I hope so. Many options for managing this disease are available and more are coming online very quickly.

Six months, eleven months or nineteen months is an eternity for the development and application of new therapies. My goal is to use every drug and therapy known to man in fighting Multiple Myeloma. If my options run out and Myeloma defeats all these efforts, at least I will know I pursued every option medical science has available. For that, I will be very grateful.

Insurance, the Scissors

Scissors. As in cut the legs out from under you. You may be under the impression that your doctor has total control of your treatment and what he says goes. Not quite. If your insurance company, and I sincerely hope you have great coverage, decides for any reason you are not eligible for a certain drug or treatment they will deny coverage. If your doctor is persuasive enough and the treatment is life or death, he may win the battle, but probably not.

Last year, Dr. Garfall wanted to put me on Venclexta/Venetoclax. I was to take four, 100 mg tablets per day. This would be my only drug and the simplicity of not having hospital visits for infusions or other drugs involved was very appealing. As previously but briefly mentioned, this drug was successful for patients that had a T (11:14) gene translocation. A translocation occurs when a piece of one chromosome breaks off and attaches to another chromosome and is common in Multiple Myeloma. But Venclexta was only FDA approved for leukemia, so my insurance company denied coverage. The retail price I would have to pay to get the drug was $122 per tablet or $14,640 for a 30-day supply. Say WHAT? Who could afford that? My Care Team at the University of Pennsylvania contacted the manufacturer, Genentech, and they agreed to bypass the insurance company and give me the drug directly at no charge. Wow. What's up with that? Perhaps they wanted approval by the FDA to charge insurance companies $14,640 for 120 pills for MM and not just leukemia. Giving it for free to MM patients would show the drug's effectiveness and speed the approval process. Whatever the reason, good fortune smiled on me twice. The drug was both free and effective. I got seven to eight months of partial remission before those pesky cancerous plasma cells found a way to overcome the drug.

I turned 65 in March of 2019. I signed up for Medicare Part A but not Part B. I was on my wife's plan through her employment. While this insurance was not cheap (about $600/month) it capped out of pocket expenses at $2500 per year. This insured a low copay for any cancer pills that could cost as much as $15,000 per month. Part D Medicare prescriptions do not offer that type of protection from high prices, so I delayed enrolling in Part B, with a supplemental and a Medicare Prescription Plan. My Cigna coverage renewal was due June 1ˢᵗ of 2021. Fearing a Supreme Court ruling that could strike down the Affordable Care Act and give insurance companies the right to deny coverage for pre-existing medical conditions, I figured it was time to switch to Medicare. I jumped through all the hoops to make this happen and the change was effective June 1 as desired.

My medical team had also reassured me there were co-pay assistance programs we could apply for to reduce the high prices for cancer drugs under Medicare prescription plans. Came time to refill my Pomalyst pills with my new $13.75 per month prescription plan. Twenty-one pills cost $3200 for the first month and $1100 every month after that. Adding insult to this injury, I only needed one refill to bridge me over to my upcoming Car-T therapy. I was not going to pay $3200 for twenty-one pills. The drug manufacturer was Celgene and they offered co-pay assistance. Unfortunately, qualifying for help was based on total household income, which they verified with a credit check. I feared we earned too much as we both collect Social

Security, and my wife is still working full time. Alternatively, they would supply this drug for free once you spent 3% of your total annual gross household income. Still expensive. The pharmacy that supplied the drug offered assistance programs, but we earned too much money. Bree Vaotogo, an RN on my Care Team at the University of Pennsylvania, sent me a message to call the Health Well Foundation. They offer grants to help pay for drugs for many diseases.

When I spoke to the nice young lady on the phone, my frustration with this entire process was evident and I just wanted to cut to the chase. I asked her directly how much you can earn and still qualify for help? Without divulging our income, I once again informed her we may earn too much, and acceptance was unlikely. I did not want to waste her time or mine any further. She had more patience than me, thankfully, and encouraged me to take ten minutes to input my information. What was the result? A grant for $11,000 that could be spent on any Multiple Myeloma medication for the next twelve months. Boy did I feel stupid and blessed at the same time. I did not want to misrepresent our income throughout this process but the prices being charged for these medications were all over the map. It may be too late at my age to show greater patience in dealing with these types of frustrating issues, but I could certainly have done a better job.

This got me thinking. On my wife's plan with Cigna, I paid a $60 co-pay for Pomalyst. According to the Cigna website which records all my treatment costs, they paid $19,774.92 for every twenty-one pill supply. YIKES! Did they really pay that much? Cancer is rampant in our society. How could any insurance company afford such an exorbitant amount of money for a drug? Something seems very rotten in Denmark as the saying goes.

Lastly, the craziest part of this issue is any drug given to you in a hospital as an infusion or in pill form will be covered by the medical portion of your insurance. However, if the medication can be taken in pill form, it is funded through the prescription portion of coverage and can lead to these enormous prices. Makes no sense to me.

Another issue. Stay on top of your insurance records. If you get a bill that you think you don't owe, be prepared for multiple phone calls, leaving voice mails that will not be returned and potentially long waits to resolve an issue. Most hospitals and doctor practices have moved their billing departments off site to companies that may handle billing for several clients. Their address will not be made available to you. Communication will be done by phone or fax. Good luck trying to get an email. That won't happen. I had a medical billing issue a couple of years ago and the person on the phone had to forward the information to another department where I was told it could take several days for a resolution and another seven to ten days to receive a fax or mail response verifying the outcome. Is it the 21st Century or 1843 when the first fax machine was invented?

Learn from My Experiences

BE YOUR OWN ADVOCATE.

Write down questions before you visit with the doctor.

Record the answers. You can use pen and paper or record the session on your phone to play back later. I have never had a doctor refuse my request to record the visit.

When you hear a word or phrase you don't understand, ask for its meaning.

When a drug name is mentioned, it won't be called Big Blue #3. Get the correct spelling. You may want to Google the drug later. If you do, the first paragraph or two may make sense and be understandable. If the scientific process relating to the drug is discussed, it will likely make no sense to you, unless you're a big smarty pants versed in biology and chemistry.

Especially early on, bring a spouse, family member or friend to your appointments. Ask them to listen carefully and take notes. A flood of information will be discussed; like filling a teacup from a fire hose. An extra set of eyes and ears will be an asset.

Bear in mind, your doctor sees many patients every day. He or she may review your history or recent blood tests for the first few minutes of the visit to get caught up. You will probably get fifteen to twenty minutes of their time. They will never start an appointment on time but being organized with your questions and concerns will help keep everything as efficient as possible. This will help your doctor and it will not go un-noticed.

Get used to needles. I can't count the number of blood draws and infusions I've had over the last six years. If a phlebotomist draws your blood, a small thin needle will be used and inserted in the crease of the elbow. I prefer to watch the needles go in and usually I can't feel a thing even though I see the puncture. IV needles are larger in diameter and longer. The initial push in will sting a little. I prefer they use a vein in the back of the hand, which allows me to freely bend my wrist and elbow. The needles are flexible, but I don't like the sensation of them bending when I flex a wrist or an elbow. Just my preference. Some infusions may take 30 minutes. I've had others that take 4 hours plus.

Lastly, if possible, try to find a doctor to treat you at a large, teaching University Hospital. These institutions will usually have multiple oncologists well versed in Multiple Myeloma. They meet regularly to discuss their patient's progress and exchange ideas for treatments moving forward. They can also attract multiple clinical trials as the pharmaceutical companies know they are well set up to administrate the complex list of protocols that must be strictly followed. Straying from the rules and regulations will present problems with FDA approval and add unwanted delays and expense to the process. And clinical trials are expensive. Many clinical trials offer room and board as well as travel vouchers for the patients. One of the trials I participated in required a three day stay in a hotel near the hospital. The drug company put me up in a $250 per night upscale Philadelphia hotel. Upon check in, the hotel manager waited on me and decided to upgrade me to a penthouse suite. No extra charge, just a gesture of kindness. The cost of trials can run as high as $400,000 to $500,000 per person. This leads to the high cost of new medications or therapies. I have been lucky to participate in several trials and will probably have more of them in my future.

Sharing My Journey with Family and Friends Through Email

THE FOLLOWING PAGES CONTAIN THE emails I sent to my Friends and Family to keep them up to speed on the progress of my illness and the steps taken to arrest the disease. Turns out I sent a lot of updates over the years and it took quite a while to pull them from my "sent mail" folder. I have listed them in chronological order and hope you will find them educational as well as encouraging. The emails begin with the knowledge something was wrong with my health, largely due to my increasing shortness of breath. This was the only warning sign of my disease and it took me too long to realize something was amiss. Here goes!

Tuesday, June 16, 2015, 9:40 a.m.

Howdy Pardners,

Echocardiogram and Stress Test went well. I did 10 minutes on the treadmill and the technician said the results were the same as my last nuclear stress test. That test went 12 minutes but the extra 2 minutes were dye injection related. Now I wait for the Dr to look at the tests and follow up. May be a few days before I hear from him. ???? Not dead yet!

Fri, Jun 26, 2015, 11:54 a.m.

All went well with my heart catheterization today. Two blockages found. One was close to the point of intersection with another artery and the Dr did not want to stent that area. If the stent protruded into the artery that branches off it could create a problem and block blood flow. If this requires attention in the future it will be done at a larger hospital with a more elaborate cardiac unit in case there are issues. The Dr did not feel this area of narrowing to be as important as the other blockage.

The 2nd blockage was farther down the line from the first blockage and that area was successfully stented. The before and after pictures showed much better blood flow, so hopefully this will relieve my shortness of breath from mild exertion. They did the catheterization through my right wrist and I have a pressure cuff on it to promote healing. The cuff should come off in a couple of hours and I should be back to full use of the wrist in a few days.

I'll be on Plavix (blood thinner) for a year to help avoid rejection of the stent and future plaque deposits. I believe a beta blocker will also be prescribed and I think that will help slow my heart rate. Not completely sure about that, however.

Thank you one and all for your emails of concern and support and especially your prayers to our creator on my behalf. How fortunate I am to live in a time of great medical technology and to be employed with health insurance to make this affordable. I am blessed beyond measure and count each of you a blessing in my life.

Tue, Jul 7, 2015, 4:41 p.m.

Here's more info on my fun with health and Dr visits:

The stent has not produced a dramatic improvement in my shortness of breath from mild exertion. There is improvement, but very little.

On top of this, the blood tests done prior to surgery showed an elevated protein count and mild to moderate anemia. Perhaps this is a contributing issue. I will see a hematologist this Thursday to start the chase down this rabbit hole.

Saw my cardiologist today. He is wondering if the narrowed artery near a descending branch which was not addressed due to possible complications from its location may need a stent to correct any remaining blood flow issues. He will do a nuclear stress test on July 15th. If the test is "positive" he will probably schedule another heart catheterization to implant a stent in the area in question. This will be done at a larger hospital with greater Cardiac Care capabilities in case there are any complications with the surgery. If the stress test is negative, he hopes the Hematologist will have some answers to my anemia and elevated protein count that will restore some normal levels of energy.

So, on we go. Thankful for health insurance and what has been great care and attention from everyone I have encountered at our local hospital and the Doctors and Nurses attending to my needs. And of course, for your continued support and prayerful concern. I am so fortunate!

Thu, Jul 9, 2015, 12:22 p.m.

To Sandra, Fred, Mary

(The heart catheterization was not conclusive in explaining my shortness of breath. Blood tests prior to the procedure identified elevated protein levels. For further investigation I will be introduced to Dr. Flavio Kruter, oncologist at Carroll Hospital Center in Westminster, MD. Dr. Kruter is one of the most respected physicians in this hospital as told to me by the nurses. If you want to know how good a doctor is, ask the nurses. They know who's the best of the best. Dr. Kruter is the first of several specialists to oversee my care and reflects the great fortune I have been afforded for top notch healers.)

Just left Dr. Kruter's office. Too early for a diagnosis so more blood tests will be ordered. My GP had blood drawn during my July 2nd visit and those results were not in my file. Dr Kruter will follow up with my GP to see what the test was for and the results before ordering more blood work. He will then send me a lab slip for any further testing he wants done.

Dr Kruter seemed more concerned about the elevated protein levels than the mild anemia. Could be thyroid issue, bone marrow issue or several other possibilities. He will progress through a series of blood tests to try and pinpoint the root cause. I will go back on July 23rd for a follow up visit. More to come.

Jul 2012015, 7:25 p.m.

Daddy,

I'm so sorry you are having such difficulty hearing over the phone. If I may, could I encourage you to get a new voice to text application for your phone? You used to have one and I think it was helpful. We talked about this many months ago and I did some research on available technology. If memory serves me, the best systems require a 2nd phone line dedicated to the device that prints the words from the caller on a separate screen. The cost would be well worth the investment if it allowed better communication. Maybe your hearing Doctor could offer some recommendations. Think about it and let me know if I can assist you.

I had to deliver some sample displays last Thursday and Friday to customers. Jinal (my Branch Manager) was very thoughtful and concerned about my lifting the display racks and boxes of samples (50-75 lbs.) and he sent a helper with me one day. Of course, I had to assist and not stand idly by. I felt fine until I got up from dinner Thursday night and the middle of my back got very tight. Lying in bed overnight made matters worse but getting up and walking around lessened the pain. I delivered more displays on Friday (against Jinal's wishes) and while I did not aggravate the condition further, it did not help matters. I went to work on Saturday and had almost no pain, but I needed some rest Saturday afternoon. Being in bed today actually makes the discomfort greater when I try to get up. The deliveries are finished, and I will not be doing any heavy lifting this week, so I hope to be much better very soon. I'm having a hard time adjusting to the fact that my age and physical condition is diminishing my ability to perform manual labor or exercise. I must lose some weight and make some form of exercise a part of my daily routine.

I will have a nuclear stress test this coming Wednesday at 1 PM. If the result is "Negative" further heart catheterization with a stent for the narrowed artery near a descending branch will probably be deemed unnecessary. A "Positive" test result will most likely suggest the need to place another stent in the concerned area. This will be done at St. Joseph's in Baltimore or the Univ. of MD hospital where greater cardiac care is available in the event of any complications during the procedure.

I am awaiting some Lab Slips from the hematologist for testing my blood. As I may have mentioned in an earlier email, Dr. Kruter seemed more concerned about my elevated protein count than the mild level of anemia. He did not elaborate on what he will be testing for specifically, but it will require a process of elimination. I'll have the blood work done as soon as I receive the Lab Slip(s) and I'm scheduled to see him for a follow up on July 23rd.

Aside from all this, life is good. Sandra, Choco and Latte are doing well and feeling good. I will email you regarding the future test results and Doctor visits as they occur. I know you are concerned and knowing you are thinking of and praying for me is a great comfort. Thank you for being such a wonderful Father and Human Being. You are the most important Man in my life. Always have been, always will be.

All my love,

Brucie

Hematologist Report

Thu, Jul 23, 2015, 9:56 p.m.

Daddy,

The elevated Protein in my blood is due to a disease called Multiple Myeloma. It is a type of cancer that begins in the bone marrow and is a cancer of the plasma cells. According to Dr. Kruter, this is a very treatable disease. I will have a skeletal scan and spinal MRI done next Tuesday to shed further light on the disease. Tomorrow morning, I will have a bone marrow biopsy done in Dr Kruter's office and he will do the procedure. Some further urine and blood tests are also being done. I will return for a follow up visit with Dr Kruter next Thursday the 31st for the results of the tests and the scheduling of chemotherapy.

I asked the Dr if this will shorten my life expectancy. He said current treatments should yield at least 10-15 more years. In some cases, a bone marrow transplant can provide a cure and they use your own marrow for the transplant. He also said 10 years is an eternity in medical research and advancements can make big improvements in outcomes.

Well, not the best news but it could be much worse of course. MJ made it through her cancer, and I will strive to follow her example. Thankful for employment and health insurance. One step and one day at a time.

As you know...I love you very much,

Bruce Lee

Biopsy Follow Up

Fri, Jul 24, 2015, 8:43 a.m.

Good morning, Papa,

Just finished the bone marrow biopsy. Not as painful as I anticipated. Only about 5 seconds of discomfort and I'd rate that a 5 on a scale from 1-10. Lab work will be performed on the marrow and reported back in time for our next visit with Dr Kruter.

The Dr is concerned about my back pain. It's no doubt related to the Myeloma and not muscular strain. We will know the extent of the progression of the disease after the skeletal scan and spinal MRI is performed next Wednesday. We meet with Dr. Kruter *on Friday the 31st for the findings.*

Hope you have a great day and fun weekend.

(A bird told me you need your windows washed. Please hire someone. NO MORE LADDERS...I need your promise on that or I will be very worried.

Re: The Day ...

Tue, Jul 28, 2015, 5:26 a.m.

To Fred

Thanks Daddy. All prayers are greatly appreciated. I hope the new voice to text machine will work perfectly. I know it's frustrating for you and I hope this will make communication better for everyone you speak to on the phone.

I'm sorry we did not do anything special for your birthday. After all, what do you give someone who "has it all"? And all the Moffatts fall into that category. We will treat you to an indulgence of your choice when next we are together.

Matthew 6: 25-34 has long been one of my favorite teachings from Jesus. It becomes even more important as we all face my cancer together. I strive each day to not worry about my illness, to remain grateful and positive and accept whatever may come. I encourage you not to worry either. Some day we will all slide into home base and be called "safe". Rounding the bases is challenging but we'll pass them one at a time.

As always, I love you to great extremes.

Jul 26, 2015

From Fred

The week has gone well for both of you, I hope.

The people at Highland, FBC Frankfort & Shelbyville, Graefenburg, St. James Episc., Victory Bap. will all be praying for you and the doctor(s).

Did I tell you that I asked Jane to listen in to my closing prayer each night? She is only two feet away from God and will be heard, you can be sure.

The phone has not arrived. Yours will ring as soon as it does.

I love you both more than you know.

Daddy/Fred

Dr Report

Jul 31, 2015, 11:00 a.m.

Hello to All and Happy Friday,

I need to go to work so here's the short version:

Bone scan and MRI were normal. No holes bored in the bones from the cancerous plasma cells. I do have a compression fracture of T11 in my spine and that is causing my back pain. This is probably related to the Myeloma. I'm going on 10mg of OxyContin for some long-term relief. If this does not heal up on its own a round of radiation to T11 can heal the area.

Marrow biopsy confirmed Multiple Myeloma. Cancerous plasma cells not following their normal life cycle and mutating rather than dying off like they should.

Two scales to measure progression of the disease. One puts me at stage one, the other at stage two. Either way this is good and shows early detection.

Treatment will be done with 2 oral medications. One is a powerful steroid I will take once a week. The other is highly regulated as it contains thalidomide which used to cause birth defects in pregnant women. I take this daily for 3 weeks and then go off of it for one week. This drug can only come from certain pharmacies and will arrive in the mail. It may take a week before all the hurdles are cleared and it arrives at our door. It must be signed for which is a pain so we will see if our pharmacy at Safeway will accept the drug for us. A 3-week supply runs about $10,000 so we will have to see what insurance is willing to pay. If the copay is exorbitant, they will look for other providers that may offer a lower cost. The nurse said a $200-$300 copay is "normal" so hopefully we can get in that price range or less.

At some point I will see another Dr that specializes in Bone Marrow transplants. This could be a "Possible Cure" but not a guarantee. Before that can be attempted the current course of treatment needs to get me in remission. Also, we are in the early stages of the disease so no need to rush into a marrow transplant.

I will see Dr Kruter monthly with blood and urine tests to track the disease and medication progress.

There's probably more but it's like taking a drink from a fire hose....too much information too fast. Sandra took copious notes, and she may add to or correct any information contained herein.

Will follow up later, but for now everything looks positive and Dr Kruter is confident this can be brought under control.

Yippee!

(Not long after my official diagnosis, we returned home one night from dining out and I got down on the floor to play with our dogs, Choco and Latte. Something snapped and I had great pain and difficulty in trying to get up off the floor. I had suffered a compression fracture, no doubt brought on by Myeloma cells boring little holes in my bones to escape my marrow and attack my organs. Healing would take several months, and the first step was radiation treatments.)

Our girls, Latte and Choco

Radiation Therapy

Aug 7, 2015, 9:39 a.m.

Good morning loved ones,

I'm still at the Cancer Center but just finished my consult with Dr. Shambert, radiologist oncologist. The cancerous myeloma cells are prohibiting the bone to heal in my compression fracture. I will undergo 10 radiation sessions specifically targeted to the problem area. Each session only takes 10-15 minutes. The radiation will kill the cancer cells and allow the fracture to heal. They need to "map out" the area to zap and that will be done in a few minutes. My first treatment will be this coming Monday. Hopefully this will do the trick and the back pain will go bye-bye. YEAH!

(My first drug used for treatment was Revlimid along with a weekly dose of Dexamethasone. Dex is a potent steroid used to reduce inflammation. Years ago, Dex was the only option for treating Myeloma. Revlimid is a derivative of Thalidomide which caused birth defects in children when taken during pregnancy. As such, this is a highly regulated drug, and every refill requires 3 interviews over the phone to review risks and proper use and handling. As you will see, the drug was not easy for me to adapt to, and lower doses had to be administered and slowly brought up to full strength. This allowed my body to adapt and eventually tolerate the drug.)

Some Good News

Fri, Aug 7, 2015, 3:36 p.m.

To Fred, Mary, Sandra

Well, I still don't have the Revlimid drug, (the expensive one) but I confirmed the cost through our insurance company, Blue Cross Blue Shield of CA. For a "specialty" drug like this, purchased through an approved provider, my maximum co-pay is $200 per prescription. Also, if I understand correctly, there is a Max out of pocket for prescriptions of $250. So, after the first or second go round I should pay nothing. Now if they will just process the paperwork and ship the drug. It will come from a Walgreens Specialty Pharmacy in Pittsburg, but the lady I spoke to there could not provide a ship date. Hopefully before next Friday. Anxious to get started.

Nice to have some good news for a change. I may die but we won't die broke!

Update

Aug 11, 2015, 11:52 a.m.

Sunday was a good day. 2nd dose of steroids and my compression fracture did not ache as much. Went yesterday for my first radiation treatment on my back. Went to sit down in the waiting room and the chair was lower than expected. In "catching myself" I twinged my back. Brief pain and then OK. The nice nurses got me off the radiation table by each one holding me under my arms and raising me up. A little twinge there but getting up is always the most difficult after lying on my back. I should have done my usual routine of lying on my side, dangling my legs off the side and pushing myself up. Lesson learned.

Came home, ate some lunch, did some computer work and took a nap. When Choco and Latte woke me up my back was in rather intense pain. At the instruction of the Cancer Center, I slithered to the car and got to the ER. They needed to do blood work and a CAT scan but attempted to deal with the pain first. Morphine did nothing so we graduated to Dilaudid. It's 7 x stronger than Morphine and after 20 minutes the pain was down from 9 on a scale of 1-10 and leveled off around a 3. WHEW! Nurse Sandra set by my side the whole time and kept me clam.

The CAT scan did not indicate any additional compression fractures but showed a slight change in the one I've had for the past 5-6 weeks. I guess that's all it took to set off a chain reaction. Next, some Valium to relax the muscles so by the time we left the ER at 10pm I was pretty loose. Slept well and had a 2nd radiation treatment today. They also gave me my first infusion of Zometa to prevent my calcium from leeching out of my bones and into my blood. I'll do this once a month. Still waiting for Revlimid (now at day 12 since first ordered) which turns out to be a chemotherapy medication. Hopefully it will arrive in the next 48 hours. Thank God I'm not sick and in need of this drug right away!

A little more discomfort as I write this but not bad. The radiation oncologist wants me to stay on Dilaudid (short term relief), Oxycontin (long term relief) and Valium 2-3 times a day. It may be several weeks after radiation before the fracture heals and my back stops hurting, so she wants me managing pain ahead of the onset of discomfort. Staying home today, but hopefully I can get out and make some sales calls tomorrow. Will see how it goes.

As expected, this road is not straight and narrow, but time, patience, medication, the awesome Doctors and Nurses along with your very kind prayers and support will someday make this but a memory.

Stay Healthy my Friends!

Aug 11, 2015, 5:56 p.m.

Mary Jane Yates (my sister)

Dear Boo Boo,

It is mighty hard to read about you being in such pain. In my experience, the Golden Rule of managing cancer is "Stay ahead of the pain!" I am very relieved that your doctor believes the same as mine did. If pain is controlled, healing can take place...mentally, emotionally and physically. This illness certainly affects the wholeness of a person and I hate that you are having to see what that's like.

It sounds like you have a wonderful team of folks helping you. Sandra and the children being your first line of defense!! You will develop a life-long love and appreciation for everyone that aids in your care, as you are already experiencing. The two gals that administered my radiation were angels...young, smart and so caring. After 28 days with them I truly felt they were my family. I became friends with an older lady whose appointments were always right before mine. She completed her radiation first and we both cried in the parking lot on her final day. So many good things come from bad. Blessings are everywhere.

I can't thank you enough for the detailed information that you are willing to share. I have been told to stop reading and researching but I'm ignoring that command. I know you are shocked that I would ever disobey! *cough! cough!*

So, here are my questions...

1. How often will you have blood work that checks on your kidneys?

Once a month meeting with Dr Kruter to review blood work.

2. With the Zometa drug, should you have a dental exam?
I was told to watch out for jaw pain and contact the Dr if the infusion causes jaw pain. I'm probably due for a clean and check soon.

3. Will you need a blood thinner while taking the Revlimid?
I'm on a Generic for Plavix as a result of the stent placement so it is doing double duty.

4. Did the doc increase the strength of your Oxycontin?
No. The radiation oncologist said that the Oxy was for long term relief and it may take a couple of weeks to build in my system.

Now, in the words of our blessed Mother "Bruce always listened sweetly to whatever I had to say, then proceeded to go ahead and do whatever he wanted." So, if you don't feel like answering my assault of questions it's ok.

I will look forward to hearing your voice when you begin to feel better. For now, cheers via email.

love you all
MJ

End of Week Update

Aug 15, 2015, 1:07 p.m.

Well, I'm happy to see this week come to a close. As I mentioned earlier, my radiologist oncologist wanted me to stay on OxyContin, Valium and Dilaudid to ensure my back pain was well managed. I did that on Tuesday and Wednesday and could barely get out of bed much less go to work. So, I cut back on the drugs and was able to make some sales calls on Thursday and Friday. But I'm very happy to have nothing to do today and tomorrow but sleep, eat and watch TV. Choco and Latte did not get their run this morning, but I will make up for that tomorrow. Two days without burning some energy and they will bounce off the walls which can be quite hilarious but detrimental to the furniture.

The good news is that the Revlimid arrives today. Sandra is picking it up at the local Walgreens and I'll take my first dose before bed. It contains thalidomide which aids sleep but falling asleep is my greatest talent. Too bad it doesn't cause weigh loss from eating cake and ice cream or add 20 yards to golf shots. Those would be much better side effects!

One more week of radiation treatments on my compression fracture and hopefully it will start to heal. I'll be very happy when I can turn over in bed and get out of bed without discomfort.

Thanks to each of you and many others I don't even know who are praying for us and our doctors and nurses. It's very humbling and encouraging to feel your love and support.

I hope everyone has a great weekend and enjoys the beautiful weather. After all, it's the small simple stuff that often makes the biggest difference.

Aug 19, 2015, 1:31 p.m.

From Fred/Daddy

How is my boy today? Better than yesterday, please, Lord! This myeloma business is really tough, isn't it? Along with good doctors, the right medicines, lots of prayer, a loving and helpful wife, it takes a tough and determined Bruce, right? Well, you've got 'em all, so things are going to get better. Just cannot be soon enough to suit me.

I love you and Sandy and Choco and Latte. May this be a better day for you!

Daddy

Aug 19, 2015, 5:18 p.m.

Dad,

Sorry to report another tough day. Started with terrible constipation. Took meds after radiation and got another low-grade fever with cold chills. Slept for 2 hours and the fever broke. Got more cold chills around 4pm. Shivered under the covers and I am now feeling better. (5pm). My stomach is mildly irritated from the radiation, so eating is difficult too. YUK! Hopefully I'll improve this weekend after the radiation treatments are done. The one positive...my back is hurting less. Count my blessings one by one. Less back pain and my family are great blessings!

The Latest, Greatest and Other Stuff

Sun, Sep 20, 2015, 6:25 p.m.

I got a muchly needed vacation from the Chemo Pill Revlimid week before last. No fevers or cold chills and that was a welcomed relief! Energy still very low as my anemia does not seem to be improving. Shortness of breath continues, and I'm constantly amazed at how easily I become oxygen challenged; a Revlimid and Myeloma side effect. A "shot" is being sent to my insurance company for approval that is supposed to help with my anemia and energy. The drug will take 4 weeks to be effective but the sooner I get it the sooner it may be of help. My stomach is touch and go with occasional queasiness and I started a new prescription to reduce stomach acid and repair any damage from the radiation effects. My back pain has returned but not quite the same; centered laterally around my right kidney and not as much on my spine. It feels more muscular oriented than compression fracture based. I was doing some stretches but stopped as they were uncomfortable and perhaps hurting more than helping.

I've been regularly whining to Dr Kruter's assistant, Dana Sandoval, about my symptoms and she has been very empathetic and responsive. My next visit with Dr Kruter is not scheduled until Oct 6th as he is very busy and has some vacation time scheduled. Dana felt that was too far off and got me in to see him this past Tuesday. Dr Kruter is very happy with the results of Revlimid and Dexamethasone (Sunday steroid). My numbers are improving, and he stated that my symptoms from Revlimid are unusual. The majority of his patients on this drug do not experience the symptoms I am going through, but of course every person is different in reacting to medication. I'm on a lower dose for the 2nd round; 10mg vs 25mg. After 6 days on the lower dose, I'm doing OK. I've been able to get to work each day for the last 2 weeks; a BIG improvement even though I can't give all the effort I'd like. Hopefully the lower dose will still be effective as it is much easier on my symptoms.

So the plan is to stay on Revlimid and see how I tolerate the lower dose. Dr Kruter will most likely raise the strength of the drug moving forward; round 3 at 15mg, round 4 at 20 mg, etc. If the symptoms return, we will change to a different regimen of treatment. This will involve twice weekly injections and twice weekly chemo infusions. I'm ready to switch now but the Dr wants to stay the current course.

As I've mentioned before, the high dose steroid I take on Sundays gives me my best 24- hour period. The anti-inflammatory effects are very beneficial. Last Sunday however I could not get to sleep and probably only did some light napping from 2-4am. This was also my first round of the lower dose of Revlimid after a week off the drug. I blamed the Revlimid for the lack of sleep, but the Dr. thinks it may be the dexamethasone steroid. This only happened once on my first Revlimid dose at 25 mg so I was hopeful it was again a one-time occurrence. To be cautious, I took my steroids yesterday instead of today as going to work on a Monday morning with no sleep is not a lot of fun. Turns out the Dr. was correct. I napped from 4am to 6am this morning and as I write, I am still wide awake. I took 2 Excedrin PM around 2am but got no real assistance from the pills. I now know for the first time in my life how miserable insomnia can be. I have a new respect for the sleeping challenged like my wife. She has weened herself off sleep aids to her credit but has some trazodone (non-addictive) she will share with me tonight.

So that's all the current news that's fit to print. I'm doing better overall but look forward to getting rid of some continuing nagging daily symptoms. I believe this will not be a quick fix and I'm trying to be patient and take the long view. I am fortunate to be in Dr Kruter's care and trust him to take the best course of action moving forward.

I remain a very blessed person, fortunate to have good health care insurance, great Doctors and nurses and such wonderful friends and family. (That means YOU!) There is an army of people praying for me, most of whom I've never met. How cool is that? Very humbling and appreciated. Not every day can be the best day of our lives but it's the small simple things that add up to great memories and getting the most from each day. I hope you are having a multitude of simple pleasures.

On Sep 22, 2015, at 8:22 p.m.

Da,

Today was my first bad day emotionally. My back started hurting again yesterday and I could not get myself out of the house. I watched an old Billy Graham sermon and the tears just happened. Not sure why or what triggered the reaction. I think I just needed to grieve. The prospect of death is a certainty for us all so I can't say my mortality was the issue. Just so many feelings of being blessed but not balancing that with contribution to others. It's so hard to deny self and live for Christ. I so much admire you and Mother for the lives you have led and the help you gave to those in need. You remain my Hero and I could not be prouder of who you are and all your accomplishments. I love you beyond measure!!! I am so happy to be your son.

Sept 23, 2015, 1:08 p.m.

Hi Brucie:

Thanks for your message of last night, which I have just read at noon on the 23rd. First and most important, how I wish I were with you right now so I could put my arms around you and hug you and kiss you and cry with you. It is very normal for you to wonder, "Am I going to die from this thing?" That fear for you has come to my mind more than once, then I grab hold once again the positive message from my family doctor, Ron Waldridge II, from your own doctor and also from people who have had the same disease. We probably face serious injury or death every time we drive a car. However, that is not likely, while something like cancer or a heart attack appears more likely. Although we recognize, for whatever reason, that God does not heal everyone, we do pray and at the same time seek all the best medical care possible. We chuckle in remembering my father's words, "Life at best is very brief, it's like the falling of a leaf, it's like the binding of a sheaf, be in time," yet the message is correct.

Your more-than-kind words about your mother and me are no more true of us than they are of you. Every member of our total family (yes, including my beat-upon brother Jimmy(is, has been, and will be, a fine and moral person, kind, generous, helpful, believing in God and devoted to his purposes. And, if judging we must, my son Bruce and his dear Sandy as well need have no fear when measured against any and all the rest. I know, because I've been a preacher!

Myeloma is a really tough thing to have happened to you, which you "deserve" no more than the innocent baby recently born to Zak and Kristy Yates. We try to build into our lives as many safeguards as possible – insurance, proper diet, check-ups with the doctor, a bit of exercise and good habits, even prayer – and even so, it sometimes seems that life can be a crapshoot. I wonder many times. Why in the world have I been so very fortunate, health-wise and in every other way imaginable? Then I realize, all could change before nightfall.

You are already working splendidly with your fine doctor and his regimen for you. Always popular, you are being prayed for by hundreds of people (at least); example: I've seen Carolyn Hyatt at Kroger's several times lately. Her very first word is "How's Bruce?" And then the second; "I pray for him every day." Knowing her, I believe those prayers are heard by a loving and capable Heavenly Father.

Darling Bruce and Sandy, we'll keep on fighting the good fight, trying our best (and glad for some fun along the way).

More love than you can count or weigh,

Daddy

New and Improved

Sep 27, 2015, 4:33 p.m.

Greetings and Salutations,

It's been a good weekend and we got off to an early start. Sandra's Birthday was Friday, and I took the day off. We drove to Deep Creek, MD where Sandra's long-time friend Elaine has 2 beautiful cabins. The original cabin is a two-bedroom unit and very nicely done. We stayed in the newer, bigger and more elaborate three-bedroom cabin next door. Both cabins are on the highest point of the area with views overlooking the Lake in the distance. Decadent and lovely to be sure. Elaine & Jim, Don & Kris, Bruce & Sandra comprised the attendees.

Friday was a sub-par day for me with some back pain and mildly upset stomach. I also felt "hot" but did not have an elevated temperature. Sandra equates this to menopause so maybe it's just hormonal effects from my medications. I prefer to call this Man O Pause and it may be an apt description. I started a Fentanyl patch this week for some consistent pain relief and I put on a new one every 72 hours. Sandra put a new patch on Friday night and it took greater effect than the first application. I awoke early Saturday morning around 4 am, lying still in bed taking assessment of my condition. Sleep was intermittent so I was still tried. Back pain was gone. Hot feelings/Man O Pause, gone. Stomach settled, no nausea. I was afraid to move. Haven't felt this normal in weeks. Thank you, Fentanyl!! Took my weekly steroid dose at 6 am, looking forward to the improvement it usually brings.

Upon rising I was a little wobbly on my feet. Whatever is in the Fentanyl Patch had me a little buzzed but I'm not complaining. I was able to be more social for the rest of the weekend and my only fear was the insomnia my weekly steroid dose has introduced. My Dr. prescribed Ambien for a sleep aid last week but that made me sick. His assistant, Dana, suggested I try Benadryl. I took 2 capsules last night and slept soundly from 10:30 pm to 6:45 am. I'm on a roll. Hope it continues. Shortness of breath is still an issue, but I take every opportunity to stay motionless and prone. Energy is very low, but I start a shot of some kind tomorrow that should give me a boost. Not sure what the drug is called, but it supposedly takes a few weeks to kick in and I will get this shot every 3 weeks. That assumes the insurance company will finally approve the drug. I'm scheduled for the first injection tomorrow at 9:45 am but I got a call that the insurance company has not cleared the way. I'll be contacted by 9 am to let me know if I should show up for my scheduled appointment. I'm past all my deductibles and the insurance company is now footing all bills. I think they'll pony up, but they are always slow to do so.

They say it's darkest before the dawn. Last Tuesday was a dark day for me; first one I've had. I can't tell why but my emotions got the best of me. I think I just needed to grieve the loss of health and the potential, but not certain, shortening of my life. I could not get out of the house and a few sessions of tears swept over me. It was a relief and by Wednesday and I felt better. And now, there's some dawn on the horizon. My symptoms and side effects have improved greatly and it's wonderful to be alive, more sharply focused on the important things in life, less worried about the stupid things we easily stress over. The future looks brighter and I'm going to stay the course to remission and hopefully a bone marrow transplant and the death of Multiple Myeloma.

Thanks again for your support, prayers, emails, love and concern. It means so much.

Thursday, October 15, 2015, 8:39 a.m.

Greetings Friends and Family,

The past 2 weeks have been much easier on my symptoms and side effects. I cycled off the chemo pill Revlimid last week and start a new 3-week cycle at the same lower dose today. The lower dose has greatly lessened the side effects of fevers and cold chills, a welcomed absence from my daily routine. Dr. Kruter was on vacation for a week and this has pushed my next visit out a bit. I'll see him this coming Monday the 19th and I'm anxious to learn if the lower dose of chemo has slowed the improvement in reducing my elevated proteins and enzymes associated with Myeloma. I'm open to switching to injections and infusions even though I would have to take time twice a week to receive treatment in the Cancer Lounge. Dr. Kruter has indicated this course of treatment to be equally effective to Revlimid, but if I can tolerate a higher dosage without side effects it's worth a try.

My compression fracture is still not healed (may take many more months) but there is no pain most of the time. Bending, stretching or twisting will sometimes remind me to limit my range of motion as I get a twinge telling me not to pass go or go to jail. I've never been a big fan of manual labor so the limitations while often frustrating are not life altering. Some golf would be nice but that will have to wait until next Spring or Summer.

I've had my 2nd injection of Procrit which is supposed to signal my marrow to create more red blood cells. I will get this injection every week and I'm told it will take 4-6 weeks to feel any effect. Hopefully this drug will work as my major issue right now is a lack of oxygen and energy. My hemoglobin count is around 8.4 and should be in the 12-18 range, I think. I'm 61 years old but a couple flights of stairs and I feel 101. I huff and puff but could not blow out candles on a cake; certainly not 61 of them!

All in all, I'm doing much better and enjoying the lack of symptoms and side effects. Hopefully, my medications are still effective at a high level and beating down my cancer. I'll report the findings after my visit to the Doctor on Monday.

Much love and happiness to each of you and thanks for your continued prayers, good thoughts and well wishes....

Bruce

Tuesday, October 20, 2015, 6:34 a.m.

(The time has come to consult with a Multiple Myeloma specialist and work toward a bone marrow transplant. This procedure is a vital component of the accepted protocol for managing this disease. Dr. Kruter will send me to see Dr. Ashraf Badros at the University of Maryland Hospital in Baltimore he is a nationally and internationally known specialist in MM.)

Sandra and I met with Dr. Kruter yesterday. Most of my side effects are gone or greatly diminished. My hemoglobin is up to 9.7 from a low of 8.4, but my lack of energy and shortness of breath form mild exertion remains. My sleep patterns have changed so I wake up every 2-3 hours and have trouble getting into REM stage. After a lifetime of falling asleep quickly and sleeping through the night I can now appreciate the frustration of anyone not blessed with great sleep habits.

Dr. Kruter is tracking the level of a protein in my blood called IGG. The abnormally high level of this protein is a key indicator to Multiple Myeloma. My IGG level was at 6500 when originally diagnosed. Revlimid has reduced that level to 4800 and Dr. Kruter is pleased with the progress. 1600 or near about will be considered partial remission so there's still work to do. I am 5 days into my 3rd cycle of Revlimid at the 10 mg dose. The lower dose has eliminated the fevers and cold chills and allows me to function better and get to work each day. However, 10mg is considered a "maintenance" level dose and moving forward the strength will be increased to hopefully accelerate the road to remission. With some luck, my body will adapt to the drug and higher dosages will be better tolerated. If not, we can switch to injections and infusions of chemo but that will require twice weekly visits to the Cancer Lounge. I'll opt for the inconvenience over side effects if the choice presents itself.

In November, Dr. Kruter will schedule me for an appointment with a colleague, Dr. Badros at the University of MD Medical Center. Dr. Badros is a Nationally Recognized Myeloma Specialist and has been a key participant in many new therapies and clinical trials. He will evaluate my current course of treatment and progress as well as explore the possibility of a bone marrow transplant once remission is achieved. This form of transplant will involve extracting my own healthy marrow cells from my blood, then using chemo to kill (?) my bone marrow and finally re-introducing my healthy marrow cells for a potential cure. I'm not sure if the word cure is appropriate but hopefully there is some chance of eliminating the disease. Recovery from this procedure is about 2-3 months according to Dr. Kruter during which time I will have very little or no resistance to infection. Sounds like fun.

So overall, the news is all good and I am very grateful. All in all, I am a Lucky Boy and I continue to be most grateful for your prayers and concern!

(The following is on an even more personal note. When my Sister and I were 7 and 8 years old, my Father's Pastorate, First Baptist of Paris, KY, held a revival. Sam Gash was the guest speaker for the week. He had a wonderful sense of humor and his preaching tied together the lessons and feelings Mary Jane and I had been experiencing in our Christian up bringing. We both made professions of faith and were baptized by our father during a Sunday night service. Although very young at the time, I have never doubted that conversion experience. My cancer caused me to reflect and examine the shortcomings of my life as a Christian and believer in God, His Son and the Holy Spirit. I felt the need to reaffirm my profession of faith publicly and could think of no better way than to ask my father to baptize me a 2nd time. I'm so glad we could do this and I hold the proud distinction as the only person my father baptized twice.)

Re: This Afternoon and Until Now

Mon, Oct 26, 2015, 3:35 p.m.

Father,

You are my one and only, Father, Pastor, closest Friend. I so look forward to seeing you. I can't explain the emotions I feel when I think of your baptizing me a second time. No other ritual, done by anyone else, could be as important. I feel so blessed and fortunate and am left wondering why I have it so good and others have such difficulties and disappointments in life. I hope Jesus will be smiling as I reaffirm my faith and count it some gain toward the debt I owe him. I have received far more than I have given.

I hope you got some sleep and feel rested today. I'm sure Betty Jean's piano concert was tremendous.

Love abounding,

Your proud son

(Betty Jean Chatham is a concert level pianist and we were so lucky to have her as a member of our church in Shelbyville, KY. Her husband, Don Chatham was our family doctor and they are another example of dedicated Christian servants using their gifts in service to others)

Oct 26, 2015, 12:37 a.m.

Fred

Dearest Son,

Mary Jane, behind the wheel, choked up for a minute when I told her the nature of our phone conversation on your second baptism; I'll not drop out of the sky of immeasurable love and excitement for a long time.

The piano concert at Broadway Baptist in Louisville was well attended and, of course, nobody can touch Betty Chatham at a grand piano (or any other kind, for that matter). Betty can be funny; between one of the pieces, she addressed the crowd: "At First Baptist Church, Shelbyville, I worked with 17 ministers of music. A few of them had talent." There was a roar from the audience.

I got to bed on time and for some while just had lots of good thoughts and thank yous, staring wide-eyed, finally remembering somewhere that if you cannot sleep, get up and read or do something rather than just lying there. So here I am, able to sleep in if needed before calling Pastor Dave Charleton for an appointment to schedule your baptism. (You can see the time it is here right now).

There will be much thought and some writing down beginning tomorrow. I'll send you more e-emails after I talk with Pastor Dave. Right now, I'm hoping our time to be at the start of the 11:00 service, with perhaps a bulletin insert of explanation. Your OK will be needed on everything.

So, dear boy, this promises to be a terrific happening in the life of our whole family.

"You are my beloved son, in whom I am well pleased."

And more love to Sandy,

Daddy

Oct 29, 2015, 4:22 p.m.

Fred Moffatt

Hey Guy:

Our Sunday bulletin is tri-fold, thus three panels, each one about 4" x 11". Here is my suggestion for an insert, subject to your and Dave's approval.

BAPTISM:
"We are buried with Christ by baptism into death, in order that just as he was raised from the dead by the glory of the Father, we too might live a life made new." (St. Paul, Romans 6:4)

Many of you know of my son Bruce and his present struggle with multiple myeloma, a cancer that starts in the bond marrow. He is gradually doing better. On Sunday evening of October 25, as usual each week, he and I talked by phone between Maryland and Kentucky. In the conversation he said he wanted to be baptized again and in a subsequent email wrote, "I can't explain the emotions I feel when thinking of you baptizing me a second time. I am so blessed and fortunate and have it so good while others face such difficulties and disappointments in life. I hope Jesus will smile as I reaffirm my faith and count it some gain toward the debt I owe him. I have received far more than I have given."

On the following morning I called Pastor Dave to ask if this would be all right. His replay was brief and to the point: "Fred, do anything you wish." Oh gee, what if every church had a pastor like ours!" Family members present today include Bruce's wife Sandy, his sister Mary Jane Yates and her husband Joe and her son Chip Snipes . . . and every one of you.

Thanks be to God for this day, this place, and your live, your concern and your prayers.

All the News

Mon, Nov 9, 2015, *3:55* **p.m.**

Greetings one and all,

I'm sitting in the Cancer Lounge getting my monthly infusion of Pamidronate, so I thought use this time to check in. Pamidronate strengthens my bones and prevents the calcium in the bones from leeching into my bloodstream. The process with this drug takes about 3-3.5 hours from start to finish. A similar drug called Zometa only takes 1 hour from start to finish but my insurance company won't approve that drug due to cost. I spoke to the hospital Pharmacist and she originally indicated that the drugs cost about the same. I asked her to check that again today so I could call my insurance company and see if they would reconsider the faster infusing drug. Turns out she mis-spoke on the cost. Pamidronate costs

$40, Zometa is $900. I think I'll pass on asking the insurance company to reconsider.

I'm also due for a Procrit shot today to boost my red blood cell count. My hemoglobin is up to 10.0 and hematocrit is at 31.7 today, so the ratio is good enough they won't give me the shot. I guess that's a good thing except I'd really like more healthy red blood cells. Maybe next week.

Overall, I'm doing very well at present. My compression fracture is not causing any pain and I may try to hit some golf balls this weekend when we visit Cheryl and Cliff in Philadelphia. (My Sister & Brother-In-Law). I'm on my 7 day break from the Chemo Pill Revlimid, and the last cycle did not present any fevers or cold chills, due in large part to a much lower dose. I start another 21 day cycle this Friday and Dr. Kruter is stepping up the dose from 10mg to 15mg. Hopefully my body is adjusting to the chemo and raising the dose will be well tolerated. My only major issue continues to be shortness of breath and lack of energy but I am also noticing some small improvement in this area as well. Not enough improvement to suit, but better. So, no need to whine or complain at present.

Some bad news. Some of you have heard me speak of Ben Witter. Ben was the most amazing human being with a golf club I have ever seen. He made his living traveling the world putting on Power Golf and Trick Shot Exhibitions. He was a multiple time survivor of Cancer in his jaw, but on last Thursday he lost his final battle with the disease. He was only 51 years old and leaves behind a wife, 5 daughters and 1 son. Since I left the golf business Ben and I did not see or speak to each other very often. He has been on my mind lately, due in large part to my own cancer, and I thought about calling him to see how he's doing and let him know of my condition. I waited too late and hate that I did not act in time. Superior athletes can be shallow and self-absorbed; or so it has been my experience in some instances with golfers. But Ben was equally amazing as a golfer and a human being. I shall miss him and make a greater effort not to postpone connecting with people when the thought arises, a bitter but important lesson.

Again, again, again I thank you for your prayers, thoughts and concern. How blessed I am with riches greater than gold and the good fortune to know each of you and so many other people I don't know that have added me to their conversations with God. I hope you are in good spirits, good health and surrounded by friends and family that make life so worthwhile.

(Our time in Westminster, MD is coming to an end as you will note in the next email. Dr. Kruter has been my local oncologist and he has been fabulous. Our new home will be in Annapolis, MD and commuting to see Dr. Kruter will be difficult as it's an hour plus drive away. Two things stand out in my memory about him. First, my wife always enjoyed accompanying me on visits to Dr. Kruter. Why? He's got movie star good looks. Second, after one of my visits with him, our conversation was not particularly encouraging and when I stood up to leave, he gave me a hug. I will never forget this kindness. I'm sure most doctors try to keep their emotional distance from their patients as a form of self-protection when bad outcomes occur. That Dr. Kruter is willing to invest himself more personally in my care speaks volumes about him as both a person and a healer.

Annapolis Here We Come

Nov 15, 2015, 6:54 a.m.

Good Morning loved ones,

Well Sandra has finally found a house in Annapolis and the location could not be better. 2032 Fairfax Rd, Annapolis, MD 21401. Sandra had never been on this street until she saw the listing; I have yet to go there. Fairfax Rd is the first left off of Chinquapin Round Rd as you head toward West St. The house is 3 minutes from Heritage Baptist Church for further perspective. Sandra likes every house on this cul-de-sac which is quite wooded and private. The house sits on a 1 acre lot with 1/2 acre fenced. Choco and Latte will have a much larger playground! Best of all the back of the property is all wooded and will not require landscape maintenance. For what needs attention, I will probably invest in a Zero turn riding mower to make quick work of my historically poor love affair of grass mowing. (Maybe Sandra will like the mower so much that she'll enjoy participating in this activity too!)

Speaking of my dear wife, this location will be awesome for her. Now instead of an early morning commute to beat traffic and still have a 1 hour drive to work, she will be 5 minutes from her West St office. Instead of a drive home of 1.5 hours in heavy traffic, she can get home in the same 5 minutes. This will, on average, save her 2-3 hours of driving every day. Now she can work 5-10 more years bringing home the bacon doing what she loves and eliminating the driving she hates. YEAH!!! And my drive to the office will be about 45 minutes instead of 1 hour and locate me more centrally to the accounts I call on. A win-win for both of us.

The house can be lived in as is but we need to make some improvements. There is only one bath on the main level and 3 bedrooms. (Large unfinished basement and attic but no 2nd story). We want to combine two bedrooms into a Master Suite, Bath and Walk-in Closet just like we did in our current home.

Very exciting stuff. I can live anywhere, in any home, but getting back to Annapolis is great; love that town! That Sandra likes the house and will be so much closer to her work and friends is awesome. If she outlives me, she will be in a much better place and that thrills me. Make you plans for a visit and of course we will keep you posted as events unfold. Life is GOOD!

Much love.

Happy Holidays and All the News

Sun, Dec 13, 2015, 8:36 p.m.

I hope your Thanksgiving was great (ours certainly was with a visit to KY to see family) and you are looking forward to a Merry Christmas and Happy New Year. We have purchased a house in Annapolis and will go to settlement Dec 23rd. Now we just need a buyer for our current home. Our Christmas and New Year are looking to be very exciting. Lots of home improvements before we move into our new home and Sandra is in full gear with the remodeling plans.

My Multiple Myeloma has continued to improve but not as quickly since the dose of Revlimid was lowered. My last cycle was increased from 10 mg to 15 mg without any side effects other than my lack of energy and low aerobic capacity. This seems to be a constant companion. Tonight, I start a new 3 week cycle at the full strength of 25 mg. Hopefully, my body has adjusted to the chemo and the fevers and cold chills from my first cycle of 25 mg will not be repeated.

My hemoglobin has been steady for several weeks at 10.2 to 10.5 which is good news. Normal is 12-18, but the shot I have been getting to boost these numbers is very expensive so the insurance company won't pay for the shot unless I fall below 10.0. Happy the numbers are holding steady but I wish they would continue the shot until I get to a more normal range. I could certainly use the increase of healthy red blood cells.

My weekly steroid dose continues to rob me of 1 night of sleep and I'm also going to blame my weight gain on the steroid as well. I'm at 220 pounds and that's way too many pounds to carry around. I started to cut back one day last week and reduced my calorie consumption to about 1500 calories. The next day I was so hungry I could have chewed off a finger. Not wanting to lose a digit, I opted to eat more food. WOW, such will power. But maybe my body has enough to put up with and I'll do better when I no longer take the drugs I need right now.

I'll see my Doctor again on Dec 30th and hopefully the increased dose of chemo will show a larger decrease in my blood protein and IgG levels. (Immunoglobulin G (**IgG**), the most abundant type of antibody, is found in all body fluids and protects against bacterial and viral infections) The protein goal is 1600 and considered remission. I'm at 3900 now if I remember correctly; down from a high of 6500.

Thanks to each of you for your continued prayers and well wishes. They are not taken for granted and greatly appreciated! I hope you have a Joyful Holiday Season in the coming weeks.

Getting Better

Sun, Feb 7, 2015, 3:45 a.m.

Greetings and Salutations,

It's been many weeks since I last gave a Multiple Myeloma update, so your vacation is now over. I finished my 2nd round of full strength chemo pills last Monday and I'm pleased to say the side effects have been minimal. Dr. Kruter wanted 2 cycles on the full dose before running the blood numbers and my visit with him Jan 28th showed good results. (3 weeks on the pills then one week off = 1 cycle) My protein levels were 6500 in July and they are now around 3300. A lot of cancer cells have been killed and I am now in 1 of 3 general categories of remission:

1. A 50% reduction in Protein Levels is termed a Good Remission. Kinda like a kiss on the cheek.

2. Getting closer to 1600 for Protein Levels is a Partial Remission. Aimed for the lips, slid off and got part cheek part lip.

3. 1600 is normal for Protein Levels and this is a complete remission. Full frontal, on the lips, got a dizzy kind of feel-

ing kiss. Ooh-La-La! (Unfortunately, not a totally accurate or best definition of remission and complete remission.)

I've made very good progress but still have a lot more cancer cells to kill. And this will become harder to do as the numbers improve. At first, there are so many cancer cells, the medication can easily hunt and destroy. But as the cancer cells diminish, it's harder for the medication to kill what's left at the same initial rate of destruction. (This could be a movie. Start with Kissing, move to Killing) Unfortunately, Complete Remission does not equate with Cured. There will still be cancer cells present, but not enough to elevate my Protein to an abnormally high level. And here's where the difficulty lies. Modern medicine has many drug therapies and techniques to achieve remission. What is not known is how to keep patients IN remission. I've spoken to people whose initial remission lasted 1 year and others 10 years and counting. Like everything else in Life, it's wait and see what happens. Relapse is greeted with new drugs and maybe a bone marrow transplant (hopefully no transplant as I hear the recovery is quite brutal) but happily, achieving remission is not a one and done proposition.

Hemoglobin (red blood cell count) is steadily above 10.0. This is still below normal but high enough that I won't be getting any more Procrit shots to raise the level. The shot is very expensive so the Insurance Company deems me good enough to get through the day. I'm still anemic and easily out of breath but doing OK. Fortunately, my sales job does not require a lot of 100 yard dashes. Driving a car, talking to people and typing do not require great aerobic endurance. Life is Good!

My once-a-week steroid dose produces increased hunger and lack of sleep. But last night, now today, I changed the hours of rest. Fell asleep at 8:30 PM, woke up at 12:30 AM. (Usually, I sleep from 230 or 330am to 630am) Maybe I'll get a nap in a few hours but overall, it's not a big issue. I have all day today to rest up and I'll get back to 7 hours sleep tonight.

My compression fracture feels healed. No pain and I can get in and out of bed normally without issue. (That used to be a big issue) I can do more lifting without problems too but I'm not pushing to see what my limits are.

I'm really doing very well at present. My Dr., Nurses and medications have all been first class and have me going in a good direction. But above all that, your concern, emails, cards, positive thoughts and prayers spoken on my behalf by you and others, many of whom I've never met or even know their names has been as important and meaningful as any drug. I am so grateful for each of you and appreciate your support through this in more ways I can say.

Thank you so MUCH!

Updates and Decisions

Apr 5, 2016, 3:30 p.m.

Greetings and Salutations,

We have a lot going on and it's an exciting time. I hope this finds you equally busy but perhaps in a state of less excitement in some regards.

We move on Thursday from our Westminster Home of the past 13 years to Annapolis. Sandra has worked herself to exhaustion remaking and remodeling 2032 Fairfax Rd and she has performed miracles to say the least. We are really looking forward to being in Annapolis again and eliminating Sandra's 3-hour round trip daily commute. I will be more centrally located as well, which will help me with my work. (Still no buyers for our current home so we could definitely do without that excitement)

I have been holding steady health wise and my drug regimen has continued to improve my "numbers" on a slow but steady basis. Overall, I show a greater than 50% improvement on protein levels in my blood along with light chain amino acid progress and with something known as M Spikes - myeloma gamma globulin. A large peak, or M spike, marks large amounts of protein and this too has improved by about 50%. On a scale of 1-10 I'm about a 5 overall.

These levels of improvement prompted a visit to Dr. Badros at the Univ. of MD hospital in Baltimore. Dr. Badros only works with Myeloma patients and is nationally recognized as a leader in this field of cancer. My Oncologist, Dr. Kruter, works in close partnership with Dr. Badros and he referred me to him for consideration of a Bone Marrow transplant.

Here are some things we learned:

Multiple Myeloma is a chronic disease, well treated with many therapies but is not considered curable. The median survival rate is currently around 10 years. (50% of patients live more than 10 years, 50% less than 10 years)

Myeloma is like Wack-a-Mole (my definition, not the Medical Industry) The disease pops up and a regimen of drugs act like a hammer to pound the Mole back into the ground. Eventually, the Mole pops up again but a different hammer is required to knock it back underground. Fortunately, there are many "Hammers" available. 15 new cancer drugs just came on the market and 3 of them treat people with relapsed Myeloma. There are no new therapies or drugs for the initial treatment of Myeloma.

Evaluation for and undergoing a Bone Marrow transplant is part of the normal regimen for treating this disease. The window of opportunity is best about 6-8 months after initial treatment with Revlimid and Dexamethasone. A 50% improvement in blood results is required and I pass that test. But the window of opportunity is getting short. Long-term use of Revlimid has negative effects on stem cell production and healthy stem cells in the bone marrow are necessary for a successful transplant. Many patients get 2-5 years of remission from a bone marrow transplant and knocking the "Mole" into remission is always the primary goal. If successful, life expectancy is improved.

Of course, there are risks and inconveniences to this procedure. First, I am being switched to new drugs. Revlimid has run its course and will not get me closer to better blood numbers. I will get a weekly injection of Velcade along with Cytoxan and continued use of the steroid Dexamethasone. Dr. Badros feels 2 cycles of this regimen (1 month = 1 cycle) will greatly improve getting closer to a better level of remission. After these 2 cycles I would undergo 2 weeks of testing (heart, lungs, kidneys, etc.) and once deemed able to survive the procedure (no guarantees) we move forward. I will also self-inject myself for

2 weeks with a drug to step up the production of stem cells in the bone marrow. The new stem cells will be harvested, enough for 2 transplants in case the first on doesn't take and replaced in my blood stream a day or two following a high dose of chemo that will kill everything in sight. If everything goes perfectly, I'll be out of the hospital in 2-3 weeks and recuperating at home waiting to regain some energy and rebuild my "near zero function" immune system. There are a lot of "ifs".

Will I do this? Not sure. I'm not too excited about the potential for improvement versus the potential for complications. Everyone responds differently to this dramatic procedure and there are lots of risks with no guarantees of long-term success. Plus, missing at least 2 months of work and more likely 3 or even 6 months of employment is not appealing. For now, we will move forward with the new drug therapy and see where we are at the end of the 2 cycles prescribed by Dr. Badros. This will give us time to learn more, talk with other people who have gone through this and weigh the positives and negatives. We met with 3 different people today and while the details above are not brief, they are greatly condensed based on the information we received. Like my good Texas buddy Jim Bell says, it's like filling a teacup from a fire hose!

Spring is almost here. Renewal and regeneration await us. Ain't life GRAND! I believe it is and I'm so grateful for the many undeserved blessings in my life. I count each of you as one of those many blessings. More news to come and hopefully it will all be good.

Enjoy every day....

We're In

Fri, Apr 8, 2016, 7:39 a.m.

To Mary, Fred

Well, we are finally in our new house. The movers unloaded the last piece of furniture at MIDNIGHT. Yes, 12 AM! Yikesy, smiksey.

It is now 7:34 am and we are on our 2nd cup of coffee discussing furniture placement. I'm sure we (mostly Sandra) will whip the house into shape in a very short period of time. We need to do some clean up at Marbeth Hill but our house cleaner is going there today and she will make a good head start. We have a showing on Monday at 3pm so maybe this will be THE ONE.

I hope your day is wonderful. I'm taking off work today so I'll have a 3-day weekend to help with the unfolding of our "way too many" possessions.

Ain't life interesting!

(While we were moving from Westminster to Annapolis, my Dad was also moving from his home to an assisted living facility. Being strongly independent, Mary Jane and I were very surprised when he announced his intention to make this move. The move was strictly his idea and it gave us some peace of mind that he would be in a safe environment with no responsibility for cooking and cleaning. So glad we did not have to push him in this direction and proud that he was willing to make this change.)

Dr Visit

Wed, May 4, 2016, 7:09 p.m.

Greetings from a cool, gray & rainy Annapolis, MD,

Sandra and I met with my Oncologist, Dr. Kruter today. After 3 weekly doses of the 2 new chemo drugs my protein levels have gone from 2700 to 3100. Wrong direction. However, the Doctor said it's too early in the course of these drugs to draw any firm and fast conclusions. I will stay the course and he will check the blood results on my next visit; May 23rd.

What we learned that we did not know is that the Plasma in my bone marrow has to be 5% or less for them to use my own stem cells for a transplant. Above 5% a donor is required and that is a more risky procedure with greater chance of complications. MM is a cancer of the plasma cells so the greater they are reduced the greater the chance of a successful transplant. When I was originally diagnosed, the plasma cells in my bone marrow were at 80%. The only way to measure this is with a bone marrow biopsy and that will be done again if I start showing significant improvement in my blood tests moving forward.

Even if I don't qualify for a BMT, Dr Kruter emphasized that the various drugs available to treat me can still be very successful. But for people under 65 in otherwise good health a BMT is a preferred course of treatment. A successful BMT can provide long term remission when successful.

I have a couple of more months to stay on these drugs and hopefully see the improvement they are looking for. It appears to me that a BMT will not be recommended if I can't achieve the results they need in the next 60 or maybe 90 days maximum. There is a window of opportunity and it won't stay open forever. Time will tell and at this point I don't know what to wish for on the BMT issue. I shall leave it to my Doctors, medications and my Creator's direction. During this time, I shall try to play more golf as I contemplate the future and take each day as a gift.

I hope your days feel like gifts.....presents are so much fun!

Bruce

June 15, 2016, 10:42 a.m.

Good morning, Mr. Moffatt,

Hope all is well. I wanted to follow up with you since you last saw Dr. Badros. He recommended you receive additional cycles of treatment with Dr. Kruter and then reassess the disease response. I wanted to see if you were still considering transplant as an option and if so, if you are interested in coming to the pre transplant class on 6/29/16. You had mentioned that you are moving homes, so I'm sure you are busy. Hope the move went well.

Looking forward to hearing from you.

Sherri
Transplant Nurse
University of Maryland Medical Center

Following Up

June 15, 2016, 11:11 a.m

Sherri,

Thank you for your follow up. Dr Badros switched my Chemo Meds and my Protein Levels have gone up instead of down. While on Revlimid my Protein levels reduced to 2700. After 6 or 7 weeks on Velcade and Cytoxan my protein level is at 3300. Dr Kruter will most likely change the Velcade to another chemo injection in the next week or two. At this point I don't know if I will be a candidate for a BMT or not.

I see Dr Kruter on the 24th and I will try to get his opinion concerning this issue. He has told me that my Plasma cells in my bone marrow must be at 5% or less to do a BMT. I believe I will need a much lower protein level to achieve that goal and only a BM Biopsy will confirm the level of Plasma cells.

I'll get back to you when I know more.

Catching Up

June 16, 2016, 9:11 p.m.

It's been several weeks since I last inundated you with my personal issues and it's time for another assault. But before I relay the mundane details, I'd like to share a few thoughts:

Our new home in Annapolis is quite amazing thanks to Sandra. We want to finish in a bedroom and bathroom in the basement, and that will complete the interior remodeling. We have plans for several upgrades to the exterior of the house and some landscaping improvements but those items will be future projects.

We finally have what appears to be a solid buyer for our Westminster home and settlement is set for early July; maybe sooner. We look forward to paying one mortgage instead of two.

We have had some good Moffatt family time in Annapolis recently with a visit from my Father, Cousins and spouses, Sister, her husband and their new Black Lab Puppy. (Is there anything better than a Dog???) We are looking forward to more family time with the Kerr/Cheston side of the family next weekend in Philly. And Mary Jane (my sister) and I just returned from Indianapolis and the wedding of my 2nd Cousin Patrick Kanne to his new bride Kari.

On top of all of this, the weather is warm and Sunny. Could life be better? Well, actually it could. Our wonderful Congressmen and Senators could stop talking and do something about Gun Violence. Sorry to interject Politics, but how can a country as great as the USA fail to value human life above the "ability", not the "right", to buy a gun? Our Constitution is a wonderful document but it was written 229 years ago. Maybe some new amendments are in order. I wish the people could vote on legislation. At least something would happen then.

Onward. (Aren't you glad). I saw Dr. Kruter on Wednesday. The new Chemo treatments are not having the desired effect. While on Revlimid, my protein count reduced from 6500 to 2700. (1600 yields remission) Eight weeks on Velcade and Cytoxan have taken the count up to 3500. A new treatment is awaiting approval from the Insurance Company. As Dr. Kruter said, "We don't go to the bathroom around here without approval from Insurance Companies". Given the reversal of direction, I asked Dr. Kruter if I might not be a candidate for a Bone Marrow Transplant. He answered that he felt confident they could find the right combination of drugs to improve my blood work and achieve the necessary results to make the BMT a reality. If he's correct, I'm looking at a two or three month vacation from work while they destroy and rebuild my bone marrow. Not what I want, but maybe what I need.

The new chemo drug is Carfilzomib, aka Kyprolis. (Thank goodness they're easy to spell and pronounce???...I could never be a Doctor) This will be administered through an IV on consecutive days with six days off between infusions; Day 1 & 2, day 8 & 9, 15 &16, etc. I will also go back on Revlimid and continue with the steroid Dexamethasone. Side effects so far have been fairly mild and manageable. Hopefully that trend will continue.

So that's all the news that's fit to print. I hope this finds you enjoying the beautiful weather and time with friends and family. Please call your Father on Sunday (I know I will) or have some special time of remembrance. I also hope your children will call and speak to you Fathers on this list. And please root for Phil Mickelson to complete the modern-day Grand Slam in golf. He'd be the 6th person in history to win all 4 Majors in Golf and his record of 6 finishes in 2nd place deserve a win.

With love and gratitude for each and every one of you...

Referral Please

Thu, June 23, 2016, 6:32 p.m.

Sherri,

Dr. Badros and Dr. Kruter have switched my Chemo from Velcade to Krypolis which requires an IV infusion on consecutive days. Since we have moved to Annapolis, going to Westminster 2 days in a row will be difficult. I would like to get my chemo treatments in Annapolis while I continue to see Dr. Kruter once a month in Westminster. I have been informed I will need an initial consultation with a Dr. in Annapolis before treatments can be scheduled. Dr. Kruter did not know of anyone to recommend. Can you or Dr. Badros suggest a Doctor for me to see in Annapolis for a consult?

Thank you,
Bruce Moffatt

On Jun 24, 2016, at 9:53 a.m.

From Sherri

(Now I will be introduced to another amazing physician, Dr. Arun Bhandari. Dr. Bhandari guided our governor, Larry Hogan, through his cancer treatments into complete remission. He is yet another world class doctor that provides me with the best care possible. I am so lucky to have such great Doctors and nurses. Read more about him at https://www. cohamed.com/our-physicians/arun-bhandari-md) Here is a beautiful quote from him:

"You are braver than you believe, stronger than you seem, smarter than you think, and twice as beautiful as you'd ever imagined. Don't let cancer cause you to sell yourself short or forget your worth. Don't lose hope. When the sun goes down, the stars come out. Be thankful for this day. Difficult roads often lead to a beautiful destination. Cancer changes your life, often for the better. You learn what's important, you learn to prioritize, and you learn not to waste your time. You tell people you love them. You are loved. You are wonderfully made. You are beautiful. You are a masterpiece. God has a great plan for you. REMEMBER: you're not dying from cancer .... You're LIVING with it. AMEN!"

Infusions

Mon, Jul 11, 2016, 11:45 a.m.

Howdy Cowpokes,

Maggie from Dr Bhandari's office just called to schedule my chemo treatments in Annapolis. We are finally approved by Blue Cross Blue Shield and my treatments moved from Westminster to Annapolis. And it's only taken about 3 weeks to coordinate the details! (sarcasm intended)

I prefer Thursday and Friday to start my infusions allowing the weekend to recover from any side effects, but Thursday is booked up. We will start tomorrow and Wednesday at 8am and see how I tolerate the new drugs. If I need to switch to Thur/Fri that can be worked out down the road.

I get a hydration IV first that will take about 45 minutes. Then the Krypolis infusion (new chemo drug) and that takes about 30 minutes. I will also get my lovely steroid Dexamethasone via IV instead of pill form; 20 mg on Tuesday and another 20 mg on Wednesday. Dr Bhandari feels it is important to administer the Dex along with the **Kyprolis.**. So, I may be wide awake for 2 nights instead of one and go to work sleepy eyed on Wed and Thur. Time will tell.

I will also start back on Revlimid, the chemo pill previously effective in killing cancer cells. I'll take that at bedtime every day for 3 weeks and then one week off. Same schedule for the **Kyprolis** infusions....back to back days a week apart for 3 weeks and then 1 week off.

Lastly, I think, is my Zometa infusion. I get that once a month to strengthen my bones. I was supposed to get that last week in Westminster but cancelled the appointment in order to start this drug in Annapolis too. It was not on the chart for tomorrow so that will have to get processed for approval and hopefully it will be added to Wednesday's appointment. Wow...you really have to pay attention to your treatment schedule. It seems the Dr's and the nurses are too busy to do it all for you on a consistent day in day out basis. It's all complicated but for now the train is back on the tracks and ready to leave the station. Destination unknown but we'll see where it takes us.

Choo, Choo . . . . . .

Bruce Lee

Mon, Jul 11, 2016, 1:31 p.m.

From Fred/Daddy

Boocie:

You are so very thoughtful to give us the blow-by-blow description of your upcoming train ride of medicines. I join you and Sandy in gratitude for the Insurance OK and for these various treatments having been transferred to Annapolis. You are soon going to feel the positive results, I am confident. With God as your main benefactor plus Sandy and MJ and me, and many others, things are going to work out. You are being lifted in the daily prayers of many, so "we do not lose hope," as the Apostle Paul it, and he surely knew what he was talking about.

"Heavenly Father, thank you for your love and care and for our confidence that if you are for us, who can stand against us? There are lots of things I do not know, but one of the deepest assurances of my very soul is that you know Bruce and Sandy and hold them in your powerful hand. Please continue to do so, blessing his doctors and every pill and shot and even surgery to the purpose of bringing him back to perfect strength and health, for the sake of all of us who love him and for the overarching sake of savior, the Lord Jesus. Thank you. Amen."

Daddy/Fred

P.S. I hope your ears were burning; MJ just stopped by and we had a good visit, speaking mainly about what a fun guy you are!

Weekend, Yahoo!

Sat, Jul 23, 2016, 11:52 a.m.

To Fred, Mary

Daddy,

I'm happy to report that I have the weekend off. The new Meds are taking a greater toll on my overall energy so I hope that means the cancer cells are getting a thorough lashing. I get my 3rd week of treatment next Tuesday and Wednesday and the following week will be free of chemo infusions. Not sure if I will continue with the steroid dose during the week off. They will draw blood and run a complete profile during my week off and Dr Bhandari will see me Aug 5th to review the results. Here's hoping for some improvement in my protein levels and other markers related to the Myeloma.

Anne Pace is throwing a surprise birthday party for her husband Mike tonight at Brio. He turns 70 and I'm sure we'll have fun at his expense. We're also playing golf with them tomorrow at Old South CC. They have been good friends for a long time but they decided to take up permanent residence in Clearwater Florida around the same time we moved back to Annapolis. Too bad. We will miss their company!

I hope you are staying inside in the cool air. It's a scorcher here but I'll take the heat over the cold any day. I'll speak to you tomorrow at our regular time assuming you have no social engagements that could interfere with our routine.

All my best, to THE BEST!

Appointment with Dr Badros

Fri, Aug 12, 2016, 6:44 a.m.

Sherri,

I started my 2nd cycle of Kyprolis and Revlimid and the ever-present Dexamethasone yesterday. Dr. Bhandari elected not to do a full Myeloma blood profile after the 1st cycle for some reason but he feels the cocktail is working. To that end he wants me to schedule an appointment with Dr. Badros for early September. My next week off the Meds will be Aug 29 to Sept 1. I assume a blood profile will be ordered during that week or shortly thereafter in order to measure the effectiveness of the medications. Can you schedule an appointment for me with Dr. Badros or send me a phone number so I can do that myself? Sept 5-8 is open for me but we will be out of town on Sept 9.

Thank you.

Myeloma Update

Thu, Sep 1, 2016, 9:25 a.m.

I just finished my visit with Dr. Bhandari and got the results of the last 2 months on Carfilzomib, Revlimid and Dexamethasone. The previous chemo drugs from May and June pushed my numbers the wrong direction and my protein levels increased from 2700 to 3658. The new Meds have reduced the protein levels (IGG) to 1458; lowest number in 13 months. I was originally told that 1600 was considered remission, but Dr. Bhandari considers this a good partial remission. (They keep moving the Goal Posts so the End Zone is just a little farther away)

More importantly is the M-Spike level. This number shows the amount of Myeloma Protein in the blood. I believe that is basically measuring the amount of Myeloma Cancer cells in the body. On July 5th that number was 2.5 grams per deciliter. Now it is at 1.1 which Dr. Bhandari was very encouraged about. The goal is to get this number as close to Zero as possible. 0.0 to .3 reflects a very low presence of cancerous plasma cells and gives a Bone Marrow Transplant a much higher degree of potential success.

Sandra and I travel to Baltimore today for a 1pm appointment with Dr. Badros, the Myeloma Specialist. Dr. Bhandari believes he will want me to stay on the current medications for 2 more months in an effort to get the M-Spike number as close to Zero as possible. If true, I can avoid the BMT and hospital until at least November. That will give me some time to hopefully enjoy some cooler temperatures, play some golf and get some much needed things done at work. If I have to be in the hospital and spend a couple of months recuperating it might as well be during colder weather.

Lastly, I must admit, the BMT will be a welcomed opportunity. The side effects of chemo are not debilitating but I sure would like to get my breath back and not feel as tired. So, we keep on course and wait for the next review. If I learn anything new from Dr. Badros I'll follow up with what should be a shorter dissertation.

Love and kisses to all......

Dr Badros

Thu, Sep 1, 2016, 2:51 p.m.

As expected, I will stay on the current cycle of meds for 2 more months in an effort to reduce my M-Spike as low as possible; hopefully to 0.0. Dr. Badros was concerned that the Cytoxan and Velcade administered in April and May allowed my numbers to go backward. He said they are very powerful and effective Myeloma drugs and this could indicate I have some very strong cancer cells. (Why do anything halfway?) But the good news is I have responded well to the current regimen.

A BMT is not a sure thing for the next step. After my next 2 months of treatment, I will not receive any chemo for a month. During this time, I will undergo testing to make sure my vital organs are up to the rigors of a transplant. I will also get injections of Neupogen, self-administered, for 2 weeks to increase production of stem cells. Assuming all this goes well, I would enter the hospital in early December.

The next step (still as an outpatient procedure) is to collect a minimum of 500 Million stem cells or more. They will put me on a machine that circulates my blood out and back into my body. Stem cells are heavy and the machine will recognize them and they will fall into a collection bag. The process is called apheresis. This could happen in one 2-3 hour procedure or it could take 2-3 attempts to collect the required amount. If they can't get enough stem cells, no BMT. You ask, why could they not get enough? The longer I stay on chemo and Revlimid the harder it is to make healthy stem cells. I've had 8 rounds of Revlimid and 10 is usually the most you can have and still produce healthy stem cells. I'm in the window of opportunity for the next 2 months on Revlimid.

Assuming a BMT is a go, I enter the hospital and receive the drug Melphalan to eradicate my bone marrow. A day or two later they re-infuse me with the collected stem cells for a reboot. 14-18 days in the hospital and then home for the rebuilding of my immune system. Probably 3 months before I'm ready to return to work.

Sandra and I will attend a class in the near future that goes into greater detail of the timelines, procedures and scheduling. The last reminder I received was that Myeloma is a chronic and not curable disease. If all goes well I could get 2-5 years of remission from a BMT but when and if there is a relapse, there is a host of drugs to reverse the cycle and achieve another remission. And with all the research going on I may live long enough that a cure is discovered. I am fortunate to live in this age of great research and discovery in Medical Science. I am a lucky boy.

Bruce

News from Bruce

Fri, Sep 2, 2016, 8:59 a.m.

Good Morning Dear Ones,

We just left Dr. Bhandari's office. My protein level is at an all-time low of 1174. That's an improvement from 1458 two months ago and down from 6500 when originally diagnosed July 2015. I'm in a "normal range" and that's good news.

Unfortunately, my M-Spike only improved from 1.1 to .9. The M-Spike is the measure of Myeloma cells in the blood and they want that as close to Zero as possible. Dr. Bhandari could not give me a definitive number for the M-Spike which would signal a green light for the BMT. I see the specialist, Dr. Badros, next Wednesday and he will decide if he wants to proceed to the transplant or continue with more chemo. My guess is that it will be difficult to lower my M-Spike much further as two months of really strong chemo only improved my M-Spike a very small amount.

The real deciding factor will come from a bone marrow biopsy. I believe they want the actual level of Myeloma cells in the marrow to be less than 5% to give the best chance of a successful BMT. I don't know if Dr. Badros will do a biopsy next Wednesday or not. I'm guessing he'll want another month of chemo and try to get the M-Spike number lower before doing the biopsy. Time will tell.

So the news isn't all bad or all good. I'll have more to share next week and we will go from there. Hope your day is full of sunshine and happiness. We press on.

Brucie

Chemo Free...For Now

Nov 2, 2016, 7:43 p.m.

Greetings friends and family,

I hope this update on me finds you in good health and happiness. I have finished my 4th month of the latest and most powerful chemo with good results. I stress powerful because it has really put me down on Sundays of late. Fortunately, Monday through Saturday is OK and I function well. My blood profile has shown dramatic improvement on Kyprolis, Revlimid and the very fattening steroid Dexamethasone; all time high of 240 lbs. this week. YUK! Time to get lean.

Sandra and I spent the day at the University of MD Hospital in Baltimore. First, a lengthy class on the steps and expectations leading up to and after a Bone Marrow Transplant. Then some dental X-rays and exam, followed by a meeting with a Social Worker for information on support groups and in- patient programs at the hospital. Finally, and most importantly, a visit with Dr. Badros, the Myeloma Specialist. The short version is that I am in Partial Remission. This reflects improvement of greater than 50% but not 90% which is the threshold for Complete Remission. Dr. Badros feels my blood profile has improved enough to move on to a Bone Marrow Transplant. The official green light will be determined after a Bone Marrow Biopsy next Tuesday which will give a more definitive look at the composition of my Marrow as well as the amount and strength of the Myeloma Cancer Cells still present. He does not anticipate any major hurdles.

The good news is NO MORE CHEMO, NO MORE STEROIDS for 2 months! November will involve more testing of heart, lungs, kidneys, etc. to make sure there are no conflicting issues with vital organs. In early December I'll receive some low dose Cytoxan (chemo) followed by 8 days of Neupogen injections (self-administered) to increase stem cell production. Stem cells will then be harvested from my blood, stored and frozen. The actual transplant could start mid to late December, but Dr. Badros will not be available, so admission to the hospital for the BMT will be my New Year's gift.

Actually, every day is a gift and I am looking forward to more energy and increased lung capacity in the next 60 days. I've forgotten what "normal" feels like, but hopefully that feeling will return, if only briefly. The BMT will keep me in the hospital for 14-18 days followed by 2-3 months of recovery at home. But if I have to be confined to home and limited outside activity, January, February and March are 3 good months for asylum.

Only time will tell, but a successful BMT could give me 2-5 years of remission. Better yet, some people have maintained remission from a BMT for 15 years and counting. There are no cures yet, but there are many options for therapies to regain remission after a relapse. There is light at the end of each tunnel and it's not always a train.

Thanks to each of you for your support, kind words of caring and prayers on my behalf. The Holiday Season is upon us and I hope your time will be filled with family, friends and great happiness. I know mine certainly will be.

Nov 8, 2016, 4:22 p.m.

Hello Mr. Moffatt,

Gina is working on your schedule for pre transplant testing and then to see Dr. Badros. We have you on schedule to start the mobilization process (apheresis) on 12/5/16 with Cytoxan followed by neupogen injections. Please see the attached calendar and let me know if this will work. I know you had your bone marrow done today so Dr. Badros will have that when he sees you. Please let me know when you will be seeing your cardiologist for clearance so we can get that note to Dr. Badros when he sees you.

I will be placing an order with your specialty pharmacy for neupogen or biosimilar medication. If you get a call in the next few weeks you can let them know you will set up delivery after you see Dr. Badros for consent.

Looking forward to getting started.

Sherri

Sherri Bauman RN MS
Transplant Nurse Coordinator
University of Maryland Medical Center
Greenebaum Cancer Center

Sunday	Monday Dec 5	Tuesday Dec 6	Wednesday Dec 7	Thursday Dec 8	Friday Dec 9	Saturday Dec 10
	730AM report to Stoler Pavilion. You will have labs drawn and receive Cytoxan. Coordinator will meet with you to re-view meds and teach neupogen injections. At least 6 hours in infusion lab today.	Begin Neupogen Injections at home and oral medications	Continue Neupo-gen Injections at home and oral medications	Continue Neupogen Injections at home and oral medications	Continue Neupogen Injections at home and oral medications	Continue Neupogen Injections at home and oral medications
Start hydrating approximately 2 liters of water.	Stay hydrated and empty your blad-der every 2-3 hours around the clock.	Stay hydrated and empty your bladder every 2-3 hours around the clock.	Continue TUMS 1 tablet 4 x a day	Continue TUMS 1 tablet 4 x a day	Continue TUMS 1 tablet 4 x a day	Continue TUMS 1 tablet 4 x a day
		Start TUMS 1 table 4x a day				

Sunday Dec 11	Monday Dec 12	Tuesday Dec 13	Wednesday Dec 14	Thursday Dec 15	Friday Dec 16	Saturday Dec 17
Continue Neupogen Injections at home and oral medications **NOTHING BY MOUTH AFTER MIDNIGHT TAKE MEDICATION WITH SIP OF WATER** Continue TUMS 1 tablet 4 x a day	INJECT NEUPOGEN AT HOME **8 am Report to Stoler Pavilion for labs.** **9 am report to Interventional Radiology to have line placed 2nd fl Gudelsky (glass elevators)** Continue TUMS 1 tablet 4 x a day and oral medications. **Need transportation home**	INJECT NEUPOGEN AT HOME **7:15 AM Report to apheresis lab room** S9C02 (Rotunda elevators) for labs and stem cell collection You will receive instructions for next day. Prepare to be in apheresis for 6-8 hrs. **The number is 410-328-7508** **Will teach you how to flush your line today** Continue TUMS 1 tablet 4 x a day and oral medications **Need transportation home**	INJECT NEUPOGEN AT HOME **7:15 AM Report to apheresis lab room** S9C02 (Rotunda elevators) for labs and stem cell collection **Continue Neupogen Injections and oral medications** Prepare to be in apheresis for 6-8 hrs **The number is 410-328-7508 if you are running late.** Continue TUMS 1 tablet 4 x a day Need transportation home			

Sunday Dec 18	Monday Dec 19	Tuesday Dec 20	Wednesday Dec 21	Thursday Dec 22	Friday Dec 23	Saturday Dec 24
This week restaging labs & follow up with doctor (24h urine if myeloma patient	ADMISSION TO BE DETERMINED					

The Neupogen is given daily until apheresis is complete. Your **dose is 1080 mcg per day**. You will need to inject **TWO 300 mcg** prefilled syringes and **ONE 480 mcg** prefilled syringes each day in the AM. DO NOT MISS A DOSE.

Do not use Ibuprofen, Tylenol or aspirin during mobilization unless directed by your physician. Claritin over the counter may be used for pain.

Oral meds should be taken for beginning the day you start Neupogen until stem cell collection completed.

- Acyclovir 800 mg by mouth in the morning and in the evening

- Levofloxacin 750 mg by mouth once a day

- Prochlorperazine 10 mg by mouth every 6 hours *as needed for nausea*

- Take your temperature four times a day after chemotherapy until apheresis. If your temperature is **100.4 degrees or higher, call the emergency numbers IMMEDIATELY,** regardless of time of day.

- Remember to bring snacks with you on the day of apheresis.

- **Increase your fluid** intake for 24 hours before receiving the Cytoxan chemotherapy and for 48 hours after you have completed the Cytoxan Chemotherapy.

Oral Medication Schedule:
Levofloxacin/Antibiotic: 1 tablet once a day until stem cell collection is completed
Acyclovir/Antiviral: 1 tablet twice a day until stem cell collection is completed
Prochlorperazine/Anti-nausea: As prescribed for 36 hours following Cytoxan infusion.

Calendar of Events

Wed. Nov 9, 2016, 5:37 a.m.

To Fred, Mary

Good Morning, or Perhaps Not...

So hard to imagine our country has elected a person of such low moral character to be President. I wonder how Bernie would have fared had he secured the Democratic Party nomination? We'll never know and now we face the most unchartered future of our lifetimes. I fear for the U.S. for the first time in my life.

Moving off my soap box, I have attached the calendar of events that reflects the steps leading up to my BMT in January of 2017. Feel free to ask any questions you may have. You'll see Neupogen injections scheduled for 8 days in a row. Neupogen is the drug that will stimulate the growth of new stem cells necessary for the Transplant.

The Bone Marrow Biopsy taken yesterday went well. Injections of lidocaine were given to numb the area. I don't recall Dr. Kruter injecting lidocaine into the bone itself when he performed the first Biopsy, but that was done yesterday. Sticking the needle into the bone was the most uncomfortable part, but once numbed, the insertion into the marrow was mostly a sensation of pressure without much pain. My next visit with Dr. Badros is not scheduled until Monday, Nov 28th. That may be my first opportunity to get the results of the biopsy. If there are complications from the biopsy, I'm sure I will hear from him in the next week or two.

I hope your coming day goes well and is full of happiness in spite of the poor choice made by our fellow countrymen.

Bruce Moffatt

(For me, the Bone Marrow Biopsy has not been as painful as anticipated. The process involves numbing the tissue around the point of entry; the back portion of the pelvis which provides a wide area of access. Once the tissue is numb, more lidocaine is injected into the bone. This produces a sharp pain from the needle in the bone but only lasts a few seconds. A tool is then used to punch into the bone and secure a section of the bone. Pressure is felt but it's not painful. Needles will then be used to extract both solid and liquid marrow. Some patients experience pain when the extraction occurs, but that was never the case for me. I never knew this until Mary Sanchez, Nurse Practitioner for Dr. Garfall at the Univ. of PA Medical Ctr, explained it. She and Dr. Garfall were debating who would do this procedure one day. I asked Mary if doing these biopsies bothered her. She said it did and the reason was that some people felt pain during the extraction phase and inflicting pain is hard on the caregiver as well as the patient. I never thought of that. Mary is a perfect example of the health care workers I have come to know. They care deeply about their work and their patients. What a gift they are. I've had this procedure done about 10-12 times and it's not a big deal. During periods when medications have stopped working and my cancer is on the rise, I have had as much as 95% of my marrow to be myeloma cells. In spite of this, I have not suffered organ failure, fevers or infections. Something in my constitution enables me to tolerate high levels of this disease so far. Just lucky in this regard I guess.)

We Are Tired

Wed, Dec 14, 2016, 5:52 p.m.

Good evening Moffatts,

I am now severed from my daily work for MSI and have filed Disability Papers and Leave Of Absence forms. So fortunate I will be paid while I miss work; I think about 60% of salary.

Last night was tough. About 10:30 lying in bed my lower back had sharp pains. It felt like I slipped a disk and I could not find a pain free position. While on Neupogen to increase stem cell production, I am not supposed to take aspirin, Tylenol or Ibuprofen. I had some Oxycontin and Valium left over from my compression fracture last year and called the hospital to see if I could take them. I got approval but they had little to no effect. Dr. Badros approved me to take 1 ibuprofen tablet this morning which I thought would be insufficient to stop the searing pain. WRONG. It was magic. The pain was gone in 45 minutes. WHEW.

So off we go to the hospital for the Hickman Port insertion in my chest. We got there at 8:15 and left about 2:45. Sandra and I had almost no sleep last night so we are exhausted to say the least. We should sleep tonight.

I return to the hospital for aphaeresis tomorrow. They will use my new port to draw my blood out and through a machine to collect my stem cells. The filtered blood then cycles back into my port through a 2nd line. The process takes about 6 hours and if they collect enough stem cells, I will not have to go back on Friday to continue the process. Here's hoping for one and done.

I hope your day has contained less drama that ours. How nice to be pain free!

Love, your Son and Brother

Aphaeresis under way through the Hickman Port. The port is installed during a surgical procedure under anesthesia. One line takes the blood out, another line returns the blood to me. A machine separates the stem cells and are frozen with the help of a special program and **preserved** *in liquid nitrogen at −196°C or -320.8 Fahrenheit.* They collected 11 million stem cells. (Actually 1 Billion plus as I learn later on) Enough for 2 BMT's in case I need a second attempt in the future. (Sorry for the goofy look on my face and unshaven appearance. My sister got the "photographic" gene.)

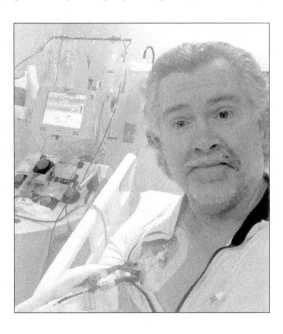

Happy Holidays

Dec 20, 2016, 5:22 p.m.

I hope this finds you well and ready for a Merry Christmas and Happy New Year. My road traveled for the last 18 months has finally reached its next stop to a hopeful remission; an Autologous Bone Marrow Transplant. Having survived and well tolerated most of the side effects of multiple chemotherapy drugs, the various cocktails have lowered the cancerous plasma cells in my marrow below the threshold required to move forward. The last push involved a high dose of chemo to "clean out my marrow" followed by 8 days of self-injected Neupogen. Neupogen helps ramp up stem cell production and these cells will be harvested, frozen and given back to me for the transplant. The process for capturing my stem cells is Aphaeresis. The Hickman Port implanted in my chest is hooked to a machine that draws out my blood, circulates through a centrifuge, separates the stem cells into a collection bag and returns the blood back to me. The process sometimes takes 2 days at 7 hours per day. Fortunately, they collected 1 billion stem cells the first day which is enough for 2 transplants. We hope this high collection rate indicates the presence of strong, healthy cells. Medical science is AMAZING.

December 13th was my last day to work and I have gone on disability as provided by my company, MS International. I cannot say enough good things about this company. They have been so understanding and supportive and I am so grateful to work for them.

I will enter the University of MD Hospital in Baltimore on Dec 27th. I will receive the very potent chemo drug Melphalan on the first day which will completely wipe out my bone marrow. A few days later, I will be infused with the stem cells previously harvested. From there, the magic of the perfectly designed human body will take over. The stem cells will sit in my lungs for a couple of weeks and then migrate into my bones and regrow new marrow, hopefully free of cancer. I'll experience some sickness and probably lose all my hair. I'll be sure to send pictures of my bald head. Maybe it will be an improvement!

I will remain in the hospital for 14-21 days. Then, two to three months at home while my immune system strengthens. Post BMT is uncertain. Some people receive remission for 1-2 years. Others have achieved remission for 15 years and counting. Of course, we hope for as long as possible.

I am so ready to get this done and look forward to a more energetic and active 2017. I cannot adequately express my gratitude to each of you for all of your prayers and support. We are all at our best when helping and focusing on others. I shall do my best to give back in 2017 all the expressions of love and concern I have received in 2016.

I hope this Christmas Season and New Year brings you much joy and happiness. Thank you for all you have given and done for me.

Bruce Moffatt

Oops!

Sun, Dec 25, 2016, 4:46 a.m.

Sherri,

I hope you have a Happy Holiday today and I'm sorry to bother you. My seasonal allergies flared up again yesterday with a dry hacking cough. That usually signals the final phase but last night my throat got sore and I had some cold chills. I just took my temperature and its 100.1. I'm sure everything is closed today and hopefully this will taper off by Tuesday morning. Should I take anything for the fever or just stay in bed with fluids?

I've laid low for the last week; mostly indoors. But the outside temperature changes seem to have made something Bloom or some mold to pop up and get me. I surely hope this will not delay the BMT.

Let me know what you think.

Thank you,
Bruce Moffatt

Test Results and Other Stuff

Wed, Dec. 28, 2016, 8:44 a.m.

Good Morning,

Got the test results back yesterday and to my surprise I tested positive for Influenza A; the Flu. Sure seems like my annual breakout of a sinus allergy with the same symptoms but the Flu it is. The Dr sent a prescription for Tamiflu. Two tablets a day for 5 days. Assuming my fever and congestion are gone in the next 5 days I'll get admitted for the BMT one day next week.

Now if I can just avoid any other health issues.....

Fri, Dec 30, 3016, 7:06 a.m.

Good Morning Papa,

Thank you for your Good Night email. I slept well last night with a couple of coughing spells that woke me briefly. Fevers are long gone and I'm on the mend. I see Dr. Badros this coming Wednesday. If he deems me fully recovered and non-contagious, I'll be admitted to the BMT Ward after our visit.

A point of clarification if you please. At some point I may have misled everyone with the word "surgery". There is no surgery, as it is commonly defined, for an Autologous BMT. I have a Hickman Catheter Line imbedded in my upper right chest. This line will be used to infuse the chemo into me which will eliminate my bone marrow. A few days later, the same line in my chest will be used to return the stem cells collected 2 weeks ago. No anesthesia, no surgery and hopefully only a short period of illness following the high dose of chemo. My hair is starting to come out on my comb and brush, so I may lose all my hair following the chemo.

I'm being a little technical, but the word "transplant" should be substituted for the word "surgery". I just don't want to give you or anyone else the wrong mental picture of the procedure.

Love,
Bruce Lee

And my hair did eventually fall out!

Not Yet

Wed, Jan 4, 2017, 6:56 p.m.

Greetings in the New Year and I hope you're off to a great start in 2017. I'm stuck in a holding pattern but that will change in the near future, I hope.

I was all set for entrance to the hospital for my BMT on Dec 27th. Unfortunately, I got the Flu the Saturday before so admission was delayed. Today was the next target date and we met with Dr. Badros to get the all-clear. I still have some minor congestion in my lungs which concerns the Doctor. Evidently, I'm at greater risk for pneumonia to develop if I am not 100% healed. The drug Melphalan will be given on day 1 in the hospital to eliminate my bone marrow. This will greatly compromise my immune system and as such opens the door to pneumonia if I still have lingering effects of the Flu. While the chances of this are slim, Dr. Badros does not want to take even the slightest risk. With no immune system, any virus or illness becomes a major problem.

So, now the target date is next Monday, January 9. I will be admitted to the hospital and Dr. Badros will check to make sure I'm good to go. He feels pretty confident I should be fine by then and we will finally get this process started. I will continue my sequestered lifestyle for the next five days and try to dodge germs of all kinds.

With any luck, my next email will be from the hospital. I anticipate some unpleasant side effects for a few days but I promise to spare you the details. If I can return to some form of "normal" health and energy, that positive will far outweigh some short-term negatives.

Best wishes for a prosperous and Happy 2017. I am confident my 2017 will be a big improvement over 2016 and I am so grateful for your prayers and support during this process.

Love in high doses . . . .

It Begins

Mon, Jan 9, 2017, 10:39 a.m.

Here's my new home. Getting chemo later today, so the game is finally afoot.

I'm already a special case!

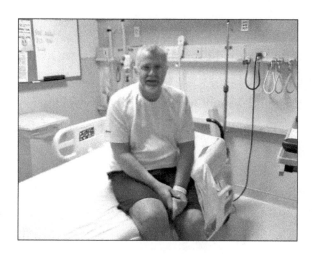

Mon, Jan 9, 2017, 3:03 p.m.

Just informed they want to move up my stem cell replacement form Wednesday to tomorrow. No good explanation offered. They are mixing my chemo now and I'll get it ASAP rather than the scheduled 5pm time. They need at least 24 hours between chemo and stem cell infusion and I have been told this is not a problem. I'll get my chemo by 3:30 today and stem cells tomorrow around 3:30 or 4:00 PM.

Just swallowed my pre-meds. Zofran to prevent nausea and my old friend Dexamethasone. That's the steroid that keeps me awake.

And away we go......(Jackie Gleason)

Thank you,
Bruce Moffatt

(I was confused about the timeframe between receiving Melphalan to destroy my marrow and the now one day interval of giving me back my stem cells. Wouldn't the Melphalan still be in my system and destroy the newly introduced stem cells? Well, it won't, because those stem cells sit in my lungs before being released into the blood stream and work their way into my bone marrow. By the time this happens, Melphalan will no longer be a danger to cell destruction. Two issues come to mind. How AMAZING is the human body to react in this fashion? Almost as if some divine, omniscient being knew this would someday be needed. Secondly, who was smart enough to figure this out and orchestrate the method of delivery along with the drug to accomplish this purpose? WOW!)

Stem Cell Progression

Wed, Jan 12, 2017, 5:27 p.m.

Good evening Friends and Family,

At long last I was admitted this past Monday, the 9th, to the University of MD Hospital in lovely downtown Baltimore to begin my Bone Marrow Transplant (BMT). As promised, they delivered my high dose of chemo (Melphalan) on day one around 5pm. The chemo will require 7-10 days to take full effect and produce some unwanted side effects. When they occur, medications can be administered to help with the severity but they will mostly likely just have to run their course. Saturday or Sunday should hold a few surprises but I'm optimistic for overcoming any unpleasantry. Enough of that; here's the interesting part.

Yesterday, (Jan 11th) at 9:15 AM, my previously harvested and frozen Stem Cells were given back to me. They came to my room in a Nitrogen Vapor container in a frozen state. Three minutes to thaw and a small bag of cells was infused into the Hickman Catheter Line implanted in my chest. Three more bags were used and by 10:15 it was finished. I was told they collected 13 Million stems cells during aphaeresis on Dec 15th. I now have learned the number was actually 13 Million per kilogram of body weight. I have surged to a little over 113 kg in weight which puts the Stem Cell Count around 1.5 Billion. WOW. Glad I didn't have to do the counting. Half were given to me and the other half are available if needed, but that is not likely.

The chemo is continuing to clear out my marrow and make a nice clean home for the new Baby Stem Cells. The chemo only stayed in my body for 24 hours but it magically contin-ues to cook, seek and destroy.

Next miracle of the human body. The new Stem Cells will somehow not be affected by the chemo. They were introduced long enough after the chemo to stay safe, even though the chemo has yet to reach its full potential of assassination. The Stem Cells spent the 1st 24 hours swimming around in my lungs; completely unnoticed by me. Now they are migrating to their new home in my bones which will take several more days. Once they find their destination, the chemo will have cleaned house and my immature baby stem cells will move in. They will divide into white and red blood cells and hopefully healthy plasma cells as well. (Myeloma is a cancer of the plasma cells) Before they mature, my counts will go down to near zero and introduce a new level of tiredness. Once they start rebuilding new marrow, I will gain energy and when the correct blood count levels are reached, I will be shown the door. Exit will hopefully be no later than Jan 25th.

As you already know, I am not an atheist. The miraculous way my body can adapt and heal at such a complex and intricate level greatly reinforces my belief in a divine source. Per chance you disagree, I am not offended. God loves atheists too.

When you receive my next dissertation, I expect to be feeling much better and headed home to my 3 girls. I look forward to sharing that good news ASAP!

Much, Much Love and appreciation for each of you.

The Slow Climb

Fri, Jan 20, 2017, 10:33 a.m.

Loved ones,

Uncomfortable last night but evening medications helped me sleep and I feel better today. My white count is no longer at 0.0 but has only risen a small amount to less than 0.1. Hopefully the number will show a better increase tomorrow.

I can't go home until the white count goes up and stays steady for a few days.

My platelets are low so I'll get a platelet transfusion later today. This is a common occurrence I'm told. My hemoglobin is still good so a blood transfusion is not necessary at this point. With luck I may avoid a blood transfusion and that too is OK by me.

The rash on my back is still rather angry. However, Sandra brought some Benadryl spray and Sarna anti-itch lotion in yesterday that has been approved for use. The Sarna lotion seems to be minimizing the itching.

Feeling pretty good so far today. I tend to go downhill around 4pm but perhaps that will not happen today. The food is borderline awful and I've lost 8 pounds. Only 40 more to go. Lack of appetite is a new and unusual experience.

MJ, send us some photos of Pat and the winter scenes of Mobridge. I hope he is continuing to do well and you and Joe can enjoy your time in the vacation spot of our youth.

Love and kisses....

Come on 2000

Sat, Jan 21, 2017, 8:47 a.m.

Good news,

Dr. Badros, man of few words, thinks I can go home this coming Monday or Tuesday. Music to my soul! My white count went from less than 100 yesterday to 200 today. Moving in the right direction. 2,000 is the normal white cell count and I hope daily improvement will get me to 2,000 quickly. I'll keep you posted on the daily counts.

Maybe Tomorrow

Jan 23, 2017, 3:38 p.m.

Hello kiddies,

Very tired today and not sure why. White cell count has doubled again from the previous day and is now at 1,000. That's very good.

My platelets (clotting cells) are only at 9 and they want them at 30. Received a platelet infusion of twice the normal volume today. I hope this yields the bump they need. If not I'll get another infusion tomorrow.

So it's possible I could get another infusion tomorrow, get to the desired number of 30 and then be sent home. More likely I'll be sent home on Wednesday if I have to get more platelets. Boo Hoo....I want to go tomorrow if possible.

The Infectious Disease team has carefully examined the rash on my back every day. It is itching less and I take that as a sign it is clearing up. Two Dr's put my pustules under close examination and will return to scrape a couple off for lab testing. Local anesthetic and perhaps a stitch after removal. They had to look really hard to find a couple of good samples. Not sure why they have waited so long to do this, but they are obviously being very cautious not to send me home with a festering problem.

Daddy, we have rain today so the plumbers could not work. As soon as they finish their part Sandra will have a better handle on completing the new bedroom and I'll be in touch with travel dates and plane schedules. We are both playing the waiting game: me to get home and you to get to Annapolis.

Looking Good for Today

Tue, Jan 24, 2017, 10:16 a.m.

Da and Sista,

They are removing my Hickman line today. They will draw blood again at 1PM. If my white cell count has stayed steady at 1700 or gone up I can come home. If it goes below 1700, I will have to stay another day. I'm betting on the white count to go up to 2000 and Sandra can come and fetch me. If discharged it will be around 4pm. I'll let you know more as I find out.

Hip, Hip, Hooray! (Or so I hope and pray)

Moving Forward

Tue, Jan 24, 2017, 2:35 p.m.

My blood was drawn at 1:20 pm. As long as the white cell count is 1700 or higher I'm good to go. Hope to have the results by 3pm.

Two Dr's. from Interventional Radiology came to my room to remove the Hickman Catheter in my chest. They removed the stitches and proceeded to try and pull it out. No luck on the 1st and 2nd try. And he pulled hard too. Some tissue had grown around a cuff in the line so some pincers were used to pull the tissue away. Two more pulls and tissue trimming without success. It finally came free in the 5th attempt. I can't say it was terribly painful but it was uncomfortable. The tissue trimming was sharper and a little painful. So happy to be free of the line and the "IV Tree" that has followed my every step for 2 weeks.

News Flash.....my white count went up from 1700 to 2000 and my platelets went up from 38 to 40. YIPPIE...I'm going home TODAY! I'm so happy I'm tearing up. Such a lucky Boy.

I love you guys!!!

Home Again

Tue, Jan 27, 2017, 10:21 a.m.

Greetings one and all,

I'm happy to report that after a 16 day stay in the BMT Ward at the University of MD hospital I returned home this past Tuesday. On the bright side, I could not have received better care from the Doctors and Nurses. I am very fortunate to have top notch professionals tending to me and my illness. On the flip side, lying in a hospital bed for 16 days with no energy, a few uncomfortable side effects and waiting for the next side effect to appear is not much fun. If you feel time is moving too fast and you don't know how the days, weeks and months have flown by, just check yourself into the hospital. Time will slow down!

The chemo I received on the first day of admission stayed in my system for 24 hours. However, it continued to kill everything in sight for about 10 days. 48 hours after chemo, I received my stem cells harvested on December 15th. They required 7-10 days to make their way into my bones and start dividing into white, red, platelet and plasma cells to rebuild my marrow. How they were not destroyed by the chemo and how they continue to rebuild my marrow is beyond my comprehension. Such a miracle, the human body.

I was told my internal working system has been reset to that of a newborn or infant. (Like I need another reason to be called infantile) . But the analogy feels accurate. I have zero energy, a very fast heart rate (my major concern) and a very finicky stomach and intestinal tract. My white cells (immune system) continue to increase each day and I return to the hospital 2-3 times a week to analyze my blood and maintain progress. It will take 6-12 months for a complete recovery. However, I hope I will be strong enough in the next 2 months to return to work. Until then I will be sequestered at home. I cannot be around anyone that has so much as the sniffles much less a cold or flu. At this point a fever or infection will put me back in the hospital. I am highly motived to avoid that outcome.

Thanks again and again to each of you for your concern and support. It is humbling and greatly appreciated.

Bruce Lee

A Mixed Review

Feb 17, 2017, 10:07 a.m.

Happy Friday one and all.....

We are anticipating temperatures in the 60's for the next 4-5 days. Winter seems to be in hibernation and only our dogs Choco and Latte will miss freezing temperatures. Of course, we have no snow as I purchased a snow blower last year and that seems to have changed the pattern of precipitation from the past several years. Still, I'm sure it will come in handy someday.

Sandy and I met with Dr. Badros yesterday for our first follow up since the BMT performed on January 11th. First, my recovery is going very well with no major complications. I have not needed any blood or platelet transfusions since leaving the hospital which is not the case for most BMT patients. My "numbers" continue to improve each week, headed in the direction of "normal" for almost all of the factors tracked in my blood profile. I still suffer from shortness of breath and an elevated heart rate and these issues continue to be somewhat of a mystery. My Cardiologist has doubled the dose of Metoprolol (a Beta Blocker) in hopes of reducing my resting heart rate. He feels the issue is related to the chemo and transplant, but Dr. Badros pointed out that I had these symptoms from the beginning of this process so something else may be involved. Dr. Badros is going to set me up with a Cardiologist on staff at the University of MD hospital for a second opinion. Fixing this issue is currently my #1 priority. I need to get some exercise as I have turned into the poster child of a couch potato.

You may recall from a couple of previous emails my mention of the M-Spike number. M-Spike is a measure of the cancerous Myeloma cells in the Bone Marrow. For about 16 months, several series of drugs were administered to reduce the presence of cancer cells. I showed a strong resistance to getting rid of these abnormal cells. Eventually my M-Spike reduced to 1.3 and at that point we moved forward with the stem cell collection and transplant. A complete remission reflects a number very close to or at 0.0. My current M-Spike is at .8 which is only a partial remission. Obviously, I would have preferred a better outcome considering the magnitude of the transplant process, but a partial remission is better than no remission. And as Dr. Badros pointed out it's better to maintain a partial remission over time than to achieve a complete remission only to relapse a short period of time later.

I will return to the hospital in 30 days for more blood work analysis and a 3rd Bone Marrow Biopsy. My M-Spike may continue to reduce during this time and the biopsy will give the most accurate assessment of my marrow and cancer cells. Having completed the required protocol of various chemotherapies and the BMT, a new direction for treatment is now possible. Dr. Badros will most likely get me into a clinical trial of some type to see if better results can be achieved. There are many trials available incorporating advance therapies. I know the measles virus has been slightly altered and introduced to patients with MM. The virus wakes up the immune system to the presence of the cancer cells and kills them using the body's own defenses. Amazing stuff.

So as with most things in life, this could be better or could be much worse. We will move forward, grateful for each day and focused on the opportunities for improvement that await our exploration. My Mother used to say we come from good "Pioneer" stock. Perhaps her words were prophetic and I can help Pioneer a treatment with good outcomes for this disease. Time will tell.

As always, your thoughts, prayers and support are so greatly appreciated. Thank you for all you mean to me. Bruce Lee

Happy Tuesday to Yous

Mar 21, 2017, 11:44 a.m.

Hello Dear Ones,

I saw a new cardiologist this morning, Dr. Peter Reyes, and I was very impressed. He will be my "go to guy" moving forward.

Dr. Reyes explained that the increased protein in my blood over the past 2 years may have caused the heart muscle to become very stiff. Without the proper elasticity, the heart cannot pump efficiently and the "backup" of blood will cause the heart to beat faster in order to keep circulating my blood supply at the necessary levels. Finally, something and someone that makes sense.

I'm to have a Cardiac MRI this Friday and Dr. Reyes was pleased this had already been scheduled. In order to get the results ASAP, Dr. Reyes gave me his cell phone number and asked me to call or text him Monday morning to remind him to get the test results. As soon as he reviews the data he will call me to discuss the findings. This is the first time in my life a Doctor has given me his cell number. Wow. Amazing. I like this guy.

If the heart muscle has stiffened, Dr. Reyes will refer me to a specialist for treatment. He knows the Head of the Cardiopathy Department at the hospital and can arrange for me to see her. Needless to say, I am encouraged at long last about resolving this issue.

I see Dr. Badros on Thursday to review the results of last week's blood draw and bone marrow biopsy. I hope my M-Spike has dropped further but if not I'm sure a new course of treatment will be outlined.

The bone marrow biopsy was my 3rd one. Unlike the first 2 done in the Doctor's office, this was done in the Interventional Radiology Department. I was sent to an operating room where they used twilight medication to relax me, an X-ray machine to locate the best spot to invade and a drill to bore into the bone. The medication was probably not necessary as I was exhausted from the 3 hour wait past my appointment time. They had 2 emergency cases to deal with and that pushed everything back. So even though the twilight medication is not full blown anesthesia, I went out like a light and never felt a thing. I'm sure there will be many more bone marrow biopsies in my future and even though this method is more time consuming and expensive I'd be happy to keep this procedure over the punch and scrape method used in the Doctor's office.

I hope this finds you both well, happy and bouncing about. More to follow on Thursday after my visit with Dr. Badros.

Love you muchly.

Hello Again . . .

Thu, Mar 23, 2017, 5:09 p.m.

Howdy Pardners,

BTW, ("By The Way" for the happily uninformed) where have all the good Westerns gone? No wonder our country is in such bad shape. No Roy, no Gene, no Big John, no Clayton Moore, no Will Hutchins, no Richard Boone, no James Arness, no Chuck Connors, no Shane (my favorite) and so many others. Yes, they used guns but only on the bad guys and they were always "Straight" with truth and justice. We could sure use some of that! Come on Hollywood and TV, get with it.

Now that I've fixed all our problems here's my latest update. We saw my Cancer Doctor (Dr. Badros) today and it's mostly all good. My partial remission is holding steady with no improvement or decline in the last 30 days. In order to keep the Myeloma in the corral, I will start a new regimen with Pomalidomide and the dreaded steroid Dexamethasone. (At least the dose of Dex will be cut in half so maybe I can finally lose some weight). I don't have to see Dr. Badros again for 3 months so here's hoping the new therapy keeps a lasso tightly noosed around those Maverick platelet cells.

Dr. Badros cleared me for swimming so I will start with this non-load bearing exercise tomorrow. We have a very nice Olympic Aquatic Center nearby and I'm looking forward to some low stress activity.

The last, but most urgent problem for me is my elevated heart rate. Just sitting in a chair, doing nothing, my pulse rate is between 105 and 115. I saw a new cardiologist, Dr. Reyes, last Tuesday and he impressed me. I'm getting a Cardiac MRI tomorrow morning that will hopefully give some answers. This test was set up several weeks ago and Dr. Reyes was happy it was already scheduled. He asked me to call or text him on Monday to remind him to get the results ASAP. He gave me his personal cell phone number and not his office number. WOW. No Doctor has ever volunteered his cell number. Very impressive or just plumb loco; I'm going with impressive. If this issue gets resolved, I can hopefully return to work soon. Lying around the house with our dogs isn't terrible but retuning to a full paycheck has its upside.

So that's all the news from this Bronco wannabe. Spring is here, the days are longer and the weather is getting warmer. It's all good!

Happy Trails to You....until we meet again,

Work Release for Bruce Moffatt

Tue, Apr 11, 2017, 8:20 a.m.

(Back to the old grindstone and happy to do so)

Dr. Badros,

My employer would like a note clearing me to return to work. My heart rate issue is still unresolved but Dr. Reyes feels I can return to work as well. I will report back to work on Monday April 17th. Can you have a note approving my return to work on April 17th uploaded to the My Portfolio Portal or emailed to me? My email is bruleemoff@gmail.com.

Thank you,
Bruce Moffatt

Back at Work

Mon, Apr 17, 2017, 7:02 p.m.

Papa,

All went well today. One of the ladies that sells tile for us made a "Welcome Back Bruce" banner and hung it over my desk. Everyone was very kind and happy to see me. My Branch Manager, Jinal Shah, who has been so supportive is in NJ for meetings and won't get back until Thursday. However, he called to welcome me back and encourage me to ease back into work slowly. His boss, our Section VP, is Ryan Wiener. Ryan also called to express his happiness for my return. Great people running a great company.

My energy and stamina are improving but my heart rate is still higher than I would like. I think as I lose weight and continue to recover from the BMT my heart will grow stronger too. I no longer have to deliver our samples and showroom tower displays which were quite heavy and time consuming. My days will involve desk work, driving to customers and speaking with them. Nothing strenuous and that's another well timed blessing for my state of being. So fortunate!

Of course my best fortunate is being born to the two best parents a child could ever ask for. Everything I have and everything I am, is a product of that great stroke of luck.

All my love forever,
Brucie

Apr 26, 2017, 8:37 p.m.

From Fred

Dear Lord,

"Oh, wow! Something else! Can it be? "Anyway, we know that You love Bruce, and from the moment he was created, and as a little boy, loving the western style and the cowboy boots that Grandfather Pat bought him each summer when we went to South Dakota. I can easily picture him in my mind's eye. And know that You have seen him and watched over him every moment until this one. "Now my prayers join his and Sandy's and Mary Jane's and Joe's in all the earnestness and love that is humanly possible. Please be with the two of them and use the skill and experience of his doctor so that everything will be done exactly right- whatever that should be- that his complete healing - which has been going forward - shall go further in perfect fashion until he is whole and well and strong again. "I dare to ask this, one father to Another, knowing you care and also have the power. Please. "Thank you. Please again."

I do not believe any father could love a son more than I love you. And Sandy.

Daddy

Back to Work

May 14, 2017, 6:09 a.m.

Good Morning All and Happy Mother's Day,

I hope all you wonderful Mothers are being well pampered today. How I wish my supercalifragilistic Mother was still here with us, but I will celebrate her life today through all the fabulous memories she gave our family.

I started back to work April 17th and have functioned well. My company, MS International, has switched my position from Product Promoter for the Kitchen and Bath Industry to Architect & Design and Commercial Sales Representative. As such 2 new priorities are in order. I have to learn a lot more about our tile and flooring products (hundreds and hundreds of options) and I get to start all over building a book of contacts and relationships. WHEW! Starting over. Just what a 63 year old person wants to do. Can't complain though, MSI is the best company I've ever worked for and they have treated me better than I could possibly expect in dealing with my Cancer and BMT.

After a 3 week + delay for insurance and human ineffectiveness, I finally received my new "maintenance program" medications. Pomalidomide (chemo pill) and good old Dexamethasone (Steroid). No side effects so far other than a lack of sleep from the Dex. Fortunately, I only take Dex once a week so I save it for Saturday mornings. I don't sleep well that night but by Sunday night I get a better rest which makes Mondays at work less Zombie like. I'll see my local Oncologist this Friday for blood test follow up and the Myeloma Specialist in a couple of weeks. Hopefully, my partial remission is holding fast and I can continue to lead a more normal life. So grateful for that!

Not wanting to rely strictly on pills, I took the plunge into juicing. If you haven't seen the movie, "Fat, Sick and Nearly Dead" I highly recommend you give it a look. You will find it on Netflix. The movie spawned a movement called Reboot with Joe. While perusing the Reboot with Joe website I found a nutritionist that guides people through the various juicing programs. Isabel Smith lives in Manhattan and I called her up. She has worked with Cancer patients and has designed a program specifically targeted to my needs. I prepare my 4, 20 ounce juices every morning and consume them throughout the day. Heavy emphasis on veggies and lower amounts of fruit. Cancer loves sugar so we're not giving it what it wants. I add some protein powder and Coconut water to the juice and that's my daytime sustenance. For dinner, a protein and non-starchy vegetable. No cravings, no hunger to speak of. While in the hospital I ballooned to 249 pounds. I'm currently at 228 and continue to lose weight at 1-2 pounds a week. The flood of nutrition from the juicing and loss of weight can only be good for my overall health. My pants are loose but I'm at that in-between size where I can't quite step into the myriad of clothes in the basement from thinner days. I think I have about 4 sizes of pants to fall back on as I get smaller. At least I won't have to buy new clothes. To keep my pants from falling off I've switched to suspenders. EUREKA! Why did I not wear these before? So nice not to have to tug up my pants all day long. I may never go back to belts.

Sandra is in full swing Designing and Building for the top 2%. Business is good and everyone wants their work done yesterday. Choco and Latte continue to add joy to our everyday lives. Choco has a cracked tooth that needs to come out. There goes $1000.00. I'm getting my first crown and that's only $700, but insurance is covering about $500-$600. It's good to be a Dentist no matter how many legs the patient has.

And it's good to be leading a more normal existence. I can't say I'm fully recovered from the BMT but my energy is much better and my elevated heart rate is coming down. No marathons in my future but I can work a pretty full day and play some golf on the weekend. I am so thankful for the improvements and of course, thankful for all your support, prayers and positive energy. Your kindness cannot be accurately measured but it has and will continue to be one of the greatest life blessings I have ever received. There really are silver linings in dark clouds.

Love to all, kisses for the women...(KOTL for Duanne)
Bruce Lee

B Moffatt Heart Rate

Dr Badros,

I saw my Cardiologist on June 13th. An EKG showed my HR at 77 bpm; much lower than when I saw you last. After much discussion, Dr Reyes felt whatever had created the HR issue was no longer a problem. I'll see him again in 6 months.

Below is a record of my recent monitoring. As you see, my HR is much improved. While we may never know what created the issue, I'm happy to report the improvement that has "miraculously" reversed itself.

Sat. 6/17.	4:35am.	118/67.	*71* bpm
Sun. 6/18.	4:08am.	118/65.	72 bpm
Sun. 6/18.	11:50am.	124/83.	82 bpm
Mon. 6/19.	4:45am.	105/70.	67 bpm
Mon. 6/19.	8:45pm.	115/70.	81 bpm
Tue. 6/20.	4:30am.	120/65.	65 bpm
We'd. 6/21.	8:00pm.	110/66.	76 bpm
Thur. 6/22.	4:30am.	106/66.	70 bpm

Thank you,
Bruce Moffatt

A Beautiful Day

Sep 10, 2017, 10:36 a.m.

Good morning and a very pleasant Sunday to all,

It's a picture perfect day in Annapolis as I sit on the front porch with Choco and Latte lying in the yard, Queens of all they survey. I wish the same could be said for our friends in Texas and Florida and I hope everyone is safe and sound.

I had my 2nd 3 month follow up with Dr. Badros on Thursday. The blood results were good with my partial remission holding steady. No increase in the level of cancer, which is probably the best to be hoped for. But no good deed goes unpunished and the Pomalyst that is keeping the cancer in check is also making me very tired and easily short of breath.

As you may recall, I had a very elevated heart rate for a long time and that has self-corrected. I think it was a side effect of Carfilzomib/Kyprolis that helped reduce my M-Spike prior to the BMT and the more potent chemo I received in the hospital to wipe out my marrow. Very grateful for the lower resting heart rate!

Dr. Badros is going to reduce the dose of Pomalyst from 4mg to 2 mg in an effort to give me a better level of energy. Here's hoping for some noticeable improvement. I'm still required to take my weekly dose of Dexamethasone (steroid) and it too has its own set of side effects. But lest I complain too much, I have no pain and I'm able to work and stay employed. So all in all, it's very good to be me.

We now have a beautiful swimming pool and patio in the back yard. Choco and Latte enjoy their daily swims and we get a big kick out of all their antics in the pool. The house exterior is getting a new paint job and that will hopefully be the end of our home improvements. Please come and visit at your earliest convenience!

My next appointment with Dr. Badros is January 4th, 2018. Until then, Happy Thanksgiving, Merry Christmas and Happy New Year. I know that sounds premature but my how time flies. We'll be singing Carols and toasting the New Year in short order.

With gratitude for each of you....
Bruce Lee

Follow Up Question

Thu, Jan 4, 2018, 12:15 p.m.

Dr. Badros,

Sorry to bother you but I was rather stunned when you commented I almost died from my BMT. (Bone Marrow Transplant). Was it my elevated heart rate, rash and diarrhea the basis of this assessment or were there other factors I was not aware of? Naturally, I'm alive and kicking now and delighted to get a vacation from Dex. Any further light you can shed on my reactions to the BMT will be appreciated.

Thank you,
Bruce Moffatt

Updates

Oct 18, 2018, 8:29 p.m.

I saw Dr. Badros today for an update on my blood results drawn last week. The results are not good and in fact he said they are quite bad. There is an infection fighting component in the blood labeled IgG. The top end of normal is 1400 mg/L. Mine is over 3400. My urine results show signs of potential kidney failure so that has to be address quickly. Dr. Badros has always told me I have Refractory Myeloma and the word refractory means "does not respond well to treatment". He admitted the results are confusing because I look the picture of perfect health. And I feel as good today as I have since my diagnosis 3 years ago. Go figure.

Pomalyst, following my BMT, has kept my cancer stable for 18 months but those crazy plasma cells that turn cancerous have overcome the effect of the drug. Time to move on to other drugs. I report to my local oncologist, Dr. Bhandari, tomorrow. He will perform a bone marrow biopsy by punching a hole in my pelvis in my lower back and collect some marrow for further analysis. I've had this done several times and while it's not a fun procedure it's not as painful as I originally expected. My new cocktail will include Dexamethasone again, the hated steroid. Kyprolis had a very good effect on my cancer level prior to my bone marrow transplant so I will go back to that drug. Two other drugs will be added as well: Velcade and Darzalex.

I pressed Dr. Badros on some questions which he was reluctant to answer. My guess is that these drugs will be quite potent and may create side effects that wear me down and make working difficult. Of course, we won't know that until we see how I react to these drugs. Dr. Badros said I will stay on this regimen for 4 weeks. If the results are not what he wants the next step will be a clinical trial.

For now everything is up in the air and I'm so sorry to give you this news. I was to have cataract removal Oct 31st and it was suggested to cancel the surgery. I asked if I could fly to KY for Thanksgiving and the answer was, let's wait and see. (Blood clots are an issue when flying in a plane). If at all possible I hope we can at least drive to KY and that will remain a top priority.

So. YUK huh? I can't say I'm completely surprised. My reading on Multiple Myeloma paints this picture of remission, relapse, remission, relapse. We must hope for the best but also be prepared for a Hail Mary if the standard protocols fail. Perhaps I'll go into a clinical trial of new, cutting edge research and become the first person cured of MM. Somebody has to be first so why not me?

Fear not. All will be well. How grateful I am for my loving, happy family! You each give me strength.

Brucie

Biopsy Done

Mon, Oct 22, 2018, 5:25 p.m.

Hello Daddy and Sissy,

The bone marrow biopsy took place in Dr Bhandari's office today. He is my local oncologist and a very nice man. I've had this done 3 times before and this one was more involved. Due to the abundance of Myeloma cells in the marrow he had a hard time getting the volume of liquid in the marrow he wanted to extract. So instead of in and out with one sweep in the marrow, he went in about 10 times. Fortunately, this was all done though the same incision or point of entry. Not pleasant but not excruciating either. More a feeling of uncomfortable pressure.

Results from the lab will take 7-10 days and I'm unsure what the point is. We already know the number of Myeloma cells is high so what bearing this more accurate method of measuring will have in my treatment evades me. But I'm sure they have a purpose.

Now we wait for the insurance company to approve my medications. Infusions may start on Wednesday and Thursday, but I prefer Thursday and Friday if possible. The first round will take 7 hours each day. After that, I expect the weekly infusions to only take 60-90 minutes.

Insurance Delays for Bruce Moffatt

Wed, Oct 24, 2018, 8:58 a.m.

(It would be nice if my Doctors we ultimately in charge of my healthcare, but it's the insurance companies that have the last word)

Katrina,

I cannot get clearance from the insurance company to start my new chemo treatments. I had a bone marrow biopsy on Monday with Dr. Bhandari in Annapolis. He is my local oncologist. They have sent a Pre Determination request for my medications to Blue Cross Blue Shield. BCBS is my provider since Oct 1st. They are showing my old insurance with United Healthcare as the primary insurer. I paid United Healthcare a one month COBRA payment to cover the gap of insurance until I was eligible with my new employer. No one seems to be doing anything about this. Evidently it is up to me to tell BCBS I am no longer with United Healthcare.

Further, there is a scheduling problem with even getting my treatments started at Dr Bhandari's office. Even if approved today for the drugs, they are not giving infusions on Friday and I'm told the earliest they can attend me may be Tue/Thur of next week.

I was not able to get my Pomalyst refilled earlier this month and no doubt that was because of the issue with BCBS and United Healthcare. So ,I have not been on any cancer fighting drugs for over 3 weeks. Dr. Badros said he was very concerned about the rapid decline in my blood results and that I need to start treatment ASAP. Getting started has no positive outlook at present. Can you help with this? Can I start treatment at your hospital Thur/Fri, Fri/Sat or even Sat/Sun. I'm getting frustrated and nervous about this.

Thank you,
Bruce Moffatt

Request from Bruce Moffatt

Tue, Oct 30, 2018, 11:39 a.m.

Dr Badros,

It's been 10 days since I met with you and still no progress on getting my new medications approved. A very nice lady at Blue Cross Blue Shield of Texas says my approval is marked for Nov 7th. This is after I asked the receptionist at Dr Bhandari's office to have him call BCBS at a special number I was given to get this marked as urgent. I was told his billing department has marked this urgent but I do not know if he called personally.

My impression from our conversation was that my health is in jeopardy and I should start treatment immediately. If I misunderstood the severity of my cancer please let me know.

Unfortunately I was just informed that you cannot call and get this expedited since your name was not listed on the application for approval. I am now calling Dr Bhandari's office again to ask them to call and get this escalated. This is very frustrating.

Thank you,
Bruce Moffatt

The Latest

Thu, Nov 1, 2018, 9:52 a.m.

Good morning all,

Maggie, a nurse in Dr Bhandari's office, just called to tell me BCBS has denied the treatment medications Dr Badros has requested. Maggie believes that it is the combination of the medications they are objecting to and not any particular drug on the list. Dr. Badros may have recent information that the combination of Darzalex and Kyprolis has been recently combined for relapsed MM but the insurance company has not seen those drugs used together so they are denying coverage.

Dr Badros has been sent a message about this and now he will have to revise the treatment and start a new approval process. Hopefully, this will not take 2 more weeks.

I am sending Dr Badros an email and asking him to confer with me to see how quickly we can start some form of treatment. I'll let you know more as this opera unfolds further.

Thank you,
Bruce Moffatt

More Info

Thu, Nov 1, 2018, 11:02 a.m.

Dr Badros called me and he has spoken to Dr Bhandari. They are submitting a new list of drugs to BCBS that are more readily acceptable for my treatment. I'm not sure which one of the 3 chemo drugs will drop off and which ones will remain. He anticipates I will start treatment next Monday or Tuesday at Dr Bhandari's office in Annapolis. If that is not the case and he can get me started sooner at U of MD hospital he will try to start me there.

Breaking news to follow as it happens.

At Last

Fri, Nov 2, 2018, 6:11 p.m.

Hello most precious ones,

Well, I'll start my new medication infusions on Monday. Dr Bhandari had a "peer to peer" conversation with a Doctor at BCBS. The approved treatment is now 2 chemo drugs instead of 3. Kyprolis, which greatly suppressed my cancer prior to the Bone Marrow Transplant, is out. The new drug Darzalex is in along with Velcade. And of course, I will go back on the steroids.

I have to take a Singular pill the night prior to each round of infusions. It's an asthma drug and I don't know why this is prescribed. I will receive Benadryl and other drugs an hour before the infusions. Evidently, Darzalex is quite powerful and patients often have reactions during administration. It will be given very slowly and stop when and if a reaction presents. I start at 7:30 am on Monday and Tuesday and the infusion process will last all day for both days. Hopefully, I can return to work on Wednesday.

Teresa, the GM at my new job, and other employees have been fabulous and offered help and concern. So lucky to be at Cosmic Stone.

So lucky to be of Moffatt/Morrison blood. How can this cancer survive my Scot/Irish lineage? If our ass of a President gets a 2nd term, I will be looking for a home in Dundee and this is your invitation to come along.

A Skelp in the Lug to Trump

The Next Step

Sat, Nov 3, 2018, 8:57 a.m.

Happy Saturday Friends and Family!

Cool and rainy here, but the rain should clear and I'll try to play golf with my friend Phil this afternoon. Try is the operative word as golf only gets more difficult the longer you play. Speaking of difficult:

Dr. Badros prescribed a new treatment for me on October 18th. I had a Bone Marrow biopsy on Monday Oct 22nd. All necessary paperwork was sent to the insurance company with an expected approval within 2-3 days. The application was marked Urgent and Critical. No approval was forthcoming. Phone calls to my Dr and to Blue Cross Blue Shield provided no information other than a possible 10-14 day approval process. Good thing this was marked Urgent and Critical.

This past Wednesday word came down that my drug regimen was denied by BCBS. The 3 chemo drugs ordered are all approved for Multiple Myeloma, but they did not like or recognize the need for all 3 drugs to be used simultaneously. So my Dr spoke to the BCBS Dr and the prescriptions were changed. Approval came yesterday and I start infusions on Monday and Tuesday. It appears that Doctors are not really in charge of your health and treatment. That belongs to the insurance company. I wonder why Dr. Badros and Dr. Bhandari went to medical school and then specialized in oncology and MM. So, my resurgent myeloma went about 2 weeks without treatment. No big deal, right?

Darzalex seems to be the powerful drug of choice. Infusions will happen over a 7-8 hour period on Monday and Tuesday along with other drugs. About 50% of patients have adverse reactions to Darzalex, so there may be some stopping and restarting to manage symptoms. After the initial dosing, future weekly treatments should only take an hour or two. Should be interesting. Regardless of all the delays and red tape, I'm looking forward to getting started and kicking my M-Spike (Myeloma level in the bone marrow) back down to less than 1.0. It's been at .6 to .8 for over 18 months and its level two weeks ago was 2.3.

Infusions will continue for 4 weeks and new blood work will reveal the results at the end of the cycle. If no progress is made, I will move into a clinical trial, but I'm confident the new treatment will re-suppress the cancer.

Thanks for reading, thanks for praying, thanks for caring and thinking about me. In addition to each of you in my extended family, my boss, Teresa Burruss (GM) and co-workers at my new employment have been fabulous and supportive beyond expectations. The world is full of wonderful people...like you.

Blood Work

Tue, Dec 4, 2018, 11:41 a.m.

Pappy and Sissy,

The Univ of MD Hospital (where I see Dr Badros) has a program called My Portfolio. This program keeps a record of my treatment and blood test results to which I have access. I was able to view the results of last week's blood draw and the results were not as hoped for. The chemo regimen I have been on for the past month did not tamp down the Myeloma cells and they have in fact continue to grow to higher levels of concentration. Today is my normal day of infusions, but I showed the results to Dr Bhandari (my local oncologist) and he agreed there was no point in continuing with the current treatment. So, I skipped out of the office and went to work. At least I won't lose a day of pay and suffer sleeplessness from the steroids.

I see Dr Badros (MM Specialist) tomorrow at 2:30. He will propose a new treatment which may be one of the 11 Clinical Trials he oversees for Relapsed and Refractory Multiple Myeloma. This could potentially involve the latest technique to "engineer" my white blood cells to recognize a specific protein on the Myeloma cells which sends a message to my immune system to destroy the cancerous cells. This bypasses chemotherapy and provides a road map for my own immune system to kill these pesky cancer cells. Of course, there are other drugs and techniques used in these experimental trials, so I'm sure Dr Badros will steer me into the best program for my particular and resistant form of MM.

I will update you as soon as I know more. I'm very hopeful one of these trials will produce some level of remission and avoid the side effects that come with the toxic chemo drugs.

The Plot Thickens

Thu, Dec 6, 2018, 7:45 a.m.

Good morning,

I hope you are adjusting to our coldest season with less daylight, less sunshine and the potential for snow. It's always nice to get a snowfall and one or two of these events can be fun. However, if we continue with the record precipitation we received in Maryland this year, the "fun" of snow could be short lived. Happy to report I bought a snowblower 3 years ago after a 22" blanket fell and it has not been used much since purchased. Hopefully it will see some use this year but not too much.

As you may recall, the combination of chemotherapy drugs my Doctor prescribed 6 weeks ago was denied by Blue Cross Blue Shield. We had to settle for a different regimen the insurance would approve. My particular form of Multiple Myeloma is very aggressive and does not respond well to treatment. The drug Darzalex has a good record of success for this type of MM, so my local oncologist kept the Darzalex and dropped Kyprolis from the list to get some treatment started. I was concerned about this choice as Kyprolis beat down my cancer successfully in 2017 which allowed me to move forward with a bone marrow transplant. Unfortunately, the treatments I received over the past 4 weeks have not been effective and the level of cancer has increased.

Of particular concern is the large increase of an antibody component in the myeloma cells called Kappa Free Light Chain. Normal levels are 20mg/liter. Mine are at 4,114 mg/liter. Left unchecked this could lead to kidney failure and the beginning of the end so to speak. Happy to report my kidney function is fine and with any luck, Kyprolis will perform as expected and significantly lower this threat.

Moving forward, I will no longer get treatment from Dr Bhandari in Annapolis, my local oncologist. I will receive my new infusions and future treatments at the University of MD hospital in Baltimore, where Dr Badros (MM Specialist) can more closely monitor my progress. Application for my new cocktail of chemo and other drugs has been submitted to the insurance company. So ,we again go through the 5-7 day approval process. If the insurance company balks, I'm confident Dr Badros will bend them to his will. His staff tells me he has the reputation of getting what he wants for his patients.

The drugs I've discussed so far are a short term measure to reign in the cancer. Dr. Badros has 1 spot left for a clinical trial under his purview and he will attempt to enroll me in that program. This could take 2-3 weeks for approval. This trial uses a "marker" of some type that attaches to the myeloma cells and a chemotherapy drug that seeks out the marker, attaches to the cell and destroys it. Sounds like a video game. Dr. Badros will also start now to enroll me in another clinical trial if needed in the future. This uses CAR-T Immunotherapy protocols. Here, my own T Cells (a type of white blood cell that fights infections) are harvested, genetically modified to recognize a specific protein on the myeloma cells, multiplied and given back to me. This wakes up my immune system which previously has been unable to recognize the cancer and will now go to work destroying the disease. Amazingly, it appears the cure may be inside me; it just needs to see the disease to kill it. Johns Hopkins Hospital in Baltimore has a trial of this type and to be considered I will need to be evaluated by them prior to enrollment.

So, lots of options moving forward. Lots of side effects and potential complications too but that is to be expected. I am very lucky to have Dr. Badros as my doctor. He is one of the top doctors in this field and has connections to all the latest cutting edge drugs and programs. And another bright spot, the Insurance companies have no say in the clinical trials. The trials are funded independently and do not require insurance funding if I am accepted into a program.

I'm expecting good results in both the short and long term progress with my disease. But in addition to science, technology and physicians, I'm grateful for your prayers and support. Keep up the good work and I look forward to giving you equal credit for my next report of positive outcomes.

Enjoy each day and be kind to everyone.

1st Infusion of New Medications

Dec 11, 2018, 7:37 p.m.

Howdy Partners and Partneretts,

I arrived at the Univ of MD cancer center at 7am today. Infusion started around 7:45 and some people at the front desk failed to show for work, so check in was slow. The single receptionist was bright, humorous and very apologetic which removed my lack of patience for standing in line; one of my many faults. Amazing what a smile and some empathy can do.

I received a double dose of Kyprolis with an hour of hydration before and after the poison was dripped in. I would have been out the door by 11am, but I had to call the insurance company to find out if the 2 chemo drugs taken in pill form, will ever arrive at my doorstep. Ashlyn, my infusion nurse, helped me arrange the very complicated dosing schedule for the remaining weeks in December. Blood draw on Dec 26th and results with Dr Badros on Jan 3rd. The pills arrive tomorrow so I'll see how I react to another set of possible side effects; they all sound worse than the disease. I've had Kyprolis before and it worked wonders. Wished we did this 4 weeks ago instead of Darzalex. If I can tolerate the new regimen, I have high hopes to return to at least a partial remission. If not, on to Clinical Trials.

I left for work around Noon and got 6 sales calls accomplished. Some promising, others need a follow up from Guido for an offer they can't refuse. I only had to miss a half day of work and vacation hours will cover my absence. Send me the MONEY!

Started feeling less vigorous on the 1:15 drive home. As soon as I entered in the door, I had some serious cold chills and loss of appetite; a first in the Moffatt Men's Clan no doubt. Amazing how my body delayed the reaction until I got home.

I'm resting comfortably under 3 blankets and a UK Hooded sweatshirt, gym shorts and socks. (Mother would be proud I'm wearing socks in bed)

That's it. I'll spare other people form this update until I know some more details after the blood work results. Feel free to share this with anyone you think has an immediate need or interest to know. Not trying to exclude anyone, just trying not to wear people out with my issues. If you want fewer updates let me know. No bruised ego.

Love to all...especially the girls, but boys too.

The Latest but Not the Greatest

Thu, Jan 3, 2019, 6:25 p.m.

I hope your Holidays were Merry & Bright. For the Moffatt family, it was not the best of times as we had to say our final goodbye to my sister's husband Joe Yates. Joe was a brilliant man, an activist in his community, attorney and outspoken liberal democrat, father to 2 children, grandfather to 3, step-father to my nephew Chip and devoted husband to my sister. Joe left us too soon and he will be remembered and missed for a long, long time.

I saw Dr Badros today and the news is not great. Myeloma cells have many parts and my bad actor is the Kappa Free Light Chain. A healthy level is 19 mg/Liter and my level had risen to over 5000 mg/Liter. This can lead to kidney failure but fortunately my kidneys are still working fine.

I will have another Bone Marrow Biopsy next Tuesday and start more infusions of the drugs recently used. Cytoxan will be dropped from the mix as it may be the cause of my low platelet count and the reason one infusion had to be cancelled. New labs will be drawn after the 3rd infusion on Jan 22nd and we'll see what the results are.

The next option, if needed, is to put me back in the hospital and give me 4 high power chemo drugs to wipe out my bone marrow. They saved a batch of stem cells from my 1st Bone Marrow Transplant and those will be given back to me to re-grow my marrow. We hope this very aggressive treatment will stall the disease but a long term remission may be out of reach.

A new introduction to the mix is the search for Chromosome 17 Deletion. I believe the Bone Marrow Biopsy will reveal whether or not Chromosome 17 is present. This Chromosome is only present when Myeloma cells exist. It allows a marker to be attached to the cancer cells and the body can then use that marker as a guide to destroy the myeloma cell. Without Chromosome 17, the cancer cells cannot receive the marker and the body will not discover and kill the cancer. (The accuracy of this description is my distillation of a 2 minute video on the subject Sandra's friends found on the internet. I think it is somewhat accurate).

Dr Badros said he cannot get me into any clinical trials. Not much explanation but my guess is he suspects I am missing Chromosome 17 so these types of immunotherapy treatments that hold a lot of promise for MM will not work if Chromosome 17 is absent. So, the future isn't completely dark but it is not great either. Ever wanting to know the worst, I asked how long I would live if I do not get good results from these treatments. The answer was less than 6 months. I hate to share this but I think it is important to strive for the best and anticipate the worst. I am certainly hoping the 6 month time frame is wrong (by a lot) but we need to be prepared for disappointment.

I will see my local oncologist, Dr Bhandari, tomorrow and get his view on the information. As luck would have it, our friend Peter Bertrand is a brilliant Physician in his own right and he has graciously agreed to go with us to see Dr Bhandari. Peter will be a big asset in helping us understand the flood of information and understanding the possible steps moving forward. I will also ask for a 2nd opinion from another Myeloma Specialist; perhaps someone at Johns Hopkins which has a great reputation for treating the most difficult cancers and other diseases.

So, there it is. The "Fat Lady" isn't singing but I think she is clearing her throat. Please do not worry, it is a wasted emotion. We cannot know the future in this life but we have a promise of a better life after this one. I take great comfort in that belief and knowledge.

With love and appreciation for each of you and the unnumbered many who have offered petitions to God on my behalf.

Bruce

Your Advice Please

Sat, Jan 5, 2019, 10:43 a.m.

Dr. Badros,

I still see Dr. Bhandari once a month as he wants to keep track of my status and treatments. He suggested yesterday that I ask you about a recommendation for a 2nd opinion. He said you would know who might be a leading research Doctor that would have experience with my particular issues. Dr Anderson at Boston University Medical Center was someone Dr Bhandari thought might be a good option, but he said you are better connected in the specialty of MM and can make the best recommendations.

Please know I have every confidence in you and cannot adequately express my gratitude for the care you have given me. Since I appear to be losing this battle, I just want to make sure I take advantage of every opportunity.

A new turning point in my life is unfolding. Dr. Badros met with us and said he could not get me into any clinical trials and my options were running thin. Maybe 6 months left to live and this was quite shocking. This was a big change from the visit we had recently with him. And not much information was shared as to this change of direction. I wrote about this to my Friends and Family list. In response to that email Daniela Hoehn was about to enter my life and I think there was some measure of divine providence in this. Daniela has extended my life and she is one remarkable person.

Some Better News

Jan 11, 2019, 7:12 p.m.

Greetings and Happy Friday,

It's been a busy week with several new developments. The first new wrinkle is that I have had to admit I can no longer perform the physical requirements of my job. I will reluctantly work my official last day this coming Tuesday, Jan 15th. I've signed up for Social Security and I look forward to receiving a little bit back against the sums paid in. My free time will come in handy as a new window has opened after a door appeared to close during my last Doctor review; keep reading....

Our friends Scott and Cheryl Donnelly know Daniela Hoehn, MD, PhD Director Oncology, for a pharmaceutical company. Cheryl suggested I call Daniela and see what she can offer as insight to my disease and what options are available with the Physicians she calls on for new therapies and clinical trials for Multiple Myeloma. Well, Daniela is a whirlwind of energy and knowledge. Within a few days I had Physicians at University of Pennsylvania, Mount Sinai in New York and Columbia University Medical Center in New York offering to see me to review my medical history and consider me for their clinical trials. This goes to prove that "who you know is more important than what you know". Thank you, Scott and Cheryl for introducing me to Daniela. The window you opened is a debt I cannot repay.

Since my Sister in Law and Brother in Law (Cheryl & Cliffe Cheston) live in Philly, it seemed logical to set my first appointment at the Univ of Pennsylvania. So, Sandy and I met with Dr. Alfred Garfall today at 1:00. He reviewed my medical history, asked a lot of questions and gave us over an hour of his time to explore possibilities. Dr. Garfall believes I will be a good candidate for a couple of the clinical trials at his hospital. Of most interest is a BCMA Bi-Specific Antibody Therapy. Basically, a drug is administered via infusion that identifies a B-cell on the surface of the myeloma cell. The drug also attracts the Killer T-cells in my immune system to the B-cell and destroys the myeloma cell. Cutting edge. No guarantee but very promising results. In addition, there is a clinical trial with a new form of chemotherapy as well as several types of Car-T Immunotherapy programs. No need to bore you with the details on these therapies, but it's so nice to have access to more options and potential remission of this cancer.

So, I may be spending more time in Philly with new drugs, a new Doctor, a new hospital and enjoying the hospitality and gourmet cooking at the Cheston household. I'll keep you apprised. Thanks for being "who I know"!

Hope you have a great weekend!

Improvements

Fri, Jan 18, 2019, 8:22 a.m.

Good Friday Morning,

I had my 2nd appointment with Dr. Garfall at the Univ of Pennsylvania Medical Center yesterday. He drew my blood last Thursday and the results are showing improvement. The Kappa Free Light Chain that was out of control at 5300 mg/L is down to 1800 mg/L. (Normal is about 20mg/L.) Since that blood draw I have had another round of drug infusions so the current level may be even lower. This is good news and will hopefully minimize the risk of kidney failure associated with this issue.

The Plan: Complete the current cycle of drug infusions; 2 down 1 to go. Since there seem to be good results, continue with another 3 week cycle starting Feb 5th. Take 2 weeks off to get these drugs out of my system and then start the clinical trial Dr. Garfall is doing with a new Phase 1 drug test. Dr. Garfall is one of 5 physicians conducting this trial in the world. His 1st patient has had no side effects and is getting very good results. I could enter the trial the end of Feb or early March.

There is a balancing act for my blood profile to allow me to start the trial. The drugs I'm on suppress my platelet count and it will need to rise to an acceptable level in order to enter the trial. A 2 week vacation from the chemo will hopefully achieve that without letting my cancer levels elevate too much. On the flip side, my recent Bone Marrow Biopsy showed my plasma cells in my bone marrow to be 90% myeloma cells. Only 10% are healthy plasma cells. I'm not sure how much progress my current treatment can make at reducing the Myeloma cells, but the clinical trial should open up a shooting gallery for my Killer T-cells to send the Myeloma cells to their grave. A more pleasant act of violence I can't imagine.

How blessed am I? Trending toward good results after my introduction to Daniela Hoehn who has made this connection to Dr. Garfall possible. Could all the prayers and support from each of you and so many others both known and unknown to me also play a part in this? You betcha. (The Great Physician is no doubt helping my other physicians.) I am so grateful to have these options and be trending in a good direction.

Until next time....much Love and Thanks!

Dr Number 3

Jan 30, 2019, 9:52 a.m.

Good morning all,

Sandra and I took the train Monday to NYC for our Tuesday appointment with Dr. Chari at Mount Sinai Medical Center. Dr. Chari is another top Multiple Myeloma specialist recommended to me by Dr. Daniela Hoehn at Janssen Pharmaceutical. Really enjoyed the train as it reminded me of travels in my younger days to see my Grandfather and Uncle in South Dakota. So much more relaxing than airplane travel.

Our visit started with a 90 minute review of my medical history with a Physician Assistant; extremely detailed and accurate. Dr. Chari was excellent and offered a review of the standard MM drugs I have been on and those not yet used. He also gave descriptions of clinical trials he is conducting for both Car-T therapy and BCMA Bispecific protocols. (These are the 2 leading clinical trial protocols used to attack MM.) Of special interest was the fact that most BCMA trials can create an environment in which a future Car-T immunotherapy would not be effective. He does however have a new Bispecific trial whose formulary will not interfere with a Car-T program. This helps with the decision of which trial to start with in order to not eliminate future treatment options; Car-T first, BCMA when the Car-T is no longer effective.

What's next? My current chemotherapy is working and lowering my cancer levels so the plan is to stay the course. (Don't fix what isn't broken.) A key to getting into any clinical trial is to catch the cancer levels just after reaching a low point and the cancer is starting to increase. In order to track this, I will ask for weekly re-staging labs instead of the current monthly schedule for these specific blood test markers. Another important factor is getting my hemoglobin and platelet levels increased; chemo is suppressing these levels and they need to rise to acceptable levels to get into a trial. Another potential therapy is a sort of mini bone marrow transplant. Drugs will be used to eliminate or nearly eliminate my bone marrow again. My stem cells re-served from the 1st transplant may be used to help boost new marrow or may not be used depending on which of 2 methods is employed. This should give a remission or partial remission for 6-9 months and enhance the prospect for clinical trials.

So, I have gone from what seemed to be very minimal options for kicking down my cancer to enough options to be confusing as to what to do next. Dr. Chari summed up the path forward by saying this is a one-day-at-a-time process. Track the disease and make decisions as changes occur. When the current course of treatment stops working, evaluate the numbers and move to the next best treatment and try to eliminate or correct any issues that could prevent using the next best protocol.

The visit yesterday took much longer than anticipated so we missed our 4:30 pm train home. We took another train at 6:25 pm and got home at 10:15 pm. A long but worthwhile day. NY is too big, too congested and too expensive for my taste. However, if my best treatment option at some future date is at Mt. Sinai with Dr. Chari, I'll go there for as long as needed. If you happen to have a nice brownstone or apartment in Manhattan with a spare bedroom please let me know.

I'll be happy to sign a document stating your rent requirement is a charitable contribution for a tax deduction.

Tomorrow we meet with Dr. Badros (current MM specialist) to follow up on my latest blood tests and discuss the opportunities at Penn Medical Center and Mt. Sinai and future treatment considerations. Friday, I see my local oncologist, Dr. Bhandari to keep him up to date on this maze of information. Also, on the horizon is to find a Cardiologist Oncologist. This is a fairly new specialty that attempts to evaluate and mitigate adverse effects chemotherapy has on the heart. I still have a very elevated heart rate that conventional thinking says is not related to the Myeloma. Getting my heart rate under control would be a very welcomed improvement.

My Doctor dance card is approaching maximum capacity. That's actually a good thing and I am fortunate to have access to these physicians and their options for helping me hang around a little longer. So many people have much bigger problems and do not have access to so many options. All in all, I'm a very lucky boy.

Thanks for your continued support. Stay safe, stay warm, stay grateful.

Another Doctor

Tue, Feb 12, 2019, 8:41 p.m.

Good evening all,

I saw Dr. Boccia (Bo shay) yesterday. I got his name from a co-worker of Sandra's, Julie Patronic. Julie must be a good friend to the Doctor as he saw me very quickly after her introduction and request for an appointment. Lucky again for me.

This visit was not as detailed as with the Penn and Mt. Sinai visits, but all their notes and results were available to Dr. Boccia so he already knew my history. Dr. Boccia is doing Car-T therapies and the earliest he would have a slot for me is in April. Of greater importance, he told me that doing a BCMA Bispecific trail with Penn will not eliminate me from a future Car-T trial with him should the need arise. There has been some conflicting information on this issue, so it's a relief to know I will have a future option after the trial at Penn when and if it becomes ineffective.

The trial at Mt. Sinai would require weekly visits to NYC for 20 months, which amounts to 80 round trips from home. I would have to make the 4-5 hour drive up the day before my infusions and return home the next day after receiving the infusion. Gas, tolls, a place to stay overnight and parking fees would quickly add up in addition to the effort and inconvenience required. I'm due for a phone visit with the Physician Assistant at Sinai to review the details but barring some more compelling reasons I think I'll start with the trial at Univ of Penn Hospital. Since the drug used at Sinai does not target the same cell or protein on the myeloma cell targeted by BCMA and Car-T, perhaps it can be saved for a 3rd option down the road.

I get another infusion of the current chemo drugs tomorrow assuming my platelet count is high enough. I was weaker today than normal and more short of breath than ever. I think the Farydak drug may be the cause, but I don't have to take it this week so maybe I'll rebound a little.

If all goes according to current thinking, I will start the clinical trial at Penn in early March. I'll need to go up for a battery of tests on my heart, lungs, kidney functions, etc. and I expect to pass everything they throw at me. Here's hoping for some good cancer assassination.

GPRC Clinical Trial Consent Form

Feb 13, 2019, 5:05 p.m.

Dennis,

Thank you for taking time to speak with me today. In order to make a final decision on which trial to select, please confirm or correct the following information as I understand how it applies to the trials offered at Mt. Sinai.

First: JNJ-64407564 also known as GPRC5D (G Protein Receptor C Group 5 Member D) This treatment is a new approach which will attach to a T Cell and a protein labeled GPRC5D, bring them together and allow for the destruction of Myeloma cells. This is different from current BCMA trials, in that it does not attach to a B Cell on the Myeloma cells. As a first step trial, this leaves open the opportunity to move to a BCMA trial at a later date if necessary. Starting with BCMA as currently written by the supplier, will negate consideration for GPRC5D after BCMA has been used. Per our conversation, an amendment to this restriction is currently being written and if approved, starting with a BCMA trial may not exempt me from GPRC5D. The GPRC5D trial is a 20 month long program requiring a weekly infusion regimen. This means 80 round trip visits to Mt. Sinai from my Annapolis home with expenses for travel, tolls, overnight accommodations and parking fees to be 100% my responsibility. All this assuming I tolerate the drug, avoid serious side effects and see positive results.

Second: Car-T trials. You have a potential spot in a Car-T trial opening with an admittance date around March 15th. This trial involves removing my T-Cells, "re-engineering" them to recognize Myeloma cells and giving them back to me. Let the killing begin! This trial will take 6-7 weeks to administer and what I assume will be monthly or quarterly follow up visits to check on the efficacy of the process. How is that handled? Starting with your Car-T trial will allow me to move to a GPRC5D if needed at a future date. Additionally, the supplier for the Car-T trial will reimburse me for the cost of travel and lodging which is an important consideration for me financially.

These are my two options at Mt. Sinai. If I understand correctly, starting a BCMA or Car-T trial at another hospital will currently exclude me from any Car-T or GPRC5D you are conducting. Is that correct? Also, the BCMA trial offered to me at Penn is JNJ-64007957 a BCMA xCD3 Duo Body Antibody trial. I believe Janssen Pharmaceuticals is the supplier for both this BCMA trial and your GPRC5D protocol. If the afore mentioned amendment which could open the door to using GPRC5D after a BCMA trial is adopted will I be able to use your GPRC5D trial following the Janssen BCMA trial used at Penn?

As I mentioned during our phone call, I have family in Philadelphia so travel distance is less of an issue and room and board is free. Dr. Garfall at Penn has a patient sailing through their BCMA trial with no side effects and very good results. No guarantee for me but better than hearing he went blind or died from Cytokine Release Syndrome. So, please let me know if my recap of your trials and requirements is accurate and please correct any errors or add additional information you deem necessary.

Thank you for your patience as I attempt to make the best all round decision for my next step in kicking down my MM.

GPRC Clinical Trial Consent Form

Wed, Feb 13, 2019, 5:26 p.m.

Daniela,

I'm still leaning to the BCMA trial at Penn as I am not looking forward to 80 round trip visits to NYC for the GPRC5D trial. Below is an email I sent to Dr. Chari's Research Coordinator, Dennis Ramdas. We spoke on the phone today and I felt the need to write down as many details as possible and have Dennis review my notes for accuracy. This will help me with a final decision as there may be an amendment coming from your company regarding qualifying for GPRC5D after BCMA has been used.

Also, I saw Dr. Ralph Boccia (Bo shay) at his Germantown, MD office Monday morning. He has a trial that will have a slot for me in April, but more importantly, I will not be excluded if I start with the BCMA trial at Penn. So, this gives me an option after BCMA. His Sponsor is Cartesian Therapeutics in Rockville, MD. It is a Phase 1 Autologous CD8+ T-cells Transiently Expressing a Chimeric Antigen Receptor Directed to BCMA. Protocol 241-59-88 #20180034. Happy to send you the Informed Consent Form for more details if you are interested in what the competition is doing.

Sorry for the lengthy email. I know you are super busy but I want to keep you in the loop. No need for an immediate reply on your part. Thanks as always and I hope you are doing well and having some fun. All work and no play = no good!

GPRC Clinical Trial Consent Form

Feb 17, 2019, 4:19 p.m.

Daniela,

I hope you're having a good weekend and getting a chance to turn off the emails and intensity of your work life. Based on the information in Red Ink below, I have decided to start with your BCMA trial at Penn with Dr. Garfall. This will be much easier from a travel and financial standpoint as I have free room and board with my Brother In Law/Sister In Law.

In addition, I will also be eligible for your GPRC-5D trial at Mt. Sinai if I do not experience Cytokine Release Syndrome above Level 3 with BCMA. This leaves a door open to a future treatment when and if the BCMA trial becomes ineffective.

The Car-T trial has one slot open and I may not qualify for, or be the best candidate for, the opening. Even if I do qualify, I will have to be on a bridge chemotherapy regimen for 4-8 weeks while my re-engineered T-cells are replicated in a lab. I would not receive my new T-cells until the end of April or early May. Considering the aggressive nature of my disease, I would like to get started with the BCMA which is scheduled to begin soon.

Dr. Garfall has asked that we skip this coming week infusion of Carfilzomib, Dex and Faradyk. I'm sure this is to give my platelets a chance to recover. They were at 38K/mcl last week. I'm sure the time off will elevate them as my last free week resulted in a level of 84K/mcl. I report to Penn on Feb 26th for a Bone Marrow Biopsy and perhaps other testing. I'm scheduled for infusion on March 4th & 6th.

I have no idea if starting with the BCMA is the best option from a "remission" standpoint. All 3 trials have no guarantee of outcome. I do know that the 3 options presented to me would not be possible without your assistance. I can't thank you enough for all your help and support. I hope you and your husband will be able to come to Annapolis for a long weekend lounging by our pool and letting us wine and dine you. You pick the date and we'll make it happen.

Thank you for EVERYTHING!

GPRC Clinical Trial Consent Form

Tue, Feb 19, 2019, 5:29 p.m.

Dennis,

Thank you for all your assistance in helping me understand the particulars for the Car-T and GPRC-5D clinical trials at your hospital. I have decided to start with the BCMA Bispecific trial at Penn for a variety of reasons. Based on current information, I will still be able to qualify for your GPRC-5D trial later provided I do not have a CRS reaction above level 3 during the BCMA trial. This leaves a future option in case the BCMA trial becomes ineffective at some point.

Please share my gratitude with Dr. Chari for the opportunities presented to me and the generosity of everyone's time and efforts to assist me with my disease. Our paths may cross again in the future and that gives me great optimism for continuing the fight against Multiple Myeloma.

Another update

Feb 28, 2019, 7:53 AM

Good Morning All,

I am sitting at BWI airport waiting for my plane to Louisville, KY. My 91 year old Father is not doing well and I need to see him ASAP. His decline started with a Urinary Tract Infection which created havoc with his state of mind and has led to a problem swallowing. He has not had food or fluid for several days. His ability to recover from this set back does not appear likely. Dad has led an incredible life and it may well be his time to validate his faith in God to which he has devoted his life. I asked him some time ago if he had any doubts about the existence of God. (No matter how deeply you believe, there exists no proof here on earth). I expected him to say he was 99.999% sure that God exists, but that was not his answer. He said he was 1,000% sure of the existence of God and the truth of His Word. How encouraging. How typical of his confidence and faith. Your prayers for my Dad will be greatly appreciated.

I will fly back home this Sunday and travel to Philly in the afternoon to stay with my Brother and Sister in Law, Cliffe and Cheryl Cheston. I report at 6:45 am on Monday to the Univ of Pennsylvania Medical Center to begin my clinical trial for Multiple Myeloma. I will receive priming doses of the experimental drug on Monday and Wednesday and remain in the hospital for observation. If there are no complications I will be discharged on Friday and return every Monday for further dosing.

This new drug is in the early stages of administration. Only 45 people around the world have received this drug and I am the 5th person to enter this trial at Penn. Results so far have been very positive, with many participants achieving a partial remission and some with a complete remission. I will continue with weekly infusions as long as the treatment shows good results.

Entering this trial would not have been possible without the help of Scott and Cheryl Donnelly. They know Daniela Hoehn who works for Janssen

Pharmaceutical and Daniela made the introductions to several doctors on my behalf for consideration in the various clinical trials those Doctors are conducting. My undying gratitude to Scott, Cheryl and Daniela.

And of course, as always, my gratitude for each of you for your prayers and support as Sandra and I move forward with treating this disease. I have been and continue to be blessed beyond measure.

It's Been a Rough Week

Mar 5 , 2019, 9:07 a.m.

Well, I'll get right to the point. Our Father died this past Saturday March 2nd at 4:15 pm. I flew to KY on Thursday Feb 28th and Dad recognized me and was still capable of speech but had difficulty forming the words. Two days earlier his speech was 100% normal. By Friday he was largely incoherent and suffering from terminal agitation. My Sister engaged Hospice and every good thing you've heard about that organization is true. They were extremely helpful. Once properly medicated Dad's body relaxed but he was no longer able to communicate.

Unfortunately, something in the KY air triggered my allergies and I grew quite ill. (It actually turned out to be the H1N1 flu and it put me down hard.) I was not able to be at Dad's bedside when he left this world but Mary Jane was there and she held her phone to his ear for my final goodbye. Our Father was an accomplished Minister and Preacher, loved and appreciated by people from all walks of life. We will miss him but take comfort knowing he is with our Mother, the love of his life. I can only imagine his joy of reuniting with his parents, brothers and friends in addition to seeing face to face our creator upon whom no one living has ever been so privileged. I look forward to joining Mom and Dad at some distant point in time.

I needed to get home on Sunday in time to drive to Philadelphia and stay with Cheryl and Cliffe. I was to report at 6:45am to begin my Clinical Trial at Penn Medical Center. Dr Garfall had prescribed a Z Pack and this would hopefully get me on the mend. Southwest mysteriously cancelled my Sunday morning flight and had only late evening flights with layovers. I changed my itinerary to fly to Philly and avoid driving up from home. Every flight I booked got delayed. I got to bed at 1:15 AM after Cliffe fetched me from the airport. Cheryl delivered me safely through the winter storm at 6:45 am as scheduled. (Chestons to the rescue!) The trial drug was administered at a low dose and I'll receive a higher level dose tomorrow. No side effects so far. If all goes well, I'll be discharged Friday and return every Monday for more infusions.

Next on the calendar is a return flight to KY for Dad's funeral. Dr Garfall cleared me for travel after next Monday's infusion and shorter hospital stay for observation. The service will be on Saturday March 16th:

http://www.halltaylorfuneralhomes.com/obituary/fred-t-moffatt-jr

A more complete obituary to follow in a few days.

To end on a happier note. I subconsciously started looking for something to replace my lack of physical energy with something fun to do without great effort. In my youth that was a motorcycle. So, with great tolerance and understanding Sandra agreed to my new hobby: 2007 Big Dog K9 Chopper.

Frighteningly powerful and 9' long I am proceeding with great caution. I will take a rider safety course the end of March or early April. The Thrill is BACK. Leather up.

Love you all…

Thank you

New News

Wed, Apr 3, 2019, 7:46 p.m.

Good evening,

First, I want to thank everyone for your cards, emails and kind words of support in the recent death of my Father. He was 91 years old, a minister and preacher of the Gospel for 60+ years and touched many, many lives. I miss him. He was my Father, Pastor, Preacher, the man I esteemed above all others and my best friend. He sowed the seed of faith in me and I look forward to the day I shall see him again.

On the Myeloma front, things are not going as hoped. I have had 4 treatments of the clinical trial study drug and all of the important markers for my cancer are trending in the wrong direction. Dr. Garfall (Univ of Pennsylvania Medical Center) has suggested I go back on the chemo regimen that was having success at reducing my cancer levels. I will resume that combination of drugs with my local oncologist, Dr. Bhandari. I will most likely not resume care from Dr. Badros (the Myeloma Specialist) at the Univ. of MD Medical Center as the infusions can be done by Dr. Bhandari here in Annapolis. Dr. Garfall at Penn, will continue working with me, track my progress and look for other trials for me to join. He has a Car-T trial that is opening some new spots and he may attempt to enroll me. For now, I need to go back to what was previously working and get some improved markers.

So, this is a setback, but I can only hope returning to the previous treatments will produce good results and other options will present themselves in the near future. The fight goes on and all options will be vigorously pursued. Please continue to keep me in your thoughts and prayers which have been such a source of encouragement and gratitude to me.

All my love to all of you,

Checking In

May 12, 2019, 7:05 a.m.

Greetings and Happy Mother's Day to all. I hope this is a fun and relaxing Family Day for everyone but especially for all Mothers. I certainly hit the jackpot with my Mother and I hope you feel the same for your Mom.

The past 3 months have been eventful but unproductive in Myeloma suppression. First off, we decided to no longer use Dr. Badros, the Myeloma Specialist at the University of MD. He diagnosed me last December as being unable to qualify for any clinical trials anywhere at any time with only a couple of treatment options moving forward. He felt I might have as little as 6 months left to live.

Thanks to the Donnellys and Daniela Hoehn, I was put in touch with other Myeloma Specialists with greater hope and treatment options. The main obstacle to clinical trials was my low platelet count, but after 2-3 weeks off chemo my platelets increased to a sufficient level for trial options. I completed a 4 week trial at the Univ of Penn Medical Center in April which unfortunately did not produce good results. Dr. Garfall oversaw my treatment and we were very impressed with him.

He is now my "go to" Myeloma Specialist. My prior chemo treatment made good headway suppressing the cancer, so Dr. Garfall suggested I return to the same protocol. About 7 weeks had passed without any successful treatment and I was anxious to get back to something that was working.

Rather than commuting every week to Philly, I used my local Oncologist, Dr. Bhandari, to oversee my chemo treatment. It took him 2 weeks to get me started which I found frustrating. At the end of my 1st treatment cycle he had not ordered the re-staging labs that show the various markers for the cancer levels. I was scheduled to see him last Thursday and I would press for the blood work required for assessment. His PA felt the tests weren't necessary as a full profile had been done April 2nd at Penn. So now I'm 9-10 weeks without any successful treatment and no urgency to get results from the 1st cycle of chemo. Frustrating.

But on Tuesday, before my Thursday meeting with Dr. Bhandari, my phone rang. It was Dr. Garfall checking in on me. This was an unexpected and emotionally uplifting gift. A Doctor calling me to see how I'm doing; imagine that. But this wasn't just a "how's it going" call. Dr. Garfall wanted to know if I would be interested in another clinical trial. Only 2 scoops of Mint Chocolate Chip ice cream could compare to this unexpected turn of events. I'm all in of course.

The new trial drug will put a marker on the Myeloma cells, but instead of trying to attract my own T-cells to the cancer, the killing action will be done with interferon. Interferon has been around a long time, but at the higher doses needed for success it is very toxic. The study drug will attempt to focus the interferon on only Myeloma cells and avoid healthy cell destruction.

I go to Penn on Wednesday for blood work, another bone marrow biopsy, echocardiogram, etc. My platelets may be too low to start right away, but I should be good to go within another week or two. Infusions will take place every other week. If successful, the dosage will be increased and I may only need infusions every 3rd week. Another dose increase could occur with infusions once a month.

I continue to receive unexpected blessings but that is nothing new. I have had good fortune all my life and often undeservedly so. I believe your prayers, concern and support have much to do with my "luck". I am forever in your debt and I look forward to a future email with some use of the word "remission". Hope springs eternal!

No Drug Infusion Today

Mon, June 24, 2019, 9:08 a.m.

Good morning,

I'm at Penn and the blood draw shows my platelets are still too low for an infusion of the study drug today. I had 4 full doses of Dexamethasone last week (YUK!) in hopes of raising my counts but they only went up from 29 to 34 thousand. Need to get to 50 thousand. I'm headed back home and will return next Monday. Hopefully, the platelets will recover and I can get back on the drug. The Myeloma is not reducing but is holding steady. The good news is that the Kappa Free Light Chain is coming down sharply and that's a big bonus.

My Sister arrives next Sunday for a visit, so I'll come up on Monday and hope to get infused. I may stay over Monday night and get a blood draw early Tuesday morning before heading back home. I'll keep you informed of course.

Hope you're enjoying the fabulous weather and having lots of fun!

Clinical Trial #2

Jul 9, 2019, 10:31 a.m.

Summer has arrived and I hope you are enjoying the warm weather. I can't handle the really hot weather like I used to, but that's just one item in a long list of "used to". Still, it's a great time of year and we have had some fabulous weather and enough rain to keep our grass very green and the pool filled without using our own water supply. Love the sunshine!

I'm about 7 weeks into the new study drug that uses interferon as the bullet for myeloma cell death. Results so far are mixed. The level of myeloma is only holding steady, but the drug is having a positive lowering effect on the Kappa Free Light Chain (KFLC). This is a protein on the myeloma cell and left unchecked can lead to kidney failure. Kidney failure would not be a good thing and end any access to clinical trials and severely restrict other treatment options. Normal levels of the KFLC are 20mg/Liter. At one point last year I was over 5,000mg/Liter. Chemo treatments helped reduce this number and the new study drug has reduced the amount from

3400mg/L to 2100mg/L. This is great news and my Doctors at Penn Medical Center are very pleased.

But there's always a BUT. The trial drug is tough on my KFLC and also tough on my blood profile. Platelets, neutrophils, white and red blood cells and hemoglobin are all suppressed. To receive the drug, my platelets are supposed to be no lower than 50,000 per microliter of blood. (Normal levels are 150k-450k.) My platelets dropped to 28k and I had to miss 2 infusions because of this. I get an infusion every other week so I went 4 weeks without treatment. Fortunately, my doctor petitioned the study drug company and the platelet restriction has been removed. I received an infusion this past Monday and will continue infusions without interruption. Evaluations on the efficacy of the trial will be ongoing and I hope to see more good results now that I'll receive treatments as scheduled. If the myeloma starts to dial back along with the KFLC, that would be fabulous.

Lastly, this past week has been a low point for how I'm feeling. My energy has been near zero and some mysterious and severe back pain came on suddenly and left almost as quickly. An X-ray did not show any fracture or compression and 2 doses of hydrocodone and a muscle relaxer relieved the pain and required no further medication.

I'm home now with nothing pressing on the schedule for this week. I feel better today than yesterday and hope the trend continues. I will do as little as possible to encourage progress. So, now I will rest from tapping on my keyboard and you can rest from reading this lengthy update.

Love to each of you. Enjoy the Summer!

Time for My Next Novella

Tue, Jan 7, 2020, 4:33 p.m.

Greetings and Happy New Year,

2020. Really? Not just a reference to hindsight is it? I hope your Christmas and New Year celebrations were fun and low stress. Having no children and able to indulge ourselves with conspicuous consumption throughout the year, Sandra and I did not exchange gifts, cards, flowers or anything of monetary value. Time with friends and family made our Season Bright!

The first week of the new year has been interesting. On New Year's Eve my seasonal allergies flared up. I was not up to a lunch date with friends, so Sandra had to attend solo. On New Year's Day my right ear started to ache in the late afternoon. By midnight I could stand it no longer and we made the "trip of last resort" to the ER. Bullous Myringitis was the diagnosis. Blisters on the outer ear drum with fluid pounding away behind the ear drum. Very painful. The first dose of Tylenol helped for 3 hours. No relief from the 2nd dose, but the antibiotic given in the ER kicked in around 4 am and the pain started to subside. (Two weeks to 3 months for a full recovery. Hoping for the 2-week schedule.)

Jan 2. I was supposed to travel to Philly for an infusion day. Too tired and too sick to make the trip. Received a lab slip for a blood draw to check my platelets and neutrophils. Results were good so the infusion was re-scheduled for Wednesday Jan 8. Just so happens I'm having a small basal cell carcinoma removed at Penn Medical Center on the 7th (today), so I'll spend the night in a hotel and get back on track with my study drug infusion tomorrow. The drug has been holding my cancer at steady levels. My doctors tell me I have about twice the level of Myeloma I should be walking around with, but my kidney function and other markers are not contributing to infection or illness. They want to stay the course until things get worse. If we move to a different treatment we can't go back to this one. At some point, maybe soon considering current events, a change will be necessary. On deck is a pill called Venetoclax in combination Kyprolis. Kyprolis is the only chemo product to give me a significant response in lowering my cancer. Of course, the combination has risks and side effects. Nothing ventured, nothing gained as my Mother always told us.

Still Jan 2. The clothes dryer died; repair man inspected on the 3rd. $500 to repair. We bought a new one. The original price quoted was wrong and the sales lady called asking for another $230. I requested the same price, so a different model was approved. Installation was done yesterday without further drama.

Jan 3. Our Chocolate Lab, Choco, had a soft tissue sarcoma removed in November. Our Vet referred us to a Cancer specialist, and he determined we needed a second surgery to obtain larger "clean margins". Paid $1100 for tests and diagnosis. $3500 for the potential follow up surgery. Our Vet was confident she could perform the operation, so we put our trust in her and only had to spend $800. (Same price as the first surgery.) I dropped her off at 8 am, Jan 3rd. (Choco is recovering marvelously and is already back to full steam ahead.) If you're considering Medical School, I would suggest Veterinary Medicine. The patients don't complain and the money seems pretty good.

Still day 3 of the New Year. Our Yellow Lab, Latte, had been off her game for several days; sullen and quiet with no energy or interest in her usual antics. She was examined at 5:30 pm with no discernable issues from blood tests or a physical exam. By 6:30 pm Choc, Latte, Sandra and Bruce were headed home. (Antibiotics and pain pills have Latte back to her love of life.)

Jan 4, 5, 6. No drama (I think...I'm a little confused), just exhaustion. Will see what today and tomorrow has in store.

So, here's my take on all of this. First, no pity party please. I can't imagine what someone with Bullous Myringitis would do without access to care. The pain is intense and unrelenting. Sleep is impossible. What would someone who has cancer and no health insurance do? Many would be too proud to ask for help and suffer with pain and a shortened life span. My life, my health and my access to care is no more important than any other person's access to life saving and pain-relieving options. Why am I so fortunate?

Well, I started life White. Fabulous Parents. Good education. Always able to find employment and earn a good living. I never go to sleep wondering how I'll pay my bills or where my next meal comes from. I have a beautiful and talented wife who loves and supports me. (She is my HERO!) I have 2 dogs that show me what true, unconditional love is and bring me joy every day of my life. We've had a lot of unexpected expenses in the last 2 months. Sandra received a nice year-end bonus as a reward for the skill and dedication she brings to her job. Coincidence??? Great financial timing like this has been the case so many times during my 65+ years. 13 months ago, my Myeloma Specialist in Baltimore gave me 6 months to live and no possibility of qualifying for drug trials. Scott and Cheryl Donnelly introduced me to Daniela Hoehn and Daniela got me hooked up with Dr. Garfall. Dr. Garfall has put me in 2 trials and has more planned when current medications fail. Talk about good luck. Divine providence? Not sure why life has been so good to me. I have received far more than I have given. I am so grateful. Thank you for your love and friendship. God is good.

Sending you love and best wishes for a Great 2020!

Your Car-T Trial

Thu, Jan 9, 2020, 10:51 a.m.

Daniela,

Long time no talk. I hope this finds you well, having a great life and continuing your marvelous contributions to improving life for those of us with blood cancer disorders.

The first trial I did with Dr. Alfred Garfall at Penn was one of your BCMA therapies. After 2 cycles, there were no signs of success so the program was stopped. I went back to Kyprolis, Dex and a new pill, Farydak. Dr. Garfall called me several weeks later and invited me to join a trial sponsored by Tekata using an interferon based product. While a good response was not achieved, the drug has had a good containment effect on my cancer and reduced my Kappa Free Light chains which were out of control. We went to every 3 weeks for treatment instead of every other week a couple of cycles ago and this gave my platelets and neutrophils enough time to recover to good levels. My last 2 treatments were at a double dose which upped the drug to .4mg/kg. of body weight. I have had no complications and the Light Chains are doing better. Prior to infusion they are around 3000 mg/L and lowered to around 2,000 mg/L or even less. Still too high, but no signs of kidney failure, infections or illness. M-spike remains around 2.6 to 2.8.

The discussion has continued to center on taking the risk of a new therapy, which may or may not be effective and therefore eliminating the containment I'm experiencing with the current treatment. I pressed Dr. Garfall about the next steps yesterday. A few options were discussed but he felt my options were becoming more limited. I reminded him of a Car-T trial he previously mentioned and it jogged his memory. Evidently, a new 20 person study will open soon (probably February) using your product, Cartitude. YEAH! My understanding is my T cells will be re-engineered and have a chemotherapy product attached which directly targets myeloma cells. He said 90% of prior participants have had a good response. SIGN ME UP!

I know you're very busy, but if you have time for a chat on this protocol, I'd love to converse with you. I look forward to hearing your voice and catching up on life, work and play.

Hoping To Start Your Trial

Wed, Feb 19, 2020, 8:41 p.m.

Daniela,

I need a new drug...ala the Huey Lewis song. The one I've been on since May only controlled my disease and did not give a response other than suppressing my Kappa Free Light chains in a see/saw fashion. It recently stopped working all together.

As my good fortune has it, your BCMA and Car-T drug is starting a phase 2 trial at Penn. Dr. Garfall feels I should qualify for the Group C contingent. I'm getting my veins tested tomorrow in case I need a port and an echocardiogram. Should know by Friday if I pass Go and start aphaeresis next Wednesday. The results of this study seem amazing so I hope to be admitted.

Without you, this opportunity would not be possible. You remain my HERO and a God send.

I Need A New Drug

Feb 23, 2020, 1:17 p.m.

Greetings all,

Credit the Huey Lewis song for my subject line as it is appropriate for my current condition. The trial drug I've been on since last May has not reduced my cancer level but has contained the growth. Its major benefit was a see/saw action on lowering the dangerous levels of my Kappa Free Light chains than can result in kidney failure. For the first time, it failed to have a lowering effect following my last infusion. However, as luck would have it, a new combination Car-T and BCMA trial is opening and I'm a prime candidate for acceptance. This study drug protocol has had 90%-100% response rate. Some participants have received complete remission but everyone has had some level of remission. As with all experimental therapies there are risks. Two recipients had their re-engineered T cells get overly aggressive and died. But that's only 2 out of 100+ people. A risk I'm more than willing to take.

During testing this past Thursday it came to light that my platelet count was too low to enter the study. Big Bummer, but Dr. Garfall has other options and the Car-T/BCMA protocol may only be delayed and can be revisited. I've had some mild lower back pain recently but no problem driving home from Penn Hospital on Thursday. By Friday mid-day, the pain worsened and Dr. Garfall was very concerned this was related to my myeloma. He wanted me to return to the Univ Penn ER for testing and evaluation. Sandy came home from work and off we went.

Got admitted to the hospital after 24-30 hours lying in the ER. Back pain had me nearly immobile. Morphine helped a little, dilaudid worked better but put me in a zombie state. Once admitted to the hospital I received a more complete protocol of pain relief medications and as I write this I am in much better condition. No pain and able to walk and get out of bed. I have also started a 4 day regimen of high dose chemo drugs that will knock down the myeloma. May lose my hair, but it will grow back. Doctors will confer tomorrow on the course of action moving forward. May get 10 days of radiation therapy on my lower back to help heal the lesions from the myeloma. Hopefully radiation will be done in Annapolis.

So, this is all the news that's fit to print at the moment. If all goes well, the chemo will have a dramatic lowering of my cancer and I'll be back on track for the Cartitude study. (The effectiveness of this program has already garnered a nick name: Car-T with an attitude = Cartitude) But I've got an attitude too. An attitude of gratitude and perseverance. I'm so grateful for my Doctors, nurses and medications to combat pain and disease. And for all the support and prayers on my behalf of each of you. How would someone with my level of disease and pain made it through this recent cycle without Health Insurance? I persevere because I have hope of beating this disease for as long as possible and using every new tested and untested medication. But most importantly, my perseverance is from my faith. I don't know exactly what the life after this one will be like, but I think it will be unimaginably awesome. When that time comes, we will all probably why we took so long to get there.

A Quick Update

Well, I get to go home tomorrow morning. My fourth 24 hour, three drug Chemo Infusion will end around 10:00-10:30 p.m. tonight, I will have the IV removed and get a shower. Can't wait for the warm soapy water. The Chemo plus five pounds of daily saline for the first 2 -3 days added 16 pounds of weight to my already larger than preferred frame. So, I hope to pee a lot and get back to where I started weight wise.

The chemo is very tiring and it will continue to attack my cells for another week or two. I'll be taking it easy and try to regain some energy at a safe pace. With more good luck, my blood counts will recover and I can get back to the Cartitude trial that has had such great success with prior victims of this disease. Median time of remission has been 20 months and that's an eternity for new research and development of the next breakthrough.

Thanks for your kind and loving emails during this time of relapse and recovery. Your prayers and support are as powerful as any drug and I am eternally grateful to each of you.

Update

Thu, Mar 12, 2020, 6:45 a.m.

The strong chemo I received continues to do its work. My platelets got dangerously low, so I was sent to Anne Arundel Medical Center (local hospital) last Wednesday for a platelet transfusion. For some reason I was sent to the ER and had to have blood type cross/matching prior to infusion and the process took 6 hours. Next, I needed a red blood cell transfusion on Friday. I was so exhausted, I had to force myself to get cleaned up and head to the Donner Pavilion for a transfusion. My temperature was checked and I had a 102 degree fever. I had no idea I had a fever. A doctor surmised I probably picked up some type of infection while in the ER. Continuous antibiotic infusions, 2 units of red blood cells and other meds got my fever under control and by Sunday afternoon my white cell count, hemoglobin level and lack of infection from a 48 hour blood culture let me go home. So happy to get out of the hospital. Being tied to an IV, lying in bed full time and eating hospital food makes going home sweet home like winning the lottery. Fortunately, Sandra was at my side breaking the monotony and bringing some outside food and beverage which greatly lessened the boredom. How lost I would be without her.

My hair has started falling out in large measure, so Sandra gave me a buzz cut. What little hair is left may also fall out and I'll be completely bald for the 2nd time. Happily, my hair will grow back. I'm getting daily blood draws to get a very close monitoring of my blood counts. Transfusions will be ordered as necessary to keep me from getting dangerously low platelets and red blood cells. I'll see Dr. Garfall at Penn Medical Center next Tuesday. A blood draw for a complete Myeloma profile will be conducted and it will show how the chemo has affected my level of Myeloma. Results will take several days, but I'm hoping for a big reduction in the Myeloma in my marrow. When my platelets recover to a level of 50k or better, I can enter the Cartitude trial that has had such great results to date. My current platelets are at 22k so recovery may take several weeks.

My current main objective is to avoid any infections or viruses. I seldom leave the house and wear a mask when I do. Visitation for my local friends is discouraged, especially if you have an ailment or have been in contact with someone who has. As my blood profile improves, I hope to be a more social person and I'll update my progress as it happens.

I hope my next email has some very good news. Thanks as always for your support and prayers.

Another Update

Thu, April 30, 2020, 10:56 a.m.

Greetings Boys and Girls,

I hope everyone is safe and sound during these stressful times and avoiding the Corona Virus. I'm staying home except for blood draws and chemo infusions. Sandra is largely working from home and doing all the shopping and running necessary errands. We are very fortunate.

It's been a year of setbacks with little progress for my cancer levels but that is changing. My doctor has been telling me about the drug Venetoclax (pill form) when combined with Kyprolis (chemo) infusions has had good success. The Car-T trial I have previously mentioned closed due to Covid just as I was ready to get started. MAJOR BUMMER! We will fall back on Venetoclax and Kyprolis. Venetoclax is FDA approved for Lymphoma but not for Myeloma, even though it has shown good results. Naturally, my insurance company denied coverage. Retail price for the pills is $12,000/month. I applied to the manufacturer of the drug for financial assistance while my care team at Penn reached out to them citing my specific cancer markers that make me especially prone to benefits from this drug. Happily, the manufacturer is providing the pills directly from their pharmacy free of charge. Never look a gift horse in the mouth, but what a confusing process. Lucky me.

I just got the blood test results from my 1st 3 week cycle of Kyprolis and about 8 days of Venetoclax. Two critical markers

I focus on show good improvement. My M-Spike (Myeloma level) has dropped from 3.2 to 1.7. Kappa Free Light Chain was 2545 in March and has dropped to 1072. (Great news for avoiding kidney failure.) There's still room for improvement but I'm thrilled to finally see my numbers get better.

Well, I'd count my blessings, but the list is too long for publication. Please know I include each of you in that list. Thanks for your care, prayers and friendship.

Bruce Moffatt

2020 Looking Better

May 28, 2020, 3:01 p.m.

Yes, that's a strange subject line considering all the less than favorable events in the first 5 months of this year. The Corona Virus has changed the world and the repercussions will be felt for a long time to come. I hope each of you is safe and doing everything possible to protect yourself and others. On a much smaller scale, my year to date has also been less than optimal. Terrible ear infection, Myeloma meds stopped working and I contracted a virus in February at the ER during a platelet transfusion (4 days hospitalized). An explosion of my lower back vertebrae required another hospital stay along with 96 hours of chemo. Hair lost but it's slowly coming back. (Full mustache already grown in.) Extreme shortness of breath and my long-time friend, elevated heart rate, remain in effect. No pain so things could be much worse.

Now for "2020 Looking Better". I started a new pill, Venetoclax, 8 weeks ago in addition to re-starting the chemotherapy drug Carfilzomib. My M-Spike (measure of Myeloma in the marrow) has dropped from 2.8 to 1.2. The dangerous Kappa Free Light chains are reduced to 1385 mg/dl which is actually within the standard range for the first time in well over a year. These numbers put me in the defined category of a "Partial Remission" which I have not achieved since my Bone Marrow Transplant in 2017. Hallelujah and Thank You JESUS!!! (I think my parents, now both in heaven, have ganged up on God and his Son demanding some improvement...how else is this possible???) And this improvement has happened very quickly with a disease that does not usually respond with such a dramatic change in my case. This could mean my cancer will abate even more as treatment continues.

My side effects remain a nagging issue, partially due to the meds, but they should improve as my body adjusts to a lower level of cancer. I don't expect to run any marathons, but maybe I can do more exercise (walking primarily) and even playing some golf or swimming a few laps in our pool.

Even with all of these dramatic improvements, my immune system remains very compromised. Sheltering at home, social distancing and wearing a mask are still required. The Corona virus presents a serious threat if I should be so unlucky to contract the illness. Dr. Garfall feels I can pretty safely enjoy outdoor activity as long as I stay 6 feet away from others and masks are used. Indoors with other people for extended periods of time is a higher risk and not encouraged.

To repeat myself from many of my previous email updates, "I am a lucky boy" and getting luckier all the time. Obviously, drugs, Doctors, nurses and my wife (nurse Ratched; my #1 Hero) bear great responsibility for my care and improved health. Your friendship, prayers, encouragement and support are not lost in that equation.

With a grateful heart, thank you beyond all measure.

Still Improving

Fri, Jul 24, 2020, 10:09 a.m.

Howdy and Happy Friday,

I hope you're staying out of this oppressive heat wave and avoiding Covid 19. I continue to dodge another bullet:

According to the American Cancer Society (ACS), these are the average survival rates for Multiple Myeloma by stage:

Stage 1: approximately five years.
Stage 2: approximately three to four years.
Stage 3: approximately two to three years.

The 5 year anniversary of my official diagnosis will be in a few days; July 29th. I was originally diagnosed as Stage 2 on one scale and Stage 3 on another scale. I am beating the odds and appear to have a good shot at continuing that trend.

The drug Venetoclax reduced my cancer M-Spike from 2.5 to 1.2 about 6 weeks ago. This was a huge improvement. Blood drawn last week has shown the M-Spike to now be at

.65. This is truly amazing. My cancer has not been this low since my Bone Marrow Transplant in January 2017. PLUS, my dangerously high Kappa Free Light Chains were around 5,000 mg/L a year ago and at best fell to 1600 mg/L with treatments. (Normal is around 19.4 mg/L.) Now, they are 176 mg/L. The fear of kidney damage is enormously reduced.

I'd dance a jig or skip down the street, but I'm still short of breath with an elevated heart rate. (Resting heart rate is improving however!) As a substitute, I'll just repeat how lucky and grateful I am to have these results and your continued prayers and support for the past 5 years and counting. I hope to bore you with this refrain for many more years to come.

I Still Need A New Drug

Thu, Nov 12, 2020, 2:05 p.m.

Subject title stolen from Huey Lewis but appropriate for my current therapy. Hope this finds you well and less disturbed than me about the decay of our democracy. Enough on that as I already wear my feelings on my left sleeve for all to see.

The pill Venetoclax has given me 7 months of much safer levels of Myeloma. I was even able to get off Kyprolis chemo infusions which made me low on energy and short of breath. I went back on Kyprolis briefly to hopefully stop my cancer markers from ticking up but it was to no avail. Onward we go to the next new thing.

Dr. Garfall thinks my next best option is an FDA newly approved drug called Belantamab Mafodotin-blmf. Simple name, hard to forget don't you think? This is a monoclonal antibody created in the lab to attach to specific types of cancer cells. These antibodies "call" the immune system to attack and destroy the cancerous cells and can even prevent the growth of the cells. They target the B cell on the Myeloma cell. I will receive an infusion every 3 weeks at the Univ of PA Medical Center for treatment. I'm very much looking forward to seeing Dr. Garfall again on a regular basis as my current treatment was in pill form and did not require trips to Philly. PLUS, I get to see all my girlfriends in the infusion lab who make my stay an invigorating experience. Cancer ain't all bad! Such great Doctors and nurses. I am lucky.

Side effects? Of course. Chief among them is eye problems. The drug can cause loss of vision, blurriness, dry eye and corneal ulcers. Braille anyone? I hope not. I will get a thorough eye exam prior to each infusion. Any changes in the eye and treatment can be halted until the condition passes. Interestingly, patients that have success with this drug continue to do well even when the treatment is discontinued to address any side effects. There is a 50/50 chance of success and those that do well usually do so for a long period of time. All the other disclaimers include problems with kidneys, liver, platelets, white and red blood cells, nausea/vomiting, etc. A previously unheard of side effect is the irregular or permanent stopping of sperm production. Way too late for me to worry about that! And I thought that was what led to blindness. Silly wives' tales.

I may start treatment as early as next week if the insurance company cooperates and I can fit into the busy schedule at

Penn. Otherwise, the week after next. Hope lives on. God is good. You are too....

With a grateful heart....

Next Drug Up

Wed, Jan 6, 2020, 2:35 p.m.

Happy New Year,

I hope everyone is being careful and staying free of Covid. These are challenging times, unseen in my lifetime and I hope we can protect ourselves and one another with responsible actions to keep everyone safe. As our Governor Larry Hogan says, wear the damn mask. Good advice.

My latest treatment for Myeloma, Belantamab, has been a bust. In addition to not curbing the growth of the cancer it has slammed me harder than any treatment to date. I could barely get out of bed and felt like I had no blood in my body. I'm not a fan of horror movies but Belantamab made me feel like a zombie; dead man walking.

Fortunately, another trial drug is available and I will begin the required testing next week to pave the way for my first dose. Previous treatments targeted the B Cell on the Myeloma cell along with a chemo drug to kill the cancer. Neither has worked. The new drug from Genentech targets a different cell and will summon my own killer T-cells for the destruction of the bad actors. Hopefully, this will be more effective.

I will receive 3 escalating doses over a 3 week period to start. Each dose will require a 72 hour stay in the hospital to watch for any potentially dangerous side effects. Assuming the drug is well tolerated, following doses will occur once every three weeks. So again, as in the past 5+ years, I am blessed to have options. Fortunate to be privileged with health insurance and the care and guidance of top doctors and nurses. How I wish this was the standard of care for everyone and perhaps we will achieve that someday.

In closing I will ask those of you who pray to pray for our friend Duanne Puckett, now approximately 68 years old. As a popular, vibrant and beautiful teenager, Duanne was in a car struck by a drunk driver. She has been a quadriplegic ever since with some limited use of her arms. But she has accomplished more with her life than most people with full use of life and limbs. Always happy, always upbeat and encouraging Duanne, has been a force of nature. Editor of a local newspaper, involved in her community and always more concerned for others than herself. Now retired, Duanne drives herself around Shelbyville, KY in her wheelchair equipped van to visit friends in nursing homes or assisted living facilities. She spent many hours visiting my Father when he resided at Amber Oaks. Duanne has been on blood thinners and they got out of control last Friday and caused a bleed in her brain. Rushed to intensive care, the Doctor was not encouraging of her prognosis. But true to form, Duanne is fighting back and surprising the experts with her recovery so far. If all goes well, she will get out of intensive care and eventually sent to a rehab facility for further improvement. She will not be able to drive anymore and may require full time live-in help. But if anybody deserves some good fortune it is certainly due to her. I know of no other person who has handled such an unfair and undeserved limitation with such courage and grace. May God bless and heal Duanne.

Doctor Doctor Gimme The News

Feb 13, 2021, 6:31 a.m.

And a lot of news there is to give. First and foremost, thanks to everyone for your prayers for our friend/adopted sister Duanne Puckett. Duanne is home, electing to forego further medical treatment and rely on Hospice Care to assist in moving from this life to the one we believe will be infinitely superior. I commend her decision, typical of the brave and fearless way she has embraced her life. Her physical absence from us will be painful, but I prefer to imagine her looking at the face of God with a transfigured body, free of braces, with no wheelchair in sight and surrounded by her family and friends that have been patiently and excitedly awaiting her arrival. What a great day that will be. Please continue your prayers and support as Duanne faces this new and wonderful beginning.

My drama continues with many twists and turns. It's been at least 4 months since any medication slowed the growth of myeloma. A recent bone marrow biopsy showed my marrow packed with 95% myeloma cells and only 5% healthy plasma cells which convert into the necessary red and white cells to sustain a good blood profile. Dr. Garfall observed again that the amazing thing with this is I am not seriously ill with fevers and infections and maintain a healthy appearance in spite of these high levels of disease. So, I've got that going for me.

Feelings of uncomfortable heart compression began several weeks ago. EKG's, an echocardiogram and a nuclear stress test were passed with flying colors. No answers. Nitroglycerin tablets eased the pressure and then the pains decided to stop. Goodbye and good riddance.

In preparation for the new clinical trial, I had a brain MRI. Good news again! Brain material was discovered. A 4 cm lesion called a meningioma also showed up. Normally benign, follow up scans will be used to check it is not growing or require treatment. Hope we can avoid opening my hood to turn off the "check engine" light.

Jan 26th. The new Genentech clinical trial begins. First dose is a tiny .3 mg in a 4-hour infusion followed by a 72-hour hospital stay for observation. No problems, easy sailing. Even saw a slight improvement in a couple of blood markers related to disease progression.

Feb 2nd. Dose increased to 3.6 mg with a 72 hour hospital stay. Bring on the rain. High fevers, delirium, fell, could not get up. (Never thought I'd say, "help I've fallen and I can't get up".) Very foggy and confusing. Oddly, this was considered a good thing as evidence the drug was working. An infusion of Dexamethasone and tocilizumab quickly reversed these symptoms and stopped the process known as Cytokine Release Syndrome (CRS). Cytokines communicate with cells to regulate the immune system response to inflammation and infection. CRS can become life threatening if left unregulated. The medications quickly restored normalcy and I was free to go home at the end of my 72 hours stay for observation. Oddly, my Kappa Free Light Chains which had reduced 200 points after the 1st dose, went up 1200 points with the 2nd dose. Confusing and unexpected.

Feb 9th. 3rd escalating dose. Now we jump to a full dose of 160 mg. My temperature is not considered a fever until it reaches 100.4 or higher which would trigger the meds necessary to halt the CRS process. I only reached 99.4 so the drug was considered safe and treatment would continue as scheduled. HOWEVER, the inflammatory response triggered a tumor flare on my spine. This tumor flare happened a year ago with a spot on my lower spine and put me in more pain than I ever experienced. An MRI revealed a new tumor on T-10 & T-11 vertebrae. As with the pain from last year, the only effective relief is the steroid Dexamethasone. As much as I dislike side effects of Dex, it is a miracle cure for inflammation and the only relief from bone pain. But they did not want to give me Dex as it would calm down the response from the clinical trial drug. Opioids do not touch bone pain but the Palliative Care Team kept giving me morphine, dilaudid and OxyContin even though these drugs gave ZERO relief. So, I got to lay in bed for about 13 hours in agony. Dex was finally approved and within 2 hours the pain was completely gone. Relief lasted for 36 hours and then the pain returned. The approval process repeated and it was another 10-12 hours before Dex was delivered. It came just in time to allow me to tolerate lying flat on my back on the hard table used for CT scans and MRI's. I now wait to see if the pain returns a 3rd time requiring another lengthy approval process for Dex.

I'm staying in the hospital to receive 8 treatments of radiation on the spinal tumor. Radiation will break up the tumor and remove the threat of intrusion on my spinal cord. If all goes well, I should go home next Saturday. Another full dose of the study drug is scheduled for this coming Tuesday. Hopefully it will be well tolerated and the spinal tumor will stay calm. Most importantly, I hope the drug is providing a good response for my cancer levels. TBD.

While recent events have been challenging and at times confusing, I remain 100% confident in my Doctors and Nurses at Penn. It's difficult to imagine a hospital where I would receive better care from a more advanced and knowledgeable staff of professionals. They give me care, options and continued hope for life extending treatments. This will come to an end at some point as it will for everyone. At that point I shall fully anticipate that new life eternal promised. I wonder if I could drag along a wheelchair for Duanne just to be a smart ass?

Till my next essay, peace, love and joy and thanks again and again for your prayers and support.

Today I Start My Book

February 15, 2021, 12:17 a.m.

I'm in my hospital room at the University of Pennsylvania Medical Center in Philadelphia, PA. It's cold outside. A steroid injection is calming the pain in my lower back and hips but preventing sleep. I have six more days of radiation treatments to destroy the tumors on my spine and I am attempting to overcome my procrastination habits to take print to paper and share my journey of living with Multiple Myeloma.

Guess what? There is much to be hopeful about.

More Twists and Turns

Feb 21, 2021, 2:44 p.m.

Happy Sunday. Today is our 18th Wedding Anniversary and Sandra will be making my Mother's Beef Stroganoff recipe over brown rice with Sister Schubert's rolls (out of this world) and garlic infused wilted spinach. AND, having finally removed our wood burning stove, the chimney company has completed the steps necessary to restore our fireplace to its natural condition. We will celebrate in front of a roaring fire, with delicious food, happy that Ted Cruz is not invading our space to pamper himself away from the misery his constituents are facing. (sorry, couldn't resist)

My introduction to the new clinical trial is complete. Well mostly. I went through the 1st 3 escalating doses with some fevers and delirium after the 2nd round. This was a good sign the treatment was working though very disconcerting when happening. The 3rd dose was at full strength and received Tuesday Feb 9th, followed by my last 3 day hospital stay for observation. All went well for a while.

The short version. The study drug creates inflammation when calling my T-cells to kill myeloma cells. This "inflammatory response" triggered a previously unannounced myeloma tumor on my spine to press against my spinal cord and create intense pain. How bad? I could not sleep, eat or find relief in any position. I actually ate nothing for a 24 hour period which is a first for me. To control the pain, I received Oxycontin, dilaudid and morphine in ascending order. Not a whiff of relief. Opioids do not work on bone pain, but my arch enemy Dexamethasone works miracles and will completely remove the pain in 1-2 hours. Simple, yes? No. Dex reduces inflammation and could have a negative effect on the success of the study drug while eliminating my pain. Clinical trials are complex and their protocols must be strenuously followed. Bringing Dex into the picture requires an exception to the process and getting approval takes 10-12 hours. It was bad enough tolerating 10-12 hours of pain the first time, but this process repeated 3 more times and each occurrence followed the same exception process with a 12 hour wait for relief. I also argued for a fentanyl patch to solve the problems as fentanyl had relieved my bone pain from a compression fracture in 2015. It worked and since it's an opioid, it would not interfere with the study drug. No luck. I lost the argument as it was feared it would probably not work, hard to adjust the dosage as it takes 24-36 hours to get fully activated and might present dangerous side effects while I'm at home 2 hours away from the hospital. Bummer. I'll try anything that might blunt the pain from these tumors.

With the discovery of my tumor on T10 & T11, I was prescribed 8 radiation treatments to reduce the tumor and its adverse effect on my pain threshold. I had a myeloma tumor last year on my L2 vertebrae and that decided to act up again as well. Mid spine, lower spine, hips and hip flexors took turns flaring up and thankfully, they did not all dance at the same time. My 3 days stay for observation turned into an 11 day stay and I'll be going back to UPenn on Monday and Tuesday for 2 more radiation treatments.

A final twist: two days after receiving my last full dose of the study drug, Dr Garfall called to tell me 3 of my most closely watched cancer markers had all shown excellent levels of improvement. The drug is WORKING! This worry about the Dex diminishing the study drug's efficacy is limited at best. Although frustrating, I understand the complexity of clinical trials and their need to follow strict rules and procedures or risk a loss of FDA approval. I just wish the exception process to giving me Dex could take 2 hours instead of 12 hours. Big Baby.

It's Friday Feb 19th. I had radiation at 8:30 am and was back in my room by 9:00 am ready to be discharged. I got out at 3:15 pm. Hospitals are harder to get out of than get into. I hurried to the parking garage and jumped in my Honda AWD truck with newly installed winter tires and wheels. Ready, set, go, and a loud warning beeper comes on indicating an object close by. I pulled out around the post next to me but the blaring continued. I got out to check the truck. Someone had backed into the front passenger side and destroyed the front end. I could not get the alarm to stop ringing and envisioned a 2 hour drive to Annapolis in full auditory assault. Happily, the alarm stopped at speed above 10-15 mph.

I'm thrilled to be home with my bride and our children, Choco & Latte. My hip flexors have been very sore but I was allowed to take Dex this morning and I'm feeling a lot less discomfort. Two more radiation treatments and a couple more weeks of the radiation continuing to "cook" and my tumors should be controlled. My next infusion will be on March 9th with the expectation the study drug has continued to kick my cancer in its gluteus maximus.

Thanks for hanging in with me. I hope future follow up on my condition will not require such lengthy explanations. This treatment gives me a lot of hope as do each of you.

Goodbye Duanne

You are loved and will be missed.

This is lengthy but worth your time.

Duanne Bondurant Puckett, 70 passed away on February 21, 2021. She was a native of Shelbyville KY, the third daughter of Jesse and Ella Puckett, who preceded her in death. Duanne "married" a wheelchair in 1967, following an auto accident on February 25th when a drunk driver didn't stop at the traffic light and rear-ended the Volkswagen in which she was a back-seat passenger. Her spinal cord was severed, but family and friends would say nothing could sever her zest for life.

After nine months in the hospital and physical rehabilitation center, Duanne returned home and completed her senior year at Shelbyville High School where she was a member of the Class of 1968, who started school in 1956 when Shelbyville began integrated classes. Duanne loved sharing the history of a friendship that stemmed from a teachable moment in that first-grade class:

"Our teacher, Nellie Miller, always asked you to stand up front on your birthday so the class could sing. I shared a birthday with Larry McNeal. His nickname was Snookie. Mine was Doodie. He was chubby. I was skinny. She asked us to hold hands. I nearly fainted because he was a boy! Never occurred to me to be flabbergasted that I was white and he was black. When we turned 40, Larry called me on our birthday – a tradition we continued until he passed away. A new tradition continued after his passing because from that year forward his mother, Mary Ann McNeal, would call me!"

She was a storyteller of history in the community and in stories she wrote for local newspapers and magazines. Duanne always credited her interest in joining the Shelby County Historical Society in 1971 to Rufus Harrod. Her other beloved historians were newspaperman Bennett Roach and researcher/author Brigadier General R.R. Van Stockum. Duanne always stressed the importance of dates and names in articles and on photos, because of the influence from her other historian, Betty Matthews. It was Betty who challenged Duanne to label every family item in the house with its origin – history for future generations. She loved to share the stories behind each treasured piece in her home. Her family will continue to keep the stories alive. She also learned much of the Puckett family and community history from her father, who served as a Shelbyville city councilman, mayor, city clerk and industrial foundation leader.

Duanne was a longtime member of the Shelbyville First Baptist Church before She started attending Centenary United Methodist Church in 1988. During her membership, she helped with Vacation Bible School, Children's Sermon Moment, Redwoods Women's Ministry and Sanctuary Sunday School class as a teacher. Duanne loved to share how God had not planned for her to be in a wheelchair, but He did plan to give her loving parents, devoted sisters, terrific friends and true grit to face whatever came her way.

A community fund drive was held in 1997 to purchase Duanne a van converted with a ramp to provide her independence once she acquired a motorized wheelchair. She no longer needed family and friends to push, carry and lift her in order to participate in her many activities. Family and friends know she replaced her wheelchair tires more often than individuals replace their vehicle tires.

Duanne often said she was a graduate of the "School of Hard Knocks", because after her accident and graduating from Shelbyville High School, she did not go to college. Shelby News owner/publisher Bob Fay actually checked with her English teachers before offering her a job as a reporter in 1971. That position led to a column "From the Desk of Bug" – a ladybug nickname to which she was referred until her death. She took on other roles after February 1972 when The News merged with The Sentinel to become The Sentinel-News. She was named classified advertising manager 1974, family living editor 1976, news editor 1982 and editor 1986.

Duanne's writing was recognized with awards from the Kentucky Press Association and Society of Professional Journalists. She received the first President's Community Service Award from Landmark Community Newspapers Inc. in 1989. In 1988, she was inducted into the Kentucky Journalism Hall of Fame after 27 years as a journalist, including 10 as editor.

She eventually went to work as community relations coordinator for Shelby County Public Schools. Duanne had always dreamed of being a teacher; however, colleges lacked accessibility in 1968. In her role with the school system, she was able to "teach" in classrooms with history lessons, writing resources and reading assistance. Even after retirement you could often find Duanne rolling down the hallways of Painted Stone Elementary heading toward the classroom of one of her nephews or her niece. There she would share her love of reading and the magic that can be found within the pages of a book. Because of her accident, she was often called upon to stress the horrors of drunk driving before students headed for prom. Many students approached her or wrote to her throughout her life thanking her for the inspiration she provided to them while students.

Duanne retired in 2013 and went to work as chief writer for Shelby Life, a monthly magazine. Through her gift of story-telling, she shared features on people of all ages and all walks of life.

Because of her hometown involvement, Duanne was named the Shelbyville Citizen of the Year in 2014 and the Distinguished Citizen of the Year by the Lincoln Heritage Boy Scout Council. She had previously been recognized by the Shelbyville Business & Professional Women's Club Young Careerist and Woman of Achievement, Ky. Farm Bureau Federation Communication award, Service Award from Shelby County Dairy Industry, Women ""History Maker"" award from the Kentucky Commission on Women, and the Shelby County Chamber of Commerce Small Business Advocate of the Year Award. She was also one of the found-ers of Leadership Shelby, a program to identify present and future community leaders. She served as program chairman and President and was an Alumni of the Year award recipient.

In 2009, Duanne and others formed Friends of Grove Hill to clean and restore older monuments at the cemetery. Photos would show Duanne in her wheelchair, leaning over as far as she could in order to make an inscription visible. She was known to say, "If I can do it, you can do it" when volunteers were being recruited. She helped organize walking tours with "Stories Behind the Stones", where she often could be found in costume portraying interesting characters from the past. Although some may have found it depressing, you could often find Duanne and whoever she was treating to lunch having a picnic in her van parked near the cemetery chapel on pretty days. She found comfort in the history in the monuments and knowing her loved ones were resting nearby.

Her other interests were being an avid reader and member of the Brown Bag Club at the Shelby County Public Library, which worked with Duanne and Victoria Schreiner to collect books for Reading Reindeer, a program that started in 1988 and continues to distribute free books to children in the community. However, Duanne's greatest love was her family. She was a devoted daughter, sister, aunt, great-aunt and cousin. Her family knows she was put on this earth to be a stable force in her family and a true example of a Christian. Her nieces and nephews were blessed with their many adventures around Shelby County, numerous crafting activities at her dining room table, countless move-watching dates and her always cheering them on from the sidelines (camera in hand). Duanne is survived by her sisters, Terry Puckett Long (Kent), Marsha Puckett James who served as her lifelong companion and caregiver (Gay Guthrie), a nephew, Harry "Chip" Long III of Florida; a niece Dawn Harrod (Mike) of Shelbyville KY; great-nephews, Jesse Harrod, Samuel Harrod and Reece Harrod; great-niece Emme Harrod; surrogate sisters, Mary Jane Yates and Pam Gray, both of Shelbyville; surrogate brother, Jack Brammer; countless friends and cousins.

Visitation and Services will be held at a later date. Expressions of sympathy can be made in the form of donations to the Van/Ramp Ministry at Centenary United Methodist Church, PO Box 38, Shelbyville KY 40066.

If you're feeling a little "inferior" after reading about Duanne, join the club. What an amazing woman with accomplishments and honors most of us with functioning arms and legs could not achieve. Duanne is as fine a human being as I have ever known. She was always bright faced and smiling with an unstoppable interest in others. She led a life of service to others while us "others" should have ministered to her. She was a true Christian of the highest order.

Duanne and I had a special connection. I had returned to Shelbyville for a visit on a weekend when my parents were being honored by the First Baptist Church where my Father had served as Pastor. Dad was the primary speaker on Sunday morning and after the service I approached Duanne to say hello. As was customary, I went to give Duanne a kiss, but as she turned her cheek toward me, I decided at the last moment to kiss her full on the mouth. When our lips parted, the look on her face and the 12 shades of red she turned were priceless. From then on, every communication between us referenced

KOTL and when we met in person every greeting was with a Kiss On The Lips. How I shall miss those moments.

Another One Bites the Dust

Thu, Apr 1, 2021, 4:22 p.m.

Happy almost Easter,

I hope this finds you well and vaccinated against Covid 19. I got my 2nd Moderna shot today, so in 2 weeks I'll be as fully protected as possible. Or almost. Because my immune system is severely compromised, Dr. Garfall has encouraged me to still wear a mask, avoid crowds and maintain social distance. He did say however it would be safe to not use a mask if everyone in our group was vaccinated and in an outdoor environment. This means pool parties and cookouts at the Moffatt house are open to all vaccinated comers. Hurry up warmer weather.

The past 5 months have probably been the most difficult since I was diagnosed in 2015. The pill Venetoclax worked great last year at tamping down my cancer and I had a great run of almost feeling normal. But it stopped working around October and every treatment after that has been ineffective. Left unchecked, my cancer has steadily increased my short-ness of breath, lack of energy and elevated heart rate. The recent myeloma tumors on my spine that required an 11 day hospital stay and 8 radiation treatments, helped to further increase my nearly vegetative state. On the brighter side, Dr. Garfall noted that in spite of these high levels of myeloma, I do not suffer from organ failure, frail or fractured bones or infections and other forms of disease. Something in my constitution is able to tolerate higher disease levels than most people with this illness. Some people have far less myeloma spread throughout their body, but the cancer cells might concentrate in one specific area and cause greater damage. My myeloma cells seem to be equal opportunity terrorists and are distributed throughout my bone marrow in all my bones. Comforting to have that working for me.

Next up is my first Car-T therapy. HALLELUJAH! This type of treatment has had the best success rate of all clinical trial studies. The leader in Car-T is nicknamed Cartitude: "Car-T with an attitude " and is produced by J&J Pharmaceuticals. In trials it had a 100% response rate with a median effective rate of 27 months. I was about to start this treatment last year, but Covid stopped the program. Cartitude is still closed to newcomers and will probably get FDA approval late this year or early next year. To my good fortune, Celgene Pharmaceuticals got FDA approval for their Car-T treatment last week. It has a 74% response rate and I'm so lucky to have this as an option. Amazing timing. Coincidence? Blessing for sure. I'll take it.

What is Car-T you no doubt are asking? A type of treatment in which a patient's T cells (a type of immune system cell) are changed in the laboratory so they will attack cancer cells. T cells are taken from a patient's blood through aphaeresis. Then the gene for a special receptor that binds to a certain protein on the cancer cells is added to the T cells in the laboratory. The special receptor is called a Chimeric Antigen Receptor *(CAR)*. Large numbers of the CAR T cells are grown in the laboratory over a 5-6 week period and given back to the patient by infusion. T-cells have many identical T-cell receptors that cover their surfaces and can only bind to one shape of antigen. When a T-cell *receptor* fits with its viral antigen on an infected cell, the Killer T-cell releases cytotoxins to kill that cell. So simple, yes?

Because this is recently approved, it will be several weeks before I can begin the process. In the meantime, I will start taking Venetoclax again in hopes that the time off the drug will create a reset and my cancer will respond again to its effectiveness. This will be combined with Pomalyst, a pill I used successfully as a maintenance drug after my bone marrow transplant and an infusion of a new drug, Empliciti (Elotuzumab). Hopefully, this cocktail will tamp down my cancer until we can start the Car-T therapy. With luck, my new myeloma killer T cells will be given back to me by late June or early July. Time in the hospital for observation may be required but probably no more than 5-7 days, I hope. Monthly blood tests will probably be required, but once I get the new T-cells that's it. Let the myeloma destruction begin and continue on its own. If the myeloma starts growing, more Car-T cells may be given again to continue the efficacy. Not sure about that, but perhaps.

So, here I am again. Another door slams shut and a window opens. There is no cure for myeloma, but I am so fortunate to have multiple options for even temporary disease containment. If I can hop, skip and jump to temporary fixes, maybe I'll make it to a longer lasting therapy under development or even, dare I say, a CURE? It may not be deserved but it would certainly be welcomed.

Spring is a time of renewal and also one of our most important and promising holidays, Easter. I pray you find as much encouragement and peace in the message of Easter and the hope it gives beyond the life we know.

Peace and love.

A Long Slow Summer

Sun, Jun 6, 2021, 10:42 a.m.

Well, I usually look forward to a long, slow summer, clinging to daylight, blue skies and lots of fun things to do and places to go. I fear this summer will not live up to those expectations but may yield benefits worth the inconveniences.

My current treatment of Venetoclax (pill), Pomalyst (pill) and Empliciti/Elotuzumab (infusion) has steadied my cancer levels but produced only small amounts of improvement. Of course, anything halting the growth of myeloma is a good thing. In addition to the high level of myeloma I have sustained over the years, inflammation is now at an all-time high. My resting heart rate is around 105-110 bpm and minimal activity will raise that number to 150 bpm. With my heart working that hard for oxygen I can easily feel I'm suffocating and have to sit down to catch some breath. The exception to this issue is the 40mg of Dexamethasone I receive as a pre-med to my weekly Elotuzumab infusion. Dex is an anti-inflammatory and it will lower my heart rate and give me a couple of days of energy allowing me to do something other than sit or lie down to be comfortable. So why not get Dex every day or at least every 2nd *or 3rd day to relieve these symptoms?* Dex also suppresses my white blood cells which fight infection. As they are already low, more Dex could lead to infections and more complications. Rock, Paper, Scissors.

Time for a new drug and it's called Abecma. (Ah beck ma) This is the first FDA approved treatment using Car-T therapy. Here's how it will occupy my summer:

Tomorrow, June 7
I will have my veins evaluated for the upcoming aphaeresis procedure which will extract a few million Killer T-cells from my blood. These cells will be shipped to a lab and engineered to recognize and kill myeloma cells. (The process takes about 5 weeks). If my veins are up to the task, they will simply use an IV in each arm to circulate my blood through a machine to capture the cells and then return the blood through the other arm. If my veins need help a port of some type will be embedded to handle the flow of blood.

Thursday June 10
Apheresis performed. Should take 5-6 hours.

Friday June 11 to July 13th. My window of freedom for the summer. Weekly infusions may continue along with the pills but for 6 days a week I'll be at home.

July 14
If everything is on schedule, I'll be admitted to the hospital for 3 days of Lymphodepleting chemotherapy. Some T-cells have to be depleted to make room for the new ones.

July 20
I receive my newly engineered T-cells and hope they start killing myeloma cells ASAP. It's likely they will get overly aggres-

sive and produce Cytokine Release Syndrome or Neurotoxicity. Left untreated these can be deadly, but treatment is available to stop this process before it gets out of control. 7 days or more of observation will require me to stay in the hospital.

Now the difficult part. I have to stay within 1 hour of the hospital for 28 days following my T-cell infusion. I live 2 hours away, so I'll impose once again on my Brother and Sister-in-Law to tolerate my presence in their Philadelphia home for some or all of this period. There is assistance in this program for hotel and meal expenses so if they need a break, I can scurry off to lesser accommodations. I'm hoping I can get clearance after a couple of weeks to head home due to no further reactions to the dangerous side effects.

I save the worst for last. Once I get my new T-cells on July 20th, I'm not supposed to drive a car FOR 8 WEEKS! Please, just shoot me. The last pleasure I can indulge in that doesn't choke the life out of me and it's gone too. I may not be following this restriction to the letter but there may be some Uber rides in my future if I have to rush to the hospital at 2am with a fever.

OK. The benefits. 75%-80% of people in clinical trials with Abecma received a response rate yielding some level of remission. On average, the remission lasted about 12 months; some shorter, some longer. If it works for me, I'll probably be free of other medications. Follow up visits and blood work will probably be once a month. And a 12 month remission may get me through to next summer with some golf and travel in my future. This also allows time for the next new treatment to come on board. If Abecma stops working some new and effective options will be available and the cycle will continue.

For all my whining about the weeks ahead, I'm lucky to have this opportunity at a time when I need it most. In spite of the inconveniences, I'm constantly aware of how fortunate I am to receive cutting edge therapies at one of our nation's top hospitals under the care of Dr. Garfall and the nurses that provide the highest level of care I can imagine. Perhaps someday, we as a nation will value every individual as worthy of the same level of care and treatment to which I have access. What a proud day that would be for America.

Thank you for your continued thoughts and prayers. I hope my next report will be full of very good news and your summer will be the best one ever!

Change of Communication

June 24, 2021

I'm hitting the pause button on emails to Friends and Family. You have just read an outline of implementing Abecma. It will be a lengthy process which may or may not go off without a hitch. So rather than send everyone a day-by-day accounting, I'll use this space to detail events as they unfold. Updates to F&F will follow in hopefully digestible bites that don't cause anyone to become comatose from too much information.

Happy Friday,

Starting the Abecma T-cell therapy will be quite involved. So rather than send everyone a day-by-day accounting, I'll use this space to detail events as they unfold over time. Updates to you (Friends & Family; F&F) will follow in hopefully digestible bites that don't cause anyone to become comatose from too much information. As you read along, I'm off to a bad start on brevity.

Thursday June 24, 2021

A great start to the day. Some Dexamethasone at 9 pm last night finally tamped down the pain in my neck. I arose at 4 am, as is our custom, and packed food for a day-long visit to UPenn. I jumped in the 12-year-old Porsche at 6 am, 57 degrees, favorite jacket for warmth, top down, music blasting and took a fabulous 2-hour drive to the hospital. What a pleasure. Something about driving a great car, a little wind in your face and the calm of driving through the countryside and even in the big city is so invigorating for me. I could have driven hours more. The only thing better is to do this at night, surrounded by darkness, pierced only by the illumination of headlights. Like being in a safe but speedy cocoon. If only the speed limit was much higher.

Pain in my right shoulder from a myeloma lesion that was successfully mitigated many weeks ago with radiation has returned. It has also migrated to my neck which is a more serious area for issues and treatment. I had a CT scan at 9am, will have an MRI on my neck at 2pm, and radiation on my shoulder at 3:30pm. Dr. Jones, radiology oncologist, will wait to determine neck treatment post MRI. On the bright side, we should be able to address these issues BEFORE starting with my Car-T scheduled events. Now if I can just convince Dr. Garfield to let me take Dex for this bone pain I'll be happy. Maybe a low dose of only 8mg every 72 hours as needed. Fingers crossed.

Oops. Following his reading of the MRI on my neck and spine, Dr. Joshua Jones wants to speak to me. Radiation scheduled for my shoulder will not happen today. Probably not great news. Dr. Jones entered the room and was in a very calm but serious state. Turns out he was very smart to do a complete MRI on my neck and entire spinal column before jumping into radiation. A myeloma tumor or lesion (pick your terminology) has encapsulated some vertebra in my neck. These pesky cancerous plasma cells have eaten through the bone and are pushing spinal fluid (the last protection for the spinal cord) out of the way, pressing on the spinal cord resulting in intermittent but very painful effects. Left untreated, the spinal cord could be severed and loss of all bodily function and movement could occur from the neck down. How pleasant. Dr. Jones stated this was discovered early and the odds of spinal cord issues are greatly diminished. He asked for my reaction, and I had to giggle a little. I explained that I came to terms with my disease years ago. This is just another bump in the road and similar events that have cropped up and handled BEFORE they became uncontrollable. I told him I was so lucky to have discovered this early and thanked him for his good judgement which has no doubt extended my life and avoided a very catastrophic outcome. He appeared a little surprised at my reaction but probably relieved to not have a crying and upset patient to deal with.

Here's the plan. Radiation for 7 of the next 8 days on my neck and another spot identified on my lower spine. Shoulder pain is probably coming from a pinched nerve and should abate with healing from the neck tumor. Radiation today, Jun 25th, will take place around 5 or 6 pm. Sandra and I will head for Philly around Noon to stay with her sister overnight. I will return to UPenn for an early Saturday morning treatment. No radiation on Sunday. They were able to schedule early to mid-morning treatments for Monday through Friday. As treatment will take less than an hour, I can commute from home each day.

As I look back, I see a trend that has often occurred. First the Porsche. Leaking seals in my front differential for the all-wheel drive were secured and repaired last week. A slow leak in the right rear tire could not be found and fixed. I got 4 new, highly rated summer tires giving me the best ride and grip available. The car is good to go. Further, the required abstinence from driving for 8 weeks after receiving my T-cells has been mitigated by daily 4 hour commutes up and back to the hospital for 8 days. And the weather report shows no rain and warm temperatures for the coming week. My love of driving has been bolstered.

Second. Can you imagine if this problem surfaced during the Abecma T-Cell therapy? Abecma has serious side effects of its own and my high level of disease is not a welcomed environment for avoiding CRS and Neurotoxicity. Adding spinal cord issues to the mix would not be optimal.

Third, my beautiful Sister arrives from KY for a visit tomorrow. We will be home in time to greet her and all my treatments next week are scheduled early in the day (no small feat considering the hospital's busy schedule) and I'll get home every day in time to enjoy her company.

Lastly. Remember the concern that Dex will lower my already low White Cell count and blood clotting Platelets? My blood draw today showed my white count and platelets at their highest level since contracting myeloma. Dr. Garfall has agreed with Dr. Jones to give me 8 mg of Dex twice a day to relieve the dangerous inflammation created by my tumors. And Dex will contain the pain. This is no small turn of events by itself.

Luck? Providence? Prayer from so many of you and others known and unknown to me asking for good outcomes? I can't provide a provable answer, but the trends indicate something other than good luck to me. So fortunate I am.

I had hoped I could deliver the coming weeks events in smaller digestible bites. I see failure right off the get go. Thanks for hanging in and reading my lengthy emails. Your support and encouragement continue to be one of the most powerful forces in my life. I could never thank you enough or repay that debt I owe.

More to follow to be sure.

Radiation Begins

Friday June 25, 2021

Today was a good day overall. I summoned the strength to run errands to 6 different places. This would usually require rest for the remainder of the day, but we had places to go and things to do. So, for the first time, Sandra and I jumped in the Porsche together and headed to Philly for radiation on my neck this evening, a night stay with Cheryl & Cliffe and a 2nd treatment at 8 am Saturday morning.

The weather was excellent. 80 degrees, sun shining, a perfect top-down motoring day and the first time we enjoyed this together. We avoided I95 North and headed over the Chesapeake Bay Bridge for a more scenic and less trafficked route. Once we were in the flat open country of the Eastern Shore, we seemed to be the only car on the road. Tunes were blasting and Sandra even commented that the sound was amazing. The Love Theme from Dances with Wolves queues up from my Spotify list. It's a beautiful and somewhat haunting melody. As I listen a calm overcomes me. I'm happy. contented. Life has been so good to me and continues to do so through times of struggle. I could have allowed a few tears to roll out, but I resisted. My soul was full of good feelings. I told this to Sandra later and choked up a bit. She squeezed my hand. We can remember the past and quess at the future, but we can only live in the present. This was one of those special moments in my life.

We arrived at Sandra's sister's house and after getting out of the car I realized every bump and dip in the road had sent small shock waves up my spine and into my neck. Man was it tight and uncomfortable. After about an hour it was time for me to head to the hospital. Waze routed me away from interstate and major roads with heavy traffic. The slower speeds helped my neck and most of the pain was gone.

The first treatment took about 45 minutes. Future applications will be half that time. My head and neck were firmly locked into place with my neck resting on a hard plastic bridge to keep my chin up and prevent movement. No problem during the procedure. When I got up from the table, the pain in my neck returned and was worse. Back at the Cheston's it was all I could do to keep my head up while I ate some dinner. Into bed to find a comfortable position and some sleep. The day did not end as pleasantly as it began but that's living in the present.

Saturday June 26, 2021

Feeling less neck pain this morning. Black coffee and some fruit for me and we were out the door by 6:50 am. The drive to the hospital was easy and uneventful. Arrived at 7:45 as instructed and the 2nd treatment started at 8 am. The machinery is amazing, like something 100 years from the future. I have been tattooed with small marks to indicate the focal points of the radiation beams. I get dragged or pushed into just the right positions for the radiation to hit those marks. Several rotating heads whirr and track around me until they are in their designated places. The beam of radiation releases and hums slightly as it passes through body tissue unharmed and focuses the killing energy on the tumors. How can it do that? So amazing.

We're in the car and headed home. Skies are overcast and it looks like rain, which does happen a few times. No top down today. Well, until there is an accident on the Bay Bridge, and we sit in traffic for over an hour. Suns out, top down for a while. We get home and I'm spent. Bed rest is helping my neck and we are awaiting the arrival of my darling Sister and her dog Martha. ETA 4:30 pm. It will be so good to see her.

Sunday June 27, 2021

It's 4:30 am, the dogs are fed and we're sitting on the patio surrounded by darkness except for the pool lights and the reflecting string of lights that surround the outer perimeter of the far side of the pool. Black coffee and the strawberry and blueberry tart Pat Bertrand made for us is a perfect start to the day. As the sun comes up, we do a little pool maintenance and patio clean up in anticipation of some friends coming over for a visit. But as the heat rises, I run out of gas and head for bed. I need the rest.

Later in the day I need to gas up the Porsche for an early departure tomorrow for my next radiation treatment. But there on the garage floor is another large leak of gear oil from the front differential. The anticipated pleasure of top-down motoring to UPenn and back every day evaporated. Easy come, easy go. Still a bummer. Cars are not a good investment but I do enjoy them so much.

Monday June 28, 2021

The drive up and back home was painful. Every bump and dip in the road sent shock waves to my spine and neck. The Dexamethasone I was counting on to relieve pain and inflammation doesn't seem to be working. Treatment went off without a hitch and I was back home by 11:00. Some good quality time with my sister and the ability to find a low stress position on the sofa for my neck and shoulders helped pass the day. Not looking forward to my commuting for the rest of the week if the neck pain persists while driving.

As the evening wore on my neck and shoulders were locked tight. Dr. Joshua Jones is the Radiologist Oncologist overseeing my treatment, but his assistant sent me back a note he was out of the office this week. Fortunately for me, Dr. Garfall has entrusted me with his direct cell number which I make every effort not to abuse. This was bad enough that I needed his help. We connected by phone and as is his custom, he did a thorough review of my issues. He had communicated with Dr. Jones about my condition, so he was not totally in the dark. After exploring all the issues, we added a 15mg tablet of morphine to my Dex dose and low-grade Fentanyl patch. Dr. Garfall is one smart cookie, and he has a tremendous way of analyzing a problem and communicating in understandable terms. He is never in a hurry to move on. I'm so lucky to have him in my corner. I took my meds and went lights out.

Tuesday June 29, 2021

I awoke this morning without the pain in my neck and shoulders. Still stiff, but so much better. I think the morphine may have helped. To make the drive to UPenn as easy as possible, I abandoned the preferred scenic route and drove up via I95. The roads are much smoother and the less bumps and dips the better, but traffic can be heavy and unpredictable. I further committed to drive more slowly, and to not exceed the speed limits. I was alone in that regard as everyone zoomed past me all day long. This paid dividends as I no longer cried out like a whimpering baby each time I hit a bump in the road. My neck was so much better. Pain is a good thing as it alerts us to problems that could turn out to be a serious health issue. But the best part of pain is when it stops.

Radiation went well and I was headed home returning in the same fashion as I arrived. I stopped at the cleaners to pick up some laundry. I was the only customer in line until another gentleman came in. I said hello and we chatted for a moment. He noticed the University of MD logo on my shirt and asked if I went to school there. Yes, I did, undergraduate degree in Law Enforcement and Criminology. He did his undergrad and master's there before receiving his degree elsewhere in Theology. Theology? I'm familiar with that word being the son of a minister, so I asked if he was a Pastor. Yes, he was. My clothes were ready for pick up, so I grabbed them, said nice talking to you and headed for my car. I waited. Why pass up this moment? When he came out, I called him over to my car for better introductions. His name is Pat Packett and he is the Lead Pastor at Chesapeake Christian Fellowship. I explained I have been looking for a church but covid and an upcoming treatment for multiple myeloma is getting in my way. You're dealing with cancer, he asked? Let me say a prayer for you now. Standing in the parking lot, we bowed our heads, he touched me on the arm and said a brief but beautiful prayer asking God for my healing and emphasizing this meeting was not by chance. What a great moment and my how I appreciate his bold faith and concern for a stranger. Is that not what Christianity is about? I'm sure our paths will cross again.

As you will read on the coming pages, do not shut yourself off from these types of encounters. They can happen naturally, unforced and result in a very meaningful connection. The world is full of good people, caring people, and these conversations can make a difference in both of your lives. This one certainly helped me.

Wednesday June 30 to July 4
What's that saying? Man plans, God Laughs. I think I made Him Giggle.

As you read above, I've got the rollout of Abecma all organized and planned out. I am finally getting a Car-T Therapy that is on the leading cutting edge for containing Myeloma. How lucky I am that the tumors on my spine were discovered now and can be addressed with radiation. Turns out the radiation is not the magic bullet I'd hoped it would be. Radiation creates inflammation as a means of stimulating healing. The effects of my 7 treatments will continue to "cook" for 3 to 4 more weeks before the tumors are completely irradicated. Oh my.

In talking to one of the radiation techs Thursday morning, I mentioned that my Fentanyl Patch, Dexamethasone and flirting with Morphine has had little effect on my back pain overall. Some days the drive up and back home is painful. Others not so bad. I failed to share that I abandoned the Fentanyl Patch last Saturday and gave up on 15mg of morphine a day or two ago. In fact, the only drug I took yesterday was Aleve which gave me complete relief. Go figure.

Realizing I was commuting from Annapolis every day, he/she squealed to a doctor that I was driving under the influence and a danger to myself and others. I received a call from a social worker and Dr. Lefaivre, (radiologist/oncologist) that afternoon. I was not to drive myself to the hospital anymore. Considering I had one treatment out of 7 left and had not killed anyone on the highway or felt the least impaired, I considered them "tardy to the party" and might have told them so. What little good these narcotics were doing for me was far outweighed by the intermittent and unpredictable bouts of pain. But being the kind, cooperative and malleable person I am, I would have Sandra accompany me tomorrow for my last treatment. (Actually, her decision, not mine)

Thursday afternoon

Dr. Garfall calls me. The lab engineering my new T-cells is not getting optimal results. Abecma has been most successful with a level of 300-450 new T-cells. (Actual unit of measure not mentioned; probably 450 mg/kg of body weight or some other complicated formula) From 200-300 the lab will send what they have and wish you good luck on a response. I'm sitting at 102 and another week's growth will need to really kick in or it's probably back to the drawing board without Abecma. God Giggles at my plans. To make matters a little worse, Dr. G suggests I may want to have a discussion with Sandra about stopping all treatment and getting off this "knife's edge" I've been living with for so long. Nay, I say Nay. I want to explore every available option and every trial drug before kicking and screaming my way across the river unknown. He was not surprised with my answer. Al mentioned a new trial targeting a different cell on the myeloma protein other than the B-cell. Abecma would be my 3rd attempt at B-cell linked therapy so maybe this other therapy will turn out to be an actual working option and avoid all the complex administration stages and potential dangers of Abecma. Now wouldn't that be special? Intervention from The Great Physician? I'll choose to look at it that way for now.

It's Friday morning and we're in the car at 5:30 am headed for Philly. Overcast and raining. No drugs in my system. I'm driving. My back and neck have discomfort but not terribly so. I get treated and will see Dr. La Riviere afterwards. He performs a neurological exam which I pass, and he's done with me. I'm getting more stiffness in my neck and upper back, so Sandra drives us home. Lowering myself into bed produced a pain in my neck. The level of pain was new and unchartered territory. On the 1-10 scale this was around 15 and a cry of hurt came out of my mouth that was also unfamiliar.

Feeling sorry for me yet? Well, some of this is of my own doing as I look back. The hospital has a palliative care division that designs a pain relief program for patients, but this is done on an in-patient hospital stay. They can closely monitor your vital signs and reactions to drugs to start with the lowest level of pain killers and work up to a level that is both safe and effective. But I saw little value in sitting in a hospital room for 23 hours a day to receive less than an hour's worth of radiation. AND my sister was in town from KY for a visit. What I should have done was be a better advocate for myself, asking more questions and a course of treatment outlined for total pain management. But they are the EXPERTS, and you'd think they would have volunteered a course of pre-determined pain management with the possible side effects from the radiation. Lesson learned. Take heed fellow cancer friends. Ask questions. Be your own best advocate!

Taking my own advice, I decided to contact an On Call Doctor at Penn to discuss pain Management on Saturday afternoon. It's a holiday weekend and I don't really want to spend the next several days self-medicating or living with unnecessary pain. I don't recall the name of this Doctor, but I got lucky that he was on call. We chatted for several minutes, and he reviewed my recent records. I was hoping for a muscle relaxer as much of my pain may be unrelated to the myeloma tumors. Without seeing me in person he was not going to add a new drug to the mix. He suggested I continue to stay off the Fentanyl Patch and restart 8 mg of Dex twice a day. It's a powerful anti-inflammatory and can only help. My history shows I've well tolerated morphine up to 45mg at a time, so I should up the 15mg to 30 mg every 6 hours. On top of that, I can take 3 grams of Tylenol or an occasional Aleve if needed. Pretty simple and guess what? It worked. The 30mg of morphine did the trick and as of now (Saturday July 3) no pain. I am a little loopy, so I won't be driving myself anywhere anytime soon. The roads are a little safer. The highways are a little safer and the road to a better outcome for my disease takes new but not unexpected turns. If only there was a GPS app for that.

Next week will be interesting to be sure as we consider all other options.

Stay safe out there.

End of The E Blast

Monday July 5, 2021

A quiet day. Reduced morphine dose from 30 mg to 15 mg at 10 am dosing schedule. I want to use as little as possible to cover pain while increasing sobriety and mobility. Taking Porsche in tomorrow morning to finally get my front-end leak diagnosed and hopefully fixed for the final time. Constipation has been relieved and now adjusting from the other direction. No more Senekot or Dulcolax required.

Monday Aug 2, 2021

Sandra and I drove to her sister's yesterday in Philly for appointments at Penn today and tomorrow. If my blood profile meets all requirements, I will begin the study drug Talquetamab. They did not pass muster as my platelets are only 39k and must be at a minimum of 50k. Yet another setback.

We had a very lengthy discussion with Dr. Garfall about how to move forward. I excluded stopping all treatment and enjoying what time I would have left free of side effects. I do well during times off treatment but there's no guarantee I'll live longer without trials and transplants than with some of the risks these treatments bring into play. I'll roll the dice on all treatments available. Here's the road map:

First: We will give Talquetamab another week. I'll get a platelet transfusion today and start a daily pill named Promacta/Eltrombopag which should help boost my platelets. Since this is a pill, my Medicare prescription plan comes into play and the cost will be exorbitant. However, my Grant from The Health Well Foundation should cover the cost. I'll come back to UPenn next Monday and if my platelets reach 50k and my hemoglobin and neutrophils hold steady we can move forward with Talquetamab. Plus, Talguetamab targets the GPRC-5D cell instead of the B cell which has not been a successful target in previous trials.

Second: If Talquetamab tanks again, I'll go off all treatment and aim to return to Abecma for a second try. This is the Car-T program that failed because my T-cells did not grow to an acceptable level during the lab engineering process. The time off of all drugs may strengthen the T-cells, and a second round of aphaeresis (extracting T-cells from my blood) may produce healthier T-cells giving me a shot at entering the study around late August. Car-T is the current leading-edge technology for fighting myeloma. There is treatment for Car-T using stem cells from a donor. This removes the risk of my T-cells failing the re-engineering process but opens the door for complications coming from a different source. I'm not currently eligible for this treatment as I have had several failed BCMA treatments, and this targets the B cells on the myeloma cells. Of course, BCMA has been extensively used in myeloma patients and it's getting more difficult to find patients that meet the criteria. This requirement may fall by the wayside and offer a future option in my treatment.

Third: No Car-T, we move to Selinexor, Carfilzomib and Dexamethasone. Selinexor is a once-a-week pill with some difficult side effects. Nausea, loss of appetite, loss of taste, weight loss. Weight loss is welcomed, the method of diet is not so great. Carfilsomib/Kyprolis is a chemotherapy infusion that has had previous success at lowering my cancer levels but is tough on my heart. By now, you're familiar with Dex.

Fourth: A Second Bone Marrow Transplant. Using the left-over stem cells from my first BMT in 2017, I would enter the hospital for a 3-4 week stay. Melphalan will be infused and wipe out all my bone marrow. My stem cells will be returned to my body and the process of regrowing my marrow begins. Risks are much greater than the first time around as my level of disease has progressed significantly. Two to three months of recovery and isolation at home will hopefully provide a window of remission for 3-6 months before the myeloma begins to regrow. During this time, I may be eligible for Car-T or other trials I was not previously able to meet due to the required levels of blood profiles or other restrictions. Dr. Garfall said the risk of dying from complications of a second bone marrow transplant increased from 1% for the first transplant to 10% for a second transplant. Still pretty good odds in my opinion.

Whew. The good news is I have options. Each contains side effects and may contribute to a greatly restricted lifestyle. They may also provide a springboard to minimizing my disease, a better daily breath of life and more time for new drugs and new treatments to develop. (By next spring, the Car-T program from Janssen may have FDA approval and it has shown to be the most effective of all Car-T therapies). For now, I'll take the uncertainty and risks of the trials over the option of doing nothing and waiting for the certainty of myeloma winning the battle of life and death. With some luck and God's continued guiding hand through this process, I hope to be sending you updates for years to come.

Your continued prayers and support are greatly appreciated more than I can express.

Monday, August 9, 2021

Sandra and I hit the road at 5:15 am for my 7:30 appointment at UPenn. As you may recall from my last report, my hemoglobin, platelets and absolute neutrophils had to meet certain minimum levels to enter the Talquetamab trial. I only hit 2 of the 3 as my platelets were still too low. What was hoped to be a long day at Penn with the beginning of a new trial, was now a return drive home.

Dr. Garfall again discussed the remaining options for treatment, including doing nothing and enjoying what time I had left free of drugs and side effects. As you may guess, that is not my preferred option. No risk, no reward. Dr. Garfall has a spot reserved for me for a 2nd attempt at Abecma. This is the FDA approved Car-T cell treatment which re-engineers T-cells to attack and kill myeloma cells. In the first attempt, my T cells did not replicate as needed in the lab and this was perhaps due to the level of disease I have maintained for the past 9 months as well as the impact of elotuzamab, pomalyst and venetoclax currently used to keep my disease in check. Aphaeresis to collect T-cells is set for Aug 25 and that will represent a 6-8-week vacation from all the previously mentioned drugs. The hope is that during the time off medications, my T cells will be stronger and respond to the re-engineering process. Dr. Garfall has had patients that failed Abecma on the first try but responded on the second and even third attempt. If successful, this will expose me to the currently best-known treatment for success in containing this disease. It will also require the most inconvenient restrictions with a 7–10-day hospital stay followed by 21 more days staying with my in-laws near the hospital and an 8-week abstinence from driving. All this will be worth the inconveniences if some level of remission is achieved.

I must admit I'm skeptical my T cells will respond after their poor performance the first time around, but I'm also hopeful I'm dead wrong on that assumption. With success the potential for 6-12 months of remission or even longer comes into play and buying that kind of time would be incredible. If this does not work, my next move will most likely be a second attempt at a bone marrow transplant. Harvested stem cells are left over from the first transplant in 2017. This transplant will be more dangerous than the first as my level of disease has increased greatly and the risk of death jumps from 1% to 10%. Not bad odds in my opinion.

A transplant will not be easy. 2-3 weeks in the hospital or longer depending on side effects. Most likely, 3 months at home in isolation while my marrow is reconstructed. A high risk of infection which could prove deadly. Even with success there is no guarantee how long before the myeloma cells start regrowing. But it will give me great satisfaction to know my bone marrow has been depleted and with it every myeloma cell in my body evaporated. I will move on to my eternal home with greater satisfaction knowing my disease suffered complete eradication for some period of time. On the plus side, if I achieve some remission and my blood profile returns to some level of "normalcy", I think that would be a great time to try aphaeresis again and attempt another T cell therapy. Surely my new T cells post-transplant will be stronger and healthier which could lead to greater success and another chance to extend some level of remission. Well, that's my plan anyway. I hope God won't laugh.

Hope is not lost, and good outcomes may still come to fruition. Never say never. Never stop fighting until I draw my last breath at which time I know a complete healing awaits.

Peace and love.

Monday Aug 1, 2021

Drove to Penn today for a CT Scan on the left side of my jaw. I experience pain when opening my mouth wide enough to eat as well as chewing food. The scan revealed some increased bone density which Dr. Garfall says may indicate a Myeloma lesion. This is a difficult area to radiate as salivary glands could become inflamed causing dry mouth and potential difficulty swallowing. The level of pain is currently low and only present when eating. Dr. Garfall prefers to wait on radiation at this time. Perhaps the 2nd attempt at Abecma will be successful and the lesion will be eradicated with the newly formed T Cells. Just another reason to hope for successful treatment of my disease.

Wednesday Aug 25, 2021

Time for the 2nd aphaeresis procedure in preparation for a 2nd attempt at Abecma. This is the therapy that re-engineers my killer T-cells to recognize and kill myeloma cells. Dr. Garfall has had several patients whose T-cells did not replicate properly the first time around, but success was achieved on the 2nd or even 3rd attempt. Here's hoping I follow that pattern for success this time..

I continue to deteriorate physically for two reasons. First, it's been almost a year since I had any medications that significantly lowered my cancer levels. Secondly, it's been about 8 weeks since all medications were discontinued in an effort to allow my blood profile to improve and achieve appropriate levels required for acceptance into clinical trials. Even so, my platelets were still too low for the Talquetumab trial, but Abecma is already FDA approved so those restrictions are not pre-requisites for starting the therapy. The lab requires 4-6 weeks to re-engineer the T-cells, so I will return to Elotuzumab, Pomalyst and Venetoclax to reduce or at least maintain current levels of myeloma. I discussed an alternate therapy of Kyprolis and Selinexor with Dr. Garfall. Kyprolis is a chemo infusion which has been successful in the past for me. Selinexor is a new drug but has some unpleasant side effects and has not produced sustained success for most patients. We agreed to save that for a future Hail Mary.

I'm at a point now where minimum exertion causes maximum exhaustion. No pain, just an inability to sustain any movement for more than 10-15 minutes. A better measure is that for the first time ever, I was unsure about driving myself to Philly and back; not my normal confidence level. So Sandra accompanied me to aphaeresis and it was a huge benefit to have her at my side. I still did all the driving but knowing she was able to take the wheel at any given time was reassuring. And having her at my bedside during the procedure was an even bigger boost to my psyche. She's a very good girl.

From the underground parking garage to the aphaeresis unit is about a half mile trek; all indoors. Sandra was my personal transport agent, using one of the myriad hospital wheelchairs to deliver me to the unit. An IV with a steel needle was inserted in a vein in my right arm at the elbow. This arm had to remain in a straight and in a fixed position throughout the procedure. The IV pulled blood from my body into the aphaeresis machine. An IV was placed in my left arm, again in a vein at the elbow joint, and returned the filtered blood back to my body. Since this needle was flexible, I was able to bend this arm but every time I did the machine beeped and I had to return to a straight arm position. The procedure took 3.5 hours and it's amazing how tired you become lying on your back in bed with both arms straight. We returned home without incident and a 2 hour nap ensued.

I'll get an Elotuzumab infusion this coming Monday and re-start Venetoclax and Pomalyst pills simultaneously. The waiting game now starts to see if my T-cells accept the planned alterations in the lab and replicate to an appropriate level of success. That's half the battle. Will it work remains to finish the battle. Only time will tell. Stay tuned.

Aug 29, 2021

Greetings Friends and Family,

I continue getting my book organized with the invaluable help of Mike and Anne Pace. I hope to end the book with a good report on the 2nd attempt at the Abecma therapy which involves re-engineering my killer T-cells to recognize and destroy myeloma cells. I'll switch to a Blog where readers of the book and you too can see how my story progresses from there. Here's the latest update on that process.

Monday Aug 30, 2021

Feeling better than last Wednesday, I drove myself to UPenn for my return to an Elotuzumab infusion. Appointment was not until 1 pm so there was no rush hour traffic. The walk from the parking garage was much shorter than the one last week to the aphaeresis unit so I was able to make it on my own steam. Since I had not had an Elotuzumab infusion for 9 weeks, they had to restart the drip at a slow rate to monitor for any negative reactions. This took 3.5 hours, followed by a Zometa, 15-minute infusion to strengthen my bones. I did not get away until 7 pm. The bright side was that there was no rush hour traffic again, and my drive home took a little less than 2 hours.

Pomalyst pills arrive tomorrow and the cost of $900+ for 21 pills will be covered by the Grant I received from the Healthwell Foundation. THANK YOU! I have Venetoxclax on hand, so I'll start that drug tomorrow also. Dr. Garfall will evaluate the performance of this cocktail in a couple of weeks. Kyprolis has been a successful chemo infusion in the past so he may switch to this instead of Elotuzumab if he thinks we can achieve a better response. Three to four weeks from now we should hear from the lab about the re-engineering success or failure of my T-cells. If we can move forward with the Abecma therapy, a new list of restrictions and requirements will begin. I'll bore you with those details when and if they come into play.

Looking forward to September, new T-cells assassinating Myeloma Cells and cooler weather. My lack of tolerance for hot weather has kept me indoors and I haven't even used our pool. Here's hoping that too will change soon.

I continue to be pain free for the most part and realize what a blessing that is. Better days are still to come for me, and I hope your days are blessed with good health and free of stress if possible.

With Love and appreciation for each of you....
Bruce

P.S. Please pray for Betty Jean Chatham in Shelbyville KY and Joe Martincic in Florida. Both of these dear friends are recuperating from recent strokes. Betty Jean is a virtuoso on piano and organ, and she remains a member at FBC in Shelbyville where my Dad was pastor for 12 years. Joe and his wife Jude played an integral part in Sandra and me meeting before they retired from Annapolis and moved south. Your thoughts and prayers for their full recovery will be very appreciated.

August 31, 2021

I'm afraid my pill taking is very boring. I tried one of those 7 day pill organizers and did not like it. So I just keep the current meds lined up in their bottles from the pharmacy on my nightstand lower shelf. In case of any confusion the labels with instructions for how much and when to take them are right in front of me. Here's my cash of pills and the current meds occupy the front perimeter. Currently I only take 6 medications of the myriad pictured below. Actually opening the bottles and reviewing the instruction labels keeps everything fresh in my mind. It works for me.

This Just In . . .

... Dr. Garfall called to tell me the 2nd attempt at re-engineering my T-cells to kill myeloma cells is a bust. The program is called Abecma and it is not in my immediate future. Six years of myeloma appear to have beaten up my T-cells to the extent they cannot accept the manipulation required. This limits my next viable option to a 2nd Bone Marrow Transplant (BMT). The first BMT was done in Jan 2017 and gave me 17 months of a good partial remission. Prior to the BMT, enough stem cells were collected for a 2nd BMT and kept frozen in liquid nitrogen. They have been transferred from the Univ of MD Hospital and await me at UPenn. This is a positive element for the 2nd attempt as those stem cells were collected when I was in better health without 5 years of myeloma beating me down. There are greater risks the 2nd time around, however.

Dr. Garfall explained that most serious procedures like heart bypass and kidney replacement carry a 2% chance of death. My 2nd BMT carries a 10% chance of dying. Doing nothing at this point yields a 100% chance of dying from myeloma so the risks are worth the effort in my opinion. I will be admitted to the hospital one day next week. Some testing will be performed and if needed some tweaks may be made to my blood profile along with an echocardiogram to measure the strength of my heart. I will be given a high dose of Melphalan which will completely eradicate my bone marrow. (Bye, bye myeloma... I won't miss you even if it lasts only briefly). 24-48 hours later my frozen stem cells will be thawed and given back to me intravenously. The fun begins.....

Major dangerous side effects that could lead to death are:

1. Uncontrollable infection. Last stop ICU.

2. Organ failure.

3. My marrow does not regrow sufficiently to produce a healthy blood profile.

Lesser but likely side effects:

diarrhea, vomiting, gastrointestinal issues, loss of appetite and an ability to keep food down requiring a feeding tube. Probably more could be added to this list but that's all I remember from speaking to Dr. Garfall.

I will be in isolation in the hospital for 3-4 weeks. If the side effects are well managed and my blood profile meets minimum standards, I'll go home for another 2-3 months of recovery.

This procedure is not considered to be a long term solution by Dr. Garfall. If all goes well, he is hopeful there will be a period of time after recovery when we can revisit T-cell therapy. My T-cells should be stronger at this point and offer a better chance of success at managing my cancer.

As you know, I'm putting a book together on my experiences with this disease. The time has come to finish the book and get it into print. I plan to start a blog where you can keep track of my progress as well as anyone who reads the book and see how my story progresses from this point. More on that later.

There are two possible outcomes in my future. First, a successful BMT paves the way to another life extending therapy and renewed health to some extent. Secondly, my time is up and I solve the great mystery. I certainly prefer option one, but I do not fear dying. I believe there awaits me a life after death that exceeds my wildest dreams. Reunion with family and friends. Looking into the face of God and HIS Son. A transformed body, free of pain or disease and so many other wonderful experiences. Should this be my fate in the near future, I hope you will join me when your time comes. Your passport is very simple: What do I need to do? "Believe in the Lord Jesus, and you will be saved" (Acts 16:31). God has already done all of the work.

With love and appreciation for each of you.

Tuesday September 28, 2021

Good evening Friends and Family,

I am currently undergoing a second autologous stem cell transplant, commonly referred to as a Bone Marrow Transplant (BMT). Stem cells held in reserve from my first BMT are being used and this will hopefully give me a window of opportunity for a healthier Marrow and yield longer term success for the next therapy in line. While I hope to receive as long a period possible for a remission of this disease, the BMT probably be used more as a bridge to that next trial or therapy that will hopefully have great success. Time will tell.

Here's the latest news on a search for some myeloma relief. Sandra and I left home today at 10:30 am for the drive to the University of Pennsylvania Medical Center. I have a 2:00 appointment to have a Pic Line installed in my arm and a 2:30 appointment with Dr. Garfall to sign consent documents. Admission to the hospital follows our visit with Dr. Garfall.

We arrived in time to eat lunch and check in early for the Pic Line. We were called early for the procedure but wound up waiting in a holding room anyway. Waiting is a common thread for anything to do in a hospital and it is very tiring.

A peripherally inserted catheter (PIC), also called a PIC line, is a long, thin tube that's inserted through a vein in my arm and passed through to the larger veins near my heart. The line has 2 leads that allows flexibility for more than 1 access to point of infusion. Chemotherapy drugs like Melphalan are highly toxic and can irritate veins. To minimize complications, the catheter is long enough to reach the heart and avoid that first 15 to 20 inches of vein structure. The procedure took about 30 minutes. Injections of Lidocaine numbed an area of the underside of my right upper arm. Ultrasound was used to "see" the vein structure so the doctor could know where to cut into a vein and guide the catheter into the correct vein as well as make the tube the correct length to reach the heart. My line was 16.5 inches.

Pic line inserted, we headed off to meet with Dr. Garfall. He reviewed all the possible negative outcomes up to and including death. Getting an infection would be a serious complication and I asked how I could get an infection in the very clean environment of my private hospital room. Turns out the infection could develop within my body. Melphalan will not only destroy my marrow but will also zap the bacteria in my gut. If this bacteria gets into my bloodstream it can travel to my organs and create an infection. Bummer.

Despite the potential deadly complications, I signed the consent forms and off we went to Admissions. I was assigned a very nice, large and private corner room with a great view. The previous occupant had just been discharged and we had to wait an hour and 15 minutes while the room was being cleaned. As noted above, waiting is tiring.

Thursday September 30, 2021

Nothing exciting today. Melphalan left to do its work and clean out my marrow.

Friday October 1, 2021

The fun begins. Stem Cells left over from the first BMT to be infused at 1:00 pm. Received saline drip for 4 hours prior and continuing for 4 more hours after the infusion. The fresh stem cells from the 2017 BMT had a preservative added to the mix while in deep freeze with liquid nitrogen. The saline solution will help the kidneys filter this out. Here's a look at the process:

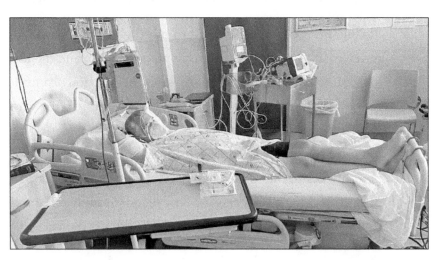

That's me, awaiting the first bag of stem cells.

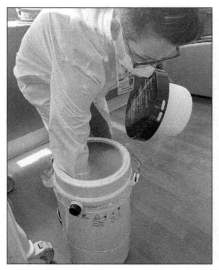

The stem cells are removed from the liquid nitrogen container (-320 Fahrenheit Yikes!), placed on a metal tray, then transferred to a warming container. The thawed stem cells are pulled from the bag and placed in my body with a syringe. The rate of delivery and side effects can be controlled. My first Bone Marrow Transplant had four bags of stem cells. Three bags were used this time, keeping one in reserve.

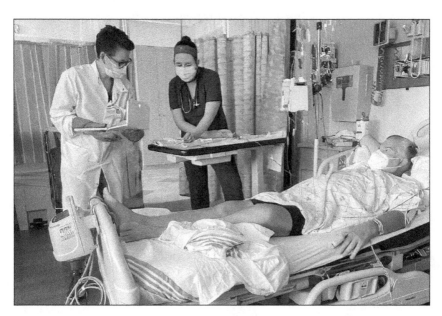

Everything went smoothly, without interruption.

Thanks team!

Now the waiting begins. Side effects likely to appear in the next few days as the new stem cells awaken the immune system. Diarrhea likely to follow and potential fevers may also pop up. Low blood counts can also be dangerous and will require attention like platelet infusions and blood transfusions. I'll be closely monitored with immediate action taken to minimize and hopefully eliminate anything dangerous. Expecting 2 to 3 weeks in the hospital followed by 2-3 months recovery at home. If all goes well, I may have some level of remission by January and be able to move more freely like your average overweight 67-year-old man. Maybe I can work on the overweight part.

What's that saying? "May you live in exciting times". Well, I do, and I'm excited for a good outcome for this treatment with more life extending therapies I can use to keep this disease in check to follow. AND as always, my gratitude for all the prayers, positive thoughts and support you have given me that mean so much.

Brucie

Encouragement and Support

ARE YOU A "PRIVATE" PERSON? Maybe a little introverted? Prefer to keep your troubles and problems to yourself? I have those tendencies. It's not easy for me to hear compliments for some self -depreciating reason. But I believe the two most important tools you possess to beating your cancer for as long as possible are to maintain a positive attitude no matter the circumstances and the support and encouragement of your friends and family and yes sometimes complete strangers.

I determined from the outset to learn as much as possible about my disease and share this information with my friends and family list. The sharing makes me accountable to maintain my positive attitude and explain some complicated information in as clear and concise a way as possible. I learn and remember by sharing through the written word. It also provides feedback and encouragement that takes many forms. As you may surmise, my Christian faith is shared by many on the F&F list, but not necessarily everyone. These fellow believers pray for me. They add me to their prayer list at their churches. This widens the list of people petitioning our creator on my behalf. My Father contacted every church he ever pastored as well as the ministers he knew personally and asked them to add me to their church prayer lists. I'm guessing thousands of people at some point have prayed for me. Complete strangers. This is simultaneously humbling and uplifting. I highly recommend you consider starting your own list of contacts and keeping them updated. The spider web of information you create can change your course of treatment by opening a window to a new doctor, clinical trial or medication that could be life extending. I would never have known Dr. Daniela Hoehn had Scott and Cheryl not read one of my emails and decided to introduce me to her. Without her contacts in the field of Multiple Myeloma, I might not be alive today. It's a real possibility.

There is yet another way you should consider sharing. I can't explain how this happens, but on many occasions, I've had an opportunity to discuss my cancer with complete strangers. A couple of examples:

I purchased a used but really well maintained, low mileage convertible sports car a year ago. My Dad infected me with the car/motorcycle gene and this 12 year old Porsche 911 has been the finest and most fun car I've ever owned. One drawback - the stereo was junk and the sound was pitiful with the top down. I knew of Westminster Speed and Sound (In Westminster, MD where we used to live) and I made the hour drive from Annapolis to explore getting an upgrade. I met with Mark Miller, the owner. In the showroom, there was a Harley Davidson motorcycle. It had clearly been upgraded for stereo sound and I mentioned how I had recently sold my Harley in favor of the Porsche at my wife's encouragement. (Best wife ever. Jealous?) Why? I had some health issues that made me tired and short of breath. I could drive a car safely, but riding a motorcycle was out of the question. He asked about my disease. This led to sharing about cancer in his family and also our mutual Christian faith. We formed a bond and an element of trust and caring. Pretty cool.

The install of a new system that met my purpose was expensive and would require 2-3 days to complete. Sandra wasn't crazy about following me to Westminster and back twice to drop off and pick up the car. Isn't there someone closer to our house? A reasonable request and I fired up the Google machine. Enter Sound Works, in Millersville, MD, twenty minutes from home. I met with Jeff, one of the co-owners. He knew Mark at Westminster Speed and Sound and vouched for his credibility. As Mark had explained, working on a Porsche required some special knowledge. Those Germans engineer awesome cars but they aren't exactly easy to perform upgrades on. Sound works was also a Porsche certified shop with lots of experience. Good to know.

At some point, an opening presented itself and I confessed my cancer to Jeff. Turns out his wife suffers from Multiple Sclerosis and is so far managing her disease well. They have three young children. Another connection and a bond of trust and empathy.

I emailed Mark Miller that I decided to use Jeff at Sound Works, strictly on a travel distance issue and thanked him for his time and willingness to share his faith with me. Mark replied with appreciation that I was truthful with him and wished more customers would do the same. This was another opportunity to share something more important than stereo speakers and the self-indulgent desire to improve a car.

Jeff did an amazing job on my new system. It was expensive, but at 75 mph with the top down, I can turn up the volume and feel like I'm in a concert hall with fabulous music to add to the joy of driving.

One More Experience

Today is June 16, 2021. We dined out with our friends Elaine Aarsand, Jim Pastor, Mary Jane and Bill Johnson. What a wonderful treat to do this on the covered deck of the Annapolis Yacht Club, overlooking the boats without wearing a mask. We have all been vaccinated and I hope you have been as well. These longtime friends are on my email list so some recent events with my journey were discussed. During the conversation a lady at the table close to me interrupted to ask if I was dealing with Multiple Myeloma. Turns out her 84 year old husband had recently passed away from the disease. I expressed my sorrow for her loss and we exchanged some information relating to his and my treatment. This was an opportunity of sharing important and beneficial information to each of us. Connecting with people is so important be it brief with a stranger or a lifelong friend. You don't have to be, nor should you be, a walking talking billboard telling everyone you meet you have cancer. But I highly recommend being attuned to opportunities to open up to people when you feel it's appropriate. Cancer is rampant. I imagine almost everyone in this country has some form of cancer in the family or has a close relationship with someone who has it, has beat it, is in remission, undergoing treatment or may have died from the disease. We need more unity in our country and while cancer is not the most uplifting way to connect with others, it may well be one of the most important ways to do so. Caring is a wonderful thing.

Following is a copy of some of the many replies I've received from the information I publish to my F&F list. There are too many to list them all so I'll try to include something from everyone, with one notable exception. Phil Lande has been and continues to be one of the best friends I've ever had. Instead of responding to my updates via email, we discuss them personally by phone. Phil is too important to me to be omitted, so let me just tell you a little bit about him and express my undying appreciation for his influence on my life.

I have never had a better friend than Phil Lande. (Pronounced Landie) We met through golf and he gave me a sales job after my departure from the golf business. He was VP of Sales for Counter

Intelligence and he taught me the countertop sales business. When we met, we both lived in Westminster, MD. I was the Head Pro at the local golf course and Phil would often ask if he could join me to play a round of golf. He often bought a small bucket of range balls and used them to chip and putt on the putting green. Then he would go to the range to hit the balls with his full swing. I never saw him play a round of golf and was suspicious he only wanted to play in my group to avoid a green fee. (Phil is both frugal and generous as I would come to know)

One evening he was on the putting green as I was going out to play with one of our members. Dave said he thought Phil was a good player and said we should ask him to join us. Phil sprinted into the shop to pay for his round. He shot one or two over par from the tips of the course with a very strong long game. He beat us both and so it began. Over the years Phil and I played a lot of golf together. Even today in a phone conversation, we reminisced about the summer evenings we played so many years ago and the idyllic setting of playing an almost empty course due to the later hours of the day. We often created our own holes playing from the tee on hole number 3 to the green of hole 7. A carry of some 200 yards over water from an elevated tee. We cemented a lasting friendship over our love for the game.

Phil has retired and moved to Greenville, NC. He is recovering from triple bypass surgery last year and like me, our age and health issues have diminished our proficiency in golf. A bitter pill for us both. If I am blessed enough to achieve enough improvement from the Car-T therapy and can play golf once again, rest assured an outing with Phil, Mike Perkowski and Craig Norford will be high on my list. We have done several buddy trips in the past and doing that again would mean the world to me. Phil is one of those rare people that will literally do anything for his friends. I'm lucky to have met him and he has had a big impact on the direction of my life. I am forever in his debt for so many things.

Beth and Phil Lande

Friends and Family Really Know How to Cheer Up a Guy!

Hi Buddy! I think of you every day and pray for you every night. I believe strongly that you will come thru this and have sun shining on you for years to come.

Best Wishes to you my Friend!
Miguel (last name)

Mike came to me through my friend Phil Lande. He lives in Memphis and is an avid and excellent golfer. He knows Phil from the countertop business as Mike is a Sales Manager for a large distribution company BPI. I've had the privilege of playing with Mike on several of our 4 man golf vacations and he has become a close and true friend. As previously mentioned I hope our traveling foursome can once again hit the road for an extend 4 day weekend (or longer) of golf till you drop. I hope my Car-T therapy will be so successful I won't be the first to drop. If I can return to a 36 hole day of golf I'm sure we can rekindle all the fun of days past.

Oh, Bruce,
I would suppose you may already be having your veins evaluated. Hoping that all goes well.

Again, I am caught not knowing what to say. It's all so much for you to handle. But I know you will do it with great courage and determination.

A prayer for you:
Our heavenly father as Bruce begins this process with the new drug we ask your guidance to his doctors. And that this drug will give him good results. We ask your encouragement to Bruce letting him feel your presence beside him. Give him strength and encouragement in the days ahead as he begins this journey. Let him feel the arms around him of all who so deeply care and love him. We ask your caring love and blessings on him in the days ahead. Amen.

Go get um, Bruce. Love you,
Pam Gray

Although only a couple of years older than Mary Jane and me, Pam was our babysitter on occasion. Our bond with her family has created strong and lasting memories. Her maiden name is Moffett, so we are separated by one letter of the alphabet. A week's stay for many summers on their houseboat in Lake Cumberland along with her parents Tom, Anne and sister Tish are some of the most fun times MJ and I ever had. Her written payer is eloquent and deeply cherished.

I don't know how you manage to spiel all this crap, it's a credit to you! As Jimmy V said, "never give up, never ever give up." Keep fighting and I'll be thinking of you.

Clyde Thomson

I met Clyde and his wife Annette through business. They are two of the finest people I know. Beyond business we share a love of dogs and golf, so what's not to like. Sometimes friendship transcends business and that's a beautiful thing. Thank you Clyde and Annette for loving me. I love you too!

Well sweet friend looks like you are hanging in there and that is good. I never you that you were such a prolific writer! Ha ha ha ha. These reports are just amazing. Please know we continue to lift you up to the Almighty although we know He already knows what is going on with you - it does make us feel better! So glad all your caregivers are on top of all that is going on with you. We have lots of folks praying for you here in Colorado - especially Carter's mother. She is the chief prayer amongst us - always has been but you might remember her and she is really struggling right now, her little heart is just not going to last much longer. She is 87. We just had a wonderful trip to Texas to see Jason and family over Labor Day. Carter was able to baptize Jason's middle Son, Henry Carter - what a glorious time that was. If you ever feel like getting on FB - the pictures are on my page and they are really neat pictures.

Well take care my friend. We love you so.
The Frey Family

Carter Frey was the Minister of Education while my Father was Pastor of the Heritage Baptist Church of Annapolis, MD. Carter and Linda had a tremendous impact on my life. They are two of the finest Cristian people I have ever known. This is from Linda.

Thanks for the update, friend. I often think about you and wonder how things are going. You're one tough dude. You'll continue to be in my thoughts this summer.

Burch Kinsolving

Burch Kinsolving lived on our street when we moved to Shelbyville, Ky during my 3rd grade year. We played neighborhood pick up baseball games together and even did some camping out when our parents allowed us to spend the night in an open field by our homes. The church moved us to a new parsonage and I lost touch with Burch for many years. He was a great baseball catcher and basketball player in High School. I was neither of those. After all these years, when Burch learned of my cancer he became one of my best advocates and encourager. What a gift. What a great man. Thank you Burch for coming back into my life and all the support you give me. Here he is with his granddaughter, Charlie.

Dear Bruce,

I just heard today about your very kind donation to our multiple myeloma research fund! On behalf of the whole myeloma team at the Abramson Cancer Center, thank you so much for the generous gift!

Our team has had an exceptional year bringing new treatments to myeloma patients. This includes work on the milestone FDA approval of Belantamab, the drug you are currently receiving for your myeloma, and initial results of Teclistamab and TAK-573, the experimental therapies you've received over the last couple years. We know, though, that we still have a lot of work to do. Donations like yours help us conduct these clinical trials and fund promising, early-stage research that translates into real prevention, treatment, and survivorship strategies for our patients. None of our vital work would be possible without partners like you.

Again, thank you for the generous gift. I look forward to seeing you at your visit next week.

Kindest regards,
Al Garfall

I included this email from my Myeloma Doctor, not to brag about a contribution but to encourage you to do what you can financially to give something back to these Doctors, Scientists and Institutions working tirelessly to discover therapies for our illness. Greatly have I received and enough cannot be given in return.

Bruce, thank you for the update. After reading these updates I can't help but to better understand what it means to "battle cancer". Not to dismiss the toll it takes on you physically but what you must be going through mentally has to be the tough part. In comparison, my life challenges seam minuscule and I just don't know how you cope. I have a great deal of respect for your optimism and hope for the best with the treatment of Abecma.

I like to think that my prayers (and I know they work) will someday end this battle for you and your loved ones. In the meantime, may Almighty God bless you during this summer's journey!

Dave Hobgood

Dave, Paul, Michael, John and Patsy.

Dave and I worked together At Frito Lay as District Managers in the 70's and 80's. Dave was outstanding, often leading our region in sales perfor-mance. Also on our unbeatable team was Denise O'Neill, Dave Turner, Larry Campbell and Jimmy Burroughs. After many years apart, it has been a real gift to reconnect with the 2 Dave's and Denise. Turns out we all now live in Annapolis. I fear Jimmy may no longer be living, but we need to find Larry Campbell. I have never worked with a team of such great talent and chemistry as these fine people.

Hi Bruce -

Thank you again for the great fun, hospitality and friendship last eve-ning. It was really terrific meeting Sandra and I truly enjoyed meeting and talking with Mary Jane. And, of course, it's always great seeing you, Denise & Marty. The meal was perfect and I loved seeing your neighborhood and your beautiful home....all so close, but yet still very secluded.

As we keep saying, it's the longtime friendships that are very often the best. So glad that we have reconnected.

Big hugs to Sandra and Mary Jane!

Let's keep in touch.

Cheers,
David Turner

Here's the other Dave, Dave Turner, I had the pleasure of working with at Frito Lay. Like Denise Dave was a management designee and we spent a hectic year or longer working at the Capitol Heights Frito Lay Distribution Center outside of Washington DC. Dave was the region Manager having been promoted from his District Manager position where we worked side by side in Baltimore. I was asked to take a lateral promotion to work as a DM for Dave in DC which was a union shop for the salesman. Brother was that a meat grinder. But we survived and lived to tell the tales which we laugh about now but moaned and cried about when they happened. Dave went on to manage the NE for Villeroy and Bach, distributors of fine dinnerware. Dave now has a pod cast called SEAT YOURSELF and delivers news and information from all over the world on the foodservice and hospitality industry. Dave is the globally known Chief Evangelist and Editor for Tabletop Journal. He is also a valued friend and reconnecting with him and his wife Linda has been a real treat.

My sweet, dear, precious, brave, funny, adorable Boo,

I still don't have an appropriate response to your recent email. There aren't enough cuss words to say, at least the ones I know...and that repertoire greatly expanded thanks to my beloved Joe. I hope prayers, in addition to medical expertise, will keep you going forward for a very long time. I so wish I could trade places with you as my remaining days are so diminished by the loss of the greatest love of my life.

I guess yours is the first face I remember other than Mother's and Daddy's. Not much to remember about North FifBenson but my vivid memory of the Brooks Street apartment in Louisville is sharing a tiny bedroom with you. I was in the rollaway bed that we had forever after and you in the crib...rocking and knocking your head. Thankfully no injury to your big brain! You were always the adorable one, generous and kind to this very day. I wish I had realized sooner what a blessing you are but better late than never. I have so often been late to the dance.

The Jewish faith teaches to concentrate all efforts and energy in conducting ourselves as children of God in this world, here and now. Gentiles believe in Hell; some Jews do but most don't. I'm somewhere in between at this point. Life is so hard but you continue to show affirmation for all that is worthwhile. As I said, what a blessing you are.

During your weeks of driving prison I will gladly volunteer to be your chauffeur. Who doesn't want to be seen in a Porsche with a hot guy??

I love you more than I can say.

Your sister
Mary Jane Yates

No explanation needed. Just one of the multitude of supportive emails for my fabulous sister.

Dear Bruce,

I feel like you are my brother because, quite simply, your sister is like my sister and your dad… well, I just wanted to marry him. They are two of the kindest, most wonderful human beings I have ever known and, since you grew up amongst them, you must be wonderful, too.

I will concentrate every day to send you the most positive energy possible and wish you freedom from this damned illness, which you handle with such grace and courage.

Love,
Leslie Brown
Former Bandmate and Long-Distance Admirer

Leslie and I are Facebook friends with carbon copy feelings on politics and many other issues. Her email to me is just another example of how someone you don't know personally can express their love and support for the journey facing you. Thank you Leslie and I hope we can meet sometime in the not too distant future.

The Energizer Bunny will be renamed Bruce...

They must be quite curious as to why your experience is seemingly unique.

We're ready for an outdoor weekend at Chez Moffatt.

You are truly one of the most outstanding people I've ever known.

Love, Cliffe Cheston

The Chestons: Cliffe, daughter Emily and son Matteo, Cheryl (sister to my wife Sandra), son Alex with daughter Clara.

One of the many supportive emails from my Brother-In-Law. Most people don't marry into an in-law family that accepts and loves you as I have been privileged to do. Thank you Cliffe, Cheryl, son Alex, his wife Sophie, Emily, her husband Ralph, Cliffe's sisters Martha and Julie for all the love and support you continue to give me.

From Emily:

Glad to hear all the pain you're going through is having the intended effect!

One of my friends is a physician in radiation oncology at HUP (Hospital of University of Pennsylvania) – Neil Taunk. If you see a handsome and very nice young Indian doc, tell him you're my uncle!

This is obviously not the same as dexamethasone but have you ever gotten an alternative treatment for the bone pain? Like gabapentin or acupuncture? Or even bisphosphonates to help slow down the bone destruction? Obviously won't take it away completely but sometimes our patients that have crazy horrible pain that we can control with fentanyl PCAs have some success with alternative therapies.

Take care and keep us in the loop.

Love, Emily and Matteo and Ralph

From Alex:

Congratulations on the progress! Your perspective and outlook through this challenge is super impressive to me. Also, thanks for sharing the specifics. It's interesting to hear the details around how this thing is treated.

Lots of Love from me and Sophie to you and your girls!
Alex

Niece Emily Cheston, married to Ralph Reidel and mother to 2 year old Matteo. Emily graduated from Williams College and was a member of their successful crew team. She moved on to Med School at Jefferson in Philadelphia and is now a practicing OBGYN. Her brother Alex lives in San Francisco with Sophie and their daughter Clara who is now 3. Alex has a successful career with Google. The Cheston's are pushing the upper limits of smart and successful as started with Mom and Dad. Who can guess the heights Matteo and Clara will reach someday?

CAR T for Bruce E – That's my new prayer for you!
It has been quite a 6 months. You are an amazing man – God's got more in store for you to do here on earth. I am glad you are here with us! Hate to see you have to go through so much. You continue to be a courageous inspiration to us! I am looking forward to outdoor time with you and Sandra!

Meanwhile, I have had COVID since Saturday. Compliments to one of my clients. Didn't realize I had been exposed, drove to PA to bury my dad and gave it to my son, Jack. Had a couple of sick with fever days, feeling better yesterday and today. Head stuffed up and no taste.

Fever gone. Jack's actually been sicker and in Virginia taking care of himself. Marty and Liam are quarantining at home – no symptoms thank God. So I will get the vaccine as soon as they tell me I can.

Big long distance hug! Stay safe and get ready for Car T Bruce E!

Denise O'Neil

You read the name Denise O'Neill in my copy of Dave Hobgood's email. Denise and her husband Marty in addition to just being great people, are two of the best business minded and successful people I know. They adopted 3 children, Jack, Liam and Lilly and as expected excel at parenthood as well. As a "Management Designee" Denise had to spend several months as a route sales driver to learn the business of driving a truck and serving Frito lay customers. At about 5' 5" tall and maybe 110 pounds, we all thought she would never last. WRONG! She rocketed to the top in Management at Frito Lay and went on the be a VP with Nabisco. One smart cookie, a logical fit for Nabisco. (Pun intended.) Denise and Marty now operate their own business consulting firm and guide companies to greater profit and success with their knowledge of best practices in running a company. A true power couple and so supportive of Sandra and me.

Bruce,

You continue to amaze us and we keep you in our thoughts. Hope you and Sandy have a nice Easter and we get to see you soon! Of course when we get vaccinated.

Xxoo
Elaine Aarsand

Elaine is a long time and close friend of my wife Sandra. They have owned several businesses together, endured the break-up of marriages, the loss of Elaine's husband Knute and remained close for about 45 years. Through thick and thin, they last. Thank you Elaine for loving Sandy and including me in your extended family.

Bruce,

As an attorney and fiction author, I've spent most of my adult life with words. This report is only the latest proof that you are a born writer who puts me to shame. As before, I encourage you to write a book about your experiences. Not only the medical explanations, which is fascinating, but also your outlook, and how you remain so upbeat. Your sprinkling of humor is masterful and keeps a reader's attention who might otherwise get bogged down in the medical jargon. Your effort would help many people, including those who might be facing different challenges in life. And it would create for you a legacy that would last forever.

Oh, and as always, fingers crossed!

Mike Pace

Bruce,
We are thrilled your stay was shorter than expected. And again, you should quit your day job and write. Readers would be mesmerized by your word skills.

We're still in Utah; heading home on Sunday. Once you figure out your Skype name, let me know and we'll try to entertain you.

And I think of you often … when I'm struggling with doing something fun or not … like skiing on a snowy, cloudy, cold day or I need to walk Scout on a rainy, crappy day. And when I start to doubt my ability to get down the mountain or exercise my dog, I'll think Bruce would love to be outside doing something, anything right now. So suck it up Anne and get going; enjoy the air! Bruce, you and other friends struggling with a bump in life are constantly in my thoughts! It's a beautiful day on the mountain!

Love ya.
Annio (Anne) Pace

Mike and Anne Pace. Another power couple and close friends thanks to my marriage to Sandra. Mike is a past Assistant U.S. Attorney for Washington, a Commercial Litigator and a General Counsel to an Environmental Services Company. Author of several novels, Mike plays the piano and sax, is a dedicated golfer and a brilliant thinker. Anne is a wizard on computers and awesome at graphic arts. Anne can make knockout brochures that rival a professional printer and probably any other document they may produce. She made a video for us of our new puppy Choco 10 years ago. Complete with pictures and video set to music, it remains one of our most treasured documents. Mike and Anne have been asking me to produce this book. They continually compliment me on my writing skills to great embarrassment and exaggeration and are the key influence in my finally accepting their challenge. I hope you will find their advice to me sagacious.

Boocie,

I could not agree with Michael Pace more, who is also a wonderful and entertaining writer. Your spirit is amazing and your words should be published to help many. I've been hanging with Sandy some this week and we've been shaking our heads as you continue to inspire us all. She is so proud of you! You're "a ray of sunshine" to quote her. I marvel at how you enjoy the smallest things to the fill and I heard about your mom's chocolate chip cookies! I'm sure there's a batch in the freezer awaiting your homecoming next Saturday.

I love a hero, especially one who is my own dear friend.

Hugs and kisses,
Krissy (Kris) Jewell

Kris and Don Jewell are Psychologists who have helped so many people overcome debilitating problems and helped them integrate more effectively into their day to day lives. Serving others is a high calling and I so respect the work they do. Sandra crashed one of their parties years ago and a lifelong friendship ensued. Don is also a musician, playing guitar and singing. He is an avid gun collector, focused on firearms from the Civil

War era. Kris and Sandra are tight as bugs in a rug. I'm so happy they are my friends.

Bruce and Sandy

First and foremost- Happy 18th Anniversary from Cass and me. After virtual church at St Patrick's Cathedral this morning (and prayers were again sent your way) , I sat here doing some computer work while looking at this wonderful view of the Florida ocean and thoughts of responding to last week's update yet words were escaping me. I find that since I retired, my composition skills have slowed since I do very little any more. Then low and behold—here comes another update! So no more delays and get out the computer and write!!! The complexity of treatment is unreal and the pains you are enduring throughout are such a credit to your perseverance of the clinical trials and treatments. It sounds like there are positives and some setbacks, but hopefully the good stuff will continue and overcome the setbacks and pains will sub-side!! Our prayers from us continue for you and as many others have commented, there are a lot more than just us! Now as others have also commented, your literary writing skills may exceed that of your put-ting (ha) and there may be some Barnes and Noble in your future!!

So, enjoy the day as you described, stay safe and well and best wishes with the next round of treatment and thanks for keeping us updated.

Happy Anniversary to you guys,
Cass and Al Rager

My wife graduated High School with Al and Cass Rager, Denny and Carol Lawson and Don and Connie Saltarelli. Though living in widely scattered areas, I have been privileged to attend their high school reunions and been accept into their group even though I am younger by several years. (Yuk, Yuk.) We usually get together with these 3 couples for a 3 day golf outing somewhere within less than a 4 or 5 hour's drive and enjoy ourselves immensely. Covid ruined our plans this year, but with some luck from my new treatment I may be able to golf again and we can renew our annual golf trip.

Bless you sweet Boocie I'm so happy the drug is kicking ass! Happy, Happy Anniversary to you and your beautiful bride – I remember the wedding well – so beautiful down here in God's Country at Cuscowilla. Joe and I wish you many, many more happy and let's hope for healthy years! Much love, kisses and hugs coming your way along with many prayers!

Jude Martincic

Jude introduced me to Sandra through golf. A long term, never to be repaid debt. Anticipating a great friendship with them in Annapolis, Joe retired and they moved to Reynolds Plantation in Georgia. Bummer. Well not totally. We visited them as often as possible and got to play a lot of golf at Reynolds Plantation's 5 world class golf courses. A neighboring golfing property was Cuscowilla and we chose it for our rehearsal dinner and marriage ceremony. My Father conducted a beautiful ceremony and tied a great knot for Sandra and me. My Mother was in the early stages of Alzheimer's but she did very well over the long weekend. Sister MJ and her husband Joe were there along with Cheryl and Cliffe, their children Alex and Emily, of course Joe and Jude and a person to play an electric piano. Thank you Joe and Jude for playing such a pivotal role in our lives.

Bruce,

I cannot tell you how impressed I am with your medical lingo and understanding of everything happening. Dr. Don would be very proud.

Thank you for adding me to your email list. I've prayed for you throughout the years, but I can be more specific now. I saw that you are doing the trial with Genentech. My friend's husband works for them and she is also doing a trial that has been pretty successful. She has GBM and has beaten the odds.

I talked to Robin Nichols today and she updated me on Duanne. I love your image, which is a perfect one. I know Daddy and your dad will be right there, behind her folks, to greet her and hug on her. Her walking again is a beautiful thing to envision. I pray for MaryJane, too, as I know how much she loves Bug and how hard this must be.

Love you, Bruce and all our Moffatt's. I have saved your Daddy's voicemail on our antiquated home answering machine, along with my Daddy's and Waddy Jesse's. Just to hear their voices brings me love and joy. Know you are in my prayers.

Love,
Martha Pryor

Martha Pryor and her sister Sara Beth Farabee are two of the prettiest girls to attend school with me and still are just as beautiful. Their last name at that time was Chatham. Sara Beth was a year or two older and Martha 3 years my junior. Martha invited me to a Sadie Hawkins Day dance in high school and we had a great time. Their father Don Chatham was our family physician and their Mother Betty Jean Chatham was a concert pianist. They were members of First Baptist Church in Shelbyville, KY while my father was pastor. Betty Jean, now 93 or 94 years young, played her rendition of How Great Though Art at my Father's funeral. It brought me to tears while stirring my soul. The Chatham's are one of the many families we share a strong bond with even today that started so long ago.

Bruce buddy,

Never apologize for your extensive reports. I'm in full agreement with your correspondent "glebebay" about the concept of sharing your journey and reflections in the form of a book. I agree that such would be a super encouragement to people. Your tremendous positivity could be so healing. People who even come anywhere near the journey you have taken just do not generally have the inner strength, well-honed tools, and the absolute faith you project so realistically.

I was thinking the other day that I had not heard from you for a while and started to write. I hope you know how proud your parents and dear Sandy are of who you are (including your heavenly Father, including the extra number of years my best friend Fred had with you, even after Lady Jane left us, as you have dealt with this daily, hourly challenge). Another reminder - you are always (weekly) on the printed and then spoken prayer list in our Sunday morning church service. (Can you believe the dear Boskydell Baptist Church has tolerated me now for 18 years?) Then I pray for you daily in my private prayers.

Here's another feather you can put in your cap (if there's room for anymore!). Your clash and then battle for this large number of years is currently feeding my soul. At the first of November 2020, our grandson Connor (age 12, Mary Ellen's son) suddenly began having brief seizures, throwing up, and blurred vision. He also had several "fits" of anger totally unlike his fun and positive personality. They live in Gainesville, Florida, and Shands Hospital at the university is considered one of the top 5 hospitals in the South. Quick trip to the ER and then admitted for overnight. A few days later, same scenario, two days later, admitted to pediatric ICU. After brain and spinal scans they determined that he "might" have a very debilitating and rare illness labeled MOG (you know how those go - the med names are so long they just reduce it to initials and you still don't know what it is). He was in ICU for a week, then step-down ICU for several more days with them still trying to determine what was going on and the seriousness of it. The scans (repeated at least two more times), revealed brain stem swelling and spinal problems, and later even some brain damage. Meanwhile, his grandparents who live in southern Illinois were praying, fretting, and trusting God. It's a long story, but some of the best neurologists in the South have yet to get to a solid diagnosis

- have dismissed MOG then later advanced that as possibility again. After dismissal sometime in December, he was back in the hospital twice in January and went home around the first of February. Among his current medications, what seems to be most helpful to him right now are an assortment of steroids. I mention that because of your dealing with steroids. One diagnosis, that seems to have been discarded now, was that he had some kind of a melanoma.

I only share this with you to tell you how reflecting on your struggles has greatly helped me to have sympathetic understanding of what your parents, especially your dad, encountered as they moved (daily I'm sure) with your attack on your bone marrow and the development into a decades long courageous fight for you. What I'm trying, not too successfully, to say is - Bruce, dear friend, your open, honest, and shared battle with this has been a very positive resource to a grandfather who loves his sick grandson. Be blessed as you are such a blessing - and I love you, Bruce.

Steve Combs

Steve Combs was the Assistant Pastor/Minister of Education for several years during my Father's tenure at FBC of Shelbyville, KY. Steve has a great and infectious sense of humor and uses that to his full capacity in his Ministry. Steve traveled by car with his family to Annapolis from Illinois during a dangerous snow storm to speak at my Deacon Ordination at Heritage Baptist Church many years ago. Steve is one of the few men I hold in high regard as a person, a Christian and a man seeking God, striving to serve others according to the teachings of scripture.

Bruce,

You NEVER cease to amaze me. Your medical journey peppered with honesty and humor are such an inspiration. Do you share these with your Doctors? I spoke with Sandy this morning and reiterated that whatever we can do to support the 2 of you, we're around. I told her my fervent prayer is that you are going to be THE patient that guides the Doctors to find the best treatment for this disease. You are strong and I believe God picked you for this job, because he knew your faith and personality were the perfect fit. So with that I continue to pray and know that we love you.

God Bless you and Happy Valentine's Day......knowing you...you have a few nurses swooning over you.

Love, Pat Bertrand

Dear Bruce,

Sitting at my desk, and closing out my day, with a heart that is full, and tears in my eyes. You are such an amazing individual. I wish your words could reach more people; you are truly inspiring!! I will continue to pray for success with the new drug for you, and for your good friend Duanne. She is an angel on earth. Your father is smiling down on you, for your continued faith and strength. 2021 is going to be a good year. Love and hugs,

Pat Bertrand

Bruce,

Thank you for the update. The news concerning the Venetoclax Effect on the M spike and Kappa Free Light chains is indeed great. Now just don't go driving as though you are Bavaria. How's the car?

We missed you at Queenstown Golf Course but it was hot. Shot 84 and that was with an 8 on Par 4 #6 where I lost 2 balls, the only 2 I lost. Had 2 birdies, first time ever in a round. No mulligans.

Yesterday at Oak Creek seemed even hotter and the heat zapped my game.

Need to reconsider playing on days when the dew point is above 70.

I am taking it easy today.

What kind of goggles do you wear when driving the Porsche?

Peter Bertrand

Are you tired of hearing about the wonderful power couples and great friends Sandra brought to me through our marriage? Sorry but this is another fine example. Patricia harkens back to working with Sandra and Elaine when they owned the Annapolis Store, selling all things in clothing and gifts with Annapolis connections. Pat is now an interior designer working independently and sharing her talent with customers looking for fabulous interiors. Peter is a retired Dental Surgeon who still speaks at Pain Management seminars affecting patients with neck and facial/dental pain. Peter has become my new golfing buddy and we join with The Lloyd Smith Seniors on a weekly basis for a round at local courses. With my declining health I have had to give up golf but hopefully I'll return to this routine after a successful Car-T therapy. Peter is one of the most intelligent people I know and has been able to answer many of the medical questions I put to him. His explanations are always in depth and well explained. Peter is fighting his own battle with cancer. His tongue cancer has been successfully resolved with surgery and his prostate cancer is being treated with good success. It involves multiple deliveries of chemo through catheterization so I'm not ready to trade his cancer for mine as of yet. Thank you Pat and Peter. We love you and cherish our relationship.

Hi Bruce!

I am sorry to hear the latest trial did not work out, but, as long as you are fighting back (you certainly are) you can beat this! We are praying for you every day and I have faith.

Please let Christine, Katie and me know if you need anything. Love you Bruce Lee!
Andrew

Hey cousin, so glad to hear from you and another update. Like MJ said your still an "A" even if it may not be A+ for now. I like what your doctor says and the virus option is truly remarkable.

Try not to beat yourself up too much about feeling like a couch potato...I have stellar experience in that field. Granted I know it's much easier to say that then to feel it. After years of pretty much a so far incurable combination of immune system diseases and other, I so often have to rest daily, choose carefully what I can and can't do, take it easy, when I much rather be able to do more at any time. The mind says go, the body doesn't follow! I understand when we want and need to be doing more when we can't, it's frustrating. I "try" to think that physically there are some things beyond our control - which you have come to understand and explain so bravely. And pray for God's understanding and that He knows best of what's up than we do. It's amazing the vast amount of medical changes your body has been through!

Glad you will be seeing a cardiologist, sorry to hear about the issues. They can be really uncomfortable. I also take Metoprolol (for Mitral Valve Prolapse) which has helped to control symptoms. I often wonder about the Moffatt gene pool and heart health (both our fathers, Andrew, etc.) so good call. I hope all goes well and look forward to an update.

We love you very much and are sending you lots of prayers for a full recovery. Best to Sandra. Hang in there Bruce, you are a wonderful inspiration to us all!

Hugs,
Katie Gorecki

Kate Gorecki is the daughter of my Uncle, James Moffatt. Her husband Hank is a big bear of a man and someone you would always want on your side in case of trouble. Andrew is her younger brother and a very successful drummer in his cover band. He also works for the U.S. Veterans Department in an administrative capacity. Kate has had a mountain of health problems herself and has used her faith and determination to keep fighting through her pain and disability. Just more Scottish DNA like mine that keeps fighting everything thrown our way. Their Father "Jimmy" was the youngest brother to my Dad, with Don being the middle brother. Three boys with a minister father. Oh, the stories of the three rambunctious Preacher Kids. And Jimmy was always the best at being the most one in trouble.

Dear Bruce,

You are such an inspiration and a true optimist. It is wonderful to see. Sometimes it is difficult to give thanks when we are not doing as well as we want and things may not be going as we had hoped, but you continue to give thanks which is a blessing in itself. I agree with your friend who said you have gained an overwhelming amount of medical knowledge that you should be granted your MD degree. We love getting your updates and continue to keep you and Sandy in our prayers. I have seen the power of prayers and how miracles can happen as long as we keep the faith. We may not know or understand God's plan, but he is in charge!!

Hugs,
Mary Jane and Bill Johnson

MJ, Sandra, Elaine and Barbara have been close friends for 4+ decades. Bill is a retired Secret Service agent and liaison officer with the DOJ. They retired to Wilmington, NC several years ago so we don't get to see them as often as we would like.

Hi Bruce,

I am so excited for you. I join you in knowing you will be in remission soon and have a fanatic and new normal for 2017. You are always in my prayers and on my mind. I love you deeply.

Your brother from a different mother,
Gregory Whitley

Hi Bruce,

I really appreciate your very detailed and articulate reports. I am so glad you are home and with your family. It does the heart good. I have a question maybe you can answer for me. Will the chemo also kill your golf swing and then allow a new golf swing to evolve and grow into a more consistent one?

Greg

Have you ever had a friend you could count on no matter the circumstances? Someone you knew would support and love you no matter what. One, that after long intervals of not seeing or speaking to each other, could reconnect with you as if no time had passed in your relationship. Such is my friend Greg Whitley. The foundation of this bond is our faith. Greg and I were ordained as Deacons together at Heritage Baptist Church in Annapolis while my father was Pastor. We share a deep faith. We sang in the choir together, directed by Betsy Rainey, whom we loved and adored. We made every effort to make choir practice as fun and irreverent as possible. Music and laughter, what a great combination. My Mother sang in choir with us and since Greg and I were adults, she could only laugh and shake her head when we behaved more like adolescent children. Greg has a fearless and infectious personality. He can be the "life of the party" better than anyone I know. It's hard not to like Greg. Unless of course you intentionally hit into his group on the golf course. Your encounter with him may not leave you feeling warm and fuzzy. I could write in greater detail about all the things we have in common and how much we admire each other, but I think you get the picture. Greg is a Brother to me.

Bruce, finished reading your message- actually read it twice - and so appreciate your taking the time to compose all your thoughts and share this with us.. am forwarding this to Scott as he is out of the country and he asked me to keep him updated re your progress.

I believe you had visitors from out of town ?? Hope you enjoyed their company and some distractions? I have to confess that since your diagnosis I have visited more churches and cathedrals overseas that I in many years - wow, they are really beautiful and there are so many of them! Am lighting candles and saying prayers in each city I am in. Just know we love you very much and are praying you continue to improve your numbers - also please make sure the pool is completed asap. (Just my lame attempt at some humor)...

Will be in contact with Sandy and perhaps try to visit Saturday depending, of course, on how you are.

Xxxxx
Cheryl Donnelly

Scott and Cheryl Donnelly. Sandra has known Cheryl since she designed and built a home for her many years ago. Scott and Cheryl are responsible for directing me to Dr. Daniela Hoehn who, as previously mentioned, helped redirect my care and has given me greater access to clinical trials. Cheryl and Pat Bertrand frequently join Sandra for pool and margarita time in our backyard. Scott is one of the hardest working people I know. He operates an online jewelry business and works tirelessly helping friends with landscaping projects. They have also been two of my biggest supporters as I continue my battle with MM.

Miles,

You are truly an amazing man. Thank you so much for your encouragement and generous offer to publish. I'll get started segmenting my emails from my sent folder in Gmail and outline some topics for additional inclusion.

I am thrilled to hear Marjorie is doing well and getting great care. I'm sure this is a relief for you to know she is safe and comfortable. I will continue to keep you both in my prayers.

Thank you, Bruce Moffatt
Miles Kanne

Miles is husband to my Mother's sister Marjorie. Miles is yet another member of our family who possess a great mind and spirit with a gentle soul and tremendous sense of humor. Miles was an outstanding businessman and very successful as the #2 man with Cook, Incorporated. Now well into his 90's Miles is caring for Marjorie as she is burdened with dementia. They have 2 children, Roger and Sandra, both a few years younger than Mary Jane and me. We have great memories of our younger days filled with good times and laughter whenever the Moffatt's and the Kannes (pronounced Connies) got together.

Hey Bruce. I've been going past Fairfax Road a few times lately and been thinking about you. How are you doing?

Tom Rice

Tom was my tax accountant and I met him and his wife Kris while working as an Assistant Golf Pro at Eisenhower Golf Course in Crownsville, MD. His teenage son Jeff worked at the course washing carts and picking the range. Jeff is now both the Greens Superintendent and Director of Golf at Oak Creek Golf Course in Upper Marlboro MD. Their daughter Jessica is married to J.W. Thomas who also worked at Eisenhower GC. J.W. was one of the most responsible young men we ever employed and it wasn't long before he was closing out the days business and preparing bank deposits. J.W. is now an investment advisor with Ameriprise Financial. He manages our retirement portfolio and has helped us build our nest egg. From tiny seeds might Oaks grow. This is also true of rela-

tionships that seem to start small but evolve into wonderful connections of the best kind.

Hi Bruce,

You never cease to amaze us. Your outlook is never less than happy and optimistic and that will see you through this journey.

It's been an incredible menu of medications for you...choice upon choice of new drugs which breeds great hope in us all. There's truth to "living with Cancer".

You continue to be in our prayers, and it looks like you and Sandra are all set for a true Thanksgiving!

We love you dearly and send our very best,

Steve & Sheri Cates

While I was a Golf Pro in in Westminster, MD, Steve Cates came in one day to get set up to establish a handicap. I helped him with the USGA computer ins and outs of posting scores. A few days later he showed up to play golf with his wife Sherri. We had started a Friday evening "Fun Couples" group to play 9 holes and dine afterwards in the clubhouse. So I invited Steve and Sherri to join. The rest is history and they became close friends with Sandra and me. They were and are a true fun couple. Steve was quite successful repairing large pumping systems on commercial buildings and retired early from the back breaking work. Sherri is a State Farm agent and she handles all of our home and auto insurance needs. In his retirement, Steve has established a tremendous wood working shop in his garage. He can build anything out of wood and is constantly doing things around his home to update or improve its look and efficiency. Too much talent in one person if you ask me. Since moving to Annapolis we don't get to see them as much as usual but we stay in contact and they have been so supportive of me with their responses to my email postings. Just another "jack pot" couple in our long list of friends.

You Make Me A Better Man

Hey Buddy!
I know you're in pain right now, but things will get better. Things will get better!!!!

I want you to know that you are with me more and more these days. As you know, I have a tendency to lose my temper when thing go wrong, whether it be on the golf course or work, or in life.

But, these days my Brother, I think of you and what you have endured during the last 6 years and the negative things that pop up in my life don't matter as much.

You give me strength, you make me a better Man. You and God have made a profound impression on me and it's a wonderful feeling.

Thank you Handsome and thank you God!

Mike Perkowski (with wife Lisa in photo)

The Rest of the Story

WHAT'S NEXT FOR ME? I'M going to keep fighting the fight. And to quote my dear father: "Just cannot be soon enough to suit me." Dad, you and me both.

We can all hope and pray for medical advancements with Multiple Myeloma.

This book is very personal and is essentially about me and my life with Multiple Myeloma. But I hope my experiences with this terrible disease will help someone who is struggling or has a loved one who is struggling with cancer.

To continue the conversation and to keep my friends and family up to date on the Bruce Moffatt train, please follow my stories on the following blog site:

BruceMoffatt.com

Thanks for checking in from time to time.

Happy trails to you....until we meet again,

Bruce

Thank You Friends and Family

Elaine Aarsand

Pat and Peter Bertrand

Teresa Burruss

Sheri and Steve Cates

Alex Cheston

Cheryl and Cliffe Cheston

Emily Cheston

Julia Cheston

Martha Cheston

Dennis Clawson

Stephen Combs

Jason Daly

Scott Donnelly

Linda Frey

Kate Gorecki

Pam Gray

Maria Hanaway Green

Ross Green

Cheryl Hall

Dr. Hazel Hanaway

Dot Hanna

Jim Harris

Dave Hobgood

Dr. Daniela Hoehn

Stephanie Hollaway

Kris and Don Jewell

Mary Jane and Bill Johnson

Miles Kanne

Roger Kanne

Burc h Kinsolving

Jack LaCesa

Phil Lande

Joe and Jude Martincic

James Moffatt

Sandra Moffatt

Denise O'Neill

Anne and Michael Pace

Mike Perkowski

Martha Pryor

Duanne Puckett

Al Rager

Ralph Riedel

Sandra Ritter

Susan SEiller

Jinal Shah

JW Thomas

Clyde Thomson

Dave Turner

Bill Werder

Greg Whitley

Mary Jane Yates

Jen Ziemer